Economic Interdependence and War

PRINCETON STUDIES IN INTERNATIONAL
HISTORY AND POLITICS

Series Editors
G. John Ikenberry, Marc Trachtenberg, and William C. Wohlforth

Recent Titles

Economic Interdependence and War

Dale C. Copeland

PRINCETON UNIVERSITY PRESS

Princeton and Oxford

Copyright © 2015 by Princeton University Press
Published by Princeton University Press, 41 William Street, Princeton, New Jersey 08540
In the United Kingdom: Princeton University Press, 6 Oxford Street, Woodstock, Oxfordshire OX20 1TW
press.princeton.edu
Jacket art: Auguste Étienne François Mayer, *The Redoutable at the Battle of Trafalgar*, 1836. Photo: Bulloz. Musée de la Marine, France. © RMN-Grand Palais/Art Resource, NY
All Rights Reserved
ISBN 978-0-691-16158-7
ISBN (pbk.) 978-0-691-16159-4
British Library Cataloging-in-Publication Data is available
This book has been composed in Sabon Next LT Pro

10 9 8 7 6 5 4 3 2 1

Contents

Preface

THIS IS A BOOK with multiple layers, and hence one that can be read from a number of angles. First and foremost, it is exploration of the conditions under which trade and investment flows are likely to push great powers either toward peace or toward militarized conflict and war. At another level, however, it is an investigation into the ways great powers think about economic exchange, and the role it plays in their efforts to build global power and long-term security. Finally, the book constitutes a study of the relative causal salience of commercial versus noncommercial forces in the movement of modern world history. In the latter sense, it is part of a larger effort to determine just how often competing theories of war, both economic and noneconomic, effectively explain shifts from interstate peace to dangerous crises and war, or from ongoing cold wars to stable peace. By covering the essential universe of great power cases from 1790 to 1991, the book provides the first major test of the relative importance of competing causal factors across the sweep of diplomatic history. The findings of this book should thus be of interest to historians as well as international relations scholars. Yet by also considering the cutting-edge work of quantitative scholars, the study shows the larger implications of the book's argument for a broad cross-section of nations, both large and small.

Because the attempt to cover two hundred years of great power history makes for a long book, different audiences will want to read this work in different ways. Readers with a primary interest in international relations theory and political science will want to explore the first three chapters carefully, and then pick and choose cases of particular interest from chapters 3 to 8. Readers whose main interests are rooted in diplomatic history need only read the first half of the introductory chapter before plunging directly into the case studies and the discussion of contemporary Sino-American relations in the final chapter. I have placed the European cases from 1790 to 1899 near the end of the book simply because there are fewer extant documents for this period, which tends to constrain our ability to test the relative validity of competing causal mechanisms. Nevertheless, a reader with a preference for chronology could start with chapters 7 and 8, and then return to chapters 3 to 6 to cover the cases of the tumultuous twentieth century.

Like its subject matter, this is a book with a long history, and there are many people to thank. I first want to express my appreciation to those individuals who offered comments at workshops on early versions of individual chapters, and whose names I may not have known at the time or have subsequently forgotten. This includes workshops at the Center for International Affairs at Harvard University, the Belfer Center for Science and International Affairs at Harvard, the Program on International Peace, Economics, and Security at the University of Chicago, the Mershon Center at Ohio State University, the departments of political science at Columbia University and George Washington University, and the Department of Government at Georgetown University. I especially want to thank the Lone Star Forum, a consortium of Texas universities, for a weekend setting that facilitated a fertile discussion of key sections of my close-to-finished manuscript. The comments from the participants there helped me fix a number of errors just before the manuscript went out for review.

For helping me work through the bugs in the original theoretical setup, I wish to thank Bob Art, James Fearon, Hein Goemans, Andrew Kydd, Jack Levy, Charles Lipson, Michael Mastanduno, John Mearsheimer, Ido Oren, Duncan Snidal, and Stephen Walt. For valuable advice on specific chapters and my methodological approach, thanks go to Deborah Boucayannis, Tim Crawford, Mike Desch, Dan Gingerich, Eugene Gholz, David Leblang, Jeff Legro, Steven Lobell, Allen Lynch, Ed Mansfield, Kevin Narizny, John Owen, Sonal Pandya, Norrin Ripsman, Len Schoppa, Herman Schwartz, Randy Schweller, Todd Sechser, Jeff Taliaferro, David Waldner, and Brantly Womack. At the University of Virginia, I was fortunate to work with a number of smart graduate students who offered incisive comments at various stages of this book's development: Karen Farrell, Kyle Haynes, Derek King, Kyle Lascurettes, Tom Moriarty, Carah Ong, Joseph Riley, Matt Scroggs, Yu Jin Woo, and Brandon Yoder. Here I especially offer my gratitude to Michael Poznansky for his penetrating critiques across many of the book's chapters.

At Princeton University Press, I greatly appreciate the help of Marc Trachenberg and John Ikenberry, editors of the Princeton Studies in International History and Politics series, for their strong support of this project from the get-go. Eric Crahan and his forerunner, Chuck Myers, were everything one could want in a general editor. I must also thank John Haslam of Cambridge University Press for his support during the review process. Although an author can (unfortunately) only publish a book with one press, John's sustained encouragement and interest in the project will always be remembered.

Finally, I want to acknowledge the anonymous reviewers at both Princeton University Press and Cambridge University Press for extensive as well as constructive comments. Their insightful suggestions helped me correct a number of flaws, leading to what I hope is now a much-improved final product. One of these reviewers, who later revealed himself to be Frank Gavin, provided especially helpful thoughts on the broader diplomatic-historical implications of the project.

My parents, Clare G. Copeland and Barbara E. Copeland, deserve a special note of appreciation. They both passed away before they could see the book in print. But their unswerving support over the many years it took me to write it leaves me grateful beyond words. I dedicate this book to my wonderful partner, Natasha Copeland, and my two incredible kids, Liam and Katya. Simply put, you are what make life worthwhile.

Abbreviations for Primary Documents and Source Material

UNITED STATES, 1905–1991

CIA (*CWE*)   *At Cold War's End: U.S. Intelligence on the Soviet Union and Eastern Europe, 1989–1991*, ed. Benjamin B. Fischer (Washington, DC: Central Intelligence Agency, 1999).

CIA (HT)   Warner, ed., *CIA Cold War Records: The CIA under Harry Truman* (Washington, DC: Central Intelligence Agency, 1994).

CR   Warren F. Kimball, ed., *Churchill and Roosevelt: The Complete Correspondence*, 3 vols. (Princeton, NJ: Princeton University Press, 1984).

CWIHP   Cold War in International History Project. Washington, DC.

CWIHPB   *Cold War in International History Project Bulletin*, issues 1–11 (Washington, DC: Woodrow Wilson International Center for Scholars, 1992–1998).

DDEL   Dwight D. Eisenhower Library, Abilene, KS.

DSB   *Department of State Bulletin* (Washington, DC: US Department of State, various years).

FCY   Department of Commerce, *Foreign Commerce Yearbook* (Washington, DC: US Department of Commerce, various years).

FD   *The Forrestal Diaries*, eds. Walter Millis and E. S. Duffield (New York: Viking, 1951).

FDRL   Franklin D. Roosevelt Library, Hyde Park, New York.

FDRPL   Elliott Roosevelt, ed., *FDR, His Personal Letters, 1928–45* (New York: Duell, Sloan, and Pearce, 1950).

FRUS   *Foreign Relations of the United States* (Washington, DC: US Government Printing Office, various years).

FRUSJ   *Foreign Relations of the United States: Japan*, 2 vols. (Washington, DC: US Government Printing Office, 1943).

FTP   Orville H. Bullitt, ed., *For the President, Personal and Secret: Correspondence between Franklin D. Roosevelt and William C. Bullitt* (Boston: Houghton Mifflin, 1972).

HSTL   Harry S. Truman Library, Independence, MO.

JFKL   John F. Kennedy Library, Boston, MA.

JFKLNSF   John F. Kennedy Library, National Security Files.

KT   William Burr, ed., *The Kissinger Transcripts: The Top-Secret Talks with Beijing and Moscow* (New York: New Press, 1998).

LC   Library of Congress, Washington, DC.

MB   *The "Magic" Background of Pearl Harbor*, vols. 1–5 (Washington, DC: Department of Defense).

MH   Svetlana Savranskaya, Thomas Blanton, and Vladislav Zubok, eds., *Masterpieces of History: The Peaceful End of the Cold War in Europe* (Budapest: Central European University Press, 2010).

NA   US National Archives, College Park, MD.

NSA (*BC*)   National Security Archive, *The Berlin Crisis, 1958–1962*, microfiche (Alexandria, VA: Chadwyck-Healey, 1991).

NSA (*SE*)   National Security Archive, *The Soviet Estimate: U.S. Analysis of the Soviet Union, 1947–1991*, microfiche (Alexandria, VA: Chadwyck-Healey, 1995).

PHA   *Pearl Harbor Attack: Hearings before the Joint Committee on the Investigation of the Pearl Harbor Attack*, vols. 1–39 (Washington, DC: Government Printing Office, 1946).

PHST   Ronald Worth, ed., *Pearl Harbor: Selected Testimonies, Fully Indexed from the Congressional Hearings (1945–46) and Prior Investigations of the Events Leading Up to the Attack* (Jefferson, NC: McFarland, 1993).

PWP   Donald M. Goldstein and Katherine V. Dillon, eds., *The Pacific War Papers: Japanese Documents of World War II* (Washington, DC: Potomac Books, 2004).

RC   Francis L. Loewenheim, Harold D. Langley, and Manfred Jonas, eds., *Roosevelt and Churchill: Their Secret Wartime Correspondence* (New York: Da Capo Press, 1990).

RF   Jason Saltoun-Ebin, ed., *The Reagan Files: The Untold Story of Reagan's Top-Secret Efforts to Win the Cold War* (Pacific Palisades, CA: Self-published, 2010).

UECW   National Security Archive, *Understanding the End of the Cold War: The Reagan/Gorbachev Years* (briefing book prepared for an oral history conference, Brown University, Providence, RI, May 7–10, 1998).

EUROPE, 1790–1941

CN   *Correspondance de Napoléon 1er*, vols. 1–32 (Paris: Imprimerie Impériale, 1858–70).

DNL   R. M. Johnston, ed., *A Diary of Napoleon's Life in his Own Words* (Boston: Houghton Mifflin, 1910).

EHS   B. R. Mitchell, ed., *European Historical Statistics, 1750–1975*, 2nd rev. ed. (New York: Facts on File, 1980).

FPVE   Kenneth Bourne, ed., *Foreign Policy of Victorian England, 1830–1902* (Oxford: Clarendon Press, 1970).

GDD   E.T.S. Dugsdale, ed., *German Diplomatic Documents, 1871–1914*, vols. 1–4 (New York: Harper and Brothers, 1931).

GM   Henry Reeve, ed., *The Grenville Memoirs: A Journal of the Reigns of King George IV, King William IV, and Queen Victoria* (London: Longmans, Green, 1896).

HP   Norman Rich and M. H. Fisher, eds., *The Holstein Papers*, vols. 1–4 (Cambridge: Cambridge University Press, 1955).

NDR   Jeremy Noakes and Geoffrey Pridham, eds., *Nazism, 1939–1945: A Documentary Reader*, vols. 1–3 (Exeter: University of Exeter Press, 1983–88).

NL   J. M. Thompson, ed., *Napoleon's Letters* (London: Prion, 1998).

NLN   Mary Lloyd, ed., *New Letters of Napoleon I* (New York: Appleton, 1897).

JAPAN, 1870–1941

DAFP   W. J. Hudson and H.J.W. Stokes, eds., *Documents on Australian Foreign Policy, 1937–49*, vol. 5: July 1941–June 1942 (Canberra: Australian Government Publishing Service, 1982).

DJ   Kajima Morinosuke, ed., *The Diplomacy of Japan*, vols. 1–2 (Tokyo: Kajima Institute of International Peace, 1978).

HYSJE   *Hundred-Year Statistics of the Japanese Economy* (Tokyo: Bank of Japan, 1966).

JDW   Ike Nobutaka, ed., *Japan's Decision for War: Records of the 1941 Policy Conferences* (Stanford, CA: Stanford University Press, 1967).

JGEACS   Joyce C. Lebra, ed., *Japan's Greater East Asia Co-Prosperity Sphere in World War II: Selected Readings and Documents* (Kuala Lumpur: Oxford University Press, 1975).

RJDE   John Albert White, "Russo-Japanese Diplomatic Exchanges, 1901–1904," appendix 1 of *The Diplomacy of the Russo-Japanese War* (Princeton, NJ: Princeton University Press, 1964).

Does economic interdependence between great powers have a significant effect on the probability of war between them, and if so, does it decrease or increase the likelihood of conflict? As levels of trade and investment between the United States, China, India, and Russia continue to reach new heights, this question has taken on renewed importance amid worries about possible future struggles over raw materials, investments, and markets. Over the last two decades, the number of articles and books devoted to the issue has grown exponentially. And yet surprisingly, we still have no consensus regarding the link between interstate commerce and war. Many and perhaps most scholars align with traditional liberalism, concluding that interdependence is indeed a key causal factor—one that can greatly reduce the chance of military conflict between states. Other scholars, however, argue that the evidence is more equivocal, with economic interdependence being either insignificant relative to other causes of conflict or in fact tending to increase the probability of war rather than to reduce it.

This book sets out to resolve this debate. It shows that commercial factors are not only far more important to the outbreak of war than either side has previously thought, but that their impact can cut both ways. Trade and investment flows can indeed moderate the likelihood of conflict between great powers, as liberals believe. Yet interdependence can also push states into crises and wars, as the critics of liberalism contend. The real puzzle to be solved thus becomes this: When and under what conditions will the trade and investment ties between nations lead to either peace or military conflict? Some crucial work has already begun on this conundrum, with scholars employing large-N data sets to identify the additional causal factors that might interact with interdependence to incline nations toward peace or war. Unfortunately, the development of deductive theories to explain the role of the added causal variables has lagged behind the empirical analysis of their significance. In terms of empirical correlation, it now seems clear that factors such as regime type, capitalism, and levels of development play important synergistic roles in shaping the impact of economic interdependence on the likelihood of war. But we still do not adequately know *why* they play these roles—that is, what these factors are actually doing to create the causal effects we observe.

This book builds a deductive theory that seeks to answer most of the outstanding questions surrounding the issue of economic interdependence and war. The argument fuses the liberal insight that commercial ties can give actors a large material incentive to avoid war with the realist insight that such ties also create vulnerabilities that can push leaders into war. Liberals are right to assert that trade and investment flows can raise the opportunity cost of going to war, since war leads to a severing of valuable commerce. But realists are correct in their claim that commercial ties make states vulnerable to cutoffs—cutoffs that can devastate an economy that has reoriented itself to rely on critical markets and goods from abroad.

To determine whether the liberal prediction or realist prediction will prevail, we must introduce an additional causal variable—namely, a state's expectations of the future trade and investment environment. When a dependent state has positive expectations about this future environment, it is more likely to see all the benefits of continuing the current peace and all the opportunity costs of turning to war. Economic interdependence would then be a force for peace. Yet if a dependent state has negative expectations about the future economic environment—seeing itself being cut off from access to foreign trade and investment, or believing that other states will soon cut it off—then the realist logic will kick in. Such a state will tend to believe that without access to the vital raw materials, investments, and export markets needed for its economic health, its economy will start to fall relative to other less vulnerable actors. If this economic decline is anticipated to be severe, the leaders of the dependent state will begin to view war as the rational lesser of two evils—that is, as better than allowing their state to fall to a point where rising states can attack it later or coerce it into submission.

This argument—what I call *trade expectations theory*—thus links the realm of international political economy to the question of security-driven preventive wars.[1] In previous work, I have shown that the vast majority of the key major wars of history were driven by fears of decline—fears by dominant military powers that they would be overtaken by rising powers unless they initiated a preventive war sooner rather than later (Copeland 2000b). The present study goes beyond this work on preventive war in two main ways. First, instead of looking just at major or "general" wars where one great power decided to take on the system, I am interested here in great power conflicts in general, or in other words, both major wars and the more limited wars and crises that great powers might fall into. The book's argument is therefore designed to cover pretty well every form of conflict where there was a substantive chance of war breaking out between great powers. I will examine all the main cases

---

[1] For summaries and references on the now-vast literature on preventive war, see Levy 2008; Weisiger 2013.

of great power conflict, starting in 1790, encompassing those that led to actual war as well as those that led to significant struggles and crises that increased the probability of war.[2] By covering such a broad range of great power cases—including those cases that do not work well for my argument—the study can assess the overall explanatory power of trade expectations theory relative to its competitors while at the same time avoiding any selection bias that would call its value into question. I also minimize selection bias through a reexamination, from an expectations perspective, of recent large-N quantitative research (chapter 2). Because this research includes small powers and not just great powers, should the expectations logic also work here, we can be more confident that its potential explanatory power is not confined simply to actors of significant size and power projection capability.[3]

The second expansion on previous work is the detailed exploration of what actually causes actors to fear profound long-term decline—the kind of decline that can propel them into costly preventive wars or risky preventive actions that increase the chance of a spiral to war. By showing how the realities of international commerce can lead leaders to believe that they can no longer sustain their states' power positions, the theory of this book provides a vital and surprisingly pervasive causal reason for great power decline across the centuries.[4] It thus undergirds any realist argument for war and peace that is rooted in the power dynamics of the system. Indeed, if history shows that a great power's security is very much a function of its position in the global commercial system, the entire field of "security studies" will need to be reoriented away from its traditional focus on military matters and reconnected with the insights of international political economy.[5]

As I will show, in a wide variety of great power settings, the combination of economic interdependence along with expectations of future trade and investment was a critical driving force shaping the probability

---

[2] Setting up the dependent variable as a continuous one, the probability of war, rather than the dichotomous variable war/peace, offers distinct advantages. Theoretically, it obliges a theory to explain important shifts in the severity of state behavior over time, including moves from engagement to hard-line containment or from containment to the initiation of dangerous crises (or the opposites). Empirically, it avoids the risk of "selecting on the dependent variable" (i.e., considering only times of war and crisis) by forcing a study to examine periods of peace as well as severe tension.

[3] Given space limitations, I will not discuss case studies dealing with interactions between regional actors where great powers are not involved. But for an interesting application of an expectations argument to such cases, see Press-Barnathan 2009.

[4] On explanations of decline, see, in particular, Kennedy 1987; Gilpin 1981.

[5] I say reconnected because, prior to 1980, there was a less distinct separation in international relations scholarship between international political economy and security studies; in this regard, consider Robert Gilpin's (1975, 1977, 1981) early work.

of war and conflict between great powers. It was dominant in the ebbs and flows of much of nineteenth-century European geopolitics: Napoléon's war on the system; the struggles of Russia, Britain, and France over the Near East in the 1830s; the British Opium War with China in 1839; the Crimean War; the wars of imperialism in the 1880s; and the crises over Venezuela, Sudan, and South Africa in the 1890s. One theory cannot cover everything, of course. As I will demonstrate, there were also a number of conflicts during this time that had little or nothing to do with economic interdependence, such as the great power interventions in Spain and Italy in the 1820s, and the wars of Italian and German unification from 1859 to 1870. What is surprising, however, is how often trade and investment expectations drove the patterns of peace and conflict, even for cases that seem, on the surface, to have little to do with economic interdependence.

The same is true for the twentieth century. Japan's attacks on Russia in 1904 and the United States in 1941 were intimately related to Japanese fears of future access to the raw materials and trade of the East Asian theater. In the first case, Japan witnessed Russia's steady penetration into economically valuable areas of Manchuria and the Korean Peninsula. After repeated and invariably unsuccessful efforts to convince Russia to pull back, Tokyo realized that only preventive war would mitigate Japan's long-term economic and military concerns. Japan's attack on Pearl Harbor had similar causal roots, even if the specific dimensions of the Japanese problem from 1930 to 1941 were unique. The closed economic policies of the great powers after 1929 had a devastating impact on Japan's economy and Japanese views of the future trade environment. Tokyo's efforts to consolidate its own economic sphere in Manchuria and northern China, spurred by its decades-long worry about Russian growth in the Far East, led to conflicts with the Soviet and Nationalist Chinese governments. When the United States entered the fray after 1938 and began a series of damaging economic embargoes, Japanese expectations of future trade fell even further, prompting a desperate effort to acquire access to oil and raw materials in Southeast Asia. The ultimate result was the attack on Pearl Harbor in December 1941.

Germany's wars with the system in 1914 and 1939 were less a function of economic interdependence per se than of German fears of the long-term rise of the Russian colossus. Russia after 1890 and especially after 1930 was quickly building up its industrial and infrastructural power. With Russia possessing three times Germany's population and forty times its landmass, it was clear that Russia's rise to economic and then military dominance would be extremely hard to stop. As I have detailed elsewhere (Copeland 2000b), German leaders twice brought their nation into war in order to destroy the Russian state before it was too late. I show here, though, that their preventive motivations for war were strongly reinforced by pessimistic expectations about the global trading system—a pessimism that gave German leaders even more reason to believe that Germany's decline would be both deep and inevitable.

The forty-five-year Cold War struggle after World War II between the United States and the Soviet Union constitutes perhaps the most startling set of cases in the book. Scholarship almost invariably dismisses the role of economic interdependence in the explanation of the ups and downs of the Cold War, mainly because trade between the superpower blocs was so minimal. Yet as I discuss in the next chapter, economic factors can still exert a powerful causal force on great power relations even when actual trade is nonexistent, simply because needy states may have reason to expect that other great powers will begin trading with them in the future. In short, the positive expectation of future trade can moderate a needy actor's foreign policy behavior, even when current trade is low, because the actor anticipates high economic benefits into the future and has reason to want the other to carry out its commitments to increase overall trade levels. Conversely, a decision by another state to continue to deny the needy state what it desires can exacerbate present hostilities insofar as it signals a desire to keep the needy state down—that is, to prevent its economic growth and in fact encourage its economic decline.

During the period from 1950 to the end of the Cold War in the late 1980s, US decisions on trade with Russia had an often-significant impact on levels of Soviet cooperation. In the late 1950s, Dwight Eisenhower's unwillingness to relax stringent economic restrictions alienated Nikita Khrushchev and contributed to the extreme tensions of the 1960–62 period. But in the early 1970s and again in the late 1980s, Washington was more willing to commit itself to higher future trade with the Soviets. This proved critical to achieving an initial détente period and then an end to the Cold War altogether. But the destabilizing tensions of the Cold War were not simply a function of US policy toward the Soviet Union. As I show in chapter 6, the very origins of the Cold War can be traced back to US fears of a loss of access to trade and investments in western Europe, the Middle East, and East Asia—fears that began to take hold as early as 1943–44. Because of the importance of the small states of these regions to US postwar economic growth, both Franklin Roosevelt and Harry Truman were determined not to allow them to be permanently lost to Soviet Communism, even if Moscow was not deliberately seeking to pull them into its sphere. Hence Roosevelt and Truman undertook a series of provocative policies designed to consolidate the United States' postwar sphere, thereby forcing the Soviets to increase their own control over the periphery. The Cold War spiral of hostility came directly out of these initial maneuvers for postwar economic position.

The documentary evidence on great power politics after 1790 reveals the relative weaknesses of liberal and realist theories on interdependence and war compared to the trade expectations approach. Liberalism's argument that domestic-level forces get unleashed when trade dependence is low fits few of the cases. Its strongest case is the outbreak of World War II in Europe, and indeed the correlation between global protectionism after 1930 and the Nazi drive for hegemony became the basis for the postwar revival of the liberal thesis, sparked by the efforts of US secretary of state Cordell Hull. As we will see, however, liberalism cannot explain the economic concerns of Adolf Hitler prior to the collapse of the global economic system, or his strategic worries in the 1930s about Germany's future dependence on raw materials and food. Realism is particularly strong here, capturing elements of Nazi decision making downplayed in trade expectations theory. And realism is clearly superior to trade expectations theory for cases such as Japan's war with China in 1894–95, in which the initiator grabs an opportunity to start a conflict in order to reduce its ongoing vulnerability to trade cutoffs. To explain the full range of cases since 1790, though, we need to bring trade expectations into the mix. As I will show, for the cases where economic factors are primary, it is almost always a combination of commercial dependence and falling trade expectations that drives states into destabilizing crises and war.

DIMENSIONS OF THE ARGUMENT

The next chapter provides a review of the literature and detailed description of my alternative argument. In the rest of this introductory chapter, I outline some of the most important aspects of the trade expectations approach, aspects that help it to resolve a number of the outstanding issues regarding interdependence and war. The new causal variable, as noted, is a dependent state's expectations of the future trade and investment environment. It is this variable that helps unite the liberal emphasis on the gains from trade and commerce with the realist sense of vulnerability. Overall, however, trade expectations theory is founded on a fundamentally realist orientation to international politics. It assumes that great powers are primarily driven by a desire to maximize their security, and not by other goals such as welfare maximization, social cohesion, glory, or the spread of their ideologies. Thus while it sometimes aligns with the liberal prediction that commerce can give states an incentive for peace, the deductive reasoning behind this prediction differs significantly from liberalism. In liberal theory, actors are interested in absolute welfare or utility maximization, and it is the gains from trade that can make states believe that peace has a higher absolute value than war. For liberals, high levels of trade act as a restraint on what would otherwise be domestic-level reasons for going to war. War therefore occurs when trade falls and the economic constraints are taken away, allowing preexisting domestic forces and pathologies to be unleashed on the system. This is a critical point that cannot be emphasized strongly enough. Interstate trade, in the view of liberals, acts only as a constraining factor for peace. To understand what actually propelled an actor to initiate war, liberals must go to the unit level—that is, to the internal social and psychological dimensions of states.

In the trade expectations argument, states go to war not because unit-level forces are no longer constrained but instead because falling expectations of future trade make them pessimistic about their long-term security prospects. The dependent great power no longer believes that the system is working for it, and has reason to think that a preventive war or increasingly coercive policies might be able to reestablish secure access to the resources, investments, and markets that are being denied to it, or will be denied in the near future. Such a deductive logic has strong neorealist roots. It recognizes that states in anarchic systems—that is, those systems lacking a central authority—always have reason to worry about not just future military attack but also a cutoff from the sources of future economic power. Without a strong and vibrant economy, great powers cannot sustain their positions in the system (Waltz 1979; Gilpin 1981).

At the same time, however, trade expectations theory rejects the inherent pessimism of one important strand of neorealism: the offensive realist view of world politics. Offensive realism provides the basis for what I have been labeling the realist perspective on economic interdependence and war. (From here on in, I will usually refer to it as *economic realism* to distinguish it from realist contentions that ignore economic factors.) Offensive realists believe that anarchy forces great powers to constantly fear the future intentions of other states—indeed, to assume the worst about them. Such a worst-case assumption leads to the well-known offensive realist prediction that states have to maximize power as a hedge against future problems, even if they only want to survive. But the assumption also indicates that states that become dependent on others for key raw materials and markets necessarily feel highly vulnerable to a severing or restricting of economic relations. Believing the worst about another means that one believes that one will be cut off sooner rather than later. Hence, dependent states will always be seeking opportunities to attack the source of their dependence to reduce their vulnerabilities and to ensure themselves continued access to what they need for a strong economy. Indeed, because offensive realist states are obsessed with both vulnerability and losses in relative power through trade, they should refrain from trading with other great powers in the first place.[6]

My argument fundamentally rejects this offensive realist pessimism. Offensive realism is based on an underspecified view of international political economy that cannot explain either why great powers become dependent on one another or why they might remain confident about their interdependent relationship for long stretches of time. Japan, for example, began to actively trade with the great power system, including the United States, from 1870 onward. It was only some three and then seven decades later that it launched its two large-scale wars in the region (1904 and 1941, respectively). More recently, China since 1980 has been quite dependent on the system, including trade with the United States. Offensive realism simply has no way of explaining how great powers can trade for many years without going to war. Either such dependent states are highly irrational for decades on end—something that systemic realists in general would have to reject—or there is a flaw in offensive realist thinking.

The flaw in the logic of offensive realism, stated simply, is this: it fails to grant that there are any trade-offs in international politics, either in the pursuit of ends or the use of certain hard-line means.[7] Take the most obvious issue: leaders' concerns about relative gains and vulnerability. Offensive realists suggest that great powers avoid trading with each other because they might lose relative power through trade and because they might become more vulnerable to cutoff.[8] Yet these two implications of economic statecraft are almost always inherently at odds with one another. If state X and state Y are considering opening trade relations with one another, it may be clear to both that Y, the more needy power, will get a much bigger bump in its economy from trade than X. If both powers start at a hundred units of gross national product (GNP), for example, and Y gets twenty units of gain and X gets ten units of gain, state X is obviously suffering a relative loss if it goes ahead with trade. According to offensive realism, state X should have a good reason to avoid trade cooperation, while state Y should be pushing for it. Once we bring in the vulnerability question, however, the smart policy is much less apparent. If trade relations were to get established, in any subsequent cutoff, state Y would lose twenty units while state X would lose only ten units. Moreover, if state Y has become dependent on critical raw material imports from X and has retooled its economy based on these imports, it

---

[6]See, in particular, Mearsheimer 1992, 1994–95, 2001.

[7]For more on offensive realism's failure to account for trade-offs, see Glaser 2010; Lascurettes 2008; Copeland 2011a.

[8]Mearsheimer 1992, 1994–95, 2001; Grieco 1988; Mastanduno 1991. For critiques of the relative gains half of this dual thesis, see essays by Snidal, Powell, and Keohane in Baldwin 1993.

will likely suffer what realists call a large *cost of adjustment* after trade is severed (Waltz 1970, 1979). Moving from autarky to dependence on state X would not mean a simple reversion back to a hundred units of GNP should trade end. State Y might descend to ninety or eighty units of GNP, while state X might only fall to, say, ninety-five units.

In short, in any situation where the gains from commerce benefit one great power more than another, the state that is gaining relatively is almost always the one that is becoming relatively more vulnerable. And vulnerability in great power politics means that a state is more subject to coercive diplomacy (state X has "leverage" over state Y). Japanese leaders certainly understood this inherent trade-off when they contemplated economic engagement after 1870. Soviet leaders knew this when they considered establishing new trade ties with the United States after 1970. How are leaders of the needy state, our state Y, to decide what to do given this tension between grabbing the relative gains and incurring increased vulnerability? And how is the less dependent state, state X, to decide on whether to go ahead with trade cooperation when trade may help Y's relative power, but it will also give X greater ability to exploit Y's vulnerability in future bargaining situations? Offensive realism cannot answer these questions.

In the next chapter, I will show that there are many solid security-driven reasons for great powers to become dependent on one another. In short, we do not have to retreat to liberal welfare-maximization assumptions—the dominant assumptions of the modern international political economy field—to explain trade cooperation. Yet the relative gains/vulnerability trade-off is only one of many trade-offs that great powers must grapple with. An even more intense one is the trade-off that state X or Y faces between the desire to improve its power position as a hedge against future threats and the fear that an overly hard-line policy to build this position will hurt its reputation for reasonableness, leading other states to increase their military spending, form counteralliances, or most important for our purposes, impose economic restrictions to curb its growth. This is where trade expectations theory brings in the insights of defensive realism. Defensive realists found their analyses on the tragic reality of international security dilemmas. Security dilemmas exist when the efforts of a great power to improve its security situation tend to reduce the security of other great powers. Because the other states are now more suspicious about its intentions, they will respond with measures to uphold their own security positions. The initial state may find itself forced to move even more strongly in a hard-line direction, resulting in a spiraling cycle of hostility and mistrust that can eventually lead to war.[9]

[9] See, in particular, Jervis 1976, 1978, 1997; Herz 1950; G. Snyder 1984; Glaser 1994–95, 1997, 2010; Posen 1993; Snyder and Jervis 1999; Kydd 1997a, 1997b, 2005; Tang 2010; Booth and Wheeler 2008; Collins 1997; Brooks 1997. A third branch of modern

The reality of security dilemmas and the dangerous spirals that result from them give defensive realists a major tool to use against the spare model of offensive realism. Contrary to the predictions of offensive realism, states should be wary about jumping at opportunities to use military force to increase their net power or reduce their economic vulnerabilities if such actions pose a high risk of counterbalancing as well as war. Such opportunistic expansion will frequently be quite counterproductive, reducing rather than increasing a state's overall security by increasing the number of wars it faces and its chances of losing such wars. Yet defensive realists have focused exclusively on what might be called the *military-security dilemma*, neglecting a potentially equally powerful phenomenon, the *trade-security dilemma* (Copeland 1999–2000, 2003, 2011a). The military-security dilemma focuses on a state's effort to improve its security by increasing its arms spending, the number and quality of its alliances, and its territorial expanse or geopolitical positioning. Such actions, to be sure, can be highly frightening to other states, invoking counter-responses in kind.

The trade-security dilemma involves the implications of actions that states take to improve the certainty of future access to resources, investments, and markets over the long term. Great powers that become dependent on trade with other great power realms and the small independent states of the system certainly do worry about their vulnerability to cutoff, as offensive realists would assert. But typically the best way to deal with this vulnerability is not to go to war to absorb more territory into one's realm but rather to project one's naval and military power into the region of dependency. Such actions signal not only one's determination to protect one's economic access but also one's military ability to do so. Thus, great powers in history have almost invariably built up power projection capabilities in support of their growing commercial ties: the role of British and French navies and expeditionary forces after 1650; the Japanese navy after 1880 and especially after 1929; the German navy after 1895; the US navy and marines after 1890; and so forth.

Yet the very act of projecting power around the system, even if only to protect a state's commerce from unexpected threats, can also send another type of signal: that the state has an aggressive character that might lead it to use force against its supposed adversaries. This can frighten other great powers that also worry about their economic access to key

---

realism, neoclassical realism, also incorporates elements of the security dilemma. Its larger focus, however, is on how domestic politics works in conjunction with relative power to drive state behavior. For the sake of testing arguments on interdependence and war, neoclassical realists therefore can be seen as part of the liberal camp. For summaries and references, see Lobell, Ripsman, and Taliaferro 2009.

trading interests, not to mention their territorial security. Their responses can set off a trade-security spiral. If dependent state Y, for example, decides that it needs more power projection capability to deal with potential trade restrictions and cutoffs, this may cause the less dependent state, state X, to rethink the trade-off between relative gains and economic leverage. As state Y starts to look more threatening, X has less reason to accept Y's continued relative gain through trade. After all, this relative gain is only enhancing Y's ability to project power over the long term. As state X starts to introduce economic restrictions on its trade with dependent state Y, however, the latter has a reason to start to truly worry about its ability to access the raw materials, investments, and markets needed to sustain its economic growth. That is, as state Y's expectations of the future trade environment begin to fall, it has more incentive to switch to more hard-line policies to either deter X from going further or directly ensure that X's allies and the small states around X's sphere continue to trade freely with Y. Such variants on gunboat diplomacy may only exacerbate the problem, leading X to ramp up the restrictions, or even turn to complete trade embargoes to reduce Y's relative power or coerce it back to "reasonable" policies.

There is another, more straightforward way that a trade-security spiral can begin to manifest itself. If state X suddenly starts, for whatever reason, to increase economic restrictions against Y, then Y may feel the necessity to project more power into a region to ensure continued supplies and exports as well as compensate for the lost trade with X. This can then set off the action-reaction cycle discussed above: X will see Y as more hostile and more in need of containment, but further economic restrictions will only push Y more strongly into militarized behavior in order to avoid a decline in its position. This escalation process can continue to the point where X's restrictions are so severe that Y lashes out with war to avoid any additional loss in power.

In the following chapter, I will describe in more detail the conditions that set dangerous trade-security spirals into motion. For now, it is worth noting that there is a fundamental endogeneity at the heart of all great power politics that must be dealt with theoretically. State Y may undertake actions that lead state X to start to impose economic restrictions on Y, which then lead Y to even more "aggressive" actions that force X to cut Y off to an even greater extent. Endogeneity is often seen as a problem in international relations theory making since it means that the independent variables are not as "independent" as they are supposed to be: the actor that ends up launching a war may be getting itself into its own mess by what seem to be its own ill-advised policies.

The trade expectations approach seeks to turn what might seem to be a problem into an asset. I argue that it is precisely because leaders are aware of the possibility that their own behavior can lead to dangerous spiraling that they have reasons to sustain their current reputations for moderation through cautious territorial policies and continued trade. This defensive-realist point provides a simple but powerful explanation for why great powers frequently experience long periods without major strife and war. With this base in place, we can then pose one of the key puzzles of international politics: Why would great powers, notwithstanding their knowledge of the phenomenon of spiraling, decide to shift to more hard-line policies that can set their interstate relations on a new and more dangerous course? Expressed slightly differently, why do systems that have remained stable for sometimes decades suddenly deteriorate into crises and wars? This book will seek to answer this profound issue without relying on the simple trick of asserting that the executives in states X and Y have fallen prey to unit-level pathologies. In this way, we can see why a dependent state Y might decide to launch a war against a less dependent state X even when the executives of both states are rational actors just seeking to do what is best for each nation's respective security.

The puzzle of why states might fall into a trade-security spiral despite the known risks leads us to another critical question to be discussed in the next chapter: why states X and Y often have trouble negotiating a peace deal that both prefer to a dangerous crisis or war. After all, if state X's economic policies are causing dependent state Y to move to a war footing to ensure access to markets and raw materials, why does X not simply offer to moderate its policies in order to improve Y's trade expectations and hence reduce the chance of war? The bargaining model of war outlined by James Fearon and others argues that rational actors have an incentive to make agreements to avoid the mutual costs of war, thereby leaving each side better off than if war had to be fought. War can still happen, but only if actors lack information about the true balance of power and resolve or cannot trust the other to uphold its commitments within an agreement.[10]

In chapter 1, I show that the second part of the Fearon logic, the so-called commitment problem, is the primary roadblock to peace. In a variety of circumstances, state X will have good reason to doubt whether state Y is committed to long-term peace, while Y will have good reason to doubt X's true commitment to open trade and investments into the future. Chapter 1 will explore the conditions under which such doubts creep into a relationship, undermining the ability of X and Y to avoid a further spiraling of hostility and militarized conflict. When these conditions are largely exogenous to the executive leaders of X and Y—such things as

---

[10]See Fearon 1995, which also discusses the problem of issue indivisibility. See also Wagner 2000, 2007; Goemans 2000; Schultz 1999, 2001; Powell 1999, 2002, 2006; Reiter 2003.

the actions of third-party states, level of state Y's economic growth, and unwillingness of legislatures to accept executive-driven agreements—then it may be hard to find common ground between the two protagonists. A key thesis of the book, however, is that commitment problems are only likely to lead to crisis and war when economic concerns for the future make state Y's leaders believe that decline will be severe without a crisis or war. Commitment concerns, in short, are an important background condition for war within my argument. Yet the deeper problem of international politics lies with the exogenous factors that increase fears of decline by interfering with the flow of future commerce between great powers.

THE STRUCTURE OF THE BOOK AND THE ROAD AHEAD

The rest of the book will strive to elaborate and defend the assertions put forward in this brief introductory chapter. Chapter 1 is the theoretical foundation of the book. After briefly reviewing the current state of the field on the link between economic interdependence and war, I spend the bulk of the chapter elucidating the deductive logic of the trade expectations approach. Chapter 2 explores the degree to which an expectations approach can help us make sense of the seemingly contradictory findings of the large-N quantitative research that has dominated the study of interdependence and war over the last two decades. In its second half, chapter 2 lays out a new approach to qualitative historical analysis for rare events research—one that minimizes the problems of selection bias and generalizability by covering the essential universe of cases for a chosen period of time. I also discuss how qualitative research can help overcome the limitations of quantitative methods in the measuring of leader expectations about the future. Quantitative research is limited to rough proxy measures that might suggest what leaders are anticipating as they make their decisions. Only documentary evidence, however, can reveal what they were actually thinking as they took their nations into crises and wars, or sought to moderate diplomatic tensions to reduce the probability of war. We thus need to plunge into the evidence from the historical periods themselves. This is what chapters 3–8 do (with chapter 2 providing a brief summary of the overall findings). I show across a wide range of geographic and historical contexts after 1790 that the trade expectations argument strongly outperforms its two main challengers, liberalism and economic realism, in head-to-head empirical tests. The final chapter will summarize the theoretical and practical implications of the argument, including the relevance of the logic for the future of US-Chinese relations.

In the end, we will see that there are three general ways to connect economic interdependence to the likelihood of war. The first way includes all the theories that suggest wars are ultimately caused by domestic-level pressures and pathologies, even if trade can often operate to moderate the incentive states have to act on these unit-level forces. Traditional liberal arguments (including interest-group explanations) fall within this camp, as do some variants of neo-Marxism. The second way encompasses those theories that start with the offensive realist insight that states under anarchy have reason to worry about the vulnerability that comes with trade. This camp, which includes most neo-Marxists, sees interdependence not as a cause of peace but rather as a force that pushes leaders to use military might to reduce the uncertainty that comes with greater dependence. The third and final way is the trade expectations argument. Starting with the assumption of rational security-driven actors, it maintains that the effects of interdependence can cut either direction, depending on leaders' expectations of the trade environment that their states will face into the future.

There is an unexpected advantage to having our competing arguments fall naturally into these three camps. It allows the book to test essentially all the main theories that have been put forward on the causes of war over the last few decades, even as the book focuses primarily on testing the economically driven approaches within this broader literature.[11] The first camp, for instance, falls back on domestic variables to explain war and uses trade only to explain peace. It therefore begs the question of how frequently it is the case in world history that wars are actually driven by unit-level pressures and pathologies. The surprising answer of this book is: hardly ever. Across the broad sweep of cases discussed in this book, domestic factors sometimes played subsidiary causal roles as factors that reinforced or facilitated a leader's desire to get a war going, or that constrained a leader from initiating a desired conflict. But they were rarely the dominant propelling forces that pushed states into the initiation of great power wars or the crises that significantly increased the risk of such wars. To be sure, there are instances where unit-level pathologies stand out as an important contributing cause of conflict, most notably Nazi Germany in the 1930s and the Russian state up to the start of the Russo-Japanese War in 1904. Yet even here, as I will show, these pathologies existed alongside more geostrategic reasons for action, making it unclear just how necessary unit-level factors were to the eventual outbreak of war.

The wars and periods of struggle examined in this book, constituting the main cases since 1790, demonstrate that the vast majority of modern great power conflicts were started by largely rational security-seeking states worried about the future. Economic realism does a good job on a

---

[11] I do not have the space to cover all these various theories, but for references and summaries, see Levy and Thompson 2010; Cashman 2013.

certain number of these cases, including the Sino-Japanese War of 1894–95 as well as the struggles between Britain, France, and Russia over the Near East in the 1830s. But economic realism is ultimately limited by its assumption that the mere fact of dependence and vulnerability is enough to push a great power into war or militarized conflict. By supplementing the offensive realist insight regarding vulnerability with the notion that expectations of future commerce vary over time depending on the political relations of states, the trade expectations approach is able to explain a much larger percentage of the cases than economic realism on its own. It is the task of this book to demonstrate the theoretical and empirical power of this approach.

CHAPTER ONE

Theory of Economic Interdependence and War

THE INTRODUCTORY CHAPTER laid out the basic dimensions of the trade expectations approach and how it could be applied to the history of the modern great power system since 1790. This chapter constitutes a more in-depth look at both the existing literature on interdependence and war and the theory of trade expectations itself. My overall goal is a simple one: I hope to show the advantages of viewing the world through the lens of the trade expectations logic in order to demonstrate that it clears up most of the logical problems that have bedeviled current scholarship. In subsequent chapters, we can then see whether the new approach is actually confirmed by both large-N quantitative analysis and detailed historical case studies.

My main concern with the extant literature is not that it is wrong but rather that it is underspecified. By not examining the role of expectations of future trade and investment on the calculation of decision makers, the literature is trapped in deductive models that are static and backward looking. Existing scholarship almost invariably assumes that it is some factor existing in a snapshot of time—either in the present moment or in the recent past—that is driving leaders to do what they do. Leaders enjoy the past and current gains from trade, and are peaceful (traditional liberalism); they see their present vulnerability and they worry (economic realism); they underestimate the other's present resolve and they push too hard (signaling arguments); they have long-standing unit-level grievances and pathologies that get unleashed when trade levels fall (traditional liberalism again). Such are the basic causal orientations of the current theories on interdependence and war. My approach is fundamentally different. In a very real way, it does not matter in the least whether past and current levels of trade and investment have been low, as long as leaders have strongly positive expectations for the future. It is their future orientation and expectations of a future stream of benefits that will likely make the leaders incline to peace. Likewise, it does not matter whether past and current levels of commerce have been high if leaders believe they are going to be cut off tomorrow or in the near future. It is their pessimism about the future that will probably drive these leaders to consider hard-line measures and even war to safeguard the long-term security of the state.

What this chapter is asking for, in short, is a basic reorientation of the thinking about interdependence and war away from theories of comparative statics and toward dynamic theories that incorporate the future within their core deductive logics.[1] It is only by capturing how leaders really think, something that necessarily involves estimates and assessments of future possibilities and probabilities, that we can build causal theories that actually work in the real world. As we will see, existing scholarship either completely ignores the impact of future variables in constructing their deductive theories or it makes implicit, fixed assumptions about how the future will unfold. Liberal arguments about trade, for example, almost invariably assume that the economic cooperation that is going on today will continue to flourish into the future as long as both sides have an incentive to punish defections, simply because rational actors will see that the absolute benefits of working together (the "mutual cooperation" or CC box of basic game theory) are greater than the benefits of trade conflict (the "mutual defection" or DD box). Realist arguments, on the other hand, assume that dependent great powers know that others will eventually cut them from access to vital goods and markets, given the incentives in anarchic systems to play the game of great power politics hard.

These assumptions are simply indefensible stipulations about the future that have no place in a properly specified dynamic theory. Such a dynamic theory would recognize both the deductive and empirical point that leaders' level of optimism or pessimism regarding the future will vary greatly over time, depending on a whole host of more ultimate causal factors. It is then the task of good theory to specify what kind of factors are likely to play important roles in shaping estimates of the future, and how these factors are logically likely to act—either alone or in concert—to drive leaders' beliefs about the future security of their states. If this is done properly, we should be able to understand how great powers in

[1] The field of macroeconomics has made such a shift in thinking with the advent of rational expectations theory and the related efficient markets hypothesis (for a summary and references, see Sheffrin 1996). While this literature, like my argument, posits that individuals are rational calculators of future developments and do not make systematic errors in forecasting, in rational expectations theory this assumption applies only for the *average* individual across thousands or often millions of actors. The expectations theory developed in this book, since it seeks to explain the actions of particular leaders rather than aggregated macroeconomic phenomena, starts with the bolder assumption that each individual leader in question is a rational forward-looking estimator of future trends. Given the complexity of international relations and the uncertainty this engenders, officials within a polity may reasonably disagree about the exact future values of certain parameters (e.g., the other state's level of commitment to open trade over the next ten years). But these officials are not offering systematically biased estimates based on ideological or personal distortions or domestic pressures from below. Such assumptions can be later relaxed after the theory's logic is established in order to see the effects of such unit-level phenomena on real-world events.

the real world will react when the boundary conditions and parameters of their existential situations change without notice or without their full control. And if, when we open up the documents, we see great powers actually planning and reacting within historical cases as the theory anticipates that they will do, then we know we are on to something.

The task for the rest of this chapter is thus to provide this theoretical foundation for subsequent empirical analysis. I begin with a brief overview and critique of the current state of the literature. I also discuss the tricky question of why great powers would ever trade in the first place if they are driven primarily by security fears. This will set the stage for a more detailed explication of trade expectations theory. This process will take up most of the rest of the chapter. At the end of the chapter, I offer a quick review of how to test competing theories and a summary of my overall approach, drawing from an explanatory diagram that the reader may want to refer to as the chapter proceeds (figure 1.1). A discussion of my research method along with the value of quantitative approaches for the study of interdependence and conflict will be reserved until chapter 2.

Overview of Existing Theories

The theories of international relations that explore the relationship between economic interdependence and war can be grouped according to three broad categories: liberalism, realism, and neo-Marxism. Many scholars might immediately contend that we should be moving beyond broad paradigmatic isms to focus on specific causal arguments, and I agree.[2] In what follows, therefore, I will examine the specific causal claims that theorists make about how interdependence shapes the likelihood of war in world politics. Yet the broad labels of liberalism, realism, and neo-Marxism can still prove useful in grouping together theories that share a broad set of assumptions and assertions about what actors want from their policies (their ends), which individuals or domestic groups are most influential in driving policy (who matters), and the overall functional roles that trade and investment ties play in the onset of peace or war.

Liberal theories as a whole start with the assumption that actors, regardless of the level of analysis, are interested primarily in achieving material benefits for themselves. In short, actors seek to maximize utility defined in terms of the net material gains from peaceful commerce or war. The foundational model of liberalism, in this regard, is the "opportunity cost" model of trade and war. It begins with the premise that the

---

[2]The argument against isms, having floated through the field for more than a decade, is nicely summarized in Lake 2011.

state is a unitary, rational actor seeking to maximize the overall welfare of the nation as a whole. Trade provides valuable benefits, or gains from trade, to any particular state, as economic theory since the time of Adam Smith and David Ricardo has recognized. Any state that is dependent on trade should therefore seek to avoid war, since peaceful trading gives it all the benefits of close ties without any of the costs and risks associated with military conflict. In other words, the opportunity costs of waging war are high when trade levels are high, and this serves to restrain actors who might otherwise have an incentive for war.[3] This straightforward logic supplied the foundation for the first wave of statistical correlational analyses in the field—studies that generally found that the higher a state's trade level was relative to its GNP, the more peaceful its relations were with other states.[4]

Subsequent liberal theorists have expressed their dissatisfaction with the presumption that the state is a unitary actor, arguing that one cannot understand the causal processes underpinning the large-N finding that trade usually leads to peace without disaggregating the nation-state itself. Hence, over the last decade a number of scholars have opened up the black box of the state to explore exactly how a liberal commercial peace could arise, and what that might mean regarding the conditions for peace overall. Beth Simmons (2003), for instance, suggests that we examine how interdependence creates groups within polities that have a vested interest in maintaining the status quo. Jonathan Kirshner (2007) asserts that open international financial flows makes bankers into a particular

---

[3] This reasoning, which can be traced back to Baron Montesquieu and Richard Cobden, was first fully developed by Norman Angell (1933, especially 46, 59–60, 87–89, 103–5) just prior to the First World War. Richard Rosecrance (1986, 13–14, 24–25) provides the inspiration for recent liberal versions of this thesis, contending that modern conditions push states to be "trading states" versus "territorial states" obsessed with military expansion. There is no incentive, in his view, to wage war in highly interdependent systems, since "trading states recognize that they can do better through [trade] . . . than by trying to conquer and assimilate large tracts of land." For recent discussions and extensions of the opportunity cost logic, see Mansfield 1994; McMillan 1997; Mansfield and Pollins 2001; Owen 2012; Stein 1993; Crescenzi 2005; essays by Jack Levy, Beth Simmons, Erik Gartzke, and James Morrow in Mansfield and Pollins 2003. For an argument emphasizing the impact of the changing nature of global production on the costs of military expansion, see Brooks 2005. On the relation between commercial liberalism and other forms of liberalism, see Moravcsik 1997; Keohane 1990. Constructivists have largely ignored the question of trade and war. Alexander Wendt (1999, 344–49), however, offers a link between liberal arguments and constructivist concerns. Interdependence, acting as a "master variable," can get cooperation going for material, self-interested reasons. Over time, Wendt suggests, this cooperation can foster changes in identity and value systems that help sustain the emerging peace.

[4] See especially Polachek 1980, 1992; Gasiorowski and Polachek 1982; Gasiorowski 1986; Oneal and Russett 1997, 1999, 2001; Oneal, Oneal, Maoz, and Russett 1996.

influential vested interest group, with bankers almost invariably wanting peace instead of war.[5]

Patrick McDonald (2007, 2009) has provided the most developed argument for the importance of domestic vested interests. He seeks to show that it is only a specific type of trading state that tends to have lower rates of militarized conflict—namely, the liberal capitalist one. McDonald maintains that capitalist states that operate through liberal economic institutions such as private property and competitive market structures are generally less aggressive. Exporters that have a vested interest in keeping peaceful trade going will operate as a powerful domestic group, exerting a strong check on any illiberal policy elites that happen to be running the state. Conversely, in more mercantilist states that do not respect private property or open trade, illiberal leaders with possibly aggressive intentions will have more autonomy to do nasty things, both because the export class is smaller and because higher tariffs supply them with more revenue to fund war.[6]

Both the initial liberal argument and its subsequent domestic-level offshoots revolve around the idea that trade provides high material benefits to certain groups of people—either the society as a whole or particular vested interests—and war therefore is avoided because of its high opportunity costs, namely, the loss of these benefits. Recently, formal modelers have sought to go after the opportunity cost logic while still upholding the overall liberal insight that high interdependence should tend to move the system toward peace. The essence of their critique is clear-cut. In any situation of asymmetrical interdependence, the high opportunity costs of war should give the more dependent state, state Y, a big reason to avoid war. But the less dependent state, state X, knowing Y's desire to avoid war, has an incentive to coerce it into making concessions through the use of military threats. Whether interdependence will lead to less militarized conflict or in fact more is thus indeterminate when we consider the opportunity cost reasoning on its own. The modelers agree that state Y will be more peaceful. State X, however, will

---

[5] Arguments based on vested interests can be traced back to the work of Ruth Arad, Seev Hirsch, and Alfred Tovias (1983; see also Domke 1988). For the effects of globalization on domestic factions and regional grand strategies, see Solingen 1998.

[6] Erik Gartzke (2007) supports the thesis tying capitalism to peace, although he offers a less straightforward causal argument for why such a result should obtain. Gartzke suggests that capitalist states tend to be more developed, meaning their firms must emphasize peaceful production over territorial control. Such states also have groups that share similar across-border interests and are able to help leaders send costly signals of resolve (more on the latter below). For a recent debate on the capitalist peace, see McDonald 2010; Gartzke and Hewett 2010; Russett 2010; Mueller 2010.

likely be more aggressive, precisely because of Y's unwillingness to risk the current benefits of peace.[7]

In place of the opportunity cost logic, these critics offer another deductive reason for the liberal prediction that trade should be associated with peace. Drawing on insights from the bargaining model of war, they contend that wars are generally the result of the private information that actors have about the resolve of other states—that is, their willingness to pay the costs of war.[8] High interdependence helps to foster peace by increasing the number of tools that states have in their toolbox for sending "costly signals" of their true resolve. Leaders of states that are dependent on trade and investment flows can deliberately impose sanctions that hurt their own people, thereby signaling that their nations are willing to suffer high costs to achieve their objectives. This should eliminate any underestimations of their resolve. In an environment of strong commercial ties, therefore, aggressive opportunists in the system will know not to push too hard, lowering the risk of an inadvertent spiraling into war.[9]

The economic realist argument seeks to turn the liberal perspective on its head. All the arguments we have seen so far can be classified as liberal since, in whatever their form, they begin with the assumption that interdependent actors are interested in maximizing their net material gains/utility and will have good absolute gains reasons not to fight when interdependence is high. Realists reject this starting point. In anarchy, realists assert, leaders must be primarily concerned with maximizing the security of the states for which they are responsible (Grieco 1988; Mearsheimer 1994–95). Given this, interdependence will only *increase* the chances of militarized conflict and war as interdependent states scramble to reduce the vulnerability that dependency brings. States concerned about security will dislike dependence, since it means not only that access to valuable export markets and foreign investments might be reduced by adversaries bent on hurting their relative power positions but also that crucial imported goods such as oil and raw materials could be cut off should relations turn sour.

Such uncertainty about their economic situations, realists assert, will push great powers to war or the use of military coercion to lower their dependency as well as to ensure the continued flow of trade and investment. As Kenneth Waltz (1979, 106) puts it, while actors in domestic politics have little reason to fear specialization, the anarchic structure

[7] See Morrow 1999, 2003; Gartzke 2003, 2007; Gartzke, Li, and Boehmer 2001; Stein 2003. For an alternative view linking trade, information, and peace, see Reed 2003.

[8] See, for example, Fearon 1995; Wagner 2000; Goemans 2000; Schultz 1999, 2001; Reiter 2003.

[9] Morrow 1999, 2003; Stein 2003; Gartzke, Li, and Boehmer 2001; Gartzke and Li 2003 (Morrow and Stein emphasize more the trade side of the equation, while Gartzke and his colleagues focus on financial flows).

of international politics forces states to worry about vulnerability, compelling them "to control what they depend on or to lessen the extent of their dependency." It is this "simple thought" that explains "their imperial thrusts to widen the scope of their control." John Mearsheimer (1992, 223) observes that states requiring vital goods, fearing cut off, will seek "to expand political control to the source of supply, giving rise to conflict with the source or with its other customers."[10] The Waltz and Mearsheimer thesis is founded on the assumption, most often associated with offensive realism, that states in anarchy must assume the worst case about the present and future intentions of the other. As such, when states find themselves in situations of dependence, they are forced to grab opportunities to reduce their vulnerability through war, at least when the chance to do so arises at low cost.[11]

The final group of arguments involves the neo-Marxist theories that link growing interdependence to war. Vladimir Lenin ([1917] 1996) has famously declared that capitalist trading states are more likely to engage in war against peripheral states in order to find cheap raw materials, export markets for their mass-produced goods, and places to invest surplus capital. The competition between capitalist great powers resulting from this struggle for colonial empires will eventually lead to war in the core system.[12] Most post-1945 neo-Marxists scholars of imperialism have adopted this reasoning in one form or another.[13] At its core, the neo-Marxist logic challenges the liberal domestic-level claim that capitalist sectors and firms dependent on the global economic system have a vested interest in peace. While agreeing with liberalism that such groups are driven primarily by the material gains from commerce, neo-Marxists contend (implicitly borrowing from realism) that the need for secure trade and investment ties makes these groups worry about their future control over their economic partners. Hence, powerful capitalist groups within the state will put pressure on political elites to project military forces into

[10]For a realist-based argument focusing on how population growth and accelerating resource consumption increase pressures to expand, see Chouchri and North 1975.

[11]For an argument that states only use force when the benefits of action are greater than the costs, see Mearsheimer 2001, 37. Many realists, of course, would contend that when push comes to shove, commercial factors are much less salient than straight power variables, or at least that the concerns of some realists regarding the protection of access to vital goods and markets are overdrawn (see Buzan 1984; Gholz and Press 2001, 2010). Because of this divide within realism, I will continue to use the term economic realism to refer specifically to the camp of realists that believes dependence on vital goods and markets is indeed an important source of conflict in the international system.

[12]When Lenin's famous book is summarized, scholars often emphasize only the J. A. Hobson (1902) aspect of Lenin's argument—namely, that capitalist states seek places to invest their excess financial capital. Lenin, however, noted all three aspects mentioned above as self-reinforcing causes of military expansion.

[13]For comprehensive summaries, see Cohen 1973.

important regions, and use direct occupation or neocolonial coercion to ensure continued trade and investment flows.[14]

Despite the realist flavor of the neo-Marxist approach, it does differ significantly from economic realism and the theory that I will put forward below. Neo-Marxists see economic elites and interest groups pressuring political elites into war to further their narrow material concerns. Economic realism and trade expectations theory, on the other hand, maintain that political elites are autonomous actors who choose policies based on what is good for the security of the whole state, not based on the greedy interests of a few.[15] This distinction in causal logic must be kept in mind when we look at the historical cases, given that neo-Marxism, realism, and trade expectations theory all expect that commerce will lead to war under certain conditions. Because the correlational prediction is frequently the same, the only way to test the superiority of one explanation over the other is to examine whether the specific causal claims of the theories were confirmed by the evidence.

COMMENTS ON THE MAIN THEORIES

The theories we have seen so far are, for the most part, deductively sound. They put forward causal logics that on the face of it sound plausible and could indeed play themselves out in the real world. It seems self-evidently

---

[14]Kevin Narizny, while not dealing directly with the question of interdependence and war, does offer a variant of the neo-Marxist logic that has relevance here. Narizny argues that different economic sectors within a society will have differing preferences toward aggressive or peaceful grand strategies, depending on the benefits or costs that the sectors are experiencing as a result of global economic engagement. He aligns with Lenin by suggesting that those sectors with strong ties to the periphery will generally have quite imperialist or interventionist sentiments. But he also holds, contrary to Lenin, that those economic groups with ties to the core powers are most likely to be peaceful internationalists (largely for liberal opportunity cost reasons). See Narizny 2007, especially 16–30. Because Narizny's argument, with its focus on the politics of interest aggregation, is designed to apply mainly to advanced democracies (specifically the United States and Britain), I will only occasionally have the chance to test his claims in the post-1790 cases that I study.

[15]My thinking here draws from Krasner (1978), who refers to the above characterization of neo-Marxism as the "instrumental Marxist" approach to foreign policy. He notes that there is also a structural Marxist logic that while assuming that state policies are still designed to help the parochial interests of the few, posits that political elites are autonomous and indeed can act against the short-term desires of firms for the long-term good of capitalism. As Krasner observes, it is difficult to test realist theories against structural Marxist ones, given that both agree that political elites do not bow to domestic pressure, and given that structural Marxists may describe what looks like policies for the good of national security as policies for the good of capitalism. Because of this empirical problem, I will largely ignore the structural Marxism in my historical work, concentrating instead on the value of instrumental Marxism relative to its competitors.

true, for example, that actors that are receiving high benefits from staying at peace will want to avoid war, whether those actors are states as a whole or individual interest groups. Yet it also seems clear that actors that feel vulnerable to the loss of those benefits and the potential impact of large adjustment costs will want to project military power against the source of vulnerability. Both liberals and realists have a point. They just have not specified the conditions under which they might be right. The theory of trade expectations outlined below will help to resolve this problem.

The fact that liberals and realists are both on to something was demonstrated by the very divide that existed in the large-N quantitative scholarship by the end of the 1990s. On the one side, serving as standard-bearers for the liberal cause, were Bruce Russett and John Oneal, two scholars who seemed to show through a number of publications that trade dependence is on average strongly correlated with more peaceful behavior.[16] On the other side, in support of realism, Katherine Barbieri (1996, 2002) revealed that when the data from the late nineteenth and early twentieth centuries are included in the large-N analysis, and when different specifications of the key independent variable (trade dependence) are used, interdependence more often than not has led to more conflict and war, not less. This liberal-realist divide puzzled scholars for a few years, until the obvious conclusion began to emerge: interdependence can lead to both peace and war. Because the work of Russett and Oneal as well as Barbieri considered only general patterns and averages across thousands of data points, their analyses, through the use of different time frames and variable specifications, were inadvertently picking up the fact that interdependence, depending on the conditions, can push states to either moderate their behavior or take more aggressive actions.

Over the last decade, this fact has led to a veritable cottage industry of new and more complex large-N analyses, with most of them seeking the holy grail of that extra condition or set of conditions that determine whether interstate commerce is peace inducing or war inducing. Much of this work, as I discuss in chapter 2, has been extremely useful to the field as a whole, and has in the process challenged many of our cherished beliefs about the role of other noneconomic variables. The work of Patrick McDonald (2004, 2007, 2009, 2010) and Erik Gartzke (2007; Gartzke and Hewett 2010), for instance, has demonstrated that trade and investments between nations usually only have a dampening effect on war when those nations are advanced capitalist states. Michael Mousseau (2000, 2003, 2009) and Havard Hegre (2000) have reinforced this finding from another angle, suggesting that it is the overall level of economic

---

[16] See Oneal and Russett 1997, 1999, 2001; Oneal, Oneal, Maoz, and Russett 1996; Oneal, Russett, and Davis 1998; Oneal, Russett, and Berbaum 2003.

development that makes commerce peace inducing. Christopher Gelpi and Joseph Grieco (2003a, 2003b) have argued that trade's effects are conditioned on the existence of regime type: democracies with high trade are more peaceful, but autocracies are often made more aggressive by trade. Edward Mansfield and Jon Pevehouse (2001) have indicated that trade's restraining effect on war is conditioned on the existence of regional trade pacts and institutions.[17]

The statistical work supporting these new findings is solid. Yet as I discuss further in chapter 2, the theoretical arguments used to explain the correlational findings are still underdeveloped and, in the absence of case studies, largely speculative. In short, we still do not know *why* these correlational results obtain when well-designed statistical studies such as these are undertaken. This chapter will provide this theoretical explanation, and chapters 3–8 will show its veracity through detailed case studies.

Before turning to the trade expectations argument, however, I need to say a word about the two other broad approaches—the signaling argument and neo-Marxism. Unlike the liberal opportunity cost logic and realist vulnerability argument, the deductive logics of both approaches suffer from internal tensions that make them unlikely to have much causal force in the real world. The signaling argument begins with the idea that the more dependent actor, state Y, will be pushed around by the less dependent actor, state X, given that X knows that Y does not want to give up the valuable benefits of peace. Yet the argument then goes on to suggest that because of its high dependence, Y has more tools to use in its effort to make costly signals of its resolve. These two elements work at cross-purposes. State Y may be more flexible in its ability to show its resolve. But it is also less likely to be resolved in the first place, given its fear that a war would end the trade benefits that it currently receives. The net result is a wash: we cannot know ahead of time which of these effects will prevail, even if the reasoning is right about the way interdependence helps the signaling process.[18]

---

[17] See also Mansfield, Pevehouse, and Bearce 1999–2000. Other additional variables that condition the trading peace included the types of goods traded (Reuveny and Li 2009; Dorussen 2006), the geographic distance of the trading partners (Robst, Polachek, and Chang 2007), and the availability of alternative trading partners (Crescenzi 2005).

[18] Note that the signaling argument assumes that within a crisis, when Y's leaders knowingly cause economic harm to their own state, leaders in X will always see this as a signal of Y's true willingness to escalate the crisis to actual military conflict. This is a problematic assumption. A citizenry's willingness to absorb some loss in material welfare (lower standard of living, loss of jobs, etc.) should say little about its desire to risk lives in a war. Indeed, economic sanctions in the absence of military mobilization might show a distinct lack of willingness to go further, as German and Italian views of British and French sanctions in the

Neo-Marxism also contains a tension that should limit its applicability. As David Landes (1961) noted half a century ago, the neo-Marxist logic for how capitalism leads to actual imperialist aggression (as opposed to, say, mere gunboat diplomacy) requires three things to be true. First, the business class must be united as a group, or at least have one part of it that is cohesive enough to act as a unit. Second, this class or subgroup within the capitalist economic elite must agree that military aggression against other states is in fact the best means to further its economic ends. Third, the business class or a subgroup within it must have a great deal of influence over the political elites—enough to be able to push these elites to choose war even when the action will cost the lives of thousands or perhaps millions of the nation's citizens.

Each of these elements is a necessary condition for the neo-Marxist argument to have sway. If any one of them does not hold, the argument should fail to have causal force. And there are reasons to doubt that they will indeed hold. There are few groups other than broad umbrella organizations (for example, the national chambers of commerce) that can bring firms with diverse interests together. Much more likely is the fragmentation of firms into lobbying groups representing particular sectors, such as mining, oil, and manufacturing. Such diverse interests will be unlikely to agree on even a broad policy for tariff reform or infrastructural subsidies, let alone for a policy of war.[19] Moreover, the neo-Marxist logic requires us to assume that elected leaders within capitalist democracies will risk the lives of the population—and thus their own chances for reelection—just to satisfy the needs of an especially energized sector of the economy. Such an assumption might work for small-scale actions, such as low-level US interventions during the Cold War (Guatemala 1954, Panama 1989, etc.).[20] This book, however, is about wars between great powers or the crises that increase the chance of such wars. And here the costs and risks to the nation are high enough to make almost any politician pull back from the initiation of any war designed solely to protect the parochial material interests of a few. We will see in my empirical chapters that

---

1930s indicate. Gartzke's (2007; Gartzke, Li, and Boehner 2001) assertion that the flight of investors from financial markets sends a signal of resolve is particularly problematic. Investors in state Y are fleeing markets because they fear economic loss. If they haven't the courage to stay the course in the realm of mere material well-being, why should state X's leaders believe they will pay the blood price of actual warfare?

[19]Neo-Marxists must assume that when different capitalist groups work at cross-purposes, the prowar faction will be particularly powerful or influential. There is no basis for making such an assumption a priori.

[20]Small-scale interventions are of course neo-Marxism's best cases, but as Krasner (1978) shows, even here the national security logic of realism is usually driving the process.

except in a few cases, neo-Marxism provides us with little insight into the causes of great power conflicts.

TRADE EXPECTATIONS THEORY

The trade expectations approach, as I have noted, is designed to resolve the fundamental tension between liberalism and realism, and in doing so, offer a causal logic that not only explains the correlational results of recent large-N analyses but also a vast amount of modern diplomatic history at the same time. It gains its leverage through the introduction of an additional variable—a dependent actor's expectations of the future trade and investment environment—that determines when high dependence will push states toward either relatively peaceful behavior or hard-line policies and war.[21] The introductory chapter laid out the core argument and some of its more important dimensions. My goal here is to show exactly how the argument works and add conceptual depth to the main deductive logic.

The trade expectations argument accepts the liberal point that trade and investment flows can lead to peace by giving states an incentive to avoid militarized conflicts and war. Yet at its foundation, as I stressed earlier, the theory is fundamentally realist rather than liberal. It starts with the assumption that leaders of states whose behavior we are trying to explain are primarily concerned with protecting the long-term security of their countries and that they operate in a realm of essential domestic autonomy. It then asks how any dependent state Y will be predicted to act given changes in the external conditions of its existential situation. The dependent state's policies, as it seeks to maximize its security, will shift only in response to these external conditions. All unit-level variables within Y that might have salience for liberal and neo-Marxist scholars— including welfare- or profit-maximization drives, pressure group politics, and desires for reelection—are assumed to have no influence whatsoever on state Y's decision making or behavior.[22]

---

[21] The argument is designed to cover both trade and investment flows between great powers, even though, for simplicity's sake, I call it trade expectations theory. Yet because investments abroad are also a form of trade—state Y's investors provide capital to state X or W in exchange for the promise of future interest payments or branch-plant profits—the trade label does capture the larger concept in question, which is the existence of commercial transactions between nations.

[22] More specifically, as in an earlier work, I treat assumptions as potential causal factors that could vary, but that are set and held constant at certain values in order to establish a consistent deductive logic. For the full list of the assumptions I am adopting here, see Copeland 2000b, 29–31. These assumptions include states as rational unitary actors that

   Such a theoretical starting point is designed to keep the deductive logic "pure." That is, it allows us to see how dependent states will operate in response to conditions even when they only want to survive the rough-and-tumble of anarchic great power politics. When it comes to actual cases, of course, the leadership of any particular state Y that we are interested in explaining will have many competing forces working on it, including the factors outlined by liberals and neo-Marxists. By assuming state Y is driven only by rational security maximization, however, we allow a direct test of trade expectations theory's value versus its competitors: if it has explanatory and predictive power, we should see liberal and neo-Marxist variables having less causal salience in history than those outlined by the new approach. Balanced documentary analysis will undoubtedly reveal that domestic variables within Y sometimes had causal importance in explaining shifts to hard-line behavior across the historical cases. But if factors external to Y usually drove its behavior, and domestic variables are shown to be only occasionally determinative, then the advantage of building deductive theories with an assumption of rational security maximization is demonstrated.[23]

Political Economy Preliminaries

Before I turn to a detailed analysis of the argument, one question must be addressed up front. If this is a theory of great power politics, shouldn't we expect that great powers will rarely trade heavily with other great powers or their spheres, and hence that interdependence will fall out as a crucial variable? Neorealists often make the argument that while interdependence is more likely to lead to war than to peace, it is usually not as

---

are cost and risk neutral; states that are geographically equidistant from one another and operate in a neutral offense-defense environment; and states that egoistically pursue only security maximization.

[23]I nevertheless should stress that the trade expectations argument does not dismiss the potential impact of unit-level variables within *other* states on state Y's expectations of trade and thus its likely behavior. Less dependent states X and Z, for domestic reasons, might restrict trade with dependent state Y at time t, causing Y at time t + 1 to adopt more aggressive policies to protect its economic access, thereby starting a spiral of hostility that leads Y to initiate a preventive war by time t + 5 or t + 10. Domestic politics again may "matter" as part of a full historical explanation. Yet from the point of view of the state whose behavior we are trying to explain—the increasing aggressiveness of state Y—it is still state Y's understanding of its external environment that is driving its increasingly hard-line policies. State Y is still a rational security-maximizing actor in the pure realist sense, even if it sometimes must take into account the domestic patterns and pathologies of other states as it acts to ensure its long-term survival as a great power. For more on this, see the discussion of exogenous factors near the end of this chapter.

salient a variable as relative power precisely because great powers have clear reasons not to trade with one another in the first place. This claim is founded on the dual logic that great powers have both relative gains concerns and a fear of vulnerability: they worry not only that they will lose relatively through trade cooperation but also that trade dependence, especially on vital goods such as oil and raw materials, will make them subject to cutoffs and coercive diplomacy down the road.[24] As we saw in the introductory chapter, by the way trade works, these two points are almost always at odds with one another. If state Y is getting a large relative gain from trading with state X, then it is also giving X more bargaining leverage in the future, considering that Y has a greater relative need for the continuation of trade and will be more hurt than X by any severing of economic relations. Neorealists are mute regarding how great powers deal with this inherent tension or trade-off. The relatively gaining state is also the most vulnerable one in the relationship. Should Y reject trade cooperation to minimize vulnerability, even though it means giving up the relative gain? Should X reject cooperation because it helps Y grow in relative power, even though it means forgoing a chance to "leverage" Y's vulnerability for its foreign policy ends?

The fact that such a tension exists helps explain an empirical reality that should make us automatically question the neorealist understanding of international political economy: that great powers in history do indeed trade with each other, and often at high levels. For the fifty years before World War I, for example, the great powers of Europe were regularly each other's best trading and investment partners, even when they were adversaries on the foreign policy front. Germany traded heavily with Britain, Russia, and even France, and Britain continued strong economic relations with France and Russia after 1860 despite their ongoing colonial struggles in Africa and Asia. Inter-European trade rebounded in the 1920s, and it was only after 1930 that European states retreated into more autarkic realms of imperial preference.[25] To be sure, the United States and Soviet Union did think more in neorealist terms during the first two decades of the Cold War, and trade was low between them. Yet as I show in chapter 6, this did not mean that the leaders of the two superpowers were unwilling to discuss much more active economic relations. These conversations even included the possibility of US government funding of Soviet purchases of American goods—surely the ultimate form of relative loss, since

---

[24] On the relative gains argument, see especially Grieco 1988, 1993; Mearsheimer 1994–95, 2001 (for critiques, see essays by Snidal, Powell, Milner, and Keohane in Baldwin 1993). For the point regarding vulnerability, see Buzan 1984; Mearsheimer 1992, 1994–95.

[25] For detailed trade statistics from 1860 to 1945, see *EHS*.

the less dependent state is essentially giving away its goods in the short term and receiving back only its own loaned money.

So if the neorealist view of international political economy is shot through with deductive tensions and empirical contradictions, how can we explain why great powers come to depend on each other and yet hold to the realist theoretical foundation at the heart of this study? The answer is surprisingly straightforward, and one that was traced in its outlines three to four decades ago by such realist scholars as Robert Gilpin and Klaus Knorr. Leaders of great powers understand that to sustain a strong level of military power, a state must have a vibrant and growing economy. Most important, leaders know that if other countries are industrializing and improving their technological sophistication, then they must do so too. Yet at the heart of advanced economies are three critical, unavoidable realities or, one might say, principles that push great powers to trade: economies of scale, diminishing marginal returns, and the proliferation of raw material inputs.

When economies of scale are present, as they almost always are with large industrial enterprises, it is necessary—if only to compete effectively with other firms and nations—to invest in large factories and enterprises that can reduce the per unit cost of production. Yet in building such phenomenal productive capability, firms require huge markets for their goods to make a profit, given the large fixed costs of modern industrial operations ("overhead"). Political elites understand this. Hence, it is in the larger interest of the nation to help its best and more efficient producers to find foreign markets for the country's goods. Because other great powers are necessarily wealthier than less developed states, they have a lot of purchasing power. It makes good economic sense, then—and indeed it is critical to sustaining an advanced economic base—to allow trade to occur with other great powers and not just with small peripheral states. For a leader to deny opportunities to trade with other great powers, especially in multipolar environments of many large states, would be to allow those states that *do* decide to trade to capture the economies of scale and outperform one's state over the long term.[26]

As advanced economies grow, however, there is also a good chance that they will start to experience diminishing marginal returns if they fail to trade extensively. Diminishing returns set in when firms try to expand

---

[26] My thinking here, as many readers will note, is heavily shaped by the work of Gilpin (1975, 1977, 1981, 1987). See also Knorr 1973, 1975; Davis and North 1971; North and Thomas 1973. The reason why this argument is likely to hold in multipolar environments is straightforward. In such situations, Y cannot afford to allow X and Z to trade and make absolute gains, since this would mean Y's relative loss to both states. State Y therefore has a strong incentive to get into the trading game. Yet this in turn will force V and W to trade with X, Y, and Z to avoid being left behind. See Keohane 1993; Schweller 1996; Liberman 1996b. For an argument that alliance commitments in multipolarity help great powers overcome their reluctance to trade, see Gowa 1989, 1994; Gowa and Mansfield 1993.

one element or input into the production mix without increasing all the other elements/inputs simultaneously. With industrialized great powers, the problem is usually with the "land" side of the land, labor, and capital mix: if the country does not have open access to large quantities of the raw materials that go into mass production, then adding more capital (machines) and labor (number of workers and managers) will add to production levels, but at falling marginal rates. Unless there is a techno-logical innovation that helps the country use fewer materials per product or synthesize the needed resources at low cost, the state's economy as a whole will start to experience the latter part of the famous S-curve— perhaps still expanding in absolute terms, but at increasingly slower rates of growth.[27] Since great power politics is a competitive game, this means that states that are indeed able to bring in vast quantities of resource inputs from abroad will gain relative to those that are trying to remain largely autarkic. The needs of survival in an anarchic world will thus push great powers to trade with whomever or whatever can provide them with cheap raw materials. To be sure, colonies and the small states within one's sphere can sometimes play this role. Yet given the simple fact that raw materials are not evenly distributed around the world but rather con-centrated in certain geographic areas, great powers will often by necessity have to trade with other great powers.

It is not just the reality that basic resources are frequently cheaper and in greater supply abroad that forces great powers to trade with other such powers. It is also that as economies increase in sophistication, the types of raw material inputs increase in variety. Consider, for example, the shift to the mass production of cars and airplanes after 1910 and especially after 1920. Even if political leaders only had been concerned about these items for civilian and not military use, they would have had to worry about the ongoing supply of such diverse inputs as nickel, man-ganese, aluminum, iron ore, and rubber just to get the manufactured goods out of the factory. Then of course there was the massive demand for oil to keep the factories running. Yet the greater the variety of inputs, the more likely it is that their natural source will be found outside the home territory of the great power. Moreover, as the economy grows, the more it will use up any internal sources, forcing the nation to go abroad for its vital goods.[28] Neorealists may allege that the system forces great powers to rely on themselves, to remain relatively autarkic (Waltz 1979). Nevertheless, as we can see, the very pressures to maintain a fast-growing

[27] See Gilpin 1981.

[28] Gilpin 1977, 1981; Chouchri and North 1975; Hirschman (1945) 1980. Indeed, mer-cantilist thinkers since the mid-seventeenth century have recognized that it is usually good to import raw materials from other great powers, since one uses up the other's resources first and minimizes the depletion of one's own. See Heckscher 1933.

and economically advanced economy will typically have the exact opposite effect, forcing great powers to reject autarky and instead favor economic ties with a vast number of suppliers, including other great powers. Thus we can understand why Germany would depend on France for a large percentage of its imported iron ore before 1914, or Japan would accept the United States as its main supplier of oil from 1920 to 1940.

The above economic realities suggest just three of the reasons why great powers may have to trade with other great powers.[29] But it is worth remembering that even if state Y tries to reduce its direct trade with state X, it will usually be forced by the above realities into trading with the smaller states within state X's sphere of influence or empire system. Germany therefore traded extensively with British possessions and dominions prior to the First World War (a situation that got it into trouble, as we will see in chapter 3). And the Soviet Union and its bloc allies, even before the United States opened up more direct trade after 1970, had already been trading heavily with the United States' Western European allies, often against the wishes of Washington.

We have seen that extensive trade with other major players and their spheres may be essential to maintaining the economic vitality of a great power, even though such trade increases its vulnerability, and hence the fear of cutoff and leveraged coercion. The life of a great power is about trade-offs, and this is one that great powers are frequently willing to make. To stay autarkic when other great powers are increasing their trade ties may reduce the vulnerability that comes with dependence, but it is almost always a self-defeating strategy. Given this, it is not surprisingly that we so often see a high level of intersphere dependence in world history, and why currently the only states that can "afford" relative autarky are dysfunctional failed ones such as Burma and Zimbabwe. China would not be the "new power" that it is today if it had held on to the failed autarkic policies of the Maoist era. Chinese leaders after 1979 were smart enough to see the necessity of trade, even if Waltz (1979) did not.

Theoretical Foundations

The above discussion shows why great powers, notwithstanding neorealist arguments, often become highly dependent on each other. We now need to consider in more detail how trade expectations theory can help

[29]Other reasons include the geographic closeness of great powers to each other (closeness reduces transportation costs and thus increases the incentive to trade), relative equality of size of great power economies (gravity models in economics show that the greater the equality, the higher trade will be as a percentage of GNP, all things being equal), and desire to minimize the depletion of one's own scarce and nonrenewable resources (see footnote 28 above).

to resolve the deductive problems of liberalism and realism as they currently stand. To begin to understand how trade and investment flows might shape the likelihood of war in a dynamic environment, it is best to start with the concept at the heart of our debate: economic interdependence. Liberals and realists both freely use the term "interdependence" to describe this core causal variable. It is important to note, however, that in making their deductive arguments, both derive predictions about behavior from how particular actors—typically nation-states—deal with their own specific levels of dependence.[30] This allows both camps to deal with situations of asymmetrical dependence, where one state in a dyad is more dependent than the other. Their predictions are internally consistent, but opposed: liberals assert that the more dependent state in a relationship is less likely to initiate conflict, primarily because it has more to lose from breaking ties; realists maintain that this state is more likely to initiate conflict, mainly to escape its vulnerability.

Despite this common focus on the decision-making processes of the more dependent state, liberals and realists have incomplete notions of what it means to be dependent in the first place. Liberals concentrate on the benefits garnered from trade and investment as states move away from autarky; the opportunity costs of dependence are at most the loss of benefits if trade is ended.[31] Realists emphasize something that is downplayed in liberal arguments: that after a state has restructured its economy around trade, there may be potentially large costs of adjustment should trade be later severed (Waltz 1970, 1979). A state cut off after basing its economic structure around imported oil, for example, may be put in a far worse situation than if it had never moved away from autarky in the first place.

That liberals downplay or ignore the realist concern with the costs of adjustment is evident. For instance, Richard Rosecrance (1986, 144–45, 233–36), whose writings on interdependence remain an important foundational statement of liberalism's theoretical logic, directly tries to refute Waltz's notion of dependence as a trading link that is "costly to break." He contends that "to measure interdependence in this way misses the essence of the concept." His subsequent analysis and supporting appendix underscore only the benefits that states give up if they choose not to trade (his "opportunity costs"), and makes no mention of any potentially severe costs of adjustment.[32] It is clear why liberals such as Rosecrance

---

[30] Some liberals, as we have seen, stress the dependence of particular subgroups on foreign trade and investment flows, but even here they accept that it is up to the political elites running the state to execute policies that have implications for the whole country.

[31] See, in particular, Rosecrance 1986, appendix; Baldwin 1980, 478–84, 489.

[32] I could find no sustained discussion of adjustment costs in any of the liberal articles and books referenced above, and certainly no attempt to adjust liberal theory based on this realist insight. Large-N theorists such as Russett and Oneal simply start with Rosecrance's logic, and then move quickly to the testing phase. Robert Keohane and Joseph Nye (1977)

are reluctant to acknowledge realist concerns: to do so would imply that dependent states might be more willing to go to war, as realists maintain, instead of less willing, as liberals argue.

This point highlights the liberal understanding of why wars ultimately occur. For liberals, interdependence does not have a downside that might push states into war, as realists contend. Rather, interdependence is seen to operate as a restraint on aggressive tendencies arising from the domestic or individual level. If interdependence falls, this restraint is taken away, unleashing domestic forces and pathologies that may be lurking in the background.[33] Rosecrance, for example, ultimately falls back on social chaos, militarism, nationalist ambitions, and irrationality to explain why Germany in the twentieth century would start two world wars within a generation. Because trade had either fallen (by 1939) or its benefits were not properly understood (in 1914), Rosecrance (1986, 102–3, 106, 123, 150, 162) claims that trade offered no "mitigating" or "restraining" influence on unit-level motives for war. This view fits nicely with the overall liberal perspective that unit-level factors such as authoritarianism, ideology, and internal social conflict are the ultimate causes of war.[34] The idea that economic factors by themselves can push states to aggress—an argument consistent with neorealism and my alternative approach—is outside the realm of liberal thought, since it would imply that purely systemic forces can be responsible for war, largely regardless of unit-level phenomena.

It is clear that liberals, by their very way of defining dependence, have made economic ties between great powers only a force for peace and not an explanation for war. To explain what propels an actor into initiating a war, liberals must fall back on unit-level factors. Yet it is equally clear that realists, or at least neorealists, have minimized the positive

---

do have a useful discussion of the difference between sensitivity and vulnerability in their book *Power and Interdependence*, with the latter notion incorporating costs of adjustment. Unfortunately, the book contains no causal argument for how interdependence might be linked to peace or war. This is because it assumes that "complex interdependence" is more peaceful by definition: "it is a valuable concept for analyzing the political process" only when military force is "unthinkable" (ibid., 29, 24). Their second edition makes this explicit: "since we *define* complex interdependence in terms of [policy] goals and instruments," arguments "about how goals and instruments are affected by the degree to which a situation approximates complex interdependence or realism will be tautological" (Keohane and Nye 1989, 255).

[33]To borrow a metaphor from Plato: for liberals, interdependence operates like the reins on the dark horse of inner passions; it provides a material incentive to stay at peace, even when there are internal predispositions toward aggression. Remove the reins, however, and these passions are free to roam as they will. See Plato's *Phaedrus* in Hamilton and Cairns 1961, sections 246–56. The historical roots of this view are explicated in Hirschman 1977.

[34]Zacher and Mathews 1995; Moravscik 1997; Levy 1989; Howard 1986.

contribution to a state's economic health generated by the gains from trade. Trade expectations theory seeks to bridge this divide by founding its analysis on a more comprehensive conceptualization of dependence. It then adds the dynamic element of expectations missing in both liberalism and realism.

Trade expectations theory's deductive logic, as with liberalism and realism, centers on an individual state's efforts to manage its own situation of dependence. For the sake of simplicity, I will continue to focus on a two-actor scenario of asymmetrical dependence, where state Y needs trade with state X more than X needs trade with Y. The assumption of asymmetry means that changes in the trading environment are more likely to affect Y's decision for peace or conflict than X's. This allows us to concentrate primarily on state Y's decision calculus, given that it is the actor that most determines the probability of a war between the states (as all our main theories agree).[35]

If state Y moves away from autarky to trade freely with X, it will expect to receive the benefits of trade stressed by liberals.[36] The process of opening oneself to trade leads state Y to specialize in the production of goods in which it enjoys a comparative advantage. Yet this restructuring of the economy can entail enormous costs of adjustment should trade be subsequently cut off, particularly if the state becomes dependent on foreign oil and raw materials that are crucial to the economy's functioning. Hence, on a bilateral basis, state Y's total level of dependence can be conceptualized as the sum of the benefits received from trade (versus autarky) and costs of being cut off from trade after having specialized (versus autarky). If a state Y of 100 units of GNP, for example, goes to 110 units after trading with X, but would fall to 85 if trade were to be severed, Y's effective dependence level is 25 units (110 minus 85). This conceptual move brings together liberal and realist notions of dependence, offering

[35] Theoretically, when two great powers are relatively symmetrical in their dependence levels, we would predict more concern about trade security spirals on both sides and thus more cautious behavior all around. The positive trade expectations that would follow should have a moderating effect on the probability of militarized conflict. Unfortunately, as the case studies show, great powers in world history are rarely symmetrical in their dependence levels. Fortunately, one potential exception to this general rule is Sino-American relations today (see chapter 9).

[36] Remember that state Y can be aware of these benefits even if present trade is nonexistent, since these benefits represent the gains that would accrue to the state *if* trade levels become high in the future. Note also that these potential benefits will rise if the state becomes more "needy" over time—say, because it is running out of key raw materials at home or requires greater export penetration to exploit growing economies of scale. In a fully dynamic setup, therefore, the perceived benefits and costs of trade will be a function of the anticipated gains from trade and potential costs of adjustment into the future.

a fuller sense of what is really at stake for state Y in its interactions with state X (and after considering Y's alternative trade options).[37]

Yet in choosing between an aggressive or moderate grand strategy, state Y cannot refer simply to its dependence level. Rather, it must calculate its overall expected value of peaceful trade into the future and compare this to the value of the war/conflict option. Benefits of trade and the costs of severed trade on their own say nothing about this expected value. There is where dynamic expectations of the future must be brought in. If state Y has positive expectations that X will maintain free and open trade over the long term, then the expected value of trade will be close to that of the benefits of trade. On the other hand, if state Y, after having specialized, comes to expect that trade will be severed, then the expected value of trade may be negative—that is, close to the value of the costs of severed trade. In short, the expected value of trade can vary anywhere between the two extremes, depending on the crucial factor of a state's expected probability of securing open trade or being cut off.[38]

From this, we can see how the new approach leads us to a different set of hypotheses regarding the conditions for hard- or soft-line grand strategies. We can predict that for any given expected value of conflict, the lower the expectations of future trade, the more a dependent state will worry about its long-term security situation, and thus the greater the likelihood that it will choose hard-line policies or all-out war.[39] Yet when expectations of future trade are high and improving, the state will feel more confident about its security situation, and be more likely to prefer cooperative policies to conflict and war. Variations across time in the behavior

[37] In the above analysis, gains from trade and costs of adjustment are conceptualized as "net" gains and losses after one takes into account state Y's alternative trading partners. Thus if state Y can get everything it wants at the same price from state W, state Y has no real dependence on state X, even if X-Y trade is high in nominal terms (see Keohane and Nye 1977; Baldwin 1980, 1985). Because of Y's alternative partners, when X wants to hurt Y it must usually ask third-party states to bind themselves to a tight sanctions program. Otherwise, "leakage" from the sanctions regime will undermine the effectiveness of any leverage of X over Y.

[38] A state's *discount factor*, or the degree to which it values future versus present gains from trade or war, can effect state Y's calculation of the net value of peace. I assume that states are nonmyopic rational actors that value future gains essentially as much as present gains (i.e., they have low discount factors). This assumption sets the baseline for predicting how great powers will react to changes in the future economic environment. From there, we can relax the assumption to explain how myopic actors might respond to short-term opportunities for gain, especially if those gains can only be had through war. For a nice discussion of the time horizons literature, see Levy and Streich 2008.

[39] As per traditional military thinking, the expected value of conflict will be a function of the relative military balance, the offense-defense balance, the economic size of the country being attacked, and other such factors. For more on this, see Copeland 1996a, 20–21.

of states, therefore, should be driven by shifts in expectations of future trade environments and not just by changing degrees of dependence.

The trade expectations argument thus provides a distinct departure from the static theories of liberalism and realism. These latter approaches derive their predictions solely from snapshots of a state's level of dependence at any point in time (even as they provide only a partial conceptualization of this concept). They thereby remain inherently limited in their ability to explain the full scope of historical cases. A critic might counter that liberalism and realism do have at least an element of implicit dynamism to them, since in their empirical analyses liberals and realists sometimes refer to the future trading environment. This may be true for their studies of particular cases. But in constructing their overarching deductive logics, it is clear that the two approaches consider the future only within their ideological presuppositions. Liberals, assuming that states seek to maximize absolute welfare, argue that situations of high trade should continue off into the future as long as states are rational; such actors have no reason to forsake the benefits of trade, especially if defection from a trading arrangement will only lead to retaliation.[40] Given this presupposition, liberals can argue that interdependence—as reflected in high trade at a specific moment in time—should foster peace. Realists, assuming states seek to maximize security, maintain that concerns for relative power and autonomy will eventually push some states to sever trade ties. States in anarchy must therefore assume the worst about other actors, including their trading partners. Hence, realists can insist that interdependence, again manifest as high trade at any moment in time, drives dependent states to grab opportunities to initiate war now in order to escape potential vulnerability later (Mearsheimer 1992, 2001; Buzan 1984).

For the purposes of forging strong theories, however, trading patterns cannot simply be assumed a priori to match the stipulations of either liberalism or realism. As the last two centuries have demonstrated, trade levels between great power spheres fluctuate significantly over time. Thus, we need a theory that incorporates how a state's expectations of its future trading environment—either optimistic or pessimistic—affect its decision calculus for war or peace. This is where the new theory makes its most significant departure. By embedding this dynamic variable into the heart of the theory, the trade expectations logic undermines or qualifies much of the established thinking about interdependence and war. A dependent state's estimation of its expected value of trade, and in turn the expected value of peace, will be based not on the level of trade at a particular moment but rather the stream of expected trade levels into the future. As I

---

[40] See the appendix in Rosecrance 1986, which draws from the neoliberal institutionalist arguments of such scholars as Keohane (1984).

have stressed, it really does not matter that trade is high today, since if state Y knows that X will cut off trade tomorrow and shows no signs of being willing to restore it later, the expected value of trade and thus peace would be negative. Similarly, it does not matter if there is little or no trade at present, for if state Y is confident that X is committed to freer trade in the future, the expected value of trade and peace would be positive.

The fact that the expected value of trade can be negative even if present trade is high, due to low expectations for future trade, goes a long way toward resolving such manifest anomalies for liberal theory as Otto von Bismarck's scramble for Africa in 1884–85 and Germany's aggression in 1914. Despite high trade levels between the great powers in both cases, German leaders had good reason to believe that the other great powers were seeking to undermine this trade into the future. Hence, expansion to secure control over raw materials and markets was required for the long-term security of the German nation (see chapters 3 and 8). And because the expected value of trade can be positive even though present trade is low, due to positive expectations for future trade, we can also understand such important phenomena as the periods of détente in US-Soviet relations during the Cold War (1971–73 and after 1985). While East-West trade was still relatively low during these times, the Soviet need for Western technology, combined with a growing belief that large increases in trade with the West would be forthcoming, gave the Soviets a high enough expected value of trade to convince them to be more accommodating in superpower relations. Conversely, the failure of presidents Eisenhower and John F. Kennedy from 1957 to 1962 to make equivalent commitments to future trade with Russia exacerbated superpower tensions at a critical juncture when both sides had reasons to worry about the security of their second-strike capabilities (see chapter 6).

Of course, such examples beg the questions of why less dependent states begin to restrict the trade and investment flows of their more dependent partners despite the risks of military escalation, and why they sometimes try to ease tensions and reduce the likelihood of war by making commitments to future economic interchange. Indeed, the very fact that less dependent states have a major card to play in their pursuit of security—the offering of greater trade to more dependent actors in exchange for nicer behavior by their dependent adversaries—makes one wonder why great powers are not always holding out the carrot of commercial gains to reduce the probability of war. This issue is tied to the question of bargaining brought up in the introductory chapter—namely, why states that need each other for basic necessities and economic growth often cannot find a cooperative deal to help them avoid all the costs of great power war. The next section seeks to explain these puzzles.

Feedback Loops and the Question of Endogeneity

Up until now, this chapter has discussed state Y's expectations for future trade as though they were largely exogenous—that is, as though they were essentially independent of the interaction between the two states. This may be a reasonable assumption in many situations. State X may have a raw material that state Y needs, for example, but X's reserves of this vital good are becoming depleted, meaning that X will be less able to trade this good over the long term even if it wants to. States X and Y may also be constrained by external events that force a shift in trading practices. In the late 1930s, for instance, Japanese leaders recognized that American leaders would probably have to cut back on oil and iron exports to Japan as dwindling US reserves were needed to supply a military buildup against Germany as well as help aid Britain and the Soviet Union. Tokyo thus had certain exogenous reasons to be less optimistic about trade flows over the long run.

In many and perhaps most situations, however, leaders recognize that they can affect the beliefs of other actors by their actions. The trade expectations that drive state behavior are therefore rarely wholly exogenous; they can be affected by diplomatic interaction. This can happen in two primary ways. First, state X can send certain signals that help the dependent state Y to form a more accurate and positive estimate of X's willingness to trade at high levels into the future. Such an updating of Y's beliefs can lead it to increase its estimate of the expected value of trade, reducing its desire for conflict. Second, and equally important, state Y knows that its own behavior—the level of aggressiveness of its foreign policy—will affect state X's assessment of Y's character type: namely, whether Y is a reasonable and moderate actor, or one that is inherently hostile for security- or nonsecurity-driven reasons. This assessment will of course tend to shape X's willingness to commit itself to future trade with Y. After all, if X comes to think of Y as an aggressive actor bent on expansion, X will be less inclined to want to trade freely with Y, especially if that trade is only facilitating Y's ability to expand through a relative gain in power or through a larger absolute capacity to project power abroad.

This leads us directly to a consideration of the trade-security dilemma briefly described in the introductory chapter. At the crux of the trade-security dilemma is the problem of incomplete information—that is, the difficulty both states have in knowing the character of the other great power. In modern game theory, incomplete information has to do with the other's current type along with its incentives to misrepresent who or what it is. Thus in the popular bargaining model of war, for example, uncertainty in the model typically revolves around the inability of state Y to know X's "resolve" and vice versa—in other words, Y's and X's present willingness to take on the costs as well as risks of war should crisis escalation actually take both actors over the brink. Through such costly signaling measures as mobilization, public stands, and alliance formation, leaders on both sides can communicate their true characters, thereby helping to reveal a bargaining space that can lead to a compromise deal before war breaks out. If actors prove unable to signal their resolve, war can break out through one or both sides' belief that by pushing both actors further out on the slippery slope to war, the other will concede to its demands (will "back down").[41] Other scholars extend this work to the efforts of states to signal their current military intentions, as opposed to resolve per se.[42]

From a dynamic perspective incorporating expectations of the future, though, this is a quite-limited view of how great power politics actually works. There are two other forms of uncertainty about character type that are typically much more problematic and much more likely to lead to war. The first is the uncertainty that X and Y have about the other's *future* military intentions—namely, whether the other will have a strong desire to attack it later, perhaps many years down the road. The second is the uncertainty that X and Y have about the other's *future willingness to trade at high and largely unrestricted levels.* Here the concern is not that the other will necessarily attack me but instead that it will so constrain my growth through economic sanctions that my country will fall by the wayside, and then be subject to the slow yet steady loss of its territory and sovereignty. This second uncertainty is clearly related to the first, since if the other is deliberately causing me to decline, there is probably a higher chance that it intends to invade later, or at least carve off key pieces of my territory or sphere for itself.

In such an environment of future uncertainty, states will be looking for signs that the other is committed to being a moderate and reasonable actor into the future. If state Y is the more dependent state in the relationship, for example, then it will be keenly attentive to signs that state X is either willing to keep the current high levels of trade and investment going, or if commerce is currently restricted, that it will be likely to open it up over the short and medium terms. Yet as I have stressed, state Y, by the very nature of its higher economic needs, is the state that is almost certainly getting the relative gain from more open trade and investment flows. Thus state X will be looking for signs that state Y, as it grows and develops through the trade relationship,

---

[41] See, in particular, Fearon 1995; Wagner 2000; Schultz 2001; Reiter 2003; Weeks 2009.
[42] See Glaser 1994–95, 2010; Kydd 1997b, 2000, 2005; Montgomery 2006.

will continue to be a moderate great power with little desire to expand against X's territorial interests.[43]

This discussion immediately brings to the fore the pervasive reality of the commitment problem in international relations: the difficulty actors have in anarchy of promising now to be nice later, given that there is no higher authority to enforce the promises and prevent defection.[44] As Robert Powell (2006) has demonstrated, in an environment of dynamic power change, the commitment problem can lead to war even when there is complete information about the other's current type—that is, even when all the uncertainties about resolve are cleared up and actors know exactly whom they are dealing with in the present moment. For Powell, it is a concern about what the rising state will do in the future, after it has grown in power, not incomplete information in the present, that leads to war.

Powell's argument nicely captures one dimension of the problem of relative decline that hangs over international politics. Yet the commitment problem is only one aspect of what in reality is the much deeper "problem of the future" (Copeland 2011a). The commitment problem, in formal terms, is about state Y's leadership's inability to convince X that Y will not defect later from promises made today (and vice versa). But what X is worried about is not just that Y's current leadership might have a change of heart later once Y has more relative power. State X is also worried that Y might have a change of leadership through elections, coups, domestic instability, and the like that lead the new leaders in Y to adopt very different policies. This is the well-known problem of the changeability of actor type—the fear of backsliding and revolution—that leads realists to stress states' uncertainty regarding future intentions.[45]

The problem of the future is even more potentially profound than that, though. State Y's very growth through the economies of scale that trade engenders can also speed up the depletion rate of its internal resources, creating a positive feedback loop that forces Y to become even more dependent on outsiders merely to keep the industrial machine rolling. China over the last decade has experienced this problem, just as Germany did after 1890. Because the incentives that state Y has to project military power in order to protect trade access routes change as trade dependence grows, state Y may have a difficult time credibly convincing X that it will indeed be moderate at time t + 10 or t + 20, even if there is no question

[43] Below, for simplicity's sake, I will continue to focus on the asymmetrical concerns of states Y and X arising from their asymmetrical levels of dependence. In practice, of course, Y is also concerned about X's military intentions while X is concerned about Y's willingness to trade openly into the future.

[44] See especially Fearon 1995, 1998; Powell 2006; Reiter 2009.

[45] Jervis 1978; Mearsheimer 1994–95, 2001; Copeland 2000a, 2000b, 2011a, 2011b.

that state Y is indeed moderate now (time t). In addition, as I discuss below, states X and Y may have difficulty committing to cooperative policies simply because they remain uncertain about the future stability and character of important third parties.

The problem of the future in all its dimensions is what makes the trade-security dilemma such a complex and enigmatic phenomenon of great power politics, and such a difficult phenomenon to understand theoretically. To avert the outbreak of a trade-security spiral that can undermine dependent state Y's expectations of future trade, Y has to convince X that it will most likely remain a moderate state over the long term if it is going to make the other lean toward an open trade policy. Yet because anarchy does make states want to prepare for unexpected events, Y's efforts to increase its power projection capabilities can undermine the other's confidence in Y's future type and start the trade-security spiral rolling. State X, on the other hand, will know that trade sanctions against Y can cause it to become more hostile. This means that X, all things being equal, would like to convince Y that it will in fact remain a reliable and open trade partner into the foreseeable future. But state Y knows that X also has an incentive to cut Y off later after Y becomes overly dependent or at least to use its economic leverage to coerce Y into concessions Y has no interest in making.

What seems clear in all this is that states in international relations face tough trade-offs all along their historical paths, and that a leader's decision to lean toward either hard- or soft-line policies involves a balancing of many different factors. Offensive realism tries to ignore the trade-offs by its simplifying stipulation that states must calculate according to worst-case scenarios. States that assume worst-case do not trade with each other, and if they do happen to become dependent (for reasons unexplained), then they are forced to grab any and all opportunities to expand through military power to reduce their dependence. While offensive realists rightly emphasize that dependent states have to worry about future trade access, history shows that they are off the mark when it comes to their prediction that great powers will not trade and will constantly grab opportunities to expand. Indeed, the very fact that for long stretches of time great powers trade heavily with each other rather than simply expanding their territorial spheres shows that they are able to "trust" the other's type to at least some degree—that they are not assuming the worst.[46]

---

[46] Trust here just means that great powers have made estimates that other states have a relatively low probability of defecting against them, at least in the short and medium terms. It does not imply that great powers "like" each other or that they consider each other "friends" in anything other than the pragmatic self-interested sense that both can maximize their security by cooperating (cf. Wendt 1999, chaps. 6 and 7; Kydd 2005).

This is where my argument fuses defensive realist insights with an essentially offensive realist baseline. Offensive realists are correct to stress that anarchy forces actors to worry about the future power and intentions of others. Defensive realists, on the other hand, are right to assert that states think in probabilistic terms, looking at the *likelihood* of the other being nasty rather than nice in character as opposed to simply presuming it is the worst.[47] Defensive realism allows us to explain why purely security-seeking great powers in anarchy might still be able to sustain high trade levels with other great powers, even though all of them have reasons to worry about the future. These great powers are making trade-offs and are leaning, at least in the short and medium terms, toward the soft-line end of the spectrum. They are engaging in trade cooperation to help build their economies while recognizing that such cooperation, if underpinned by positive expectations of future trade, is helping to stabilize the peace. They are also trying to signal that their characters are moderate so that the other side will have at least a modicum of confidence in their future behavior.

What is still not clear, however, is why a stable trading system between the great powers would ever break down. That is, why would either state X or Y decide to start inclining more to the hard-line end of the spectrum despite understanding—as my rationalist logic assumes they do—that such behavior poses risks of trade-security spirals and ultimately war? This is where exogenous factors outside the control of the political elites in both X and Y play their determining roles. My interest is in explaining the behavior of the more needy state in any relationship, so I will continue to assume that dependent state Y is a rational security-maximizing state whose leaders are unaffected by any domestic-level pressures and pathologies, and thus alter their behavior only in response to changes in either X's behavior or Y's external conditions (a non-trade-related fall in power, for example). This means we need to focus on how factors exogenous to X's leadership are affecting X's ability and willingness to keep trade relations with Y open and unrestricted.

There are six primary factors that can change X's calculations of the trade-off between building a reputation as a reliable trade partner (at the cost of giving Y a relative gain) versus reducing trade with Y to curb its economic growth (at the risk of hurting Y's confidence in X as a trade partner and increasing the chance of a trade-security spiral to war).[48]

---

[47] See especially Brooks 1997; Glaser 1994–95, 2010.

[48] Chapter 2 also considers additional reinforcing factors that shape Y's evaluation of X's willingness to trade in the future, including the "democratic-ness" of X's regime type, the presence of preferential trading agreements, and X's levels of capitalist and industrial development.

Three of them involve various dimensions of the problem of third parties mentioned above. The first is the degree to which third-party concerns constrain X's ability or strategic incentive to trade freely with Y into the future. If state Y is posing a threat to state Z, and X's leaders are determined to help Z survive, then X may reduce its trade with Y in support of Z. As I show in chapter 5, President Roosevelt recognized in 1941 that he could not restore open trade to Japan if that increased the chance of Japan attacking the Soviet Union. Roosevelt needed to keep Russia strong in order to defeat the main threat to world peace, Hitler's Germany. To avoid having Russia weakened by a two-front war, he maintained tight sanctions against Tokyo to reorient Japan southward and reduce its fighting power. A US-Japanese war was the result. In situations such as this, we can certainly ask why it was that state Y was targeting Z to begin with. In terms of understanding Y's ultimate attack on X, though, Y's declining trade expectations due to X's behavior can take us a long way toward an explanation.

The second exogenous condition shaping X's trade policy toward Y is the level of domestic instability in small third parties that both Y and X need for their ongoing economic viability. If internal problems within small state F cause state X to intervene to reestablish order, this can cause Y to worry about its future access to F. The formal occupation of F by X, or even simply the informal projection of X's power into F's domestic politics, can make dependent state Y believe that F will have to reorient its trade policies away from Y and toward its new great power protector, state X. Throughout the nineteenth century, for example, Turkey had periodic internal crises caused by revolts within the European part of its empire. In many of these crises, Russia feared that it might lose its commercial and naval access through the Turkish Straits if other powers such as Austria and Britain moved in to control the Balkan states. Russia's efforts at power projection in turn troubled the other great powers of Europe, leading to destabilizing interstate crises and one large-scale war (1853–56). Domestic problems within small third parties also created the context for the imperialist scramble for Africa in the early 1880s: unrest along the Gold Coast and in North Africa encouraged France to push harder for formal control, which in turn led Britain to intervene in Egypt when civil strife broke out there. The Boer War of 1899–1902 was also partly sparked by unrest in third parties, as was the spiraling hostility between Washington and Moscow in 1943–45 that led to the Cold War.

The third exogenous factor is simply the unit-level drives of a third-party great power, state Z, whose actions against small state F cause X to intervene, which then forces dependent state Y to act. Italy after unification had strong nationalist reasons to carve out a small empire in northern Africa. When it readied itself to jump on an unstable Tunisia in 1881, the French felt compelled to jump first. These actions convinced Britain and then Germany that they, too, must reluctantly scramble for pieces of African territory or risk being left out of the game. Note that while domestic-level variables in the third-party great power start the ball rolling, our key players X and Y turn to imperialism not because of their own unit-level pathologies but instead because of their perceived need to protect their trade and investments abroad.

The fourth factor driving X's trading behavior is Y's overall level of economic growth, either because of Y's sheer economic dynamism or because of the relative gains that Y can accrue through trade. State X may be willing to allow Y to grow for a while, especially if state Y starts from a low position in the relative economic power hierarchy. But if state Y can sustain its strong growth trend year after year, Y's economic growth will start to pose an increasing threat to X, especially if it is being translated into increasing military power. And if X's leaders come to believe that Y will rise to a point of dominance simply through peaceful engagement, they will be more inclined to turn to more restrictive economic measures to reduce or contain Y's growth, despite the risks of setting off a trade-security spiral that increases the probability of war. In this sense, the level of asymmetry of dependence between X and Y can act as a crucial shaping force in X's behavior: if Y gets much more out of the economic relationship than X, then X is not only more inclined to worry about long-term relative loss through continued trade but also sees that it will pay a lesser cost in restricting X-Y trade. The increasingly harsh economic restrictions imposed on the Soviet Union, beginning in 1945, illustrate both of these mechanisms. The US government had good reason to believe that the Soviet Union would grow rapidly after World War II even without trade. Yet it clearly understood that US-Soviet trade, given Moscow's need for advanced technology, would make Russia's relative economic rise even more rapid (chapter 6). French and British fears of continued German growth after 1890 also fit this pattern (chapter 3).[49]

---

[49] Power dynamics and levels of relative dependence can also work in a positive direction. If Y is not currently rising against X in a way that would mean a dramatic loss in X's relative power, and if Y and X are both relatively symmetrical in their dependence on each other, then X is less likely to cut Y off from trade with X and its sphere, all things being equal. After all, X also needs the X-Y trade to grow, and Y is not receiving a large relative gain through trade. Polarity comes into play here, too. As I noted earlier (note 26), in multipolar systems X may keep trading with Y even if Y gets a moderate relative gain, given that X's absolute gain gives it a relative gain compared to states W and Z. In bipolar systems, relative gains concerns are more problematic, given that X has less concern about small third parties and yet also has no strong alliance partners to fall back on if Y overtakes it in relative power (cf. Keohane 1993; Schweller 1996; Copeland 1996b, 2000a).

The fifth factor involves the depletion of raw materials within X's sphere that makes X not only less able to supply Y with such vital goods but also may encourage it to compete with Y for control of third parties.[50] The primary example in the case studies is Roosevelt's recognition in 1943–44 that with US oil supplies running out, the United States had to start intensifying its competition with Russia over dominance in Iran and the Middle East more generally. This factor captures an aspect of the economic realist logic: states that anticipate future dependency on key resources will begin to maneuver now for position, and that maneuvering can cause current trade partners to worry. The realist focus, however, is on X potentially going to war because of its expected future dependency. My focus is on X's incentive to restrict other states' access to resources and how that reshapes the expectations of a currently dependent state, Y, when it considers its own future.

Sixth, and finally, X's leaders may be constrained from trading freely with Y by an exogenous factor arising from within their own state. In particular, X's executive branch may keenly want to increase trade with Y, but find that the legislative branch is making this impossible. The classic case is US-Soviet relations from 1971 to 1975. Through linkage agreements in 1972, Richard Nixon and Henry Kissinger were able to buy Soviet cooperation on a number of issues by extending US trade credits and promising more open trade. Unfortunately, the US executive, in the wake of Watergate, subsequently found itself unable to implement the policy that it wished to undertake: the US Congress negated Nixon's détente policy through a series of amendments that undermined Moscow's new, more positive expectations for future trade. We also saw a similar problem for the US executive arise with the passing of the Smoot-Hawley Tariff Act of 1930, a legislative action that damaged Japanese confidence in the United States as a trading partner and helped usher in a decade of conflict in East Asia.[51]

The above exogenous factors can work together or independently to constrain state X's ability or willingness to trade openly with state Y, thereby setting off a trade-security spiral that can lead both nations into

---

[50] This is separate from the problem of depletion occurring within state Y, mentioned above, that makes it hard for X to rest assured that Y will not be more of a hard-liner later.

[51] See chapters 6 and 4–5, respectively. I should note, with reference to footnotes 1 and 23, that the inclusion of this sixth factor does not involve the smuggling in of unit-level factors for a theory that assumes rational security-maximizing states. The executive officials in both X and Y are still assumed to be solely interested in rationally maximizing security for their respective countries. Yet sometimes domestic-level factors within the less dependent state, X, can constrain its leaders' ability to credibly commit to future trade. It is factors exogenous to Y (and X's executive), then, that are driving Y's expectations and thus its behavior.

conflict. These factors help us explain theoretically why states with no desire for war may still be unable to locate a bargain that helps them to avoid it. In their absence, however, long-term cooperation can obtain, as long as actors have reason to believe that their concerns regarding others' commitments to trade and peace in the future are not as problematic as the invoking of a trade-security spiral due to overly assertive policies now.

Summary of the Argument and the Competing Hypotheses

This chapter has added flesh to the bare bones of the argument laid out in the introductory chapter. We have seen that to explain fully the relationship between interdependence and war, we must move away from the static models of the traditional literature. It is a dependent state's expectations of the future economic environment that determines whether its policies will be moderate or hard line, peace inducing or war inducing. Yet since expectations of future trade are often also shaped by the behavior of the actors themselves, we need to specify exactly what sorts of mechanisms are likely to keep great powers on the soft-line end of the spectrum—trading relatively freely across their spheres and avoiding spirals of hostility—and what factors are likely to drive them toward conflictual actions and ultimately war.

Figure 1.1 provides a diagrammatic summary of the basic causal logic of the trade expectations argument. As with both liberalism and realism, the analytic focus is on explaining the behavior of the more dependent state in a relationship—in this case, state Y. It is state Y's behavior—either soft or hard line—that shapes the probability of war within the dyad. Building on the insights of realism, the trade expectations model maintains that state Y's policies will be a function of its evaluation of its overall security situation and, most important, estimates of its long-term power position in the system.

This is where state Y's dependence level and expectations of future trade play their main role. If Y's leaders need access to the other's sphere for raw materials, investment income, and markets, and if they have reason to believe its leaders will help facilitate that access into the future, then Y's policies toward X should be quite peaceful. State Y, anticipating the future stream of benefits, will want to avoid jeopardizing the relationship via hard-line actions that might raise the other state's mistrust of its future intentions. But if Y's leaders see X cutting Y off from access to X's sphere, or have reason to think that X will do so in the future, then the policies of Y will likely turn nasty. State X's restrictive actions, by reducing current benefits and imposing costs of adjustment on Y's economy, can cause Y to decline in economic power relative to X. If such decline kicks in, then Y's leaders have an increased incentive to launch a war against X's sphere to reestablish economic access and stabilize the state's power position.

International politics, though, is not simply a matter of responding to expected trends on key economic and power variables. It is also an ongoing bargaining game of give-and-take, gesture and response. States recognize that their soft- and hard-line behaviors send signals to other actors about their levels of commitment to moderate future behavior as well as open trade. State X's leadership will be watching Y's behavior for signs that it is an undependable state that might pocket the benefits of trade and use them for future aggression. Part of what drives X's economic policies toward Y, as figure 1.1 shows, is therefore X's evaluation of Y's character based on the latter's past behavior. If X's leaders evaluate that character negatively, then they may start to restrict Y's access to resources, investments, and markets. Such moves could easily kick in a trade-security spiral, whereby X's new, more restrictive posture on trade and commerce leads Y to undertake more assertive foreign policies against the former's sphere or third parties, which in turn leads X to further restrict Y's ability to trade freely. This self-reinforcing feedback loop could ultimately lead Y to initiate war, either against state X directly or smaller states within its sphere.

We have also seen that the awareness of leaders of the deleterious effects of the trade-security spiral should give both sides reasons to avoid overly provocative policies. Why, then, might either X or Y start to shift toward the hard-line end of the policy spectrum? One possibility is that Y observes that the general trade environment is now no longer working in its favor. Japan after 1929, for example, faced a situation where all the major powers were retreating into increasingly closed-off economic spheres. It is thus not surprising that Japanese expectations of future trade turned pessimistic. Yet in analyzing the X-Y relationship, we must focus more specifically on the factors that might cause X to reevaluate its own weighing of the relative benefits and risks of open trade with Y. This chapter laid out six main factors that can push X to restrict Y's trade access: concerns about Y's designs on a third-party great power; domestic instability in small states and X's need to intervene; the drives of a third-party great power against a small state that forces X to act; X's fear of Y's overall economic growth; X's depletion of key raw materials and its need to compete for future control of these resources elsewhere; and legislative resistance to the economic policies of X's executive branch.

As the case studies will demonstrate, these exogenous factors, alone or in combination, played significant roles in the outbreak of war. By damaging the prospects for trade, they led the leaders of Y to believe that there was little they could do through their own actions to correct

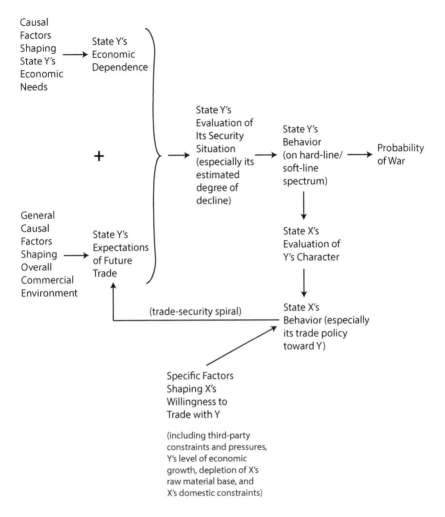

FIGURE 1.1 The causal logic of the model

the problems that were causing the deterioration of their trade relations and decline of their states. When leaders not only have pessimistic expectations of the future but also view the sources of those expectations as "givens," then they are more likely to see war as the least-of-many-evils rational choice—one that must be made sooner rather than later.

In the next chapter, I will discuss my research method and the value of large-N quantitative analysis in the study of interdependence and war. Recent quantitative work strongly supports the notion that expectations of future trade shape the likelihood that two states will fall into war or militarized conflict. Quantitative analysis is nonetheless inadequate on its own. By using proxies for expectation variables, and concentrating on snapshots of current and past data, quantitative methods cannot in the end get at what we are truly interested in: the way leaders think about the future. Thus in the remaining empirical chapters, I plunge into a detailed look at the primary cases of great power politics and military conflict since 1790.

The main goal of the case studies is to test the logic of trade expectations theory directly against its main alternatives, namely, liberalism and economic realism. The technique for testing these competing theories through historical documents is straightforward. If we see interdependence sustaining peaceful relations, but unit-level drives for conflict and war being unleashed when trade and investment levels fall, then liberalism will be supported. If, on the other hand, we see dependent actors grabbing opportunities to reduce their vulnerability and enhance the security of supply, then economic realism is confirmed. Yet if leaders focus less on present trade and investment, and more on anticipated levels of commerce into the future, and if these leaders calibrate the severity of their policies according to the optimism or pessimism of their estimates along with how these estimates shape state security, then the trade expectations approach is upheld.

We cannot expect any one theory to explain each and every case in world politics. And indeed there will be a number of cases where economic factors had little or nothing to do with the outbreak of hostilities. Still, by setting up our methodology to cover the essential universe of great power cases over the last two hundred years, we can begin to determine the relative salience of trade and commerce as causes of war across the centuries. If this book can show that trade expectations theory provides a surprisingly powerful explanation for shifts in great power behavior across time and space, even when one would predict that economic factors should be unimportant, then the value of adopting a dynamic approach to international relations will be clear.

CHAPTER TWO

Quantitative Analysis and Qualitative Case Study Research

OVER THE LAST THIRTY YEARS, the study of economic interdependence and conflict has been driven empirically by scholars who use exclusively large-N quantitative methods to test the various competing hypotheses. In fact, one would be hard pressed to find more than a handful of scholars who have ever presented even a single in-depth case study based on the diplomatic-historical evidence, let alone attempted a detailed cross-case analysis of the competing arguments.[1] The vast majority of the empirical studies focus simply on the statistical findings generated by elaborate mathematical models, and thus offer little sense of how the results might apply to particular cases or periods. The causal mechanisms that lead to peace or war will be inadequately understood if this is our sole or primary methodology, given that quantitative methods are inherently about correlations and associations between variables rather than causality per se. This book's larger purpose is to rectify this situation. Starting in 1790 with the onset of the modern postrevolutionary period of world history, the book will plunge into the documentary evidence to show the relative salience of international economic variables for the onset of conflict between the great powers. Detailed case analysis will allow us to determine to what degree great power interdependence and commercial expectations actually drive world history relative to other potential causal factors, and when they do, which of our particular economically based theories is best supported.

Yet this does not mean that the quantitative analyses do not have an important place in the study of interdependence and war. Recent studies certainly have offered a number of new and critical insights into the impact of trade and commerce on international conflict, insights that have the potential to reorient the whole field of international relations. Most important, they reveal that key variables such as trade dependence and

---

[1] Notable examples of those who do examine cross-case historical evidence include Ripsman and Blanchard 1995–96; Gholz and Press 2001, 2010; Papayoanou 1996, 1999; Bearce 2001, 2003; McDonald 2009.

the level of mutual democracy do not, on their own, have consistently significant or predictable effects on the probability of interstate conflict. Their effects are conditioned on the presence of other variables such as development levels, the intensity of contracts, and the role of institutions and high-level contacts that determine when as well as to what extent dependence and democracy shift the likelihood of militarized conflict and war. Such findings, as we will see, undermine our confidence in the foundational assertions of liberals that commerce always tends to reduce the probability of conflict or that higher degrees of shared democracy necessarily create zones of "democratic peace." The takeaway point from these recent large-N studies is a startling one for modern liberals: commerce not only can cut either way—pushing states toward peace *or* greater conflict—but the causal role of regime type can be often overridden by the powerful impact of trade and financial flows.

Subsequent chapters, through in-depth case study analysis, will show the strong historical support for these dramatic findings. I will demonstrate that the effect of economic interdependence is conditional on the expectations of future trade and financial flows that shape leaders' confidence in their long-term power positions in the system. Indeed, as the recent quantitative studies confirm, expectations of the commercial environment can drive foreign policy behavior even when trade levels between states are low or nonexistent; it is leader expectations of the future combined with the underlying need for future commerce that drive state actions. The case studies also reveal just how weak regime type is as a causal variable that pushes states into war. Even for what should be "best cases" for the liberal claim that states with pathological goals and domestic structures are the initiators of war when trade is low, the documentary evidence indicates that the external pressures of a state's economic situation are almost always more influential in the decision for conflict than unit-level propelling factors. As we will see, quantitative scholars nicely support this finding by observing that the likely basis for any democratic peace between modern liberal-democratic states is not domestic institutions or moral constraints but rather the economic structures that such states usually possess. Because large-N studies reveal correlations not causation, the exact causal mechanism that explains how and why these structures lower the risks of conflict is still up for debate between quantitativists. I will argue that the trade expectations logic provides the only coherent explanation across the diverse array of models presented in the quantitative literature.

The second half of this chapter discusses the research method used to explore the qualitative-historical cases and summarizes the findings of the six historical chapters. I look at a new approach to doing case study research when one is dealing with rare events. The phenomena I am studying in this book—destabilizing great power crises and war along with the changing probabilities of their onset across time—are fortunately rare occurrences in modern world history. Their rarity is a reflection of the complex number of factors that must come together before the events can arise. In-depth qualitative research has the advantage over quantitative methodologies in that it can unpack the exact mix of causes that go into particular cases. Yet traditional ways of doing case study work have tended to suffer from problems of selection bias and an inability to generalize beyond the cases considered. I show how the examination of the essential universe of cases across a bounded time frame and for a clearly defined set of actors can overcome these problems while focusing our attention on what is ultimately of most interest: how frequently it is the case that the factors of a particular theory are able to explain the phenomena in question, and with what degree of salience. True progress in international relations requires that scholars actively debate specific cases in order to establish general agreement as to how often and how well theories work across space and time. Toward the furthering of this end, the last part of the chapter provides a brief summary of the results of the next six chapters. This summary highlights not only the surprising salience of commercial factors in the onset of great power crisis and war but also that the trade expectations argument outperforms both the liberal and economic realist ones in explaining how such factors have shaped the likelihood of war and peace since 1790.

The Contribution of Quantitative Studies

From the early 1980s to the late 1990s, the quantitative study of economic interdependence and war revolved around one simple question: whether higher levels of interdependence lead to a greater or lower probability of militarized conflict. Little effort was expended to explore whether the effect of commerce was conditioned by the presence of other important variables.[2] In the initial stages of any new quantitative investigation, it makes sense to express the key research question in such straightforward terms. After all, one is trying to figure out whether the new variable of interest—in this case, economic interdependence—has any statistically significant effect relative to established causal variables (typically represented as *control variables* within the analysis), and if so, whether that effect is in the positive or negative direction.

[2] Early studies include Polachek 1980, 1992; Polachek and McDonald 1992; Gasiorowski and Polachek 1982; Gasiorowski 1986.

Because of the simplicity of their setups, however, these early studies were bound to come up with conflicting or overly general answers that left the field more confused than enlightened. Oneal and Russett led the liberal charge, showing that increasing interdependence (typically measured by trade over GDP) is associated on average with a reduction in the likelihood of militarized interstate disputes and war. They were also able to support the larger liberal proposition that mutual democracy and the presence of international institutions, in conjunction with economic interdependence, all help to improve the chances for peace, with each element contributing a statistically significant benefit to the overall mix.[3] Barbieri challenged Oneal and Russett's quantitative results regarding interdependence. Starting from a largely realist framework, she demonstrated that with different conceptualizations of the key independent variable, one could show that interdependence either had no statistically significant effect on international conflict or in fact increased its probability rather than lowering it, as liberals assert.[4] The decade of the 1990s ended with a fierce and largely inconclusive debate around which side, liberal or realist, was correct.[5]

By the turn of the new century, a host of scholars had come to the obvious realization that correlations between any single variable such as economic interdependence (however it is measured) and militarized conflict show only average relationships. In simple quantitative models, a great many of the data points will fall far from any "regression line," indicating that a large number of the individual cases may be exhibiting the opposite causal relationship from what any average across the data points would seem to reveal. If that were the case here, then interdependence could be cutting both ways, sometimes leading to more conflict and sometimes to less conflict. Everything would then depend on the specification of further conditions that interact with economic interdependence to determine when trade and financial flows hurt or improve the chances for peace. Yet the initial quantitative models, because they were simply adding economic interdependence measures to the established host of largely noneconomic control variables, were not able to capture these conditional relationships.

Interactive variables were needed to transcend the dead end reached in the initial liberal-realist debate of the late 1990s. Simple quantitative models examine whether causal variable A and causal variable B have

---

[3] Oneal and Russett 1997, 1999, 2001; Oneal, Oneal, Maoz, and Russett 1996; Oneal, Russett, and Davis 1998.

[4] Barbieri 1996, 2002.

[5] See, for example, the debate in the special issue of the *Journal of Peace Research* 36, no. 4 (1999).

independent and additive effects on event E. In more complex models with interactive variables, though, an interactive term A × B is introduced to see to what extent A and B potentially feed off one another synergistically to determine E's value across space and time. Depending on the signs of the coefficients, the inclusion of an interactive term, when read in conjunction with A and B on their own, can reveal conditional relationships that remain hidden in simple additive models (Friedrich 1982; Braumoeller 2004).

One of the first important contributions in this regard was Gelpi and Grieco's (2003b, 51) reexamination of Oneal and Russett's and Barbieri's data sets, this time with an interactive term capturing the possible synergy between regime type (level of mutual democracy) and economic interdependence. Using a logit estimator designed to analyze rare events data, Gelpi and Grieco first reproduced the basic results of Oneal and Russett as well as Barbieri—namely, that interdependence either has a statistically significant negative effect on the probability of a militarized dispute (Oneal and Russett) or no statistically significant effect (Barbieri). Their results are reproduced in columns 1 and 3 of table 2.1. They then went on to show how the inclusion of an interaction term between regime type and interdependence dramatically changes our understanding of the variables (columns 2 and 4).[6] When the interactive term is included, the trade dependence variable on its own stays significant, but switches from a negative to positive coefficient. The coefficient for the regime variable, democracy, remains, as liberals would expect, negative and significant, while the coefficient for the interaction term is also negative and significant. The implications of these results are profound. They suggest that interdependence only helps to reduce the probability of military conflict when both states are strongly democratic. When the level of joint democracy is low, however, growing interdependence can actually increase the risk of conflict.

Something in the simple liberal version of the commercial peace is clearly not quite right. Trade may reduce the probability of war for strong democracies. But between autocratic states, it makes conflict more likely, not less likely. Of course, as a set of computer-generated large-N correlations, Gelpi and Grieco's results beg the obvious question: Why might this be so?

[6]The dependent variable is the onset of a militarized interstate dispute. (The period being tested is not stated, but the dates given in a parallel paper [Gelpi and Grieco 2003a] are 1950 to 1992, which would correspond to Oneal and Russett's time frame; see also Gelpi and Grieco 2008.) Their democracy and trade dependence variables, as in most quantitative analyses, employ the so-called weak-link hypothesis, which uses the democracy and trade dependence scores of the state in the dyad with the lower score. In this chapter's six statistical tables, to save space I have not included peace years splines, intercepts, and log-likelihood estimates when they are provided by the authors.

TABLE 2.1 Gelpi and Grieco's Results on the Role of Democracy and Interdependence

(Dependent Variable: Onset of a Militarized Interstate Dispute)

	Oneal and Russett model	Gelpi and Grieco model	Barbieri model	Gelpi and Grieco model
Democracy and trade variables				
Higher trade	2.165	2.753	0.876	1.196
dependence	(2.533)	(2.946)	(1.243)	(1.278)
Lower trade	−59.847**	70.037**	−2.797	40.887**
dependence	(27.313)	(21.353)	(7.820)	(16.912)
Low democracy	—	−9.199***	—	−5.112**
× low dependence		(3.115)		(2.037)
Lower democracy	−0.800***	−0.0683***	−0.089***	−0.068***
score	(0.014)	(0.149)	(0.014)	(0.015)
Control variables				
States are contiguous	2.423***	2.399***	2.025***	2.010***
	(0.182)	(0.180)	(0.181)	(0.179)
Ln of distance	−0.741***	−0.735***	−0.509***	−0.516***
between capitals	(0.074)	(0.073)	(0.074)	(0.075)
Ln of the capability	−0.221**	−0.216***	−0.141**	−0.148***
ratio	(0.049)	(0.049)	(0.057)	(0.056)
Major power dyad	2.367***	2.370***	1.691***	1.731***
	(0.218)	(0.215)	(0.183)	(0.179)
Shared alliance ties	−0.431**	−0.407**	−0.256	−0.258
	(0.179)	(0.175)	(0.192)	(0.189)
Number of	28,100	28,100	12,574	12,574
observations				

Note: Gelpi and Grieco 2003a, 51, with some rounding of numbers and their four "Peace Year Splines" removed for space considerations. The number of observations is lower than the other works studied in this book, given Gelpi and Grieco's use of rare-event logit analysis. Original note in Gelpi and Grieco (ibid.): Standard errors for coefficients appear in parentheses. Huber-White robust standard errors allowed for clustering on each dyad. All tests for statistical significance are two tailed. * $p < 0.10$; ** $p < 0.05$; *** $p < 0.01$.

Drawing on a fusion of classical liberal and selectorate theories, Gelpi and Grieco (2003b, 52–54) hypothesize that democratic leaders are more responsive to the larger population, and thus are sensitive to the opportunity costs of disrupted trade. Authoritarian leaders are less sensitive to these opportunity costs, and hence less constrained from initiating crises and wars.[7]

---

[7]On selectorate theory, see Bueno de Mesquita, Morrow, Siverson, and Smith 1999; Bueno de Mesquita, Smith, Siverson, and Morrow 2003.

There is something incomplete about this explanation, though. While it might capture part of the reason why democratic states with high trade are loath to fight, it is less than satisfying as to why authoritarian states with high trade are more likely to fall into conflict than authoritarian states with low trade. Gelpi and Grieco's explanation is based, like most liberal arguments, on the constraints provided by trade that hold states back from fighting. Democratic leaders may be more sensitive to these costs and therefore less desirous of conflict when trade is high. But by their own logic, authoritarian leaders either should be slightly less inclined to conflict (if at least somewhat sensitive to public opinion) as trade rises or unaffected by trade levels altogether. Why they might be propelled into conflict *because* of increasing trade is left unexplained by such an argument.

Gelpi and Grieco (2003b, 52, 54) are not unaware of this problem. Yet to deal with it, they simply assert that realists must have it right when it comes to authoritarian states—that is, that increasing commerce heightens their senses of vulnerability to any cutoffs in trade. This is an ad hoc fallback argument that does not tell us why realism only applies to authoritarian states or under what conditions a realist-like logic might apply to democracies as well, thereby offsetting the opportunity cost reasoning. A more plausible conceptual approach—one that would offer a consistent theoretical argument across all dyads—would start with the idea that it is the economic characteristics of democracies and authoritarian states, as opposed to their domestic institutional or moral qualities per se, that drive their likelihood of military conflict.

A trade expectations approach, for example, would interpret Gelpi and Grieco's findings as follows. Democracies, because of their liberal economic structures and ideologies, are generally more oriented to free trade—or at least freer trade—than authoritarian states. As such, when two democracies have high trade they are likely to feel confident about the long-term prospects for open commerce. This should hold even when the tariffs and nontariff barriers to trade are occasionally raised, say, to punish other states for what are judged to be unfair trade practices in certain sectors. But if authoritarian states are seen, because of their economic orientations, as less committed to long-term "open-door" policies, increasing levels of trade dependence can actually increase the probability of militarized conflict. Uncertain or pessimistic trade expectations would push one or both sides to turn to military force to protect access to raw materials, investments, and markets. Adverse trade-security spirals might result that would only exacerbate mistrust and hostility. The democratic peace, in this reading, is therefore really an economic peace, based on the largely free-trading orientation that most democracies adopt. It is positive expectations about the future commercial environment that leads two democracies with increasing trade dependence to have a lower risk of a militarized conflict. And it is more pessimistic expectations about future commerce that makes dyads with authoritarian states more conflict prone.[8]

Studies by Hegre, Mousseau, Gartzke, and McDonald point strongly toward the idea that it is the economic characteristics of certain states—and what these characteristics say to the outside world—that really matter, and not their legislative or moral aspects per se.[9] Hegre and Mousseau, in separate work, show that the effects of interdependence and those of joint democracy, respectively, on the likelihood of militarized conflict are conditioned by the levels of development that two states have reached. When statistical models that include interactive terms for interdependence and development as well as democracy and development are tested, the simple arguments for the liberal commercial peace and liberal democratic peace are overturned or highly qualified. Hegre (2000, 16) demonstrates that when the interactive term of interdependence × development is added to the baseline model, the coefficients for the interactive term and for the development variable on its own are significant and negative. The interdependence variable on its own, however, while it remains highly statistically significant, reverses its sign from negative to positive. This indicates that trade dependence only helps to reduce the likelihood of military conflict when both states are highly developed nations. When there is a low level of development between one or both states in a trading relationship, higher levels of interdependence can actually increase the probability of conflict. These results are reproduced in table 2.2.[10]

Mousseau's (2003, table 1, 490, and table 2, 495) work is focused more on the possibility that it is the democratic peace, rather than the liberal commercial peace per se, that is conditioned by the level and nature of development. Nevertheless, his findings have dramatic implications for the study of economic interdependence and war. In the initial presentation of his research, he shows that once one introduces an interactive term for democracy and development, the coefficient for joint democracy

---

[8] Note that it is not that democracies necessarily create more actual trade, trade that might then be serving as an intervening variable to foster greater peace. The effect of positive expectations for future trade between democracies should hold even when current trade is low or nonexistent, given each side's anticipation of a future stream of benefits if both states stay peaceful. This point is nicely supported by the literature discussed below.

[9] For the institutional and normative arguments underpinning the traditional democratic peace research program, see especially Doyle 1986b; Russett 1993; Maoz and Russett 1993; Owen 1994; Chan 1997; Dixon 1994; Lipson 2003; Ray 1995; Gleditsch 2008. For critiques, see especially Farber and Gowa 1995; Layne 1994; Rosato 2003.

[10] Hegre's dependent variable is the onset of a fatal militarized interstate dispute over the period 1950–92. He employs a multiplicative gravity model to measure dyadic interdependence. Development is captured by GDP per capita. To save space, I have omitted Hegre's size asymmetry and peace history variables.

TABLE 2.2 Hegre's Results on the Role
of Development and Interdependence

(Dependent Variable: Onset of a Fatal Militarized Interstate Dispute, 1950–92)

	Model 1	Model 2
Development and trade variables		
Interdependence	−0.13***	0.87***
(residual from gravity model of trade)	(0.39)	(0.29)
Development: GDP per capita	−0.48***	−0.70***
	(0.18)	(0.16)
Interdependence × development	—	−0.14***
		(0.04)
Control variables		
Two democracies	0.28	0.34
	(0.40)	(0.39)
Two autocracies	0.019	−0.045
	(0.26)	(0.25)
Missing regime data	−0.91	−.076
	(0.78)	(0.76)
Contiguity	3.03***	3.02***
	(0.35)	(0.34)
Alliance	0.06	0.007
	(0.25)	(0.25)
One major power	−0.14	−0.001
	(0.37)	(0.36)
Two major powers	0.52	0.47
	(0.53)	(0.53)
Number of observations	266,094	266,094

Note: Hegre 2000, 16, with size asymmetry and peace history control variables removed for space considerations. Models 1 and 2 above correspond to Hegre's models 1b and 1c, respectively. Standard errors for coefficients appear in parentheses. All tests for statistical significance are two tailed. * $p < 0.10$; ** $p < 0.05$; *** $p < 0.01$.

goes from being negative to positive, even as the coefficient for the interactive term is negative. This suggests that joint democracy only helps to reduce the risk of conflict when both actors are developed nations. When development levels are low, joint democracy can actually increase the likelihood of a militarized conflict—a result that Mousseau confirms in a later article coauthored with Hegre and Oneal.[11] All this builds the

[11] Mousseau, Hegre, and Oneal 2003, 294–300.

case for the intriguing proposition that the democratic peace is really an economic peace, not a political one.

In his more recent work, Mousseau (2009, 61) seeks to unpack the causal reasons for why development, in correlational terms, seems to have these strong conditioning effects. He suggests that developed states are more able to foster what he calls *contract-intensive economies* (CIEs): economies where transactions are based around impersonal contracts backed by effective legal systems rather than on traditional social connections and personal contacts. When firms are conducting business within and between such CIEs, he argues, they are able to overcome problems of trust regarding the other's true commitment to carrying out its expressed obligations into the future, problems that might otherwise impede their willingness to go forward. As he summarizes it, CIEs "foster the expectation that strangers will fulfill their contractual commitments," implying that states with established CIEs will have "higher levels of impersonal trust than other nations." In his empirical tests, the interactive term, joint democracy × CIE, is strongly significant and negative, while the coefficient on the joint democracy variable, depending on model specifications, is either negative or positive, but never reaches a level of statistical significance. This implies that joint democracy is only peace inducing when at least one of the states has a CIE. The finding, moreover, is robust: the interactive variable remains statistically significant and negative even after the introduction of competing economic variables, including trade interdependence and capital openness. These results are shown in table 2.3.[12]

Taken together, Hegre's and Mousseau's empirical work forces us to fundamentally rethink the liberal notions that increasing trade and joint democracy are, on their own, factors that necessarily lead to higher probabilities of peace. Yet we must return to the well-known point that quantitative findings, in and of themselves, are merely suggestive correlations; they cannot tell us anything directly about the causal mechanisms underlying the correlations. Conjectural interpretation is necessarily required. Our common scholarly goal must be this: to discover a plausible interpretation that covers as many of the findings as possible. In short, which of the causal explanations makes the most sense of all the diverse quantitative evidence?

---

[12]Mousseau 2009, table 2. Mousseau's dependent variable is the onset of a fatal militarized interstate dispute across the years 1961 to 2001. He measures joint democracy via the weak-link hypothesis. CIE is a dichotomous variable. It is measured by a "single-state CIE" (one state in a dyad has a CIE, or neither does) versus a joint CIE, since the latter has a perfect correlation with peace and thus would bias the results in favor of his logic (ibid., 68–71).

Table 2.3 Mousseau's Results on the Role of Democracy and a CIE

(Dependent Variable: Onset of a Fatal Militarized Interstate Dispute, 1961–2001)

	Model 1	Model 2	Model 3
Democracy and CIE variables			
Democracy$_L$	−0.03	−0.02	0.02
	(0.02)	(0.02)	(0.02)
Democracy$_L$ × one-state CIE	−0.20***	−0.20***	−0.27***
	(0.04)	(0.04)	(0.06)
One-state CIE	−0.85**	−0.90**	−1.47**
	(0.30)	(0.30)	(0.53)
Development$_L$	0.05	—	—
	(0.09)		
Trade interdependence$_L$	—	−0.59	—
		(0.41)	
Capital openness$_L$	—	—	−0.15**
			(0.05)
Control variables			
Capability ratio$_L$	−0.21***	−0.23***	−0.15
Major power	0.94***	0.96***	0.84*
Contiguity	1.52***	1.56***	1.37***
Distance	−3.42***	−3.43***	−3.78***
Brevity of peace	3.14***	3.13***	3.13***
Development$_H$	−0.38**	−0.33**	−0.35**
Distance × development$_H$	0.34***	0.34***	0.37***
Number of observations	276,133	276,133	145,584

Note: Mousseau 2009, 73. The subscript L indicates the choosing of the state in a dyad with the lower level of the particular variable (with subscript H the higher level). Standard errors for coefficients appear in parentheses (Mousseau does not report them for the control variables for reasons of space). $^*p < 0.05$; $^{**}p < 0.01$; $^{***}p < 0.001$. CIE stands for contract-intensive economy. Models 1, 2, and 3 above correspond to Mousseau's models 1, 2 and 6, respectively.

Hegre's causal conjecture, borrowing from Rosecrance, is that higher development levels increase the costs of grabbing and holding territory, which might explain why higher trade only reduces the likelihood of militarized conflict when states are economically developed. This, however, can only be at best a partial explanation. Peter Liberman (1996a) has shown empirically that under a variety of conditions, even in the twentieth century, developed states can often effectively attack and then economically exploit other advanced economies. Mousseau's argument points us in a different and potentially more fruitful direction. Developed economies are typically ones based on CIE structures that encourage higher levels of impersonal trust between strangers. Given this, their expectations regarding the future commercial environment are likely to be much more positive. In the language of this book's theory, this implies that leaders in a CIE-rich environment will have much greater confidence that commercial partners will continue to have open access to raw materials, investments, and markets. Thus they will have more reason for optimism regarding their future power positions, and less reason for the initiation of preventive war or crises designed to coerce more raw material, investment, and market access at the point of a gun.

As I will now show, this interpretation is supported by a wide variety of other large-N tests conducted over the last decade, some of which directly employ the notion of commercial expectations to understand their results. Edward Mansfield, Jon Pevehouse, and David Bearce (1999–2000) demonstrate that preferential trading arrangements—a broad class of institutions that include free trade zones, common markets, and custom unions—have a statistically significant and negative effect on the likelihood of militarized interstate disputes. In a follow-up analysis, Mansfield and Pevehouse (2000, 788) show that the probability of a militarized interstate dispute is cut in half if the two states belong to a preferential trading arrangement than if they do not, and that these agreements have a conflict-dampening effect even when current trade is low or nonexistent. Drawing on trade expectations theory, these scholars offer a straightforward explanation for these findings: preferential trade arrangements "foster expectations of future economic gains" by reducing trade barriers while increasing the likelihood that participants will maintain minimal barriers off into the future. As such, they "enhance the credibility of commitments made by a state's current administration to sustain open trade with selected trade partners" even as they help bind subsequent administrations that may be more protectionist in orientation (Mansfield, Pevehouse, and Bearce 1999–2000, 98).[13] The commitment problem that makes trading states wonder about the other's true willingness to maintain open trade into the future is therefore ameliorated, if not completely eliminated.

In subsequent work, Bearce (2001, 2003) backs up these conjectures through case studies. Examining three institutions that began life as regional trading arrangements—the Gulf Cooperation Council charter

---

[13] See also Mansfield and Pevehouse 2000, 779–80. For an early, nonquantitative assertion of the need for institutions and interdependence to work together to create the conditions for peace, see Keohane 1990.

between Persian Gulf states, the Mercosur pact between states in the southern cone of South America, and the ECOWAS pact of West African states—he shows that expectations of future trade benefits helped to moderate incentives for militarized conflict.[14] This proved to be true even when interstate trade levels were initially low, with positive expectations for the future giving states a stake in the present peace. Moreover, from Bearce's perspective, it was not the mere existence of the regional pacts that helped foster better political relations. High-level meetings between state leaders and top officials were also critical to the establishment of greater degrees of trust regarding the others' commitment to future trade and peace. In a large-N study that measures the degree of high-level meetings, Bearce and Sawa Omori (2005, 664, 671) go further. They show that high-level diplomatic contacts between states involved in preferential trade arrangements prove particularly important across a wide variety of model specification in dampening the likelihood of militarized conflict. Such contacts have a negative and statistically significant effect even in the presence of such alternative variables as the degree of economic integration and levels of trade interdependence. Bearce and Omori's explanation is instructive. The more states engage in high-level contacts within a preferential trading arrangement, they suggest, the more state leaders can come to trust each other—with trust in their logic being defined as having "positive present expectations about the other actor's future behavior." As trust grows, actors come to believe that the other is indeed committed to maintaining their promises within the institutional structure.[15]

Commercial expectations also likely play a dominant role in the reality of any "capitalist peace" in world history. Such a peace has recently been asserted separately by Erik Gartzke and Patrick McDonald. Building on the idea that the democratic peace is more a reflection of economic structures than domestic institutions or liberal norms, Gartzke and McDonald seek to demonstrate that the statistical and substantive significance of joint democracy is either reduced or completely washed out once variables measuring degrees of joint capitalism are introduced. For Gartzke, capitalist states typically share higher levels of economic development, have common interests in maintaining valuable finance and trade flows, and are better able to signal their willingness to fight because the market repercussions associated with military conflict serve as costly signals of

[14] Mercosur stands for Mercado Commun del Sur; ECOWAS stands for the Economic Community of West African States.

[15] Yoram Haftel (2007) confirms the importance of high-level contacts within regional trading arrangements, while also emphasizing their ability to foster trust and mutual confidence.

their resolve. These three elements together should make capitalist states less likely to become involved in a militarized interstate dispute.[16] Table 2.4 reproduces some of Gartzke's (2007, table 1, 177) key results.[17] It illustrates that higher mutual financial openness, his primary measure of the level of market capitalism, has a negative and statistically significant effect on the likelihood of a militarized interstate dispute. Perhaps even more important, this variable's addition to the baseline model has the effect of washing out the statistical significance of joint democracy. Gartzke thus concludes that any liberal peace is rooted not in the political institutions of democracy but instead in the economic openness that is associated with liberal democratic states.[18]

McDonald also puts forward an argument for a capitalist peace, but he comes at it from a different angle. He contends that when nations have high protectionist barriers to trade and the state itself owns a large percentage of key industries in the economy, leaders with aggressive intentions are less constrained from initiating military conflicts. With government coffers flush with tariff revenue and the profits from nationalized firms, and private businesses with foreign trade interests having less say in executive decisions, leaders are more able to initiate wars and expansionist policies when they so desire. Conversely, when trade barriers are low and government-owned firms constitute only a small part of the economy, leaders will be constrained from initiating conflicts both by the lack of financial resources and backlash from private business interests.

---

[16]There are good reasons to doubt the third element of Gartzke's explanation, which reiterates the signaling argument introduced by Gartzke, Quan Li, and Charles Boehmer (2001; see also Gartzke and Li 2003). As discussed in chapter 1, there is no logical reason why either high trade or financial dependence should help a state signal its resolve to use military power in a crisis. Li himself now rejects this argument. In recent work with Rafael Reuveny, Li identifies a number of significant empirical problems with the signaling logic, including the fact that once one disaggregates overall trade into its components, certain key export and import sectors are quantitatively associated with more militarized conflict, not less. See Li and Reuveny 2009, 182–83. Their findings are supported in Dorussen 2006 and Souva 2000. Jana von Stein (2001) also shows that efforts at "economic signaling"—the use of economic sanctions to communicate resolve—are, if anything, quantitatively associated with a greater probability of a militarized interstate dispute, not a lower one. This result directly contradicts the signaling argument, even if it is nicely consistent with trade expectations theory, which would stress how trade cutoffs can increase another state's pessimism regarding its future power position.

[17]Gartzke's dependent variable is the onset of a militarized interstate dispute for the period 1950–92. His measures of trade dependence, democracy, development, and his key variable, financial openness, all employ the weak-link hypothesis.

[18]For a critique of Gartzke's methodology, see Dafoe 2011. For the view that it is foreign direct investment flows in particular that create the conditions for a commercial peace, see Rosecrance and Thompson 2003.

TABLE 2.4 Gartzke's Results on the Role of Democracy
and Capitalism ("Financial Openness")

(Dependent Variable: Onset of a Militarized Interstate Dispute, 1950–92)

	Model 1	Model 2	Model 3	Model 4
Democracy and economic variables				
Democracy$_L$	−0.064***	−0.010	−0.011	−0.017
	(0.014)	(0.014)	(0.013)	(0.012)
Democracy$_H$	0.0356***	0.0077	0.0080	−0.0022
	(0.010)	(0.012)	(0.012)	(0.013)
Trade dependence$_L$	−37.8343*	−16.9177	−5.2063	−5.4023
	(15.874)	(10.073)	(8.473)	(9.036)
Financial openness$_L$	—	−0.1877***	−0.2143***	−0.2468***
		(0.053)	(0.059)	(0.058)
Development$_L$	—	—	2.237×10^{-4}***	2.481×10^{-4}***
			(3.87×10^{-5})	(3.25×10^{-5})
Development$_L$ × continuity	—	—	-2.853×10^{-4}***	-2.776×10^{-4}***
			(4.91×10^{-5})	(4.92×10^{-5})
Interests	—	—	—	−0.9824***
				(0.201)
Control variables				
Contiguity	2.003***	0.760***	3.429***	3.740***
	(0.211)	(0.302)	(0.306)	(0.273)
Distance	−0.6108***	−0.4742***	−0.4327***	−0.4164***
	(0.084)	(0.097)	(0.093)	(0.085)
Major power	2.515***	2.030***	1.973***	1.404***
	(0.257)	(0.374)	(0.356)	(0.273)
Alliance	−0.430*	−0.238	−0.217	−0.007
	(0.203)	(0.240)	(0.232)	(0.233)
Capability ratio	−0.304***	−0.129*	−0.130*	−0.151**
	(0.055)	(0.060)	(0.058)	(0.056)
Number of observations	282,287	175,548	171,509	166,140

Note: Gartzke 2007, 177. The subscript L indicates the choosing of the state in a dyad with the lower level of the particular variable (with subscript H denoting the higher level). Contiguity, major power, and alliance are dummy variables, while distance and capability ratio are logged variables. I have omitted Gartzke's controls for region to save space. Standard errors for coefficients appear in parentheses. * $p < 0.05$; ** $p < 0.01$; *** $p < 0.001$. Models 1, 2, 3, and 4 correspond to Gartzke's models 1, 2, 4, and 5, respectively.

McDonald's empirical work seems to support these domestic-level explanations. His measures of protectionism and government ownership of the economy are both statistically significant as well as in the expected positive direction. That is, as protectionism and government ownership grow, there is a greater likelihood of a militarized interstate dispute. When no interactive terms are used, as depicted in table 2.5, trade dependence has no statistical significance. Something interesting happens, however, when McDonald introduces an interactive term, dependence × protectionism, to capture the possibility that trade's effect is conditional on the level of tariff barriers. The interactive term is positive and statistically significant (as is the protectionist variable on its own), while the coefficient on dependence is negative and now shows statistical significance. These results, as McDonald (2009, tables 4.4 and 4.5, 102–5) presents them (i.e., without the control variables), are displayed in table 2.6.[19]

How do we interpret these findings? One implication, as McDonald (ibid., 104–6) notes, is that higher bilateral trade flows may only inhibit military conflict when both states have relatively low levels of import barriers. But the findings also indicate that even "when bilateral trade is absent between two members of a dyad, higher levels of regulatory barriers still increase the likelihood of military conflict." Both of these empirical insights fit perfectly with the trade expectations argument. High protectionist barriers will propel states that are already dependent on trade toward the initiation of militarized policies or even war, knowing that such actions can help to reestablish access to vital resources, investments, and markets, thereby avoiding decline. We will see this logic unfold with a vengeance in the Japan 1941 case (chapter 5). Even when current trade is low or nonexistent, though, highly protectionist stances by state X can provoke militarized behavior by state Y if Y needs what X's sphere can offer, but believes that there is little possibility of gaining access to that sphere. This, as chapter 6 discusses, was a major causal reason for ongoing Cold War tensions between the United States and Soviet Union after 1944 up to the late 1980s.

Interestingly, McDonald's domestic-level argument has a difficult time explaining the second part of these findings. To be sure, when trade is high, large import barriers could well provide the revenue that is supposed to facilitate the aggressive policies of illiberal leaders according to McDonald's logic. Yet when trade is low or nonexistent, trade barriers such as tariffs generate little or no revenue for the simple reason

---

[19] McDonald's dependent variable is the onset of a militarized interstate dispute for the period 1970–2001. The trade dependence and democracy variables employ the weak-link hypothesis, while his variables for protectionism and government ownership use the state in the dyad with the higher level of these two factors to provide a better test of his argument that more protectionism and public ownership should increase the probability of conflict.

TABLE 2.5 McDonald's Results on the Role of Protectionism
and Government Ownership ("Public")

(Dependent Variable: Onset of a Militarized Interstate Dispute, 1970–2001)

	Model 1	Model 2
Economic and domestic variables		
$Protect_H$ (tariff levels)	0.024***	0.020***
	(0.007)	(0.007)
$Public_H$ (government ownership)	—	0.014***
		(0.004)
$Democracy_L$	–0.046***	–0.036**
	(0.013)	(0.013)
$Dependence_L$	–2.691	–3.415
	(5.442)	(5.158)
Control variables		
Power preponderance	–0.116*	–0.112*
	(0.061)	(0.060)
Great power	1.408***	1.445***
	(0.210)	(0.203)
Interests	–1.074**	–0.998**
	(0.359)	(0.352)
Allies	0.657**	0.684**
	(0.205)	(0.207)
Distance	–0.298***	–0.279***
	(0.091)	(0.094)
Contiguous	2.187***	2.211***
	(0.282)	(0.286)
$Development_L$	1.9×10^{-4}***	1.7×10^{-4}***
	(7.1×10^{-5})	(7.0×10^{-5})
$Development^2_L$	1.2×10^{-8}**	1.2×10^{-8}**
	(5.1×10^{-9})	(4.9×10^{-9})
Number of observations	87,708	85,416

Note: McDonald 2009, 102. The subscript L indicates the choosing of the state in a dyad with the lower level of the particular variable (with subscript H denoting the higher level). Standard errors for coefficients appear in parentheses. * $p < 0.10$; ** $p < 0.05$; *** $p < 0.01$. Models 1 and 2 above correspond to McDonald's columns 1 and 3, respectively (his columns 2 and 4 provide an alternative specification of the protect variable). McDonald notes that splines were added to all models, but not shown.

that trade is not flowing between the two states. By focusing only on the removal of constraining factors such as low government revenue while offering no propelling rationales for state aggression, McDonald's theory cannot explain why states that have little or no current trade might still be pushed into conflict for economic reasons. If they have a strong

TABLE 2.6 McDonald's Results on the Interaction
of Dependence and Protectionism

(Dependent Variable: Onset of a Militarized Interstate Dispute, 1970–2001)

	Model 1	Model 2
Protect$_H$ (tariff levels)	0.019.**	0.015*
	(0.008)	(0.008)
Public$_H$ (government ownership)	—	0.014***
		(0.004)
Dependence$_L$	–24.483*	–24.410*
	(14.210)	(13.353)
Dependence$_L$ × protect$_H$	3.737**	3.615*
	(1.898)	(1.850)
Number of observations	87,708	85,416

Note: McDonald 2009, 105. In his published version, McDonald does not include his control variables to save space (for the list, see my table 2.5). The subscript L indicates the choosing of the state in a dyad with the lower level of the particular variable (with subscript H denoting the higher level). Standard errors for coefficients appear in parentheses. * p < 0.10; ** p < 0.05; *** p < 0.01. Models 1 and 2 above correspond to McDonald's columns 1 and 3, respectively (his columns 2 and 4 provide an alternative specification of the protect variable). McDonald notes that splines were added to all models, but not shown.

unfulfilled need for trade, however, and each believes that the other is not likely to satisfy this need, then conflict, according to trade expectations theory, is likely. In short, a trade expectations approach can provide a parsimonious explanation for the impact of protectionism on militarized conflict that covers both dimensions of McDonald's empirical findings, including the one left unexplained by his domestic-level argument.[20]

McDonald's other main large-N finding—that higher levels of government ownership in the economy are associated with increased risks of militarized conflict—is more directly consistent with his domestic logic. States in which the government runs much of the economy through state-owned enterprises are indeed more likely to have the revenue needed to prepare for and initiate war. Yet McDonald still has no explanation for why such states might be peaceful for many years before they decide to initiate war or dangerous crises. His case studies do not help him here,

[20]Trade expectations theory's interpretation of McDonald's evidence is further supported here by the work of Michelle Benson (2007). Benson shows that positive trend lines in trade levels between states that are just starting to trade or have had previously low levels of trade have a statistically significant dampening effect on the likelihood of militarized conflict. Positive trends in trade also had a negative impact on the probability of a militarized interstate dispute for states that previously have had middle and high levels of trade (although the mid-level finding was not statistically significant).

given that he provides no examples of a state with high government ownership initiating a militarized crisis or war.[21] As we will see in the remaining chapters, there is little evidence that leaders of great powers in the two centuries after 1790 saw strong government control over public enterprises as even a necessary condition for the initiation of conflict, let alone a sufficient one. When there was the rational need for conflict, great powers of all stripes proved more than willing and able to initiate hard-line policies, even when government ownership of the economy was minimal—as it was with such states as Britain and the United States, for instance. The remaining chapters show that great powers typically started conflicts only when they saw looming threats to their future access to raw materials, investments, and markets.[22] In essence, it is declining confidence in the future commercial environment, not domestic economic structures, that best explains why states so often fall into war and militarized crises.

QUALITATIVE ANALYSIS: A NEW APPROACH AND A SUMMARY OF THE FINDINGS

The above look at recent quantitative work has shown how an expectational approach not only can supply a powerful explanation for many of the large-N results over the last decade but also explain anomalies that remain in the quantitative findings. Yet large-N analysis, even if it is the dominant methodology for testing claims about interdependence and conflict, is clearly not enough. As I discuss below, the approach has a number of important limitations inherent to its very setup, including its inability to directly measure leader expectations of the future and its difficulty in dealing with the specific causal roles played by different variables within situations of complex causality. In particular, quantitative approaches have a problem in dealing with rare events of a certain

[21] McDonald's case studies of the United States and Britain regarding Oregon in 1845–46 and Venezuela in 1895 focus on how the United States' and Britain's relatively open trade policies might have helped them resolve conflicts before war occurred. Their fall into these crises certainly cannot be explained by the government-ownership variable, since both states had low levels on this variable throughout the nineteenth century and into the twentieth century. His explanation for World War I is security driven: Germany initiated a preventive war out of fear of Russia's rise. While Russia's rise, as McDonald observes, was partly fueled by revenues generated by public enterprises, Russia was not the initiator of conflict and in fact sought to buy time for further economic growth. This is contrary to McDonald's baseline prediction for why government ownership increases the probability of conflict.

[22] McDonald's empirical result—the strong positive correlation between government ownership and militarized conflict—may be an artifact of the time period he studies: 1970 to 2001. Many of the conflicts of this period were initiated by Russia or states in the Middle East—nations with strong levels of public ownership of the economy.

kind—namely, those phenomena such as war and crisis initiation where leaders, prior to such events, are aware of their own impact on the very factors that go into the mix of variables determining the rare event.

Still, the problems that may be inherent in large-N analysis do not imply that case study research, at least as it has been traditionally practiced, is necessarily a superior methodology. This research has generally suffered from two overlapping concerns: selection bias and a lack of generalizability. Qualitative research has always had one obvious advantage over large-N work: it can reveal the causal mechanisms that join independent variables to dependent ones, thereby helping explain why factor A or factor B is associated with event E (George and Bennett 2005). This goes beyond the inherently correlational analysis of quantitative methods. Yet it also leads qualitative researchers to select cases that are particularly useful in illustrating the way these causal mechanisms work in practice. Through in-depth process tracing, qualitative scholars can show to what extent the leaders acted for the reasons posed by one theory versus another, and how salient these reasons were in the context of all the factors shaping and constraining the actors at the time. But because the goal of traditional qualitative research has been to reveal why actors did indeed act, researchers tend to fall into the trap of picking cases that do a good job illustrating causal mechanisms while ignoring cases that do not fit the model. Even when such researchers can plausibly demonstrate that the cases chosen are "hard cases" for the theory being tested, or that they conform to the dictates of such techniques as John Stuart Mill's methods of difference or agreement, there is still the problem of generalizability. We might have confidence for the cases selected, but we have no way of knowing how well the theory works or under what conditions for the broader population of cases.[23]

These related problems of selection bias and generalizability might seem inherent to qualitative case study research. As we will see, however, when dealing with rare events, it is possible, at least as an ideal, to lay out what is essentially the "universe" of cases within a particular time frame and for a certain type of actors (e.g., great powers). Setting forward this universe of cases forces a researcher to determine how well the theory or theories being tested do across the full scope of cases. In-depth analysis will still be required on cases that have the potential to support a scholar's favored theory—after all, the scholar must still convince the reader that the theory does indeed explain particular cases. Yet by framing the cases that work within the larger context, we avoid the selection bias charge while also providing a sense of how well the theory travels across space

---

[23] See King, Keohane, and Verba 1994; Collier and Mahoney 1996; Collier, Mahoney, and Seawright 2004; Brady and Collier 2010.

as well as time. And most important, from a practical standpoint this approach tells us what we want to know: how often any specific theory explains the rare events of interest and how frequently it does not. This allows us to transcend stale debates about whether particular theories or factors "matter" to concentrate on more relevant questions: *how often they matter*, and *with what relative force or salience.*

A NEW APPROACH TO THE QUALITATIVE STUDY OF RARE EVENTS IN INTERNATIONAL RELATIONS

Rare events in international relations such as the onset of crises and wars pose significant challenges for large-N researchers. The fact that there are so few positive cases of the phenomenon to be explained can play havoc with measures of coefficients and statistical significance. These methodological concerns can be mitigated to some degree by incorporating all the rare events but only a small randomized percentage of the cases of nonevents into the sample.[24] From a qualitative researcher's perspective, however, such large-N research is missing a key point: that rare events are rare for a reason. Rare events in international relations are typically situations where a complex set of factors must come together for the event to occur. Each of the particular factors is a necessary condition for the event, since without each factor the event would not happen. Yet when put together, they become sufficient to produce the event. This is the deductive logic of "individually necessary, jointly sufficient" (INJS), whereby factors A, B, and C must be included in a particular bundle of causal variables before event E can come about. And for almost all phenomena in international relations, there are multiple pathways to a specific type of event such as war or alliance formation. This means that other complex bundles of factors—perhaps A, D, and J, or D, K, L, and M—may also be sufficient for E to arise.[25]

Such complex conjunctural causality poses a problem for large-N research, given that regression analysis is designed to show the independent and additive impact of individual causal variables, not how factors might have to come together as necessary conditions before phenomenon E will

---

[24] See King and Zeng 2001a, 2001b. On the distortions created by overly large data sets, see also Braumoeller and Satori 2004.

[25] See especially Ragin 1987, 2000, 2008. See also Mackie 1980; Mahoney and Goertz 2006; Bennett and Elman 2006. The acronym that Mackie (1980, 62) uses to capture the idea that each bundle of necessary factors is sufficient on its own, but not necessary for E, is INUS—individual factors are an "insufficient but nonredundant [necessary] part of an unnecessary but sufficient" bundle of conditions. The idea that there are multiple paths to event E often goes under the name *equifinality* (George and Bennett 2005).

occur. As we saw earlier, quantitative researchers can deal with complex conjunctural causality to some degree through the use of interactive variables, with a new variable A × B included in the regression model instead of A and B being treated only separately and additively (Friedrich 1982; Braumoeller 2004). There is a limit to this solution, though. If factor A operates within a causal bundle only as a threshold condition—having to reach a certain level before it has any important causal effect, but then having little or no additional effect after that threshold is achieved—then treating A as a part of multiplicative interactive variable will create significant distortions in the results. If we as researchers do not know this threshold level ahead of time, or if leaders themselves have different estimates of the threshold level, then large-N tests will frequently see no statistical significance for interactive variables despite the fact that A and B together are indeed crucial parts of the causal story. To take an obvious example, if leaders in state Y believe they need a certain level of domestic popularity—say, at least a 50 percent positive approval rating from the public—before they can contemplate launching a successful war against state X, then this threshold will operate as a necessary condition for war. Anything below 50 percent and the leaders will have to hold off from starting the conflict. But ratings above 50 percent may have no additional impact on the leaders' predisposition to start a war, meaning that including domestic popularity as factor A in an interactive variable may lead to a statistically insignificant result for something that is in fact critical to the overall "mix" that the leader is considering. This would be especially true if leaders in states W and Z had different estimates for the domestic support threshold.[26]

There are additional problems, however, that quantitativists face in dealing with the complex conjunctural causality that is inherent to rare events in international relations. For one thing, while quantitative research can show that a factor is correlated with the emergence of a crisis or war, and can use interactive variables to capture some aspects of complex causality, it cannot say *what causal role* a particular factor played within any complex INJS pathway leading to E or not E. As scholars and as leaders, we need to know more than simply that factor A was associated with the arising of event E. We need to know whether factor A was propelling actors toward behaviors that led to E, or whether it played more of a facilitating or reinforcing role for other more primary propelling variables, or indeed whether it was constraining the actor from taking actions that might have otherwise produced E.

---

[26] For this reason, treating A and B as dummy variables within an interactive variable does not solve the problem, since the researcher must impose a priori thresholds on a continuous variable without empirical evidence and without consideration of variations among leaders.

These are terms that are frequently thrown around in academic discourse but rarely defined. A *propelling factor* is one that directly involves an actor's ultimate ends and desires or fears—its "reasons" for acting. A leader worried about the state's future power because of a trade cutoff, for example, is propelled by the fear of the future and a concern for security into initiating a crisis or war. A *facilitating factor* is one that is incidental to the actor's ends, but needs to be in place before the desired action can be carried out. The above-mentioned need of leaders to reach a threshold of domestic support before starting a war is an obvious instance of a facilitating factor: this support is not pushing the leader into war but instead must be achieved before the war can begin. A *constraining factor* is in some sense the flip side of a facilitating factor: if the public support is not there, then the leader is constrained from acting. More narrowly, though, a constraining factor is something that is pulling actors back from doing what they might otherwise want to do. We saw this with the liberal argument for why trade leads to peace—namely, that trade constrains leaders who might have unit-level reasons for wanting war by increasing the value of continued peace. A *reinforcing factor* is one that operates to make the potential effect of a key propelling factor that much more likely to occur. Take, for example, ethnic or ideological differences between dependent nation Y and the nation cutting it off from trade. Such differences might easily create an even greater desire for war, since Y has a stronger reason to fear the implications of the relative decline caused by the cutoff.[27]

When we are dealing with the complex conjunctural causality underpinning rare events, understanding the functional role played by a variable is critical. If we know that when A, B, and C come together, event E typically follows, it is important to know whether factor A was propelling state Y to war or simply facilitating the decision for war. Indeed, the very "support" or lack of support for a theory depends on it. In this book, for example, if a leader's level of domestic popularity (or lack thereof) is actually propelling the actor to start a war, and the trade environment is acting as merely a constraining or facilitating factor, then liberal and neo-Marxist arguments for war are supported. Conversely, if the trade environment is actually propelling the leader to choose war to maximize the nation's security, and domestic popularity is simply a constraining or facilitating factor, then economic realist and trade expectations arguments have potential explanatory force. Note that large-N quantitative work cannot help us here: in either scenario, all the factors

---

[27]We could also talk about *accelerating factors*—that is, ones that work with propelling factors to speed up the process that leads to event E. Knowing that the other is trying to form alliances is a classic example of something that can speed up a state's timetable for war (see Christensen 2011).

are correlated with war, and thus all the theories seem equally plausible as explanations.

Another dimension that complicates large-N work on rare events in international relations is the specific nature of the endogeneity problem. Events such as crisis initiation and war are almost always a function of the decisions of a select few individuals at the heads of states X and Y. Such leaders are usually highly aware that they hold the fate of their nations in their hands, and that many of the conditions that can increase the likelihood of crisis and war depend on their "choices," and therefore are a function of their own diplomatic and military behavior. Military and trade-security dilemmas of the kind discussed in the previous chapters are only two examples of the endogeneity concerns that leaders may be cognizant of. Quantitative methodologies have an inherent difficulty dealing with such concerns, since it is the leaders' anticipations of *future* effects that is affecting their behavior *now*. Large-N data sets, at least in international relations, can only develop rough proxies for leaders' anticipations of effects; there are, after all, no across-the-board historical surveys of leaders that can measure such beliefs. Documentary process tracing, on the other hand, does give a researcher at least some access to the inner thinking and planning of leaders as they grapple with their awareness of feedback loops and endogeneity. Moreover, in a book such as this one where expectations of the future are a fundamental variable said to be driving behavior, the best way to investigate leader expectations is ultimately through careful documentary analysis. Quantitative work of the kind studied in the first half of this chapter can allow us to infer that expectations of the future were at work across many cases, but such inferences will be indirect and thus ultimately unsatisfying. We need to go further, and that is where qualitative historical work shows its stuff.

This discussion of endogeneity and leader anticipations of the future leads to an additional point. In situations such as great power politics where a few key leaders have great influence over the destinies of nations, decision makers know that they have the ability to manipulate both the other's beliefs *and* the characteristics of their social unit—in this case, the nation-state. This means that hard-line actions such as the initiation of war can be deferred until certain domestic or international conditions have been altered to facilitate a policy shift. These two facts play havoc with large-N analyses, since they create the possibility not only of feedback loops but also of leaders deliberately shaping key parameters before embarking on important actions that bring on rare events. As a result, the posited control variables in a large-N analysis will often not be independent of one another. Indeed, they will likely move together in a predictable direction just before the rare event arises. A war that is planned in advance, for instance, will likely see the build up of military power, tightening of alliances, mobilization of nationalism and domestic support, reduction of democratic rights, and development of offensive technologies just before the war is initiated. Any correlation of these variables with the dependent variable will be overstated by the fact of prewar planning, with the real propelling cause of both war and changes in these variables likely overlooked.[28]

For all these reasons, qualitative documentary analysis is the best method for studying rare events in international relations, at least when one has access to the documents that reveal the inner decision-making process of the actors in question. In-depth documentary work provides us with a window into the thinking of key decision makers as they make estimates of future realities, grapple with trade-offs associated with feedback loops and escalatory spirals, and adjust their behavior to alter the factors that will serve their ends. Yet the way qualitative case study analysis has been traditionally approached in international relations leaves much to be desired, precisely because researchers are prone to pick only a handful of examples from the larger population of cases. This leads to the above-mentioned charges of selection bias and lack of generalizability—charges that always seem to hamstring qualitative researchers when they try to show the value of their craft relative to quantitative methods.

Yet when dealing with rare events, these two concerns are easily overcome, at least in theory, by one simple move: the consideration, across a defined period, of as many of the rare events in question for which one can get adequate information.[29] For practical reasons—including a researcher's time and the availability of documents—boundaries for research have to be established. One might examine, say, all the initial formations of great power alliances since 1870 or all the onsets of civil war since 1918. Decisions on boundaries should also be guided by methodological consider-

---

[28] In quantitative studies, this is the problem of spurious correlation between A and E due to the fact that a hidden factor F is causing both A and E. Incorporating omitted and lagged variables can deal with this concern to some degree. Still, the larger problem discussed here is that a leader's future concern about factor G at time $t - 5$ is leading to planning decisions that shape factor F by time $t - 3$, and factors A, B, and C by time $t - 1$, such that war is chosen once all these factors are "in place" by time t (when the leader has the state's ducks in a row, so to speak). It is the original anticipation or expectation at time $t - 5$—unmeasurable by large-N and therefore hidden—that is causing the reshaping of all the other INJS variables in the mix.

[29] Recent "middle-N" qualitative work in comparative politics by Steven Levitsky and Lucan Way (2010) and James Mahoney (2010) moves us quite far down this road, although their approaches are not specifically designed for the study of rare events, nor do they seek to cover the essential universe of cases for a specified time period. The closest parallel to my methodological setup is found in Stephan Haggard and Robert Kaufman (2012), although their work is designed to test a single empirical hypothesis—whether inequality is linked to regime change—rather than to evaluate the relative salience of competing theoretical arguments and their potentially endogenous causal factors.

ations, including the type of actor being studied and whether the overall time frame can be said to favor or not favor the theories being tested. In this book, I look at the onset of essentially all the significant great power crises and wars from 1790 to 1991. The choice to focus on great powers is not just a practical one (i.e., the bounding of the number of rare events and the emphasizing of cases where documents are generally available). It is also a theoretical one, given that all the theories before us are ones that assume anarchy. Conflicts between smaller regional powers might be explained by such theories. Yet the fact that these powers can be shaped and constrained in their behavior by the overhanging influence of great powers makes the tests less reliable (Copeland 2012a).[30]

The time frame of 1790 to 1991 was chosen not just because of the availability of documents. The period is also one that is quite favorable to liberal theories that have dominated the study of interdependence and war, and generally less favorable for economic realist and trade expectations approaches. If I were to concentrate on the era from 1550 to 1750, for example, a critic could easily charge that economic realism and trade expectations theory are much more likely to work with regard to the heyday of great power mercantilism. During this time, leaders thought more in zero-sum terms, and did not yet have access to the liberal economic theories of Smith, Ricardo, and modern trade theory.[31] From 1790 to 1991, in contrast, we should expect that liberal theories will do well, with leaders thinking increasingly in terms of the constraining effects of absolute gains from trade and less in terms of the outmoded arguments of early mercantilism. If liberalism does not do well during this modern period, and economic realism and trade expectations theory are supported, then there will be greater confidence that the latter theories have withstood a "hard period" for the upholding of their claims.

This approach of focusing on all the rare events within a certain time frame and for a certain type of actor may still seem to suffer from the bias

---

[30]In the above discussion, one might of course quibble with the dividing line between significant and insignificant crises. My determination of significant crises was shaped not only by the militarized interstate dispute data set but also by the common judgments of diplomatic historians. The latter is important, since the militarized interstate dispute data set often includes situations where states engaged in low-level maneuverings that historians typically view as aspects of normal great power politics, not as true crises that risk an escalation of hostility and increased chance of a slide into war. To avoid charges of bias, however, I also included in my set of cases such events as the Belgium crisis of 1830–31 as well as the French and Austrian interventions into Spain and Italy in the early 1820s. Such cases have significance to historians even though they had little to do with economic interdependence and trade expectations, and even though they did not create any appreciable increase in the likelihood of conflict between great powers.

[31]For the application of trade expectations theory to key cases of the mercantilist age, such as the Anglo-Dutch wars of the seventeenth century, see Moriarty 2007.

of "selecting on the dependent variable"—that is, choosing cases based on the fact that event E occurred.[32] There is a simple way to mitigate this concern. In addition to examining the immediate outbreak of a crisis or war, we can look at the periods leading up to the crises and wars of interest, to see if the planning for conflict, levels of tension, and probabilities of war changed as the core independent variables changed.[33] Of course, because crises and wars are a function of complex bundles of factors, and because leaders will seek to manipulate these factors to facilitate the initiation of conflict under optimal circumstances, we cannot expect changes in individual independent variables to drive changes in conflict levels. Even if such variables are propelling factors, they are nested within sets of necessary facilitating factors that must be in place before leaders would be rational to start a crisis or war. Qualitative research thus needs to be subtle, looking at how the core independent variables specified by the main theories interacted with other supporting factors to either keep the peace or bring on conflict.

The above approach to rare event research has important implications for the way scholars orient themselves to the study of "evidence." It is a self-evident point that rare events in international relations and comparative politics, such as crises, revolutions, and wars, will be a function not of a single complex bundle of INJS conditions but rather different bundles of factors operating with different causal force at different places and times. That is, even when we think in terms of complex conjunctural causality, we must still think in terms of multiple pathways to event E. Recognizing this starting point requires a critical shift in research focus. We must give up any search for a single "master explanation" for rare event E across time and space. Instead, we must look at the competing theories in terms of the competing bundles of variables said to drive E. Then we can look to see *how often* it is the case that a bundle from one theory will do a better job explaining the arising of E than a bundle from a competing theory.

Yet we must also move beyond stale debates in both quantitative and qualitative research where scholars seek to show that a factor or set of factors "matters" within a larger causal picture—in quantitative work, the demonstrating of statistical and substantive "significance" relative to established control variables; in case study research, the showing of a factor's importance in select cases. Given that almost every factor identified in political science can be said to sometimes matter, any useful research

[32] King, Keohane, and Verba 1994; Collier and Mahoney 1996; Collier, Mahoney, and Seawright 2004.

[33] This is equivalent to using process tracing "within" a case to determine the relative level of congruence between changes in independent variables and the dependent variables of interest. See George and Bennett 2005; Bennett and Elman 2006; Munck 2004.

agenda must revolve around the issue of how frequently a factor plays a critical causal role (propelling, reinforcing, etc.) within the complex causality that is producing event E.

More specifically, in this book I am interested in answering three key questions. How often is it the case that variables related to economic interdependence were important to the onset of crisis and war across the 1790 to 1991 period? If interdependence is indeed causally important, how frequently is it the case that the variables and causal logic of trade expectations theory do a better job explaining the onset of conflict than the variables and logic embedded within liberal arguments and economic realism? And given that factors having nothing to do with interdependence may be also at work in specific cases, what is the relative salience of a theory's mechanisms compared to the factors posed by competing noncommercial theories? By covering the essential universe of cases during the specified time frame and scrutinizing the cases using documentary analysis, we can get a good handle on each of these three questions. As I summarize in the next section, economic interdependence not only plays a far more significant role in modern great power conflicts than has been previously appreciated but within those cases where interdependence is key, trade expectations theory and economic realism also do a solid job in explaining the vast majority of the cases.[34]

---

[34] In evaluating whether the approach laid out here makes sense, it is instructive to realize that for rare event research in the medical field, researchers follow a methodology similar to the one proposed above. Consider one particularly tragic example: the problem of sudden unexplained death (SUD) in teenagers and young adults. Young people who suddenly die of heart attacks, strokes, and other ailments are extremely rare—in the United States, between one and five per hundred thousand patient-years. To get a handle on causality, medical researchers stress the importance of in-depth study of the rare events themselves. By performing autopsies on SUD patients, these scholars can calculate the percentage of the total number of SUDs across a defined time period and region who died from particular medical conditions (arrhythmia versus myocardial infarction versus pulmonary embolism, and so forth). They may then consider the role of background conditions such as physical activity and heat indexes, say, with SUDs in competitive athletes. The primary interest is on what different bundles of factors might produce the rare event, and how often it is the case that the event is caused by bundle one versus bundle two versus bundle three. See Puranik et al. 2005; Tester and Ackerman 2007; Marini et al. 2001; Basso et al. 2000; Maron, Gohman, and Aeppli 1998. Likewise in rare event research in international relations, our focus must be on careful "autopsies" of the cases themselves. The international relations field has the advantage that when the documents for the actors exist, scholars can examine the period of lead-up to the rare event and not just its immediate circumstances. This allows them to determine how the propensity of actors to fall into a rare event changed as the core independent variables changed, and how actors acted to alter the conditions that would increase or decrease this propensity.

A Summary of the Findings

This section provides a broad overview of the results of the in-depth historical documentary work that is detailed in chapters 3–8. It serves two main purposes. First, it provides the reader with a handy reference tool for remembering the key findings of each of the forty case studies. Second, it offers a summary that can be dissected according to the guidelines for rare event qualitative research outlined above. We can determine, at least as a first cut at a broad swath of history, not only how important economic interdependence is to the ups and downs of great power conflict but also the role and salience of the trade expectations logic versus its competitors. Moreover, because the historical chapters cover essentially all the great power cases of crisis and war between 1790 and 1991—including ones having little to do with economic interdependence—the forty cases give us direct insight into the relative significance of systemic versus domestic-level factors for international politics at the highest level.

Table 2.7 lays out the results from these forty case studies. Each case can really be thought of as a "case period," since I investigate the years and months leading up to a major event in great power relations (a crisis, a war, or in the case of US-Soviet relations, the ending of the Cold War) as well as the event itself. The first two columns of table 2.7 provide details on each case period in terms of the years investigated, great powers involved, and main issue being considered. A clear dividing line between case periods can, of course, be hard to establish. Three criteria were used to mark out the case periods. For one, the period had to be marked by a particularly salient issue or important event. Thus the wars from 1790 to 1815 are separated into two case periods, the French Revolutionary Wars and Napoleonic Wars, given that the battles of the first were directly related to the fall out of the French Revolution while those of the second were driven by the hegemonic calculations of a single French leader. This criteria alone, however, is not sufficient, considering that conflicts can revolve around a single large issue for decades, such as the British and Russian concerns for dominance in the eastern Mediterranean from 1820 to 1880. If a turn to a new dramatic event involves new great powers or has a distinctly different geographic focus, I treat this turn as a distinct case period. The period 1943–45, for example, is broken into two case periods: one for the US-Soviet dispute in 1943–44 over the control of Iranian oil and another for the US-Soviet struggle over the postwar European order in 1943–45. The first of these is of interest because of its distinct regional character. The second not only has a different regional focus but also ended up leading to the larger

TABLE 2.7 Summary of Findings

Period (chapter)	Key great powers and main issue	Key puzzle/outcome to be explained	Primary propelling factors	Supporting factors	Importance of economic interdependence (and best theory)
1790–1801 (chap. 7)	1. France versus Britain/Prussia/Austria over French regime type	General war in Europe after French Revolution	Ideological divide and fear of spread of revolution	France's large population, heightening ideological threat	Negligible
1801–1815 (chap. 7)	2. France versus Britain/Prussia/Austria/Russia over hegemony in Europe	Return to general war in Europe by 1803–5	French fear of British trade restrictions tied to long-term rise of industrializing Britain	Napoléon's personal drive for glory as reinforcing factor	Strong (trade expectations theory best)
1815–23 (chap. 7)	3. France, Austria, and Russia over regime type in subsidiary states	Willingness of great powers to intervene militarily in periphery	Ideological concerns for stability of monarchical regime type	Geopolitical gains in position for France and Austria in Spain and Italy	Negligible
1823–30 (chap. 7)	4. Britain versus Russia over eastern Mediterranean	Russo-Turkish War of 1828–29 and Russia's moderate peace terms	Russian concern for economic access into Mediterranean and fear that Turkey would collapse	Russian and British concerns for spheres of influence in Near East	Moderate to strong (trade expectations theory and economic realism best)

1830–31 (chap. 7)	5. France versus Britain over Belgium	Why crisis, and why it remained at low level	French seeking cheap opportunity to revise 1815 settlement	Domestic pressures on French government for foreign policy gain	Negligible
1830–40 (chap. 7)	6. Britain versus France/Russia over eastern Mediterranean	Why British intervened in support of Turkey in 1839–40 crisis	British concern about French penetration into Near East trade	British desire to contain Russian influence over Turkey	Strong (trade expectations theory and economic realism best)
1830–40 (chap. 7)	7. Russia versus France/Britain over eastern Mediterranean	Why Russia acted so moderately, supporting Turkey in 1839–40 crisis	Russian concern to keep Turkey alive as best assurance of access into Mediterranean	Russian concern for reputation for resolve relative to British influence in region	Moderate (trade expectations theory and liberalism best)
1830–40 (chap. 7)	8. France versus Britain/Russia over eastern Mediterranean	Why France backed Egypt against Turkey/Britain	French desire to increase economic penetration of Levant	Domestic pressures on French government to counter British economic growth	Moderate (economic realism best)
1830–39 (chap. 7)	9. Britain versus China over opium trade into China	Why Britain initiated war in support of the nefarious opium trade	British fear of loss of triangular trade between India, China, and Britain	British merchant support as facilitating factor	Strong (trade expectations theory best, with some support for economic realism)

TABLE 2.7 (Continued)

Period (chapter)	Key great powers and main issue	Key puzzle/outcome to be explained	Primary propelling factors	Supporting factors	Importance of economic interdependence (and best theory)
1840–56 (chap. 7)	Britain versus Russia over the future of the Ottoman Empire	Why Britain and Russia fell into Crimean War despite past cooperation regarding Turkey	Russian and British fears of loss of trade access through Turkish straits	Reinforced by Russian, British, and French reputational concerns in Near East	Strong (trade expectations theory best)
1856–60 (chap. 8)	Italy/France versus Austria over the question of Italian independence	Italian Wars of Unification	Italian nationalism and Napoléon's desire to revise 1815 settlement	Reinforced by personal glory drives of Cavour and Napoléon	Negligible
1860–66 (chap. 8)	Prussia versus Austria over future of Schleswig/ Holstein and German territories	Austro-Prussian War as part of German Wars of Unification	Prussian security-driven need for more territory; Prussian nationalism	Perhaps reinforced by Bismarck's personal drive for glory	Negligible
1866–70 (chap. 8)	Prussia versus France over future of Spain and the German territories	Franco-Prussian War as part of German Wars of Unification	Prussian need for more territory and Prussian nationalism; French fear of decline versus Prussia	Perhaps reinforced by Bismarck's personal drive for glory	Negligible

1871–75 (chap. 8)	14. Germany versus France over rise of French military power	Why Germany brought on "War in Sight" crisis in 1875	German fear of the military rise of a revanchist France	Facilitated by Bismarck's strong domestic position	Negligible
1875–78 (chap. 8)	15. Russia versus Britain over the future of the Ottoman Empire	British-Russian crisis of 1878 over outcome of Russo-Turkish conflict	Russian desire to increase control of Black Sea area and British fear of economic losses	Pan-Slavic domestic pressures on Russian government and British concern for reputation	Moderate (economic realism best for Russia; trade expectations theory best for Britain)
1878–85 (chap. 8)	16. France versus other great powers over control of Africa	French moves to increase formal control of West and North Africa	French fear of declining economic competitiveness and future loss of markets	Reinforced by geopolitical concerns regarding the new German Empire in the east	Strong (trade expectations theory best)
1878–85 (chap. 8)	17. Britain versus other great powers over control of Africa	British moves to increase formal control of Egypt and parts of Africa	British fear of new French colonial presence in North Africa and loss of trade via Egypt	Reinforced by increased importance of India as market for British industrial goods	Strong (trade expectationsn theory best)
1878–85 (chap. 8)	18. Germany versus other great powers over control of Africa	German moves to increase formal control in West and East Africa	German fear of France and Britain "closing door" on German trade with Africa	Side benefits of increased prospects in German elections of 1884	Strong (trade expectations theory best; liberalism captures reinforcing effect of domestic incentives)

TABLE 2.7 (*Continued*)

Period (chapter)	Key great powers and main issue	Key puzzle/outcome to be explained	Primary propelling factors	Supporting factors	Importance of economic interdependence (and best theory)
1894–95 (chap. 8)	19. United States versus Britain over Venezuelan border	Crisis due to US intervention in British-Venezuelan border dispute	US fear of British economic penetration of South America and loss of access to raw materials	Reinforced by increased importance of overseas markets to US economic growth	Strong (trade expectations theory best for United States; economic realism best for Britain)
1897–98 (chap. 8)	20. France versus Britain over control of Sudan	Crisis due to British efforts to counter French at Fashoda	French desire to increase east-west trade penetration and British efforts to stop it	British need to show resolve against any challenges to its imperial realm	Strong (economic realism best for France; trade expectations theory best for Britain)
1894–99 (chap. 8)	21. Britain versus Germany over South Africa	British efforts to reduce and destroy Transvaal Republic, leading to Boer War	British fear of German economic penetration of Transvaal and Transvaal's future control of South Africa	Overall sense of British economic decline relative to Germany and United States	Strong (trade expectations theory best)

Period	Case	Event to be explained	Situation/Opportunity	Domestic facilitation	Strength of theory
1880–95 (chap. 3)	22. Japan versus China over control of Korea	Outbreak of the Sino-Japanese War of 1894–95	Opportunity to increase Japan's control over Korea's development	Facilitated by domestic consensus within Japan on need for low-cost expansion	Strong (economic realism best)
1895–1904 (chap. 3)	23. Japan versus Russia over control of Manchuria/Korea	Outbreak of the Russo-Japanese War in 1904	Russia's growing threat to Japan's economic access to Manchuria/Korea plus Russia's military buildup in Far East	Domestically driven hard-liners in Russia reinforcing Russian government's strategic reasons for avoiding concessions	Strong (trade expectations theory best)
1905–22 (chap. 4)	24. Japan versus China/Russia over control of northern China and Manchuria	Japan's demands on China in 1914–15 and move into Siberia in 1918–19	Opportunities to increase Japan's economic penetration of China and Far East	Facilitated by domestic support within newly democratic Japan for low-cost expansion	Strong (economic realism best)
1922–31 (chap. 4)	25. Japan versus China/Russia over control of northern China and Manchuria	Why Japan did not grab rest of Manchuria in 1928, but did in 1931	Japan's positive trade expectations from 1922 to 1929, then impact of Great Depression and new US tariffs	1931 move facilitated by domestic consensus in Tokyo	Strong (trade expectations theory best; liberalism has partial success explaining Japanese restraint in 1928)

TABLE 2.7 (*Continued*)

Period (chapter)	Key great powers and main issue	Key puzzle/outcome to be explained	Primary propelling factors	Supporting factors	Importance of economic interdependence (and best theory)
1931–37 (chap. 4)	26. Japan versus China over Japan's role in northern China	The outbreak of the Sino-Japanese War in 1937	Domestic pressures on Chiang Kai-shek by 1936–37 to fight Japan not Communists	Facilitated by Chiang's temporary capture in December 1936 by Maoists/nationalists	Negligible for Sino-Japanese War (but trade expectations theory does capture Japan's interest in North China)
1938–41 (chaps. 4 and 5)	27. Japan versus United States over Japan's policies toward China and Russia	Why Japan attacked United States in 1941 rather than attacking Russia, as Japan had been planning since 1936	US trade sanctions driven by Japanese preparation for war against Russia	Reinforced by Japan's high dependence on outsiders for raw materials needed for war with Russia	Strong (trade expectations theory best)
1900–1914 (chap. 3)	28. Germany versus Britain/France/Russia over hegemony in Europe	Why Germany brought on general war in Europe	Increasingly negative trade expectations exacerbating German fears of the rise of Russia	Significant German military superiority relative to other great powers	Moderate to strong (trade expectations theory best)

1919–39 (chap. 3)	29. Germany versus Britain/France/Soviet Union over hegemony in Europe	The outbreak of World War II in Europe	German concerns about access to trade and raw materials tied to fear of long-term rise of Russia	Hitler's personality and Nazi-Soviet ideological divide as reinforcing factors	Moderate to strong (economic realism best for Hitler's logic; trade expectations theory best for explaining cooperation of traditional military)
1943–44 (chap. 6)	30. Soviet Union versus United States over control of Iranian oil	Why Soviet Union sought greater influence in Iran despite risks to wartime alliance	Soviet fears of being shut out of Iran's oil development by United States and Britain	Soviet geopolitical fears of foreign invasion through Caucasus if no Russian military presence	Strong (economic realism best for US behavior; trade expectations theory best for Soviet behavior)
1944–45 (chap. 6)	31. United States versus Soviet Union over postwar order in Europe	Why United States by 1945 turned to protocontainment of Soviet Union, including refusal to continue strong economic relationship (origins of Cold War)	US fears of Western Europe falling to Communism and threatening US access to European trade, tied to fears of long-term rise of Russia	Russia's historical neomercantilist ideology tied to Communist economic spheres logic, reinforcing US fears of cutoff if Western Europe goes Communist	Strong (trade expectations theory best for both US and Soviet behavior)

TABLE 2.7 (Continued)

Period (chapter)	Key great powers and main issue	Key puzzle/outcome to be explained	Primary propelling factors	Supporting factors	Importance of economic interdependence (and best theory)
1945–46 (chap. 6)	32. Soviet Union versus United States over nature of postwar Iranian state	Why Soviet Union refused to leave northern Iran despite wartime agreement	US shift to protocontainment policies in 1945 made Moscow less inclined to cooperate	Russian historical geopolitical fears of foreign invasion through Caucasus	Moderate to strong (trade expectations theory and economic realism best)
1946–48 (chap. 6)	33. Soviet Union versus United States over nature of postwar German states	Why Soviet Union sparked crisis over Berlin in 1948	US/British policy of reuniting western sectors of Germany threatened East German economy	Marshall Plan's expected impact on the revival of Western Europe and German economies	Negligible (Soviet fears of decline in European position not driven by economic interdependence)
1948–50 (chap. 6)	34. Soviet Union versus United States over control of Korean peninsula	Why Soviet Union ended up giving green light to North Korean invasion in June 1950	US new policy of building up US political/military presence in Far East	South Korea's advantage over North Korea in population and economic potential	Negligible (Soviet fears of declining position in Asia not driven by economic interdependence)

1950–53 (chap. 6)	35. United States versus Soviet Union over the future of Iran	Why United States acted to overthrow Iranian regime despite known risk of superpower escalation and war	Clear risk of Communist takeover of Iran and the subsequent Soviet advance to oil-rich Persian Gulf	Facilitated by British support for hard line against current Iranian regime	Strong (trade expectations theory best)
1954–56 (chap. 6)	36. United States versus Soviet Union over Suez Canal and the future of Egypt	Why United States was so restrained during Suez Crisis despite apparent threat to traffic through canal	Lack of Communist threat to Egyptian government and its clear incentive/ ability to keep traffic flowing through canal zone	Increasing US concern for public opinion in developing states reinforced the wisdom of acting moderately	Strong (trade expectations theory best)
1956–62 (chap. 6)	37. United States versus Soviet Union over question of global strategic stability and the risk of nuclear war	Increase in strategic instability and risk of war despite Soviet efforts to forge trade-based détente	Mutual fears of loss of second-strike capability and US concern that trade would help Soviet relative power	Ideological divide reinforced fear of a first strike, increasing perceived need to establish a strong strategic position	Moderate to strong (trade expectations theory best)

TABLE 2.7 (Continued)

Period (chapter)	Key great powers and main issue	Key puzzle/outcome to be explained	Primary propelling factors	Supporting factors	Importance of economic interdependence (and best theory)
1963–74 (chap. 6)	38. United States versus Soviet Union over question of global strategic stability and the risk of nuclear war	Decrease in superpower tension and risk of war by 1972–73 via détente process	US decision to lower trade restrictions and offer credits in exchange for better Soviet behavior	Solidification of stable second-strike capability on each side and clear reality of new mutually assured destruction world	Strong (trade expectations theory best)
1975–83 (chap. 6)	39. United States versus Soviet Union over question of global strategic stability and the risk of nuclear war	Renewal of superpower tension and risk of war (the coming of "the second Cold War")	Destruction of the trade-based détente due to congressional politics in aftermath of Watergate scandal	Pressure from hard-liners within Soviet leadership who were against increased cooperation with United States	Moderate to strong (trade expectations theory best)
1984–91 (chap. 6)	40. United States versus Soviet Union over question of global strategic stability and the risk of nuclear war	Decrease in superpower tension and the ultimate end of the Cold War altogether	United States willingness to promise lower trade restrictions in response to more cooperative Soviet behavior	Severity of Soviet bloc decline left Russia with little choice but to make concessions to secure trade/technology	Strong (trade expectations theory best)

Cold War conflict that dominated the next four decades of great power history.[35]

A final criterion—the relative degree of independence of events—was used to ensure that the years of struggle between two or more great powers were not divided up too finely. It would make little sense, for instance, to treat the series of great power wars from 1803 to 1815 as "separate" case periods, since they were all shaped by one overarching factor: the hegemonic aspirations of Napoleonic France. Treating them as independent events would create a bias in favor of whichever theory does a good job for the 1803–15 period as a whole (giving it more "hits" than it deserves). The same is true for periods of peace that may involve multiple crises or disputes all tied to one larger geopolitical question or issue. From 1905 to 1914, for example, the Germans and their Austrian allies were involved in a series of crises over great power control of Morocco and the Balkans region. These crises, and whether they escalated or not, were all bound up in the larger issue of the German-Austrian alliance's future position within the global economic and strategic system, as I show below and elsewhere (Copeland 2000b, chapters 3 and 4). Treating these individual crises as independent cases would again distort the results in favor of the theory that does the best job explaining World War I.[36]

The results in table 2.7 are designed to be self-explanatory, so I won't go through them in any detail. Columns one and two describe each case period in terms of the key great powers in the struggle and the main issue animating the time period. The third column outlines the main historical outcome or puzzle for each case period that requires explanation, such as the outbreak of war between Japan and Russia in 1904, or why the

[35] Each case period assumes that one of the great powers is the primary initiator of the conflict for the time frame in question. When we see different great powers each taking independent steps to initiate conflict or insert itself aggressively into a region, though, I treat the decision making of each great power as a separate and important case period that needs explaining in its own right. As such, for the 1830–40 struggle over the eastern Mediterranean and the 1878–85 period of "New Imperialism" in Europe, I explore the separate impulses behind expansion for the British, French, Russian (1830–40), and German (1878–85) states.

[36] For similar reasons, large-N quantitative studies generally take the beginning of a war or crisis as the starting point of a distinct case, and do not count subsequent events within an ongoing war or crisis as separate cases (unless the escalation or duration of a crisis or war is of distinct interest). Such studies, however, usually treat the actor-years or dyad-years prior to a crisis or war as "independent" observations that go into the sample, even when history suggests each of the years is driven by a common overarching factor, such as Hitler's preparation for war against the system from 1933 to 1939, or US concerns for secure second-strike nuclear capability from 1956 to 1962. Moreover, these studies rarely address the question of whether crises that fall close together in time, such as the five Balkans crises from 1911 to 1913, should be considered as separate cases or examples of a single larger phenomenon.

Soviet Union sparked a crisis over Berlin in 1948. The fourth and fifth columns lay out the primary factors that went into the complex mix of variables that led to the main outcome for each case period. Column four is the crucial one here. It summarizes the findings on the primary propelling factor or factors that drove the great powers into conflict, or in the case of 1963–74 and 1984–91, helped them achieve a dramatic lessening of tensions.[37] Column five depicts some of the supporting factors that served as reinforcing, facilitating, or constraining variables within the larger causal mix.

The sixth and final column provides the short answers to the first two of the three questions posed above. It tells us whether commercial variables were important in the case (question one), and if so, which of the main theories does the best job of explaining the causal role of these variables (question two). By assessing the significance of trade and finance within the case period on a scale from "negligible" to "moderate" to "strong," this column, when read in conjunction with columns four and five, also indicates the relative salience of the commercial variables within the overall mix of factors driving the events (question three).

Table 2.7 thus offers the reader not only a quick overview of the findings of the chapters to follow but also a means of assessing how often economic interdependence matters and how frequently each of our main theories can explain the case periods at hand. As is to be expected in situations of complex causality with multiple pathways, there are many case periods that have little or nothing to do with economic interdependence per se. In ten of the forty cases, I found no real documentary evidence that interstate trade or financial variables drove the events of the case period. In such situations, none of the variables of our main theories had causal salience relative to noncommercial factors.[38] Yet what is surprising, at least for traditional international relations scholars who tend to downplay the importance of commercial variables, is just how

---

[37] I do not cover the occasional détentes of the multipolar period from 1790 to 1945, for the simple reason that they were almost invariably the result of self-interested balancing against a common great power threat (e.g., British-Russian cooperation against France in 1839–40; British-French-Russian alignment against Germany before 1914). The détente of the early 1970s and the ending of the Cold War in the late 1980s are of unique interest, given that they take place without the provocation of a hostile third party.

[38] Terminology is important here. I tend to talk throughout the book about particular theories lacking salience, rather than being disconfirmed or falsified by the evidence. The latter terms are really only appropriate when the evidence shows that the leaders acted for reasons directly contrary to the way a theory argues leaders should act. In almost all the cases I have studied, leader behavior does not contradict the deductive logics of our main theories. Instead, leaders simply find themselves propelled and overwhelmed by noncommercial factors or alternative economic logics, meaning that a particular theory may lack salience within the larger mix of factors causing the rare event E.

often interdependence was indeed important.[39] In thirty of the forty case periods, or 75 percent, economic interdependence played a moderate to strong causal role in shaping the events. This does not mean, of course, that commercial variables were the only factors driving the events, and columns four and five give a sense of some of the other propelling, reinforcing, and facilitating factors at work within the cases. Still, the fact that interdependence had salience in three out of four case periods is prima facie evidence that the economic dimension of great power politics cannot be ignored.

Turning to the cases where economic interdependence was important, we see that trade expectations theory does well in head-to-head tests with its competitors. Trade expectations theory finds support in twenty-six of the thirty cases (86.7 percent), while economic realism is supported in eleven of thirty cases (36.7 percent) and liberalism in three of thirty cases (10 percent).[40] What is most surprising about these results is just how poorly commercial liberalism performed across the two centuries considered.[41] Even for the three cases in which liberalism was supported— Russia's moderation in the 1839–40 eastern crisis, Bismarck's decision to turn to imperialism in 1883–84, and Japan's restraint over Manchuria in the late 1920s—it did not cover the case period on its own but instead worked only in conjunction with trade expectations theory, with each explaining differing aspects of the events. And for what should have been "most likely" cases of unit-level factors being unleashed as trade falls— German and Japanese behavior up to World War II, the Berlin Crisis of 1948, and the outbreak of the Korean War in 1950—liberal arguments could not explain the driving forces for conflict.

Trade expectations theory and economic realism sometimes worked together within specific cases, such as the Venezuelan Crisis of 1895–96, with trade expectations theory explaining the behavior of one great power and economic realism the behavior of the other.[42] Economic realism did

[39] This is especially true for realist scholars who emphasize military power, but also for liberals focused on the pacifying role of democratic regime type. See Buzan 1984.

[40] The percentages add up to more than 100 percent because, within particular case periods, competing theories sometimes do well for different great powers or capture different elements of the decision-making process (e.g., the propelling versus reinforcing dimensions).

[41] Neo-Marxism did not explain any of the cases well, although it had some subsidiary value for dimensions of two cases: the British-Chinese Opium War of 1839 and the German plunge into imperialism in 1884–85. Because of its poor performance and to save space, I do not discuss neo-Marxism in table 2.7, but it is considered as a competing argument in chapters 3–8, when appropriate.

[42] Note that I follow diplomatic historical convention, and do not consider the United States a great power until after 1890 and the build up of its modern global navy. The Spanish-American War of 1898 is not included in the data set here, given that Spain was not a great power. In my follow-up book on US foreign policy (Copeland, forthcoming), I show

well on its own for three important case periods: France's behavior in the eastern Mediterranean in 1830–40, the Japanese war with China in 1894–95, and Japan's moves against China and Russian Siberia from 1914 to 1922. Trade expectations theory, however, proves significantly stronger than economic realism across the broad sweep of case periods. It provides a strong explanation on its own for fourteen of the thirty cases involving economic interdependence, and its logic is at least as salient as economic realism for the nine cases where both trade expectations theory and economic realism help explain the events of the case period.

Needless to say, readers may disagree with the exact way that I characterize the case periods along with the propelling forces driving great power behavior. The proof is in the pudding, and it will be up to me to demonstrate in the following six chapters (and my follow-up volume on commerce and US foreign policy) that the documentary evidence justifies my understanding of each of the case periods. Within the context of the methodological setup outlined above, though, dissenting opinion is not a problem but instead a healthy and indeed necessary part of a research program's long-term intellectual progress. It is only through back-and-forth discussion that the international relations field can reach relative consensus on the cases in this book, or on cases that are added from other time periods. And it is only through increasing consensus that we can say that there has been an "accumulation of knowledge" in international relations.

The case studies that follow, therefore, are first steps in an extended process and are meant to provoke scholars into debates that will hopefully achieve this long-term accumulation of knowledge. They are not designed to provide definitive interpretations of the case periods—an impossible task given the amount of documentary evidence available for the complex events discussed herein. This being said, I am still confident that readers will find the historical chapters not simply provocative but also plausible and even convincing. For each case period, I set my arguments against the main historical interpretations of diplomatic history, including both economic and noneconomic contentions. When the evidence suggests that economic interdependence had little causal role in the case period, I cover the events in short order, summarizing the key factors to ensure a broad picture of the overall salience of systemic versus unit-level variables across the forty cases. Yet when interdependence is important, I slow down to examine in depth the documentary evidence for the competing theories of interdependence and war. In this way, we can see not only the extent to which these theories explain the particular case periods

---

the value of applying trade expectations theory to this conflict as well as the conflicts of early nineteenth-century North America, including the War of 1812 and Mexican-American War (1846–48).

but also the way their factors work with noncommercial variables to bring about the results. This allows us to reject or support certain key noneconomic interpretations of history put forward by diplomatic historians and political scientists as I focus on the competing economically based logics from chapter 1.

In the end, the diplomatic historical work of chapters 3–8 reveals the overriding importance of systemic variables and security fears in the ebb and flows of world history. Liberalism's view that unit-level forces that favor conflict get unleashed when trade falls is rarely upheld. The great powers in these cases were almost always driven primarily by their fears of the future and the implications of external changes for their long-term security. Even in case periods where economic interdependence had no causal role to play, unit-level variables operated more as external factors that heightened leaders' senses of national insecurity than as direct propelling forces "from within."[43] Ideological differences between monarchy and republicanism, for example, played critical roles in the 1790–99 and 1815–22 periods, but largely because they caused insecure leaders to worry about the future stability of their states.[44] To be sure, in a number of the cases unit-level drives for status ("glory") and wealth ("greed") were important supporting factors in the outbreak of conflict. And who would want to deny that the personal motives of Napoléon, Bismarck, or Hitler played a role in leading such individuals to bring war down on their neighbors? Yet as the historical chapters suggest, such unit-level factors operated largely as reinforcing factors to the more salient external forces that propelled these actors and their supporters into conflict.[45]

I will close this chapter with the self-evident observation that my interpretations of the cases of chapters 3–8 are unquestionably shaped by my own theoretical framework. There is no escaping the impact that theoretical frameworks have on the filtering of one's view of reality—not for this scholar, not for any scholar. The only thing one can do, therefore, is to seek to be as self-conscious as possible about such potential biases, and

---

[43]For the role of external unit-level factors in the other as causes of a state's increased threat perception, see Walt 1996.

[44]For a discussion of ideological distance as a systemic variable driving states' estimate of external threat, see Haas 2005.

[45]The only case I found where domestic motives were *the* primary propelling force for conflict was the Sino-Japanese War of 1937–45. But contrary to the common view that Japan initiated the war, the new evidence discussed in chapter 4 shows that only Chiang Kai-shek sought all-out war, and did so to hold together his shaky coalition and maintain his position as head of the Nationalist Party. In a broad sense, this case aligns nicely with the liberal worldview. Since trade between Japan and China had been rebounding for the years before the war, though, the economic side of liberalism detailed in chapter 1 is not supported.

minimize distortions through the objective handling of documentary evidence and a careful methodological setup. By examining the universe of great power cases for a hard period (1790–1991), for example, this book was forced to deal with cases that do not work well for trade expectations theory. Moreover, I deliberately included potentially marginal cases such the Belgium Crisis of 1830–31 as well as the French and Austrian interventions of 1815–22 in order preempt charges of historical bias.[46] Yet the evidence from the following chapters nonetheless shows the surprising power of the trade expectations logic across a wide variety of settings and time periods. Notwithstanding my efforts to address counterarguments, my assertions for such controversial cases as US-Japan 1938–41 and the origins of the Cold War may still strike some readers as too one-sided. My hope, however, is that by the end of the book, even skeptics will not be able to return to well-known historical cases without a new appreciation of the role of trade expectations on the course of world history. And if such skeptics jump into the fray to adjust the interpretations in a way that builds a new consensus for each case period, or indeed to bring in new case periods to widen the historical scope, then a true accumulation of knowledge within the international relations field may yet be in sight.

[46] See footnote 30 above.

CHAPTER THREE

The Russo-Japanese War and the German Wars for Hegemony, 1890–1939

THIS CHAPTER EXPLORES THE ORIGINS of three of the four most important wars of the first half of the twentieth century: the Russo-Japanese War of 1904–5, World War I, and World War II in Europe (the Pacific War is covered in subsequent chapters). These three wars had more than just a chronological connection to one another. The Russo-Japanese War helped solidify the diplomatic and economic alignments of the great powers in the decade before 1914, while the disaster of the First World War clearly set the stage for the rise of Nazism and the outbreak of yet another global war a generation later. I have covered the two world wars started by Germany in some detail in a previous book, so I will not repeat that analysis here.[1] Rather, this chapter will focus on providing a fairly comprehensive account of the causes of the Russo-Japanese War, confining the discussion of the world wars to the economic determinants of those conflicts.

As we will see, trade expectations theory outperforms its main competitors for the Russo-Japanese conflict and First World War. In both cases, declining expectations of the future trade environment were critical to the overall fear of decline that drove Japan in 1904 and Germany in 1914 to initiate war. The high dependence of Japan and Germany on foreign markets and raw materials was not enough on its own to push these states into war in their respective regions. For a full account of these conflicts, economic realism's argument that dependent states grab opportunities to reduce their vulnerability must be supplemented with a dynamic view of actor expectations. Liberalism has great trouble with the two cases. In the Far East after 1880, both Russia and Japan were increasing their economic connections with China and Korea, and yet these connections only increased their drives for conflict. World War I is even more problematic for liberalism. All the great powers were trading at high levels, even with their main adversaries. Systemwide dependency,

---

[1] Suffice it to say that my earlier work (Copeland 2000b) shows the extent to which the exogenous rise of Russia to future superpower status put strong pressure on German leaders in both wars to reduce Russia before it was too late.

however, did not keep the peace. Yet once a dependent Germany's increasingly pessimistic expectations regarding the global economic system are brought into the picture and tied to German fears of the rise of Russia, the role of economic factors in the start of the war becomes clear.

World War II in Europe is a more complicated case. From the mid-1920s onward, Hitler thought in economic realist terms: he saw Germany's small size and concomitant dependence as a source of long-term vulnerability within the larger struggle for existence among the great powers. But the Great Depression along with the retreat of Britain, France, and the United States into closed economic realms made the true implications of German dependence obvious for all to see. Falling trade expectations after 1930 thus proved essential in the building of support for war among the traditional military and Hitler's Nazi ministers. Both economic realism and trade expectations theory therefore find at least partial confirmation in the World War II case. Liberalism again comes up short, though, even with what might appear on the surface to be one of its best cases. Liberalism seems to have the correlation right: as trade levels fell after 1930, growing domestic pathologies within Germany were no longer restrained by the benefits of trade. Yet as the evidence shows, German dependency was indeed a propelling force for war, and for reasons explained by realism and trade expectations theory. So even if unit-level variables, particularly Nazi ideology, need to be included in any comprehensive explanation of the origins of World War II, it is clear that German leaders and officials did not see economic interdependence as a force for peace but instead only as a problem for the German state.

For all three of the main cases in this chapter, the trade expectations logic nicely supplements historical arguments that emphasize the preventive motivations for war. For Japan in 1904, Germany in 1914, and Germany in 1939, there was tremendous uncertainty and concern regarding the ability of the state to maintain its position in the system in the face of a rising power. And in all three cases, this rising power happened to be Russia, the only Eurasian state that had the potential power base of territory, resources, and population needed to overwhelm the system over the long term. This chapter shows that falling expectations for future trade were instrumental in the overall pessimism that drove the Japanese and Germans into war. In a global environment of growing economic constraints, war was seen as the only way to gain the resources and markets believed to be necessary for future national survival. Yet the trade expectations argument does not work well across the board. As we will see, economic realism outperforms trade expectations theory for a smaller-scale war that was part of the background to the Russo-Japanese War: the Sino-Japanese War of 1894–95. A crisis in Korea in 1894 gave the Japanese leadership the opportunity it needed to reduce its economic vulnerability on the Korean Peninsula. It was this exogenously arising opportunity, not falling expectations of trade per se, that propelled Japan into initiating war with China over Korea's future.

THE ORIGINS OF THE RUSSO-JAPANESE WAR

Almost every scholar of the conflict agrees on the broad outline for an explanation of the Russo-Japanese War of 1904–5. Japan initiated the war as a response to the growing penetration of Russia into what the Japanese saw as their most important strategic region—Manchuria and the Korean Peninsula. Japanese leaders were reluctant to initiate a war against such an established great power, and thus sought with great effort to find a diplomatic way out. But Russia's unwillingness over three rounds of intense diplomatic discussions to offer concessions that would reassure Tokyo about these territories forced Japan to attack before Russia got any stronger.[2] There are no real debates among historians as to these basic points. The areas where debates remained heated, however, are the following: To what degree did domestic political divisions within Russia contribute to Saint Petersburg's inability to provide adequate concessions in a timely fashion? What indeed were the driving forces behind Russia's push into Manchuria and Korea that made a Japanese preventive response in some form so inevitable? Did Japan fear simply that Russia might use Korea to attack the home islands, or were Japanese fears equally, if not primarily, about losing access to the markets and raw materials needed for economic growth and hence long-term security?

I show below that the fear of losing access to the markets and resources of Manchuria and Korea was at least as important as the immediate security threat posed by a Russian takeover of Korea. In this sense, there were two key and interconnected propelling causes of war in this case: the impact of an economic cutoff on Japan's future economic position and the geographic threat to the home islands posed by a Russia that controlled Korea. Domestic politics and personal ambitions played almost no role in the Japanese decision for war. All the key leaders and officials hoped for and wanted a diplomatic solution—one that would have established clear spheres of influence between "Russian" Manchuria and "Japanese" Korea, and still have allowed Japan to keep trading with Manchuria and China. Despite pressure from right-wing groups calling for war, it is clear that the Japanese government would have chosen a

[2] See Nish 1985; White 1964; Beasley 1987; Malozemoff 1958; Ito 2007; Okamoto 2007; Schimmelpenninck van der Oye 2005; Stolberg 2007; Warner and Warner 1974; Westwood 1986. For summaries and additional references, see Streich and Levy 2011.

negotiated solution that guaranteed these objectives. This is therefore a case where the initiator of war was responding almost exclusively to external threats, and where those threats were in large part economic ones. This provides strong support for the trade expectations logic, especially as that logic fed into Japanese worries about long-term decline vis-à-vis Russia. And since this is a case where rapid modernization and partial democratization did create pressures from below for war, the fact that these pressures proved so insignificant to the decision-making process means that many domestic-level arguments, including those underpinning economic liberalism, fail this "most-likely" test of their logics.[3]

Where domestic-political forces might still play a part is not with the initiator of war but rather with the state that ends up provoking the initiator—namely, Russia. Consistent with the sixth exogenous factor from chapter 1, I show that domestic divisions and infighting within Russia did have some role in exacerbating Japanese mistrust of Saint Petersburg's economic and military intentions in the region. Overall, though, domestic politics within Russia were not as critical to the start of the war as many scholars have come to accept.[4] This was for one simple reason: for most of the 1891–1904 period, there was a strong consensus among Russia's elite that Manchuria was critically important to the country's economic and strategic future. By 1903, despite the increasing likelihood of war with Japan, even the most moderate of the czar's advisers were adamant about Russia maintaining economic and political dominance over the region, backed by Russian troops. To retreat in the face of Japanese concerns, they believed, would have compromised Russia's own long-term economic and strategic position in the system.

Disagreements among the Russian elite that did emerge centered on Korea, and here certain moderates did seem willing to offer Japan a limited sphere of influence. But there was still general agreement that Japan must not threaten Russian commercial and naval access through the Korean-Japanese straits, especially given that Russia's ports on China's Liaodong Peninsula were its only ice-free ports in the east. Japan's inability to provide adequate assurance on this concern was a critical roadblock in the negotiations. In short, Russian diplomacy before the war—despite how it is often portrayed—was not merely a function of incompetent bumblers and aggressive officials who led Tokyo to believe that Russia had unlimited regional ambitions. Rather, Russian hard-line posturing reflected a deep belief that Russia had a lot to lose should it yield to Japanese demands. Most significant, if Russia failed to consolidate its

---

[3]See, in particular, Mansfield and Snyder 2005. On most-likely tests, see George and Bennett 2005.

[4]For references, see Nish 1985.

hold on Manchuria or protect the sea lanes to Liaodong, it would be vulnerable to the commercial expansion of a Japan now allied with Russia's longtime "Great Game" adversary: Britain. Japan's growing industrial efficiency threatened Russian efforts to penetrate China's vast market. And Tokyo's alignment with Britain and its adherence to the Anglo-American open-door policy meant that Russian products might be pushed out of both China and Manchuria should Russia fail to dominate Manchuria (Davis 2008–9). In this sense, Russian intransigence arose out of a deep-seated fear of losing the nation's own economic and strategic position in the Far East.

In the final analysis, therefore, the Russo-Japanese War is a conflict infused with deep tragedy—perhaps the most tragic case studied in this book. Neither side could fundamentally change its policies without hurting its long-term economic growth and thus national security. Japan could not permit Russia to continue to penetrate an area so vital to its trading future, while Russia could not allow Japan to gain a forward position that would undermine Russia's vital economic and strategic interests in what it also considered to be its backyard. The fact that both powers were industrializing and trying to catch up to more technologically sophisticated states only made matters worse. Both knew that they needed readily available markets for their low-cost manufactured goods and, especially for Japan, cheap raw materials to ensure the continued competitiveness of their exports. With Manchuria and Korea smack-dab in the middle of the two great powers, neither state could afford to give way on the key issues of economic and naval access to the two territories. A clash of arms, then, was largely inevitable.

Economic realism and its emphasis on the need to seize opportunities to reduce dependence goes some way toward explaining this conflict. Both Japan and Russia needed to penetrate Manchuria and Korea to sustain their industrial growth, and both were looking for opportunities to expand. Trade expectations theory, however, fills in the gaps left by realism. It shows that the two sides saw themselves trapped in a trade-security spiral of a particularly intense kind: both actors were seeking to contain what they perceived to be a growing economic threat, yet by projecting their political and military power into the Manchurian-Korean region, they increased the very mistrust and fear of cutoff that was fueling their power projections.[5] The trade expectations approach, because of its dynamic nature, can also nicely explain how the powers' mutual dependence on Manchuria and Korea ultimately progressed from mere geopolitical struggle to actual war. Russian military growth, tied to Saint

[5]This case thus represents a rare double hit of the fourth exogenous factor from chapter 2.

Petersburg's traditional mercantilist economic policies, increased Tokyo's fears that if it did not act before Russia became permanently entrenched in the region, access to vital resources and markets would be reduced or cut off. Because London and Washington would not use force to defend the Chinese open door but instead had signaled they would not oppose Japan's effort to do so, Japanese leaders knew they could attack without worrying about third parties and that no one else would take on the growing Russian state if they did not. By the end of 1903, it was truly a "now or never" situation for Japan's economic and political security.

Background of the War

The deeper roots of the Russo-Japanese War go back a few decades. Both Russia and Japan in the late nineteenth century were states determined to catch up—not to each other, but instead to the other more advanced great powers of Britain, France, and Germany. Japan began its modernization and industrialization program soon after the restoration of the Meiji emperor in 1868. The "two pillars" of this program were captured in the Japanese phrases *fukoku kyohei* and *shokusan kogyo*—slogans promoted by the new ruling elite and usually translated, respectively, as "rich country, strong army" and "production promotion." As Richard Samuels (1994, 36–42) explains, the first phrase connoted the sense that national strength and security rested on growing national wealth, while the second phrase stressed the necessity of industrial and technological development as the basis for this wealth. Without the government's active involvement in the indigenous growth of Japanese industry, fueled initially by imported Western technology, Japan would be vulnerable to coercion and attack from other states, as China's recent history illustrated so well.[6] Russian elites similarly recognized the importance of modernization after Russia's disastrous performance in the Crimean War. Serfdom was ended in the early 1860s, and through the 1870s and 1880s, czars Alexander II and Alexander III accelerated Nicholas I's earlier efforts at industrialization through high tariffs and government subsidies.

Both nations began to see a takeoff phase in their industrial development by the 1880s and especially in the 1890s. Yet this caused elites in both states to worry about how they could sustain high growth rates as the more advanced powers reacted. In particular, both sets of elites understood that long-term growth depended on access to Far Eastern markets and raw materials, especially in China and Korea. Markets for exports of their inexpensive manufactured goods were critical to raising

[6] See also Beasley 1987.

the foreign currency and species needed for the import of the technology as well as raw materials necessary for low-cost production. Neither state, however, could compete in Europe against the more efficient, higher-quality British and German industrial machines. But because of geographic proximity, Russia and Japan had much lower transportation costs for East Asian markets. They could thus expect to outcompete the European great powers in certain niche markets, particularly low-quality textiles and cheap industrial goods.

As we will see in chapter 7, Russia had been actively trying to displace Britain in the China market since the 1830s. Under Alexander III, a new bid for a commercial presence in the Far East was initiated. In 1891, Alexander authorized the building of the Trans-Siberian Railway to join Vladivostok to Moscow and Saint Petersburg. In 1892, under the leadership of the highly capable finance minister Sergei Witte, Russia embarked on a new active Far Eastern policy—one tied directly to an accelerated industrialization policy. Witte's overall strategy was one of *pénétration pacifique*: through an efficient railway system that brought low-cost Russian goods into Manchuria and Korea, Russia could beat the British at their own game. Although Britain still controlled two-thirds of the China trade in 1890, Russia could undersell its products in the north, where British goods had less of a presence. Once established there, Witte's plan was to continue the economic steamroller into China proper. The growing export trade would fuel Russian industrial growth at home, giving Russia the additional economies of scale needed to compete with Britain on a more global scale (Schimmelpenninck van der Oye 2005, 31–45).

Needless to say, the other great powers were not happy about Saint Petersburg's new policy. Historian William Langer (1960, 172) nicely summarizes their reaction:

> The construction of the Trans-Siberian Railway was regarded throughout the world as a portentous departure in Russian policy; as an event bound to transform the whole Far-Eastern question and at the same time to modify the whole framework of international relations. Japan as well as China watched the Russian plan with deep apprehension. In Tokyo it was feared that if the Russians once completed their system of communications it would no longer be possible to resist their advance with anything like even chances of success.

Tokyo's fears were exacerbated by the success of Russian industrialization. By the early 1890s, Russian industry was growing at approximately 8 percent annually at a time when most states were still mired in the depression that had afflicted the European economy since 1873. Witte was able to hold down military spending to plow extra capital into the industrialization program. But the compounding growth of Russia's economy led to absolute increases in annual military outlays from approximately 240 million rubles at the start of the 1890s to around 380 million by the decade's end. Much of this extra spending went into the modernization of Russia's military technology, increasing the state's battlefield and power projection capabilities (Fuller 1992, 362–84).

Japan responded to these developments by increasing its efforts to control Korea and by trying to penetrate the China market with its own goods. Japan had done the system a service by forcing Korea, the isolated "Hermit Kingdom," to open up to trade in 1876. At least initially the bulk of the imports into Korea came from Europe; in 1882, for example, 76 percent of Korean imports consisted of European textiles. Japanese efforts at economic penetration, though, succeeded beyond anyone's dreams. By 1892, a mere decade later, Japan dominated the market, providing 87 percent of Korea's imported goods.[7] Nevertheless, there were reasons to worry about Japan's ability to sustain this dominance. In 1885, during a standoff with Russia over Afghanistan, the British had seized Port Hamilton, a port on an island off the southern Korean coast, to counter an expected Russian takeover of a neighboring Korean port. Britain did leave two years later. But for Tokyo, the incident showed just how easily the Great Game between Russia and Britain could spill over into struggles for territory near Japan.[8] Japan therefore had to be ready to assert its rights—if necessary, with military power.

Also of concern was Korea's notoriously unstable domestic situation, a fact that invited intervention by its neighbors. China had historically seen Korea as a vassal state, and in the 1880s and 1890s still believed that it was primarily responsible for Korea's internal order. In late 1884, domestic unrest caused by factional infighting led Beijing to send troops into Korea. Tokyo responded with troops of its own. The standoff was quickly resolved when both sides agreed to withdraw their forces. Japan, however, made it clear that it would not tolerate future Chinese threats to its economic sphere. Japanese senior minister Ito Hirobumi told the Chinese viceroy that while China's ties to Korea were largely historical and sentimental, Japan's interests were driven by economic necessity, including Korea's value as a supplier of food to Japan (Langer 1960, 170).[9]

In May–June 1894, much more severe unrest broke out in Korea, spurred by the rebellion of an antiforeign group, the Tonghaks. The crisis again led to the speedy dispatch of Chinese troops to Seoul and the

---

[7]Beasley 1987, 45. See also Langer 1960, 170.

[8]Langer 1960, 169; Cumings 1997, 114.

[9]Figures on rice imports for the 1880s are hard to find, but we know between 1896 and 1901, rice from Korea hovered between 26 and 51 percent, respectively, of Japan's total rice imports. See Duus 1984, table 9, 171.

surrounding areas. In the 1884 crisis, Japanese leaders had felt too weak to fight a war against China. This time, given Japan's new military strength, they saw an ideal opportunity to push China permanently out of Korea. By doing so, they could force reforms on the Korean government that would accelerate trade between Japan and Korea. War broke out between China and Japan in early August, and by year's end, Japanese forces had won a decisive victory, largely through the quick occupation of Korea and an attack on China's Liaodong Peninsula. In the peace that followed, Japan acquired Taiwan, imposed a large indemnity on China, and forced it to further reduce trade barriers to Japanese goods. But the intervention of Russia, aided by France and Germany, compelled Japan to give up its claim to the Liaodong Peninsula along with its great harbors of Port Arthur (Lushan) and Dalny (Dalian).

The Sino-Japanese War of 1894–95 should be seen a precursor to the Russo-Japanese War a decade later. It is apparent, as W. G. Beasley (1987, 55) shows, that Japan did not enter into the war expecting territorial gains. Rather, Japanese officials realized that if things continue on the established pattern, with Korea refusing to modernize and China intervening at its pleasure, internal turmoil would make it impossible for Korea to play its designated role in Japan's economic development. It might even lead to a foreign takeover, as the Russo-British standoff of 1885–86 had intimated. Mirroring US and Soviet thinking about client states during the Cold War, Japanese officials believed that they needed to reform Korea from within—if necessary, through a temporary occupation and reworking of its government—in order to ensure its proper economic connection to the metropole. As the Japanese consul in Seoul summarized in a dispatch on June 26, 1894 to Tokyo regarding Korean reform, Japanese aims in Korea were "to conclude a treaty under which Korea accepts Japanese protection, then intervene in Korea's domestic and foreign affairs, so as to achieve progress and reform, leading to wealth and strength; for thereby we will on the one hand make Korea into a strong bulwark for Japan, while on the other we extend our influence there and increase the rights enjoyed by our merchants" (quoted in ibid., 48). Earlier that month, Prime Minister Ito Hirobumi and Foreign Minister Mutsu Munemitsu had initially believed they might be able to work with China to subdue the rebellion while compelling Korea to institute necessary economic and political reforms (DJ, 1:33). On June 22, however, Beijing rejected a proposal for joint cooperation. Later that day, the Japanese cabinet decided that Japan must undertake reform in Korea whether China approved or resisted Tokyo's actions (see ibid., 1:37, 38–39).

This decision was taken despite a warning on June 14 from the Japanese minister in Seoul, Otori Keisuke, that should Japan move forces into Korea, Russia might intervene militarily (ibid., 1:37). But Korea was now simply too critical to Japan's future to allow it to fall into chaos and disorder. As Japan's foreign minister told the Chinese envoy on June 22, Japan's interests in Korea, "arising from [proximity] as well as commerce, are too important and far-reaching to allow [Tokyo] to view with indifference the deplorable condition of affairs in that Kingdom" (ibid., 1:40). This was not merely a justification for Japanese aggression. The correspondence between Japanese officials in Seoul and Tokyo from late June until war was declared on August 1 was overwhelmingly dominated by one theme: what kinds of reforms had to be forced on the Korean government to ensure Korea could resist Chinese and foreign intervention as well as trade freely with Japan.[10] In the peace agreement with China of April 1895, the Treaty of Shimonoseki, Japan wisely allowed Korea to maintain its independence, albeit one that would be strongly shaped by Japanese desires. Although this moderate outcome was in keeping with Tokyo's fears of great power military intervention, it was also entirely consistent with Japan's prewar aims of building a stable and independent Korea that would remain a crucial Japanese trading partner.

The Sino-Japanese War can thus be seen as Japan's first defensive response to growing external concerns about the stability of its trade relationships. Economic realism nonetheless edges out trade expectations theory as an explanation for this particular case. Because the failure to act would have likely hurt Japanese-Korean commerce, this war is certainly consistent with trade expectations theory's overall predictions. Yet Japan's concerns about Korean instability had been ongoing since the mid-1880s and were not that much higher in 1894 than during the unrest of 1884. What made the difference in Japan's response across the two dates was its increased military power coupled with its much higher dependence on Korea for markets and food imports. Japan's destabilizing moves in June–July 1894—moves that risked war not only with China but possibly with Russia, too—were taken because an opportunity to reduce the country's ongoing vulnerability had suddenly presented itself. This is strongly consistent with the economic realist logic. Expectations in 1894 that future unrest in Korea would hurt Japan's trade certainly helped to bolster the sense that hard-line actions were necessary. Still, the opportunity to lower Japan's economic vulnerability was the main propelling force behind the provocative policies adopted, with declining trade expectations playing mostly a reinforcing causal role.

The 1895 Triple Intervention of Russia, France, and Germany as well as the subsequent events of 1897–98 helped sow the seeds of Japanese mistrust over Russian long-term intentions. By the terms of the Treaty of Shimonoseki, China was to have leased the Liaodong Peninsula to Japan

[10] See documents in *DJ*, 1:41–73.

for a twenty-year period. The combined pressure of the three powers, however, compelled Tokyo to hand the peninsula back to China. Russia's actions over the next three years revealed its own designs in the region. In 1896, a chastened China gratefully signed an alliance with Russia that was directed solely at Japan. In return for Russian military support in the event of another war with Japan, Beijing agreed to grant Russia the right to build a railway across Manchuria to Vladivostok—one that would be protected by Russian "guards" (i.e., soldiers). The Chinese Eastern Railway would be funded by the newly established Russo-Chinese Bank, which would pool French and Russian capital together to build the line in the shortest possible time. Then in March 1898, Saint Petersburg carried out the ultimate betrayal. Completing a diplomatic project begun in late 1897, Russian officials forced Beijing to lease the Liaodong Peninsula— with its ports of Port Arthur and Dalny—to Russia. This outraged Japanese officials. Here was the very state that had forced Japan to give back the peninsula to China now grabbing it for itself (Nish 1985, 22–34).

The extension of the Trans-Siberian Railway into Manchuria and now the Liaodong Peninsula fit perfectly with Witte's overall plan for the Far East. Not only would the Chinese Eastern Railway shave eight hundred miles off the trip to Vladivostok compared to the track that went around China; the extensions south also would position Russia perfectly to compete for the China market. Because Vladivostok was ice bound for four months of the year and was on the other side of the Korean Peninsula, it was poorly positioned to help Russia increase its China trade. The Manchurian line would allow quick, low-cost penetration of Chinese markets, taking trade away from both Britain and Russia's newest economic competitor, Japan (Warner and Warner 1974, 151–53). Witte believed deeply that "finances are the nerve of war" and only economically strong states do well in the "unceasing struggle to acquire commercial influence" over weaker states (quoted in Schimmelpenninck van der Oye 2007, 33–35). He also understood that the railway would have important strategic implications, including the efficient projection of coercive power against the Chinese capital.[11] Notwithstanding Witte's later efforts to distance himself from hard-liners, his thinking in the late 1890s clearly reveals that the Manchurian railway was part and parcel of his larger scheme to control northern Chinese commerce, and if necessary, use military force to back it up (Stolberg 2007).

Initially, the Russians supported the new Manchurian railway with soldiers to staff the stations and protect the tracks. The Boxer Rebellion in summer 1900 changed all this. The Boxers, a rebel group determined to push the great powers out of China, did not just attack foreigners

[11] See Tang 1959, 38–39, drawing from a March 1896 memorandum.

in Beijing and neighboring territories. It also launched attacks directly against the Manchurian railway and Russian troops protecting them. When the great powers agreed in July to intervene to defend their subjects, Russia used this as an excuse to send 170,000 soldiers into Manchuria to occupy the whole province (Hopkirk 1990, 508). This action was worrisome not just to Japan but also to two other states that along with Japan, had pledged themselves to maintaining open commerce in northern China: Britain and the United States. US secretary of state John Hay had officially announced the US adherence to an open-door policy for China in September 1899. Unfortunately for Tokyo, Hay also made it clear during the Boxer crisis that Washington would be unwilling to use force to maintain trade access to Manchuria. Britain also showed little interest in opposing Russia. This left only Japan to force Russia out of its new possession.

The period from 1899 to early 1900 had already been a rocky one for the two countries. Notwithstanding an informal agreement in April 1898 that seemed to imply Russia's recognition of Japan's "predominant" commercial position in Korea, Russia had been trying to make inroads on the Korean Peninsula (Nish 1985, 46–47). To protect its trade and naval routes from Vladivostok to Port Arthur, Saint Petersburg in 1899 renewed its effort to acquire a land concession at Masampo harbor on Korea's southern shore. In March 1900, Russia anchored its squadron near Seoul, and within days successfully coerced Korea into leasing land at Masampo for the recoaling of Russian ships. Japan responded by mobilizing its navy. In pushing the port concession, Saint Petersburg understood the risks. Foreign Minister Mikhail Muraviev had written in January 1900 that Japan would oppose Russia even if it had no support from powers such as Britain. Admiral Pyotr Tyrtov answered Muraviev's memorandum by arguing that Russia needed a Korean port to protect communications between Port Arthur and Vladivostok. In the end, though, neither side was ready for war, and the crisis petered out when Japan learned of the limits that Korea had placed on the Russian lease (Langer 1960, 691–92). Yet the dispute underscores that even before the Boxer Rebellion, Tokyo had reason to worry about Russia's long-term plans for the region.

The occupation of Manchuria in summer and fall 1900, given the size of the Russian operation, was seen as an even more serious threat to Japan's position than the Masampo lease. Through late 1900 and into 1901, Tokyo used both direct diplomacy with Saint Petersburg and indirect diplomacy via the other great powers to convince Russia to leave Manchuria. Saint Petersburg responded by pressing Beijing to accept a permanent Russian military presence in Manchuria to protect Russia's railway and commercial interests—in essence turning the province into a Russian protectorate.

This move greatly concerned Tokyo. For one thing, Japan's growing trade with Manchuria through its only open port, Niuchuang, was now threatened. This port in southern Manchuria had been opened in 1861 through British and French pressure, but during the 1890s Japanese merchants and citizens had flooded the city until they made up more than 85 percent of the approximately ten thousand foreigners stationed there. Russia's occupation of Manchuria also reinforced the long-standing fear that an action by any one European power to formally control parts of China would lead to an all-out scramble for colonial provinces, with Japan being left on the sidelines—as the initial scramble for ports in 1897–98 had already portended. On top of all this was the problem of Russia's future intentions. As Katsura Taro, Japan's new prime minister, argued, Russia would now try to extend into Korea and would not stop "until there is no room left for us" (quoted in Beasley 1987, 77).[12]

It is important to show, to counter the view that the czar and his officials were simply crazed imperialists, that almost all of Nicholas's top advisers were driven more by the fear of losing Manchuria than by any glory and greed associated with its absorption. As Eva-Marie Stolberg's (2007) detailed work reveals, a broad swath of officials during the 1898–1903 period, from Russian transport ministers and foreign ministers to Russian generals, were worried about the defense of the poorly populated Siberia region. Controlling railways and warm-water ports in Manchuria, they believed, was a vital frontline defense against Japanese along with other foreign traders and immigrants.[13] It had been future foreign minister Vladimir Lamsdorf who had argued strongly in November 1897 that if Russia failed to grab Port Arthur, the English would do so first. The czar's brother-in-law, Grand Duke Alexander, had contended in 1899 that Russia needed to build a dominant position in northern Korea to prevent Japan from taking over the whole country (Fuller 1992, 373).

Most revealing of all was a pessimistic memorandum on Russia's future military challenges written for the czar by War Minister Alexsei Kuropatkin in 1900. Kuropatkin accepted that "in all likelihood" Russia would have to fight Japan in the near future. Yet as William Fuller (1992, 375–79) notes, he took little comfort in the prospect. The vast majority of Russian soldiers were stationed in the west, and for Kuropatkin, that was how it should stay. Russia must always remember that its primary enemy was Germany, not Japan or Britain. It therefore should avoid territorial grabs in Asia. Yet Kuropatkin saw the tragic dilemma underlying Russia's pursuit of greater economic power. It had no choice but to continue penetrating Manchuria, just as it had to seek control of the Turkish Straits.

[12]See also Nish 1985, 14–15, 65–66.
[13]See also Fuller 1992, 362–93.

These actions, though, he told the czar, touched so deeply on the interests of other states that Russia would have to prepare for a daunting struggle against a coalition of great powers, including Britain, Japan, Germany, and Austria.

Kuropatkin's 1900 memorandum recommended that the czar pursue a moderate course in the Far East—the same advice he would give right up until the start of the Russo-Japanese War. Still, his logic implied that Russia had to maintain a strong military presence within Manchuria. Thus we see that even Russian officials who strongly preferred a focus on Germany were forced by Russia's economic situation into advocating the domination of China's north. And this was despite the recognition that a costly war with Japan would drain resources away from Europe.

In the face of Russia's strong need for Manchuria, the years from 1901 to 1903 were filled on both sides with a growing sense of impending doom. Japan tried a variety of diplomatic options to persuade Russia to leave Manchuria, or at least commit to open access and a Japanese sphere of influence in Korea. Even moderate Russian officials, however, could not sacrifice two things: Russia's preponderant hold over the Manchurian economy, and its right to secure commercial and naval access through the Korean Straits. Given this, and given Russia's growing military and economic strength in the region, it was becoming increasingly clear that finding any negotiated solution to the impasse would be difficult.

Japan's main strategy in 1901–2 to avoid war was to form an alliance with Britain to compel Russia to exit Manchuria. Talks with Britain began in April 1901, at a time when Russia was pressing China to accept a permanent Russian presence in Manchuria. They were concluded in January 1902, with the treaty made public on January 30 and its terms two weeks later. Given the need to signal resolve to Russia, the Japanese had insisted back in November that the terms be announced publicly. Britain, initially reluctant, came to accept this demand (*DJ*, 2:34–35, 68). The treaty's preamble was revealing: the agreed-on objectives of the treaty were to maintain "the independence and territorial integrity of the Empire of China and the Empire of Korea," and secure "equal opportunities in those countries for the commerce and industry of all nations." In the second and third articles, Britain and Japan agreed to enter into any bilateral war only if a third party became involved (ibid., 2:65–67). Practically speaking, this meant that Britain would come into a Russo-Japanese conflict only if France supported Russia. But Britain's acceptance of these clauses—its first binding alliance commitment since the Napoleonic Wars—sent a strong signal to Saint Petersburg. Here was Russia's Great Game enemy joining forces with Japan to show its dedication to the open door for China—a concept that Japan had now officially signed on to. In mid-February 1902, nicely timed to coincide with the announcement of the treaty's terms, Secretary of State Hay communicated US support for the two other open-door states by lodging a protest against Russia's supposed plan to create an economic monopoly over Manchurian commerce (White 1964, 90).[14]

The alliance, at least at the start, had its intended effect. The Russians were shocked by its announcement, seeing the alliance as a major diplomatic setback (Nish 1985, 129). Perhaps not surprisingly, Russia suddenly became quite conciliatory. On April 8, 1902, Saint Petersburg and Beijing announced the terms of an agreement requiring a three-stage pullout of the Russian army from Manchuria over eighteen months coupled with the restoration of the pre-1900 status quo. The first stage involved the withdrawal from the southwestern section of the province west of the Liao River, which included the treaty port of Niuchuang. This was to be completed within six months—that is, by October 8, 1902. The second stage, to be completed by April 8, 1903, concerned the middle section of the province. In the last stage, northern Manchuria was to be vacated by October 8, 1903. Russia would retain its lease over the Liaodong Peninsula and be allowed guards to protect the railway lines. Both the Japanese and British governments hailed the pullout agreement as a victory for open-door diplomacy (ibid., 141).

Their mutual optimism was not to last. By October 1902, Russia had evacuated the southwest section of Manchuria west of the Liao River—although not the city of Niuchuang. Witte, however, had insisted on an escape clause in the April agreement making Russia's pullout contingent on a situation in which "no disturbances [arose]" during the evacuation (quoted in ibid., 140–41). This gave the Russians ample wiggle room to renege on the agreement if they changed their minds. On April 18, 1903, just ten days after having begun a pullout from Niuchuang and Mukden—the former a holdover from the first zone of retreat, and the latter the key city from the second zone—Saint Petersburg reversed itself. It presented seven new demands to Beijing that would have to be met before the evacuation could continue. Before receiving a reply, Russian forces quickly reoccupied Niuchuang and Mukden.

The seven demands made it clear that the Russians had no intention of ever relinquishing economic and political control over Manchuria, even if Russian troops actually pulled back to their pre-1900 positions. The first required the Chinese to agree that "no free port [was] . . . to be established in the [area] evacuated." The second required that Russians be the only foreigners allowed to work in northern Manchuria. The fourth demand

[14] As Hay told Japan's ambassador on the day that the terms were revealed, Washington was "deeply grateful" for the notification and that the treaty's purpose was "entirely in accord with the desire of the United States" (quoted in *DJ*, 2:73).

stipulated that all customs revenue generated by the single currently free port, Niuchuang, be paid into the Russo-Chinese Bank. This meant that the considerable revenues generated by port duties—and paid mostly by the Japanese merchants who dominated Niuchuang's trade—would not go to China but rather to the bank established by Saint Petersburg to fund Manchurian railway construction. Finally, the seventh demand required that China agree not to alienate any portion of Manchuria to any foreign power (other than Russia, of course) (ibid., 146).

Needless to say, Beijing could not accept such demands and still claim sovereignty over Manchuria. Four days later, China rejected the new demands, refusing any discussions on the matter until Manchuria had been evacuated (ibid., 149). Historians agree that Saint Petersburg's decision to renege on the 1902 agreement was the single most important action leading to Japan's preventive attack in February 1904. As we will see, Tokyo went through three rounds of diplomatic exchanges in 1903 to see if any negotiated solution could be reached to avoid war. None of these talks would have been necessary had Russia honored its agreement, pulled out of Manchuria, and accepted open commercial access for foreign powers. Hence the fundamental puzzle that must be answered in explaining the Russo-Japanese War boils down to this: Why did the czar and his advisers decide in late 1902 to early 1903 to abandon an evacuation agreement signed less than a year before, and then impose demands that they knew would be almost impossible to accept?

This question is critical to addressing the issue of whether glory- or greed-crazed imperialists somehow hijacked the Russian state, driving Japan into war by their unwillingness to make adequate and timely concessions. This is the explanation adopted by many observers of the war. Accepting that Japan was forced into a preventive war given Russia's diplomatic intransigence and continued military buildup in the region, they argue that hard-liners such as Alexander Bezobrazov and Yevgeni Alexseev bent the ear of the czar, leading Russia to a "new course" of assertive foreign policy that made war essentially inevitable.

In its specifics, this reasoning aligns with neo-Marxist and liberals arguments focusing on the powerful propelling forces of greed and self-delusion.[15] Bezobrazov, a retired general who had developed a strong friendship with the czar, had a direct financial stake in the timber and

---

[15]It is important to reiterate that the argument that Russian policy was driven by domestic factors does not hurt trade expectations theory per se, since it was still Japan, not Russia, that initiated war, and it did so in response to forces external to the state. Were such an argument valid, it would represent an example of the sixth exogenous factor of chapter 1 (domestic politics in the other) driving the behavior of a dependent state. My goal in what follows is simply to show that this explanation is not historically valid and that the deeper reasons for war are much more tragic than the domestic argument would imply.

mining concessions that Russia had acquired in northern Korea in the late 1890s. He and his followers could not afford to allow Japan to draw Korea into its sphere, even if Japan conceded Manchuria to Russia. They thus distorted Nicholas's thinking to convince him that no concessions on Korea or Manchuria could be made. Admiral Alexseev, the commander of forces in the Far East and diplomatic point person after May 1903 for all direct discussions with the Japanese government, was not part of the so-called Bezobrazov group of low-level officials who did the former general's bidding. But Alexseev did believe, so the explanation goes, that Japan was too weak to attack Russia and that concessions would hurt Russia's position in the region. Given this, he misled the czar and his officials as to the risk of war while shaping the negotiations to prevent any real concessions from being made.[16]

Despite the popularity of this domestic-political explanation, it faces one intractable problem—a problem identified by John White in the early 1960s.[17] In a phrase, the timing is off. The key decisions for the shift in foreign policy that would later be dubbed the "new course" by historians were taken during the waning months of 1902 and early months of 1903. This was long before either Bezobrazov or Alexseev had any real role within the Russian government, or were given official positions of any significance. Indeed, in the first round of internal discussions leading to the reversal of the decision to withdraw from Manchuria, held in November–December 1902 at Yalta and Saint Petersburg, both Bezobrazov and Alexseev were completely out of the loop (the former was deliberately isolated and then sent to the Far East, and the latter was sitting in Port Arthur as Liaodong fleet commander). And there is almost no evidence that either Bezobrazov or Alexseev had any influence on the heated conversations that continued from January 1903 up to March, when the final decision to reverse the pullout was made by Nicholas and his advisers.[18]

So who *were* the advisers guiding the discussions and providing policy advice for the czar during the critical months of November 1902 to March 1903? Perhaps surprisingly, they were the same ones who early in 1902 had pushed for the April agreement committing Russia to a return to the pre-1900 status quo—most prominently, Finance Minister Witte,

---

[16] For summaries and references, see Nish 1985, chap. 11, 248–51; Schimmelpenninck van der Oye 2005.

[17] Even the war's most accomplished historian, Ian Nish (1985), adopts some aspects of this explanation, although his overall account is quite balanced.

[18] A third individual sometimes mentioned as a crucial member of the hard-line faction, Rear Admiral Aleksei Abaza, was not appointed to his key position—secretary of the new Far Eastern Commission—until mid-1903, long after the important decisions had been made. See Nish 1985, 165.

Foreign Minister Lamsdorf, and War Minister Kuropatkin. These were the three individuals who Bezobrazov disparagingly referred to as the "mangy triumvirate," the three who had been thwarting his desires regarding Korea since the late 1890s (Warner and Warner 1974, 157–58). As White (1964, 50–51) and Nish (1985, 145) show, it was Witte, Lamsdorf, and Kuropatkin who dominated the talks during winter of 1902–3. Not coincidentally, these discussions began soon after Witte had returned in November from his two-month fact-finding mission to the Far East. On November 9, 1902, the czar met with Witte, Lamsdorf, and Kuropatkin at his winter home in Yalta, with Interior Minister Vyacheslav Plehve, a Witte compatriot, also in attendance. The details of the conversations are not clear, but what we do know is that there was unanimous agreement from all present, including Witte, that Manchuria must be annexed to Russia or at least made dependent on it. The details of this policy reversal would be hammered out over the next four months of intense discussions in Saint Petersburg. But by November 9, the key decision had essentially been made: Russian forces would remain in Manchuria and evacuate only if China agreed to a new set of conditions that left Manchuria completely dependent on Russia. A reversion to the pre-1900 status quo—the premise behind the original withdrawal agreement of April 1902—would no longer be in the cards.

Why the change in policy? Since the documentation is thin here, we can only speculate. Perhaps the czar's key advisers never had any serious intention of implementing the 1902 evacuation treaty, as Witte himself argued in 1904 once out of power (Nish 1985, 142). This explanation seems implausible for two main reasons. First, we know that Russia did meet the requirement to pull out of the area west of the Liao River by October 8, 1902, and was in the process of retreating from the second-stage area when the policy was officially reversed. It would be strange to go this far with an evacuation that one had never intended to carry out. Second, these seasoned advisers would understand that agreeing to a pullout and then deliberately reversing oneself twelve months later would send a terrible signal to other great powers, particularly Japan and Britain. It would say that Russia could not be trusted to stand by its agreements— which is exactly how the Japanese and British saw the new policy after its April 1903 announcement.

The only explanation that seems plausible, given that all the main players are the same, is that Witte had collected new information on his fact-finding tour of Manchuria revealing just how problematic the situation had become. Perhaps the tour had shown that Russia would likely lose its dominant position in Manchuria should it return to the pre-1900 status quo, either through heightened domestic insurgency or the economic penetration of Japan and Britain. Japan in particular had become a major economic threat, given its highly efficient production of low-cost textiles and advantage in transportation costs over Britain, the traditionally dominant exporter to China. Such a defensive line of thinking would have meshed with the czar's established mind-set: in 1901, in talking to a German envoy, he had argued that he didn't necessarily care if Russia controlled Manchuria; he simply did not want any other power to do so (ibid.).

Regardless of what changed the minds of Nicholas and his advisers by the time of the Yalta meeting on November 9, everything that followed fit nicely within the new plan of action. It was agreed at Yalta that Bezobrazov, who was not at the meeting, would be sent off on a long fact-finding tour of the Far East, almost certainly to neutralize any influence that he and his supporters might have over a notoriously indecisive czar (ibid., 165). He played no role in the discussions and planning over the next three months. The next major meeting, consisting mostly of foreign affairs officials, occurred in Saint Petersburg on January 24, 1903. It was agreed that Manchuria would be evacuated only if adequate guarantees for Russia's interests in the province were agreed to by China. A follow-up conference was held on February 7, attended by a broad array of individuals responsible for Far Eastern policy, both in foreign affairs and the military. Foreign Minister Lamsdorf argued that recent Japanese proposals—including the long-standing Japanese suggestion that Russia and Japan create two spheres of influence, with Russia taking Manchuria and Japan taking Korea—had to be rejected given that Russian "national interests" unavoidably touched on Korea. After dialogue on whether concessions might harm Russia's access to the port of Masampo, the talk turned to Manchuria. The majority, following War Minister Kuropatkin's lead, agreed that Russia should postpone the second stage of evacuation set for completion on April 8 (White 1964, 50–53).

On April 8, the last meeting before the presentation of the new demands was held. This was the first and only meeting in which the Bezobrazov group played any significant role—and only through the personage of Rear Admiral Aleksei Abaza, not Bezobrazov, since the latter was still in Manchuria. The topic of conversation was Korea. Abaza argued that the Yalu timber concession—a concession in which the Bezobrazov group had a direct interest—should be kept and developed, since it made good economic sense and would help protect Manchuria's southeastern flank. He also proposed that the war ministry organize to defend Russian enterprises in Manchuria and Korea, and that Far Eastern administrative functions be consolidated to reduce interdepartmental disorder. The question of withdrawing from Manchuria was not on the table, for one simple reason: the decision to renege on the 1902 agreement had already been made (White 1964, 54–55).

In the face of the above chronology, it is clear that the assertion that greedy imperialist forces hijacked Russian foreign policy and drove it into war cannot be sustained. The key decision of the whole prewar period—the decision not to withdraw from Manchuria and to raise new demands against China—evolved completely under the guidance of the old triumvirate, with neither the Bezobrazov group nor Alexseev playing any discernible role. Abaza's argument for the reorganization of the Far Eastern administrative structure did lead to its centralization in mid-May under the command of Alexseev in Port Arthur. But this reorganization process was the natural result of the decision to stay put in Manchuria rather than a direct cause of war. Had the Russians exited Manchuria as promised, no intense diplomatic discussions with Japan would have been necessary in the first place. In the end, the only possible causal tie between the Bezobrazov group and Alexseev and the outbreak of war in February 1904 lies with Alexseev's admittedly poor management of the final five months of negotiations in late 1903. Yet the fact that the main proposals on both sides went through Saint Petersburg, and were accepted or rejected by the czar's inner circle, not by Alexseev, indicates that the responsibility for Russia's intransigent position after May 1903 must be laid on that inner circle. And as we have seen, there were good strategic and economic reasons for not pulling out of Manchuria and not allowing Japan to control access through the Korean Straits. The final fruitless efforts at diplomacy in 1903 would reveal just how important these reasons were.

The Last Months of Negotiation and the Start of the War

Once it became clear by April–May 1903 that Russia was hunkering down in Manchuria and would not be easily dislodged, the Japanese government had to make a choice: plan for an early war or seek a new diplomatic way out. It decided to do both: to try to find the basis for a new agreement that would protect Japan's economic and strategic interests, but also prepare for a preventive war should Russia prove unmovable. Given the difficulties in attempting to convince Saint Petersburg to renew its 1902 commitment to evacuate Manchuria, the cabinet returned to elder statesman Ito's plan of *man-kan kokan*—a plan first broached in the late 1890s. This strategy called for Tokyo's recognition of Manchuria as part of Russia's sphere of influence in return for Saint Petersburg's recognition of Korea as within Japan's sphere.

A meeting of the general staff on June 8 concluded that Russia's failure to withdraw from Manchuria "must give rise to grave alarm in Japan for the future." Japan should work with Britain and the United States to compel Russia to leave. But if the other powers declined to help and Japanese negotiations proved fruitless,

> Japan should achieve her objects by armed force. . . . The present is the most favorable time for this purpose, being in mind the superiority of our forces over Russia, the fact that the Trans-Siberia [Railway] is incomplete, [and] the existence of the Anglo-Japanese alliance. . . . If we let today's favorable opportunity slip by, it will never come again. (quoted in Nish 1985, 157)

A number of division chiefs remained opposed to the man-kan kokan concept of trading Manchuria for Korea. This opposition was resolved in an important cabinet conference held on June 23 in the presence of the emperor and certain key elder statesmen, including Ito and Inoue Kaoru. The participants agreed that Japan should make some concessions on Manchuria in view of Russia's already-superior position there. Japan, however, should use the current crisis to "resolve the [long-standing] Korean problem," including making sure that the Korean government did not cede any part of its territory to Russia.[19]

This was in essence the man-kan kokan compromise of 1903, and its acceptance by the cabinet and emperor was most likely the result of two memorandums drawn up separately by Foreign Minister Komura Jutaro and Chief of Staff Oyama Iwao, and circulated prior to the conference. Komura's memo stressed that in light of the situation in the Far East, Japan had to focus on national defense and economic development. In this regard, Korea demanded the government's immediate attention. Korea was like a "dagger pointing at Japan's heart," and Russia's recent moves were "leading eventually to her domination over Korea." Negotiations with Saint Petersburg had to revolve around the following principles: preservation of the territorial integrity as well as commercial openness of China and Korea; mutual recognition of the rights that each state held in Manchuria and Korea, and the right to send forces to their respective regions; and Japan's special right to assist Korea in carrying out internal reforms. Oyama's memo also emphasized the importance of Korea to Japan's national security, and urged the government to negotiate the Korea-Manchuria exchange with Saint Petersburg while Japan was still militarily superior.[20]

Formal discussions with Russia began on August 12, when Japan presented (in English) a proposal outlining a six-article agreement that would supersede all previous agreements between the two nations. In essence,

[19] See *DJ*, 2:99; Nish 1985, 159.

[20] For the quotation from Komura's memo, see Nish 1985, 159. My summary of both memos is drawn from Okamoto 1970, 76; Nish 1985, 159; Beasley 1987, 80.

Tokyo was asking for four main things: Russian respect for the territorial integrity of China and Korea along with the commercial equality of all great powers in these countries; recognition by Russia of Japan's "dominant interests" in Korea in return for Japan's recognition of Russia's "special interests" in the railways of Manchuria; a mutual understanding that neither would obstruct the other's industrial and commercial enterprises in their respective spheres; and the right of both states to send troops to their sphere to suppress disturbances (RJDE, 351–52).

Much to Tokyo's frustration, Saint Petersburg sat on the proposals for almost two months before replying with its own set of eight treaty articles. This Russian counterproposal of October 3 (also in English) was a sign of things to come. Saint Petersburg would only agree to respect the integrity of Korea, with mention of China noticeably missing from any of eight articles. Russia would recognize Japan's "preponderating" interests in Korea, and would not "impede" Japan's commercial and industrial undertakings in that country. Moreover, Japan could send troops into Korea to protect its interests, but only after informing Russia and in numbers not to exceed those needed for the job—with the troops leaving as soon as their mission was accomplished. Saint Petersburg also introduced two new articles that proved problematic. Tokyo would have to agree not to use Korean territory for "strategic purposes" or "undertake on the coast of Korea any military works capable of menacing the free of navigation in the Straits of Korea." It would also have to set aside the northern part of Korea (above the 39th parallel) as a neutral zone into which neither state could introduce troops (ibid., 351–52).

This was hardly a conciliatory response on Russia's part. Despite evident Japanese concerns, China and Manchuria were simply left off the table. And while Japan's economic interests in Korea were recognized, Tokyo had to accept a neutral zone in the north that would allow Russian timber and mining enterprises to penetrate the area, backed as they already were by Russian soldiers. The demand that Japan not fortify the Korean coast clearly reflected the long-standing Russian worry about continued trade and communication through the Korean Straits.

In a further sign of Japan's good faith desire for a negotiated solution, when Tokyo replied on October 30, it did not merely reject the Russian demands out of hand but rather sought to offer further compromises.[21] The Japanese did keep pressing for Russian recognition of the territorial integrity of both Korea and China, with Japan and Russia having "spheres of special interest" in Korea and Manchuria, respectively. But they included a new article promising not to build any military works

---

[21] These compromises were hammered out in two internal conferences held in Tokyo on October 14 and 24. See Okamoto 1970, 98.

on the Korean coast that might menace Russia's freedom of navigation. And instead of simply dismissing the idea of a neutral zone in northern Korea, they proposed a neutral zone extending for fifty miles on either side of the Korean-Manchurian border (RDJE, 352–54). Once again, the Russians were slow in responding, and when they did on December 11, they offered almost no concrete compromises. Any mention of China and Manchuria, whether in terms of China's integrity or mutual spheres, was studiously avoided. Instead, Saint Petersburg again focused solely on Korea. The two new Russian demands—that Japan not use Korea's coast for strategic purposes or military works, and that northern Korea remain a neutral zone—were left exactly in their formulations of October 3. This was a clear rejection of Tokyo's effort toward compromise. The Russians would not discuss the question of spheres, and by their response, appeared interested only in defining the limits on Japan's involvement in Korea in order to ensure that Russia's economic interests and its rights of free passage through the straits were protected (ibid.).

Following a conference on December 16 attended by almost all senior Japanese officials, it was decided that with time running out, Japan must be more direct in its diplomacy. A third round of proposals was presented to Saint Petersburg on December 21. In a pointed note that replaced Japan's article 1—the article seeking respect for the territorial integrity of both China and Korea—Tokyo made it clear that the causes for "future misunderstanding" could not be removed "if a large and important portion of those regions [where the interests of the two empires meet] is wholly excluded from consideration." This was a not-so-subtle signal to Saint Petersburg that the two countries might well end up in war should Russia continue to refuse to discuss the Manchurian question. Tokyo also removed the previous suggestion of a fifty-mile neutral zone on both sides of the Yalu River, likely hoping that Saint Petersburg would let its own demand for a neutral zone drop. As for the Russian demand that Japan not use any part of Korea for strategic purposes, the Japanese government said nothing (ibid., 354–55).

The questions of the neutral zone and promise not to use Korea for strategic purposes proved to be deal killers. Russian officials of all stripes, including Alexseev, were coming to realize that Japan might initiate war at any time and that the latest round of Russia's military buildup, begun in June 1903, was not yet complete. For the first time, the Russian government appeared nervous. As opposed to waiting its usual two months to respond, the Russians forwarded a new draft treaty to Tokyo in less than two weeks (on January 6, 1904). In it, Russia provided counterproposals that for the first time mentioned the words "Manchuria," "China," and "sphere of interests." The draft signaled that Saint Petersburg would agree to a new clause that had Tokyo recognizing Manchuria as being outside Japan's sphere of interests in return for Russia's agreement not to "impede" Japan from exercising its rights and privileges under current treaties with China—although this excluded "the establishment of settlements." Russia would only accept the addition of this clause, however, if Japan agreed not to use Korea for strategic purposes and accept a neutral zone in northern Korea above the 39th parallel (ibid.).

Despite the ray of hope that the new Russian proposals seemed to suggest, this was truly a case of too little, too late. Russia was still unwilling to state formally that Korea was outside its sphere of interests—the language that Japan had wanted. And Russia was still demanding a neutral zone in the area of northern Korea already penetrated by Russian businesspeople and soldiers. Furthermore, given the distrust that Russia had engendered over the last year, there was little reason to believe that Saint Petersburg would truly allow Japanese merchants and investors to operate freely in Manchuria. The Russian army, after all, had already reoccupied the one free port of Niuchuang in southern Manchuria. Russia also was rejecting the establishment-of-settlements demand—namely, the setting up of new free ports that would allow Japanese citizens to live and trade openly. Finally, Russia was still insisting that Japan agree not to use the Korean coast for strategic purposes.

On January 12, 1904, an imperial conference was held to discuss Russia's January 6 counterproposals. There was unanimous agreement that negotiations were now essentially hopeless. Because the troopships were not quite ready, it was also agreed that Japan should present one more round of proposals, mainly to buy a bit more time (Okamoto 1970, 100). On January 13, Tokyo sent Saint Petersburg a final set of suggestions that differed little from its previous proposals. Most important, Japan would neither accept a neutral zone in northern Korea nor promise not to use the Korean coast for strategic purposes. The Japanese government did, however, try to clarify Russia's apparent concession regarding Japan's economic rights in Manchuria. Russia was asked to take out the clause excluding new settlements in Manchuria, given that it conflicted with the terms of the new Japanese-Chinese commercial agreement (signed on October 8, 1903). The Japan communiqué ended with the ominous warning that Saint Petersburg needed to respond quickly, since any "further delay in the solution of the [issues before it] will be extremely disadvantageous to the two countries" (RJDE, 356–58).

Back in Saint Petersburg, there was a general mood of pessimism. Given the seriousness of the situation, a special conference was called in late January to discuss the fourth set of Japanese proposals. It was agreed that the demand for a neutral zone in Korea should be dropped. Once again, though, the article demanding that Japan neither use Korea for strategic purposes nor take measures that would threaten the freedom of navigation in the straits was retained. Russia did simplify its language over Japanese rights in Manchuria, stating that it would respect all rights and privileges obtained by Japan through treaties with China. Yet the Russian counterdraft still required that Japan recognize Manchuria as "outside her sphere of interest," while making no similar promise as to Korea (ibid.).

As it turned out, the final Russia proposals failed to arrive in time. They were sent through Alexseev on February 3 and did not reach the Russian ambassador in Tokyo until a few days later. On February 4, an imperial conference decided in the presence of the emperor to go to war immediately. The surprise attack on Port Arthur began on February 8. It is nevertheless apparent that even had the proposals arrived in time, they would have made no difference. The mistrust of Russia was so great by January, and Russian concessions so relatively minor, that only a significant set of new proposals protecting Japan's sphere in Korea and ensuring open trade access to Manchuria could have possibly stopped the momentum for war. Japanese trade expectations were now so low and the concern for Russia's rising military power was so great that war had become the only rational option.[22]

On the Russian side, a profound fear that Russia might lose economic and political control over Manchuria combined with the importance of access through the Korean Straits had united both Russian moderates and hard-liners around a policy of minimal concessions. This was not a case of ignorant or arrogant Russian officials hijacking the process while the czar and reasonable ministers sat helplessly on the sidelines. Russian moderates such as Lamsdorf and Kuropatkin did not want a war, nor did they believe the risks of Japan starting one were slight, especially after October 1903.[23] Yet they also knew that Manchuria had to be kept within the Russian sphere if Russia were to sustain its long-term industrial growth. Moreover, they recognized that free access for Russia's merchants and navy between Vladivostok and the warm-water ports on the Liaodong Peninsula was essential to the protection of its Far Eastern commerce. The fact that Saint Petersburg would ultimately concede on the neutral zone in northern Korea demonstrates that controlling Korean timber (a demand of the Bezobrazov group) was less crucial than protecting Russia's dominance in Manchuria and hence its ability to penetrate the vast China market. But because both of these two industrializing nations needed assured access to Manchuria and China, their respective connections to these areas were ultimately nonnegotiable.

---

[22] In environments of severe decline, commitment problems become much more difficult to resolve. See Copeland 2000b, 48–49, 20, 148; Powell 2006.

[23] Witte had been bumped upstairs in September and thus had only minimal influence on the final negotiations.

The Russo-Japanese War shows well how two great powers, trapped by their current and anticipated economic dependence on a common region, can get themselves into a trade-security spiral of self-reinforcing mistrust and falling trade expectations from which there is no way out. No leader or important official on either side wanted a war. Still, because of Manchuria and Korea's significance to both sides, neither could make sufficient concessions without causing a decline in its economic and geopolitical position. We have seen that the domestic factors held to be critical for both liberals and neo-Marxists played little role in the decision making of either Japan or Russia. Economic realism certainly captures the intense need for control that both powers felt. It also nicely explains Japan's opportunistic move in 1894 to fight China in order to reform Korea's government toward Japanese trade needs.[24] Yet economic realism cannot explain ongoing efforts by Tokyo to negotiate a deal that would avoid war while still preserving Japanese access to the markets as well as resources of Korea and Manchuria. Japan went to war reluctantly, and only when the threat to its economic and strategic interests in the area was obviously not going to be resolved through diplomacy. Russian intransigence may at first seem puzzling. But once we see that concessions to preserve Japan's position in Korea and Manchuria were expected to hurt Russia's economic growth, the hard-line posture that even moderate Russian officials advocated is more understandable. War can be a tragic least-of-many-evils choice for both sides. This case is a perfect illustration of that sad fact.

GERMANY AND THE OUTBREAK OF WORLD WAR I

The explanations for the causes of World War I can be grouped into three main categories.[25] The first includes all arguments that see the war as inadvertent, as a war that no state wanted but that everyone fell into through crisis escalation dynamics. Such assertions would start with the mistrust sparked by the spiraling naval and arms race after 1897. They would then stress that psychological misperceptions, cults of the offensive, and rigid military timetables led great powers to rush their militaries to the borders in late July 1914 for fear of being struck first or missing an opportunity to help an ally in need.[26] The second group of explanations rejects the idea

---

[24] Table 2.7 separates the years 1880 to 1904 into two case periods, 1880–95 and 1895–1904, giving the nod to economic realism for 1880–95 and the outbreak of the Sino-Japanese War.

[25] For an excellent overview of the most recent scholarship, see Levy and Vasquez 2014.

[26] See, in particular, Jervis 1976, chap. 3; Lebow 1981; Van Evera 1999; J. Snyder 1984.

that no one wanted war. Some states—most important, Germany—were certainly aggressive, not as a result of misperceptions and security fears, but instead because of domestic pathologies. Jack Snyder (1991, chap. 3), building on Eckart Kehr (1970), contends that Germany's desire for war reflected a strategic ideology shaped by a cartelized political system: the sharing of power between interest groups led to expansion through domestic logrolling. Most influential is Fritz Fischer's (1967, 1975) neo-Marxist argument that German leaders sought a continent-wide war to achieve economic hegemony in Europe, thereby solidifying the position of the Germany ruling classes vis-à-vis the rising working class.

The third group of explanations operates at the systemic level. For some neorealists, the war was one of miscalculation caused by multi-polarity: great powers could not afford to abandon their allies and thus a small crisis in the Balkans dragged all the states into war.[27] For dynamic neorealists, the First World War was fundamentally driven by German fears of decline. This was no miscalculated or inadvertent war. It was rather a preventive war deliberately initiated by German leaders in order to maintain Germany's power position, and hence, security in the face of territorial giants possessing much greater potential for long-term economic and military growth.[28]

In other work, I have shown what I believe to be the overwhelming evidence in favor of the dynamic neorealist perspective (Copeland 2000b, chaps. 3–4; 2014). I will not repeat here the intricate details of the July Crisis of 1914 that reveal how German leaders and officials manipulated the system into a war that only they wanted. Rather, my objective is to demonstrate how global economic factors, specifically German worries about their state's long-term access to raw materials and markets, strongly reinforced the overall pessimism about Germany's position in the system. In particular, with the other great powers moving after 1896 toward policies of economic containment, German officials had good reason to believe that Germany's long-term decline relative to huge economic empires such as Russia, Britain, and the United States could not be reversed merely by greater economic penetration of the world economy. In such an environment, war to secure the resources and markets needed to secure Germany's economic growth became seen as a necessity. Increasingly pessimistic trade expectations, in short, played a critical role in the preventive logic that drove German leaders to choose war in July 1914.

In making this argument, I draw extensively from Fischer's detailed documentary evidence on the economic determinants of World War I—evidence that is still by far the most complete. But while Fischer ends up

[27] Waltz 1979; Mearsheimer 2001; Christensen and Snyder 1990; Sagan 1986.
[28] Copeland 2000b, chaps. 3–4; Copeland 2014; Lieber 2007; McDonald 2009.

concluding that the war was a social-imperialist one designed to prevent a class-based revolution within Germany, I show that his evidence actually points toward a straightforward security logic for war. Indeed, as I have discussed elsewhere, it was quite clear that the key German leaders and officials prior to the war held that even a successful war in Europe would only increase the likelihood of revolution at home. They chose war in spite of this belief and with the primary goal of protecting Germany's long-term position in the system against the rise of the great economic empires surrounding them (Copeland 2000b, chaps. 3–4).

In the early and mid-1890s, Germany had been one of the few great powers trying to buck the trend toward protectionism. Recognizing that German industrial products could now match the goods of any state, Chancellor Georg Caprivi (1890–95) sought to expand German trade in Europe and overseas (Coutain 2009).[29] Signals sent by other powers, however, indicated their opposition to any German pénétration pacifique. The severe tariffs from the United States (McKinley Tariff, 1890) and France (Meline Tariff, 1892) were certainly worrisome. But even that bastion of free trade, Great Britain, showed after 1894 that its fear of the rise of German commercial strength would soon lead to a reversal of policy. As I explore in a later chapter, strong concerns about declining competitiveness and economic power relative to a rising Germany and United States—the fourth exogenous factor from chapter 1—had led British conservatives to talk openly of the need for much closer ties to the colonies. In December 1895, a British-supported raiding party attacked the Transvaal Republic of South Africa in an effort to inspire British residents to overthrow Transvaal's Boer government. The raid failed miserably, but Berlin naturally saw it as part of London's hostile reaction to Transvaal's new reorientation toward German trade and investment (see chapter 8).

In mid-1897, Berlin experienced an even more somber portend of things to come when Canada slapped a discriminatory tariff on non-British goods—a move directly contrary to the 1865 most-favored-nation treaty between Germany and the British Empire. Germany lodged a protest, but far from making amends, the British upheld the Canadian decision and then renounced the 1865 treaty in July 1897. It was soon after this that Joseph Chamberlain opened talks with British colonies on the possible creation of a general imperial preference system.[30] The implications for

---

[29] Note that by instituting lower tariffs, Caprivi was able to overcome the great opposition of the "iron and rye" coalition during this period. Such achievements are inconsistent with a view that sees German foreign policy as driven solely by upper-class interests (see Barkin 1970).

[30] See Kennedy 1980, chaps. 14–15. On the pervasive sense of decline that encouraged these British actions, see Friedberg 1988.

the future were clear. Even if Britain failed to formalize "from London" an imperial preference system to discriminate against German goods, it could allow individual colonies or commonwealth countries, on their own initiative, to favor British goods with unilateral policies. The effect on German trade would in the end be the same.

German expectations for future trade reflected these developments. On July 31, 1897, the Prussian minister in Munich informed Chancellor Choldwig von Hohenlohe that public opinion saw the British denunciation of the 1865 treaty as "the prelude to a close trade relationship of England with her colonies." The kaiser's marginal comments captured his agreement: "the denunciation," he wrote, "is the beginning of a revolution in the whole system of British commercial policy," and any suggestion that the target of British action was North America was "nonsense"; clearly "it is against Germany." The kaiser elaborated that "now that the superiority of German industry is recognized, [the British] will soon make efforts to destroy it," and would succeed "unless we quickly and energetically forestall the evil by building a strong fleet" (*GDD*, 2:486–87).[31]

The "main worry" of German leaders during the late 1890s, as Fischer (1975, 7) summarizes it, "remained . . . the extreme protectionist tariffs of the United States and the plans for a British customs association." There seems little question that the German naval buildup that began in 1897–98, producing a hostile sixteen-year naval race with the British, had the protection of German trade abroad as one of its critical objectives. This protection centered on the imports of not only raw materials but food as well; Lamar Cecil (1967, 149) remarks that there was widespread recognition in Germany that with its fast-growing population, Germany "could no longer subsist on native-grown foodstuffs," and a "navy strong enough to keep the sea lanes open was therefore a necessary bulwark against starvation."[32] It was also in the late 1890s that two cru-

[31] Such feelings pervaded both government and legislative circles, as Kennedy details (1980: 261–64, 297–98). In particular, many Reichstag deputies believed that "the granting of preferences by Canada (and, later, several other British colonies) to imports from the motherland marked . . . the beginning of [a protectionist] trend, the chief intention of which was to cripple the economy of Britain's most formidable rival, Germany." (Ibid., 298.)

[32] By the late 1890s, raw materials constituted about 40 percent of Germany's total import bill, with food about making up another 35 percent (Kuznets 1967, 127). The increasing dependency on food imports provided an important strategic rationale for increased grain tariffs in the 1901–2 debates on tariff reform: German industrialization and hence urbanization were proceeding so rapidly after 1890 that without greater restrictions on food imports, the country might be completely at the mercy of its grain suppliers (see Ashley 1910, chaps. 7–9; Barkin 1970, chaps. 4–6). Even *with* the 1906 tariffs in place, however, German imports of food up to 1914 grew faster than the economy as a whole (Offer 1989). All this suggests that the German move to increase tariffs by 1906 was not solely or even primarily driven by the iron and rye coalition but also by systemic fears within a more

cial concepts, *Weltpolitik* and *Mitteleuropa*, were solidified as responses to growing protectionism. Weltpolitik, as Woodruff Smith (1986, 65, 78) observes, sought "the creation of protected markets and investment areas outside Germany's borders and the attainment of secure external supplies of raw materials at regulated prices." Mitteleuropa was its continental counterpart, envisioning the development of "an organized and protected system of economic exchanges between an industrial Germany and an agricultural periphery in central and eastern Europe."

German leaders had good reason to worry about the dependability of outside suppliers. In the last decade and a half before the war, dependence on trade for vital goods increased dramatically, driven by the phenomenal growth in both population and industrial size (see Kennedy 1980, 1987). Domestic oil production, for example, had gone up 140 percent from 1900 to 1913, but still accounted for only 10 percent of total German needs. The state went from being a net exporter of iron ore as late as 1897 to relying on outsiders for close to 30 percent of its needs by 1913, despite domestic production increases of 120 percent.[33] By 1913, over 57 percent of Germany's imports were in the form of raw materials, versus 44 percent in 1903 and 41 percent in 1893 (Bruck 1938, 110).

Of great concern, of course, was the growing political-military encirclement of Germany by France, Russia, and Britain, which found its economic counterpart in the denial of German commerce around the world. Consider colonial possessions. After 1897, Britain and the United States worked in tandem to deny Germany major territorial gains in the Southern Hemisphere; despite German efforts, for instance, it received nothing from the dissolution of the Spanish Empire, and received only small parts of Samoa and China. In both Moroccan crises, 1905 and 1911, Britain helped France secure political control of Morocco at the expense of Germany's export trade and access to raw materials.[34] In fact, from 1898 to 1913, the colonial territory that Germany had been permitted to acquire was only one-seventh that of a state we prefer not to think of as imperialist: the United States (Herwig 1976, 9).

In one of the most critical new areas, the Middle East, the British again worked actively with other powers to minimize German economic penetration. In 1901, the British secured their first oil concession in Persia; by 1907, they agreed with Russia to divide Persia into spheres of influence as

---

restrictive world environment. For a discussion of Germany's naval buildup as a partial reaction to Britain's new policy toward its colonies, particularly as revealed in the South African Crisis of 1895–96, see chapter 8 below.

[33] On oil, see *EHS*, 393, 439; on iron ore, see ibid., 409, 445.

[34] James Davis (2000) shows convincingly that Germany initiated both crises primarily as a defensive response to France's increasingly bold interventions in Morocco and the implications of French moves for Germany's economic interests.

part of a campaign to restrict any extension of German power produced by its involvement in the Berlin-Baghdad Railway. As the Russian ambassador reported to Moscow in August 1910, "England is less interested in what happens in Persia than in preventing any other Power, except England and Russia, from playing any role there. This applies particularly to German and Turkey" (quoted in Dickinson 1926, 261).[35]

From 1911 to 1914, as the British navy shifted to a reliance on oil, the British ensured that no other state would have access to Persian oil reserves. By 1914, the British government had acquired a controlling interest in the previously private Anglo-Persian Oil Company. It had also worked out a tacit deal with the United States allowing it a sphere of influence over Latin American oil, in return for British domination of the Middle Eastern oil reserves.[36] By these means, the Germans were effectively shut out from any control over imports of this most critical of commodities, all at a time when internal production supplied only 10 percent of Germany's growing oil requirements.[37]

Two other areas concerned the Germans: raw materials and food. The Morocco Crises, as even Liberal Party member Gustav Stresemann acknowledged at the time, were in large part "a struggle for [Morocco's] ore deposits" (quoted in Fischer 1975, 236). As noted, Germany had gone from being a net exporter of iron ore in 1897 to being extremely reliant on imports by 1913. France played an increasingly important role here: ore imports from France had increased almost sixty times from 1900 to 1913 as Sweden, Germany's main supplier, moved to establish export quotas. German industry invested heavily in the mines of northern France, such that by 1913, it directly controlled about 10 to 15 percent of the French ore reserves (ibid., 321–22).[38]

The French government took steps to stop this economic penetration, holding up further concessions to German companies in early 1912

---

[35]While the British and Germans, despite a long-standing conflict over the railway, agreed to share control by 1913, Britain ensured that the railway would stop a hundred miles from the all-important Persian Gulf, retaining a veto over further construction (Earle 1924). This ensured that Britain, not Germany, would control any oil flowing from Persia, Kuwait, and Arabia.

[36]See Venn 1986, chap. 2; Yergin 1991, 153–63. The importance of oil for the British was clear. As Winston Churchill argued in July 1913, "If we cannot get oil . . . we cannot get a thousand and one commodities necessary for the preservation of the economic energies of Great Britain" (quoted in Yergin 1991, 160).

[37]The significance of oil would be shown in the war itself, when Romania's move to join the allied forces provoked an immediate German attack on the country (Yergin 1991, 179–81).

[38]For additional figures on Germany's phenomenal increase in dependence on others for iron ore, tied to massive gains in steel production, see Fischer 1975, 320. On the German penetration of the French ore industry, see Gatzke 1950, 30–38.

and then halting them altogether in December 1913. This came at a time when German capital in general was being shut out of both the French and Russian markets (Fischer 1975, 322–26).[39] It is therefore not surprising that German industrialists in 1913 would openly speak to the Italian minister of commerce, as he records, "of the need to lay their hands on the iron ore basis of French Lorraine; war seemed to them a matter for industry" (quoted in ibid., 326).

Expectations for the critical food trade were also deteriorating in the last years before the war. Imports of foodstuffs from 1890 to 1913 grew at an average of 4.8 percent a year, significantly faster than the overall economic growth rate of 3.9 percent. Avner Offer's evidence supports the point that the Anglo-German naval arms race reflected in large part fears on both sides that the other would blockade imports to starve the adversary into submission. British plans for such a blockade were well advanced in the last decade before the war, and as Offer (1989, 322) relates, "[the] threat to Germany was a real one."[40] A 1907 German naval office report indicated that about 74 percent of Germany's imports came by sea, either directly or indirectly. In 1908, a German naval diplomat argued that Germany must endeavor "to possess a fleet which is powerful enough to make [a] blockade of our coasts impossible" (ibid., 325–26, 335; see also chaps. 15–21).

The above analysis demonstrates that German leaders after 1897 were worried about great power economic as well as political-military encirclement. In particular, there were fears that the British would move to restrict German commerce around the world. One might contend, however, that since Britain never actually introduced tariff walls or imperial preference before the war, German leaders should have had positive trade expectations with this state. Despite its surface plausibility, what this claim ignores is how any forward-looking decision maker would have reacted to the significant growth in protectionist sentiment in England after 1896. In short, while Britain did not abandon free trade, the Germans had cause to think that Britain was likely to abandon it in the near term.

As Ross Hoffman (1983, 225) shows in detail, the British public and government officials alike were greatly alarmed by the growing German economic challenge after 1895. In his words, "Hard times, the evident stagnation of some British industries, the widened area of world competition, the rise of German shipping . . . all conspired to produce a high

---

[39]On the French endeavor to build up its Russian ally through massive loans, which went hand in hand with its efforts to restrict the role of German finance around the world, see Feis 1931, especially chaps. 8–9.

[40]Britain by 1913 was importing about four-fifths of its wheat and flour. By 1906, Germany was importing about 20 percent of its annual grain consumption, and in total tonnage, its imports were second only to Britain (Offer 1989, 93, 230).

measure of national apprehension." From 1897 on, a strenuous debate over tariff reform took place throughout England—a debate that "provoked great alarm within Germany" (Kennedy 1980, 305). Chamberlain was spearheading this attempt to move toward imperial preference. In 1897, as British colonial secretary, he initiated a series of imperial conferences involving the white dominions and colonies to discuss tighter economic and political integration. By the second such conference in 1902, he put forward the idea that Britain "would grant the white colonies favored access to its markets, in return for stronger military and politics bonds" (Offer 1989, 264).

The idea of tariff reform was a dominant element in the three general elections in Britain before the war—one in 1906 and two in 1910. The party leading the charge for imperial preference, the Unionist (Conservative) Party, lost all three elections. But it is important to note that the Unionists had essentially the same number of seats in both 1910 elections as the Liberals, and indeed garnered a greater percentage of the popular vote than any other party.[41] The Liberals was able to form a government only by a coalition with the Irish Party. While the members of the Irish Party overwhelmingly favored protectionism, they joined the Liberal coalitional government to secure their dominant objective of Irish home rule (Curtiss 1912, part 6, chap. 1).

In short, by 1910, it did not take much for the German leadership to realize that a majority of British politicians favored the creation of a closed economic empire, and that it would only be a matter of time before protectionism won out. As Albert Ballin wrote to the kaiser in spring 1910, "Tariff reform and a Zollverein [customs union] with the Colonies are the catchwords that are on everybody's lips, and the anti-German feeling is so strong that it is scarcely possible to discuss matters with one's oldest friends, because the people over here have turned mad and talk of nothing but the next war and the protective policy of the future" (quoted in Hoffman 1983, 292).[42]

---

[41] In both 1910 elections, the Unionists received about 46–47 percent of the vote, with the Liberals getting about 43–44 percent. In the 1906 election, the Unionists received 44 percent of the vote versus 49 percent for the Liberals (Lloyd 1993, 9–22). Given the closeness of the 1910 elections and general movement in popular vote toward the Unionists, it would not have been irrational for German leaders to think that the protectionist forces would win the next election, whenever it was held.

[42] Hoffman (ibid., 252) continues that "the standing threat of a tariff war . . . was a serious obstacle to any lasting accord with Germany." The "innumerable utterances" made at this time in the British press against the German economic challenge also had the "inevitable effect" of stiffening the British government's commitment to the Triple Entente against Germany. Hoffman also observes that tariff reform was seen as "weapon with which to liberate England from the hazards of German naval and imperialist rivalry, for the idea got abroad that the adoption of protection by Great Britain would so cripple Germany economically that she would have to abandon all hope of disputing British supremacy."

I now turn to a specific analysis of how declining expectations of future trade affected German geostrategic thinking up to the start of World War I. Much of what follows is drawn from Fischer, whose work from the archival documents is still the best in the field.[43] Fischer shows the clear relation between initial German war aims and the increasing economic anxieties of a diverse group of individuals before July 1914. The shared fear was that German industry, increasingly dependent on outsiders for vital goods, would be strangled by the growing economic restrictions imposed by Germany's adversaries. Since these powers had extensive imperial possessions, they could afford to adopt closed economic policies. Germany lacked such an alternative. As neomercantilist Gustav Schmoller put it in 1900, the Russian, British, and US world empires, "with their greed for land, their power at sea and on land, their trade," want to put all others "into an economic straitjacket and to smother them" (quoted in Fischer 1975, 35).

By 1911, after the failures of the second Moroccan Crisis, and "in response to the protectionist trends in the United States, Britain, and Russia," Germany "turned again to the idea of a central European economic area as a defensive measure" (ibid., 10). Concern for economic security was tangible, and transcended ideological and party lines. In November 1911, the business manager for the Nasa League, Manfred von Richthofen, argued that expansion was "an urgent necessity" given the small size of Germany, which needed territories "from which we can satisfy our need for raw materials" (quoted in ibid., 231–32).[44] National Liberal Stresemann stated in early 1913 that Germany must seek to "create a self-sufficient economic area, so as to make sure of our raw material requirements and to protect our exports." Ernst Basserman of the Centre Party in mid-1912, fearing isolation by economic encirclement, asserted that "our trade declines more and more in certain places where we are pushed out or where it keeps its end up only with difficulties." A Free Conservative paper in 1913 wrote that a future war must be fought for "a large piece of the earth in the immediate European sphere of power . . . which with one stroke will give us the economic independence which we need for our industrial exports, for the bread supply of our masses." Even the Social Democrat Gerhard Hildebrand would write in 1911 that "from a socialist standpoint the acquisition of colonial domains has become an acute economic necessity for Germany." Indeed, Fischer (ibid., 234, 239, 250–253) shows that

---

[43] For summaries and references of recent work on World War I, see Levy and Vasquez 2014.

[44] A year later, he maintained that "Germany needs colonies" since "it must become independent from America which may one day refuse us its raw materials, grain, copper, and cotton." To compete, Germany must seek its own "closed customs union of continental Europe," otherwise "our exports will slowly lose more and more ground and finally disappear altogether" (quoted in ibid., 236–37).

after 1906, the Social Democratic Party moved to not only drop its opposition to German colonial expansion but actually encourage it.

These views paralleled those within the government. Walter Rathenau,
who became the influential head of the department of raw materials in
August 1914, was contending by December 1913 that the German raw
material base was too "narrow" and depended on "the mercy of the
world market as long as [Germany] did not itself possess sufficient raw
material sources." In April 1914, Ballin noted that the "expansion of our
foreign markets is increasingly threatened," and in the oil-rich Near East
in particular, "we have been thrown out of the most important regions
there" (ibid., 238, 450).

The declining expectations of future trade contributed to the pervasive sense of general decline felt by the German leadership in July 1914.
Elsewhere I consider the overwhelming evidence that German leaders
initiated world war for preventive motives—namely, to forestall the rise
of powers such as Russia.[45] What is critical here is to see the economic
factors that reinforced these motives. In essence, if France and Russia
could be defeated, valuable areas in northern France, Belgium, Ukraine,
and central and eastern Europe would be brought under German tute-
lage, guaranteeing the raw materials and markets needed for future German economic power, and therefore security; without major war, the economic policies of German adversaries would push Germany further into
decline over the long term.

These aims were revealed in the so-called September Program, which
was finalized by Chancellor Theobald von Bethmann-Hollweg on September 9. The plan stated that the "general aim of the war" was "security for the German Reich in west and east for all imaginable time."
Russia "must be thrust back as far as possible from Germany's eastern
frontier," while France would become "economically dependent on Germany, secur[ing] the French market for our exports." France's "ore-field
of Briey, which is necessary for the supply of ore for our industry, [is] to
be ceded" and a "central European economic association," including central Europe, France, Poland, and "perhaps Italy, Sweden, and Norway,"
was to be formed. And while members would be "formally equal, . . . in
practice [the association] will be under German leadership and must stabilize Germany's economic dominance over Mitteleuropa" (Fischer 1967,
103–4). This blunt program for German economic hegemony in Europe
was clearly consistent with the prewar call for a Mitteleuropa, and reflected the work of Bethmann-Hollweg and his associates through the
months of July and August 1914. Rathenau, who was now in charge of
raw materials for the reich, was particularly influential. On August 1,
1914, he submitted a long memorandum to Bethmann-Hollweg arguing

---

[45] For a summary, see Copeland 2000b, chaps. 3–4; Copeland 2014.

that "only a Germany reinforced by Mitteleuropa would be in a position to maintain herself as an equal world power between the world powers of Britain and the United States on the one side and Russia on the other," and war, if necessary, would help to achieve this "essential objective" (ibid., 101, 11).[46] The date shows that the report must have been prepared during the height of the July Crisis, demonstrating that the September Program reflected prewar objectives rather than a post hoc scramble to justify the reality of war.

Of particular concern for Bethmann-Hollweg were German iron ore interests in France. On August 26, he sought information on the size of the ore deposits in French Lorraine, and soon after agreed to consider the annexation of French mines "in a final peace treaty." Aware of prewar French discrimination against German companies, in the September Program he wrote that any commercial treaty with a defeated France "must secure for us financial and industrial freedom of movement in France in such a fashion that German enterprises can no longer receive different treatment from [the] French" (quoted in ibid., 104).[47]

The importance of ensuring German long-run access to markets and raw materials was restated in an October 22, 1914, memo that Bethmann-Hollweg wrote to Clemens von Delbruck, secretary of state in the Reich Interior Office (ibid., 248). One of Germany's primary goals, Bethmann-Hollweg argued, was to open the French and Russian markets to German trade and industry. The rich iron ore region of Longwy-Briey in France was to be ceded. And Russia "would have imposed on it a long-term commercial treaty which would mean a lowering of Russian industrial tariffs" (Fischer 1975, 538).

It is important to note the widespread agreement during the September–October period that despite likely opposition from key industrial and agricultural interests, Germany needed to create a free trade zone within Europe after victory in order to compete against the remaining world powers. In a September 13 memo to Bethmann-Hollweg, Delbruck asserted that "only a Europe without customs barriers [and controlled by Germany] can effectively face the vast producing potential of

---

[46]The first part of the quote is Fischer's paraphrase; Fischer takes the words "essential objective" from the document itself. Bethmann-Hollweg was clearly impressed by the memo; he had it circulated throughout the department (ibid., 101).

[47]German territorial objectives were not confined to Europe, however. On August 25, Foreign Minister Gottlieb von Jagow asked Wilhelm Solf, the secretary of state in the colonial office, for ideas on German gains in Africa. Solf's memorandum on the subject recommended the acquisition of vast areas of French and Belgian Africa, especially in Central Africa. These suggestions found their place in the September Program, with Bethmann-Hollweg remarking, "The first aim is the creation of a continuous central African colonial empire," although the overall question of "colonial acquisitions . . . will be considered later" (ibid., 104).

the transatlantic world" (ibid., 540). In October, Alexander von Falken-huasen, counselor at the Prussian Ministry of Agriculture, wrote that economic hegemony in Europe was needed to "match the great, closed bodies of the United States, the British, and the Russian Empires with an equally solid economic bloc." Reflecting the prewar problems in securing access for German goods, he stressed that one of the key German pur-poses was to "lead the entire economic strength of allied Europe . . . in the struggle with those world powers over the conditions of the admission of each to the markets of the others" (ibid., 539).

It was also at this time that an adviser to Delbruck perhaps best sum-marized the importance of the war as a means of overcoming the pro-jected intensification of global trading restrictions. There was one "final great aim" in the war, the adviser proclaimed to his superiors, which despite "difficulties of procedure," should not be forgotten: "to create a great central European economic area which allows us to maintain our place in the economic struggle of the nations and prevents us from de-clining into economic impotence in the face of the increasingly close and assertive economic world empires—Great Britain with its colonies, the United States, Russia, Japan with China" (quoted in ibid., 539; see also Fischer 1967, 251).

In sum, we can see that increasingly pessimistic trade expectations had much to do with the overall fear of decline that drove Germany lead-ers to bring on major war in July 1914. With Britain shutting Germany out of the oil-rich Middle East and resource-rich Africa, France threaten-ing access to iron ore, and high French and Russian tariff levels limiting German growth versus "economic empires" like Britain and the United States, German leaders felt that only a major war would provide the eco-nomic dominance of Europe needed for long-term German survival. Eco-nomic realism has a problem with this case: while it can explain German fears of dependence, it cannot explain why German leaders allowed such dependence to continue for decades without it driving them into either war or a determined policy of relative autarky. Liberalism cannot explain why the high levels of trade dependence between the great powers did not keep the peace. Falling trade expectations, tied to Germany's strong need for foreign resources and markets, explain why interdependence ended up pushing Germany into war.

GERMANY AND THE START OF WORLD WAR II

There are two main camps in the modern literature on the origins of the Second World War in Europe. The "intentionalists" such as Klaus Hildebrand (1973), Eberhard Jäckel (1981), and Andreas Hillgruber

(1981) build on the traditionalist historical account that emerged in the first decade after the war's end. These authors argue that Hitler and his followers assumed power in 1933 with the intention of waging a new European war for German hegemony, and then manipulated the diplomatic and military environment to bring about this war under the best possible circumstances. The "structuralist" counterargument, led most prominently by Hans Mommsen (1979), Martin Broszat (1981), and Tim Mason (1995), is a revisionist effort to show that Hitler had no set program for German hegemony. Hitler lacked long-range goals, structuralists contend. He reacted to the domestic forces that were unleashed as he sought to rebuild the Germany economy. In particular, the economic crisis of 1938–39 led Hitler to start a war to grab the resources needed to maintain his own hold on power.[48]

There are problems with both these camps. The structuralist reasoning is the most easily challenged. The evidence quite clearly shows that Hitler did have an agenda for total war as soon as he assumed power in early 1933.[49] Moreover, it was Hitler's very efforts from 1933 to 1936 to create a military capable of offensive war by 1939–41 that caused the economic crisis of 1938–39. The structuralists have thus reversed the causal sequence: the economic crisis was the result of Hitler's desire for major war, not the cause of it.[50] Yet the intentionalist argument also has its problems. The intentionalists are right to say that Hitler planned for major war, but they are less clear as to why. Hildebrand and Hillgruber rightly specify Hitler's strategic objective as the destruction of France and Russia along with the eventual reduction of both the British Empire and United States. But they are vague as to Hitler and his followers' ultimate ends—whether they sought national security, wealth, or the spread of Nazi ideology. Most intentionalists would probably accept Alan Bullock's (1964, 806–7) conclusion that Hitler had a pathological lust for power. Yet such a conclusion is not only unilluminating (do not almost all leaders thirst for power?) but also essentially tautological: in the very act of seeking geopolitical hegemony, leaders who initiate major wars show that they "want" to dominate others.

The weaknesses of the main camps leave an opening for the three main competing theories of this book. The evidence presented below reveals the weaknesses of the liberal contention. Germany's dependence

---

[48] For full references, see Kershaw 1993, chap. 6.

[49] On February 3, 1933, just three days after becoming chancellor, Hitler assembled his top generals to explain that the most important short-term task was the rebuilding of Germany military power for the "conquest of new living space in the east and its ruthless Germanization" (*NDR*, 3:628–29; see also Weinberg 1970, 27). For the traditional military's enthusiastic response to this news, see Copeland 2000b, 125–28.

[50] For an incisive critique of the structuralist view, see Kershaw 1993, chap 6.

on the outside world for vital goods was not simply a constraint on domestic-level pathologies—a constraint that was removed as the other great powers reverted to imperial preference systems after 1930. Rather, as economic realism and trade expectations theory suggest, German dependence created a sensitivity to the nation's ongoing access to raw materials that reinforced a keen feeling of insecurity at the highest levels. As I discuss, both realism and the trade expectations approach find strong support in the documentary record. Which theory ultimately emerges as "superior" depends on whether one stresses the singular role of Hitler in the starting of the war, or the need for consensus between Hitler and the traditional military leaders who would be in charge of waging this total war. It is to this divide that I will now turn.

One basic geopolitical fact about Germany in the pre-1914 era and interwar period stands out: this was a state capable of superior military power, but its small territory possessed few natural resources compared with the great powers surrounding it. Two things fell out from this. First, Germany would always remain highly dependent on outsiders for the food and raw materials vital to its economic health, unless it expanded. Second, since the surrounding great powers were better able to fashion self-sustaining imperial realms, should they ever move in this direction by closing their borders to trade—as they did starting in the early 1930s— long-term German economic viability and thus security would be threatened. These two realities implied that Germany's potential military superiority might have to be used, as in World War I, to generate the territorial mass needed for survival against what in 1914 were referred to as the "economic world empires."[51]

The strategic obsessions of Hitler and the Nazi regime revolved around this dilemma that the First World War had failed to solve. Hitler's own views about Germany's economic and military vulnerability were shaped by talks with geopoliticians such as Karl Haushofer in the early 1920s, which in turn reflected entrenched arguments from the pre-1914 era (Stoakes 1986, chap. 5). In his 1925 *Mein Kampf*, Hitler foresaw that with Germany's small size constraining its "living space" (lebensraum), its dependence on foreign states would only increase as the population grew faster than the yields on arable land. For Hitler (1925, 131–40, 641– 55), because the colonial world was already controlled by other European powers, Germany would have to acquire new land within Europe itself. Russia was both a huge threat and an opportunity. Because its landmass and population were many times Germany's, industrialization would leave Russia predominant in Europe over the long term. But its large territory could also provide the basis for overcoming Germany's high

[51] See Copeland 1996a, 2000b, 2012b; Tooze 2006.

dependence levels.[52] By the mid-1930s, Hitler's anxieties had broaden: Germany's problem was not simply the supply of food but even more seriously, the supply of raw materials needed for industrial strength. Hitler's program for war from 1933 on was thus devoted to the destruction of Russia. In one stroke, this would acquire the land needed for vital food and raw materials, while preventing the rise of the state most likely to overwhelm Germany in the future.[53]

Even if we question critical aspects of Hitler's worldview, it is important to note not only that his strategic objectives mirrored much of pre-1914 thinking but also that without his mass appeal and the loyalty of his subordinates, Hitler could not have initiated world war. Hence, a simple counterfactual must be posed: Would Hitler's arguments have made as much sense to his followers had Germany possessed the landmass of Russia or the British Empire, or if world trade had not been disrupted by the Great Depression? Implicit in what follows is the claim that had Germany been less dependent on vital goods, and had expectations for future trade not been so pessimistic following US, British, and French efforts to create closed trading blocs, it would have been much more difficult for Hitler to pull Germany into war. The security situation of Germany would have looked less dire, thereby dampening the necessity for war.

On his accession to power in February 1933, Hitler announced to his closest associates that Germany needed to plan for a war to achieve lebensraum in the East (see Copeland 2000b, 125). The so-called Reformers, a group of economists that called for the creation of a self-sufficient "large economic area" (*Grosswirtschaftsraum*) protected by tariff barriers, guided Nazi economic policy at the time. As Jeremy Noakes and Geoffrey Pridham summarize in their collection of primary documents: "This campaign was prompted by the collapse of the international trading system in the wake of the slump, the revival of world-wide protectionism, and specifically, the creation of imperial or regional preference areas. . . . If Germany's economy was to compete with those of the United States, the British Empire, and Japan, it would need to create a rival economic bloc" (*NDR*, 2:259–60). This was akin to the pre–World War I concept of Mitteleuropa, an idea that had been actively resuscitated by the Heinrich Bruning and Franz von Papen governments after 1930 in response to the collapse of world trade (see ibid., 2:260–62).

Nevertheless, from 1933 to 1936, when Hjalmar Schacht, the president of the Reichsbank, was overseeing the economy, Germany did not proceed immediately toward autarky. Keynesian deficit spending, including mass rearmament, produced an immediate economic revival that

---

[52] For the origins of the idea of lebensraum in the pre-1914 era, see Smith 1986, chap. 5.
[53] On the planning for war against Russia, see Copeland 2000b, chap. 5.

required marked increases in the input of raw materials, which generally came from abroad. The enormous wave of protectionism that followed the US Smoot-Hawley Tariff Act of 1930, however, created a major constraint: since Germany could not sell its exports abroad, foreign currency could not be raised to pay for the imports of raw materials. By June 1934, Hitler was being told that the "raw materials situation is becoming daily more acute" and that there was a "drain of foreign exchange" (ibid., 2:270). The problem was particularly acute since much of Germany's raw materials was coming from British colonies or dominions that had entered into the British imperial preference system. Part of the New Plan of September 1934 was to reorient German trade away from the British Empire, and toward smaller European countries and South America, where supplies would be more secure (ibid., 2:274).

The New Plan solved the balance of payments problem for 1935, but world economic upheavals by late 1935 had shifted the terms of trade against Germany; import prices had risen 9 percent while export prices dropped by 9 percent. In other words, Germany had to sell 18 percent more just to import the same amount (ibid., 2:277). By 1936, Hitler decided to move toward greater autarky in preparation for the war he saw as necessary for Germany's long-term economic viability. This decision was embodied in the Four-Year Plan of August 1936. Imports were to be restricted to goods that could not be acquired within Germany, while a program to synthesize oil and later rubber was initiated.

Since the plan was opposed by Schacht and others, Hitler composed a lengthy memorandum to his key subordinates in August, explicating his rationale. Germany, he wrote, was engaged in a struggle for its very survival. Marxist Russia was the primary long-term threat, given that "the military resources of this aggressive [state] are . . . rapidly increasing from year to year." Germany's situation was dire: "We are overpopulated and cannot feed ourselves from our own resources. . . . It is equally impossible for us at present to manufacture artificially certain raw materials which we lack in Germany or to find substitutes for them." Germany needed to act to relieve its dependence on food and raw material imports, and the solution "lies in extending our living space, that is to say, extending the sources of raw materials and foodstuffs of our people" (ibid., 2:283–84).

Hitler recognized that Germany could try to satisfy its dependence by importing the necessary goods, but this required selling exports to get imports. The world economic environment was not amenable to this strategy. His chain of logic went as follows:

(a) Since the German people will be increasingly dependent on imports for their food and must similarly, whatever happens, import a proportion at least of certain raw materials from abroad, every effort must be made to facilitate these imports. (b) An increase in our own exports is possible in theory but in practice hardly likely. Germany does not export to a political or economic vacuum, but to areas where competition is very intense. Compared with the general international economic depression, our exports have fallen . . . less than those of other nations and states. But since imports of food on the whole cannot be substantially reduced and are more likely to increase, an adjustment must be found in some other way. (ibid., 2:284)

Hitler's solution was therefore to seek "100 per cent self-sufficiency . . . in every sphere where it is feasible" to save precious foreign currency for the importation of food and any raw materials that could not be found or synthesized within Germany (ibid., 2:286).[54]

The problem of raw material dependence turned out to be more intractable than Hitler had imagined. Through vast investments, Germany was able to increase production of synthetic fuel by 130 percent from 1936 to 1939. In 1938, though, still only about 10 percent of German petroleum needs was met by domestic production; the other 90 percent was coming from outside, primarily the West Indies, the United States, and Romania (Goralski and Freeburg 1987, 26). In the same year, two-thirds of the iron ore requirements came from outside Germany (EHS, 446, 410).[55] By the outbreak of war itself, Germany still relied on outsiders for fully one-third of all raw materials needs (NDR, 2:291).

Expectations for future trade were not getting any better after 1935. British and French moves toward imperial preference were solidified. The League of Nations' attempt to impose oil sanctions on Italy after its attack on Ethiopia, while ultimately unsuccessful, suggested how the "have" great powers would react should the "have-nots" seek changes in the status quo. And vital imports were sometimes suddenly cut off for no apparent reason or due to uncontrollable domestic factors in the supplying nation. In February 1936, for example, the Soviet Union stopped all oil deliveries to Germany, stating only "difficulties with foreign payments"

---

[54] In 1936, the German predicament was also well expressed by the brilliant "economic general" Georg Thomas, the head of the Armed Forces' Economic and Armament Office (and an individual opposed to Hitler's overall military strategy): "We are overpopulated, as can be seen from the fact that we cannot feed our people on our own native soil; and we are economically dependent, for we have no tropical or subtropical raw materials at our disposal. Furthermore . . . [we] have no natural boundaries . . . and, viewed from the standpoint of the national states, [this] must be characterized as intolerable" (quoted in Carroll 1968, 39).

[55] It is worth noting that this fraction is more than twice that of the pre–World War I figure; that is, despite Hitler's campaign for self-sufficiency, the depletion of domestic sources of iron ore made Germany by 1939 even more dependent on outsiders for a raw material that is one of the cornerstones of a modern industrial society.

(Yergin 1991, 332).[56] Such actions could only have further diminished Hitler's estimate of the value of the trading option.

To reduce the severity of dependence, Germany heightened efforts after 1935 to find trade partners that it could more easily control. In 1936, agreements were signed with Chiang Kai-shek to provide China with military and industrial supplies in exchange for key raw materials, particularly tungsten (Weinberg 1980, 12).[57] Trade links with Latin America and Eastern Europe were also strengthened (see Weinberg 1980, 182–83; Kaiser 1980; Hirschman 1980). In 1936, Germany intervened in the Spanish Civil War to support the side of Francisco Franco, with one of the main objectives being Spanish reserves of copper, iron, and pyrites (Weinberg 1980, 146).[58]

From 1936 onward, Hitler sought to place Germany on a self-sufficient footing in order to fight a war for long-term living space and destroy an ascendant Soviet Union before it was too late. In the last two years before the war, however, major shortages in raw materials were still being felt, especially in terms of oil and iron ore (Carroll 1968, chap. 8). By 1938, Germany was making a major effort to control Romania's oil production—Romania being Europe's largest oil producer after the Soviet Union. Romania exploited its British connection to secure a favorable deal in its December 1938 agreement with Germany, but over the next year it was drawn into the German economic orbit, mostly out of fear of German military power (Weinberg 1980, 491–94).

By this time, the critical decision for war had been made. On November 5, 1937, Hitler brought together his top four military leaders and the foreign minister for what is generally considered to be the most important "war council" meeting prior to the war (see NDR, 3:680–87).[59] The

[56]Supplies resumed only after the Nazi-Soviet Pact of 1939, and given past Soviet behavior, Hitler clearly had little reason to think that Joseph Stalin's willingness to supply him with goods from 1939 to 1941 was anything but a means to buy time for the Soviet buildup (on this, see Read and Fisher 1988).

[57]This relation was so important that even when quasi-ally Japan found itself at war with China in July 1937, Germany did not support Japan by reducing trade with China, nor did it pull out the German military advisers to Chiang. In 1938, Foreign Minister Joachim Ribbentrop moved to a more pro-Japanese position, recognizing Manchukuo, but even this action was based on the expectation that Germany would receive a share of Manchuria's raw materials. Ironically, since Japan was also resource poor, the German expectation remained unfulfilled, even after the formal Japanese-German alliance was secured (Weinberg 1980, 182–83).

[58]Capturing Spanish exports of iron ore had an additional side benefit in that it denied that ore to Britain, which had been Spain's primary customer (ibid., 150). See also Whealey 1989.

[59]Hitler himself stressed its significance, opening the meeting by stating that his position "be regarded, in the event of his death, as his last will and testament" (NDR, 3:681). The meeting notes, recorded by Colonel Friedrich Hossbach, are generally referred to as the "Hossbach memorandum."

aim of German foreign policy, Hitler began, was to solve the problem of "space" for the security of future generations. The issue at hand was whether Germany's problem could be solved by "means of autarky" or "increased participation in the world economy." The first was infeasible, since complete autarky "could not be maintained." Hitler then launched into a discussion of the trading option as a means to German long-term security. As for participation in the world economy, he said, "there were limitations which we were unable to remove. The establishment of Germany's position on a secure and sound foundation was obstructed by market fluctuations, and commercial treaties afforded no guarantee for their actual observance." He pointed out that countries that Germany formerly relied on for food were now industrializing, implying that they could no longer afford to meet German food needs, even if they were so inclined. Germany was also living in "an age of economic empires," and Hitler compared Germany to countries like Japan and Italy where "economic motives underlay the urge for expansion." Unfortunately, "for countries outside the great economic empires, opportunities for economic expansion were severely obstructed."

Admitting that the economic stimulus provided by rearmament could never form the basis of a sound economy over the long term, Hitler further elaborated the supply dilemma:

> There was a pronounced military weakness in those states which depend for their existence on foreign trade. As our foreign trade was carried on over the sea routes dominated by Britain, it was a question rather of security of transport than of foreign exchange, which revealed in time of war the full weakness of our food situation. The only remedy, and on which might seem to us visionary, lay in the acquisition of great living space.[60]

Showing the continuity with his view in *Mein Kampf*, he argued that this living space could only be sought in Europe. This was "not a matter of acquiring population but of gaining space for agricultural use. Moreover, areas producing raw materials can be more usefully sought in Europe, in immediate proximity to the Reich, than overseas" (*NDR*, 3:680–87). Germany, Hitler explained, would have to acquire territory from others through force. He then laid out three possible contingency plans, all of which envisioned war by 1943–45 at the latest, since by then German military power would have been past its peak.[61]

---

[60] Here Hitler showed that he had learned the lesson from World War I: that states may not be able to get the goods they so vitally need, even if they have the money to pay for them. See Liberman 1999–2000.

[61] "After this date, only a change for the worse, from our point of view, could be expected" (*NDR*, 3:684–85).

From this meeting, it is clear is that the two conditions outlined by trade expectations theory as determinate of war—high dependence and low expectations for future trade—were present in the German case by the late 1930s. In such a situation, even if the expected value of invasion is low or negative, the value of the status quo trading option tends to be even lower.[62] Major war then becomes the lesser of two evils, especially when the negative expected value of trade only exacerbates the anticipated decline.

While no one would want to understate important unit-level reasons for the war (Hitler's personality, the nature of the Nazi regime, its racist ideology, etc.), Germany's systemic economic situation was a fundamental cause. Like Japan in the 1930s, Germany's small territorial size, highly industrialized economy, and growing population meant that it would always be dependent on other great powers for goods vital to its long-term well-being.[63] This would be so despite German efforts to achieve relative autarky. With the world economy going through significant fluctuations, and with large economic empires such as the United States and Britain shutting off trade with have-not nations like Germany, it was not surprising that "participation in the world economy" was not seen as the means to achieve Germany's long-term security. Poor expectations of trade thus reinforced beliefs that Germany would decline over the long haul, especially relative to huge and resource-rich states such as the Soviet Union.

The above analysis supports both economic realism and trade expectations theory while it challenges much of the logic of the liberal view. In support of realism over liberalism, we saw that Germany's significant dependence on others for vital goods did indeed drive much of the fear of the future felt by Hitler and his subordinates. If we want to argue that Hitler alone was responsible for the war, then realism seems superior to trade expectations theory; after all, Hitler was obsessed with German dependence even before the world economic collapse and turn to imperial preference. Yet the evidence also strongly suggests that Hitler understood that he could not get a war going if he did not convince his bureaucratic officials and military leaders that the changes in the world economy were undermining Germany's security over the long run. Declining expectations of future trade were critical to the support needed to initiate war. This is especially true for the traditional German military. As I discuss elsewhere, almost all the German generals were in positions of authority

---

[62] While war against the smaller states like Czechoslovakia was highly profitable, Hitler had no illusions that taking on the other great powers would be without major costs and risks. On May 23, 1939, for example, Hitler told his top military officials that while Germany must aim at a short war, it "must also be prepared for a war of 10–15 years' duration" (NDR, 3:738).

[63] And dependence would only increase as Germany continued to deplete its own meager natural resources.

before Hitler assumed power. Hitler knew that they had to be convinced on geostrategic grounds that war was necessary; Nazi ideology would not do the trick (Copeland 2000b, chap. 5). Given this, Hitler's extended analyses of the closed global economic system served to reinforce the need for preventive war against the system. In particular, by attacking the Soviet Union, Germany would destroy the rising state that most threatened its future while grabbing the raw materials and fertile territory required for long-term security. On this geopolitical logic, both Hitler and the traditional military establishment could agree.

CONCLUSION

This chapter has shown the remarkable force of declining trade expectations on the decision making of states confronted with the most profound choice that leaders can face: whether or not to launch highly costly major wars against other great powers. Japan may have jumped at the opportunity in 1894 to increase its control of Korea at China's expense (supporting economic realist predictions). But Japan was clearly reluctant to enter into war with Russia in 1903–4. Through a number of diplomatic efforts, it sought to convince the czar and his advisers to reduce their efforts to control the economic as well as political affairs of Manchuria and Korea. Only when it became obvious that Saint Petersburg was not interested in a bargain that would have preserved Japan's long-term economic access to the region did Tokyo make a firm decision in favor of preventive war. Needless to say, the sheer fact of Russia's military rise in the Far East was also making Japanese officials worried about the future. Yet as we have seen, it was Russia's relentless economic penetration into the area and its long-term plans to redirect the flow of trade toward the Russian west that proved a fundamental propelling cause of war in 1904. Russian strategic interests and to some degree its domestic political pressures acted as exogenous forces that made it difficult to find a negotiated solution to Japan's concerns.

The case of Germany and World War I illustrates in the profoundest way possible how expectations of the future trading environment can be negative even when present trade levels are temporarily high. Liberal theory cannot explain why this high trade dependence did not keep the peace. Realist theory cannot explain why Germany remained dependent on the system for raw materials and markets for decades, and yet only attacked the system in 1914. Trade expectations theory, combined with a larger view of Germany's declining position vis-à-vis Russia, provides the answer. The German leadership had good reason to believe that the other powers were slowly trying to contain Germany economically, squeezing it out of the Middle East and restricting its ability to trade with European colonies. War against the system was thus required to destroy Russia before it grew any larger, and to gain control of key territories in northwestern and eastern Europe—territories that would provide a stable economic base for long-term Germany security.

World War II was basically a repeat of this causal story, although the efforts of other powers to retreat into restrictive trading realms was more a function of the Great Depression than any deliberate attempt to build their own economic power at Germany's expense. The result, however, was largely the same. In addition to needing to destroy Russia before it overwhelmed the system, Hitler and his advisers were highly conscious of Germany's poor economic prospects in the larger global system. The well-endowed powers would continue to control world trade in ways that benefited them, and kept the have-not states down. This chapter showed that economic realism on its own supplies a good explanation for Hitler's thinking in the mid-1920s: reducing Germany's high vulnerability to trade cutoffs through war was clearly a critical element in his larger geopolitical logic. Yet the deleterious impact of the Great Depression on trading practices not only reinforced Hitler's own concerns about Germany's economic future but also helped solidify the need for war among the majority of his advisers. If trade expectations across Germany had not fallen off the cliff after 1930–31, it is much less likely that Hitler could have mobilized the traditional military and nation for another round of total war so soon after the last one had ended. In this sense, falling trade expectations were both a propelling and facilitating cause for war in 1939.

CHAPTER FOUR

The Prelude to Pearl Harbor: Japanese Security and the Northern Question, 1905–40

THE BREAKDOWN OF US-JAPANESE RELATIONS that led to the Japanese attack on Pearl Harbor in December 1941 has posed many puzzles for historians over the last seven decades, but one stands out above all the others. Why would a small island nation risk all-out war with a state possessing a much larger economic capacity to wage total war, especially given that the two nations had never had a direct military clash in modern history? Japan was a military great power, to be sure, and its stunning victories in the first six months of war affirm what both Japanese and US officials knew at the time: Japan was superior in military power in the short term. But if war with the United States were to become protracted, as most Japanese officials expected, then Japan had only a small chance of emerging victorious. Why, then, would these officials embark on such a risky war when the end result was likely to be the nation's total defeat and occupation?

For most international relations scholars who have delved into this question, the answer is straightforward: Japanese leaders and officials by 1941 were no longer operating in a rational manner. They were filled with a host of irrational beliefs, including the argument that to sustain their larger vision of empire, they had no other choice but to fight the United States. And if the United States did prove to be a paper tiger without the stomach for a long war, Japan could realize its Asian empire if it could just hold out for a couple of years. Such beliefs, so the reasoning goes, were a product of domestic pathologies that arose within the Japanese state after 1930. Powerful forces in the army and navy were able to dominate civilian leaders, hijacking the state for their ideological and organizational ends. As the more reasonable leaders from the 1920s were shunted aside or coerced into submission, it was inevitable that a momentum for war would grow until a senseless action such as Pearl Harbor was perpetrated.[1] This position aligns nicely with the liberal economic logic. As trade levels fell in the 1930s because of the depression and trade barriers, there was no longer any rational constraint on the unit-level

---

[1] For the most developed expressions of this logic and further references, see Snyder 1991; Kupchan 1994; Taliaferro 2005 (Sagan 1989 offers a more rationally based argument).

drives for war within Japanese society. These drives were thus unleashed on the world in the form of a deluded effort at regional hegemony, much like the war in Europe begun just two years earlier.

The Pacific War of 1941–45 represents probably the best case for commercial liberalism among all the great power conflicts over the past two hundred years. Liberals can point to the shift from moderate Japanese policy in the 1920s when trade ties were strong and democracy was entrenched to the subsequent rise of militarism along with expansionism as the world trade system fell apart during the 1930s. And what great power in history seems more the product of internal irrationalities than Japan taking on the US giant? Indeed, it was the Japanese attack on Pearl Harbor along with the war in Europe that helped revive the popularity of the commercial liberal argument after the apparently decisive disconfirmation of World War I. Largely due to the strenuous public efforts of Secretary of State Cordell Hull, after 1941 it became more plausible to contend that had trade levels not dropped precipitously after 1930, war might have been avoided altogether (see Buzan 1984; Hull 1948).

Because of its importance to the liberal edifice, and because the case is so complex, I will spend two chapters detailing both the lead up to the final year of diplomacy (this chapter) and the ups and downs of the diplomatic negotiations of 1941 (next chapter). Overall, I assert that despite its surface plausibility, there are two major problems with the liberal argument. First, it ignores the great continuity in Japanese imperialist policy since 1880 across a wide variety of domestic situations. During the initial period of oligarchic control Japan initiated two wars, one against China and another against Russia (chapter 3). As Japan moved into the era of "Taisho democracy" after 1912, with party leaders assuming more dominance over policy, Japan occupied parts of China and kicked off a disastrous four-year intervention in Siberia against the Red Army. Even in the mid- and late 1920s, when Japanese leaders were supposedly operating according to Wilsonian ideals (the period of so-called Shidehara diplomacy), Japan expanded its influence in Manchuria and northern China, and consistently responded with hard-line actions whenever Asian economic interests were threatened. A complete explanation of Tokyo's behavior from 1931 to 1941 requires that we understand the forces behind Japanese policy from 1880 to 1930. Otherwise, we fall into the common trap of seeing Japan's behavior in the last decade before Pearl Harbor as somehow at odds with the previous half century.

The second problem for the domestic/liberal argument is a simple but neglected one: the closer Japan came to actual great power war from 1938 to 1941, the more civilian leaders and Emperor Hirohito worked together with moderate military officials to restrain as well as largely neutralize the more ideologically driven elements of the Japanese military.

Through a series of meetings and conferences that began in 1937, and that dominated the decision-making process after June 1940, Japanese officials of all stripes actively discussed the pros and cons of various options, including peaceful diplomatic solutions. The shift toward harder-line policies was done gradually and by consensus, and in full awareness of great risks to the Japanese state. Indeed, the military was not always the most in favor of war. The foreign ministry was often more hard line than the navy, while by 1940–41 almost all civilian leaders accepted the necessity of total war. Moreover, as Herbert Bix (2000) and Edward Behr (1989) have shown, Hirohito was involved throughout the process, playing his designated role as supreme commander and head of state. In the face of recent evidence, it is impossible to sustain the view that the Japanese army and navy hijacked the state for their own purposes. What we instead need to explain is why a consensus for all-out war—against either the United States or Soviet Union, depending on the circumstances—would emerge among the key military and civilian players notwithstanding the self-evident risks.

Economic realism and trade expectations theory, both founded on the assumption of rational states seeking to maximize security in an uncertain environment, provide more plausible explanations for Japanese behavior than does commercial liberalism. As Japan developed as a modern industrial power, its small territorial size made it highly dependent on others for the raw materials and food necessary to both maintain its economic growth and support its population. Yet because Japan needed to export in order to acquire these vital imports, Japan was also dependent on US and Asian markets for its goods. From 1880 onward, Japanese leaders of all the major parties and ideological inclinations were obsessed with one problem: how to ensure that Japan maintained access to the resources and markets critical to its long-term security as an emerging great power. The liberal perspective, by overlooking the fears that arise with growing economic dependence, cannot explain the six-decades-long Japanese preoccupation with trade access and its link to Japan's security policies.

Economic realism certainly captures the Japanese obsession with increasing dependence and Japan's occasional grabbing of opportunities to expand the realm of its control, such as during World War I. Nonetheless, it is still incomplete as an explanation. According to economic realism, Japan's high dependence on the system for crucial goods and markets should have led it continually into war to reduce its vulnerability. Yet Japanese foreign policy was often relatively restrained, not just in the 1920s, but also perhaps most surprisingly in 1941, when it made a sustained and genuine effort to reach a modus vivendi with Washington to avoid war altogether. A constant (Japan's high dependence) cannot explain its varying behavior over time. This is where changing expectations of the economic environment play their role. What we see after 1905 is a continuation of the strategic thinking that drew Japan into war in 1904. Whenever a threat to Japan's access to trade and investments arose in the Far East, especially in Manchuria and northern China, Japanese leaders would become more forceful in order to neutralize or eliminate the threat. Their chosen *degree* of forcefulness, however, would reflect a weighing of the level of immediate economic threat against the risks of escalation with key powers—not just the United States, but Russia and China as well. Moreover, Japanese leaders understood that such risks included not just the risk of war but also the risk of a further deterioration in the trade environment due to the increasing mistrust of Japan's intentions. The trade-security dilemma hung over Japan like no other nation, and they knew it. Thus decision makers in Tokyo would seek to maintain moderate foreign and economic policies whenever possible to minimize the chance of undesired spiraling.

Japan's policies in the 1920s remained quite reasonable for one simple reason: the global trading system had been rebounding after the economic dislocations caused by the First World War. By 1929–30, however, Japanese trade expectations began to sour. The onset of the Great Depression and signing of the Smoot-Hawley Tariff Act (June 1930) had a devastating impact on Japan's export trade. Japan's exports to the United States fell by 55 percent from 1929 to 1931, and its overall exports to the world dropped by more than a third.[2] Britain's turn to an imperial preference system in 1931–32 further undermined Japanese confidence in the global trading system. The Japanese view of the regional system was also changing dramatically. By the last half of the 1920s, China was emerging out of its decade-long "warlord period" as Chiang Kai-shek and his Kuomintang (KMT) government consolidated a power base in the south and began to move north.[3] Meanwhile, Russia in the north was reviving quickly after the turmoil of world and civil wars as well as reestablishing its geopolitical presence in the east. By 1930–31, Japanese economic interests in Manchuria and north China suddenly seemed to be under threat from all sides.

After 1930, Japanese leaders focused their efforts on new economic threats to Japan's existence while simultaneously trying to avoid an escalation to great power war. The move to absorb the rest of Manchuria

---

[2] Even by 1937, just before Washington embarked on increasingly severe trade sanctions, Japanese exports to the United States were still more than 30 percent below the 1929 figure. *HYSJE*, 292–93.

[3] Regarding the spelling of Chinese names, I will use the modern pinyin system, except for well-known individuals and organizations such as Chiang Kai-shek (pinyin: Jiang Jieshi) and the Kuomintang (pinyin: Guomindang).

in September 1931 (Japan having controlled the southern railways and Liaodong Peninsula since 1905) may have been ordered by a select group of officers in Manchuria and Tokyo. But the majority of Japanese civilian and military leaders quickly accepted it as necessary to Japan's economic health. The fact that the Japanese government accepted the army's action in 1931 but rejected a similar maneuver in 1928 must be explained by any good theory. Yet surprisingly, those arguing for a domestic-level explanation of the Pacific War rarely consider the events of 1928. I show that changes in the economic environment in northern China and the world, tied to worries about the growth in Soviet power in the Far East, provide the best rationale for the shift in Tokyo's policies by 1931.

Subsequent actions from 1932 to 1936 to establish compliant local governments in the northern Chinese provinces bordering Manchuria were a response to both the growing strength of Chiang's Nanjing government and increasing Soviet domination of the nominally independent state of Mongolia. The Japanese government could not afford to let either China or Russia harm Japan's economic future in an age when all great powers, including the United States, were shoring up their imperial realms and excluding have-nots such as Japan. By 1936, the focus of Japanese officials was on the long-term growth of the Soviet and US giants along with what this would mean for Japan's economic and territorial security. Both future superpowers were expected to constrain Japan's economic growth in Manchuria, China, and the rest of Asia. It is nevertheless important to remember, especially given what happened in 1941, that Tokyo's primary obsession, as it had been since the 1890s, was with the rise of Russia.

In 1936, civilian and military leaders, with the emperor's support, came together to prepare for a major preventive war against the Soviet Union within five years. The goal was to use a naval buildup to deter the United States in the south as the army organized the country for total war in the north. As in 1903–4, everything was driven by the need to attack Russia before it was too late, both to ensure economic access to Northeast Asia and prevent a future Soviet attack on the home islands. The economic penetration of Southeast Asia was also needed because Japan required raw materials to support a move north. The first preference, however, was for a pénétration pacifique: by augmenting Japan's naval presence, Tokyo hoped to increase its bargaining leverage with regional powers, thereby securing trade without the cost of a war.

Chiang, leader of the Chinese Nationalist Party, derailed this plan. In early July 1937, Chiang used a small skirmish outside Beijing to bring on a war with Japan. The evidence shows clearly that the vast majority of Japanese leaders did not want a war over what became known as the Marco Polo Bridge Incident. They knew that a large-scale war with China was an undesired sideshow—one that would divert valuable economic and military resources away from the preparation for the invasion of Russia. It was Chiang who sought a war, and he did so largely to shore up his faltering domestic position at home. Given Chiang's obvious determination to push into northern China, in late July Japanese decision makers reluctantly accepted that China would have to be neutralized first before the true rising threats, Russia and the United States, could be dealt with. A third-party issue had drawn Japan into a war on the continent that would exacerbate tensions with both Russia and the United States.[4]

During the war in China, Japan continued to build up both its army and navy. But until 1941, those in the navy most supportive of a "southern advance" still believed Japan could achieve an economic penetration of Southeast Asia without necessarily provoking a war with the United States. For almost all Japanese officials, the southern question remained distinctly secondary to the northern one. The strategic priority remained, as it had been since the 1890s, the control of the resources and trade of Manchuria and northern China as well as the prevention of Russia's growth in the area.

Internal support for a more militarized expansion southward gained momentum after 1939 because of the growing need for Southeast Asian resources to deal militarily with Japan's precarious situation in the northeast, especially the rise of the Soviet colossus. The United States by 1938–41 was also a long-term threat given its size and growth rates. In the short term, though, the United States was a problem mainly because it resisted Japan's southward penetration and because US economic policies were impeding Japan's effort to build up for war against the Soviet Union. As we will see in the next chapter, war with the United States would almost certainly not have occurred had it not been for the critical importance of northern China and Manchuria to Japanese security.

This chapter sets the stage for the next one. It shows the continuity of Japanese concern for the nation's economic and geopolitical position in Northeast Asia, and how Japan's foreign policies varied with changes in the level of threat to this position. Together, both chapters allow us to see the Pacific War in a fundamentally different light. It was not some deep Japanese hostility toward the United States, grounded in domestic pathologies, that inevitably led to Pearl Harbor. Rather, the Pacific War arose out of a Japanese need to protect its economic and territorial

---

[4]Given that Chiang had brought on war for internal reasons, the liberal contention might seem supported here. Unfortunately, overall Chinese-Japanese trade by 1936–37 had been restored to pre-1930 levels, after having dropped by half from 1929 to 1932 (see *HYSJE*, 292). So one cannot argue that domestic forces within Chiang's regime had been unleashed because the restraint of trade had fallen away. Rather, they were set loose *despite* the renewal of Sino-Japanese trade.

security in northeast Asia in the face of growing Chinese and Russian challenges. From a theory standpoint, the Chinese and Russian challenges represented third-party effects that interfered with the normal requirements of bilateral US-Japanese economic diplomacy. Japan's need to safeguard its interests in Northeast Asia led it to push southward to gain access to the raw materials needed for action against Soviet Russia. This led to a US response that further restricted Japanese access to resources from both Southeast Asia and the United States, leading to an action-reaction spiral that undermined confidence on both sides.

In these two chapters, I proceed in a different fashion from most political science studies of the Pacific War. Because I wish to demonstrate that Japan's foreign policy from 1931 to 1941 was rooted in a logic going back many decades, I will start by briefly discussing US-Japanese relations from the end of the Russo-Japanese War up to 1921. I will then turn to an exploration of Japanese behavior during the period of Shidehara diplomacy and late Taisho democracy. This section will show that Japanese leaders of all stripes, including Foreign Minister Shidehara Kijuro, were hardheaded realists who sought to maintain Japan's economic position in Manchuria and northern China even as they acted to reduce the risk of economic or military conflict with the great powers. The rest of the chapter will be taken up by a more detailed analysis of the tragic decade from 1931 to 1940. Chapter 5 will then look at the last year of negotiations. It will consider the primary puzzle that to this day, remains a fierce point of debate for historians and international relations scholars alike: why Japanese and US leaders proved unable to secure a peace that could have averted the disaster of the Pacific War.

THE FALLOUT FROM THE RUSSO-JAPANESE WAR, 1905–21

Tensions in the US-Japanese relationship began soon after the Russo-Japanese War. Before the war, Japan had been a member of the US-British club of open-door nations seeking freer access to Chinese markets and resources (Davis 2008–9). Theodore Roosevelt helped broker a peace in 1905 that would facilitate US economic penetration into China through the stabilization of the regional balance of power between Russia and Japan. The peace, however, gave control of the Liaodong Peninsula and southern part of the Chinese Eastern Railway to Japan. Overnight, Japan had assumed a major presence in China, for better or worse. Roosevelt and his successors reacted by adopting a largely realist balance-of-power strategy for East Asia. The initial objective was to carve out spheres and avoid clashes. In July 1905, Secretary of War William Howard Taft signed a secret agreement in Tokyo acknowledging Japan's "suzerainty" over

Korea in return for a pledge that Japan had no aggressive intentions toward the Philippines. US exports to China had just reached a new height, and on the eve of the trip, Taft spoke publicly of the four-hundred-million-person Chinese market that was now "one of the greater commercial prizes of the world." American financiers were also clamoring for more control of future railways in Manchuria and northern China (see Griswold 1938, 125; Iriye 1967, 108–10). Still, Japan's rising power created suspicions that began to undermine its foreign relations. Naval maneuvering touched off a war-scare crisis in mid-1907, leading Roosevelt in July to warn Pacific commanders of an imminent Japanese attack (Griswold 1938, 126). That year, he pointedly sent the US fleet on a "world cruise" to signal Washington's determination to defend its Far Eastern interests. By late 1907, Japan's elder statesman Ito would complain of the "unmistakable trend toward [the] isolation [of Japan]."[5]

Recognizing the risk of further spiraling, Secretary of State Elihu Root met with Japanese ambassador Takahira Kogoro in May 1908 to find a way to reduce tensions. The subsequent Root-Takahira agreement would shape US policy for decades to come. Going beyond Northeast Asia, both states agreed to respect the "existing status quo" in Asia, including each other's current territorial possessions. They also agreed to uphold the open door in China along with the independence and integrity of China. The deal thus legitimized the United States' recent imperial acquisitions (Guam and the Philippines) and Japan's new presence in Manchuria (Griswold 1938, 128–29). That President Roosevelt was accepting of Japan's control over Manchuria is clear. After Taft took over as president, he asked Roosevelt to submit an analysis of the Far Eastern situation. Roosevelt's December 1910 report argued that it was distinctly in the US interest "not to take any steps as regards Manchuria which will give the Japanese cause to feel . . . that we are hostile to them." Manchuria was "vital" to Japan, and Tokyo would not tolerate any interference. Roosevelt also astutely noted that Russia would seek to regain its lost prize, forcing Japan to prepare for a new round of hostilities (quoted in ibid., 131–32).

This realistic understanding of spheres and Japan's keen interests in Manchuria would be sustained in one form or another through all subsequent administrations. Taft, Woodrow Wilson, and those who followed in the 1920s accepted Japan's special interests in Manchuria as a given. Even after Japan's takeover of the rest of Manchuria in 1931, the US government offered only verbal condemnation. Most revealingly, the United States continued to trade in areas of China under Japanese control. For the US government, Japan's presence in Manchuria was fine as long as

---

[5] Quoted in Iriye 1967, 114; for Roosevelt's growing concerns regarding Japan, see Griswold 1938, 127.

Japan allowed US trade and investment to pass through the open door. As we will see, the event that truly shifted US policy toward economic sanctions was the Japanese occupation of southern China. It was this act's implications for US trade and the struggle against Hitler that led to US counteractions in 1938–39.

Through the 1910s, the United States and Japan remained on good terms. Taft's policy of "dollar diplomacy" from 1909 to 1912 focused on increasing the presence of the United States in China and Manchuria through American investment capital. Wilson, like the British and French, appreciated Japan's entry into World War I on the side of the Allies. Japan used the war as an opportunity to secure the German Marshall Islands and Germany's sphere of influence on China's Shantung Peninsula. The infamous Twenty-One Demands, presented to China in January 1915, focused on consolidating Japan's economic position in Shantung and China's port cities. Its main points were enshrined in the Sino-Japanese treaty of May 1915. Here economic realism does the best job explaining Tokyo's behavior: there was no immediate threat to Japan's economic position, only an unexpected opportunity to enhance it that Tokyo quickly seized. The subsequent outbreak of revolution and civil war in Russia opened up another opportunity, leading Japan to launch a disastrous intervention into Siberia in 1918. Although ostensibly part of an allied operation to defeat Bolshevism, the fact that Japan stayed in Siberia until 1922 and occupied the oil-rich Sakalin Island until 1925 shows that this was more about increasing Japanese access to Siberian raw materials than combating Bolshevism per se. Economic realism again explains this behavior nicely. Liberalism's position is particularly problematic, given that Taisho democracy was in full swing by 1914. Indeed, it was Hara Kei, Japan's first "commoner" prime minister, who led Japan into the Siberian expedition of 1918–22.[6]

During the world war, the Allies registered only minor complaints regarding Japan's new imperial expansion. In November 1917, US secretary of state Robert Lansing and Japanese viscount Ishii Kikujirō reached an agreement that reconfirmed Washington's understanding of the Far East. With Wilson's support, Lansing agreed to a secret protocol "recogniz[ing] that Japan has a special interest in China, particularly in the part to which her possessions are contiguous" (quoted in Griswold 1938, 215–16). Japan in turn recommitted itself to the open door and China's territorial integrity. Unfortunately, Tokyo's decision to stay in Siberia after the Allies departed in 1920 raised suspicions about its intentions by the time that Japan, Britain, and the United States sat down for talks in Washington in late 1921. Japan now had the third-largest navy in the world,

[6] See Griswold 1938, chaps. 5–6; Beasley 1987.

and Japanese leaders keenly recognized the need to avoid a naval race with the US giant. Despite the vigorous protestations of the navy, which argued that a ten-to-seven ratio of US to Japanese capital ships was necessary to protect Japan from a British or US attack, Japanese negotiators accepted a ten-to-six ratio in the final treaty. They also agreed to pull Japanese forces out of the Shantung Peninsula, and as part of a nine-power treaty on China, to reaffirm Tokyo's commitment to equal commercial opportunity in China and the territorial integrity of the Chinese state (Iriye 1990, 18).

Because future foreign minister Shidehara was one of Japan's chief negotiators at the Washington conference, and because the final language in the nine-power treaty incorporated Wilsonian language rejecting spheres of influence, it is often assumed that the Washington treaties of 1922 reflected a new orientation in strategic thinking. The three powers, after all, had apparently put aside arms racing and exclusive spheres in favor of peaceful economic cooperation in disputed areas such as China. While certainly a few US diplomats may have imbibed the Wilsonian champagne, Japanese officials refrained from doing so. As Akira Iriye's (1990) seminal work shows, even Shidehara himself never acted against Japan's key interests in Manchuria during his time in power. On numerous occasions Shidehara emphasized Japan's "visible and invisible rights and interests" in Manchuria. Visible rights for Shidehara were the ones confirmed by Japan's 1915 treaty with China (notwithstanding the coerced nature of the agreement). Invisible rights were the product of what Shidehara called Japan's "peculiar" relationship with Manchuria—a relationship that reflected Japan's huge capital outlays to help Manchuria develop, but also Japan's "right of survival," which demanded that the nation have access to the "untouched treasures" of the region (quoted in ibid., 111). Economic realism and, as we will see, trade expectations theory do a better job than liberalism in explaining Japan's carefully calculated policy stances through the post-1921 period.

GROWING PROBLEMS WITH CHINA, 1922–28

Given what we have already seen of Japan's entrenched imperial orientation, the relative moderation of Japanese policy witnessed during the 1920s reflects not a new Wilsonian idealism but instead a hardheaded assessment of the costs and risks of more assertive strategies. In particular, as the prospects for renewed trade with the United States and other powers brightened after World War I, the Japanese adoption of a policy of economic engagement made perfect sense. Japan could further its industrial development at a time when it was still technologically inferior to Britain and the United States, and it would avoid a costly arms race with actors possessing a greater power base from which to run them. It is worth remembering that from 1922 until the 1931 Manchurian incident, a period typically labeled as the era of Shidehara diplomacy, Shidehara occupied the position of foreign minister for only five years: from June 1924 to April 1927, and again from July 1929 to December 1931. What we thus need to explain is the striking continuity of policy across this period—why all of Japan's prime ministers and foreign ministers accepted the need for a moderate foreign policy as well as the need to restrain internal factions seeking a more aggressive posture toward China.

The domestic politics perspective within liberalism argues that this moderation arose from the democratic nature of the Japanese polity at the time (see Snyder 1991; Kupchan 1994). This is an inadequate explanation. For one thing, there were a number of men from the military that occupied the prime minister's post during the 1920s, including Kato Tomosaburo (1922–23) and Tanaka Giichi (1927–29). Their policies were far more soft line than one might expect given their backgrounds and the pressures they were under from military hard-liners. The case of Tanaka, a man who also assumed the role of foreign minister during his tenure as prime minister, is particularly instructive. He faced significant disturbances within China in the late 1920s. Yet in the end, as Iriye shows, his policy paralleled Shidehara's: Tanaka sustained US-British confidence by being careful not to annex more Chinese territory, even when he did use force to protect Japan's economic interests. Despite new challenges from the KMT, he also stopped the Japanese Kwantung Army in Manchuria from executing a military coup in 1928. What we need to explain, therefore, is why both civilian- and military-led governments were able to sustain a relatively moderate policy in the 1920s despite China's domestic turmoil. We must also explain why by 1930–31, this policy proved unacceptable to the vast majority of politicians and ministers, such that a second effort at a coup in Manchuria in September 1931 was openly embraced.[7]

If there is one key point to make about the 1922–31 period, as Beasley (1987, chap. 11) underscores, it is that the treaty port system established

---

[7]The simple argument that right-wing radicals were coercing moderates after 1930—as shown by the killing of Prime Minister Hamaguchi Yuko and other assassination attempts during the 1930–32 period—is lacking in historical perspective. Japanese leaders had been under attack before: in the early 1920s, a prime minister was killed and future emperor Hirohito was the target of more than one assassination attempt. The early 1930s were a tumultuous time in Japan, to be sure. But Japanese leaders prided themselves on resisting personal threats in order to act in the best interests of the country. Hamaguchi's assassination, for example, followed his signing of the 1930 US-British-Japanese naval treaty—an act he knew would be highly distasteful to extremists and might endanger his life.

before 1904 to facilitate great power trade with China and Manchuria was increasingly under threat as time progressed. China's revolution in 1911–12 had turned the country into a republic. But after President Yuan Shi-kai's death in 1916, the country quickly fragmented into a number of warlord states. In 1923–26, the KMT under the leadership of Sun Yat-sen and then Chiang consolidated a power base in Canton (Guangzhou) in southern China. In 1926 the KMT, working at the time with the Chinese Communist Party, began a "northern expedition" to eliminate warlordism and unite the country under the banner of an antiforeigner nationalism. Such nationalism was sweeping China, as it was the colonial world (e.g., Mohandas Gandhi's India). The KMT built a following around promises to modernize China and eliminate unequal treaties forced on China during the nineteenth century, and by 1927 it had seized control of most of southern China. From his new capital in Nanjing, Chiang allied with northern warlords and began asserting the KMT's authority over northern provinces south of Manchuria.

By the late 1920s, Japan had acquired a huge stake in Manchuria, and these political developments posed a direct threat to its interests. Japanese firms had invested over a billion dollars to tap the region's huge deposits of coal, iron, and other minerals. And with some of the richest soil in the world, agriculture was booming; the land under cultivation for soybean and grain, for example, had risen 70 percent since 1905. Manchuria was also one of the few areas of China that exported more than it imported to the non-Japanese world, meaning that sales of Manchurian products by Japanese firms brought in valuable foreign currency. By 1930, over 225,000 Japanese were living in Manchuria—an effective doubling of its Japanese population in two decades (Coox 1985, 2, 20–21; Iriye 1990, 111).

Initially Tokyo sought to respond to the KMT's growing popularity by concessions to Beijing, China's traditional capital and a city not controlled by Chiang. In tariff conferences that began in 1925, Japanese diplomats agreed to work with Washington and London to adjust the old "unequal treaties" left over from the nineteenth century. In exchange for greater tariff autonomy, the three powers sought guarantees of limited tariff increases and minimal restrictions on investment. Just before talks were to resume in January 1927, Foreign Minister Shidehara delivered an important speech that nicely expressed the two conflicting sides of his thinking. He emphasized that foreign powers should avoid intervening in China except to help China create internal stability. Nonetheless, he noted, Japan had the right to protect the lives and property of its citizens living abroad. Toward this end, Japan would continue to support local leaders within China who possessed the power to maintain order (Iriye 1990, 110–11). This was a not-so-subtle reference to the fact that since the early 1920s, every Japanese government regardless of ideology had aided the brutal Manchurian warlord Zhang Zuo-lin, the "Old Marshal," in his efforts to eliminate rivals and dominate the region. Shidehara himself had actively encouraged this policy, seeing it as critical to both promoting order and countering the KMT's influence.

In the speech, Shidehara also spoke of his hope that Chinese nationalists would be "reasonable" in their consideration of Japanese interests. Questioned as to his understanding of the term reasonable, Shidehara remarked that it would be reasonable for China to seek "coexistence and coprosperity," but unreasonable for it to threaten Japan's economic existence. And while Japan understood China's desire to revise current treaties and would be unreasonable if it used force before trying diplomacy, China must give equal weight to Japan's interests as it crafted its policy.[8] As Iriye (1990, 114) observes, Shidehara's carefully chosen language was a signal of Japan's willingness to use force to uphold its economic interests should diplomacy prove insufficient. And Japan's policy of supporting warlords such as Zhang would continue.

Tariff negotiations with Beijing broke down soon after they restarted in January 1927, and by the time Tanaka took over as prime minister in April, the situation on the ground had deteriorated dramatically. Having occupied Shanghai in March, Chiang's KMT immediately began destroying Communist allies who had helped it win the city. In late May, Tanaka reinforced Japan's military presence in Shanghai while sending two thousand troops to the Shantung Peninsula to protect Japanese citizens. Following Shidehara's statement that Japan would use force only to protect current holdings, Tanaka instructed the troops to stay on the defensive and not get drawn into the Chinese civil war. Given that US, British, and French forces were also mobilized to protect their foreign settlements, Tokyo's moves were certainly not out of the ordinary.[9]

Of more potential significance was the so-called Eastern Conference held between June 27 and July 7, and called by Tanaka to discuss Japan's China policy. Participants included individuals from all key ministries and the consul generals from crucial Chinese cities. The policy that resulted, as Iriye demonstrates, was simply a continuation of Shidehara's emphasis on protecting Japanese economic interests in China, taken up a notch to deal with new, more chaotic conditions on the ground. The participants agreed that the main priority was to protect Japanese citizens and trade, and that given China's overall economic importance, Tokyo could not afford to retreat. Japan should stay out of the Chinese civil war,

---

[8] Quoted in Iriye 1990, 114; see also Dower 1979, 68.

[9] On more than one occasion, British forces used bombing raids to give their citizens the time to flee battlefronts between the warring Chinese parties.

while working with the KMT moderates to help restore order so as to reinvigorate commerce and minimize future disturbances.[10] In line with Shidehara's thinking, with trade expectations with the outside world still strong, there was good reason to appear moderate and merely copy what the other powers were doing.

THE MANCHURIAN QUESTION, 1928–31

A puzzle that should be of great interest to international relations scholars—yet one that has been almost completely ignored—is why Japanese officials in Tokyo restrained hawkish elements in the Kwantung Army during a planned takeover of Manchuria in 1928, but almost to a person applauded a similar coup effort undertaken in September 1931. In April 1928, Chiang's million-strong Nationalist army moved north to complete the unification of the country. Tanaka dispatched additional troops to Shantung, again to protect Japanese citizens and property in the treaty ports. An inadvertent clash between Japanese and Chinese troops occurred in Tsinan in early May—the first of a series of minor skirmishes that would take place between 1928 and 1937. But with Chiang focused on defeating northern warlords and with foreign powers sympathetic to Tokyo's concerns, the Nationalists pulled back and the incident was resolved by late May (Fenby 2004, 177–78). Chiang was on a roll, however, and warlords began to bandwagon to his cause. Japan's protégé in Manchuria, Zhang Zao-lin, started showing signs that he would be less compliant with Japanese wishes and might even align with the KMT. Faced with the first serious challenge to Japan's position in Manchuria, an internal divide emerged. Tanaka along with the majority of civilian and military ministers believed Japan could work with both Chiang and Zhang. Chiang could be convinced to leave Manchuria out of his unification plans, and Zhang cajoled by the benefits of maintaining an independent base in Manchuria. As Iriye (1990, 210) summarizes it, Tanaka's government sought to "divide China through persuasion."

A hard-line coalition formed in response, unified by the view that a moderate policy would lead to the loss of Manchuria. This coalition consisted largely of young Kwantung officers and a few generals in Tokyo. But it also had supporters on the civilian side—the most famous being Yoshida Shigeru, the future postwar prime minister of Japan. Yoshida was consul general in Manchuria's capital of Mukden until spring 1928 and then vice foreign minister under Tanaka. He was considered a moderate

---

[10] See Iriye 1990, 125–56, 171–72. On the continuity of policy between Shidehara and Tanaka, see Dower 1979, 83–90.

throughout his career in the foreign service in the 1920s and 1930s, so
his position on China's upheavals is particularly useful in tempering the
naive view that all officials calling for a strong policy were ideological
hotheads. In memorandums to Tokyo between early 1927 and summer
1928, he laid out the argument for what we would now call a forceful
deterrence posture. Soft-line policies would only lead Zhang and Chiang to take advantage of Japan, sensing Japanese weakness of will. To
maintain Manchuria as an economic asset and strategic counter to the
growing Soviet threat in the north, Yoshida argued, Tokyo would have
to embark on a much more active policy, using Japan's superior military
strength to browbeat Zhang and Chiang into complying with Japanese
wishes. Japan's survival depended on continued access to food and raw
materials as well as markets for Japanese manufactured goods. Hence,
Japan must follow the example of other imperial powers such as Britain
and the United States, and act strongly to protect its external interests
(Dower 1979, 63–83).

In June 1928, the hard-liners in the Kwantung Army struck. They blew
up Zhang's train as it returned to Mukden, killing the Old Marshal. They
also arranged for bombs to be thrown at Japanese property in Mukden,
supplying an excuse for Japanese troops to intervene. The hope was that
Japan would be able to use Zhang's son, the "Young Marshal" Zhang
Xue-liang, as a puppet governor of a new Japanese protectorate. The
coup leaders' plan fizzled, however, when it failed to receive support from
either civilian ministers in Tokyo or the army general staff. The younger
Zhang quickly assumed full control of the region and proved as difficult
to manage as the Old Marshal. Japanese policy continued as before, seek-
ing to shape but not control the new Zhang while striking deals with
KMT moderates to uphold Japan's economic rights in Manchuria and
China more broadly.

Why did Japanese officials in Tokyo not seize this opportunity for
a complete takeover of Manchuria, as they would in September 1931?
Japan's positive trade expectations provide the best answer. Overall,
trade prior to the onset of the Great Depression was booming, with the
United States now Japan's leading trade partner (*HYSJE*, 292–93). Japan
was highly dependent on exports to the United States and Britain for the
cash needed to purchase vital raw materials, including oil and iron ore,
and could ill afford to upset either Washington or London. Moreover,
Manchuria seemed safe for now. Chiang had signaled that he would not
proceed north of the Great Wall. The younger Zhang was told that Japan
would support him only if he maintained Manchuria's autonomy from
China, and he seemed to accept this (Iriye 1990, 232–37). As the economic environment in both China and the world continued to look up,
and with Japan staring at clear risks of great power spiraling should it

act more fiercely, the continuation of a moderate policy made sense. The liberal argument that trade constrains domestic-level pathologies is also upheld here. Generally, though, the trade expectations approach does a better job of showing both Tokyo's concern for economic security in Manchuria and its willingness to restrain those individuals who might take economic realist thinking to its logical extreme, namely, war.

The KMT's new strength within China by 1928 gave it increased leverage in economic negotiations, and by January 1929, Beijing and Tokyo reached an agreement allowing for a gradual increase in Chinese tariffs (ibid., 246–50). Five months later Tokyo recognized the Nationalist government, and with China's domestic order now stable, the free flow of commerce seemed to be reestablished. Yet Manchuria remained a problem that Japanese leaders could not avoid. Chiang had made a calculated decision in 1928 to act moderately with all powers, including Japan, to buy time to modernize the newly unified Chinese state as well as build its power against both external enemies and the internal Communist threat. Nevertheless, he steadfastly refused to recognize the 1898 and 1905 treaties giving Russia and then Japan a long-term lease on the Liaodong Peninsula along with the right to control Manchuria's railways. The younger Zhang also appeared to be bidding his time through 1929 and 1930 as he built a power base from which he could exact revenge on the nation that had murdered his father (ibid., 227–53; Sun 1993).

To add to Tokyo's concerns, the Soviets were growing in power and seeking to spread Communism into Manchuria, utilizing their control of the northern half of the Manchurian railway system for this end. In July 1929 Zhang, with KMT support, expelled the Russians from their positions within the railway. Soviet troops crossed into Manchuria in response. The KMT and Zhang refused to reinstate the Russian employees of the railway, including its Russian director, leading Russian and Chinese forces to fight two brief battles in August and November before Chiang backed down. Foreign Minister Shidehara, who had resumed his position in July, saw the Chinese action against Russia as "a test case of China's observance of treaty stipulations." If the KMT was willing to expel Russian officials without first trying diplomatic means to resolve its grievances, this suggested a willingness to change its policies at a whim (Iriye 1990, 264–68).

The pressures on Manchuria from both north and south by mid-1929 were clearly undermining Tokyo's confidence in future trade relations with China and Manchuria. But the real blow to the faith in Japan's established strategy of economic diplomacy came with the onset of the Great Depression in October 1929 and passing of the US Smoot-Hawley Tariff in June 1930. Japanese economic problems were compounded by the ill-timed decision in January 1930 to go back on the gold standard.

Japan's exports to the United States fell by more than 55 percent between 1929 and 1931. Its exports to China, now hurt by an overvalued yen, fell by half.[11]

These dramatic changes caused havoc to Japan's ability to import the raw materials and food needed for its modern industrial economy. Moreover, the world's main economic empires—Britain, France, and the United States—were unwilling to work together to solve the global crisis, and more inclined to retreat into neomercantilist policies of imperial preference or the equivalent. Suddenly, what had been the minority view during the Manchurian Crisis of 1928—that the effort to avoid trouble and to engage the wider economic system was weakening Japan's position in China, and thus its overall security—made much more sense. As Iriye (1990, 278, 283) puts it,

> The primacy of [Shidehara's] economic policy was challenged after 1930 as the impact of the world economic crisis made itself felt in the Far East. . . . Just as the Japanese officials' plea for cooperation met with no success abroad, their ideas and policies were severely attacked at home. The collapse of the American market, the decline in trade with China, and the failure to achieve any degree of constructive cooperation with the powers in China, all meant the removal of the basic rationale for Japan's economic diplomacy. Exponents of this policy could show no tangible fruit of their strategy.

Given all this, by 1931 "an atmosphere favoring any alternative to [Shidehara's] economic policy prevailed."[12]

An alterative was soon put forward by the same elements that had sought a coup in 1928. In mid-1931, Zhang signaled to Chiang that he would accept Manchuria as part of a Nationalist unified state. For militarists, this was too much. In September 1931, they launched a coup against Zhang while he was off fighting a border war. This time the coup plotters had significant backing within the army hierarchy in Tokyo. More significantly, the cabinet of Wakatsuki Reijiro, with Shidehara still serving as foreign minister, refused to order the return of Japanese forces to their barracks. This signaled that the counteractions taken against coup plotters in 1928 would not reoccur. When Inukai Tsuyoshi took over as prime (and foreign) minister in December 1931, his cabinet followed Wakatsuki's example, waiting to see if foreign powers would react to Japan's action. The greatest concern—that Russia would intervene to maintain its position in northern Manchuria, as it had in 1929—proved

---

[11] See *HYSJE*, 292–93; Iriye 1990, 279.

[12] For a similar argument tying the global economic collapse to Japan's move against Manchuria, see Beasley 1987, 175.

unfounded. The Soviets did nothing. The League of Nations was slow to react. Its watered-down report of October 1932 was quickly shelved, and it soon became obvious that the key powers on which Japan depended—namely, Britain and the United States—would condemn Japan in public but turn a blind eye in private. Far from imposing economic sanctions, as the league report suggested, they continued their active trade with Manchuria and the puppet regime of Manchukuo established in 1932 (Beasley 1987, 193–219). As we will see, US decision makers right until the end of November 1941 continued to view Manchuria as part of Japan's sphere of influence—as of course it had been since Roosevelt's administration helped make it so in 1905.

My larger point here is a simple one. By 1931 Japanese leaders and officials, both civilian and military, had come to see that economic engagement with the system was no longer serving Japan's long-term security interests. So while in August civilian ministers were mostly unaware of coup preparations, once the coup was pulled off, they embraced it as a move that was necessary to deal with the new situation—both in Manchuria and the global economy more broadly. Thus unlike 1928, Japanese governments from 1931 to 1933 (those of prime ministers Wakatsuki, Inukai, and Saito Makoto) not only allowed the occupation to go forward but also actively moved to reinforce Japan's control of the region. In the new global reality of the early 1930s, as other great powers moved to consolidate their own economic spheres, Japanese leaders saw no other choice. As one government publication put it at the time, the "shortage of the prime necessities of life" and "instability of their supply" made Manchuria essential to national security. Even if others wanted to supply Japan, their own expanding needs meant that Japan was reasonable to "fear as to whether advanced industrial countries will long continue to supply the material to our industries which compete with their own. . . . [I]f the economic policies of advanced industrial countries should be directed towards the prohibition or restriction of the export of raw materials to this country, the blow dealt to us would be very heavy."[13]

As things played out over the next few years, no major great power other than Russia was willing to adopt anything more than a rhetorical stance against Japan. This is perhaps not surprising. In consolidating their own imperial realms, Washington and London did not want to raise too many red flags. The United States, after all, had just recently come off yet another military intervention in Nicaragua, and the British

---

[13] Imperial Government of Japan, *Relations of Japan with Manchuria and Mongolia,* document B, 141–43; this document was found in the University of Chicago library, without a publication house or date, but its contents indicate that it was published around 1932–33.

were busy fighting Gandhi's independence movement in India—things that scholars usually conveniently ignore when discussing Manchuria. Some individuals such as the State Department's Stanley Hornbeck did want the United States to switch to a containment policy against Japan. The vast majority of officials, however, feared the spiral of tension that would likely result. Furthermore, Japan's presence in the north did serve the useful purpose of dissuading Chiang from pressing for the end of the final holdover from the era of unequal treaties: the valuable US, British, and French settlements in Shanghai, Tietsin, and other treaty ports (Barnhart 1987, chap. 2). It was not until Japan's full-scale war with China in 1937 that Washington would truly start to worry about Japan's larger goals in the Far East, and how they might conflict with US economic and geopolitical interests.

CHINESE UPHEAVAL, THE RUSSIAN THREAT, AND THE DIVERSION OF THE SINO-JAPANESE WAR, 1932–37

The period from 1932 to the start of the Sino-Japanese War in July 1937 marked a return to fundamental instability within China, as Chiang sought to destroy threats to his rule from both Chinese Communists and regional leaders in the north seeking more autonomy. Chiang had a delicate game to play. Knowing he needed time to modernize China and eliminate his opponents, he continued his policy of accommodation with Japan whenever periodic border clashes threatened to escalate to war. Yet as Chinese nationalism intensified, partly driven by Chiang's own efforts to build his power base, he found himself pressured by forces within his own party to do something about Japan's occupation of Manchuria. He initially squared this circle through truces with Japan and northern Chinese leaders that bought time while seeming to keep Japan at bay. In 1932–33, Tokyo had begun a policy of supporting Chinese leaders in the northern provinces bordering Manchuria who were willing to break with the Nationalists. Japanese forces occasionally entered these provinces to reinforce these bids for independence. In May 1933, Chiang accepted the Tanggu Truce requiring that Nationalist troops withdraw from the northern part of Hubei Province (in which Beijing was located) in return for the retreat of Japanese forces behind the Great Wall. With Chiang bogged down in his fifth major campaign to wipe out the Chinese Communists, he needed to avoid opening a second front in the north. And as he wrote in his diary, the truce would also give him time for reconstruction and the preparation for later war (Taylor 2009, 99; Sun 1993, 43).

Over the next three years, Japan used this truce and Chiang's troubles with the Communists to encourage autonomy movements in Shantung,

Chahar, and Suiyuan, three northern Chinese provinces. This policy, which was supported by almost all civilian and military leaders in Tokyo, had three main goals: to establish a buffer zone against Nationalist China as it revitalized; position Japan to defend itself against a Soviet attack from Mongolia, a Soviet puppet state that regularly stationed Russian troops on its soil; and further Japanese connections with the valuable Chinese markets and raw materials of the north (Barnhart 1987; Coox 1985). By 1933, there was widespread agreement within the Japanese leadership that Russia would be the predominant future threat to Japan, as it had been prior to 1904. The Soviets had successfully completed their first five-year plan in 1932, and were well on their way to becoming *the* industrial and military superpower of Eurasia (a fact that the Germans also understood; see chapter 3). Decisive victories over Chinese forces in the 1929 Manchurian dispute had shown even at that point the growing technological sophistication of the Soviet military. Japanese decision makers became obsessed with the fear that Russian leaders would seek to complete the eastern expansion halted by defeat in 1904–5—this time under the guise of spreading Communism. In the early 1920s, with the Russian state in disarray, Japan and particularly its navy viewed the United States as an equal, if not more important, threat. By 1933–36, though, ministers and military officials across the board, aside from a few holdouts in the navy, agreed that the rising Russian state was the greatest long-term threat to Japan's economic and national security. As Bix (2000) shows conclusively, Emperor Hirohito strongly approved of this focus on the future showdown with Russia.

The key question after 1932 was not about which state constituted the main threat but instead simply about the best way to handle it. Disagreement arose within the army—and also within civilian ranks—between those favoring a quick and decisive attack on Siberia, perhaps as soon as 1936, and those believing that Japan must wait until the nation was ready for a long all-out war. The so-called total-war officers in the army pushed the latter position. They had learned from World War I that modern wars required the prewar mobilization of the whole nation, both militarily and economically. Short, decisive wars like the Russo-Japanese War of 1904–5 were a thing of the past. In 1933, the advocates of a quick war had seemed to hold sway, with Army Minister Araki Sadao pushing for an emergency plan that would have Japan ready for war by the designated crisis year of 1936. But counterarguments made by other army officials, the navy, and the ministers of finance and foreign affairs won out. With Joseph Stalin's massive industrialization program well under way, and with his deployment of modern tanks and planes to the east, it was clear that there was little chance Japan could beat the Soviets in 1936. To embark on a crash militarization of the state would only undermine

Japan's economy just as it was starting to rebuild after the steep downturn of 1930–32. Seeing the consensus against him, Araki stepped down in January 1934 (Barnhart 1987; Crowley 1966).

From then on, with the complete support of Hirohito, the total-war advocates dominated the Japanese government in both the civilian and military realms. Individuals in the quick-war faction of the army were demoted and reassigned. Seeing their waning influence, they attempted a last-ditch effort to put the nation back on a course for immediate war with Russia. In February 1936, junior officers in this faction attempted a coup. The coup leaders gained little support within the army, and when the emperor immediately expressed his outrage, their operation was quickly defeated. Over the next year, with Hirohito's approval, remaining supporters of the coup and quick-war scenario were either punished or suppressed. By the start of 1937, just before the total-war planners were to be sidetracked by an unintended war in China, there were no major divisions within the Japanese government (see Bix 2000; Behr 1989). Contrary to any domestic-level argument emphasizing division and logrolling as the cause of war in 1941, as the Japanese government moved closer to major war after 1935, it became increasingly unified (Snyder 1991). Remaining disagreements, as we will see, centered only on the tactical question of whether war against Russia necessarily required a conflict with Britain and the United States over Southeast Asia, and if so, whether a southern war should proceed or be launched simultaneously with the war in the north.

The year 1936 was thus a decisive one in the history of Japan—and was seen as such at the time. After the suppression of the quick-war faction, Japanese civilian and military ministers sought to create a consensus plan that would prepare Japan for total war. There was general agreement that Japan had to avoid war with Chiang while consolidating the economic sphere in Manchuria and northern China. This would allow the buildup of forces in Manchuria and development at home of a total-war economy capable of supporting eventual war with Russia. Evidence had been arriving that the Soviet buildup in Siberia was much faster than previously estimated.[14] Yet the army and navy still had no overarching plan to coordinate their activities. The navy took it on itself to create such a plan, knowing that Ishihara Kanji, now head of the army general staff's Operation Bureau, was seeking the navy's approval for a mobilization that would center on the war against Russia (Pelz 1974, 169). The navy document offered for discussion in April 1936 to the Five Ministers Conference, titled "General Principles of National Policy," recognized that

---

[14] In just four years the Soviets in Siberia had gone from four rifle divisions to fourteen, and now had a thousand tanks to support them; Barnhart 1987, 42.

the main external goal of the nation was "to ensure Japan's position on the continent." Specifically, the economic relationship to Manchuria and China's northern provinces had to be strengthened in a way that would "facilitate the reinforcement of defense against Russia and the economic development for both Japan and Manchuria." But the navy document, not surprisingly, also argued that Japan in the meantime must use its navy to project its power and influence southward to increase Japan's economic penetration. Importantly, the document stressed that the push southward must be gradual and peaceful to avoid provoking Britain or the United States. Nonetheless, given that London and Washington might overreact, Japan must complete preparation "for any eventuality" (see *JGEACS*, 58–60).

This document is often taken as a statement of the navy's determination to grab a bigger slice of the budget by reorienting policy to a "south-first" strategy (Snyder 1991; Pelz 1974). There is little question that many in the navy did prefer a south-first approach (Pelz 1974, 171). A study of the "General Principles" document, however, reveals that in dealing with the Inner Cabinet (the five key ministers), navy leaders only sought to show that the navy deserved equal footing with the army, and that naval preparations and a move south would *supplement* any future action to deal with the rising Soviet threat. Ishihara, the army's leading strategist and a strong supporter of the plan for war with Russia by 1941, had been pressing for a policy that included another naval limitation agreement with Britain and the United States along with a buildup of the navy only in the second of two five-year periods (Crowley 1966, 284–85; Barnhart 1987, 46). Navy leaders certainly recognized that such a policy would give them a decreasing share of the budgetary pie. Yet they also believed that a go-north policy against Russia, given the nature of total war, could not succeed without access to southern resources. The first two sections of the navy document, dealing with Japan's "fundamental policy toward nations in an important relationship to us," were devoted to Manchukuo and China. "Countries in the southern area" were delegated to the third section. Immediately after describing how these countries were critical to solving Japan's economic and population problems (the latter through emigration), the document states that Japanese penetration of the southern area "is necessary to complete our policies toward Manchuria, China, and Russia." The fourth section concerned Russia directly. It argued that "in order to restrain Russia's advance in the Far East we should make necessary military preparations" and adopt as a basic principle "a policy of active offense" (see *JGEACS*, 58–60). In short, the navy was not asking for a primary orientation south but rather only for an understanding of Southeast Asia's significance as a necessary element of a policy focused on China and Russia (Barnhart 1987, 44).

Some navy officers, despite the harm already being caused by post-1930 Anglo-American mercantilist policies, were explicit about the importance of a "Russia-first" policy. In March 1936, Commander of the Third Fleet Oikawa Kojiro wrote headquarters to underscore that the military buildup against Russia had to be Japan's top priority. He summarized Japan's strategic dilemma:

> No problem would arise if we [could advance] . . . peacefully in all directions, but when the powers are raising high tariff barriers as they are today and are preventing artificially the peaceful advance of other countries, we must of necessity be prepared and determined to use force in some areas and eliminate the barriers. . . . [Yet the] empire had not yet reached the time when we can happily bring about a collision with England and the United States. Rather than that, we should advance to the north even though it causes a collision with the Soviet Union and settle [the threat from] the north. (quoted in Pelz 1974, 170)

Only after that point, Oikawa argued, should Japan consider turning south.

In late June 1936, the army issued its own document, "General Principles of National Defense Policy," to shape the debate within the Inner Cabinet. Preparing for war in the north was the top priority. Japan must devote "all [its] strength to making Russia surrender" through war or coercive diplomacy. No mention is made of a simultaneous southern advance, but the document notes that "it will be extremely difficult to execute a war against Russia unless we maintain (good relations) with the United States and Britain, [or] at least with the United States." As a sop to the navy, the document ended by noting that once Russia had surrendered and friendship with China established, planning for possible war in the south could proceed. But it made it clear that all planning and economic mobilization in the near term had to emphasize preparations for a move against Russia (*JGEACS*, 61–62).

After further discussions, the Inner Cabinet approved a new document on August 7, aptly titled "Fundamentals of National Policy." This document is absolutely crucial to understanding all that follows in Japanese foreign policy until November 1941. This is not because its details were always followed, but because it self-consciously specified the overarching priorities and objectives that would guide the nation through the impending five years of turmoil and uncertainty.

On the surface, the document seemed to split the difference between the army and navy positions. Japan's "basic policy" was to secure its position on the continent, "and at the same time to advance and develop in the Southern area." Going deeper, however, we see the Inner Cabinet's obvious desire to distinguish preparations for an almost-certain war with Russia from the hopefully peaceful economic penetration of Southeast Asia. Policy must center on the "removal of the threat of northern Russia," and this would require "pay[ing] attention to friendly relations with the world powers." Thus as Japan expanded its sphere southward, it should avoid provoking other countries while increasing its power "by gradual peaceful means." The larger goal, after all, was to ready the nation "to launch a major attack . . . against the armed strength of Russia," and for this end, Japan needed the navy to protect the flow of raw materials. Accordingly, an accelerated buildup would develop "armed strength sufficient to ensure naval supremacy in the Western Pacific." The objective for the south was deterrence, not war. A stronger navy would dissuade Washington from interfering in Japan's sphere of influence in Southeast Asia. The message was the same one stated explicitly in the April document: war with the United States would be a last resort, undertaken only if deterrence failed and Washington resisted Japan's economic penetration southward (*JGEACS*: 62–64).

For the next five years, until the failure of talks with Washington in November 1941, the navy remained highly reluctant to take on the United States in a long naval war. This hesitancy was even stronger in 1936, given the advantage that the United States had established as a result of previous restrictions on Japanese naval growth. The failure of naval limitation talks by the end of 1935 had ended institutional restraints on a Japanese naval buildup. Until August 1936, however, the Japanese leadership had not yet agreed that a buildup should proceed. The consensus reached on August 7 changed all that. It permitted an expansion that would, by 1941, allow Japan to initiate war against the United States and do extremely well in its first six months. Yet as we have seen, war with the United States was not the primary policy goal. The goal was the stabilization of Japan's economic position in Northeast Asia through the destruction of Soviet power in the Far East. A situation even worse than that of 1902–3 had arisen, and Japanese officials were again preparing to deal with it through war. These points must be remembered in order to understand all that follows in this chapter and the next. It is so often assumed that the Japanese leadership desired the wars with China and the United States. In fact, from the start, these wars were unwanted sideshows brought on by the need to reduce Soviet power before the economic jewel of Manchuria was lost.

By fall 1936, relations with Chiang had been relatively stable for more than three years. Periodic clashes between Nationalist forces and Japanese troops or their local puppet regimes in the northern provinces had continued unabated. The Tanggu Truce of 1933 had nonetheless held. Chiang was focused on eliminating Mao Ze-dong's Communists in northern Shangxi, while Tokyo concentrated on its buildup against Russia. Yet by summer 1937, both sides found themselves embroiled in an all-out war that would last eight grueling years. How did this happen?

Oddly enough, international relations scholars who study the Pacific War typically ignore the causes of the Sino-Japanese War, despite its critical role in the lead-up to Pearl Harbor.[15] These scholars accept that the war in China greatly increased Japan's resource needs and overall dependence on raw materials from the United States and Britain, leaving Japan vulnerable to the economic restrictions that the two countries imposed after summer 1939. They also accept that these restrictions led Japanese leaders to highly pessimistic assessments of Washington's willingness to trade with Japan into the future, thereby pushing Japan into war against the United States. But they presume that some underlying imperialist obsession with controlling all of China was what led Japan into the Sino-Japanese War and also kept it from pulling out in 1941, notwithstanding US demands that raw material exports would only be renewed if Japan left China. In this way, they can argue that pathologies within the Japanese polity led to an irrational plunge into war with the US giant.

Yet far from wanting war with China in 1937, all the key Japanese civilian and military leaders hoped to avoid such a conflict. They rightly saw it as an unnecessary and costly diversion from the plan laid down in 1936 to prepare for total war with the Soviet Union. Indeed, they believed that a war with China might risk the whole goal of destroying the Soviet power in the Far East. Thus we have the puzzle that any good causes-of-war theory must explain: Why would a minor clash at the Marco Polo Bridge on July 7, 1937 lead to total war when similar clashes from 1932 to 1936 had not? Scholars stressing ongoing pathologies within the Japanese state since 1931 cannot answer this conundrum. After all, a constant cannot explain a variable. The answer to the puzzle does not lie with anything new going on inside Japan—after the August 1936 consensus agreement, the Japanese leadership was, if anything, even more desirous of maintaining peace with China. Rather, we must look to a significant change in Chiang's attitude toward Japan. Chiang's policy of appeasing Japan to concentrate on the internal war with Mao had put him under severe pressure by 1936 to end the civil war and refocus attention on pushing Japan out of northern China and Manchuria. Chiang's Nationalists had from the beginning stood for the unification of the China, and they had rode the wave of Chinese nationalism to their presently strong domestic position. Yet in the eyes of its own followers, the Nationalist Party had not completed the task. In essence, Japan had to go, or Chiang had to go.

By fall 1936, Chiang was caught between two simultaneous pressures. On the one side, he knew that China was still weak relative to Japan: the

[15] Snyder 1991; Kupchan 1994; Richardson 1994; Taliaferro 2005.

program to modernize the army (with help from German advisers) had not been completed, and he had still not quelled rebellions within his own sphere, let alone destroyed Mao's Communists. The Machiavellian strategist in him also recognized that a war with Japan, even if he won, could weaken his strength relative to Mao, right at a point when Mao's party seemed to be growing in power and popularity. On the other hand, Chiang well understood that his policy of appeasing Japan was losing him support within his own party and the Chinese people more generally. This became particularly clear with the formation of the National Salvation Association within the KMT in early 1936. This faction dedicated itself to the expulsion of Japan from Chinese soil. The faction had built a large following in 1936 after KMT forces defeated an attempt by a Japanese-backed warlord to take control of Suiyuan Province, bordering Soviet Mongolia. Because Japanese troops had actively assisted the warlord, it had seemed that the KMT had, for the first time, achieved a significant military victory over Japan. Chiang of course knew better, understanding that this clash with a few Japanese infantry troops was not a true test of China's military ability to beat Japan. Yet he could not ignore the growing domestic pressure on him to "do something" about Japan. This pressure increased in mid-1936 when Mao, coerced by Stalin to follow Moscow's new policy promoting "united fronts" against fascism, publicly announced that he would be willing to join Chiang in a war against Japan. An armed revolt by Salvationists in the south also broke out that summer, and was put down only by military force and substantial bribes (Fenby 2004, 274–76).

Notwithstanding his shaky hold on his party and warlord allies, Chiang decided in fall 1936 to avoid war with Japan in order to embark on his sixth campaign to eliminate the Communists. Chiang asked warlords in the north to participate in the campaign, including Marshal Zhang, who had been expelled from Manchuria after the 1931 coup. When the two met in Xian in December 1936, however, Zhang betrayed Chiang, capturing the Chinese leader and holding him hostage. Negotiations assisted by Mao's emissary Zhou En-lai convinced Chiang to put aside his campaign against the Communists and formally commit to the united front against Japan. When a much-rattled Chiang returned to his capital at Nanjing, subordinates noticed the change. Chiang threw himself into the task of working with Mao to prepare for war with Japan (see Taylor 2009, 142–45). Beyond a mere commitment to a promise, Chiang's experience in December had shown him that his domestic survival was now directly dependent on ending his appeasement policy and confronting Japan (see Fenby 2004, 287). The opportunity came on the night of July 7, 1937, when Chinese and Japanese troops exchanged gunfire at the Marco Polo Bridge. By the Tanggu Truce of 1933 and a follow-up accord in 1935 (the He-Umetsu Agreement), Chiang had agreed that the northern provinces were outside Nanjing's direct control. The man on the spot, Song Zhe-yuan, commander of the 29th KMT army, thus had a large degree of autonomy in deciding how to respond. Song was just as fearful of KMT troops marching north as he was of a Japanese reaction (Sun 1993, 88). Meanwhile, the Japanese army was under strict instructions from the army general staff in Tokyo not to escalate the conflict (Taylor 2009, 145). As a result, on the morning of July 11, representatives of both armies were able to sign a cease-fire agreement allowing the pullback of troops (Crowley 1966, 327–28).

For three and a half days, therefore, this looked to be just another in a series of minor clashes quickly resolved by diplomacy. But back in Nanjing, Chiang was ready to pounce. His response, as Sun Youli (1993, 88) relates, "was swift and uncompromising, unlike in previous years." On July 9, Chiang hastily ordered four of his best German-trained divisions to cross the Yellow River to "reinforce" a 29th army that was already well on its way to negotiating a peace. He sent a message to the military commanders and governors of all KMT provinces notifying them of a "general mobilization to get ready for war." He ordered the drafting of a declaration of war on Japan. By the act of sending divisions, Chiang knew he was violating the He-Umetsu Agreement with Japan. It had specified that the area north of the Yellow River was off-limits to the Chinese Central Army. Reminded of this agreement, he remarked: "What He-Umetsu Agreement! I have torn it to pieces."[16]

The Japanese reaction during those first few days was the exact opposite. Back in the spring, there had been "high hopes in Tokyo for a new era in Sino-Japanese relations," to the point where an economic mission had been sent to Nanjing to increase trade between the two countries (Barnhart 1987, 82). There were individuals within the Kwantung Army who had believed for some time that Japan should first eliminate the KMT threat to the south before turning to the main event—war against Russia. But Ishihara, a key instigator of the 1931 Manchurian coup and now head of the army general staff's Operation Bureau, was dead set against such a move. Insisting that preparedness for war against the Soviet Union must take precedence over anything else, he worked with his fellow generals in Tokyo to keep the Kwantung China-first officers under wraps. A military clash with Russia in late June 1937 at the Amur River only reinforced the delicacy of the Manchurian situation and the need to avoid opening a second front in the south (Coox 1985, 102–5).[17]

---

[16] Quotations from Sun 1993, 88; Taylor 2009, 145.

[17] On Hirohito's dissatisfaction during the Amur Crisis with the state of Japanese military preparedness, see Bix 2000, 319.

When word was first received on July 8 that an exchange of arms fire had occurred near Beijing, civilian and military leaders in Tokyo thus unanimously agreed that the incident must be resolved quietly as well as quickly. The army's chief of staff, Prince Kanin Kotohito, sent an order on July 8 to General Hashimoto Toranosuke, the commander of the small Japanese contingent in Hebei Province, stating that the incident should be settled with all speed. Kanin told the Inner Cabinet that insofar as "the government's policy of localizing the incident" was thoroughly understood by the field commander, he would be allowed to work out a peaceful resolution on the ground. On the afternoon of that same day, the cabinet of Konoe Fumimaro, the new prime minister, approved a position paper jointly prepared by the war, foreign, and naval ministries arguing for a policy of "nonexpansion" and a "local settlement" of the issue. The next morning, July 9, Kanin relayed the key terms of an agreement that would be acceptable to Japan—the same terms that local Chinese representatives would agree to in the cease-fire accord reached on July 11 (Crowley 1966, 328–29).

It is apparent beyond all reasonable doubt, then, that during the first four days after the Marco Polo Bridge Incident, as Japan sought to prevent escalation, it was Chiang who chose to fan the flames of this specific clash, primarily to shore up his position at home. What happened after July 9 as Tokyo learned of Chiang's deployment of divisions can be told in short order. On the evening of the July 10, Ishihara reluctantly advised War Minister Sugiyama Hajime that Japan had to mobilize five divisions to counter the KMT troops already moving north. Ishihara knew that the plan for war against Russia—a war he approved of and was helping organize—required five years of peace. Yet he also appreciated arguments reaching him from field officers indicating that Chiang's unexpected move meant he now intended to destroy Japan's position in northern China and Manchuria. After Sugiyama informed Konoe of Ishihara's advice, Konoe approved the action along with the assembling of the Inner Cabinet to ratify it (Barnhart 1987, 85–86). The next day, however, Ishihara had a change of heart. Showing his trepidation over what might transpire, he asked Konoe to suspend the mobilization order, believing a localization of the incident was still possible. During the cabinet meeting on the morning of July 11, Sugiyama continued to argue in favor of deploying the five divisions, and the cabinet approved the action. But just after Konoe's public announcement of the decision, word was received of the agreement reached by local commanders that morning. Ishihara immediately suspended the mobilization order. At another Inner Cabinet meeting held at 10:00 p.m. that night, Sugiyama concurred that mobilization would not proceed if the Chinese agreed in writing to Japan's terms (ibid., 86–88).

The leadership in Tokyo was evidently still hoping for a localization of the incident, and up until July 20, this hope still seemed realizable. On July 19, with time running out on a Japanese ultimatum to pull back, local KMT commander Song agreed to Japan's terms. He was obviously looking for a way out: over the previous two days, Song had gone so far as to apologize for the incident and attend the funeral of one of Japan's generals killed in a recent skirmish. Chiang had not authorized Song's actions, though. Showing his displeasure, Chiang released a bellicose statement reaching Tokyo on July 19 that made it clear a lasting solution had not yet been found. Nevertheless, Ishihara went ahead and again suspended mobilization.

Things by this point had spun out of the control of Ishihara and his total-war officers. On July 25, new clashes broke out between Chinese and Japanese forces near Beijing. With officers from Song's own army denouncing Song as a collaborator, there was apparently no one left on the Chinese side who could secure a peace. On July 26, Ishihara reinstated the mobilization order of three divisions, and the cabinet met to approve of a new operations plan to punish the Chinese and push the KMT out of northern China. Even at this moment the objective was to win a quick war in the north and convince Chiang to leave the north as it was, namely, as a buffer zone between himself and the Japanese puppet state of Manchukuo. But after Chiang in August refused a return to the status quo ante and then sent divisions to Shanghai to eject Japan from its international settlement, the conflict quickly escalated into total war.[18]

The meaning in all this is straightforward: Japan's leadership did not want a large-scale war with China in 1937 but instead sought to focus on the buildup for preventive war with Russia. Japan's leaders can hardly be considered innocent victims, however. They did desire war on the Asian continent—but north, not south. In terms of explaining the later attack on Pearl Harbor, therefore, the Sino-Japanese War cannot be used by liberal theorists as yet another example of the Japanese leadership's pathological drives of greed and glory. If we are to truly understand what happened in December 1941, we need to keep our attention on Japan's long-standing concerns for its economic position in Manchuria and northern China as well as its fear of the long-term rise of Russia. The war with China was an undesired sideshow, and as the next chapter discusses, one that Japanese leaders were keen to conclude so that they could get back to their ultimate task: the destruction of rising Russian power in the Far East and protection of Japan's economic position in Manchuria. The final section of this chapter will show how US actions after 1937 provided an

[18] See Crowley 1966; Sun 1993; Fenby 2004; Taylor 2009.

additional diversion from this task, forcing Tokyo to consider something that had never been desired. And that was war with the United States.

Before moving on, it is worth noting that none of our three main theories work well for the Sino-Japanese War (see table 2.7). Because its origins lie in Chinese domestic politics rather than in Japanese or Chinese security drives, neither economic realism nor trade expectations theory is supported. Commercial liberalism might seem strong here, given that Chiang brought on war for internal reasons during a period when overall world trade had dropped precipitously. Unfortunately for the liberal position, Chinese-Japanese trade had been growing since 1932 as Chiang concentrated on the Communist threat (hence the Japanese optimism in early 1937 regarding potential trade talks). By 1936–37 trade had been restored to pre-1930 levels, after having dropped by half from 1929 to 1932 (see *HYSJE*, 292). So it is hard to argue that domestic forces within Chiang's regime had been unleashed because the restraint of trade had fallen away. The larger liberal view that domestic factors drive the phenomenon of war is certainly upheld. But the commercial liberal argument is not.

THE DECLINE OF RELATIONS WITH THE UNITED STATES, 1938–40

By mid-1938, it was clear that Japan had entered a quagmire from which it could not easily extract itself. Chiang had lost the key cities of Shanghai and his capital at Nanjing, but he still refused to make a peace, notwithstanding the horrible massacre the Japanese had inflicted on the latter. Much to the dismay of Japanese ministers, Japan was now diverting much of the materiel slated for the five-year buildup against the Soviet Union to a total war in the opposite direction. Yet they saw little choice in the matter. Chiang had to be defeated if Japan was to continue to dominate the economy of northern China/Manchuria and use it as a base for the coming battle with Russia. Of particular concern was the new support Moscow was giving the KMT. In an obvious attempt to keep Japan bogged down in the south so it could not go north, Stalin was funneling Soviet military supplies to Chiang, including tanks and planes. He was also sending hundreds of Soviet military advisers to organize Chiang's counteroffensives and even allowing "volunteer" Soviet pilots to fly bombing raids against Japanese positions.

In early 1937, before the Sino-Japanese War had broken out, Moscow had begun to reinforce its army in Siberia to deal with the evident buildup of Japanese forces in Manchukuo. The Soviet army was reorganized into two more efficient military districts, one in east and one in the west (with some of the latter being stationed in Mongolia) (Clubb 1971, 309–11). In July 1938, the nightmare of a two-front war that Japanese military officials had been studiously seeking to avoid suddenly seemed likely. Japanese and Russian forces clashed at Changkufeng near the Korean border, leading to a monthlong battle for control of a disputed hilltop. Japan's troops did poorly, and with its army simultaneously pushing against KMT military headquarters in Wuhan, Japanese forces retreated from Changkufeng in early August to avoid further escalation.[19]

After the capture of Wuhan and Chiang's retreat to Chongqing (Chungking), the Sino-Japanese settled into a cautious stalemate for the next three years. The Japanese continued to pound Chiang's positions with bombers, hoping to coerce Chiang into a peace. With each side understanding the difficulties of waging an offensive ground war up and down the Yangtze River valley, the size and number of actual engagements dropped significantly. By 1938–39, both civilian and military ministers in Tokyo were seeking an end to the war under terms that would reestablish the pre-1937 status quo and include protection of Japan's economic rights in China. Even with the large drop in casualties, the war was a huge economic drain on Japan.[20] It impeded preparations for war in the north and significantly increased the country's dependence on raw materials from the United States. Already by early 1938, Japan had used almost half its gold reserves to pay for the growing trade deficit, caused mainly by increased raw material demands. To make matters worse, the terms of trade were moving against Japan: with global prices for raw materials rising as militaries around the world expanded, the cost of Japanese imports increased 37 percent during 1937, while the value of Japanese exports grew only 18 percent. A May 1938 report by the Japan-Manchuria Finance and Economic Research Association noted that the China war had significantly reduced revenues from exports and was interfering with the materials mobilization plan. A follow-up report by the Planning Board in June stated bluntly that Japan now could pay for only 80 percent of the raw material imports initially planned. The five-year plan was in trouble, and radical changes were required to avert economic chaos (Barnhart 1987, 109–14).

Prime Minister Konoe appointed Ugaki Kazunari as foreign minister in May 1938 for the express purpose of negotiating a peace with China, but the talks went nowhere (ibid., 112). After the defeat at Wuhan, Chiang hunkered down at Chongqing, hoping that a war between Japan and either the United States or Russia would save China from having to negotiate a peace that would leave Japan in northern China (Sun 1993). Washington, for its part, had done little to help Chiang during the first

---

[19] See Coox 1985, chap. 10; Clubb 1971, 312–13.

[20] By 1940, Japanese soldiers killed in action in China made up one-quarter of total figure for the first year of the war (Bix 2000, 346).

year of the war. In June 1938, however, President Roosevelt initiated the first in a series of trade sanctions, announcing a "moral embargo" on military equipment. This was not a huge move; Roosevelt was merely asking firms voluntarily to restrict or halt their imports of such equipment to Japan. Nonetheless, by signaling the United States' willingness to constrain Japanese power, it did represent an important shift in policy. From here on out, Japanese trade expectations would get progressively more pessimistic. And it was this fall in expectations that would shift Tokyo from its focus on war with Russia to the contemplation of war with the United States.

On the US side, hawks in the State Department, led by Far Eastern division chief Hornbeck, were becoming increasingly concerned with two problems: Japan's military growth, and the risk that it might impede US access to Chinese and Southeast Asian trade. There is little evidence that State Department officials cared much about the ethical dimensions of Japan's brutal occupation of southern China (despite the high-sounding phrase moral embargo). The US concern was almost solely geopolitical. Japan's buildup after the collapse of talks in early 1936 threatened the United States' naval supremacy in the western Pacific. It was feared that this growing strength, combined with the exigencies of the Sino-Japanese War, might push Tokyo to block all non-Japanese trade with China. The Japanese government had been careful after the start of war in August 1937 to allow the British, French, and Americans to continue trading through their treaty-port settlements. The inadvertent sinking of the US gunboat *Panay* in December 1937 led Hornbeck and Treasury Secretary Henry Morgenthau to press for tight economic sanctions to reduce Japan's military growth. Although Roosevelt had been discussing the value of sanctions since October, when the Japanese leadership quickly apologized and offered compensation for damages, the crisis blew over. The arguments of Hornbeck's successor in the State Department, Maxwell Hamilton, and ambassador to Japan Joseph Grew held sway. They maintained that Japan would moderate its expansionism if it felt economically secure and strong enough to deter a Soviet attack. Moreover, Japan required outlets for its goods, and if it could meet these needs in China, it would return to its "natural" place within the Anglo-American sphere.[21]

Given this thinking, the moral embargo of 1938 was designed as an initial signal of US concern for its own economic position in the Far East. True economic sanctions—backed by the US state rather than voluntary and of the kind that could harm Japan's ability to sustain its five-year mobilization plan—would only begin in mid-1939. The impact of these

[21] Barnhart 1987, especially 125–27; Marshall 1995, passim.

sanctions nicely demonstrates the tragic dynamics of the trade-security dilemma described in chapter 1. As I discuss below, the more Tokyo began to doubt Washington's willingness to trade, the more it increased its emphasis on securing raw materials from Southeast Asia. As Japan supported its diplomatic push south with growing naval power, US officials started to accept Hornbeck's assertion that sanctions were necessary to reduce Japan's power projection capabilities. Such sanctions in turn only heightened worries in Tokyo that Japan would not be allowed access to the raw materials needed to end the Sino-Japanese War on reasonable terms and complete the buildup for war against Russia. From 1939 on, a spiral of hostility would ensue that would redirect Japan away from its primary task—destroying Soviet power in the Far East—into an all-out war with the United States that few in Tokyo had ever seriously contemplated, let alone desired, when the total-war buildup was kicked off in 1936.

The spiral of declining trade expectations did not go just one way, though. As the war in China intensified through 1938, US officials were becoming increasingly concerned about restrictions on US trade.[22] By early fall 1938, three concerns were primary: Japan was blocking free navigation up the Yangtze River; it was establishing a new currency in northern China that made it harder for anything but Japanese imports to enter the area; and additional Japanese monopolies were moving into China. Seeking to uphold open access for US business, Secretary of State Hull lodged a formal protest on October 1, 1938. By way of reply, Prime Minister Konoe made an address outlining Japan's vision for a "New Order" in East Asia in early November (Barnhart 1987, 131; Montgomery 1987, 407). The speech assured the United States that Japan did not intend to exercise an economic monopoly in China. But it also underscored that Japan expected China to recognize that for its own good, it must accept an independent Manchukuo and work with Japan in the fight against global Communism. This would include, presumably after a peace agreement to end the current war, the stationing of some Japanese troops in the Inner Mongolian provinces (Chahar and Suiyuan). While the Soviet Union is not mentioned by name, the speech made it clear that the common defense pact sought would be directed northward (see *JGEACS*, 68–70). (There was no mention of Southeast Asian states being part of the New Order. This would only come in mid-1940 as the Japanese leadership announced its plans for a Co-prosperity Sphere going beyond northeast Asia.)

The State Department saw the speech as a statement of Tokyo's plan to control the Chinese economy after a peace with Chiang and thus to end the open door that it had maintained even in the midst of the

---

[22] Marshall's (1995) treatment of this is the most complete.

Sino-Japanese War. These suspicions were reinforced when Hull received a statement from the new foreign minister, Arita Hachiro, arguing that the principles of the open door should be applied beyond China. The United States and Britain, Arita explained, already had spheres that allowed for economic self-sufficiency. It was only fair that Japan have access to territory "from which she could not be cut off by belligerent action of third powers" (quoted in Barnhart 1987, 131–32). Seen objectively, the foreign minister had a point: the United States and Britain could not very well demand a continued open door in China if they were using high and discriminatory tariffs to protect their own vast economic realms. After the New Order speech, however, US officials were in no mood for such comparisons, and US foreign policy moved in a distinctly hard-line direction. Even Ambassador Grew in Tokyo now believed that Japan had broken its earlier promises to maintain the open door. Hornbeck and his supporters proceeded to press for significant economic sanctions, contending that Japan was vulnerable to economic pressure and therefore would have to moderate its policy objectives (ibid., 131–33).

Konoe's failure to end the war with Chiang led to increasing difficulties as Japan moved toward the third year of the "China Incident." Congress began to jump on the "no appeasement" bandwagon in spring 1939. Several bills that would have embargoed sales of iron and steel scrap metal to Japan were put forward for consideration. This increased the pressure on Roosevelt to do something to reduce Japan's military power in the east. Roosevelt, Hull, and the majority opinion in the State Department still favored a gradual tightening of the economic screws—enough to cause pain, but not enough to push Japan into an early war for which the United States was unprepared. In July 1939 Roosevelt announced that the US-Japanese trade treaty—the treaty that had formed the basis of US-Japanese economic relations since 1911—would not be renewed but instead allowed to expire in six months. This was an important diplomatic step, since by ending the treaty, Roosevelt gave himself full discretion to impose restrictions or a full embargo on any products traded with Japan (ibid., 133–35).

Combined with the outbreak of war in Europe two months later, this action constituted a devastating blow to Japanese expectations of future trade. Planners in Tokyo quickly realized that the war would force the United States, Britain, and France—Japan's main suppliers of iron ore, oil, and other key raw materials—to reduce resource exports in order to build their militaries. And even if Japan could secure these goods, the jump in total global demand would send prices through the roof, exacerbating Tokyo's already-delicate foreign exchange problem. As Michael Barnhart (ibid., 149) puts it, by fall 1939 the Japanese nation "was about to encounter enormous obstacles in its attempts to obtain raw materials."

The impact of these developments on Japanese thinking is seen most strikingly in the army's case. In spring 1939, the army had already decided to scale back operations in China to save precious materiel for the still-anticipated war with Russia. Army leaders presented a long report to Hirohito in May arguing that with world war likely by 1942 or 1943, the diversion of the China Incident was leaving Japan unprepared for what was to come. The Planning Board's estimates at the time showed that Japan would have only two billion yen for purchases abroad during the 1939 fiscal year, down 17 percent from the adjusted 1938 plan, which itself was 20 percent below the original plan. Even before the shocks of July 1939 (the end of the trade treaty) and September 1939 (war in Europe three years before expected), the army was already being told that there were not enough resources to meet the plan for war with the Soviet Union by 1942 (ibid., 137–39). Moreover, relations with Moscow were already tense. The cease-fire after a short war on the eastern Manchurian border in July–August 1938 was still holding. The Soviet buildup in Mongolia, however, was leading to recurring clashes on the western front. In May 1939, a minor struggle began near Nomonhan, and by August it had escalated into a major battle to control the Mongolian-Manchukuo border region. The Japanese defeat in late August, after some fifty thousand casualties, only reinforced the shared belief that Japan still needed at least three more years to prepare for a decisive war with Russia (Clubb 1971, 316–18; Coox 1985, chaps. 12–13). After Stalin's August pact with Hitler, Japanese leaders knew that German expansionism would not help divert Soviet forces westward. Another truce was thus signed in September to end the Nomonhan campaign and get Japan back to the preparation for total war with Russia by 1942.

It was during summer 1939, prior to the Nazi-Soviet Pact, that the army began to press for a formal alliance with Germany to draw Soviet troops away from Siberia and Mongolia. The navy was wary of such a deal, fearing its impact on relations with the United States. Navy Minister Yonai Mitsumasa reminded his colleagues that the purpose of the Japanese navy was to deter a conflict with the United States, not to start one. Japan still required good relations with the United States to furnish the supplies needed for the buildup against Russia. By 1939, the United States was supplying approximately 80 percent of Japan's oil needs and 75 percent of its scrap iron. The southern advance strategy entailed using gunboat diplomacy to pressure Dutch, French, and British possessions to increase raw material exports. Yet the navy still had no desire for an actual war in the south, even if by projecting its influence it was willing to increase the risk of one (Barnhart 1987, 139–47).

The coming of an early war in Europe had a dramatic effect on the Japanese military's calculations. Germany's quick victories over Holland

and France in May–June 1940, and assault on Britain, shifted the Japanese army's perception of the whole Southeast Asian region. After the US-Japan trade treaty formally ended in January 1940, Roosevelt and Hull began to restrict the export of select products. These were products that were needed for the United States' own buildup, and might increase pressure on Japan to make peace with China and reinstate the open door. Army leaders in Tokyo had already agreed by early 1939 that Japan needed an honorable exit from the China Incident, albeit one that preserved Japan's pre-1937 presence in Inner Mongolia and Manchuria. By 1940, however, with trade restrictions limiting Japan's military growth in Manchuria and its ability to end the China Incident, army leaders started to see a more vigorous southern advance as critical to the nation's war plans in the north. For army leaders, such an advance, including a move into northern Indochina and an increased effort to coerce more raw material exports out of the Dutch East Indies, would have a two-pronged effect. By destroying routes through French Indochina and Burma that were transporting 80 percent of Chiang's foreign supplies, it would force Chiang to make peace. The advance would also supply the raw materials needed to continue the northern buildup and stabilize control of northern China after the peace with Chiang (ibid., chaps. 7–9).

This led to one of the more surprising developments of the prewar period—something that cannot be explained by a domestic logrolling argument (Snyder 1991). From early 1940 until mid-1941, it was the army, instead of the navy, that pushed the hardest for a military move southward—that is, for military occupation as opposed to the simple projection of naval power in support of economic penetration. This shift was advocated even though it was agreed that the risks of war with the United States would greatly increase as a result. From Snyder's bureaucratic perspective, the navy should have been the driving force of this policy, and solely to increase its share of the budgetary pie. Yet the army, supported by both the civilian leadership and Hirohito, understood that unless Japan started to go south with actual force, its position in the northeast could not be sustained.

The army's first formal push for a move south came with its issuing in July 1940 of a document titled "Outline for Dealing with the Changes in the World Situation." If Japan could break the KMT's morale with its recent offensive against Ichang, Chiang would likely sue for peace. If he did not, the document argued, it was imperative to gain military control of northern Indochina to pressure Chiang through economic means. Japan needed greater self-sufficiency in raw materials through access to additional resources in Southeast Asia, although it should try to do so without provoking war with the United States. Finally, the document stressed the importance of an alliance with Berlin, with the obvious goal of both splitting Soviet forces and deterring US interference in Japan's southern push (Barnhart 1987, 158–59).

Negotiations with French authorities to allow Japanese troops to be stationed in northern Indochina, begun in June, picked up steam after Washington announced in July an export licensing system to restrict exports to Japan of iron ore, scrap iron, and some oil products. Under Admiral Yonai's cabinet from January to early July, the army had been restrained from pushing too fast with the southern option. But after pro-army Konoe reassumed the prime ministership on July 22, Tokyo increased pressure on the French to permit the "peaceful" entry of Japanese forces into northern Indochina. With the threat of invasion hanging over them, French authorities caved in, and Japanese troops took up their positions in late September (Tsunoda 1980).

Simultaneously, the Japanese initiated a new round of aggressive diplomacy with the Dutch authorities in Batavia (Jakarta) to secure a new agreement on the export of oil and raw materials to Japan. The Japanese envoy was partially successful, signing contracts by November for two million tons of oil. At the same time, the Dutch negotiators, under US pressure, made sure that all contracts with Japan had a maximum time frame of six months. The total secured was also only a small portion of the amount originally requested, leaving Japan still dependent on the United States for most of its oil (Nagaoka 1980).

When Tokyo embarked on its new coercive strategy against the French and Dutch, army leaders still assumed that they could avoid a conflict with the United States. Because Japan had moved into northern Indochina through purportedly voluntary French agreement, they hoped Washington would not overreact. The focus was still on a coming war with Russia, not the United States. Navy leaders, on the other hand, had a more realistic grasp on Washington's perspective. They leaders knew that Roosevelt and Hull would not permit Japan to control trade with the Dutch East Indies, and would probably blockade the waters of the South China Sea to prevent Japan from exploiting such trade. A push south of the kind being advocated by the army would likely lead to a clash—one that the Japanese navy was still unprepared for.

The admirals, however, were caught between a rock and a hard place. The naval bills that had passed Congress in June 1940, building on the first Vinson bills from 1936, would soon create a US navy four times the size of Japan's fleet. Ambivalent naval leaders thus went along with the army's new southern push, knowing there was little time left to establish an economic sphere that could compete with the British and US realms. Yet the navy, aligning with the cautious Planning Board, also used the army's dependence on the fleet as leverage to exact its price: an increased allocation of Japan's limited resources to shipbuilding to establish temporary naval superiority. It also made sure in September 1940 when it accepted the Tripartite Pact with Germany that any southern move would be as peaceful as possible (Barnhart 1987, chap. 9; Copeland 2011b).[23]

The year 1940 ended with the Japanese navy and army both working feverously to prepare the nation for war, either north against Russia or south against the United States. All agreed that war against Russia to stabilize Japan's position in Northeast Asia was the highest objective if it could be initiated without war with the United States. But if the United States proved determined to continue or increase its economic sanctions, then Japan would have to push south first to ensure access to the necessary raw materials. If this move brought on war with the United States, that would have to be accepted. Yet the outcome desired by all was the avoidance of war in the south, renewal of open trade with Southeast Asia and the United States, and redirection of Japanese forces northward against the rising Soviet Union. As we will see in the next chapter, it was the inability of Tokyo and Washington to agree to a modus vivendi that would restore this trade that led Japan to reluctantly choose its second-best option—war with the United States—as a way to avoid the worst outcome, the steady decline of the Japanese state into the ranks of a third-rate power.

Conclusion

This chapter, along with testing our competing theories across the years 1905–37, has set the stage for the final descent into war by 1941. Above all, it has shown that the growing threat to Japan's economic position in Northeast Asia caused by the rise of Russia—an obsession going back to the late nineteenth century (chapter 3)—was the guiding theme of Japanese foreign policy from the end of the Russo-Japanese War to the outbreak of the Second World War in Europe. Even at the height of Taisho democracy from 1914 to 1929, Japanese diplomacy was oriented to improving and protecting Japan's position on the continent vis-à-vis Russia. Much of this early period, especially the years 1905–22, is nicely explained by economic realism. The Japanese state, regardless of the party affiliations or ideological orientations of its various leaders, continued to jump at opportunities to expand Japan's influence and control on the continent whenever it could do so under the radar of the other great powers. During World War I and its immediate aftermath, then, with

---

[23]On the navy's worries about an escalation to war with the United States as a result of a push on Indochina, see Tsunoda 1980, 255–58.

the European powers distracted by the destruction back home, Japan imposed new demands on China, increased its hold on Manchuria, and occupied parts of Siberia. Through the 1920s, however, we see that trade expectations theory does a superior job of explaining the cautiousness of Japanese decision makers in the face of growing Chinese nationalism and the rise of Chiang. Confronted with opportunities to exploit upheavals in east-central China in 1926–27, Tokyo imitated the policies of the other great powers and stayed on the defensive. When an chance arose to effect a coup in Manchuria in 1928, the central leadership in Tokyo held local military hawks back from any precipitous action. Concern that hard-line policies might cause a trade-security spiral undermining Japan's economic security nicely explains the prudent policies of this time.[24]

A distinct turn in Japanese foreign policy only came after the onset of the Great Depression in 1929, and subsequent moves by economic empires such as the United States and Britain toward closed economic spheres. Through the 1930s, beginning with the coup in Manchuria and continuing with efforts to exert more direct influence in northern China, Japan had more reason to squelch any threats to its economic position in Northeast Asia and less reason to worry about Western diplomatic and economic retaliation. With their focus still on the rise of Russia, Japanese leaders could not afford a severing of economic ties with Southeast Asia through British-US naval blockades. Hence, they continued to allow Western trade with Manchuria, and made sure, even after the outbreak of war with China in 1937, not to destroy foreign access to Chinese markets.[25] Preparation for preventive war against the Soviet Union was the number one priority. Keeping the Western great powers trading was thus a critical element of the five-year plan of 1936–41. Britain, France, and the United States, after all, had important colonial holdings in Southeast Asia, and as such, could deny Japan the raw materials needed for the buildup against Russia.

The deepest fall in Japanese trade expectations began only after 1939 with Washington's ending of the US-Japanese trade treaty and its increasingly severe restrictions on raw material exports from the United States— and with US encouragement, from the British and Dutch empires. It was these actions—as opposed to any domestically driven animus toward the United States—that shifted Tokyo toward the idea that Japan might have to initiate war south and not just north against the Soviet Union. War with the United States, just like the war with China in 1937, was always

---

[24] Commercial liberalism gets the correlation right, but cannot account for the security-driven logic behind Japanese thinking.

[25] The Sino-Japanese War itself, as we have seen, could not be explained by any of the main theories in this book.

an undesired sideshow to the main event: the reduction of Russian power in the Far East along with the protection of Japan's economic and strategic flank. Yet as we will see in the next chapter, US leaders were not going to allow Japan to repeat its 1904 attack on Russia, at least not in the midst of a European war that might allow Nazi Germany to take over most of Eurasia. President Roosevelt and Secretary of State Hull would try to convince Japan, in exchange for raw materials and help getting out of China, not to go north against the United States' vulnerable Soviet ally. Yet if talks failed to secure Tokyo's promise of good behavior in the entire Pacific region, a war south would have to be accepted. It is to these final negotiations of 1941 and their ultimate failure to avoid war that I will now turn.

CHAPTER FIVE

The Russian Problem and the Onset of the Pacific War, March–December 1941

THE PREVIOUS TWO CHAPTERS have shown just how important the rise of Russian power was to Japanese leaders of all stripes from 1895 to 1940. Chapter 4 in particular discussed Tokyo's preparations after 1935 for an all-out war with Russia, and how those plans got diverted by an undesired war with China. This chapter will focus on the nine months leading up to the attack on the United States on December 7, 1941. The puzzle is a simple one: Why did Japanese officials, despite their obsession with reducing Russian strength and recognition of the unlikelihood of winning any war with the United States, decide to take on the US giant rather than find a negotiated peace that would have avoided a costly and risky war? This riddle becomes even more profound once we realize just how earnestly both sides sought a peaceful way out. On three separate occasions—in early June, early September, and late November 1941—Tokyo and Washington almost came to an agreement that would have maintained the peace. Yet something kept getting in the way. What was this something, and why did it prove so intractable?[1]

For pretty well every international relations theorist who has studied this question, the primary obstacle to peace was Japan's unwillingness to leave China and what this said about Tokyo's larger obsession with the building of a regional coprosperity sphere. This view nicely aligns with the commercial liberal argument, insofar as domestic and psychological pathologies within the Japanese state can be said to have been unleashed during a period of reduced bilateral commerce, especially after 1939 and the imposition of increasingly severe US trade restrictions.[2]

As this chapter demonstrates, this contention is almost certainly wrong. For one thing, right from the start of talks in March–April 1941,

---

[1] This case represents, perhaps more than any other, a direct challenge to a fundamental premise of the bargaining model of war: that states fall into war when they lack information about the other's power and resolve (Fearon 1995; see also chapter 1). As we will see, both US and Japanese leaders were fully aware of their adversary's capabilities as well as willingness to fight, and yet war still occurred in spite of their best diplomatic efforts.

[2] On the supposed irrationality of Japanese decision making, see especially Snyder 1991; Kupchan 1994; Taliaferro 2005.

the US government was aware that Japan did want out of China and that it desperately sought Washington's help in finding a face-saving deal with Chiang. In return for US help, Roosevelt and Hull wanted one thing above all: a Japanese promise not to start a war somewhere else in the Pacific region, either against the United States and Britain in the south or the Soviet Union in the north. The primary objective of US policy was to defeat Hitler in Europe, and Roosevelt and Hull did not want Japan opening a second front in the Pacific should the United States enter the war against Germany. Thus Washington kept pushing Tokyo to agree to ignore its alliance obligations with Hitler, even if the United States was seen as the initiator of war against Germany. More broadly, and especially after Germany attacked the Soviet Union in June 1941, Roosevelt and Hull wanted Tokyo to commit to not attacking the north in support of Hitler's eastern campaign. After June 22, it was this latter requirement that became the key sticking point in all the negotiations. Tokyo wanted to maintain the option of going north if the Soviets were about to be defeated by Germany. The Japanese leadership therefore could not agree to Washington's final condition for peace, even if this meant the continuation of harsh economic sanctions against Japan.

As this chapter reveals, the traditional argument suffers from a profound irony. The United States had to worry that Japan would indeed get out of China, perhaps with US help, and that hundreds of thousands of battle-hardened Japanese troops would then be redeployed to the Siberian front for an attack on Russia. If this happened and Stalin was forced to fight a two-front war, the Soviet Union might lose its war with Germany. This would leave Hitler in a commanding position in Eurasia—the worst of all outcomes. Soviet survival, in short, was critical to Roosevelt's whole war plan, and the Japanese could not be allowed to interfere with it. Keeping Japan bogged down in China, as the US leadership well understood, directly served US interests. Roosevelt and Hull were willing to help Japan exit China only on one condition: that Tokyo make a credible commitment to not going north or south. In the end, it was Japan's unwillingness to commit to not attacking Russia—rather than any reluctance to leave China per se—that got in the way of a deal to avert war.

From a theoretical standpoint, this chapter supports the assertion from chapter 1 that third-party concerns can cause less dependent states to restrict trade flows with more dependent states, driving the latter into hard-line behavior and war. In this case, the highly dependent Japanese would have preferred to avoid a war with the United States. But this was only because Tokyo's main priority was to launch a decisive preventive war against Russia. From 1938 to early 1941, Roosevelt used trade sanctions on military equipment, iron ore, and aviation fuel to restrict the growth of Japanese military power without directly provoking Tokyo into a war. He was well aware that going directly after Japan's oil supply might push Japanese leaders into the ultimate act, and he wanted to be able to focus on the European war without the bother of a Pacific conflict. The sanctions gave Washington leverage: if Tokyo would commit to not redeploying forces in China for war against either Russia or the United States, Roosevelt and Hull in return would mediate with Chiang to help Japan get out of China, and would relax the economic restrictions. After Hitler's attack on the Soviet Union in June, however, the priority was to interfere with Japan's buildup against Russia and draw Japanese military resources south. This would allow Stalin to transfer the bulk of his crack Siberian forces to the German-Soviet front. The complete oil embargo of July 1941 against Japan was thus part and parcel of a larger strategy to help Russia avoid a two-front war, even as it gave Washington additional leverage in the negotiations. As I show, the traditional view—that Roosevelt was unaware of the plan to impose a total oil embargo and, due to bureaucratic momentum, could not reverse it once he found out—is a misinterpretation of the evidence. Roosevelt was intimately involved in the planning and fully informed of what was in fact an ingenious strategy to enhance Washington's flexibility in its subsequent dealings with Tokyo.

Ultimately, then, it was Washington's unwillingness to relax devastating economic sanctions that drove Tokyo to initiate a war south against the United States instead of north, as the Japanese preferred. Highly pessimistic trade expectations combined with extreme dependence on raw materials pushed Japan into war on December 7, 1941. Yet the US reluctance to make a deal reflects Roosevelt and Hull's keen sense that such a deal would send Japan north against the only US ally that stood a chance of reversing Hitler's bid for Eurasian hegemony. The United States would have preferred a deal committing Tokyo to peace both north and south. But if it could not get that—and Japanese leaders continually refused to promise not to go north—then a policy of oil sanctions drawing Japan south was preferred to a deal that left the United States out of a Pacific conflict, but only at the cost of having Japan attack United States' most important ally and key to the eventual defeat of Nazi Germany. In short, Roosevelt and Hull were forced to choose the lesser of two evils to prevent Japan from going north. And because they did, the Japanese, in the face of such pessimistic trade expectations, had to attack south to avoid economic collapse.

In what follows, we will see that neither the liberal nor realist perspective on trade and conflict is able to explain the failure of diplomacy along with the outbreak of war. The liberal focus on the pathologies unleashed as trade falls can explain neither Tokyo's effort to get out of China through US-mediated diplomacy nor its effort to avoid war with Washington in 1941. It also cannot explain the almost exclusively security-driven discussions within the Japanese state for the year before the war. Economic realism captures the strong feelings of vulnerability caused by raw material dependence that were shared by essentially all Japanese political and military elites. But it cannot capture the ups and downs of US-Japanese diplomacy in 1941, nor why Tokyo would try so hard to avert a war. As will become apparent, the fluctuations in relations over 1941 directly reflected Japanese perceptions of Washington's willingness to relax its economic sanctions. It was only after the clear failure of negotiations in November 1941 that Japanese trade expectations became so pessimistic that war seemed the only logical way out.

The chapter proceeds as follows. I begin with a look at US-Japanese talks in spring 1941. For those who see Japan's "unwillingness" to exit China as the underlying cause of the Pacific War, there is a surprise. Not only did Tokyo and Washington come close to an agreement that would have kept the peace but the United States also was prepared to sacrifice Chinese interests in the process. To get Tokyo to commit to not assisting Germany should the United States enter the European war, Washington was willing to help it negotiate a deal with the KMT that would have allowed Japan to hold on to Manchuria and maintain Japanese troops in northern Chinese provinces. In the second section, I explore why the US-Japanese agreement fell apart in late June 1941. After Germany invaded Russia on June 22, the United States feared that Tokyo would attack Siberia, knocking Russia out of the war. No agreement that might aid this attack could be allowed.

In the third section, I examine Roosevelt and Hull's willingness to restart talks with Tokyo in late August and their subsequent suspension of the talks in early September. This odd behavior is best explained by the successes of Germany's renewed offensive against Stalin coupled with the worry that Japan would use a peace with the United States and restoration of trade to facilitate its long-desired attack on Russia. The last two sections discuss the last three months of peace and aborted final round of negotiations in late November 1941. I show that US officials were highly aware that Japan's desperate economic situation, caused by the American oil embargo, was driving Tokyo into war. The key puzzle here is why Roosevelt and Hull would pursue a modus vivendi in late November, and then decide on November 26 to, in Hull's words, kick the whole thing over. The answer is not, as traditionalists would have it, that the United States received word that China objected to any deal compromising its fight with Japan. The answer is much simpler and more consistent with everything that had transpired over the previous six months. New information had arrived late on November 25 showing that the Soviets were on the ropes and Moscow might fall. Roosevelt and Hull were compelled to end negotiations in order to force Japan south, allowing the Soviets to avoid a two-front war. Only this action would give the Allies a fighting chance to save the world from Nazism.

THE FIRST ROUND OF NEGOTIATIONS, MARCH–JUNE 1941

The Japanese nation entered 1941 with a number of unsettled issues, including the nature and timing of any further advance south. The army was pushing for additional moves against the French and Dutch colonies, despite recognizing that a conflict with United States would hurt efforts to end the China Incident and develop an offensive capability against Russia. The navy and Planning Board were still hoping for a peaceful penetration of Southeast Asia. The Planning Board's pessimistic assessments through summer and fall 1940 had shown that Japan's already-severe economic difficulties would get immeasurably worse should Washington block all oil sales, as it might well do if it saw its policy failing to deter Tokyo (Barnhart 1987, 174). Japan, however, now found itself in a corner from which there seemed little way out. The China quagmire and Russian war preparations combined with increased trade restrictions had left the country without sufficient resources to either end the war with Chiang on reasonable terms or match the Soviets' massive industrial and military buildup. And yet to coerce the French and Dutch, and perhaps even the British, to join Japan's economic sphere would only cause Washington to increase sanctions or counterattack, leading to a war of attrition that Japan was unlikely to win.[3] Meanwhile, after imposing an embargo on scrap iron and aviation fuel in July 1940, the Roosevelt administration kept adding new materials to the list of restricted goods every month. By early 1941, only oil was still off the list. And this was only because Roosevelt rightly feared that oil sanctions would provoke an attack on the Dutch East Indies, given that Japan still needed the United States for 80 percent of its general oil needs and 90 percent of its gasoline (Heinrichs 1988, 7, 10–11).

By early 1941, there seemed to be only one way out of the predicament, and only one way to preserve access to raw materials and still protect Japan's security in the core region of Northeast Asia. And that was to sign a deal with Washington that would achieve two simultaneous objectives: the ending of the China Incident through US pressure on Chiang, and the reestablishment of a US-Japanese economic relationship that would end US sanctions. This solution had obvious appeal, since by re-creating the pre-1937 status quo, it would allow Japan to refocus attention on the 1936 total-war plans for the north. In late 1940 and early 1941, the outlines for a deal began to gain acceptance among key ministers and officials. The question was how to implement it in a way that did not reveal Japan's strong need to get out of southern China. If

---

[3]On the navy's pessimism regarding its chances of winning a war with the United States, see Tsunoda 1980, 258–59.

Washington felt it had a powerful bargaining position, Tokyo would have trouble securing a critical requirement for the peace, one that Konoe had stated in his 1938 New Order speech: the continued presence of Japanese troops in northern China, especially in the Inner Mongolian provinces of Suiyuan and Chahar. Troops in these areas were essential to the protection of Manchuria against Soviet forces in Mongolia, as the 1939 battle of Nomonhan made even clearer than before.[4]

Fortunately, Roosevelt and Hull were willing to talk. Since 1939 the two men had one obsession, and that was the destruction of Hitler's Germany. In 1940–41, Roosevelt was desperately trying to keep Britain in the war through economic and military aid. He was also more than willing to place US ships in harm's way in the Atlantic, hoping that a clash with Germany would bring the United States into the European war. The last thing in the world he needed was a war in the Far East. Thus when talk of a peace deal with Japan started to emerge in early 1941, Roosevelt and Hull were indeed interested. And as we will see, their bargaining behavior in the first half of 1941 was purely geopolitical in nature. They were more than willing to overlook moral issues such as the stationing of Japanese troops in northern China as long as Japan met one key demand: the United States be allowed unimpeded entry into the European war.

The Japanese government used two routes to send peace feelers. One was through Foreign Minister Matsuoka Yosuke, who sent signals in March and April 1941 that he was interested in having Washington mediate a peace between Japan and China (Tsunoda 1994, 13–14). The second, more indirect path was through a Japanese banker, Ikawa Tadao, who had ties to both Prime Minister Konoe and the White House. The Japanese army leadership took a keen interest in the venture. It authorized a staff officer, Colonel Iwakuro Hideo, to join Ikawa in Washington to facilitate negotiations and ensure army desires were well represented. Both of the two routes would be overseen by the new ambassador to Washington, Nomura Kichisaburo. The choice of Nomura was an important one, since it signaled Tokyo's willingness to make a new start. Nomura was well known for his anti-Axis leanings and had shown a strong interest in better US-Japanese relations during his time as foreign minister in 1939. Moreover, as a former admiral, Nomura would give the navy a de facto representative at the table to complement Iwakuro's presence. When Konoe through Nomura and Iwakuro offered proposals, the United States could assume that both civilian and military officials were on board back in Tokyo.

The second diplomatic path proved more effective than the first. On April 9, 1941, Ikawa presented a "Draft Understanding" to Hull detailing

[4]See Coox 1985; Montgomery 1987; Duus, Meyers, and Peattie 1989.

Japan's demands but noting its potential concessions. Hull and Roosevelt had used a March meeting with Nomura to signal their two primary concerns: Japan's continued adherence to the Tripartite Pact and its lack of economic openness regarding China (*FRUSJ*, 2:396–98). So when Hull saw the initial draft on April 9, there was much in it that was pleasing, at least as a first step. Japan pledged that the Tripartite Pact was defensive only; it guaranteed that Japanese activities in the "Southwestern Pacific" would be "carried on by peaceful means, without resorting to arms"; and it noted the desire to sign a new treaty of commerce. Japan in return wanted Roosevelt to use his office to convince Chiang to "negotiate peace with Japan." This peace, the draft stated, would include the withdrawal of Japanese troops from Chinese territory and resumption of the open door. But it would also include "recognition of Manchukuo," presumably by both Chiang and the United States (ibid., 2:398–402).

When Hull and Nomura met on April 16 to open what would become two months of intense negotiations, Hull told Nomura that the draft contained "numerous proposals with which my Government could readily agree." Hull laid out four broad principles to guide the talks: respect for territorial integrity; noninterference in internal affairs; support for the principle of equality, including equality of commercial opportunity; and nondisturbance of the status quo except by peaceful means. The Japanese ambassador noted that point four might interfere with Japan's position in Manchuria. Hull quickly made a surprising concession, stating that "this status quo point would not . . . affect 'Manchukuo,' but was intended to [apply] to the future [after] adoption of a general settlement" (ibid., 2:406–9). This was a highly significant signal. It showed that the United States was not going to let the legal or moral status of Manchuria—an area almost one-fifth the size of China—get in the way of a peace deal. In all subsequent drafts of the agreement over the next two months, the independent status of "Manchukuo" was affirmed by both sides, taking this issue off the table. Already at this early stage in the talks we see that Roosevelt and Hull were ready to operate as clearheaded geopoliticians rather than starry-eyed idealists. But this should come as no surprise: Manchuria had never impeded US-Japanese negotiations since Teddy Roosevelt had helped Japan secure its foothold there some four decades before.

As the talks proceeded through May and into early June, the US side kept reiterating three objectives. The first was advanced the hardest: Japan must distance itself from Germany. It must make a statement indicating that if the United States got into a war with Germany, even as the result of an offensive move by Washington, Japan would not invoke the defensive clause at the heart of the Tripartite Pact and respond with an attack on US possessions. The second objective was Japan's agreement to refrain from any further aggressive acts in the region after a US-mediated

China-Japan peace was arranged. The third aim was the assurance by Japan that it would reinstate the open door in China.[5]

Oddly missing from the list of demands, at least from the perspective of the traditional argument for why negotiations ended in late November 1941, is any US insistence that Japan put an end to the Sino-Japanese War and exit from China. This contention sees China as the key sticking point that led to the breakdown of talks and start of war: the United States wanted Japan to leave China before oil and other raw material exports would be reinstated, and Japan kept refusing. Yet in the April to mid-June negotiations, at a time when Washington should have been pushing its maximalist position, Roosevelt and Hull made no such demand. This was for one simple reason—a point that, once seen, completely alters one's view of the causes of the Pacific War. The reason was this: getting Japan out of China was *Tokyo's* objective, not Washington's, and Roosevelt and Hull were using this as leverage to achieve their own ends.

Indeed, from a larger geopolitical standpoint, the United States had a distinct interest in keeping Japan bogged down in China. This would keep Japan from causing havoc elsewhere, either north against the Soviet Union or south against Britain and the United States. As Hull's senior adviser Hornbeck told him on April 7, one must remember that the Sino-Japanese conflict "had become part of a world conflict." Hence,

> so long as and while Japan remains a member of the Tripartite Alliance, it would not be in the interest of the United States or in the interest of Great Britain that the Japanese-Chinese hostilities be brought to an end by any process which leaves Japan's military machine undefeated [and] intact. . . . The world situation being what it is . . . Japan's present involvement in China is to the advantage of the United States and Great Britain. (quoted in Tsunoda 1994, 51–52)

It was Tokyo that had approached Washington for help in ending the Sino-Japanese War. Through the April–June negotiations we therefore see Japan pleading for Hull's guarantee that he and Roosevelt will actively push Chiang to make peace. The only two things that Tokyo sought, in fact, were this guarantee along with reinstated US trade. The US negotiators, understanding this, held back their assurances on these two items as bait to lure Japan into an agreement on the three US demands. This back-and-forth dynamic permeated almost every discussion held over these crucial three months (see *FRUSJ*, 2:passim). As we will see, US leaders were keenly aware through all three sets of talks before Pearl Harbor that ending the Sino-Japanese War would aid Japan at the expense of US interests.

[5] For the discussions between May 2 and June 17, see *FRUSJ*, 2:411–83.

The larger point being made is straightforward, but crucial to any rethinking of the Pacific War. Roosevelt and Hull did not care about China per se. What they cared about were Foreign Minister Matsuoka's repeated statements that Japan would not relinquish its commitments to the Tripartite Pact. As the price for ending the Sino-Japanese War and allowing Japan to deploy its divisions elsewhere, Roosevelt and Hull wanted assurances that Japan would not use its renewed strength for attacks elsewhere in the Pacific, exploit China's postwar economy for its own purposes, and above all, interfere in US effort to destroy Nazism. During the first three months of conversations, the US side expressed no outrage at the immorality of Japan's war, and never demanded that Japan leave China on moral or ideological grounds. Such ideological language would be employed only after June 22 (and especially November 26), when the talks fell apart. Through the whole first round of negotiations, the United States operated in the realm of pure realpolitik. It wanted a deal binding Japan to good behavior after a Sino-Japanese peace, and made it clear that it would offer US help as an honest broker only if Japan made a credible promise to this effect.

There is not the space to discuss the details of this first round of talks, but a brief review of the efforts in May and June to revise the draft understanding will capture the essence. On May 12, Nomura presented a revised draft stating that Japan was still committed to its Tripartite Pact obligations. When Hull and Nomura met two days later, the main issue was the question of the United States' "self-defense" against Hitler. On May 16, they met again when the US side presented its suggestions for a revision of the draft understanding. In reviewing the thinking behind these suggestions, Hull once again reinforced that Washington and Tokyo had to work out what the United States would be allowed to do against Nazism for its own security. Hitler's plan of "unlimited conquest" required states to take "appropriate measures of self-protection and self-defense." This meant that the United States might indeed have to become involved in the European war "even if its territory was not attacked." Hull handed Nomura a long annex of the secretary's recent public statements about the US need to fight Germany to defend the hemisphere.

Nomura got the message. He responded that while Japan desired only peaceful relations, it might still have to carry out its obligations under the Axis alliance (i.e., if the United States initiated war against Germany). Nomura then turned to Japan's need for US mediation to end the China war. Hull's draft suggestions had indicated that Washington might play this role should a broader deal be signed, so he was able to reassure Nomura on this point (ibid., 2:420–34).

When Hull met Nomura on May 20, there was an air of optimism. The ambassador assured him that there was strong support for the revised draft from the army, navy, foreign ministry, and Hirohito. Aware that Nomura was talking about the Japanese version of the draft, Hull asked Nomura about two details that concerned him: the idea that China and Japan after a peace would build a "joint defense against Communism," and the statement that some Japanese troops would remain "in certain parts of Chinese territory" (ibid., 2:434–36).

As he went on, it became apparent that Hull was concerned not because he feared Japan might keep troops in northern China but rather because explicit statements to that effect might hurt the United States' diplomatic position and global image. Hull stressed that he was not discussing the merit of the two points; he was simply wondering whether Chiang would view them as problematic, making it more difficult for Washington to broker a peace. It would be embarrassing for the administration, he noted, to have Chiang reject US suggestions because these two points were explicitly written into a US-Japanese agreement. Maxwell Hamilton, head of the Far East Division and Hull's senior negotiating partner, subsequently added that the specific wording was important, since any agreement's chances for success depended on US public opinion and the administration's ability to counter critics.

In the subtle language of diplomacy, these comments represented a major concession. The United States had already acquiesced to Japan holding on to Manchuria. Hull and Hamilton were now indicating that the stationing of Japanese troops in northern China was not a deal breaker. If Tokyo wanted to bring it up with Chiang, fine. But it would be up to Japan and Chiang to decide the nature of China's postwar reality. All the US side wanted was language in the US-Japanese agreement hiding the fact that Japanese troops might indeed remain in the north. Hull told Nomura that he wondered whether it would be possible "to cover these two points under some broader provision, such as a provision which would call for special measures of protection for Japanese nationals and property interests against lawlessness in areas where special measures for safeguarding the rights and interests of nationals of third powers were necessary" (ibid., 2:434–36). In short, Washington would not challenge Japan's stationing of troops in the north. Knowing that Tokyo wanted to highlight its right to do so, however, Hull was suggesting vague language that would signal this right (under the cover of protecting citizens of third parties) without making it look like Washington had betrayed the Chinese.[6]

When they met the next day, Hull plunged back into the topic of Japanese troops in China. Once again his goal, far from trying to force Japan *out* of northern China (let alone Manchuria), was to accommodate Japanese wishes while protecting the administration's image. Using

[6]With Japan showing no signs of readying for war on Russia, Hull could make this concession without worrying about the impact on the European war.

sympathetic language designed to persuade, he suggested that Chiang's forces might work with Japanese troops to protect areas where "special arrangements" to safeguard third-party nationals were needed. In any schedule for the troops' departure, forces occupying the provinces of northern China could "come out last." A commission also could be established to study the problem of keeping order in these areas. In making such suggestions in the most diplomatic way possible, Hull was again signaling that he did not want the issue of Japanese forces in northern China to derail US-Japan talks (ibid., 2:437–39).

Negotiations that day went well. Hull reiterated that the central purpose of the talks was to guarantee a regional peace. A "mutually acceptable tentative formula" was agreed on that found its way into the subsequent US draft—namely, the principle that "the controlling policy underlying this understanding is peace in the Pacific area." Both sides pledged not just to maintain this peace but also that they had no "territorial designs in the area mentioned" (ibid., 438). This was a positive development. Back in Tokyo, though, the mercurial Japanese foreign minister threw a wrench into the works. On May 26–27, Hull received a flurry of reports from Grew and others that Matsuoka was again stating strongly that if Washington started a war with Germany, Japan would have to respond according to Article 3 of the Axis pact (see *FRUS* [1941], 4:224–38). When Hull met with Nomura on May 28, Matsuoka was the first topic of conversation. Given Matsuoka's many statements on Japan's obligations under the Tripartite Pact, Hull remarked, it was essential for Tokyo to clarify its real policy. After all, the United States might soon be drawn into the European war "through action in the line of self-defense."

Nomura tried to reassure Hull that Matsuoka's statements were designed for domestic consumption and the foreign minister sincerely desired peace with the United States. It would be difficult to eliminate draft language that talked about Japan's adherence to the pact, Nomura observed, since the Japanese government would then be in a difficult position vis-à-vis Germany and pro-Axis forces inside Japan. But his government "would make its own independent decision and would not be dictated to by Germany" regarding Japan's obligations under the alliance. Nomura was essentially asking Hull to go beyond the exact wording of the Axis document, and trust that Japan would look the other way should the United States and Germany fight (*FRUSJ*, 2:440–41).

At the meeting of May 28, Hull again broached the question of the withdrawal of Japanese troops from China, politely asking Nomura to "indicate what the Japanese Government had in mind." Nomura noted that the general withdrawal might take as much as two years. He then introduced a new element that must have taken Hull by surprise. Nomura explained that the evacuation "would not include troops retained in China under the provision of cooperative defense against communistic activities. He contemplated an arrangement being negotiated with China similar to the Boxer Protocol under which Japanese troops would be stationed for an indefinite period in north China and Inner Mongolia." For the first time, Nomura was stating explicitly that in any peace with China, Japan planned to keep forces in northern China for an undefined period. Had the nature of the Sino-Japanese peace been terribly important to Hull—as his outward behavior in late November 1941 might suggest that it was—the secretary should have ended all negotiations at that point. He did not. Instead, he simply commented that this might make a permanent friendship between China and Japan difficult. Continuing in the sympathetic mode used the week before, he even spoke of Washington's own recent past interventions in Latin America (!) and how the US "experience" there had shown that a policy of employing troops did not pay. The subsequent discussion made it clear that Hull's concerns revolved solely around the question of his role as broker should the Japanese seek to remain in northern China permanently (ibid., 2: 440–43).

That US leaders had no strong objections to Japanese forces staying in northern China and Manchuria—contrary to the traditional view that it was the fundamental divide that led to war in 1941—is confirmed by what followed over the next three weeks. On May 30, Hull sent Hamilton to meet with Iwakuro to clarify Japan's thinking regarding the maintenance of troops in northern China. Iwakuro told Hamilton that the troops were absolutely critical to Japan's effort to prevent the spread of Soviet Communism. Sketching a map of northern China, Manchuria, and Siberia, he indicated the specific Chinese provinces where Japan needed to keep forces to protect against the "the entry of communistic elements" from the Soviet puppet state of Mongolia. When asked how many troops would be stationed there, he replied one-fifth to one-tenth of the current number. When questioned about the length of their stay, Iwakuro responded that it would not be permanent but instead only long enough "[to protect] against communistic activities from external sources."

Despite these revelations, Hamilton pushed on with his agenda. He reiterated that the question of Japanese troops mattered only insofar as Washington had been asked to mediate a China-Japan peace. Hamilton asked Iwakuro whether it might be possible to "work out a formula" whereby the stationing of Japanese troops in China after a peace would not be mentioned in the US-Japanese agreement. He even offered one possible strategy for Tokyo to consider. The document could state that in any China-Japan peace, the evacuation of Japanese troops in the north could be "left to the last." Then Japan, "shortly before the due date of [the] completion of [the] evacuation," could propose to China that it consult "in regard to measures called for by any situation that might exist, including any situation [involving] communistic activities." The two sides bandied ideas back and forth on how to word such a delicate matter within the draft. With it getting late, Hamilton suggested that they leave the exact wording for now and work on it independently (ibid., 2:444–45).

The incredible nature of Hamilton's suggestion may not be fully evident at first glance. Here was Hull's second in command not only stating that Washington would accept language obscuring the issue as to when Japanese troops in northern China would leave, as significant as this concession was. He was actually giving the Japanese advice as to how they could use future concerns about "communistic activities" to skirt any commitments made to China regarding a fixed withdrawal date!

That Hamilton had Hull's full confidence when he made these suggestions is shown by the US revised draft of the agreement presented on May 31. In section 3, on "action toward a peaceful settlement between China and Japan," the US text for the first time formally accepted that Washington would approach Chiang to encourage him to make peace with Japan. In addition, the United States accepted most of the eight items from the Japanese draft of section 3. The two main changes made by Hull were important signals of the evolving US perspective. Item 6 on the withdrawal of Japanese forces from Chinese territory after a peace did add the phrase "as promptly as possible." Yet by saying nothing about a specific time frame, the United States was giving Japan flexibility on this question. This allowance was linked to a crucial change on item 2. Here, the United States reworked the Japanese draft, which had simply called for "joint defense against communism," to read:

> 2. (Cooperative defense against injurious communistic activities— including the stationing of Japanese troops in Chinese territory.) Subject to further discussion.

This was the first written confirmation that the US side would accept the possibility of Japanese troops staying in northern China under the guise of fighting Communism and protecting foreigners (including US citizens). In line with the Hamilton-Iwakuro talks, Hull was now agreeing to discuss the issue until a mutually agreeable wording or "formula" was found (see ibid., 2:446–51; cf. ibid., 2:422–23).[7]

Hull had a price for his concessions, however. The May 31 draft retained the annex that he had put forward on May 16 and knew was strongly opposed by the Japanese. This was the annex that provided long

---

[7] The United States also adjusted item 3 on economic cooperation to note the importance of commercial nondiscrimination, thereby reinforcing Washington's interest in open-door access to China.

excerpts from Hull's speeches on the need for US involvement in Europe for its own "self-preservation." The secretary again wanted it to be clear that any US entry into the war against Hitler should not be considered an offensive action, regardless of how Washington got involved. In section 2 on the "attitude of both governments toward the European war," he thus excised a paragraph from the Japanese draft stating that Japan's obligations under the Tripartite Pact remained in place. In a concession to Japanese sentiments, Hull kept Tokyo's line indicating that the purpose of the Tripartite Pact was defensive and designed to prevent the participation in the European war of nations not presently involved in it. But he immediately added, "Obviously, the provisions of the Pact do not apply to involvement through acts of self-defense." For the United States, the main objective was to keep the peace in the Pacific to allow Washington to focus on defeating Nazism. If China had be convinced to accept some Japanese troops on its soil to achieve this end, so be it (ibid., 2:446–51).

The negotiations in the first half of June went well. Japanese diplomats were able to assure Hull that Japan, notwithstanding recent statements by Matsuoka, did indeed accept the United States' right to self-defense, even if this meant a US entry into the European war (see ibid., 2:454–70). Japan's willingness to compromise showed in its revised draft agreement, dated June 8, but presented to the United States on June 9. The basic thrust of the US draft of May 31 was kept, with revisions confined largely to adjustments of language. US changes to the critical section 2 on attitudes toward the European war were allowed to stand, including the line that Washington's perspective on the war would be determined by considerations of "self-defense" (*FRUS* [1941], 4:256–59).[8]

The Japanese compromises seemed to do the trick. For the next two weeks, the talks went smoothly, revolving around the specific wording of what was now taken as the common baseline document: the US draft of May 31, as adjusted by Japan on June 8. There was still some discussion regarding the all-important question of Japan's commitment to the Tripartite Pact, but it was limited and moderate in tone. The focus was on more secondary issues, in particular the question of US access to China's economy after a Sino-Japanese peace. In their revised draft of June 15,

---

[8] The line "Obviously, the provisions of the Pact do not apply to involvement through acts of self-defense" was taken out, but Iwakuro carefully explained to the Americans that day that this was merely to avoid adverse public reaction at home, and that the US right of self-defense was so universally recognized that this line seemed superfluous (*FRUSJ*, 2:468–70). Sensitive to Japanese concerns, the US side did not hold up negotiations over this line, suggesting instead that Japan state that the purpose of the Tripartite Pact was defensive and designed to prevent the "unprovoked extension" of the European war (ibid., 2:478, 471–83; *FRUS* [1941], 4:260–74). Japan formally accepted this language on June 21, the day before the German attack on Russia (*FRUSJ*, 2:488).

the Japanese negotiators finally conceded that commerce in the Pacific region would conform to the principle of nondiscrimination—something Hull had been pushing for since March (*FRUSJ*, 2:472–76). Subsequent talks centered largely on the specifics of nondiscrimination in China, with the Japanese accepting that US trade could flow freely, but arguing that Japanese mining companies be given some preference due to the significance of raw materials to Japan's economy (ibid., 2:476–83). That the conversation could concentrate on such details reveals just how far the negotiations had come on the big issues that had dominated the early talks. The two countries seemed headed for a peace deal, and both negotiating teams knew it.[9]

THE BREAKDOWN OF NEGOTIATIONS AND THE SUMMER OF DISCONTENT

Everything fell apart with Germany's surprise invasion of the Soviet Union in late June. Both Washington and Tokyo had been aware for months of Germany's massive buildup on the Soviet border. Until the invasion began, however, US opinion was divided as to whether Hitler was preparing for war or only trying to coerce Stalin into additional concessions. Germany's war with Britain, after all, was still ongoing. But once the German attack on Russia began in earnest on the morning of June 22, US officials agreed that this single act changed everything. If Germany were to beat the Soviet Union and push it back behind the Urals, as many observers anticipated, then Germany would be the first empire to truly dominate the Eurasian landmass.[10] It would then be extremely difficult to dislodge, even if Britain stayed in the war. From this position, Hitler could then mobilize for the destruction of his final main adversary, the United States (Tooze 2006).

Since the early spring, when reports of a possible German attack began to gain credence, Roosevelt and Stalin had begun to work on repairing US-Soviet relations (see Heinrichs 1988, 54–56). Yet the German invasion in June suddenly made the relationship between the two future superpowers the most important "axis" in the world. For the next six months, the allied effort to prevent a Soviet collapse would be Roosevelt and Hull's number one preoccupation, with everything else seen through its lens. This would include the US relationship with Japan.

---

[9]Indeed, the very language of diplomacy had changed. Both sides by mid-June would talk in terms of "the present understanding" and "now pending" agreement, with US concerns centered mainly on whether hard-liners such as Matsuoka might try to undermine the emerging deal. See Nomura's diary, June 15 and 19, in *PWP*, 142–43.

[10]On the expectations that Germany would likely win, see Sherwood 1950, 304–5.

Roosevelt and his closest colleagues knew they had to act quickly if Russia were to survive. On July 24, the president publicly announced that Washington would do everything possible to provide aid to the Soviet Union. Two days later Sumner Welles, the acting secretary of state, told the Soviet ambassador that "any request" that Moscow might make for material assistance "would be given immediate attention." In the three days after the Soviet attack, Roosevelt unfroze $39 million in Soviet assets to facilitate purchases of US goods. By June 30, the Soviets had requested $1.8 billion in military equipment and industrial hardware (*FRUS* [1941], 1:769–70; Herring 1973, 9–10). The US problem in meeting these requests was a simple one, though: not only was the $7 billion allotted to the first lend-lease appropriation for Britain almost exhausted, but isolationists and anti-Communists in Congress opposed giving any material assistance to Soviet Russia. Roosevelt therefore worked behind the scenes to purchase Russian gold, giving Moscow the cash needed to buy US goods until he had secure a political deal on lend lease. He also agreed to send his closest adviser, Harry Hopkins, to Moscow by the end of July to assure Stalin that much more would be on the way.[11]

Yet Roosevelt also still had to deal with the possibility of war in the Pacific. This section will examine Japanese decision making through late spring and summer 1941 as the German-Soviet struggle began to dominate all events. Along the way, I will provide a window into the internal debates within the Japanese polity—debates that set Foreign Minister Matsuoka against the majority of the Japanese cabinet and military. This section will also show how Roosevelt and his officials sought to deal with growing information from various sources suggesting that Japan was gearing up for a war against the Soviet Union.

It must be reiterated that the vast majority of Japanese ministers and military officials had been keen to reach an agreement with Washington during the spring negotiations. Leaving southern China and reestablishing US trade were both essential for any future military move north. The main stumbling block, as the United States had gathered through decoding Japanese diplomatic transcripts (via the "Magic" program), was in fact Foreign Minister Matsuoka. Matsuoka was already well known as a strong supporter of the northern option, and had been instrumental in securing the Tripartite Pact back in September 1940. During thirteen intense Liaison Conferences between mid-April and mid-June 1941, called to coordinate civilian and military decision making, Matsuoka displayed a stubborn unwillingness to make any deal with Washington if it meant relaxing Japan's military obligations under the treaty. As the internal debates unfolded, it became clear that he did not oppose a US-Japanese agreement per se—after all, some form of agreement was essential to his

---

[11] Herring 1973, 10–11; Kimball 1991, 22–36; Sherwood 1950.

cherished goal of attacking the Soviet Union. He nevertheless believed that Japan could not fight Russia without Germany taking on the Soviets, and that Tokyo needed to maintain a good relationship with Hitler. Herein lay the tension. As Navy Minister Oikawa Koshiro pointedly told Matsuoka on April 22, if Japan made German acquiescence a precondition to any US-Japanese deal, Japan could not achieve the key purpose of such a deal: the ending of the Sino-Japanese War (*JDW*, 19–24).

In late May, word arrived that the Dutch East Indies would not likely extend a six-month trade agreement covering tin, rubber, and oil exports (ibid., 36–43). By the May 29 and June 11 meetings, when it seemed the Dutch would probably start cutting Japan off, Matsuoka advocated a strong stand. Army Chief of Staff Sugiyama countered that in the view of both the army and navy, confronting the Dutch East Indies would probably draw in Britain and the United States. As such, Japan should end the Dutch East Indies talks and accept whatever raw materials it could get (ibid., 43–51).

What these internal debates up to early June reveal is that the army and navy, far from seeking war in the south to satisfy organizational needs or out of some crazed paranoia, were responding rationally to developments as they arose. They were seeking to restrain their emotional foreign minister from taking steps that would automatically throw Japan into a war with the United States. For Japanese military and civilian officials, the overarching goal remained the securing of a deal with Washington to help end the China war and reinstate the raw material imports needed for the northern buildup. For all concerned, including Matsuoka, war with the United States was still an undesired last resort.

On June 25, three days after Germany's invasion, the first Liaison Conference on the implications of the German-Russian war was held. Another split opened up between Matsuoka and the military, this time over whether to strike the Soviets right away or wait. Matsuoka argued that with Soviet Siberian troops being sent west, Japan should strike north immediately. Army and navy leaders both opposed this, asserting that any decision depended on conditions in China, the north, and the south, and if Japan attacked the Soviet Union prematurely, "the United States will enter the war" (ibid., 56–60). In five follow-up meetings over the next six days, it was agreed that Japan did not have the capability to go both north and south simultaneously, and so must prepare for both options and see how the situation develops. A firm decision to attack Russia, as Prime Minister Konoe summarized on June 30, could be made only after consideration of the "the world situation," meaning, most important, the state of talks with Washington (ibid., 60–75). Since these talks might still bear fruit, making a move north that much easier, Japanese leaders recognized the value of waiting.

An Imperial Conference was held on July 2 to secure Emperor Hiro-hito's approval of a document titled "Outline of National Politics in View of the Changing Situation"—in view, that is, of the German attack on Russia. Reflecting the consensus of the extended cabinet, the document noted that Japan would not immediately enter the German-Soviet war but instead continue its buildup against Russia while pursuing negotiations with the United States. Then, "if the German-Soviet war should develop to the advantage of our Empire," Japan would use armed force to "settle the Northern Question." As this buildup was going on, Japan would push into southern Indochina, to both secure rubber and tin for the northern operation as well as prepare for a strike that might be needed against the Dutch East Indies. In carrying out this southern advance, the document underscored, Japan would not be deterred by the possibility of war with Britain and the United States, even if, as Navy Chief of Staff Nagano Osami told the gathering, this was not the desired outcome.

It was up to Privy Council President Hara Yoshimichi to speak on Hirohito's behalf (by Japanese tradition, the emperor, being "above" poli-tics, did not speak at such conferences). From Hara's words, it was appar-ent that Hirohito was concerned about a war with the United States and wanted to make sure the focus was kept on the Russian problem. The Ger-man war with the Soviets had given Japan the chance of a lifetime: "Since the Soviet Union is promoting Communism all over the world, we will have to attack her sooner or later. Since we are now engaged in the China Incident, I feel that we cannot attack the Soviet Union as easily as we would wish. Nevertheless, I believe that we should attack the Soviet Union when it seems opportune to do so" (ibid., 77–90). Such a stance was per-fectly consistent with Hirohito's anti-Soviet views since the mid-1920s. And as Bix (2000) has shown, he took his role as the supreme commander of Japan's military seriously. So when Hara spoke again near the end of the meeting and invoked "the Supreme Command," it was evident to all that Hirohito knew exactly the direction he wanted to see Japan take:

> I think that the Government and the Supreme Command are in agree-ment on this point: that is, we will try our best to avoid a clash with Great Britain and the United States. I believe that Japan should avoid taking belligerent action against the United States, at least on this oc-casion. Also, I would ask the Government and the Supreme Command to attack the Soviet Union as soon as possible. The Soviet Union must be destroyed, so I hope that you will make preparations to hasten the commencement of hostilities. I cannot help but hope that this policy will be put in to effect as soon as it is decided.

War Minister Tojo Hideki immediately jumped in to say that he shared Hara's (i.e., the emperor's) opinion, although the continuing war with China was still a constraint. Army Chief of Staff Sugiyama then spoke of the need, given Soviet current superiority, to build up the army in Manchuria. Yet with Soviet forces being shipped westward and Germany doing so well against the Red Army, he argued, Japan could be ready for war against Russia in as little as two months. Until then, Japan should continue to negotiate with the United States and Britain. The navy signaled its consent (as Sugiyama remarked) by remaining silent. When the conference ended, the note taker recorded that "the Emperor seemed to be extremely satisfied" (*JDW*, 77–90). This was not surprising. Hirohito now had both military and civilian officials on board for his primary objective, the single overarching objective of Japanese leaders for four decades: the destruction of Russian power in the Far East. Within days, the army moved to mobilize 850,000 men and an unprecedented 800,000 tons of materiel to Manchuria by the end of July (Barnhart 1987, 213).[12]

Back in Washington, Roosevelt was made aware through Grew's reports and the Magic transcripts that the Japanese government was intensely debating whether to go north or south. On July 1, Roosevelt wrote Petroleum Coordinator Harold Ickes to say that the question of ending oil exports was a delicate one, given information he had received on Japan's political situation. Ickes had been arguing that all oil exports to Japan should be ended given severe US gas shortages. Roosevelt, however, had known for over a year that an oil cutoff would likely lead Japan to strike south, and he needed peace in Asia to focus on the war in Europe. He thus told Ickes,

> I think it will interest you to know that [the Japanese] are having a real drag-down and knock-out fight amongst themselves and have been for the past week—trying to decide which way they are going to jump—attack Russia, attack the South Seas (thus throwing in their lot definitely with Germany) or whether they will sit on the fence and be more friendly with us. No one knows what the decision will be but, as you know, it is terribly important for the control of the Atlantic for us to help to keep peace in the Pacific. I simply have not got enough Navy to go round—and every little episode in the Pacific means fewer ships in the Atlantic. (*FDRPL*, 1173–74)

As will become increasingly clear, by "peace in the Pacific" Roosevelt meant peace in the whole Pacific region, north and south. Already by late June, Roosevelt and Hull had shifted gears in order to deter a Japanese attack against Russia as well as the south. On June 22, the day of

---

[12] Because of the tension southward, not all these troops and materiel would arrive in Manchuria.

the German attack, Hull met with Nomura and came right to the point. He wanted to know whether "Matsuoka's intention was . . . to have [Washington] subject China to pressure to come to an agreement with Japan," so that Japan was then "free to take action with reference to the European war." This was a thinly veiled reference to a possible Japanese attack northward to support Germany's invasion of Russia, justified by the "defensive" clauses of the Tripartite Pact. Nomura cagily replied that Japan did not want war with the United States, but could not "bind itself in advance with regard to some future eventuality" (*FRUSJ*, 2:492–94).

That Roosevelt and Hull along with their subordinates were worried about a Japanese move north is demonstrated by their behavior after June 22. On June 23, Hamilton wrote a memorandum for Hull noting that some in Tokyo might argue that Germany's attack gave Japan the freedom to move south, but others will urge "that this is Japan's opportunity to remove the Russian menace to Japan and that Japan should attack Russia." Japanese thinking would follow the second line, not the first, he maintained. Thus while the main purpose of the proposed US-Japan agreement was to "preserve the peace in the entire Pacific area," Washington might not be able to deter Japan from going north. The US problem was simple but profound. Japanese leaders understood that going south against British and Dutch holdings would lead to war with the United States, but they didn't believe the United States would respond to an attack on Russia. Tokyo would therefore be eager for a peace deal with Washington. Yet because such a deal would increase Japan's ability to go north, Hamilton concluded, the United States had less desire for such an agreement (*FRUS* [1941], 4:276–77).

A lengthy paper written for Hamilton and Hull that day by subordinate Max Schmidt supported Hamilton's contentions. Titled "The Effects on Japan of the Present War between Germany and Russia," it claimed that Japanese leaders "cannot be expected to forget what they have for many years considered as the Russian dagger pointed at the heart of Japan." While Japan might still decide to go south, any further military adventures were "far more likely . . . to be in the direction of action against Russia" (ibid., 4:983–84). Two days later, another subordinate produced a report reinforcing these concerns. German successes on the battlefield would be "an impellant to Japan to move against Siberia." This posed a huge problem, since it would leave the Soviets fighting a two-front war that would shorten the period they could resist the Nazis. To help defeat Hitler, Washington should try to "immobilize Japan as regards an attack upon Siberia and as regards an attack against Singapore or the Dutch East Indies." To achieve this, the report offered a fateful recommendation: "[increase] restrictions upon the export of petroleum products to Japan," while freezing Japanese assets (ibid., 4:278–80).

On July 2, Willys Peck, from Hamilton's Division of Far Eastern Affairs, provided a more Machiavellian set of ideas. Peck also believed that given Hitler's recent successes, it was "on the whole more probable that Japan will decide to invade Siberia than continue her southern expansion." Under these circumstances, "one fact stands out as indisputable," namely, that it was

> more than ever urgent that China's resistance to Japan shall be intensified [and] to the end that more and more of Japan's armed striking force shall be immobilized and dissipated in the "China Incident." . . . The advantage of this situation to the United States seems clear. By encouraging China to ever greater efforts against Japan, by dragging Japan into deeper and deeper involvement in the China hostilities, the United States can work powerfully toward the achievement of some of her principal objectives, among them the maintenance of the status quo in the Far East, the preservation of our rubber and tin supplies, [the] aiding of Russia against Germany, and the aiding of Britain.

Peck's recommended policy of sending China more lend-lease aid was straightforward realpolitik: in helping the Chinese achieve their ends, he contended, "we shall be taking the most effective course open to us of achieving our own ends" (ibid., 4:288–89). Peck's arguments aligned with ideas that Hornbeck had been championing since March. So as Hull's senior adviser on political relations, Hornbeck felt free to pen a note next to Peck's line about Japan being more likely to go north than south. He wrote: "Contingent on German success or lack of success in Russia" (ibid., 4:288n62). Hornbeck was making sure Hull and Roosevelt recognized that Japan's desire to attack Russia would rise should Germany appear to be winning, and US policy would have to adjust accordingly to deter a move north. As we will see, Hull and Roosevelt well understood this concern.

Given all these dire analyses, it is not surprising that US diplomacy took a decidedly hard-line turn after June 22. We have already seen that Hull that day signaled his worry to Nomura about Japan using a peace with China to take action elsewhere. On June 27, Welles instructed Grew in Tokyo to tell Japanese leaders that it was the fixed policy of the US government "to aid Great Britain and other nations" in their fight against Hitler. With Britain and Russia the only two powers left against Germany, this was an obvious reference to Roosevelt's new commitment (announced three days earlier) to do everything possible to help the Soviet Union, including supplying aid through Vladivostok. Washington was now aligned with Moscow, and Japan must know this fact (*FRUS* [1941], 4:987).

Roosevelt and his associates attempted to deter Japan from going north in other important ways. Probably the most explicit was Welles's follow-up telegram to Grew on July 4. Grew was instructed to give Konoe a message sent at "the specific request of the President." It read:

> The Government of the United States is receiving reports . . . that the Government of Japan had decided to embark upon hostilities against the Soviet Union. As the Government of Japan is aware, the Government of the United States had earnestly desired to see peace maintained and preserved in the Pacific area. . . . It goes without saying that embarkation by Japan [upon such] a course of military aggression and conquest would render illusory the hope which this Government has cherished and which it understood the Government of Japan shared [namely,] that [the] peace of the Pacific might not be further upset.

The message concluded with the hope that the reports were not based on fact, and that Washington would deeply appreciate Konoe's assurance to that effect (ibid., 4:994–95).

This message to Konoe came as close as Roosevelt dared, given isolationist and anti-Communist sentiment in Congress, to an explicit deterrent commitment to Russia. Not surprisingly, it arrived only two days after the Imperial Conference that had decided to prepare for a northern advance within two months, should conditions permit. Roosevelt and Hull had learned of the conference through Grew and Magic, and the US ambassador in Paris affirmed this gathering's focus on the northern option. The ambassador had information indicating that a decision was reached in Tokyo "in favor of a move against Russia." The "so-called northern party seems to have 'won out' . . . and has been strongly supported by German influence in Tokyo." This dispatch came just after a telegram from the ambassador in China, suggesting that the Chinese had received reliable information that "an attack by Japan on Siberia is certain" (*MB*, 2:56–57, appendix; *FRUS* [1941], 4:994–96).[13]

When Grew got back to Hull and Welles on July 6, it was clear that Konoe was playing for time. Konoe had avoided seeing Grew, so Grew sent a hard copy of Roosevelt's message through an intermediary. Konoe's two-sentence note back thanked Roosevelt and stated that Matsuoka would provide a response. Grew opined that the president's message had probably reopened internal debates as to the advisability of the course

[13] That US officials were taking the new situation seriously is shown by two actions on July 3. Chief of Naval Operations Harold Stark sent a message to subordinates warning that "[Japan's] neutrality pact with Russia will be abrogated and a major military effort will be [made] against [Russia's] maritime provinces," probably at the end of July, "though [the] attack may be deferred until after collapse of European Russia." He asked that principal army commanders and the British chiefs of staff be informed of this situation (*PHA*, 13–14:1396). Across town, Welles told the Soviet ambassador that he had information that Japan had decided to break its neutrality pact and attack Russia soon after (*FRUS* [1941], 1:787).

marked out in the Imperial Conference—one that "envisages an attack on [the] Soviet Union" (*FRUS* [1941], 4:997–98). In short, from Grew's perspective, US diplomacy was having its intended effect: to get Tokyo to rethink any decision to move north.

Despite Grew's cautious optimism, the fact that Konoe was unwilling to say that Japan would not go north was undoubtedly troubling. Moreover, his passing of the buck to Matsuoka—the individual known to be the most in favor of the northern option—was not a good sign. When Matsuoka handed Grew a formal reply on July 8, these concerns were only increased. The statement read that Japan had always had a sincere desire for peace and had "not so far considered the possibility of joining the hostilities against the Soviet Union." This hedging of bets was repeated in Matsuoka's July 2 statement to the Soviet ambassador (which Grew attached as an annex), affirming that Tokyo did not "at present" feel compelled to modify its policy toward Russia (*FRUSJ*, 2:504).[14]

It was apparent that more had to be done to protect the United States' most valuable ally from a two-front war. On July 14, the administration chose to take the highly unorthodox step of demanding that Japan change the makeup of its government. That day, again incapacitated by illness, Hull had Hamilton deliver a blunt message to Nomura asking whether Tokyo was willing to assert control over "elements" in the government that "supported a policy inconsistent with the policy of peace" (*FRUSJ*, 2:505–6). Given Hull's known concerns about Japan's foreign minister, the message was clear: Matsuoka had to go if Japan expected any sort of deal with Washington.

The normally mild-mannered Nomura, plainly taken aback, told Hamilton the next day that the United States had no business raising questions about particular individuals in the Japanese government. Hamilton disclaimed any idea that Washington was trying to interfere in Japan's internal affairs. The goal was only the achievement of peace, not just between Japan and the United States, but "among all countries in the Pacific area" as well. Nomura's reply was not reassuring. For the first time since the negotiations had begun in April, he referred to Japan's encirclement by hostile powers and that Japan might be forced to "take appropriate precautionary measures" such as the United States had done recently in occupying Iceland (ibid., 2:506–9).

Back in Tokyo, however, Hull's remonstrance was having its desired effect. Army, navy, and civilian leaders had been concerned for some time about Matsuoka's undiplomatic stance toward Washington and

---

[14] On the Japanese awareness that the German-Soviet war has led many in the United States to believe that Japan would now undertake "her long-cherished policy" of a northward advance, see Nomura's diary, July 8, in *PWP*, 150.

tenacious adherence to the Tripartite Pact. Given this consensus, Konoe decided to use a procedural trick to both satisfy both US demands and get rid of a difficult colleague. On July 16, he secured the resignation of the cabinet. Two days later, the emperor authorized Konoe to form his third government, and Konoe asked every cabinet member to rejoin him—except Matsuoka.[15] With Matsuoka out and Toyoda Teijiro in as foreign minister, Konoe could proceed with his larger plan: to make a peace with Washington that would give Japan the time and resources to prepare for war in the north.

For the United States, Matsuoka's dismissal was a good sign. But Konoe had still not committed to the status quo, either for Russia or Southeast Asia. Something else was needed, especially as it became evident through US intelligence that Japan was gearing up to occupy the southern half of Indochina. This something was the final weapon in the economic arsenal: tight restrictions on all oil sales to Japan. The way the story is typically told is that the licensing restrictions announced on July 25 were only to punish Japan for its move against southern Indochina. Roosevelt did not intend for them to turn into a complete cutoff of all oil sales, but he became a victim of bureaucratic overzealousness. In this way, Roosevelt inadvertently pushed Japan into all-out war by depriving its economy of its most vital resource.[16] This story would fit nicely with the trade expectations argument, since it suggests that Japan might not have attacked Pearl Harbor had Washington not ended oil exports.

These elements of the traditional account are nevertheless only partial truths at best, and as such, they obscure the larger dimensions of Roosevelt's global strategy. There have always been two big problems with this account. First, it assumes that Roosevelt, who had known for a year that sanctions on general oil products (as opposed to specialty items like aviation fuel) would almost certainly drive Japan to attack the Dutch East Indies, could have allowed lower-level bureaucrats to formulate the details of oil policy without his direct oversight. Second, it asserts that Roosevelt returned from his Atlantic conference with Winston Churchill, realized that the bureaucrats had turned the sanctions into a complete embargo, and then did not have the courage to correct this mistake immediately, despite knowing of its implications. In essence, we are asked to believe two things at odds with everything we know about this consummate politician: he was of both weak intellect (he didn't understand the licensing arrangement) and weak character (he couldn't reverse the complete embargo for fear of seeming soft on Japan or upsetting his underlings).

[15] See Ike's summary notes, in *JDW*, 103–4.
[16] For references and a summary, see Sagan 1989.

There is clear evidence, however, that Roosevelt did in fact know and understand the exact details of the licensing arrangement before he left to see Churchill, and approved them. On July 18 Roosevelt told Ickes, who was still keen on an oil embargo, that he agreed with Hull that such a move would precipitate a Japanese attack on the Dutch East Indies. At a cabinet meeting that day, the president ruled out a complete embargo, but agreed that the United States should freeze Japanese assets and limit US sales of oil to Japan to "normal" amounts—that is, pre-1939 levels (Barnhart 1987, 225–28).[17] Over the next six days, a program was developed by the State Department with the following characteristics. Japanese firms would first have to ask for licenses for specific amounts from the department's Division of Controls. To then receive the oil, the firms would need a second license from the Foreign Funds Control Committee (chaired by Assistant Secretary of State Dean Acheson) in order to release the funds to buy it.

This complicated series of bureaucratic steps had one great appeal to Roosevelt and his secretaries when the cabinet met on July 24 to discuss the matter. Whereas a full embargo, announced as a "regulation," would merely stop all oil purchases until it was rescinded, the licensing system would give Roosevelt and Hull maximum flexibility to increase or decrease the level of economic pressure on Japan, depending on Japan's behavior and US objectives (ibid., 230). The system would also achieve the key tactical objective recommended by the Division of Far Eastern Affairs back in late June: to keep Japan uncertain about US oil policy (*FRUS* [1941], 4:278–80). With reports in late July that Russia was starting to slow the German juggernaut and would probably survive until winter, such a policy would reinforce any Japanese reluctance to go north while still giving Tokyo the hope that oil could be reinstated if its behavior improved (Heinrichs 1988, chap. 5).

Roosevelt and his cabinet approved the licensing recommendation at their July 24 meeting. The next day the White House released a statement. By its very wording, it is obvious that this statement was designed to create confusion and hence uncertainty as to what the United States was really up to. It mentioned the new licensing system, but said little about how this system would actually work, noting only that the measure "brings all . . . trade transactions in which Japanese interests are involved under the control of the [US] Government" (*FRUSJ*, 2:266–67). The statement thus signaled that the US state would now dictate every

---

[17]Roosevelt and Hull's concerns were reinforced the next day by a navy report sent through the president's Chief of Naval Operations Admiral Harold Stark. It recommended against an oil embargo, noting that "the shutting off [of] the American supply of petroleum will lead promptly to an invasion of the Netherlands East Indies." *FRUS* (1941), 4:836–40.

aspect of Japanese-US trade, down to the smallest detail. But it left the Japanese with little clue as to how to get the bureaucracy to actually approve of oil sales.

The British and Dutch were as puzzled as the Japanese as to what the United States was really announcing on July 25. Still, to ensure maximum economic pressure, they immediately renounced their trade treaties with Japan (see Heinrichs 1988, 135–36). Back on July 8, President Roosevelt and British ambassador Edward Halifax had talked about the importance of using oil sanctions to keep the Japanese guessing (see ibid., 134, 141). Roosevelt quickly saw that the new strategy was working. On July 26 he sent a letter to Churchill through his personal assistant Hopkins, who was on his way to Moscow to discuss US aid for Russia. Roosevelt instructed Hopkins to tell Churchill that "our concurrent action in regard to Japan is, I think, bearing fruit." Revealing how much Roosevelt already knew about Japanese decision making (via Magic) a mere day after the freeze announcement, the president went on to say that "I hear their Government [is] much upset and no conclusive future policy has been determined on" (CR, 1:225). The coordinated sanctions policy was already pushing the Japanese to rethink the wisdom of further expansion, either north or south.

Even if it is clear that Roosevelt fully understood the strategic logic behind the new policy, one might still argue that he thought the sanctions were only partial when in fact hard-line bureaucrats were acting to turn them into a complete embargo on all oil exports. Yet this part of the traditional story is also a distortion. Roosevelt's time frame was this: he planned to meet Churchill at Argentia from August 6 to 9, leaving Washington just before August 6. On July 30, George Luthringer of the Office of the Adviser on International Economic Affairs submitted a long memorandum on the execution of the licensing system to Acheson and his boss, Hull. In the first main section, it noted that for the immediate future—specified in brackets as "approximately two weeks"—there should be absolutely no indication of what Washington's general policy was. During these two weeks, a complete two-way embargo would be imposed: no license applications on exports *or* imports would be granted. But in the "intermediate period" that followed, Japan would then face a trial period in which Washington could adopt "a cautious attitude . . . with respect to trade with Japan." Some export and import trade might be reinstated, including a limited amount of petroleum exports to Japan, but this would depend on "general political developments in the Far East" (FRUS [1941], 4:844–46).

This document was commissioned by Acheson to reflect the conclusions of an Interdepartmental Policy Committee meeting held the previous night (ibid., 4:844n13). It shows that the intention right from the beginning was to completely shut down all US-Japanese trade—not just exports, but imports as well. This would send the clearest possible signal that Washington could hurt Japan if it wanted to. Yet by avoiding any sign that this was part of a new general policy, Tokyo would retain enough hope that it could get the trade reinstated if its behavior improved. Once again, we see a deliberate policy at the highest levels to create uncertainty and anxiety in the Japanese government, and nonetheless retain the flexibility needed to negotiate a peace.

But was Roosevelt aware of this Machiavellian strategizing at the highest levels before he left for Argentia? He certainly was. On July 31, with Hull again out sick, Welles sent the president a long memo on the execution of the sanctions policy, providing in essence a summary of Luthringer's report, yet also incorporating other details discussed internally over the previous week. Welles told Roosevelt that some Japanese applications for export licenses had been submitted, but "[for] the time being, [Acheson's] Foreign Funds Control Committee is holding these applications *without action*." It was desirable, Welles continued, that this committee along with export-control authorities "be given instructions as to the policy you desire it to follow." He described a list of embargoed goods that the Foreign Funds Control Committee would continue to deny. With regard to petroleum products, though, depending on developments, Welles noted that it might be worth reinstating trade in gasoline and lubricating oils at "normal" 1935–36 levels—that is, prior to the increase in Japan's oil purchases caused by the China Incident. Just to make sure Roosevelt got the point, Welles ended by saying that the committee would "continue to hold without action" all oil-export applications and subsequently grant licenses "only in accordance with the policy to be initiated by export control"—that is, after instructions from the president (ibid., 4:846–48). Roosevelt approved of Welles's recommendations by noting: "SW [Sumner Welles] OK. FDR" (ibid., 846n16).

Thus we see that Roosevelt left for his conference with Churchill perfectly aware that for two weeks, all sales of oil products to Japan would be ended. And he knew that it would be up to him to decide what policy would replace this total embargo. The strategy was indeed a brilliant one. The fact that Japan would get no oil for two weeks would shake Japanese leaders out of their complacency. Yet by retaining the flexibility to reinstate oil sales after two weeks simply by allowing license applications to go through, Roosevelt could reward Japan for any improved behavior without much damage to his reputation as a reasonable negotiator. The fact, too, that Luthringer's memo explicitly stated two weeks as the time frame for the immediate period is instructive: two weeks from the imposition of sanctions (July 25–26) was when Roosevelt was slated to return from his Argentia meeting. Roosevelt would have time to discuss the issues with Churchill, observe what Japan was doing on the diplomatic or military fronts, and then make a final decision as to whether to persist with the complete embargo. The real story, then, is the exact opposite of the one traditionally told: far from Roosevelt leaving for the conference believing sanctions were only partial, he knew from the beginning they were total, and it was up to him to decide whether such an interim policy should be continued.[18]

The Japanese government, believing that the oil embargo was only re-lated to the July move into southern Indochina, sought to appear accom-modating. In a note delivered to Hull on August 6, Nomura proposed both that Japan would go no further than Indochina and all troops there would be withdrawn after the peace with China. The note expressed hope that in return, Washington would reinstate normal trade relations and even help Japan secure raw materials from Southeast Asia (*FRUSJ*, 2:549–50). Hull, however, came to the meeting ready to signal the United States' tough new posture. Instead of reading the note, Hull stuffed it unceremoniously into his pocket. Two days later he handed Nomura a reply stating that Tokyo's proposal was "lacking in responsiveness" to Roosevelt's earlier suggestions (ibid., 2:546–53). The president received Hull's reports of the exchange while he was at the Atlantic Conference. On August 11, the last full day of meetings, he decided to give Churchill a copy of Japan's August 6 proposal. The two agreed that Japan would have to promise not to station additional troops in Southeast Asia and withdraw the ones now in Indochina before Washington would accept Tokyo's terms. If the Japanese government refused, Roosevelt was to in-form it that "various steps" would have to be taken, even if they resulted in war (*FRUS* [1941], 1:356–60).

The two then considered whether the warning should include a state-ment covering any aggressive steps by Japan against Russia. Welles reit-erated that the main US goal was to keep the peace in the entire Pacific region, regardless of whether Japan intended to go north or south. Hence, the statement Roosevelt should make to Nomura should be "based on the question of broad policy rather than premised solely upon Japa-nese moves in the Southwestern Pacific region." This of course had been Roosevelt, Hull, and Welles's thinking all along: to deter not just a Japa-nese move south but also north. Roosevelt agreed with Welles's sugges-tions, reasoning that this strategy would help prevent further Japanese aggression for at least thirty days (ibid., 1:356–60). The "thirty days" remark shows just how pessimistic Roosevelt had become regarding Ja-pan's short-term intentions: while he might not be able to deter a Japa-nese attack on Russia, he might still be able to buy a month. With the

---

[18] For evidence that reinforces this argument, see Heinrichs 1988, 141–42, 246n68.

Soviets still on the ropes in the west, a month might be just long enough to preserve the Soviet Union through the winter. The global strategy to defeat Hitler thus demanded one more effort at negotiations with Japan.

THE ABORTED EFFORT AT A SECOND ROUND OF NEGOTIATIONS, AUGUST–SEPTEMBER 1941

That Roosevelt still wanted peace in the Pacific region is shown by his behavior over the next three weeks. True to his word, on August 17, soon after returning to Washington, he called Nomura to the White House. Having signaled Konoe's interest in a summit meeting over a week before, Nomura now stressed Konoe's strong desire for such a meeting at some midway location, perhaps Honolulu. Roosevelt replied that before discussions could continue, it was necessary to clarify the US position. He read and then handed the ambassador a long statement reiterating Washington's new deterrence posture. Japan had continued to deploy its forces around the Far East and had occupied southern Indochina, the document noted. The president wanted Tokyo to know that if Japan took any further steps as part of a policy of "military domination . . . of neighboring countries," Washington would be compelled to take "any and all steps" to safeguard US security in the region (*FRUSJ*, 2:556). As he and Churchill had agreed, Roosevelt was now explicitly extending the US deterrent to the whole region, including the Soviet Union (one of the "neighboring countries").

Roosevelt then turned to the question of Japan's desire to restart negotiations. He read and handed to Nomura a separate statement that began by bluntly declaring that any resumption of talks would require an agreement covering "the entire Pacific situation." Five of the next six sentences repeated this refrain—any deal had to involve all the countries in the Pacific region. If, after an agreement, any of these countries were menaced, Washington would immediately extend assistance to them. Following this stick, Roosevelt dangled the carrot: through a peace agreement, Japan could secure everything it wanted, including the "satisfaction of its economic needs." Tokyo, however, must furnish a clearer statement of its present attitude and plans. Nomura replied that he would communicate Roosevelt's views to his superiors, adding that they were "very desirous" to preserve the peace between the two countries (ibid., 2:557–59).

Roosevelt was still determined to leave no stone unturned to secure peace for the entire Pacific region. While we might dismiss Roosevelt's diplomacy at this stage as designed only to buy time, it was that and much more. A peace deal with Japan protecting both the north and south would achieve his primary objective: the freedom to pursue a war with

Germany without the diversion of a second front, and with Russia and Britain free to focus solely on the European theater. As such, on August 18, Roosevelt met again with Nomura in a secret meeting (with only Hull present) to confirm his interest in negotiations. He told Nomura that it might be difficult to meet in Honolulu, given the overseas flight, but that perhaps the summit could be in San Francisco, Seattle, or even Juneau, Alaska, if that worked for Konoe (*MB*, 3:26–29, appendix).[19]

Back in Tokyo, things were coming to a head. The US oil embargo had had a dramatic cooling effect on those wanting an immediate invasion of Russia. As Barnhart shows, even those most inclined to a northern move agreed that a southern advance was now necessary. War in the north was always dependent both on Germany's success in the west and adequate raw materials. Two reports in the first week of August confirmed that a northern attack before the snows began in October was unwise now. The first report by the General Staff Intelligence Division predicted that Russia, displaying more resilience at this point, would now not surrender in 1941, and perhaps not even in 1942. The second report by the Army Ministry's Equipment Bureau stated that given the Western oil embargo, without the oil fields of Southeast Asia, Japan could not fight the Soviets with any degree of confidence (Barnhart 1987, 239). Roosevelt's nicely timed oil licensing system had had one of its desired effects: it had ended all talk about an autumn attack on Russia. On August 9, all operations planning for the attack was temporarily suspended and instead redirected toward southern preparations. While the army led this charge, the navy was in agreement. With no oil imports, both army and navy analyses estimated that Japan had only two years of stocks remaining, even if it undertook no major military operations (ibid., 240–41).

Declining expectations of future trade had shifted the Japanese focus from north to south. The main issue during the August Liaison Conferences was now not strategy but rather the inevitability of war with the United States. Konoe had secured army and navy support on August 7 for the idea of a direct summit with Roosevelt. Everything depended on the terms, though: the army signaled that it wanted peace with the United States, but only if Roosevelt agreed to allow raw materials to flow into Japan unimpeded. At the August 26 conference, participants concurred that Japan should respond to Roosevelt's latest démarche in a reasonable way to help persuade Roosevelt to proceed with the summit (*JDW*, 85–112).

On August 28, Nomura met Roosevelt and handed him two documents. The first expressed the desire for "the peace of the Pacific" and thus "urgent necessity" of a summit meeting. The second signaled some

[19] As this meeting was kept secret from State Department officials, there is nothing about it in the *FRUS* series.

of the concessions Japan might be willing to make. Japan would be willing to withdraw its forces from Indochina "as soon as the China Incident is settled or a just peace is established in East Asia." Moreover, Japan would take no military action against Russia "as long as the Soviet Union remains faithful to the Soviet-Japanese neutrality treaty and does not menace Japan or Manchukuo. . . . In a word, the Japanese Government has no intention of using, without provocation, military force against any neighboring nation" (*FRUSJ*, 2:572–75).

These were significant changes in Japanese policy. By including the line regarding a just peace in East Asia (i.e., a US-Japanese agreement), Tokyo was now indicating that it would not make the ending of the Sino-Japanese War a precondition to a pullout of Indochina. More important, for the first time the Japanese government was willing to promise that it would not attack the Soviet Union unless provoked. Japan, in essence, was recommitting itself to its April 1941 nonaggression pact with Moscow, notwithstanding the pressure being placed on it by Berlin to attack Russia's eastern front. Hull had reiterated the significance Washington placed on this assurance just five days earlier, at a meeting on August 23, when he told Nomura point-blank that should Japan "project herself into the Russian-German situation," there would be no chance at a US-Japanese agreement (ibid., 2:567).[20] Clearly Tokyo had got the message.

Given the war that broke out in December, one might conclude that Japan had no intention of honoring these concessions, and Roosevelt and Hull knew this. This view is too simple on two counts. For one, the Japanese intention was indeed to honor the Japanese-Soviet pact for at least six months, given that the earliest feasible time for a move north was now seen as February 1942. A peace deal that reinstated trade would help Japan prepare for this northern war.

Roosevelt and Hull also plainly saw the Japanese statements on August 28 as crucial, at least in terms of buying time for the United States' own buildup and perhaps as a way to keep the Pacific peace. That night, at Hull's request, Nomura came to Hull's apartment to talk about the specifics of both the reinstated "informal" negotiations and a subsequent summit meeting. What is most significant is not the details discussed but instead that Hull proceeded as if it were already a given that the negotiations and summit meeting would go ahead. The meeting's tone was similar to the May–June meetings—so much so that when Nomura reintroduced the notion that Washington act as intermediary to end the China war, Hull again accepted that Washington would play this role, provided

[20] Just prior to this line, Hull had sarcastically told Nomura that the stationing of large armies by both Japan and Russia along the Manchurian border must be the two countries' way of preserving the Soviet-Japanese neutrality pact.

Chiang was willing. The US position was remarkably reasonable. Hull spoke of his willingness to "work together" to make the most of China's potential as a trading nation, and the conversation itself revolved around the agreed assumption that Japan would pull its troops out of Indochina *after* the China Incident was resolved—as opposed to such a withdrawal being a precondition for US help in facilitating a Sino-Japanese peace, as Roosevelt had emphasized earlier in the month (ibid., 2:576–79).

Despite this promising restart of the aborted talks from June, six days later everything fell apart. On September 3, Roosevelt called Nomura into the White House and presented two statements to him. Before any summit could go forward, he stressed, the Japanese government had to show that it stood "earnestly for all of the [four] principles" that Hull had used as guidelines for talks back in April. Yet even if the Japanese were somehow able to prove their adherence to such vague principles—including respect for territorial integrity, noninterference, and commercial equality—Roosevelt added another condition. The US government would have to first "discuss the matter fully" with the British, Chinese, and Dutch to secure their acceptance of any deal (ibid., 2:588–92).

These two new conditions were deal killers, as Roosevelt certainly understood. The first one was bad enough. Whereas discussions over the previous two weeks had pragmatically revolved around the June draft agreement, Roosevelt was now forcing Japan to meet the unstated standards of four obscure principles. In diplomacy, this is an old technique designed to signal lack of interest in the horse-trading needed for a deal. The second condition, on the other hand, was completely new. Roosevelt had never before indicated that he required the approval of even the British before proceeding, let alone secondary allies such as the Chinese and Dutch.

Back in Tokyo, Foreign Minister Toyoda was clearly worried after receiving Nomura's meeting report (*MB*, 3:64–68, appendix). Later that same day (September 4, Tokyo time; September 3 in Washington), Toyoda called in Grew and explained that Konoe wanted to "leave no stone unturned" to secure a summit meeting. Toyoda gave Grew a memorandum summarizing seven concessions, drawing Grew's attention to parts (c), (d), and (e). Here, the three main sticking points over the last six months—Japan's adherence to the Tripartite Pact, the stationing of troops in China, and the issue of the open door—were eliminated in one stroke. Should the United States get involved in the European war, Japan's interpretation of the Tripartite Pact would be "independently decided." (Toyoda emphasized several times how different this was from Matsuoka's position.) Japan would also remove its armed forces from China as soon as possible after a Sino-Japanese peace, while restrictions on US firms in China would end. These concessions had been cabled to

Nomura, Toyoda mentioned, but he underscored the importance of Grew transmitting them immediately to Washington (*FRUSJ*, 2:593–94, 608).

The next day (September 4, Washington time) Nomura rushed a new version of the draft agreement to Hull, incorporating the concessions. The section on the Tripartite Pact, borrowing from an undiscussed draft Japan gave Hull the day before Germany's attack on Russia, stated that the pact was defensive only, designed to help prevent an "unprovoked extension" of the European war. The word unprovoked was critical, since it marked Japan's willingness to ignore any obligations to Germany should the United States enter the war. (Japan could claim that US entry into the European conflict had been provoked by German expansionism.) In section 5, Japan accepted the principle of nondiscrimination in trade. In the section on China, Japan agreed to withdraw from Chinese territory "as promptly as possible" after a Sino-Japanese peace, and within a maximum of two years. Clause 2 on the stationing of Japanese troops in northern China, as the document noted, had been "entirely dropped" to accord with US wishes (ibid., 2:597–600, 608, 488).

These concessions were sweeping, to say the least. A comparison with the US draft from early June shows Japan now complying with Washington's desired wording for almost every section of the document. In fact, the new document went further than the US draft on the troops issue. In June, the United States had agreed to discuss the stationing of troops in northern China to fight Communism and had simply asked for troops in southern China to leave "as promptly as possible." By dropping the stationing question entirely and specifying a two-year maximum for withdrawal, Japan was communicating its willingness to withdraw completely from all of China (excluding Manchuria) after two years (ibid., 2:597–600; cf. ibid., 2:446–49).

Notwithstanding these concessions, Hull, in his meeting with Nomura, put up roadblocks every step of the way. He restated the need for Allied approval before proceeding. To Nomura's point that Washington now should not fear Japan's adherence to the Tripartite Pact—the primary US issue for the whole April–June period—Hull said that this would create difficulties with the Senate if there were no "explicit assurances" on these items (ibid., 2:595–96). These were clearly bogus reasons for not seizing the most important set of Japanese concessions to date. Indeed, Hull didn't even try to exploit Tokyo's obvious desperation to push his demands further, as most good negotiators would do. He simply refused to continue bargaining.

What was going on here? Why would Roosevelt and Hull become intransigent just when the deal they had been seeking for half a year was within their grasp? This is a key question, given that Roosevelt and Hull's actions effectively shut down serious negotiations until mid-November.

The oil embargo that could have been reversed by an agreement was continued, which of course only reaffirmed Japan's already-pessimistic expectations for future trade. Roosevelt and Hull's decision to abandon the summit and negotiations made war essentially inevitable in the absence of new negotiations. So why did they do it?

There are few explanations in the literature on this conundrum, largely because scholars tend to presume that neither side by August–September was really that interested in a deal.[21] The above discussion shows beyond doubt that a lack of interest was not the problem. In August, Roosevelt had still wanted a deal so he could concentrate on Hitler and buy time for his naval buildup. The Japanese military and civilians wanted to avoid war with the United States so they could use raw material imports from the south and the United States to facilitate a war against Russia.

Because there are no documents revealing Roosevelt and Hull's thinking during the first days of September, we must rely on circumstantial evidence and logic.[22] One plausible explanation is that a number of factors interacted to convince them to shift to an intransigent stance. Three factors seem most salient. First, the existence of secret talks regarding a possible summit had leaked out in both the Japanese and US press around this time. For hard-liners in both Japan and the United States, such talks were anathema. This may have led Roosevelt and Hull to believe that continuing the talks were too politically dangerous, or that Konoe would no longer have enough support at home to ratify any agreement.

It is also possible that Roosevelt and Hull, given new evidence that Japan was preparing for a war in the south sooner rather than later,

---

[21] Even a careful historian like Barnhart (1987, 232–33) breezes quickly through the August–September negotiations.

[22] Hull's (1948) own recollections are a wonderful example of dissimulation on this issue. At every step of the way, his recounting of events is the exact opposite of what actually happened. He does admit that he and Roosevelt desired a peace deal in late August, and then changed their minds in early September. Yet he claims that his about-face was a result of Japan only wanting to adhere to vague statements of principles (ibid., 1024). In fact, it was Tokyo that had made potentially game-changing concessions. Hull (ibid.) states that while the negotiations in early September were proceeding, Konoe's government "narrowed the concessions it had originally been willing to make." It was Washington that had in actuality done just that. Hull (ibid.) asserts that the very holding of a summit "would cause China grave uneasiness" unless agreement had already been reached to protect China's sovereignty, even though Tokyo had finally confirmed that all troops would leave China proper within two years. Overall, Hull (ibid., 1025) argues, he and Roosevelt could not make an agreement at the "expense of our principles and interests" as well as those of China, notwithstanding the fact that his diplomacy until that point had nothing to do with ideals and everything to do with realpolitik. Such consummate lying by a former secretary of state gives us prime facie evidence that he and Roosevelt were covering up something that had it become known, would have greatly damaged their reputations and that of the United States.

suddenly decided that negotiations were no longer useful and that Japan would only use such talks to buy time. Grew was sending reports from Tokyo in late August noting that Japan seemed to be mobilizing for war (see *FRUS* [1941], 4:408–19). More significant, the Japanese civilians and military held an important Liaison Conference on September 3 that affirmed a consensus that Japan, pending Hirohito's approval at an Imperial Conference, had to attack south should diplomatic efforts fail (*JDW*, 129–33). Since this conference was held on September 2, Washington time, there was a day for Magic and other intelligence tools to learn of this meeting along with what had transpired.

Finally, in late August the Germans renewed their offensive against the Soviets in an all-out effort to destroy Stalin's army before the onset of winter. The German army had been forced to halt in early August and for three weeks had remained in place on a line running from the Baltic through the middle of Ukraine. But on August 22, Germany began a full-scale drive toward Leningrad, the Caucasus, and ultimately Moscow. Reports began to arrive in Washington in late August and early September that the Russians were not doing well and were retreating (Heinrichs 1988, 146–79; Clark 1965, 109–49). With Roosevelt and Hull fully aware since June that Japan's decision to go north depended on German success on the western front, this news could not have been pleasing. As Roosevelt had remarked to Ambassador Halifax in mid-August, the Japanese "were more influenced by the sway of battle in Russia than by regard for the United States."[23] The thinking behind Roosevelt and Hull's sudden ending of negotiations thus probably mirrored their thinking in late June: with Japan now more likely to attack Russia, any deal allowing a diversion of troops north and renewal of raw material flows had to be scotched.

All three of these factors may have contributed to the about-face on September 3. There are good reasons, however, to believe that the first two were not nearly as salient as the third. The idea that Roosevelt and Hull would stop negotiations because the existence of these talks had been leaked seems suspect. The concessions offered by Tokyo on September 4, if codified in a final agreement, would have been a huge public relations coup for Roosevelt. It would have demonstrated that coercive diplomacy, including oil sanctions and a military buildup, could pay big rewards, not only in keeping the peace, but in renewing trade with China, too. As for the argument that Washington ended negotiations because of new evidence on Japan's preparations for war, this also seems suspect. It is unlikely that it was Grew's reports regarding increased Japanese

---

[23]The quotation is a paraphrase of the original Halifax memorandum to London on August 18 (Heinrichs 1988, 161).

mobilization that caused the shift in US behavior. After all, this news was consistent with what the United States had known for two months: that Japan, after the Imperial Conference on July 2, was mobilizing for total war either north or south, depending on subsequent conditions. A somewhat more plausible notion is that Roosevelt and Hull received information about the September 3 conference, and believing war essentially inevitable, decided to end negotiations.

Discussions at this conference did in fact reveal a growing desperation in Japanese thinking. Navy Chief of Staff Nagano began the conference by noting that "the Empire is losing materials: that is, we are getting weaker . . . [and] the enemy is getting stronger." With the passage of time, "we won't be able to survive." Japan had to try diplomacy, he continued, but if this should fail, a decision for war must be made quickly. He was not optimistic about the chances of victory. Japan might do well in the opening months, yet even with an initial decisive battle, "it would be a long war," and one that Japan, with its small resource base, was unlikely to win. Sugiyama then spoke of the need to achieve Japan's diplomatic objectives by October 10 at the latest. His reasoning had nothing to do with weather or logistics, and everything to do with the army's true objective: destroying Russia. Japan could not carry out large-scale operations in the north until February. "In order to be able to act in the North," he explained, "we have to carry out operations quickly in the South. Even if we start right away, operations will take until next spring. Insofar as we are delayed we will not be able to act in the North. Therefore, it is necessary to move as quickly as possible [in the South]." Agreement was reached that day that Japan had to give diplomacy a chance. If there were no results by October 10, though, the leadership would then "immediately decide to commence hostilities." The ministers also agreed to ask the emperor for an Imperial Conference three days later to approve this plan of action (*JDW*, 129–33).

Had the details of this important conference been picked up by Magic, it might have contributed to Roosevelt and Hull's decision to abruptly end negotiations. But even if they had gotten wind of this conference, there is still a puzzle.[24] What information from it would have driven them to stop the negotiations? It is highly improbable that the news of the decision to begin a move south after October 10 would have done it. After all, this decision explicitly depended on Konoe's diplomacy failing. So if Roosevelt and Hull had wanted to prevent a move south, driven by resource scarcity, they should have *increased* their efforts to sign a deal giving Japan some oil and raw materials. Only this would have improved

---

[24]I found no Magic transcripts discussing the conference in the usual sources (*MB* and *PHA*), but that of course doesn't mean they don't exist.

Japanese trade expectations and averted a tragic plunge into Southeast Asia. At the very least, it would have bought time for the US buildup—something, as we will see, that the US military desperately wanted.

If Roosevelt and Hull had received details on the conference, the thing that would have been most worrisome was Sugiyama's comment that the army was still actively anticipating action against Russia as early as February. Japan, like the United States, had undoubtedly learned of the renewal of the German offensive on August 22 and its initial successes. If Roosevelt and Hull had learned of Sugiyama's remark, they could only assume one thing: any US-Japanese agreement helping Japan to end the China war and restore trade would mean that hundreds of thousands of troops as well as millions of tons of resources would be sent north for the offensive against Russia.[25] As such, a deal with Japan would have been the last thing Roosevelt and Hull wanted.

Yet even without information about the September 3 conference, news from the Russian front would have been upsetting enough to cause Roosevelt and Hull to suspend negotiations. Knowing that the decision to go north depended on Germany's advance toward Moscow, and that Japan had gone from two hundred thousand to around six hundred thousand troops in Manchuria as a result of the July buildup, Roosevelt and Hull had good reason not to help Japan reinforce its northern army any further (see *PHA*, 13–14:1346–47). This does not mean, of course, that the pair was deliberately trying to draw Japan into an attack on Southeast Asia. Indeed, over the next three months, they both continued to be preoccupied by the need to get into the European war and avoid war in the Pacific. A two-front war had always been seen as highly problematic, and the imminence of it in November would bring them back to the idea of a temporary modus vivendi with Tokyo to buy at least six more months of peace. In early September, however, Roosevelt and Hull could not afford to facilitate a Japanese attack on the one state, Russia, that was critical to winning the war against Hitler.

To see this, we need to look briefly at the larger geopolitical context during late summer 1941. Other than provoking a war with Germany in the Atlantic, sending as much military and economic aid to Russia as possible remained Roosevelt's primary geopolitical objective. For an hour on August 1, he angrily lectured cabinet members, particularly Secretary of War Henry Stimson, for their foot-dragging on this issue. With information confirming his hopes that Russia could hold Germany back until

---

[25] Such concerns might explain Hull's comment to Nomura on September 4 that he opposed Japan's "station[ing] of troops for anti-Cominterm purposes" and "desired a complete evacuation" of such troops (Nomura's diary, September 4, in *PWP*, 177–78). This was contrary to his position in early June, before Germany's attack.

winter, he told the cabinet that whatever the United States could supply to Russia must be there by October 1, "and the only answer I want to hear is that it is under way" (quoted in Herring 1973, 13–14). He was even willing to sacrifice the United States' own military buildup to achieve this end; he ordered Stimson to send the promised aircraft immediately, even though there were no planes to replace them (Henrichs 1988, 139–40).

Through August and into September, Roosevelt continued to berate his subordinates about the slow pace of Russian aid. Huge supply problems were arising as the US economy suddenly prepared for total war. The president was trying to give the Russians everything they asked for. But with shortages pervasive and the anti-Soviet legislators in Congress trying to bar the extension of lend lease to Russia, Roosevelt was in a bind (Herring 1973, 13–17). Hopkins's trip to see Stalin in late July–early August had been a success: the two states were now in a de facto alliance, with Hopkins reassuring Stalin that aid was on its way. Yet there was little Roosevelt could really do for Russia in material terms in the short run. From the larger strategic perspective, however, there was certainly something that the president could do, and that was to keep Japan from opening up a second front in Siberia.

The need to end negotiations with Japan would have been reinforced by the wording of the above-mentioned statement of concessions presented to Grew late on September 3 (Washington time). In listing seven things Japan would agree to do, Toyoda had drawn Grew's attention to items (c), (d), and (e)—the parts discussing the Axis pact, troops in China, and open door, respectively. Items (b) and (f), in contrast, while they seemed to be important concessions, contained a glaring omission. In item (b), Japan promised that it would not resort without justifiable reason to military actions against any regions "lying south of Japan." In item (f), Japan promised that its activities "in the Southwestern Pacific Area" would be carried on only by peaceful means and according to the principle of nondiscrimination (*FRUSJ*, 2:608).[26] For anyone who knew anything about Japan's recent internal discussions, such language would have raised immediate red flags. Here was Japan promising to keep the peace in the south, leave China, and observe economic nondiscrimination, but making no explicit assurances regarding its all-important neighbor to the north, Russia. The very fact that Toyoda would not have tried to dissimulate by presenting his concessions as covering the entire Pacific area suggests that he either hoped any US-Japanese agreement would last past early spring 1942 (the projected date for the northern invasion) or was constrained by army leaders from making a larger concession.

---

[26] While this *FRUS* document has a September 6 date on it, it was the same one given to Grew three days earlier in Tokyo and immediately passed on the Hull.

Regardless, Roosevelt and Hull would have easily read between the lines, thereby recognizing that the Japanese government's desire for peace in the south was masking its larger plans for war in the north.[27]

Logic and circumstantial evidence thus point to one primary explanation for why Roosevelt and Hull abruptly ended negotiations with Japan on September 3–4, despite having restarted them in earnest only a week earlier. It seems that the only thing that could have propelled them to shift policy—especially given the known risks of ending Japanese hopes for renewed trade—was the new victories of the German army on the Russian front and their anticipated impact on Japanese decision making. The two other factors—the leaking of the existence of secret talks and evidence about Japan's buildup for war—were too weak on their own. At best, they served only to reinforce US fears that Japan was preparing to go north and would need US raw materials to do so.

The Final Months of Peace, September–November 1941

Almost everything that occurred over the next two and a half months, right up until mid-November, was driven by the US decision in early September to end negotiations. Japanese leaders knew that war was inevitable if talks were not restarted. Japan's whole economic structure, plus the maintenance of its fleet and modern army, depended on oil and raw materials. Without access to these resources, Japan would decline so precipitously that it would become vulnerable to whatever power decided to pick it off in the future. The September–October Liaison and Imperial Conferences made these facts perfectly clear to any official who was not already keenly aware of them.

At the critical Imperial Conference of September 6, held two days after Washington's change of heart, Hirohito was asked to approve a document stating that Japan would take "all possible diplomatic measures" to get trade restored by October 10. If these measures failed, however, a decision to commence hostilities would be made immediately. And this was no longer just an attack on the Dutch East Indies, as the army had previously wanted. It would be war against "the United States, Britain, and the Netherlands."

Konoe began the conference by outlining the general problem. Given the coordinated policies of the US, British, and Dutch governments,

> if we allow this situation to continue, it is inevitable that our empire will gradually lose the ability to maintain its national power. . . .

[27] On Hull's constant berating of Nomura from early September to late October regarding the increasing presence of Japanese troops on the Soviet border, see footnote 35 below.

[Japan] must try to prevent the disaster of war by resorting to all possible diplomatic measures. If the diplomatic measures should fail to bring about a favorable result within a certain period, I believe we cannot help but take the ultimate step in order to defend ourselves.

Navy Chief of Staff Nagano then told Hirohito that Japan could not delay a decision for war for long. Otherwise, the dwindling of oil supplies "[would] cause a gradual weakening of our national defense." Meanwhile, the United States was quickly building up its military strength. By mid-1942, "America's military preparedness will have made great progress, and [it] will be difficult to cope with her." War would have to be waged now, should diplomacy fail.

Nagano spoke candidly of the low probability of victory. Even if Japan had initial successes, the United States would fight a prolonged war using "her impregnable position, her superior industrial power, and her abundant resources." Japan did not have the means "to make [the Americans] give up their will to fight." The only hope lay in Japan establishing a strong position early in the war and then waiting on "developments in the world situation." These utterances are significant considering how often scholars claim that Japanese leaders entered the war believing it would be short, or that the United States did not have the will to fight more than a year or two.[28] Nagano not only dispelled such illusions but also implied that only if the United States got bogged down in a war with Germany (the "world situation") would Washington seek some sort of peace, and even then only after a long war in the Pacific. He ended by reiterating that Japan must spare no efforts to find a way to avoid war. But it also could not allow itself to decline, only to face an aggressive opponent later and with less power. His remarks nicely captured the tragic choice that would hang over Japanese ministers for the next three months: either allow decline and trust that adversaries would not destroy Japan, or attack now, hoping for a negotiated peace after a prolonged war.

Sugiyama spoke up to agree with Nagano about the problem of decline. Yet he went on to reassure the emperor, whose enthusiasm for a northern advance was known to all, that Japan was still continuing preparations for war against Russia. By spring 1942, a full-scale attack could be launched to take advantages of any "changes in the Northern situation." His remarks reiterated what the group already took for granted: the nation's core objective was the destruction of Soviet power. The northern operation would go ahead even if there was peace in the south. Conversely, if war in the south happened, southern raw material bases had be to secured quickly to facilitate the northern spring offensive.

---

[28] For such an argument and references, see Snyder 1991.

Suzuki Teiichi, director of the Planning Board, informed Hirohito that the country's only problem lay in its access to raw materials. Japan's economy had developed through trade, he reminded the emperor, and depended on foreign sources for its vital goods. Due to Anglo-American economic sanctions, though, Japanese national power was declining day by day. It was thus "vitally important" for Japan's survival that it "establish and stabilize a firm economic base." There were no illusions about what Japan would have to face. If it went to war in the south, Suzuki cautioned, its short-term productive capacity would be halved. And even if the raw materials of Southeast Asia fell easily into Japanese hands, it would take two years to make full use of them.

Given this sobering assessment, it is unsurprising that Hara was not happy with the solutions offered by Konoe and his colleagues. Speaking for the emperor, he told the group that in a time of such poor US-Japanese relations, conventional diplomacy was no longer enough and every possible means should be taken to resolve the situation. The emperor had been led to believe that diplomacy and military preparations were to be undertaken simultaneously. Yet as he read the policy documents, it seemed that the emphasis was on war, not diplomacy. Navy Minister Oikawa quickly tried to reassure Hara that diplomacy had equal importance, as the prime minister's determination to visit the United States showed. On this basis, Hara (i.e., the emperor) gave his consent to the policy proposal. Nevertheless, at the end of the meeting, Hirohito took the highly unusual step of voicing his concerns. He read a poem composed by his grandfather, Emperor Meiji: "All the seas in every quarter are as brothers to one another. Why, then, do the winds and waves of strife rage so turbulently throughout the world?" This statement was swiftly understood as an imperial censure of any tendency to favor war over diplomacy. Every possible effort for a peaceful solution would have to be made before war with the United States would be sanctioned (*JDW*, 133–51).[29]

The ministers' subsequent actions showed that they got the message. But it was now apparent that if Washington refused to meet Japan halfway, war would have to begin sooner rather than later. The pressure to attack south if diplomacy failed was coming from two sources. One was the simple fact that the US navy would be much stronger in another year, leaving little hope of even a stalemated victory. The other was the army's constant point that the military operation in the north had to start after February 1942, meaning that raw materials from either the United States (through diplomacy) or Southeast Asia (through war) had to be acquired before then. Many scholars have noted the strong preventive motivations of Japanese thinking by fall 1941.[30] Yet they overlook

---

[29] For the documents presented to Hirohito, see ibid., 152–63.
[30] For references, see Sagan 1989; Taliaferro 2005.

the larger geopolitical picture: that from Tokyo's perspective, it was still even more critical to stop the rising Russian colossus than to prevent the growth of the US giant. Destroying Russia by taking advantage of the German-Soviet war had been the emperor's primary goal at the July Imperial Conference, and would remain the overarching Japanese aim through fall 1941, as the continued buildup in Manchuria confirms.

In the five Liaison Conferences in September, discussion focused on the state of diplomatic negotiations with Washington. Because Nomura's dispatches had downplayed the roadblocks to a deal that Roosevelt and Hull were now putting up, Japanese ministers maintained an overly optimistic picture of the true state of relations.[31] Only on October 2 did Nomura finally tell his foreign minister that the negotiations were deadlocked and the chances of a summit were remote. At the Liaison Conference two days later, both the army and navy chiefs of staff argued that Japan now had to move immediately to war. War Minister Tojo, who over the previous six months had shown himself to be a strong supporter of the emperor's desires, was more cautious. Because this matter was "extremely critical," he warned, Japan had to avoid any quick decision and give the matter more study (*JDW*, 179–81).

At the next conference (October 9), navy leaders were now reticent about war, too (see ibid., 181–84). By October 12, however, two days after the deadline for a deal and with nothing to show for all his hard work, Konoe knew he was in trouble. At a private meeting that day with just the foreign, war, and navy ministers (Sugiyama was excluded), Konoe tried to persuade Tojo that there was still hope for negotiations. Tojo was not convinced. He agreed with the army that war was the logical choice and Konoe should resign, to be replaced by a leader that could, if necessary, take Japan into war. Both men concurred on the choice of Prince Higashikuni Naruhiko as an individual who, as both a blood relative of the emperor and army officer, could achieve the unity needed for the crucial next steps. But Hirohito, not wanting a relative to be associated with taking Japan into war, surprised Tojo by asking him to become the new prime minister. Tojo was seen as the individual who could control the army and ensure that the emperor's wishes were carried out.[32]

With reluctance, Tojo accepted his assignment, and appointed Togo Shigenori as foreign minister. By this point, resource shortages were already playing havoc with Japan's military buildups both north and south. At the Liaison Conference on October 27, Finance Minister Kaya

---

[31] On the proceedings of the five Liaison Conferences from September 11 to 25, see *JDW*, 167–78. For Nomura's dispatches from early September to mid-October, see *MB*, 3:73–163, appendix.

[32] See diary notes of Kido Koichi, lord keeper of the privy seal, in *PWP*, 126–28; Barnhart 1987, 253–54.

Okinori began the meeting with the key issue: "the acquisition of vital materials." Suzuki explained that by the end of 1942, Japan would have exhausted all of its stockpiles. Restrictions on both civilian and government resource allocations had already been imposed. If further restrictions were required, "the productive power of the country will decline." Tojo, speaking now as both prime minister and war minister, replied that the army was making its preparations "with emphasis on getting ready for the Soviet Union," and would still be able to attack Russia in 1942 despite the shortages, as long it were given the same allocations as before (*JDW*, 190–93).

Follow-up conferences on October 28 and 30 focused on the possibility of using synthetic oil to overcome Japan's supply problem, and whether southern operation could begin as late as March 1942 to give more time for diplomacy. Suzuki argued forcefully that Japan could not produce enough synthetic oil to overcome the oil shortage. The army, citing material shortages, rejected any delay past November. There were also discussions on whether Japan should simply accept the US demands. All participants except Foreign Minister Togo agreed that Japan would fall to the status of a vulnerable third-rate power if that came about. Thus three—and only three—options remained for future discussion: Japan should "avoid war and undergo great hardships" (i.e., accept the status quo); Japan must begin a war in the south immediately; and Japan should "decide on war but carry on war preparations and diplomacy side by side." The participants agreed to meet on November 1 to make a final decision (*JDW*, 193–99).

What is perhaps most surprising about these late October meetings is that option number three was still on the table. The September 6 Imperial Conference had agreed that if there was no diplomatic solution by October 10, a decision for immediate war would be made. Yet here it was late October, with former army general Tojo now in the prime minister's spot, and everyone but the army leaders was hesitating. When the group reassembled on November 1 for what would be a historic seventeen-hour debate on Japan's future, the army leaders found themselves outvoted and had to accept another postponement of the final deadline for a war decision—this time to November 30. Proposal number three—to continue war preparations but keep striving for a diplomatic solution—had won out.

The discussion on November 1 of the first option nicely illustrates how actors in severe decline worry about the future power and intentions of rising states. If Japan put off war, Kaya asked, and "three years hence the American fleet comes to attack us, will the Navy have a chance of winning or won't it?" Nagano replied that nobody could answer that question. Kaya then asked whether the United States would indeed attack Japan. Nagano answered that he wasn't sure, but that the "chances are

50–50." Kaya and Togo suggested that it was unlikely that the United States would attack. Nagano's response was that "the future is uncertain; we can't take anything for granted." And in three years time, he noted, the United States would be that much stronger.

In the middle of the long conference, as it was becoming clear that option three would win out, Tojo (backed by Togo) turned to the army leaders and asked them to make an important promise. If Japan was going to make one final diplomatic effort, "you must give your word that if diplomacy is successful we will give up going to war." In the subtle give-and-take tradition of Japanese decision making, this was a highly unusual and almost-brutal request. Tojo and Togo were essentially asking army leaders—in front of the whole group, no less—to put their honor on the line and refrain from pushing the nation into war should Washington prove accommodating.

Not surprisingly, the discussion suddenly took a nasty turn. Army Vice Chief of Staff Tsukada Osamu quickly responded that this was "impossible"; such a promise would throw the Supreme Command into confusion. Sugiyama jumped in to support Tsukada. Navy Minister Shimada Shigetaro then inquired if it might be acceptable to negotiate up until two days before a war started. Tsukada shut him down: "Please be quiet. What you've just said won't do." A heated debate followed. The group decided to take a twenty-minute recess, during which the army came to accept a compromise suggestion that negotiations continue until five days before war was to begin. By doing so, the army was essentially agreeing to Tojo's demand that it accept a peaceful solution if one could be arranged before the deadline. The note taker summed up the mood of the room as this marathon seventeen-hour conference came to an end:

> In general, the prospects if we go to war are not bright. We all wonder if there isn't some way to proceed peacefully. There is no one who is willing to say: "Don't worry, even if the war is prolonged, I will assume all responsibility." On the other hand, it is not possible to maintain the status quo. Hence one unavoidably reaches the conclusion that we must go to war [should diplomacy fail]. (ibid., 200–207)

The significance of the above exchange between Tojo and his former military colleagues lies not in its unusual frankness but rather in the fact that it is the final nail in the coffin for all arguments suggesting either that the military hijacked the Japanese state and drove it into war, or that some cultural or ideological dementia had overtaken the Japanese leadership prior to the attack on Pearl Harbor.[33] As in previous Liaison

---

[33] See especially Snyder 1991; Kupchan 1994.

Conferences, the discussion was open and wide ranging, revolving around what would be best for the Japanese state instead of what was best for some organizational group or individual. And when army leaders proved intransigent, they were coerced into accepting that a diplomatic solution, even at this late date, was still the preferred option. A rational lesser-of-two-evils decision for war might still have to be made on December 1. But the prime minister and his foreign minister, acting in the name of the emperor and state, were still in control. The military obeyed them, and not vice versa.

On November 5, another Imperial Conference was held to secure Hirohito's approval for the decision agreed to four days earlier. Diplomacy with Washington would revolve around two proposals, A and B. Proposal A was based around the US version of the draft agreement from early June. As it had on September 4, Japan would again promise to "act independently" on the Axis question and accept the open door. On the third big issue—that of China—Japan would again agree, as it had on September 4, to leave China as soon as possible (within a maximum of two years) after a Sino-Japanese peace agreement and withdraw from Indochina immediately after that agreement. Yet unlike the September 4 draft, which had removed Japan's request to station troops in northern China, the Japanese now returned to the idea of leaving some troops there for a "necessary period," presumably to fight Communism as per the June draft (*JDW*, 209–10; cf. *FRUSJ*, 2:600). The United States, one will recall, had made a concession on the question of troops in northern China when things were going well in early June. But in the face of current US intransigence, this was now likely to become a major stumbling block.[34]

The backup plan, proposal B, was designed as a temporary modus vivendi should proposal A prove too hard to negotiate given the limited

[34] It is important to note that in the November talks, the Japanese did not adopt the position that they were unwilling to leave China or would leave China only after twenty-five years, as is sometimes thought. The twenty-five-years figure was discussed at the November 5 Imperial Conference, but it referred only to the question of troops in northern China, not to those that would leave southern China. Moreover, this figure was to be used only for initial bargaining purposes, and only if Washington wanted to know how long Japan envisioned keeping troops in the north (*JDW*, 209–10). In short, by offering proposal A, the Japanese were making it perfectly clear they still wanted out of the China Incident with US help (their goal since April). The main US concern from September to November was not the Japanese troops that had occupied southern China *after* 1937 but rather those that might remain in the north from the *pre-1937* period (see the following footnote). This subtle although critical distinction must be kept in mind to understand the US-Japanese talks of mid- to late November. In the end, Hull made "leaving China"—that is, all of China including the northern provinces *and* Manchuria—a key US demand. But he made this demand—one that was far more extreme than his position in early June—only after he and Roosevelt had decided against a modus vivendi on the morning of November 26.

time frame. It proposed that the two sides simply go back to the pre–July 1941 status quo: Japan would get out of southern Indochina, and the United States would restore most of its oil exports. It was this proposal that would tempt Roosevelt and Hull briefly to the bargaining table again in November.

When the November 5 Imperial Conference started, Tojo began by telling Hirohito of the November 1 decision to pursue both diplomacy and military preparations. Togo then noted that diplomacy was currently deadlocked, with Washington unwilling to make any concessions. These two presentations were followed by Suzuki's long analysis of the resource problem. Expectations of future trade were pessimistic: "the probability that we will experience increased difficulties in obtaining materials is high." In fact, Japan might be drawn into war, "even though we wish to avoid it," to secure its supply. This was not just a question of keeping Japan's military strong. Suzuki detailed a long list of materials critical to Japan's domestic needs that were also unobtainable due to the Anglo-American embargo. Because the United States had free access to raw materials and Japan did not, he concluded, "differences in defensive power" would open up over time.

Finance Minister Kaya reinforced this gloomy picture, observing that without raw materials, the national economy would collapse no matter how perfectly the government managed it. Sugiyama followed with a detailed analysis of the military situation. With the US arms buildup, the power balance was becoming increasingly unfavorable. As for the north, Sugiyama underscored that the Russians had suffered massive losses on the German-Soviet front, and had sent forces westward from Siberia equal to thirteen infantry divisions, thirteen hundred tanks, and a similar number of airplanes. In the short term, then, Russia would not attack Japan's army in Manchuria. Given that it was being reinforced by US aid, there was still a future danger. Thus Japan "must conclude its operations in the South as quickly as possible, and be prepared to cope with this situation"—namely, strike north.

It was at this point that Hara spoke up on Hirohito's behalf. He commented that despite the September 6 consensus—that Japan would concentrate on negotiations with Washington—to his regret no agreement had been signed. Togo informed him that US concerns regarding the Axis pact had been resolved, since Japan had agreed not contest any US entry into the European war. The China question, however, had become the main stumbling block. The United States was now balking at Japanese requests to station some troops in northern China after a peace deal with Chiang.[35]

Hara turned to the specifics of proposals A and B. Japan had to settle the China Incident, he stressed. So it seemed odd to him that plan B had said nothing about China per se. Togo noted that given the short time remaining, a quick agreement was unlikely under plan A. Even the much simpler plan B was unlikely to succeed. Hara then turned to the military "to explain what will happen if negotiations break down." The key issue was Japan's ability to defeat the US navy. Nagano said that in the short term, Japan did have a measure of superiority. The US fleet was bigger overall, but with 40 percent of it in the Atlantic, Japan had a 7.5 to 6 ratio in its favor. Yet even if Japan won an initial decisive battle, "war will continue long after the Southern Operation."

Hara then summarized the emperor's perspective in a long statement. It was still essential to try to get an agreement, he emphasized. But with little prospect of a diplomatic breakthrough, if Japan missed the present opportunity to go to war, "we will have to submit to American dictation." The country must therefore accept a decision for war should diplomacy fail. With his remarks indicating Hirohito's approval of the plans, the meeting quickly came to a close. Before it did, Tojo summed up the situation. There was still some hope for success in the US-Japanese negotiations, he contended, since the United States needed time to complete its buildup. He somberly noted the uneasiness felt around the table regarding the prospect of a protracted war. On the other hand, how could Japan let the United States do as it pleases? "When I think about the strengthening of American defenses in the Southwest Pacific," he declared, "the expansion of the American fleet, the unfinished China Incident, and so on, I see no end to difficulties. . . . [Still] I fear that we would become a third-class nation after two or three years if we just sat tight." The participants filed out of the conference knowing that unless a diplomatic miracle occurred within three weeks, Japan would be embarking on its most dangerous venture since the Meiji Restoration (*JDW*, 208–39). Yet aside from perhaps Sugiyama, not one person in the meeting expressed any degree of optimism regarding Japan's chances for even a stalemated victory. All knew the risk of defeat and national destruction was high. Nevertheless, in the face of a continued US embargo and Roosevelt's unwillingness to accept

---

[35] Togo does not mention this, but from September 3–4 onward, US officials had continually berated Nomura about Japan's deployment of troops against the Soviet Union. Nomura had made it clear to his superiors that this was Washington's number one concern and the main stumbling block to any deal. See Nomura's dispatches to Tokyo for September 4, 11, 17, 22, and 30 and October 9, 14, 16, and 27, in *PWP*, 177–96.

the deal for China that had emerged in early June, the Japanese saw no other option but to go south. War was quickly becoming a true lesser-of-two-evils choice.

THE FINAL NEGOTIATIONS

From the above, we can see that the real puzzle surrounding the last three weeks of November was not why Japan was preparing for total war in the south but instead why Roosevelt and Hull were still unwilling to make a deal to avert the impending disaster. Ever since negotiations began in April, the pair had been seeking to avoid a Pacific war so they could concentrate on the war against Hitler. By early September, Japan had conceded to their primary initial concern: Tokyo would operate "independently" of the Axis should the United States enter the European war. With Roosevelt, Hull, and the military all wanting to avoid a draining war in the Pacific—especially one taking place before the US buildup was complete—one would think the rational strategy was at least to buy some more time through a compromise.

In fact, Roosevelt and Hull did decide, for good geopolitical reasons, to seek such a deal. The two key military advisers, Army Chief of Staff George Marshall and Chief of Naval Operations Harold Stark, had been arguing for weeks that Japan was being driven into war by the oil embargo. With US forces not yet ready for war, they wanted an agreement that would give the United States at least an extra six months. The president was sympathetic to this reasoning. In an hour-long meeting with Stimson (diary, in *PHA*, 10–12:5431) on November 6, Roosevelt told Stimson that he was "trying to think of something which would give us further time." By mid-November, with Japan's desperate situation plain for all to see, Roosevelt decided to proceed with a modus vivendi strategy. In a handwritten memorandum to Hull on or about November 17, he said that the United States should "resume economic relations—some oil and rice now—more later," and it could again agree to play the role of intermediary to "introduce [the Japanese to the] Chinese to talk things over" (*FRUS* [1941], 4:626).

In return for US help, Roosevelt told Hull, Japan had to accept two things. First, consistent with long-standing US concerns, Japan must agree not to invoke the Tripartite Pact even if the United States got into the European war. Tokyo was unlikely to put up a fuss here, since it had already accepted this condition in early September. The president's second condition, in contrast, was much harder to secure, and quite revealing of his deeper worries. Japan had to promise to "send no more troops to Indo-China or [the] Manchurian border or any place South—(Dutch, Brit., or

Siam)" (*FRUS* [1941], 4:626; Heinrichs 1988, 208, 258n95). Once again, we see that Roosevelt was not just concerned about a southern advance but also a move north. He could not accept a deal that helped Japan exit China and kept the peace in the south if it only meant the redeployment of forces for an attack on Russia. This concern had been the root of the demand in previous negotiations that Japan promise to keep the peace in the entire Pacific region. Roosevelt now wanted something much more explicit. Japan not only had to agree not to attack Russia; it had to agree not to put additional forces in the north. His inclusion of Manchuria on the list of restricted countries could only have had one purpose: to get Japan to commit to peace with Russia while providing a simple mechanism—no further troop movements from either southern China or the home islands—to verify compliance.

By mid-November Roosevelt knew he was in a bind. Defeating Hitler was still the main priority. Through the fall, Roosevelt had continued to put US ships in harm's way in the Atlantic in order to spark an incident that would spiral to war. Hitler refused to take the bait. Notwithstanding Roosevelt's frustrations, the revisionist thesis that the president, seeing Berlin's unwillingness to escalate, sought a backdoor to war with Germany by provoking a war with Japan is without foundation.[36] Not only is there little direct documentation supporting it, but there is also one decisive fact against it: Roosevelt and Hull actively contemplated making a deal with Japan three times over six months—in early June, late August, and finally and most significant, late November. If one wants to provoke an adversary into attacking to get into a war elsewhere, one does not expend significant energy finding a way to satisfy its demands.[37]

Roosevelt's goal was exactly the opposite of what the revisionist thesis supposes: he wanted to avoid all conflict in the Far East if Japan would accept his two (and now only two) conditions—to delink itself from Germany, and remain peaceful everywhere in the Pacific and, most important, in the north vis-à-vis Russia. It is self-evident why this scenario was his first preference. It allowed him to focus solely on the European war while ensuring that Russia could play its key role in defeating Nazi Germany.

In international politics, however, one cannot always achieve one's first preference, and Roosevelt knew he might have to choose between

[36] For references and a reworking of this argument, see Trachtenberg 2006.

[37] The revisionist thesis has always had one underlying flaw: it assumes that it was obvious to the United States that Hitler would declare war on the United States should Japan attack the United States in the Pacific. By the terms of the Tripartite Pact, though, neither Germany nor Japan was under any obligation if its ally was the clear aggressor against a third party. In retrospect, it seems obvious that the Pacific War got the United States into the European war. But this could not have been anticipated with any degree of confidence prior to December 7, 1941.

two far less desirable options. The first was simply a war with Japan where the Japanese struck south to gain access to the raw materials being denied to them. The second was a compromise deal with Japan along the lines of his note to Hull, but one that Tokyo broke in order to attack Russia. Getting the Japanese to agree to not moving additional forces into Manchuria might help bind Tokyo to a regional peace. A severe form of the commitment problem nevertheless hung over any deal.[38] In the end, Tokyo might decide to build up in Manchuria secretly or just attack Russia with what it had already deployed there.

Thus Roosevelt, in even considering a modus vivendi, was entering into a delicate and risky diplomatic game. If Japan agreed to his terms, he could accept the deal and hope that Japan lived up to its promises. Then if and when his Atlantic scheme or some other ploy proved successful and the United States found itself at war with Germany, his first preference would be realized. Yet the downside risk was clear. Renewing trade with Japan and helping it end the China Incident might lead to the worst of all outcomes: a Japanese war with Russia at a time when the Soviet Red Army was the only real barrier between Hitler and the German domination of Eurasia.

Roosevelt was perfectly aware of his military's desire to buy time. On November 5, the war department sent him a memorandum noting that the US navy was presently "inferior to the Japanese Fleet" and incapable of offensive operations. With the United States and Britain still reinforcing the Philippines and Singapore, they would lack the capacity to deter Japan until early spring. The chiefs of the army and navy (Marshall and Stark) thus agreed that war between the United States and Japan "should be avoided while building up defensive forces in the Far East." The "primary objective" of US policy, after all, remained the defeat of Germany, and any war with Japan "would only greatly weaken the combined [US-British] effort in the Atlantic against Germany" (PHA, 13–14:1061–62). The importance of buying time would be a constant refrain of Marshall and Stark through the remaining days of November (see Trachtenberg 2006, 120–21).

The president also understood the fragile nature of the Japanese-Russian peace that had held despite German advances. Roosevelt knew Japan was readying for war, but was waiting for a decisive German victory and possible Sino-Japanese peace before taking the plunge. From early July through November, Roosevelt received a series of top-secret estimates the Far Eastern situation directly from the war department.[39] The

---

[38] See my discussion in the first two chapters; Fearon 1995.

[39] These reports were generally sent via Brigadier General Sherman Miles, acting chief of staff of the G2, the army's planning and information-gathering division.

July 17 report indicated that in spite of its Manchurian buildup, Japan might stay on the defensive, given that "the major part of the Japanese Army . . . [was] pinned down in China." The August 16 report stated that Japan had increased its strength in Manchuria to six hundred thousand troops (from an original two hundred thousand in May), yet was unlikely to attack in the short term because Germany's offensive had "gone awry." The analysis of September 5 reiterated that Japan would refrain from war against Russia until peace with China had been secured. The September 23 evaluation concluded that Tokyo probably sought a summit to hide preparations for an all-out northern attack "timed with the expected Russian collapse in Europe" (*PHA*, 13–14:1342–57).

The October 2 report to Roosevelt was the most remarkable of the bunch. Should the Sino-Japanese War end, it asserted, Japan would free up twenty-one divisions and a thousand aircraft, most or all of which would be diverted to Manchuria. Tokyo would then initiate war if either Russia collapsed in the west or Japan achieved superiority due to transfers of Soviet troops westward. Given this, Washington should exploit the continued China quagmire to prevent a Japanese move north.

> The initial feeling of revulsion over this apparent utilization of China as a cat's paw in our plan of strategy will be alleviated by an examination of the situation of the anti-Axis powers in the light of cold reason. Our objective is the destruction of Nazism, and all-out aid to those powers actively engaged in resisting its aggressive drive for world domination. Russia is, as a matter of expedience, an ally in this cause. We must, among other things, do what we can with what we have at our disposal to aid Russia in her struggle with Germany. Any action on our part, therefore, which would liberate Japanese (pro-Axis) forces for action against Russia's rear in Siberia would be foolhardy.

The document did note that Washington might use a summit to buy time for its own buildup. Most important, however, was the immediate objective of "weaken[ing] Hitler in every way possible." In any negotiations, then, Washington had to ensure Tokyo showed "substantial evidence of sincerity, not to attack Russia in Siberia." Only such a guarantee would free Russia, psychologically and militarily, for stronger opposition to Nazi Germany (ibid., 13–14:1357–59).

Given the above, it is impossible to accept the idea, critical to almost every historical argument, that Japan's refusal to leave China in late November was the key reason for US unwillingness to renew the oil trade. US officials well understood that ending the Sino-Japanese War was Tokyo's objective, not Washington's, and that Washington had a strong interest in keeping Japan bogged down in China. For if Japan invaded Siberia, the war with Germany would then be as good as over, with Hitler the head of a new Eurasian superpower.[40]

But did Roosevelt himself really understand the significance of these startling analyses? He certainly did. On October 10, Roosevelt told British ambassador Halifax that he feared that Japan would attack Vladivostok (Heinrichs 1988, 191). Five days later, on October 15, he wrote to Churchill that the situation with Japan was "definitely worse and I think they are headed north" (*CR*, 1:250). The next day, October 16, he held a meeting with his top advisers at the White House. From diary notes made by Stimson (LC, October 16, 1941), we can see that Roosevelt was now actively considering the necessity of drawing Japan into war. The United States, the president argued, faced the delicate question of the "diplomatic fencing" that had to be carried out by Washington "so as to be sure that Japan was put into the wrong and made the first bad move." Not coincidentally, Chief of Naval Operations Stark sent a telegram to his Pacific and Atlantic commanders that day stating that Japan was unlikely to make a deal with the United States, and as such, "hostilities between Japan and Russia are a strong possibility." He went on to suggest that because the United States and Britain might be blamed for Japan's economic situation, there was also a risk that Japan might attack them. The commanders were advised to engage in preparatory deployments, but to avoid maneuvers that "constitute provocative actions" (*PHA*, 13–14:1402). Such language indicates not only that the main US fear was of an attack on Russia, not Southeast Asia, but also that Japan had to be allowed to strike the first blow.

The information gathered by the war department after October 16 only reinforced the worry that Japan might attack Russia soon, despite the onset of winter in Manchuria. The department's October 21 analysis to Roosevelt stated that the Soviets possessed air superiority, but this could be quickly altered "by [Japan's] shifting from China . . . the bulk of [its] air forces." On the ground, Japanese troops now numbered 684,000 to Russia's 682,000. If more Siberian troops were moved westward and the Kwantung Army achieved a two-to-one superiority, it was "highly probable" that it would take the offensive. If this rose to a three-to-one ratio, the probability "will become a certainty" (ibid., 13–14, 1360–61).

Given this desperate situation, the report argued, Washington had to do everything possible to maintain Russia's military equality. Two policies

---

[40]Fear of German hegemony was reinforced by the internal release of the Joint Board's Victory Program on September 11, 1941, which stressed that if Germany ended up controlling Eurasia, it could then prepare for the "the eventual conquest of South America and the military defeat of the United States" (Trachtenberg 2006, 118–19; see also Stoler 2000, chaps. 2 and 3).

stood out. The first, a continuation of the cat's-paw strategy, was to increase aid to China to allow it "to continue to pin to the ground . . . the bulk of the Japanese Army." The second was to help Russia by bolstering aid to Soviet armies in both Europe *and* Siberia, meaning a funneling of more lend-lease aid through Iran and Vladivostok (ibid., 13–14:1360–61). A follow-up report to Roosevelt on November 1 noted that Japan now had thirty-three divisions in Manchuria—a large jump from the nineteen divisions of early September, and a quadrupling of the eight divisions there prior to Germany's invasion of Russia. The Japanese might still increase southern troop levels, the report suggested, but this action might hurt the northern army and cause Japan to "'miss the bus' when [its] chance comes for [the] invasion of Siberia" (ibid., 13–14:1361–62).

By mid-November, therefore, Roosevelt found himself walking a geopolitical tightrope. He could only negotiate toward a modus vivendi that might give him his preferred outcome—total peace in the Pacific even if the United States entered the European war—at the risk of sending Japan north against Russia. Throughout the first half of November, encouraging reports were arriving indicating that Germany's push toward Moscow had been halted (Heinrichs 1988, 201). Then on November 13, Grew forwarded a report strongly maintaining that Japanese leaders were reaching the end of their economic rope. Without the renewal of raw material imports, Japan's economy "[could not] withstand the present strain very much longer," meaning Tokyo "must accept the inevitable or fight" (*PHA*, 19–20:4051–57). It was likely this information combined with the sense that Russia might survive the winter that led Roosevelt to reverse policy and support a compromise deal on November 17. With Japan deterred a bit longer in the north, Roosevelt could buy time for his southern buildup.

This was now the third time since March that Roosevelt had restarted US-Japanese talks in hopes of reaching an agreement to keep the Pacific peace. Just like the other two instances, he would subsequently decide to end them abruptly, this time on November 26, much to the frustration and mystification of the Japanese diplomats (and US military). It is crucial to remember that there is no way to explain Roosevelt's on-again, off-again interest in a negotiated peace by any version of the "backdoor-to-war" thesis. If he was manipulating Japan into war to get the United States into the European war, then he should have kept the pressure on throughout November (and through spring and summer, for that matter).

In fact, the only riddle left to explain is why Roosevelt would push for an immediate modus vivendi, reach a consensus on the need to secure one with his top advisers on Tuesday, November 25, and then reject the idea the very next morning. For anyone studying the Pacific War, this about-face on November 26 is the single most puzzling event of the whole March to December 1941 period. Roosevelt's unwillingness to proceed with a modus vivendi seems even odder once we consider the exact sequence of events. The president knew from discussions with Nomura and his associates that Tokyo desired a modus vivendi should a broader agreement based on the May–June and August–September talks not pan out.[41] This of course was plan B from the Imperial Conference of November 6: Japan would return to the pre–July 1941 status quo, pulling out of southern Indochina if Washington reinstated at least part of US oil exports. Thus when Roosevelt sat down at noon on Tuesday, November 25 for an hour-and-a-half meeting with Hull, Stimson, Stark, Marshall, and Navy Secretary Frank Knox, he knew almost exactly what the Japanese would both propose and accept. The draft agreement settled on by the end of the meeting emphasized Japan's removal of forces out of southern Indochina. In return, Washington "[would] permit the export to Japan of petroleum . . . upon a monthly basis for civilian needs" (*FRUS* [1941], 4:662–64). Stark and Marshall, who had been pressing Roosevelt for a month for such a deal, were delighted. They left town Wednesday afternoon believing that the two sides would avoid war for at least a few more months, giving the military time to expand its presence in Hawaii, Guam, and the Philippines.[42]

When Roosevelt and Hull met early the next morning, Wednesday, November 26, they decided, in Hull's words, to "kick the whole thing over." Without consulting the other participants of the Tuesday meeting, they also decided to immediately call the Japanese diplomats into the White House to break the news to them. That afternoon, Roosevelt told Nomura and his associates that there would be no modus vivendi and in fact Tokyo must now agree to ten US demands before oil would be renewed (*FRUS* [1941], 4:645–46). Because Magic had made known the November 29–30 deadline for a Japanese decision to attack, Roosevelt and Hull had not expected to meet with Nomura until Friday or Saturday. So to ask him to come in Wednesday afternoon, not to secure a deal, but to lay down ten demands that they knew would be unacceptable, is certainly odd behavior.

That Roosevelt and Hull understood that the Japanese leadership could not possibly accept the ten demands is quite clear. Nomura and his colleagues on Wednesday afternoon, despite their shock, did not reject the ten demands but instead stated only that they would relay them to Tokyo. Yet the next day, the war department sent a message to the Pacific command telling it straightforwardly that diplomacy was now

[41] See Nomura's dispatches to Tokyo on November 20 and 22, in *PWP*, 205–7.

[42] The military's more relaxed attitude is shown by the notes of the Joint Board meeting held Wednesday at 11:35 a.m., presided over by Stark and Marshall. The discussion revolved solely around military preparations in the Pacific Rim (*PHA*, 15–16:1641–43).

essentially over, war was possible at any moment, and were it to occur, "the United States desires that Japan commit the first overt act" (see *PHA*, 13–14:1328–29; Prange 1981, 402–3).[43]

So the puzzle remains: Why would Roosevelt and Hull suddenly end any chance of a diplomatic solution on November 26, when only the day before they had agreed to pursue one? Obviously something must have happened between 1:30 p.m. on Tuesday and the Roosevelt and Hull meeting on Wednesday morning to change their minds. To try to explain the riddle, historians have generally focused on the roles played by the Chinese and British leaders on the night of November 25. There is evidence that Chiang communicated to Stimson on the night of November 25 that he was upset about the possibility of a deal with Japan. In Chiang's memorandum, written to Chinese envoy T. V. Soong and passed by Soong on to Stimson, Chiang wrote that the morale of the Chinese people would collapse if they believed that Washington was sacrificing their interests. If the Chinese army then fell apart, "[such] a loss would not be to China alone" (*FRUS* [1941], 4:660–61). Historians speculate that this message changed Roosevelt's calculation: he realized that he could not maintain China as an ally if he made a deal with Japan.[44]

This explanation is reinforced by the British leadership's reaction to a possible US-Japanese deal. Early on the morning of October 26, Churchill wrote to Roosevelt, noting that he had read Halifax's dispatches regarding the proposed modus vivendi. There was only one point that disquiets us, Churchill told Roosevelt: "What about Chiang Kai-shek? Is he not having a very thin diet? Our anxiety is about China. If they collapse, our joint dangers would enormously increase" (*FRUS* [1941], 4:665). Combined with Chiang's message, so the reasoning goes, Roosevelt and Hull had no choice but to end the effort to reach a compromise (Dallek 1979; Kimball 1997).

From a theoretical perspective, it is perfectly in line with the trade expectations argument to accept the traditional historians' take on the events of November 25–26. After all, it suggests that an exogenous third-party issue—the survival of China as an ally—compelled Washington to maintain a hard-line policy. And it was this policy that confirmed Japan's negative expectations for future trade, making war inevitable. Yet the "Chinese-connection" assertion must be called into question. It was another third-party issue—the now-familiar one of Russia's survival in its war with Germany—that was almost certainly the key to Roosevelt

---

[43] According to Marshall, the language of this message came directly from Roosevelt himself (*PHA*, 1–3:1310).

[44] For references and one of the better versions of this argument, supported with Chinese sources, see Sun 1993, chap. 7.

and Hull's about-face. In what follows, I lay out the evidence for this alternative perspective. But it is worth remembering that whether one accepts the Chinese-connection thesis or Russian-connection argument, both uphold the book's contention that third-party constraints can drive two states into war over economic issues.

The problems with the Chinese-connection thesis are threefold. First, Roosevelt and Hull had known for months that Chiang was upset about the prospect of a US-Japanese agreement, believing it would reduce US aid. Chiang's panicky telegram on the night of November 25 was not telling them anything new. Indeed, for the previous four days, ever since Hull briefed the Chinese and British ambassadors about a possible modus vivendi, the Chinese government had been registering its disapproval.[45] In particular, on Monday, November 24, the day before Roosevelt's inner circle met, Hull was told of Chiang's "rather strong reaction" to the modus vivendi, believing that Washington was now inclined to appease Japan at China's expense (*FRUS* [1941], 4:646–47). In light of known Chinese anxieties, why would Roosevelt and Hull proceed with the compromise idea on Tuesday and then kick it over the next morning?

The second problem is simply that Chiang's concerns were not valid, and thus could have been easily placated by subsequent US behavior had Washington and Tokyo made a deal. The US drafts of the proposed agreement from November 21 to 24 made it clear that Japan would have to reduce force numbers in northern Indochina even as it pulled out of southern Indochina. The November 24 draft in fact specified that Japan could only keep a maximum of twenty-five thousand troops in northern Indochina after the agreement—a number deemed by the US military as too small for a successful attack on the Burma Road (the main conduit for supplies to Chungking) (ibid., 4:643). Moreover, the draft made absolutely no promise that US aid to China would not increase. In short, by stabilizing China's southern frontier, keeping the Burma Road open, and allowing Washington to sustain its aid to Chiang, Washington would be actually *helping* China's ability to fight Japan, not hurting it.

It is evident that Roosevelt understood these points and had little tolerance for Chinese concerns, as shown by his meeting with Soong on Wednesday, November 26. Early in the morning that day, just before throwing over the modus vivendi, Roosevelt had been on the phone with Hull when the latter mentioned Chiang's anxious telegram from the night before. As bystander Henry Morgenthau (FDRL, November 26, 1941), Roosevelt's treasury secretary, recorded in his diary, the president breezily replied, "Well, send [the Chinese envoys] in to see me today and I will

---

[45] For the record of the Saturday briefing and Hull's dismissive reaction to Chinese objections, see *FRUS* (1941), 4:635–40. See also Heinrichs 1988, 209–10.

quiet them down." When Soong met with the president that afternoon, Roosevelt led him to believe that a deal with Japan was still being considered, even though he and Hull had already rejected it many hours before. Stringing Soong along, Roosevelt told him that "he thought Chiang Kai-shek was much too excited." Any modus vivendi would help keep supplies flowing to China along the Burma Road, Roosevelt argued, and would buy three to six months to get ready in the Philippines (ibid., FDRL, November 27, 1941).[46]

One might believe that it was Churchill's intervention that made the difference, since the United States needed Britain on its side regardless of the validity of Chinese concerns. But this notion also has little foundation. Halifax had made it clear to Hull before November 25 that the British were anxious to avoid a two-front war in the Pacific and that London strongly supported the modus vivendi. Churchill himself had been signaling for months that he did not want war in the Pacific. So the only "new" piece of information was the passage in Churchill's letter of November 26 asking if Chiang was on too thin a diet. Historians regularly quote this passage to support the notion that Hull suddenly realized that neither the Chinese nor British would support the deal. Hull's (1948, 1080–82) own memoirs argue along these lines.[47]

Once we examine the surrounding content of Churchill's letter, however, it is apparent that this letter could not have been decisive. Prior to the section on Chiang's thin diet, Churchill tells Roosevelt that he has read Halifax and his foreign secretary's assessment of the proposed modus vivendi. He goes on to say, "Of course, it is for you to handle this business and we certainly do not want an additional war." Only then does he introduce the phrase "there is only one point that disquiets us" as a precursor to discussing Chiang's thin diet. The larger context thus makes it plain that Churchill is giving authority for any decision over to Roosevelt and his main priority is, like the president's, to avoid a two-front war. Churchill's language is muted and circumspect. By saying "there is only one point," he is deliberately moderating his tone to indicate that he is only making a suggestion. And by highlighting Chiang's thin diet, he is underscoring the importance

---

[46] The fact that Morgenthau obtained this information from his meeting with Soong on Thursday afternoon shows that the Chinese envoy still believed that the modus vivendi was on the table more than twenty-four hours after it had been kicked over. Roosevelt had not only misled him on Wednesday but also clearly still had no interest in telling him the truth even the next day, despite having already met with Japan's diplomatic team. If Chiang's worries had been critical to the Wednesday morning flip-flop, one might think the Chinese embassy would have been the first to be reassured.

[47] Given the calculated fabrications contained in Hull's memoirs regarding the April–September negotiations (see note 22), the very fact that he jumps on the Chinese and British letters as the cause of his flip-flop should raise red flags as to the explanation's validity.

of material aid for China rather than trying to reverse any US decision regarding a deal with Japan. Churchill had no reason to communicate opposition to a deal that he as well as everyone else knew was the only way to avoid a Japanese attack south at that point. So the idea that Hull later propagates—that he went to Roosevelt on the morning of November 26, and told him that given China's opposition along with "the half-hearted support or actual opposition of the British, the Netherlands, and the Australian Governments," the modus vivendi should not be presented—is pure fabrication (see Hull 1948, 1082). The British, Dutch, and Australians were already on board, and given their geographic vulnerability in Southeast Asia, understandably anxious to secure a peace.[48]

The third and final problem with the Chinese-connection argument is the most straightforward: it cannot explain why Roosevelt and Hull torpedoed possible negotiated deals on two previous occasions (in late June and early September). There is an evident pattern here—a serious US interest in an agreement and then the deliberate undermining of promising developments—that the argument about Chiang cannot cover. We have seen that the most likely reason for the two previous terminations of talks was Russia's situation vis-à-vis Germany and whether Japan would exploit a Russian setback to attack Siberia. Could this again be the best explanation for the about-face on November 26?

Although we will probably never have complete smoking gun evidence for Roosevelt and Hull's change of heart that Wednesday morning, the need to keep Russia alive in the global struggle against Nazism is the only explanation that fits all the available evidence, and certainly the only one that aligns with the evidence for the two previous shutdowns in talks. Roosevelt and his advisers, as we have seen, had been obsessed for months with the possibility that Japan would go north. Within this context, the information on Russia's situation that arrived on the night of November 25 could only have been seen as deeply troubling. Back in early November, the German campaign that had begun in late August had finally been halted just a few hundred miles outside Moscow. For a few days Hitler had held his forces in place, and it looked as if he might pull them back to stabilize supply lines and wait for better weather. But instead of retreating, Hitler engaged in yet another perilous roll of the dice. On November 15, he began a new major offensive to take Moscow

[48] Indeed, they were upset when they found out that Hull had *not* presented the deal to Tokyo, since they knew they would be the front line of the war to come. See, in particular, the Australian documents on this period, detailing the efforts of Australian and British diplomats to get diplomacy back on track after November 26 (*DAFP*). For British and Australian efforts on November 30 to persuade Hull to buy time via diplomacy, see *PHA*, 19–20:3690–91.

before the full depth of the Russian winter set in. For the next nine days, the front line ebbed and flowed in what had become the most crucial single battle of the war so far. On the night of November 25, however, new information came in indicating that the Germans had scored major victories that day. They had moved within thirty-one miles of the city, and were making a beeline for the Moscow-Volga Canal in the north and Oka River in the south. If either fell, the road to the Soviet capital would be open. Hitler was throwing everything he had into the struggle to take Moscow, knowing that if Stalin had to retreat behind the Urals, the war would be essentially won.[49]

As Morgenthau's diary notes reveal, Roosevelt had become highly concerned with these developments by the early morning of Wednesday, November 26. That morning, Morgenthau went to the White House to discuss recent US efforts to increase the flow of lend-lease goods to the Soviet Union. Catching Roosevelt in the middle of his breakfast, Morgenthau handed him a memo. The news was discouraging. The number of ships that had delivered goods to Russia during November was less than a third of the planned amount. Yet to Morgenthau's surprise, the president did not want to talk about the "Russian matter." This, for Morgenthau, "makes me believe he knows the situation is bad." (It was just after this that Roosevelt spoke on the phone with Hull, telling him he would "quiet down" the Chinese.)

At this point in his notes, Morgenthau reminds himself of the essence of the proposed modus vivendi (which at that point had not yet been kicked over). His spare summary is instructive in terms of what it mentions and what it leaves out. He writes that the United States is to unfreeze Japanese assets to allow Japan to buy as much oil as it needs for industrial uses and export as much as it wants. In return, the "Japanese are to agree not to attack Russia in Siberia." Nothing more is mentioned. Morgenthau was well informed about the state of US-Japanese relations. Nevertheless, he makes no mention of a US demand to "get out of China"—surely a strange omission if Japan's exit from China was the United States' primary concern in these tense November days.[50]

---

[49] See Heinrichs 1988, 213; Clark 1965, chap. 9; *PHA*, 19–20:4473–74. On the administration's fear that Moscow would fall, see George Marshall's testimony before the Pearl Harbor congressional hearings, in *PHA*, 1–3:1148–49.

[50] Morgenthau's diary that day also summarizes information that Soong had told him of a recent meeting between Hull, Soong, and British, Australian, and Dutch ambassadors. After the envoys were given details of the modus vivendi, Halifax mentioned he would have to consult with London. Hull "became very annoyed and said that it was up to the English to accept the proposal without any comments, which seems to me [Morgenthau] rather high-handed." This is further proof that Hull and Roosevelt had little interest in allied opinion, and were determined to act according to their own strategic imperatives.

Near the end of the meeting, Morgenthau's diary relates, the phone rang again. This time it was Eleanor Roosevelt on the line. After some banter about the resignation of a lower-level official, Eleanor asked him about how things were going. Roosevelt replied, "Everything is terrible. The Russian situation is awful. Moscow is falling." The British might also lose Libya, he continued. The situation, the president told his wife, "looks very bad." Roosevelt seemed so worried by the course of events, Morgenthau observes, that he couldn't finish his breakfast.[51] The meeting wrapped up, and an hour or so later Hull arrived to see the president. It was in that one-on-one meeting that Roosevelt and Hull made their fateful decision to toss out the compromise and slap the ten demands on Japan that made war inevitable.

While perhaps not quite a smoking gun, Morgenthau's diary notes are highly suggestive, to say the least. His notes are essentially the only contemporaneous documents available to shed light on the early morning of November 26, 1941.[52] They show a president who had little concern for Chiang's objections to a possible modus vivendi, but who was deeply anxious about the imminent fall of Moscow. Scholars clinging to the backdoor-to-war thesis might claim that the new information Roosevelt was receiving on Russia simply reinforced that he had to get the United States into the European war, and quickly. Notice, though, that even an immediate US entry into the war would have done nothing to help Russia in the short term, had Japan still gone north. The war for Eurasia would have been decided long before the first US soldier touched foreign soil.[53] Germany would then have been able to redirect troops southward

[51] All the above quotations and summaries are taken from Morgenthau's diary, FDRL, November 26, 1941. One source for Roosevelt's information, aside from increasingly pessimistic reports in the *New York Times* (Heinrichs 1988, 213), was likely a military intelligence report written late on November 25. The report expressed new doubt about the city of Moscow's ability to resist the German onslaught, noting that Russians officials were for the first time signaling their worry over the situation (*PHA*, 19–20:4473–74).

[52] Stimson's diary records his conversations with Roosevelt later that morning, after Hull had already informed Stimson that the deal would not be presented. But we have apparently no other documents revealing Roosevelt and Hull's thinking prior to their decision to reject the modus vivendi and present Japan with ten demands that afternoon. Interestingly, Stimson himself was not told that the decision was final until he talked to Hull the next morning. Stimson immediately phoned the president, who led him to believe that Roosevelt and Hull had only presented the Japanese with a "magnificent statement." He found out only later that this was not a "reopening" of US-Japanese talks but instead their essential termination. See Stimson's diary notes for November 26 and 27, in *PHA*, 10–12:5434–35. It seems clear from this that Roosevelt and Hull were trying to make sure that no one, not even a close associate such as Stimson, could act to reverse their decision.

[53] For this reason, even after severe setbacks in early 1942, US military strategy continued to focus on fighting hard enough in the Pacific such that Japan would not be able to attack Siberia. This effort knowingly diverted US resources from the European theater,

to finish the job of capturing the vast oil potential of the Middle East (as Roosevelt's concern about the British in Libya suggests). If the continental balance of power was to be restored, Communist Russia had to be saved from a two-front war. There was no other option. Japan had to be drawn south to keep it from going north.

CONCLUSION

The analysis of this chapter provides strong support for the thesis that third-party factors can lead states into a downward trade-security spiral that forces them into severe economic restrictions and war. Neither the Americans nor the Japanese wanted war with each other when negotiations restarted in April 1941. The Americans wanted to fight Germany, not Japan, and the Japanese wanted to end the China conflict so that they could regroup for the long-desired war against the rising Soviet colossus. By early June, a deal had been hammered out that appeared to satisfy both sides. But after Nazi Germany struck Russia on June 22 and began its steady push toward Moscow, Tokyo would not commit to staying out of the German-Soviet war. Roosevelt and Hull kept hoping they could achieve their first preference—namely, peace in the Pacific as the United States entered the European struggle. By late November, however, it seemed clear that any deal with Japan to restore the oil flow would likely only send Japan north against Russia. Roosevelt and Hull thus reluctantly decided to keep the embargo on, knowing that pessimistic trade expectations would force Japan to make a plunge toward the oil-rich Dutch East Indies and into war with the United States.[54] As undesired as such a conflict was, it would at least help preserve the Soviet Union as an ally, giving the United States a fighting chance to save the world from Nazi tyranny.

It is important to see that this explanation for the Pacific War not only aligns with the evidence but also covers the anomalies that exist for alternative explanations. Economic realism can explain Japan's concern for its high dependence. It nonetheless cannot explain the Japanese desire to resolve their raw material supply problem through diplomacy, nor why Japan would switch from diplomacy to war by late November 1941. The constant of high dependency cannot explain a variable. For liberals, the Pacific War should be one of their best cases: as trade

---

but by keeping the Soviets in the war, it prevented the German domination of Eurasia long enough for the United States to complete its build up for total war. See Stoler 2000, 72–97.

[54]There is no evidence, by the way, that Roosevelt knew about the impending attack on Pearl Harbor. But he certainly anticipated the strike on the Philippines.

levels fell from 1939 to 1941, preexisting domestic pathologies should have been unleashed. Yet even the strongest argument for the role of domestic politics—Snyder's (1991) notion that parochial groups, specifically the army and navy, hijacked the Japanese state and pushed it into war because of internalized imperial myths along with self-created domestic pressures—faces deep problems. For one thing, civilian leaders and Hirohito were very much involved in the decision-making process, with all top officials working hard to create a consensus for war. Moreover, many in the military, particularly in the navy, were reluctant to fight the United States, and as such, actively supported efforts to secure a deal that would restore Western oil exports. Finally, the documentary evidence shows overwhelmingly that the primary motive for war with the United States was the fear of long-term decline caused by the double whammy of economic sanctions and the US naval buildup. There is little proof that Japanese officials felt any pressure from the general population or lower-level military officers to start a war with the United States. And if they had felt such pressure and were just unwilling to express it, they would not have sought a negotiated peace across nine months of on-again, off-again talks.

Purely historical arguments fare no better. The backdoor-to-war thesis that sees Roosevelt manipulating Japan into war in order to get into the war in Europe falls apart in the face of one key fact: Roosevelt and Hull worked hard to get a peace deal for the Pacific and almost made such an agreement on three occasions. The argument of this chapter shows why they would pursue such a deal. It also demonstrates why they would have to repeatedly scuttle it, even at the risk of a US-Japanese war, when Tokyo refused to commit to not going north. The traditional assertion that Roosevelt and Hull kicked over the final negotiations because of Chiang also proves unsustainable. Chiang's concerns were well known and largely immaterial, since Roosevelt and Hull were more than prepared to keep supplying China with economic and material aid in the event of a modus vivendi with Japan.

In the end, the war between Japan and the United States cannot be viewed as overdetermined by a mix of powerful forces. Rather, it was driven by one primary cause: Japan's increasingly pessimistic trade expectations in a situation of high dependence. All other factors can be seen to have had little salience or acting merely as facilitating conditions. Needless to say, when we look at the war in its broader context, Japanese leaders—civilian and military as well as the emperor—are hardly blameless. Had they been willing to give up their four-decades-long drive to reduce Russian power in order to protect Japan's economic and strategic position in Northeast Asia, a deal for peace in the Pacific could have been made. Yet in explaining the total war of 1941—and why it was launched against the United States and *not* against the Soviet Union—we must turn to Roosevelt and Hull's decision to impose as well as maintain a complete embargo on oil and raw materials despite knowing that they were pushing Japan into war. The two understood full well that by manipulating Japanese trade expectations in either a positive or negative direction, they held the fate of the Pacific region in their hands. Still, the force of circumstances—the importance of keeping Russia in the fight against the greatest menace the world had ever seen—led them to make a lesser-of-two-evils choice for war in the south to avoid a war in the north.

In the final analysis, we can say that they made the right choice, both on moral and geopolitical grounds. The only irony is that by creating the conditions for Hitler's eventual defeat, they also set down the conditions for a future bipolar struggle between Russia and the United States that would consume the next half century of world history. The country that Roosevelt helped save in 1941 would become the United States' main rival and long-term threat a mere four years later. Great power politics, however, often requires that distasteful means be used to avoid having to face a disastrous outcome. And it is hard to argue that the destruction of Hitler's Germany was not an end that justified any means.

CHAPTER SIX

The Origins, Dynamics, and Termination of the Cold War, 1942–91

THE GOAL OF THIS CHAPTER is a broad, probably overly ambitious one. I will try to sweep across five decades of post-1941 great power politics to examine one simple question: What was the relative causal importance of economic interdependence and changes in commercial expectations to the ups and downs of Cold War history? This chapter provides a detailed but summary answer to this question. A companion book on commerce and US foreign policy offers a more complete explication, and readers keen on post-1941 US statecraft will want to consult that volume as well (Copeland, forthcoming).[1]

At first blush, it would seem self-evident that economic interdependence could have had little to do with the origins of the Cold War or the crises and tensions that pockmarked its history until the late 1980s. After all, US-Soviet trade from late 1946 onward remained at very low levels given what seemed to be strong geopolitical reasons for not trading, particularly US fears that trade would promote Soviet relative economic growth. It would seem, then, that economic interdependence drops out as a causal variable that might explain not only the start of the Cold War but also its occasional though intense crises and its final termination in 1989–91. Indeed, both realists and liberals usually completely ignore the economic aspects of the US-Soviet relationship from 1945 to the 1980s, presuming that consistently low or almost nonexistent trade could not possibly have had much of a role in explaining variations in the intensity of the Cold War struggle. The two camps thus tend to fight over the relative salience of other variables: realists stress the significance of power and nuclear technology in shaping arms-racing dynamics along with the competition for territorial position, while liberals argue for the importance of ideological and domestic motivations as well as the role of international arms control regimes.[2] When it comes to the underlying causes of the Cold War itself, liberals typically align with the traditionalist ar-

---

[1] For a summary of the eleven case periods covered below, see table 2.7.

[2] The literature here is too vast to cite, but for a general overview of the two sides' positions and references, see Buzan 1984.

gument that Moscow's drive to spread Communism led to the spiral of hostility between the two wartime allies. Systemic realists generally adopt the postrevisionist view that both sides brought on the Cold War spiral out of fear of the other side's present and future territorial intentions. Yet the economic dimensions of great power politics have typically played little or no role in either camp's analyses.[3]

To garner any insight into the role of economics in the Cold War, one has had to fall back on so-called revisionist scholars—that is, scholars who argue that the United States started and sustained the Cold War in order to prop up capitalism as well as ensure US control of foreign markets and raw materials. Revisionists have uncovered crucial documents that force us to rethink the nature of the US-Soviet conflict.[4] Unfortunately, they are led off track by their neo-Marxist starting point. By typically presuming that US elites sought global domination to increase the wealth and power of their capitalist class, revisionists ignore the profound national security implications of economic interdependence that arose for the United States as World War II wound down and a new era began. Moreover, their focus on Western capitalism leads them to miss a key fact: Russia also had strong economic needs that made its leaders quite concerned about Soviet ties with new spheres of influence in Eurasia and Africa along with the United States itself.

This chapter seeks to rectify the lacuna in the international relations field by showing the truly powerful impact of commercial factors on the dynamics of US-Soviet relations after 1941. The problems with realist and liberal thinking about economic interdependence are starkly revealed by the Cold War case. The theoretical logics for both camps are based on the actual present trade between great power spheres. But in situations where current trade is low or nonexistent, leaders' expectations of *future* trade and commerce can be still critical to their decision-making processes. So even when there is little present trade, if a state needs what the external system has to offer, the other's commitment or lack of commitment to providing future economic benefits may be critical to a leader's assessment of the state's future security.

---

[3]For overview articles on debates regarding the Cold War's origins, see Gaddis 1983; Jones and Woods 1993; Leffler 1994a. Neoclassical realists, because of their emphasis on unit-level factors, have typically sided with liberals (Kydd 2005; MacDonald 1995–96). Marc Trachtenberg (1999) provides a systemic realist account stressing the impact of the competition over the control of postwar Germany. The only realist scholar focusing a great deal of attention on economic factors is historian Melvyn Leffler (1984, 1992, 1996a, 1996b), and my perspective has been strongly influenced by his writings.

[4]See, in particular, Kolko 1990; Paterson 1973; Williams 1962; Hearden 2002; Gardner 1972, 1993, 2009.

The first half of this chapter will discuss the start of the Cold War and crises of the early Cold War period (1945–56). The origins of the Cold War itself are deeply rooted in both sides' concerns about economic developments within their own and the other's sphere coupled with their expectations for future trade and commerce. The Soviets in the last years of World War II had become highly dependent on US lend-lease aid not only to fight the war but also to rebuild their devastated country as the Nazis retreated. They therefore looked to US willingness to keep trade and loans flowing as signs of Washington's attitude toward economic cooperation in the postwar era. The United States was also concerned about the postwar trade environment, but for quite different reasons. Some US officials, following Secretary of State Hull's lead, did believe that freely flowing global trade might help keep the peace, largely for Wilsonian reasons (Layne 2006). Yet as Melvyn Leffler has forcefully shown, the question of US access to markets, raw materials, and investments was driven more by realpolitik logic: without such access, US officials believed that US power would decline, leaving the country vulnerable to the rising Soviet colossus. To maintain power preponderance and security into the future, then, it was critical to ensure continued access to the states of the Eurasian periphery—states that held the bulk of global production and resources outside Russia and the United States per se.[5] This overriding concern, present from the start, would overshadow the whole of the Cold War era, making American expectations sensitive to any political or economic developments that might threaten the future economic viability of the US sphere.

The second half of this chapter will examine the economic determinants of the various efforts after 1956 to moderate the tensions of the Cold War and perhaps end the conflict altogether. Both sides by the mid-1950s understood the horrors of thermonuclear war, and had good reasons to find ways to increase trust and to avoid the arms buildups and crises that might push the superpowers into actual war. Yet despite two major attempts to secure a stable détente—an initial effort in the late 1950s and a more promising one in the early 1970s—Washington and Moscow failed to find a true end to the Cold War until the late 1980s. Why did these early attempts prove ephemeral (and indeed often seem to lead to greater hostility), and why did the policies of the 1980s finally "work"?

Because there were so many factors, not just commercial ones, shaping the behavior of the superpowers, this chapter's goal is not to prove that the trade expectations approach provides a definitive answer to the questions posed above. Rather, I seek to show the underappreciated and often surprising significance of economic factors in both the causes of conflict and the creation of a lasting superpower peace. While not denying the

[5] See especially Leffler 1992; see also Leffler 1984, 1994b, 1996b.

importance of realist and liberal factors such as power, ideology, and domestic politics, I demonstrate how expectations of future trade at important moments significantly exacerbated the intensity of tension and risk of superpower crisis. We will see, for example, that trade concerns interacted with military fears to undermine the chances for peace during the most dangerous period of the modern nuclear era—from 1956 to 1962. We will also see just how important trade expectations were to the unwinding of Cold War hostility, both in the early 1970s and 1980s.

THE BEGINNING OF THE COLD WAR

The causes of the Cold War can be traced to the trade and financial expectations held by both the Soviet Union and United States as they emerged from World War II. Four years of German occupation had left the Soviet Union in tatters, with thousands of villages flattened, a quarter of its industrial capacity destroyed, and twenty-seven million dead. To rebuild, Moscow desperately needed to keep US trade and loans flowing after war's end (Congress having approved lend-lease aid only for wartime). It also needed reparations from Germany, and a reorientation of Eastern Europe toward Russia and away from traditional trading partners in Western Europe. Finally, it wanted access to potential oil supplies in Iran, given Russian import needs. By 1944–45, the Soviets were worried: Would Washington facilitate or hinder the realization of these ends?

US concerns, especially by April–June 1945, were of a different sort. Washington feared that war-devastated peripheral states, even without Moscow's active encouragement, would fall to Communism. The Americans knew that any small state that "went Communist" would likely realign its foreign-economic policy toward Moscow's sphere, seeing the Soviet economic model as the wave of the future. And precisely because of Russia's great needs, Moscow would welcome such states and then sever their commercial ties with the West.

The threat of fragile peripheral states in Western Europe going Communist was real. Communist groups that had played critical roles in wartime resistance movements were poised to exploit domestic conditions to seize power—by either the rifle barrel or ballet box. Key states such as France, Italy, and Greece were particularly vulnerable. Through 1945, US leaders looked to Eastern European states as litmus tests of future Soviet economic policy, and did not like what they saw (Leffler 1992). The Americans could understand why Moscow needed to keep Poland, the historical invasion route to Russia, so firmly within its grasp. But Russia's tight neomercantilist policy toward Romania and Bulgaria in 1945 suggested that if other European states fell to Communism and were pulled into the Soviet sphere, the US economy would be severely undermined.[6] Should these effects snowball across Eurasia, the Soviet Union might find itself the dominant global superpower without having to fire a shot.

Given these threats, any responsible US statesperson had but one option: contain Russia's growth by restricting its access to trade and loans while redirecting US goods to the faltering Western economies, notwithstanding the risks of provoking a trade-security spiral. I show that US leaders began to take such measures as early as April–June 1945—a good two years before the Marshall Plan and Truman Doctrine were announced. The United States also built up a strong position in the Middle East to help reduce Russia's influence in this vital region. These shifts in behavior were already well under way by the time of President Roosevelt's death in April 1945. US policy from May to August 1945, however, took a decidedly hard-line turn, driven by one major fact: by spring 1945, it was clear to every key official, including Truman, that if Washington did not act forcefully to rebuild Western Europe, states in the US sphere would soon start falling to Communism.

The emerging threat to US access to resources and markets was thus a fundamental cause of its switch to harder-line policies by mid-1945, and the subsequent spiral into Cold War hostility. This was not the only cause, though. Also important was the simple need to maintain the United States' ongoing power preponderance given Russia's vast potential for future growth. There is overwhelming evidence that through the summer of 1945, Truman liked Stalin and believed he could do business with him. Yet he also worried that if the United States did not act to constrain Russia, it would grow significantly, and future Soviet leaders might not be as restrained in their behavior. Because I have detailed this evidence elsewhere, I will not repeat it here.[7] Rather, my goal is to extend this work by showing that Truman and his advisers in 1945 were equally worried about the economic implications of the immediate loss of peripheral states to the beguiling appeal of Soviet Communism.

As for the age-old question of who started the Cold War, let me make my position clear up front. In terms of simple chronology, the United States was the first to shift to a grand strategy designed to reduce the strength of the other side. By July–October 1945, US leaders had surrounded Russia with air and naval bases, made a firm decision to deny atomic secrets to Moscow, initiated the rebuilding of Western Europe (including Russia's archenemy Germany), ended aid to Moscow, restricted

---

[6] For a detailed look at the importance of Romania and Bulgaria through 1945, see Copeland, forthcoming.

[7] See Copeland 2000b, chap. 6, which draws on the seminal work of Leffler (1984, 1992, 1994b, 1996b).

reparations from Western Germany, and sent US marines into China and Manchuria to prevent Communist consolidation of these critical areas.[8] Russian policy, on the other hand, remained cautiously inward looking, and for a good geopolitical reason: the Soviets needed to appear reasonable to buy time to rebuild their devastated society.[9]

This chapter thus challenges the traditionalist and liberal thesis that it was Soviet aggression in 1945–46 that forced Washington by 1946–47 to switch to a hard-line containment posture. But my argument should not be seen as putting moral "blame" on Truman for starting the spiral of hostility we now call the Cold War. Truman did exactly what was required of him given the uncertain circumstances he faced, including the unknown future intentions of Russian leaders. Furthermore, Truman's pessimism regarding the future system was shaped by the nature of the Soviet state—its mercantilist economic practices and authoritarian structure. From a theoretical perspective, however, Russia's Communist regime type can be said to have had only an indirect impact. It was not Soviet "aggression" in 1945–46 that sparked the Cold War (more expansionistic Soviet behavior came only after the US policy shift). It instead was the US worry that revolutions would lead to further losses to the closed Soviet economic sphere combined with the concern that Moscow's intentions might not stay moderate that led to the hardening of US behavior. In this sense, both states can be held "responsible" for the Cold War, but for different reasons: the United States because it was the first to turn to hard-line policies known to be provocative; and the Soviet Union because its regime type and intrasphere economic policies undermined US confidence in the future.

Roosevelt and the Iranian Oil Crisis, 1943–44

In the first decade after World War II, the notion emerged that Roosevelt had been a naive leader who had allowed Stalin to expand his empire at little cost. While many international relations scholars still hold to this view, it has little remaining sway among historians. With the seminal work of Warren Kimball (1991, 1997) and Robert Dallek (1979), we can now see that Roosevelt was far more the Machiavellian realist than the Wilsonian idealist, and indeed saw himself that way. To centralize power, he would allow factions to fight and then mediate between them. In

---

[8] For a detailed discussion of these actions, see Copeland 2000b, 149–75.

[9] I set aside here the much-debated question of whether "deep down" the Soviets still had expansionist future intentions (see, for example, Gaddis 1997). The point is simply that in concrete terms, Stalin was moderate in his behavior through 1945, and was seen as such by Truman and his key advisers.

diplomacy, he would avoid hard-and-fast statements of doctrine, thereby increasing the flexibility needed to realize his postwar agenda. He was the master of subtle deception that came in the form of a jovial cajoling and affable willingness to bargain even at the expense of stated principles. As he described himself in mid-1942, "I am a juggler, and I never let my right hand know what my left hand does. . . . I am perfectly willing to mislead and tell untruths if it will help win the war" (quoted in Kimball 1991, 7).

Roosevelt's larger strategic objective from 1943 to 1945 was a simple one: build a peaceful postwar order through the recognition of clear Soviet and American "spheres of responsibility." In particular, by reassuring Moscow that Eastern Europe would be within its sphere and no longer a conduit for invasion, the Soviets would have an incentive not to interfere in the US sphere (ibid.). But Roosevelt also hedged his bets. In December 1942, he asked the military to investigate the United States' postwar basing needs. The Joint Strategic Survey Committee sent him a report in March 1943 arguing that overseas bases were essential to US security, given that international institutions could not be counted on to keep the peace.[10] In November Roosevelt approved JCS 570, which stressed the importance of bases in West Africa, the Pacific, Iceland, and Japan as well as on the East Asian mainland to the countering of any rising and future Russian threat (Sherry 1977, 44–47; Copeland 2000b, 152–53).[11]

For Roosevelt, however, the question of bases went beyond merely projecting air power to keep Russia cooperative. In February 1944 he told Hull to push the state, war, and navy departments to examine how overseas bases could be used for naval and ground forces as well.[12] Since his time as assistant navy secretary under Wilson, Roosevelt had internalized the Mahanian view that states must project global power to both maintain security and build power through access to foreign markets and raw materials (Ninkovich 1994, 101; Mahan [1890] 1987). His fateful decision in 1943–44 to build a web of overseas bases was driven by both military concerns and the more general need to improve US commercial ties around the world.[13]

---

[10] "Post-War Military Problems—with Particular Relations to Air Bases," NA, JSSC 9/1, RG 218, CCS 360 (12–9–42), sec. 1.

[11] Roosevelt's thinking was shaped by a remarkably prescient analysis presented to the president in January 1943 by adviser William Bullitt, his former ambassador to the Soviet Union. Almost two years before similar arguments by Averell Harriman and George Kennan, Bullitt stressed the importance of using the United States' superior military power and economic largesse as tools to keep the Russian "amoeba" from extending its tentacles beyond its current sphere of influence (*FTP*, 576–90).

[12] "Supplemental Instructions to the State Department concerning Post-War Military Bases," NA, JCS 570/4, RG 218, CCS 360 (12–9–42), sec. 2.

[13] This dual vision extended to Roosevelt's interest in building a system of international airports to serve the US air force and facilitate global commerce (Kimball 1991).

Roosevelt's concerns about economic access came to a head over the issue of which great power would control Iranian and Middle Eastern oil after the war. During the interwar period, US oil firms had entered the Middle East in a big way. While Britain dominated Iranian oil through its government-owned Anglo-Iranian Oil Company, US firms by 1942 controlled a quarter of Iraqi oil, half of Kuwaiti oil, and the majority of Saudi oil concessions. But the future was uncertain. Britain and Russia had occupied Iran in August 1941, splitting it into spheres. Although the US army entered Iran in 1942 to help manage lend-lease shipments to Russia, the dominating presence of the British and Soviet armies led US officials to worry that Moscow and London might seek to extend their influence, either within Iran or toward US-dominated areas such as Saudi Arabia.

The problem facing the Roosevelt administration by 1942 was a simple one: domestic oil supplies were peaking but demand was skyrocketing, driven by the United States' industrial recovery and the needs of its now-huge overseas military machine. The trends were not encouraging. In October 1941, a State Department study had concluded that the US's proven reserves were declining faster than new reserves were being discovered. If the trends continued, the United States, the world's largest oil producer, would move from a position of net exporter to net importer. The study concluded on a prescient note: as the United States becomes a net oil importer, its foreign policy "will probably become more aggressive and will come more and more to resemble Great Britain's policy of the past thirty years" (quoted in Miller 1980, 49). A subsequent study by the Board of Economic Warfare in July 1942 reinforced the value of increasing the US foothold in the Middle East, given that the region's reserves were probably as great as those in the United States (at a time when the United States produced almost two-thirds of the world's crude) (ibid., 55, 57–58; Yergin 1991, 395–96).

Given such assessments, it is not surprising that Roosevelt decided in 1943 to make Iran his "test case" for the policy of protecting US access to postwar resources, notwithstanding the risk of hurting Moscow's expectations about its own access (RC, 650–51). The Soviets and British in 1941 had divided the country into northern and southern spheres. Britain's main goal was to safeguard Anglo-Iranian Oil Company oil in the south, while the Soviets hoped to exploit the potential oil resources of northern Iran. Wartime oil production had proved inadequate, and Moscow needed to seek new sources outside the country (see Yegorova 1996). In late 1942, the Iranians asked Washington to increase its involvement to counterbalance the Anglo-Soviet presence. In January 1943, a State Department report recommended that Washington strengthen Iran's political and economic organizations to prevent instability as well as ensure its independence vis-à-vis Britain and Russia. Iran, it argued, constituted a test of Atlantic Charter principles, especially the protection of sovereignty and trade openness (Kuniholm 1980, 156–63; Rubin 1980, 20).

Hull enthusiastically forwarded these recommendations to Roosevelt, noting both the idealistic and self-centered reasons for acting. The United States had a vital interest not only in establishing a lasting regional peace but also in ensuring that "no great power be established on the Persian Gulf opposite the important American petroleum development in Saudi Arabia" (quoted in Kuniholm 1980, 159–60). By US actions over the next two years, it is clear Roosevelt strongly concurred with Hull's conclusions. Washington quickly became heavily involved in the direct running of the Iranian state. Most surprisingly, and notwithstanding Iran's nominal status as an independent sovereign state, US officials, with the shah's approval, were appointed to major positions in the Iranian government. Most important of these was Arthur Millspaugh's insertion as Iran's director general of finance. In this role, Millspaugh not only guided Iranian economic reforms; he oversaw the use of US military advisers in the reshaping of Iran's army, too (Kuniholm 1980).

At the Tehran Summit in November 1943, Roosevelt convinced Churchill and Stalin to accept the Tehran Declaration reassuring Iranians that full sovereignty would be restored after the war. By that point, US advisers were fully entrenched, backed by thirty thousand US troops. Roosevelt now saw Iran as a test case for his postwar vision of stable peripheral states connected to an open global economy. While in Tehran, Roosevelt had told his roving ambassador Patrick Hurley to prepare an analysis on Iran to guide US relations with weaker nations. Hurley's January 1944 report stressed the need to fight Soviet and British "imperialism" in Iran, and ensure that free enterprise took root in the country, as per Atlantic principles. Should this plan work, Iran would serve as a template for Washington's dealings with all nations fighting monopolies, oppression, and imperialist aggression (ibid., 168–69).[14]

Roosevelt forwarded Hurley's analysis to Hull, noting that he was "rather thrilled with the idea of using Iran as an example of what we can do by an unselfish American policy" (quoted in Kuniholm 1980, 169). Considering it was Hull who, in early 1943, had first told Roosevelt that Iran was important from a selfish perspective to protect the United States' Saudi interests, this was obviously a disingenuous statement. But Iran had already become much more than a mere buffer for Saudi Arabia. In December 1943, the Iranians sent formal invitations to two US oil companies to begin negotiations on the first US oil concession in Iran. Despite warnings from US officials in Tehran that such negotiations might harm allied unity, the firms were allowed to start the talks.

[14]On Roosevelt's language on Iran as a test case, see *RC*, 650–51.

The British immediately got wind and pressed Tehran to be included in any new concessions. By February 1944, Moscow was concerned enough to send word to Iranian officials to remind them of its "prior rights" to northern Iranian oil (McFarland 1980, 341). The scramble to secure new oil concessions in Iran, sparked by US action, was now on.

Initially the Soviets were a side player in this scramble. Until September 1944 the United States' main competitor was Britain, the traditionally dominant player in Iranian oil politics. Through the first half of 1944, in fact, Moscow was loath to get directly involved. The Soviet government had received an analysis of the oil resources of northern Iran in January 1944 that recognized Iran's strong potential but also cautioned that more geologic exploration was needed, requiring both large investments and the likely annexation of part of Iranian territory (Yegorova 1996, 2–3).

The signing of the Anglo-American Oil Agreement in early August 1944, though, changed Soviet calculations. The agreement established rules for comanaging Anglo-American global production—some 80 percent of the world's total—to ensure stable prices and distribution.[15] For Moscow, however, it smacked of a deal to divide global oil into US and British spheres of influence. Lavrenty Beria, deputy chair of the Council of People's Commissars, sent a report to Stalin on August 16 stating that Britain and the United States were working together against Russia, specifically "to prevent the transfer of the oil fields of Northern Iran [into Soviet hands]." Moscow must insist on participation in the Tehran talks "to defend Soviet interests in the sphere of international oil affairs" (quoted in Yegorova 1996, 3). In September, Moscow sent a high-ranking envoy to Iran to negotiate a Soviet concession. The Oil Crisis of 1944 had begun.[16]

The declassified Russian documents show, as Natalia Yegorova (1996, 3) summarizes in her seminal analysis, that Moscow was concerned not only with immediate security (the Caucasian land-invasion route) but also its ability to "participate on a par in the postwar competition . . . for the right to possess the new oil fields of the Middle East." It was the new threat of an Anglo-American condominium, just when Soviet dependence was rising, that led the Soviets to jump into the scramble, notwithstanding the clear risks of a spiral.

What happened in response is instructive. On October 11, just days after Moscow's official request for a concession, the Iranian government announced that it was postponing all negotiations on new concessions until after the war (ibid., 6). Washington supported the decision, and for good reason. Although it delayed a US concession, it would prevent

---

[15] Yergin 1991, 402–3; Painter 1986, 64.
[16] So named in Kuhiholm 1980.

concessions going to either Britain or Russia while their soldiers exercised predominant influence in Iran. By waiting until all foreign troops had left—by agreement, they were to be gone within six months after the war's end—Washington stood a better chance of shaping Iran's postwar development and its oil trade. With the United States' economy globally dominant and its firms technologically superior, Iran would naturally gravitate to its economic sphere if given a choice. Conversely, Moscow's only bargaining tool was the presence of Soviet troops in the north and the implied threat that they would not withdraw until an oil concession was offered.

The details of the fall 1944 crisis need not detain us. The Soviets reacted angrily to the postponement of negotiations. They encouraged the Communist Tudeh ("Masses") Party, established through Comintern support in 1941, to organize strikes and demonstrations—pressure tactics that would frighten the Iranian government while sheltering Moscow from direct responsibility. Yet the tactics failed to sway the majority in the Majlis (parliament). To reiterate Iranian determination, the Majlis passed a law in December making it illegal for government officials to engage in even informal talks about oil concessions. By early January 1945, with Moscow needing to avoid further escalation prior to Yalta, the crisis petered out. The Soviets would not push hard for an oil concession until early 1946, at a point when US-Russian relations had already taken a dramatic downward turn.

The 1943–44 struggle over Iran suggests two important conclusions. First, it was Washington's effort to insert itself into the running of the Iranian state and the slicing up of oil concessions that caused Moscow to act. The decline in Soviet expectations regarding their economic position had turned British-US competition over Middle East oil into the first superpower crisis of the emerging Cold War era. Trade expectations theory thus does a good job explaining Soviet behavior and the onset of the crisis.

This is not the whole story, however. Roosevelt and Hull knew the risks of seeking more influence in a country viewed by Russia and Britain since 1907 to be part of their geopolitical spheres. American leaders went in with their eyes open, meaning we need an explanation of US and not just Soviet behavior. This leads to the second conclusion: economic realism ultimately covers US behavior better than trade expectations theory. The Americans saw a threat, but it was more the threat of anticipated future oil dependency than fear of immediate British and Soviet moves to restrict US oil access. The Roosevelt administration worried that the British and Russians would gain undue influence in Iran if Washington did not act. All this was happening just when Roosevelt was seeking to encourage peripheral states to join the global economy. As economic realism would predict, by grabbing an opportunity to project power into the

Iranian power vacuum, US leaders believed they could reduce Soviet and British influence while securing access for their own state—and despite the risks of sparking a trade-security spiral. As a result, the Middle East became the center of a geopolitical competition that would continue until the present day.

EUROPEAN INSTABILITY AND THE START OF THE COLD WAR STRUGGLE, JANUARY–JULY 1945

By January 1945, Roosevelt's policies had left the United States in a highly favorable position—one that would allow his successor to begin shifting to a protocontainment stance by late June–early July. The United States now had a string of bases around the Eurasian perimeter, and it had helped resurrect the Iranian state to block further Soviet penetration. Moreover, by rejecting extreme versions of Morgenthau's plan to break Germany into small agricultural provinces, Roosevelt had laid the basis for integrating Germany's coal and industry into the larger Western European economy. It was this integration that proved essential to preventing Western Europe's fall to Communism. At Yalta in February, Roosevelt conceded what he could not prevent: Moscow's hold over Eastern Europe. But Yalta allowed him to get Stalin's assurance that he would not insist on a Soviet role in Italy's recovery. Stalin also agreed to enter the Pacific conflict three months after the European war ended, thereby minimizing American military losses that might hurt US postwar power. Stalin's terms were moderate. In return for recognizing the KMT as China's legitimate government and agreeing to hand Manchuria over to Chiang after Soviet troops withdrew, he sought only the use of a warm-water port on the Liaodong Peninsula and a role in running the trans-Manchurian railway (see Plokhy 2010; Harbutt 2010).[17]

Two main economic issues nevertheless hovered over US policy discussions from January to September 1945. The first was a Soviet request for a six billion dollar postwar loan to facilitate Russia's rebuilding process. The second was Western Europe's devastated economy and the fear that simple hunger and cold might cause its states to fall to Communism, either through elections or revolution. Two other economic issues were tied to these primary concerns: the reparations policy toward Germany, and question of US access to Eastern European trade and investments.[18]

[17]Truman and Stalin confirmed this arrangement for the Far East the day before the Potsdam conference began in mid-July (*FRUS* [1945], Potsdam 2:43–46:1585–87).

[18]For coverage of the latter two in detail, see Copeland, forthcoming.

On January 3, 1945, Soviet foreign minister Vyacheslav Molotov met with US ambassador Averell Harriman to request a six billion dollar loan to enable Russia to rebuild its industrial structure (*FRUS* [1945], 5:942–43). From spring 1944 onward, Harriman had been pushing Roosevelt to use postwar loans as a diplomatic tool. In Harriman's oft-repeated language, Washington should adopt a "firm but friendly" stance, exacting political concessions as a "quid pro quo" for US loan guarantees.[19] Roosevelt accepted this view, telling the new secretary of state, Edward Stettinius, on January 10 that it was "very important that we hold back on [the loan] and don't give them any promises of finance until we get what we want" (quoted in Herring 1973, 170). Agreeing with Stettinius that the issue should not be raised at Yalta, Roosevelt studiously maintained his silence when the conference began a month later (Paterson 1973, 39–40; *FRUS* [1945], 5:967–68). The loan would not be approved during his remaining time in office, and Truman's administration would delay dealing with it until 1946, at which time the idea was finally rejected for good. Needless to say, for a Soviet nation that had borne the brunt of Nazi aggression, this was a major disappointment as well as an early sign of the United States' emerging economic grand strategy.

Yet the most important event in 1945 that would directly shape US policy and, as such, Soviet commercial expectations was the realization in April that Western Europe was suffering an economic crisis of epic proportions. On April 4, 1945, Harriman warned Roosevelt that Western Europe's situation was giving Moscow an ideal vehicle to trumpet the superiority of its economic system. If the United States did not act soon, all of Europe might fall to Soviet domination. Thus US policy should shift to one of "taking care of our Western allies . . . first," and only after that "allocating to Russia what may be left." More than two years before the Marshall Plan, Harriman saw what had to be done. To stop Communism's spread, Washington must use economic aid "to reestablish a reasonable life" for peoples who shared the United States' liberal values (*FD*, 39–40).

Harriman's report did not have its full impact until mid-April, when Assistant Secretary of War John McCloy returned from Europe to inform his colleagues that the conditions were far worse than thought, especially in Germany. In his diary on April 19, Stimson noted that Germany's situation was "worse than anything probably that ever happened in the world. I had anticipated the chaos, but the details of it were appalling" (quoted in Leffler 1996b, 16). US officials knew that without a viable Germany, the whole operation in Europe would be compromised. Western European homes and factories needed German coal, especially if Russia restricted exports from Eastern Europe. McCloy and Stimson used their frequent

[19]See Paterson 1973, 35–36; Herring 1973; Harriman and Abel 1975; Martel 1979.

meetings with Truman in April to keep him informed of European developments as well as warn him of the implications of inaction. One report to Truman was particularly direct, declaring that "there is complete economic, social, and political collapse going on in Central Europe, the extent of which is unparalleled" since Rome's collapse. Countries such as France and Belgium "[could] very well be torn apart by the collapse now in effect over [central] Europe" (quoted in ibid., 16–17).

The new president was clearly absorbing these concerns and adjusting his behavior accordingly. On April 20, Harriman told Truman that a "workable basis" for US-Soviet relations was still possible, but Washington had to adopt a strong posture, which it could do because Moscow "needed our help in order to reduce the burden of reconstruction." Truman agreed, stating that he intended to be "firm but fair" to get 85 percent of what he wanted.[20] Two days later, Truman began two days of talks with Molotov. While pleasant on day one, on the second day Truman forcefully argued that Stalin must uphold his Yalta promises on Poland, and that without this, Congress was unlikely to approve of any legislation providing economic aid to Russia.[21] Through straightforward linkage politics, he was now making it clear that to receive valuable postwar aid, the Soviets would have to start playing ball in Eastern Europe.

Despite his new rhetoric, Truman at this stage still sought US-Soviet postwar cooperation. His objective regarding Poland was quite moderate. Truman knew as well as anyone that he could not prevent Soviet domination of the country. Given this, over the next two months he pushed Stalin to make enough cosmetic concessions on Poland's internal makeup to keep domestic public opinion on Truman's side. Presumably Stalin, after hearing Molotov's report, would see that placating public opinion was key to the securing of postwar loans. In late May he sent Hopkins to Moscow. He told Hopkins before he left that he wanted a "fair understanding" with Stalin, and Hopkins should make Stalin aware that what transpired in Eastern Europe "made no difference to US interests" except in terms of the larger peace structure. Hopkins should try to get Stalin to make some gesture, "whether [the Soviet leader] means it or not," to "keep it before our public that he intends to keep his word" (quoted in Maddox 1988, 65).[22]

---

[20] "Memorandum of Conversation," HSTL, April 20, 1945, Papers of HST, PSF: Subject File Foreign Affairs, Russia: Molotov.

[21] "Memorandum of Conversation," HSTL, April 23, 1945, Papers of HST, PSF: Subject File Foreign Affairs, Russia: Molotov. See also *FRUS* (1945), 5:256–58.

[22] This aligns with Chief of Staff Admiral Leahy's advice to Truman that Washington should focus simply on giving Poland the "external appearance" of independence (Leahy Diary, LC, April 23, 1945).

Contrary to many accounts, Poland was not the deal breaker that led to the spiral of Cold War hostility. Indeed, the very agreement that Hopkins reached with Stalin in June 1945 demonstrates that Truman's primary concern was getting a fig leaf for domestic consumption. Stalin agreed to include London Poles in the interim Polish government until elections were held, but only as a minority part of the government. In early July, Truman publicly announced with "great satisfaction" Washington's recognition of the new Polish government. He did this even before he received any guarantee that elections would be held (they never were) and before recognizing the other Eastern European governments under Soviet control. More telling still, Truman made no objections in July when Stalin proceeded to try sixteen leaders of the Polish opposition.[23]

The true point of contention that would divide the two superpowers and lead to the Cold War was something broader and more geostrategic. This was the question of Western European stability and its link to Stalin's economic plans, both for the Soviet Union and Eastern Europe. Washington would not only have to divert money and goods away from the emerging Eastern bloc toward Western Europe but it would see Stalin's policy of binding states such as Romania and Bulgaria to Russia as a clear sign that East-West trade could not be used to prop up Europe's Western half. As with so many cases in this book, it was the political realities of third parties that would lead to declining relations between great power protagonists.

Already by the end of April, US policy was becoming more at odds with Soviet interests as Washington scrambled to address Western Europe's economic crisis. On April 30, the White House issued a long press release detailing a new internal report on Europe. The situation was grave. The "future permanent peace of Europe" depended on restoring this region's economy, and the US economy itself would be deeply affected unless Western Europe could trade. Furthermore, "a chaotic and hungry Europe is not fertile ground in which stable, democratic and friendly governments can be reared."[24] Truman's message was obvious: without active US assistance, Western Europe might soon be lost to Communism.

As a first act, lend-lease aid would have to be diverted from supplying Washington's key wartime ally—the Soviet Union—to the countries of Western Europe. On May 12, Washington announced the immediate ending of all lend-lease aid to Russia. Traditionalists might argue that this action could not have been seen as terribly unfriendly, given that the blanket denial of all aid was reversed the next day and US goods for

[23] See *FRUS* (1945), Potsdam 1:735; Davis 1974, 237–48; McJimsey 1987, 386; Trachtenberg 1999, 12–14.

[24] HSTL, April 30, 1945, Papers of HST, Office File 426 (1945–46).

Russia's anticipated war against Japan were reinstated. As we will see, however, the Soviets correctly interpreted US behavior as indicating a disturbing shift in US strategic thinking.

On May 9, Secretary of State Stettinius had written his undersecretary, Joseph Grew, to contend that programs to assist what were already being called Western allies should have priority over aid to Russia, and that the United States should immediately curtail lend-lease shipments to Russia. US policy should be one of "firm[ness] while avoiding any implication of a threat" (*FRUS* [1945], 5:998). On May 11, Stimson met with Truman to convince him of the need for "a more realistic policy" regarding lend lease—namely, that this aid should end. Truman was "vigorously enthusiastic," telling Stimson (diary, LC, May 11, 1945) to write up a memorandum on the subject. After talking with Stimson, Grew later that day presented Truman with a report underscoring that Washington was formally committed to keep some aid flowing until June 30—that is, supplies for a Soviet entry into the Pacific War. Yet all other lend-lease deliveries to Russia should end immediately and the goods "diverted to the approved supply programs for Western Europe." Truman formally approved the memorandum.[25] The next day, after internal debate within the committee managing lend lease, it was decided to interpret the Grew memo aggressively and instantly stop all shipments to Russia. Later that day, not only were ships at ports unloaded and those at sea turned around, but even goods slated for the Pacific war were blocked, too (Herring 1973, 204–5).

The Russian embassy reacted immediately. When Harriman and Assistant Secretary of State William Clayton got word, they secured Truman's permission to countermand the order and allow supplies already loaded or at sea to proceed to Russia. Clayton explained to the Russian ambassador that the total cutoff had been a bureaucratic mistake that was now corrected (ibid., 205–6). But the sense that US policy had shifted was reinforced by a memorandum that Grew sent to the Soviet embassy that same day, May 12. It stressed that future lend-lease deliveries had to be "justified" based on Soviet military need and "in the light of competing demands for such supplies in the changed military situation." (The actors making competing demands were obviously the Western Europeans.) The Russians were then told bluntly that any future aid—including goods for Moscow's entry into the Pacific War—would not be covered by formal contract but instead simply provided to meet new military situations "as they arise" (*FRUS* [1945], 5:1027–28). The message was clear: the Soviets would get no more aid to facilitate reconstruction in Western Russia, and

<hr />

[25] HSTL, May 11, 1945, Papers of HST, PSF: Subject File, 1945–53, Foreign Affairs, Lend Lease; see also *FRUS* (1945), 5:999–1000.

lend-lease assistance for the war against Japan would be dispensed on an ad hoc basis—that is, at Washington's discretion.

As the above shows, the May 12 incident was not merely some administrative snafu. While the officials that day certainly went too far, there is little question that Truman and State Department hard-liners were pushing US policy in a new, significant direction. Lend lease was now going to be used to help struggling Western European states, most of which had played little or no role in the defeat of Nazism. The damage to Soviet expectations was significant. As George Herring (1973, 206) summarizes it, the "sudden, drastic, even rude, stoppage of shipments on May 12—without warning and without consultation—needlessly antagonized the Russians at a critical juncture in Soviet-American relations."

There is little doubt that Soviet perceptions of US economic policies were certainly hurt by the May 12 incident. This quickly became apparent when Hopkins met with Stalin in late May. After controlling the first day's proceedings, Hopkins on the second day asked if Stalin had any concerns.[26] Stalin began by stating that recent US moves had created a "certain alarm" regarding Washington's attitude now that the European war was over. One of the most obvious examples, Stalin continued, was the curtailment of lend-lease aid. If the United States was no longer able to supply such aid, that was one thing. But "the manner in which it had been done had been unfortunate and even brutal." If the refusal to continue lend lease was designed to "soften [Russia] up," then the Americans had made a fundamental mistake. Hopkins obfuscated, arguing that the May 12 cutoff was only a "technical mistake," not a "decision of policy," and there was no attempt "to use [it] as a pressure weapon." Stalin refused to be placated. It was the action's form that he objected to, and if only proper warning had been given, there would be no ill feeling. In a rare admission of the Soviet need for what the United States had to offer, he noted that such a warning "was important to [the Soviet government] since [its] economy was based on plans" (FRUS [1945], Potsdam 1:31–41).

One might dismiss Stalin's words as simply an effort to guilt Washington into restoring the flow of what were, after all, essentially free goods. Yet Stalin's admission that lend-lease goods were critical to Soviet planning and his larger recovery effort suggests that the Soviets were genuinely shocked as well as angered by the May 12 cutoff along with what it signified about the future. Through late May and June, the Soviets

---

[26] On the first day, which focused on Poland, Hopkins told Stalin, per instructions from Truman, that even though US public support was declining for Russia, Truman wanted to work with Moscow. Stalin indicated that the Polish issue could be easily solved, and over the next week the Soviet leader made the cosmetic concessions that Truman sought (FRUS [1945], Potsdam 1:24–31).

continually complained to Harriman about their inability to secure criti-cal lend-lease goods and the diversion of aid to Western Europe.[27] The State Department had no intention of moderating its policy, however. On June 26, Grew told the Russians that lend-lease supplies not only had to be justified by military requirements but also could now only be secured by "cash payment." If the Soviets could not purchase the goods, Wash-ington would take steps "to protect the interests of the United States by diverting machinery and equipment to other requirements"—meaning, most obviously, Western Europe (*FRUS* [1945], 5:1027–28). Hence by late June, Moscow understood that even lend-lease goods destined for the Pacific would be diverted to states in the US sphere playing little or no role in the war against Japan. Grew did not mention whether these states were more able to pay cash for such goods, for the simple reason that he knew they would be receiving them under the old lend-lease terms—free of charge. The new policy of building up the Western sphere at the ex-pense of the Soviet recovery was clearly well under way.

Let me now turn briefly to the role played by Germany in the harden-ing of Truman's foreign policy between April and July 1945. The redirect-ing of lend-lease aid and delaying of loans to Moscow were only two steps in the larger strategy to prevent Western Europe from slipping into the Soviet sphere. Equally important was the need to reestablish trade be-tween Germany/Eastern Europe and the Western European states.[28] On May 16, Stimson held a critical meeting with the president on Germany—a meeting that Truman (1955, 235–36) would later recognize as a turning point in US policy. Stimson told Truman that

> all agree as to the probability of pestilence and famine in central Eu-rope next winter. This is likely to be followed by political revolution and Communistic infiltration. Our defenses against this situation are the western governments of France, Luxembourg, Belgium, Holland, Denmark, Norway, and Italy. It is vital to keep these countries from being driven to revolution or Communism by famine.

The immediate problem was that a food shortage would likely begin by summer 1945 and get much worse by the coming winter. It was there-fore critical to make sure Germany was allowed to rebuild its industry and play its necessary role in the European economy. The fate of eighty

---

[27]See, for example, Grew's "Memorandum for the President" from early June, in Papers of HST, PSF: Subject File Foreign Affairs, Reports: Current Foreign Developments; *FRUS* (1945), 5:1018–20. Harriman himself wrote Hopkins on June 21 that he was "gravely concerned" over delays and hoped Hopkins could use his connections (i.e., to Truman) to rectify the problem immediately (*FRUS* [1945], 5:1020).

[28]For the importance of Eastern European trade, see Copeland, forthcoming.

million Germans along with their ability to form a wealthy and democratic society, Stimson stressed, would "necessarily swing the balance on
[the European] continent." Given what Germany had just done to Europe, reintegrating it into Europe was a touchy issue, requiring Russia's
cooperation. A revitalized German industry would need Eastern European food, and the Soviet army, after all, was sitting on the best agricultural lands of Central Europe. Washington "must find some way of
persuading Russia to play ball" (Stimson diary, LC, May 16, 1945).

After that meeting, a new and radical policy shift was implemented.
The nation that had just plunged Europe into the bloodiest war in world
history was now to be quickly reintegrated into the European economy
and allowed to restore its industrial base. For a Soviet government that
had been promised at Yalta a weak and subdivided Germany as a necessary foundation for Russia's long-term security, this was a highly problematic shift in US policy, to say the least. But with Truman now on
board, there was no going back. On May 22, Truman sent a letter to the
war agencies in Europe noting that the future peace of Europe depended
on restoring the economies of liberated countries (Leffler 1996b, 17). On
June 24, he wrote a detailed letter to Churchill arguing that the "coal
famine" that threatened Europe meant that every effort had to be exerted to increase German coal exports. "I believe that without immediate
concentration on the production of German coal we will have turmoil
and unrest in the very areas of Western Europe on which the whole stability of the continent depends" (FRUS [1945], Potsdam 1:612–14). In a
meeting on July 3, when Stimson (diary, LC, July 3, 1945) reiterated the
importance of rehabilitating Germany, Truman said that was exactly the
way he thought it should be.

Part and parcel of the new policy was a decision to deny the Soviets
reparations from the western half of Germany. At Yalta, Stalin, Churchill,
and Roosevelt had agreed that Germany would be forced to pay twenty
billion dollars in reparations—ten billion of which was to come from the
Western zones to help the Soviets rebuild. Through June and into July,
however, knowing that reparations would undermine Germany's ability
to play its new role in Western Europe, US officials made it clear that any
reparations from Germany's western half would be forthcoming only after
it had paid for necessary imports. The Soviets could see that this principle could be used to justify no reparation transfers at all. They fought
back, but Washington refused to budge.[29] At the Potsdam conference in
July, after much discussion, the Russians were forced to concede. Despite
Molotov's willingness to reduce the ten billion dollar figure down to two
billion—but as a guaranteed amount—the final agreement specified only

[29] FRUS (1945), Potsdam 1:477–79, 491–93, 510–11, 528–37; Copeland, forthcoming.

a figure of 10–15 percent of Western Germany's surplus industrial production (i.e., after imports) (Copeland 2000b, 155–56). The agreement essentially ensured that there would be little coordination between the Western and Eastern German zones. The Soviets could take what they wanted from Eastern Germany—a policy that of course would only hurt their sphere's overall strength. But they would receive little from the West. Since the West held most of Germany's industrial strength, this was a major blow to Soviet efforts to rebuilt Russia's industrial infrastructure.

As Carolyn Woods Eisenberg (1996) observes, Washington's policy constituted a clear breach of the Yalta commitment regarding reparations, which was designed to recognize the great sacrifice made by Russia in defeating Nazi Germany. Now, just three months after Hitler's defeat, Washington was helping to build up the western part of Germany as well as what were now called the United States' Western European allies. To be sure, the financing that was supplied to Germany and the other Western European states was not ultimately as substantial as the billions of Marshall Plan dollars that flowed to Europe after spring 1948. Still, because it bypassed Congress and was not held up by legislative wrangling, it was immediate and decisive in reversing the economic chaos threatening to undermine the Western sphere. The West would be saved from the specter of Communism. If the Soviets found as a result that their economic recovery was impaired, they would just have to learn to live with it.[30]

THE CRISES AND TENSIONS OF THE EARLY COLD WAR, 1946–56

As we have seen, declining expectations regarding future trade with Western Europe if it fell to Communism played a critical role in driving US actions that in turn greatly damaged Soviet expectations about future trade and credit coming from the West. The United States, as a result, must be seen as the superpower most causally tied to the onset of Cold War tension, even if one can applaud Truman's actions as the prudent response to a deteriorating situation. Stalin had hoped to use negotiations through the first half of 1945 to rebuild his nation and consolidate his sphere. But by the fall, he began to react to Washington's strategic shift. We first see Stalin's change of policy with regard to Far Eastern questions. After Hiroshima, Truman had not only used US marines to help Chiang retake Manchuria. He had acted to exclude Russia from the occupation of Japan's four main islands, despite the fact that Moscow's entry into the

---

[30] Elsewhere I detail Truman's strategy at Potsdam in mid-July to press Stalin to open Romania and Bulgaria to trade to help stabilize Western Europe and avoid its Communization (Copeland, forthcoming).

war gave it a claim to share in occupational duties. With Japan having attacked Russia in 1904, 1918, and the late 1930s, Stalin had reason to fear a renewal of Japanese militarism. So he had Molotov demand a role in Japan's occupation at the foreign ministers' meeting in September. Secretary of State James F. Byrnes held firm, however. In October, Stalin told Harriman that if Moscow was denied its rightful role regarding Japan, it would be forced to pursue a "unilateral course" in Asia. Harriman, worried that US policy had become too hard line, warned Washington that US intransigence would only heighten fears that the United States was using Japan to contain the Soviet Union.[31] His warnings were ignored, setting the stage for the first crisis of the Cold War era.

The Iranian Crisis of 1946

It was soon after tensions flared over the Far East that Stalin began to take a more assertive stance with regard to the long-simmering question of Iran. In late 1944, one will recall, Tehran had postponed discussion of oil concessions until the great powers removed their troops as promised—that is, within six months after the war's end. US troops were largely gone by December 1945. The Soviet forces, though, were still in the north by year's end, and seemed to have no intention of leaving by the early March deadline. For Moscow, the reality of the situation was clear: while the United States and Britain could promise large infusions of advanced technology and connections to world markets, the Soviet Union had few bargaining tools in its favor. Its only point of leverage was the threat to continue military occupation until Tehran agreed to an oil concession. Thus from late November 1945 onward, Moscow blocked all efforts by Tehran to quell unrest in the Soviet-occupied northern provinces while refusing to remove Soviet troops until a concession was granted (Yegorova 1996).

The maneuvering turned into a low-level crisis in March 1946 when the Iranians, with US support, presented their case to the UN Security Council. The Soviet delegates walked out of the proceedings. A few weeks later, on April 4, Moscow and Tehran signed an oil agreement promising an oil concession in the north in return for a troop evacuation. By May 9, Soviet forces had been withdrawn. US officials celebrated what they saw as the first use of hard-line pressure to coerce a Soviet pullback from a key strategic area. Yet in reality, as Yegorova's work shows, the results obtained were close to what Moscow had been seeking for almost two years. Moscow was still importing oil in 1945–46 from Eastern Europe,

---

[31] For more detail on US Far Eastern policy, see Copeland 2000b, 159–61, 169–70.

and was still far from achieving the strong export position in oil and natural gas it would enjoy by the late 1950s. The agreement of April 1946 was certainly not a clear-cut victory for Moscow. But it did seem to ensure that the northern provinces would have a Soviet rather than British-US presence into the future (ibid.).

This crisis, like the Iranian one of 1944, was fundamentally the result of great power maneuvering for economic position in the postwar world. As in 1944, Washington wanted to block Soviet penetration of Iran as it increased its own control in the region. The State Department emphasized to Truman through summer and fall 1945 what it had told Roosevelt for two years: that Saudi oil—what one report to Truman called "a stupendous source of strategic power, and one of the greatest material prizes in world history"—had to be protected (*FRUS* [1945], 8:45–48; Leffler 1992, 80). While Washington was ultimately prepared to give London primary control of Iran's oil, it could not allow Russia to have any role—military or economic—in such a pivotal state. Yet Moscow's fears of being denied access to Iranian oil made it essential to maintain at least some presence in the country. Trade expectations, therefore, were driving both sides to struggle over Iran's future. The economic realist perspective also has some validity here, since both superpowers saw Iran as a power vacuum that had to be filled. That Iran in the end reneged on its promise of a concession does not mean the Russians did not believe in April 1946 that they had secured economic access and could withdraw Soviet troops. Indeed, the crisis resolved itself precisely because Tehran had played on Soviet expectations of *future* access in order to achieve an agreement that undercut Moscow's only bargaining tool—its military presence on Iranian soil. Once Soviet troops were gone, Iran could break the agreement and seek better deals from the West, knowing that Moscow would fear that reoccupation might spark a larger war. Tehran won this round. But as we will see, the Soviets were not through with Iran by any means.

The Berlin Crisis and Korean War

The years 1947–48 saw another jump in overall Cold War hostility. In February 1947, the British government informed Washington that it could no longer support Turkey or Greece given its severe budget deficit. The Truman Doctrine of March and Marshall Plan of June borrowed directly from the strategic logic set down in 1944–45: if the Soviets were able to pull peripheral nations such as Turkey and Greece—or worse, Western European states—into their sphere, the United States would lose access to the trade and investments needed to sustain long-term power. Diplomat George Kennan's arguments in 1946–47 about the importance of US dominance over the "military-economic potential" of Eurasia only reinforced these fears (Leffler 1992, 143; Gaddis 1972). As Leffler (1992, 146) puts it, while Truman had domestic reasons to couch his doctrine in stark ideological terms, the intensified crusade to protect the periphery was driven by "deeply rooted geopolitical convictions that defined national self-interest in terms of correlations of power based on the control of critical resources, bases, and industrial infrastructure." In April 1947, for example, the State-War-Navy Coordinating Committee (forerunner to the National Security Council [NSC]) stressed the significance of global economic and military aid. "It is important to maintain in friendly hands," the committee report argued, "areas which contain or protect sources of metals, oil, and other national resources" and that represent "substantial industrial potential" (ibid., 147–48).

Russia was an authoritarian state that had been practicing hard-core neomercantilism for 150 years. The United States, conversely, was a democratic state that could not simply coerce allies into handing over goods or accepting US products. Peripheral states could only help sustain high US economic growth through ongoing trade ties. Yet by 1947, it was apparent that many states around the world could no longer afford to trade: they simply lacked the dollars to buy US goods. Western Europe was a case in point. In 1946, the Western Europeans imported approximately $4.4 billion of US goods, but exported only $900 million back. Bridging loans had helped in the short term. But by early 1947, US officials expected that the Europeans would have to reduce US imports by as much as 80 percent unless larger cash infusions were provided. Greater central planning and relative autarky would follow, and perhaps Communist revolutions. As the State Department's committee on the European Recovery Program noted, Western European states falling to Communism would set up restrictive trade treaties with Russia. The Soviets would then leverage this trade to control the region's vital resources. Scandinavia, North Africa, and the Middle East, given dependence on Europe, would then have to follow suit, radically shifting the overall economic balance of power in Russia's favor (ibid., 159–63).

The Marshall Plan and Truman Doctrine were, as Truman famously remarked, two halves of the same walnut; both were essential in the maintenance of US economic and geopolitical strength over the long term. The Berlin Crisis of 1948 arose out of this general context of economic competition, although it was not directly a function of economic dependence per se. Because I have covered this case elsewhere (Copeland 2000b, chap. 7), I will only briefly summarize its security-driven roots.

By winter 1947–48, Germany's importance to Western European recovery loomed larger than it had even in 1945. At the London Conferences of January–March 1948, Britain, France, and the United States agreed to unite their German occupation zones, and hand control over to an independent West German government.[32] For Moscow, this was highly problematic. A resurgent West Germany not only posed a long-term military threat but in the short term, large flows of refugees from the Soviet zone had been increasing the economic strain on the overall Eastern bloc. When Britain and the United States announced currency reforms in mid-June 1948 as a preparatory step to creating a unified West German state, the Soviets reacted. They blockaded all ground traffic to Berlin, hoping this would pressure the West into reversing its recent decisions. The United States understood that the Soviet Union was reacting defensively to Western moves. As Moscow ambassador Walter Smith wrote to Washington in July, the Soviets desired "a return to [the] status quo," and would forgo a battle for Berlin if the London agreements were canceled (*FRUS* [1948], 2:984–85).

In discussions over the next two months, the constant Soviet demand was for the agreements' reversal, but Washington held firm. By June 1949, the Soviets ended their blockade and accepted the new status quo, ending the first Berlin Crisis. Economic factors were a primary force in the Soviet initiation of the crisis. Moscow foresaw that the unification of Western Germany would cause a relative loss of economic power for Russia. But it was not Eastern German dependence on trade with the West that made the Soviets fear the London agreements. They simply knew that these agreements would create a strong West Germany, improve Western growth, and fuel the exodus of East German citizens to the West. In short, fears of economic decline drove the process, but these worries were not a function of interdependence per se.

Berlin 1948 is a problematic case for liberalism. US-Soviet trade levels had been plummeting. US exports to Russia had dropped from $3.5 billion in 1944 during the height of lend lease to $149 million in 1947, and a mere $28 million in 1948 (*FCY*).[33] With economic realism, such low trade by 1948 would make dependence fall out as an important variable. With liberalism, in contrast, the ending of any economic restraint on Soviet behavior should mean that at least in the short term, unit-level drives such as greed and ideological expansion should become the primary propelling forces behind Soviet actions. Yet it is clear that Moscow was reacting out of security fears, desiring only a return to the status quo prior to the London agreements. The case also poses problems for trade expectations

---

[32]On the London Conferences, see *FRUS* (1948), 2:867–86.

[33]Because data are reported only yearly, the low figure for 1948 is partly the result of the crisis itself. But even if we assume trade fell to zero after the start of the crisis in June, the fact that only around $28 million in exports was sold to Russia in the first half of the year shows that monthly figures had already dropped precipitously before the crisis began.

theory. Falling Soviet expectations for future trade should have pushed Moscow into trade-related expansion to recoup economic losses caused by US sanctions. Soviet coercive behavior, however, was focused on the economic implications of the London agreements for Eastern Germany and the Soviet bloc, independent of East-West trade per se. The fact that security fears were determinative of Soviet action aligns with the assumptions of trade expectations theory. But the case shows that in certain situations, other sources of decline can overwhelm trade expectations in relative salience.

The next big crisis of the Truman era was the outbreak of the Korean War in June 1950. As with Berlin 1948, if we were to rely only on correlation, the Korean War might appear to be a good case for both trade expectations theory and liberalism. The former would see declining Soviet trade expectations leading to security fears that pushed Stalin to accept the risks associated with a North Korean attack. The latter would stress that the low trade level reached by 1949–50 helped unleash preexisting pathologies in the Soviet regime. Yet the evidence suggests that changing superpower trade was not part of Stalin's calculus over Korea in 1949–50. Thus like the Berlin case, the trade expectations argument lacks salience, even if it is not wrong per se. Still, the traditional view of the Korean War, which sees Stalin grabbing an opportunity to expand once Washington placed South Korea outside the US defense perimeter, seems to fit liberalism nicely. In the low-trade environment reached by 1949–50, Soviet greed and ideological motives were unleashed as the economic restraints on Soviet behavior were removed. The fact that the Communist bloc was seeking a distinct territorial gain in 1950, while in 1948 Stalin was only trying to counter Western moves, lends even more credence to the perspective that Moscow was aggressively seeking to expand Communism's scope for reasons going well beyond "security." While Korea 1950 seems like the only good case for economic liberals across the entire Cold War era, new evidence from Soviet archives suggests that Stalin was driven more by defensive motives than by greed or ideological ends.

Trade did indeed keep falling after Berlin, from $28 million in US exports to Russia in 1948 to $7 million in 1949, to a mere $700,000 by 1950 (FCY). This reflected Washington's imposition in 1948–49 of formal barriers to US-Soviet trade and the establishment with Western allies of the infamous CoCom restrictions on East-West trade. As Michael Mastanduno (1992) has argued, these actions were pure economic warfare: the United States and its allies were seeking to block the sale of almost any product that might increase Soviet economic and thus military power. This declining trade, though, had apparently no impact on Stalin's decision making regarding Korea.

Arguments for the Korean War typically center on Secretary of State Dean Acheson's important foreign policy speech on East Asia on January 12, 1950 as the trigger for war. The speech was designed to describe a new intensified program of containment for East Asia. A "defense perimeter" existed from Japan through the Philippines, he noted, with Washington committed to defending the states within it. According to most accounts, by leaving South Korea outside the perimeter, Acheson gave the Soviets and North Koreans a green light to invasion. Extended deterrence cannot operate, after all, if the United States refuses to commit itself to a state's defense.[34]

The Soviet documents nonetheless indicate that Moscow was already switching to a more hard-line policy in Asia ten days before the Acheson speech and in fact saw the speech as a sign that Washington was becoming *more* involved in East Asian affairs, not less. Mao had arrived in Moscow in mid-December 1949 with the hope of negotiating a Soviet-Chinese alliance, only to be told bluntly that he should expect no such thing. All the senior Russian officials then summarily ignored him until a bizarre Soviet volte-face on January 2. That day, out of the blue, the Soviets reversed themselves and agreed to work toward the immediate conclusion of an alliance. This dramatic shift cannot be explained as some bargaining tactic. The Soviets arriving at Mao's door that day (Molotov and an associate) did not ask for anything in return but instead merely caved to Mao's primary demand. And they did so despite the obvious risks of inflaming US-Soviet relations—the concern that had previously been holding them back. The best explanation for the policy shift seems to be the startling revelations in the *New York Times* on January 1, 1950 that Washington was embarking on new hard-line policy in East Asia. At the time, the *New York Times* was the dominant US newspaper for foreign news, serving as a critical source for Soviet leaders. Its primary reporter was James Reston, an individual known to have personal connections with key players such as Acheson and Truman. The front-page article by Reston on January 1 provided leaked details on a December 29 NSC meeting in which Truman approved of a more aggressive Far Eastern containment policy.

According to Reston, the new strategy was designed to "widen the breach" between Stalin and Mao. It would also stop Communism in Southeast Asia and establish via treaty US military bases in Japan.[35] As part of the deal, Truman would likely allow Japan to remilitarize. Next to Reston's piece was another article discussing General Douglas MacArthur's address to the Japanese people, in which he suggested that

---

[34] For the seminal version of this argument, see George and Smoke 1974.
[35] *New York Times*, January 1, 1950, A1.

with Communism on the march, Japan could not be expected to accept complete disarmament.[36] The direction of the shift seemed clear. As yet another *Times* article that day opined, Washington was embarking on "a more vigorous Oriental policy," with Japan as its critical link.[37]

Such news, given past Japanese aggression, would have been enough to push the Soviets to change direction and agree to a Soviet-Chinese alliance. Such an alliance would keep China in the Soviet fold and help deter US attacks from future bases in Japan.[38] Supporting this interpretation is the fact that no other changes in US or Chinese behavior occurred between late December and January 2 to explain the shift in Soviet behavior. By the process of elimination, we can say with fair confidence that it was Stalin's fearful reaction to the revelations in the *New York Times* that provoked the policy change.

Yet if Stalin was reacting defensively, then the January 12 speech still seems like a puzzle for any theory emphasizing Soviet security concerns: if South Korea was placed outside the US defense perimeter on January 12, why would the Soviets worry about this tiny nation? It now seems clear, however, that the Soviets did not even know Korea was outside the perimeter when they formulated their key decisions in January. Since the text of Acheson's speech was not released for eleven days, Moscow had to rely on US press reporting, with the *New York Times* once again the best source. The *New York Times* article on January 13 covering the speech mainly focused on Acheson's charges of Russian imperialism in East Asia, specifically against China. Russia was trying to annex four northern areas of China in an act, Acheson said, that must bring on the Russians "the hatred and righteous anger of the Chinese people." Such statements supported the previous reports in the *New York Times* that Acheson and Truman were striving to divide China from Russia.

The article later briefly covered Acheson's discussion of the so-called defense perimeter running from Japan to the Philippines. Acheson commented that with regard to other parts of Asia, "no person can guarantee these areas against military attack." After North Korea's attack on June 25, critics and historians used such lines to argue that Acheson had given Moscow a green light to invasion.[39] Yet Acheson went on to stress that should any area outside the perimeter be attacked, this would invoke

---

[36] Ibid.

[37] Ibid., A20.

[38] The alliance document, released February 14, 1950, emphasized the need to prevent the revival of Japanese aggression as well as imperialism from any state collaborating with Japan (see Goncharov, Lewis, and Xue 1995, 260–61, doc. 45).

[39] I have not found any statement by analysts prior to June 25 interpreting Acheson's speech in this way. For a discussion about the fact that no one except the South Korean ambassador was concerned, see McLellan 1976, 210–11.

"the commitments of the entire civilized world under the Charter of the United Nations." In short, even if the Soviets had believed Korea was outside the perimeter, this statement would have been a red flag: at this time the United States clearly dominated the United Nations, often using it to promote US interests in Korea.[40] To say that the United Nations would resist any aggression was close to saying, from Moscow's point of view, that the United States was committed to Korea.[41]

But here is the real shocker: the *New York Times* (January 13, 1950, A1) mistakenly reported Acheson as saying that "in the southern part of Asia, unlike Japan or Korea," the United States was just one of many nations that would provide assistance through the UN mechanism. Thus, according to the *New York Times*, South Korea was actually *inside* the defense perimeter! The newspaper's reporters continued to hold to this position through winter and spring 1950, even after the complete text of the speech was released.[42]

A detailed record of Molotov and Mao's conversation on January 17 shows that the Soviets did indeed have a different impression of Acheson's speech than is commonly supposed. Not only did Molotov make no mention of the defense perimeter or Korea, he was totally preoccupied with Acheson's hostile remarks on Russian imperialism. Mao said that he was puzzled by the speech: was it a "smoke screen" to facilitate a US occupation of Taiwan? Molotov replied that "the Americans [were] trying, with the help of slander and deception, to create misunderstandings" between Russia and China. He asked Mao to denounce the speech as an "insult" to China. Mao agreed to do so. The Russian fear that Washington might detach China from the Soviet bloc, as it had with Tito's Yugoslavia, is tangible. It is thus not surprising that on January 22, Stalin made yet another unilateral concession, telling Mao he would jettison the 1945 agreements so distasteful to Chinese leaders (the ones giving Russia a port in Manchuria and joint control of its railways) (*CWIHPB*, 8–9:232–35).

Acheson's strategy had backfired: instead of detaching China from Moscow, the secretary's comments had led to a Russian-Chinese alliance and increased suspicions of US intentions. The Korean Peninsula now had more direct salience for all involved. Back in March 1949, Kim Il Sung had first appealed to Stalin to support a war on South Korea. Stalin had rejected the idea, telling the North Koreans "that they need [to

[40]Dobbs 1982, chaps. 5–7; Lee 1995, chap. 2; Cumings 1990.

[41]Indeed, given South Korea's ambiguous status—a creation of the United Nations but not yet a member—Acheson could hardly have said otherwise. The United Nations was thus the perfect cover to protect the fledgling state while maintaining the posture of impartiality.

[42]*DSB*, vol. 22, January 23, 1950; Cumings 1990, 423–38.

exercise] caution" (ibid., 5:5). The Soviets pushed Kim to achieve victory through subversion, not war. In September 1949, Kim again sought a go-ahead, since the southern insurgency was failing. He was again told to exercise caution (ibid., 5:6–8).

Through fall–winter 1949–50, the South completed its annihilation of the insurgency. Then on February 9, after appeals from Truman, Congress approved another $60 million in economic aid for South Korea in addition to the $60 million already earmarked (*New York Times*, February 10, 1950, A1). On March 7, Truman asked Congress for another $100 million for South Korea for fiscal year 1951, starting July 1, 1950. Translated into current dollars, these were significant injections of aid: the equivalent of more than $1.4 billion by July 1, 1950, and another $1.1 billion thereafter. Acheson told the Senate Foreign Relations Committee in early March that this assistance symbolized US support for emerging democracies. Moreover, "it was generally recognized . . . that [the United States] had 'special responsibilities' in South Korea" due to the 1943 Cairo Conference "just as it had [with] Japan" (ibid., March 8, 1950, A6).

The US public commitment to South Korea was not only strong; it was growing. For Stalin, who doubted North Korea's ability to survive, this could only have suggested one thing: if he continued to hold Kim back from war, South Korea would grow to dominate the peninsula (see Goncharov, Lewis, and Xue 1995, 140). It had twice North Korea's population, and with US economic help it would surely overtake it in the long term. Yet in the short term, according to embassy reports, North Korea had significant military superiority. As historian Charles Armstrong (2003, 238–39) relates, in Kim's view South Korea "was vulnerable at the moment, but might be more formidable in the future," and as such, needed to be defeated now.

By mid-March, Stalin had made up his mind. On March 18, he wrote Kim directly to inform him that he could now supply the arms needed for an attack. A few days later, Stalin agreed to meet Kim in Moscow to finalize the details. Kim had his go-ahead by mid-April for the war, pending Mao's approval. On May 13, Kim met with Mao in Beijing, telling him that he had received a directive from Stalin "that the present situation had changed." Puzzled by this abrupt policy shift, Mao asked the Soviet ambassador for clarification. Stalin wrote Mao directly the next day, confirming that he had told the North Koreans that given the changed international situation, they could proceed with reunification (*CWIHPB*, 4:61). Kim left Beijing with Mao's approval, and on June 25 the invasion of South Korea began.

The origins of the Korean War thus appear to be quite similar to those of the Berlin Crisis of 1948. The Soviets acted more out of fear than from a desire for gain or to exploit a perceived Western weakness. Stalin had been cautious about a North Korean attack from April 1949 onward. But with new evidence that the United States was poised to increase its Far Eastern military presence and build its sphere's strength through aid to frontline countries such as South Korea, the Soviets had to act. The evidence offered here only briefly summarizes the documentary support I provide elsewhere (Copeland, forthcoming). It shows, however, that fear of the future rather than greed or ideological motives was primary in the Soviet leadership's thinking. The argument that falling trade can unleash domestic pathologies is called into question, notwithstanding that Korea constitutes a "most-likely" case for liberalism. Yet the case, as with Berlin 1948, also demonstrates that the trade expectations argument can lack salience when other powerful determinants of decline are hanging over a decision maker.

The Iranian and Suez Crises, 1951–56

The Iranian Crisis of 1951–53 and Suez Crisis of 1955–56 should be analyzed together. Both were part of a larger geostrategic struggle over the Middle East, and unlike the Berlin and Korean crises, dependence and trade expectations did play important causal roles in shaping US behavior. There are many commonalities across the two cases. Both crises were fundamentally about the flow of Middle Eastern oil. And as in so many of our cases, it was exogenous third-party concerns that drove the great powers. Iran and Egypt were led by nationalistic leaders wanting control over something of significant value to a US ally: in the Iranian case, the British-owned Anglo-Iranian Oil Company; and in the Egyptian case, the British-dominated Suez Canal Company. Moreover, in both cases there were worries that Soviet ties to the key leaders in power might permit Moscow ultimately to deny US access to the region's oil and its most important producer, Saudi Arabia. Finally, when the crises reached their heights in 1953 and 1956, respectively, the United States was led by the same individual, Dwight D. Eisenhower, supported by almost the exactly the same set of advisers, including the influential secretary of state John Foster Dulles.

Yet despite these similarities, US responses to the two crises were radically different. In the Iranian case, Eisenhower authorized a coup against the government. In August 1953, a military general with active Central Intelligence Agency (CIA) support overthrew the Iranian leader Moham-med Mossadeq—a risky move that could have sparked a larger superpower escalation. Eisenhower's behavior in the Egyptian case was much more moderate. He rejected any effort to overthrow the government, and took a strong stance against any intervention by Britain, France, or

Israel—the states most interested in using force. When these states did in fact attack Egypt in late October–early November 1956, Eisenhower joined Moscow in condemning their actions in the UN Security Council, and then applied economic sanctions so devastating that Britain and France soon ended their occupation.

What explains why the US government would adopt such different stances to deal with two seemingly similar problems? To my knowledge, there is no political science work comparing the two cases on this issue. And while historians of US Middle East policy have covered these crises thoroughly, they typically treat them separately and fail to answer the posed question. I show that differing trade expectations for the future, filtered through fear of Soviet advances in the Middle East, explain the differing US responses across the cases. In both instances, US elites were wary of overreacting to the nationalizations undertook by the particular governments of the time. They worried that a strong response in support of Britain would only fuel anti-Western hatred, hurting the United States' position just as Moscow was posing as the champion of "anti-imperialist forces" around the world. In Iran, however, the domestic situation was in chaos by 1952 as British oil sanctions destroyed Iran's economy. By the end of Truman's presidency, there was a tangible fear that if Washington failed to act, the country would fall to Communists already aligned with Moscow. With Iran and its oil in their control, the Soviets would then be poised to go after other regional actors whose oil went largely to the United States and continental Europe. Given this threat, Eisenhower chose to implement a plan for Mossadeq's overthrow first discussed in the waning days of Truman's presidency.[43]

In the Egyptian case, in contrast, there was never any serious risk that Communists would seize control of the government. Egypt's president, Gamal Abdel Nasser, was certainly viewed as an unpredictable leader who employed Arab nationalism to build his domestic and regional popularity. But there was no evidence that Egyptian Communists were strong enough to overthrow him. Indeed, despite accepting military and economic aid from the Soviet bloc, he had successfully repressed the Communist Party at home. When Britain began pushing for military action to counter Nasser's announced nationalization of the Suez Company, therefore, Eisenhower saw the risks as much greater than any benefits. A British-led attack or coup effort would enflame Arab sentiments across the Middle East, and if Washington was seen to support such moves, its reputation would be greatly damaged. Moreover, Nasser was acting quite moderately: he offered compensation for the nationalization of the Suez

---

[43]On the continuity between the Truman and Eisenhower presidencies regarding Iran, see Gavin 1999.

Company; assured the world that the canal would be kept open; and in September, proved that Egypt could pilot ships through the canal without European help. In short, from Eisenhower's perspective, Nasser did not pose a threat to European or US oil, even if the president and his secretary of state personally disliked the leader and what he stood for.

The British strongly disagreed with Eisenhower's assessment and believed the threat to trade was high. Yet Eisenhower saw more clearly than London that Nasser had every interest in keeping trade flowing— especially since he needed the canal's revenue to fund his Aswan Dam project. The Egyptian situation was therefore quite different from Iran in 1953, where the threat to oil was real. Different expectations of future trade across the two cases explain nicely the different postures assumed by the US government. As we will see, economic realism and economic liberalism fail to explain either case, let alone the variation between them. Contrary to economic realism, the United States was dependent in both cases, yet it acted only in Iran, and only when things got bad. And US behavior was propelled by security fears, not the unit-level factors that liberals propose.

The US postwar obsession with the Middle East, as we saw earlier, can be traced to Roosevelt's concern with growing US energy dependence and renewed Russian interest in the region. After India's independence in 1947, the impending collapse of European imperial influence around the world foreshadowed an ominous new chapter in the superpower struggle. In September 1948, the CIA distributed its first major analysis of this new situation. The report's opening paragraphs sketched the logic that would guide US thinking about the so-called third world for the next three decades. The breakup of the colonial system had "major implications for US security, particularly in terms of possible world conflict with the USSR." If the United States did not play its cards right, it could easily be "[deprived of] assured access to vital bases and raw materials in these areas." The Soviet Union, as a noncolonial and newly industrializing power, was effectively positioned to "champion the [anti]colonial cause," meaning that emerging states might align with Moscow, "adversely affect[ing] the present [East-West] power balance" (*CIA [HT]*, 219–34).

Given this new reality, Washington had to act carefully with regard to growing Middle East nationalism or else it would be seen as "just another imperialist power." In 1948–49, major Middle Eastern oil producers, including Iran and Saudi Arabia, began to renegotiate agreements with foreign multinationals to increase their share of oil profits. In July 1949, Tehran and London's Anglo-Iranian Oil Company negotiated an initial deal seen by most Iranians to fall far short of Iranian demands. The Majlis refused to ratify the agreement. In June 1950, the issue was referred to a special committee chaired by Mossadeq, the leader of the

National Front, a coalition of nationalist groups. In November, the committee repudiated the agreement, announcing that only nationalization would secure Iran's interests (Painter 1986, 172–73).

The Truman administration was concerned that Britain's refusal to accept even limited nationalization would cause unrest that Moscow could exploit via the Communist Tudeh Party. A July 1950 memorandum to Truman from R. H. Hillenkoetter, CIA director, stated the problem starkly. Soviet forces were "in a position to overrun Iran without warning." Should things get worse and Tudeh assume power, the Soviets would gain access to Iran's great oil resources, and be positioned to penetrate the rest of the Middle East and the Indian subcontinent.[44] And things did indeed begin to deteriorate. Prime Minister Ali Razmara, who had supported a go-slow approach, was assassinated on March 7, 1951. Eight days later, the Majlis voted to nationalize the Anglo-Iranian Oil Company. On April 28, Mossadeq was chosen as Iran's new prime minister, and three days after that the new law went into effect with the shah's approval (Painter 1986, 171). London rejected the nationalization, kicking the crisis into high gear.

Truman's position over his last two years in office remained consistent. Britain should accept nationalization to avert unrest that might bring the Communists to power, but Iran should provide compensation as well as assure British and US companies that they could still sell Iranian oil around the world. Iran and the Middle East had simply become too important to the world economy. A January 1951 National Intelligence Estimate noted that if Middle Eastern oil were cut off, not only would the United States suffer "substantial rationing" but Western Europe would have its industrial expansion halted, too, leading to "profound changes" in its economic structure.[45] The latter implication was of particular concern, given that Washington's primary goal since 1944 had been to stabilize Western Europe to prevent it from going Communist.

Through summer 1951, Truman attempted to broker a deal between Iran and Britain via envoy Harriman, but London and Tehran remained intransigent. Churchill's return to power in October only made things worse. Exports of Iranian oil had already fallen off, but Churchill acted to ensure Iran could not sell oil to non-British oil companies. By year's end, a total blockade of Iranian oil was in place. This would have an

[44] "Memorandum for the President," HSTL, July 27, 1950, Papers of HST, PSF: Intelligence File, 1946–53, Central Intelligence.

[45] "The Importance of Iranian and Middle East Oil to Western Europe under Peacetime Conditions," NIE-14, HSTL, January 8, 1951, Papers of HST, PSF: Intelligence File, 1946–53, Central Intelligence Reports. See also an undated NSC memorandum circulated sometime probably in March making similar points (*FRUS* [1952–54], 10:12).

absolutely devastating impact on the Iranian economy through 1952 and into 1953.

The Truman administration was now caught between a rock and a hard place. Through 1952, Truman would continue his efforts to broker a British-Iranian agreement. The diplomatic discussions went nowhere, however, and Iran continued its descent into domestic chaos (Yergin 1991, 465–66). In August 1952, Secretary of Defense Robert Lovett began to push for a dramatic change in policy. With Britain no longer powerful in the region, he argued, the United States must accept new political, economic, and military commitments to prevent Iran from going Communist (Leffler 1992, 483). By fall 1952 Acheson and Truman, fed up with British and Iranian intransigence, came around to Lovett's point of view. When the two met with president-elect Eisenhower on November 18, Iran was second on the agenda. Acheson told Eisenhower that both London and Tehran were being "wholly unreasonable," and their standoff had led to the "very grave disintegration" of Iran's political structure. Acheson vaguely stated that he and Truman were therefore "going forward under the President's authority to consider what [Washington] alone might do to solve the problem."[46]

What Acheson did not tell Eisenhower is that the State Department was already gearing up to implement Lovett's radical shift in policy—one that would leave no options off the table, including military force. The day after meeting Eisenhower, Truman met with his NSC. The defense department's deputy secretary, filling in for Lovett, told Truman that it was now necessary for the United States "to proceed unilaterally . . . to get Iran back on our side." While he hoped nonmilitary measures would work, his department had already reached tentative conclusions on the feasibility of military options (*FRUS* [1952–54], 10:526). The next day, a NSC document on Iran, NSC 136/1, was issued for Truman's approval. The loss of Iran to the Soviet bloc, it contended, would allow Moscow to seriously threaten Middle Eastern oil. Thus, if Communists try to seize power, the United States should support the non-Communist side via actions that included "military support" (ibid., 10:529–34). Planning for a covert operation began that November through contacts with the British government, such that by the first month of Eisenhower's administration, London and Washington had agreed on the details of a coup plan and had selected Teddy Roosevelt's grandson, Kermit Roosevelt, to oversee its implementation (Painter 1986, 189–90; Rubin 1980, 77–79).

The deteriorating situation in Iran and threat to oil had, by the end of the Truman administration, caused it to shift toward risky military

---

[46] "Memorandum of Meeting at the White House between President Truman and General Eisenhower," HSTL, November 18, 1952, Student Research File (File B), Oil Crisis in Iran, 1951–53.

and subversive options. While everyone still hoped the problem could be solved without war, the final section of NSC 136/1 showed the true seriousness of the problem. Should Moscow move forces into Iran, Washington would have to assume that "global war is probably imminent." It would then have to "[take] action against the aggressor . . . in the manner which would best contribute to the security of the United States" (*FRUS* [1952–54], 10:533–34). With the resources of not just Iran but also the whole of the Middle East at stake, the United States was ready to go to war should Russia try to muscle its way into the region.

The end of the story can be told in short order. Even before Eisenhower (1963, 160–61) came into office on January 20, 1953, he was already working on a solution to the problem. London and Washington had a coup plan in place by February. By early March, it was clear that even if Mossadeq managed to hold on to power, he could only do so with Tudeh support.[47] At a NSC meeting on March 4, Dulles told Eisenhower that if Iran succumbed to Communism, "there was little doubt that in short order the other areas of the Middle East, with some 60% of the world's oil reserves, would fall into Communist control." The talk around the table was extremely pessimistic. The secretary of the treasury asked Dulles if he already believed Iran would go Communist. Dulles replied affirmatively, prompting Eisenhower to argue that US forces could be moved into neighboring states. The risks were obvious. If the United States was compelled to move forces into Iran itself, Eisenhower noted, Moscow would invoke its 1921 treaty of alliance, and "then we would find ourselves at war with Russia." Yet if the United States failed to act, he "feared that the United States would descend to the status of a second-rate power" (*FRUS* [1952–54], 10:692–701).

In April, a million dollars was sent to CIA operatives in Tehran to bring about Mossadeq's fall. In mid-July, Kermit Roosevelt entered Iran from Iraq to finalize arrangements for "Operation Ajax." Street demonstrations in mid-August were going in Mossadeq's favor, and the shah fled the country. But on August 18–19, with CIA help, General Fazlollah Zahedi was able to arrest Mossadeq and assume control of the state. The shah returned triumphantly to Iran, and the Soviets wisely chose not to contest the outcome. Within two years a consortium made up of US, British, and Dutch oil firms agreed to share profits with Iran's nationalized oil company, thereby paralleling similar recent deals with other key oil-producing states, including Saudi Arabia (see Kinzer 2003; Yergin 1991).

The Iranian Crisis was ultimately resolved without an escalation to regional war, or worse. Yet both Truman and Eisenhower were willing to risk such an escalation to prevent Moscow from gaining a foothold in the Middle East. Third-party instability had created a situation where a

---

[47] See memorandums on March 1 and 2, 1953, in *FRUS* (1952–54), 10:689–92.

negotiated solution had become highly unlikely. Declining expectations of future trade, tied to the West's growing dependency on Middle East oil, drove the increasingly severe policies of both presidents. With dependence levels constant, economic realism cannot explain the shifts in US policy. Liberalism cannot explain US leaders' risk-taking behavior during a period of high dependence, or the fact that security objectives were predominant. That the world avoided a war has more to do with Soviet caution, perhaps facilitated by Stalin's death in March 1953, than with US restraint. Truman and Eisenhower were preparing themselves for a big fight, and economic fears for the future were determinative.

The Suez Crisis of 1955–56 mirrors the above, with the United States again finding itself in a crisis because of Britain's unwillingness to accept the loss of a Middle Eastern asset. On June 26, 1956, President Nasser of Egypt announced the nationalization of the Suez Canal Company, the organization that had run the canal for almost eighty years. The British government under Prime Minister Anthony Eden instantly began to organize a military response, drawing into its plan the governments of France and Israel. Some two-thirds of all oil consumed by Western Europe passed through the canal. The British were worried that if they allowed Nasser to grab the waterway, not only would Britain's economy suffer, but its regional position would deteriorate rapidly as well.[48] Eisenhower tried to restrain Eden from taking military action, but Eden was hell-bent on safeguarding European control of the canal. When the Israelis launched a preventive attack on October 29, 1956, British and French forces invaded the canal zone soon after. With the Soviet bloc supplying arms to Nasser through Czechoslovakia, Premier Khrushchev felt obliged to hint that Britain and France might be hit by Russian missiles should they not retreat. In late November, London and Paris did decide to end their occupation. Yet the deeper reason for their exit was not Russian coercion but instead the economic devastation created by Eisenhower's refusal to send Latin American oil to Europe or support their rapidly falling currencies. As with Iran 1953, however, the situation was a highly dangerous one. One misstep by either side—say, a US decision to support Britain's use of force, followed by a Soviet decision to deploy conventional forces in the area—could have easily spiraled to a full-scale superpower confrontation.[49]

The question before us is why Eisenhower chose such a moderate stance in this crisis despite the apparent challenge to the economic health of the Western world. Eisenhower and his secretary of state were indeed

[48] Given space limitations, I will not cover British decision making during the crisis, but suffice it to say that declining trade expectations were a determinative force.

[49] My summaries above and below are drawn largely from Hahn 1991; Freiberger 1992.

concerned about developments in Egypt after the 1952 military coup that overthrew King Farouk and put a regime of generals in his place. Colonel Nasser emerged as the sole leader by early 1954, and then proceeded over the next two years to establish an image as head of pan-Arab nationalism and a driving force behind the so-called nonaligned movement. For Eisenhower and Dulles, nonalignment in a struggle of such importance as the Cold War was more than mere nuisance; it was a betrayal of the US cause. Nevertheless, the stakes were too high to simply write Nasser off. By February 1955, the new Soviet politburo (now known as the presidium) under the leadership of Khrushchev and Nikolai Bulgarin was determined to increase Soviet influence in the south. Moscow began an "economic offensive" (so named by Washington) to draw away key third world states through the promise of aid and trade. Moscow's initial focus was on newly independent states in Asia, including India, Burma, and Indonesia. But in mid-1955, Khrushchev and Bulgarin turned their attention to Egypt as the one major Arab state not in the clutches of either Washington or London.

An Israeli attack on the Egyptian-controlled Gaza Strip in early 1955 combined with Britain's formation of the Central Treaty Organization convinced Nasser of the need to increase Egypt's military strength. In September 1955, he shocked the Western world by announcing a major arms purchase from Czechoslovakia. The US government was worried, but unlike the Israelis and British, still believed that Nasser was a rational leader who would keep his radical nationalism within bounds. Moreover, Eisenhower and Dulles thought they had much bigger fish to fry: as long as Nasser continued to repress Communism within Egypt and did not directly threaten commercial access through the canal, he could be tolerated. Seeing that Nasser was setting Moscow against Washington to get the best deal, Eisenhower decided to play the game. When Nasser signaled that he wanted massive foreign funding for the building of the Aswan Dam, Washington was supportive. In December, Dulles indicated that the US government would provide a substantial loan to supplement what the US-dominated World Bank had already offered.

By that point, the United States' Cold War strategy had undergone a visible shift in focus. Until late 1955, the series of Basic National Security Policy papers that oriented US foreign policy had still placed primary emphasis on the strategic military struggle and competition over Europe. On October 3, though, the State Department distributed a memorandum arguing for a new policy direction. Because the Soviets saw general war as irrational, they were now concentrating on the "nonmilitary competition" in the developing world, especially in the Middle East and Latin America. To counter this, Washington had to increase efforts to foster economic growth in these areas. This new view would be incorporated into revisions of the Basic National Security Policy document undertaken over the winter and approved on March 15, 1956.[50]

We can thus see why Eisenhower and Dulles became so keen to maintain relations with Nasser in late 1955–early 1956, notwithstanding his pan-Arab nationalism and purchase of Soviet bloc arms. Unfortunately, Nasser played his hand too hard: he was unwilling to make peace with Israel, continued his buildup, and signaled he would turn to Moscow for economic aid should Washington continue to hold up US and World Bank assistance for the Aswan Dam. His recognition of Communist China and announcement of a new arms deal with Poland in May 1956 were the final straws. National Security Council and State Department officials now agreed that the carrot of US and World Bank money could not dissuade Egypt from aligning more closely with the Soviet bloc. On June 19, Dulles told the Egyptians that the United States could not supply aid for the dam, nor would it encourage the World Bank to do so. A week later, on June 26, Nasser announced the canal company's nationalization in a highly charged speech in Alexandria, noting that monies raised through transit fees would be used to fund the dam (Hahn 1991, 203–10).

Nasser's move took Eisenhower by surprise. On the morning of Friday, July 27, he held an emergency meeting with CIA director Allen Dulles and Undersecretary of State Herbert Hoover Junior (Dulles being out of town). Hoover asserted that Nasser's move violated international law and might result in interference with the canal through which two-thirds of Middle Eastern oil passed. Eisenhower agreed, stating that "we and many others have a concern over [the canal's] operations," and Washington should issue a statement that it viewed the matter "with grave concern" (FRUS [1955–57], 16:5–6). Soon after the meeting, Eisenhower received a letter from Prime Minister Eden, emphasizing that Egypt was incapable of running the canal and Britain was developing a military plan to counter the threat to the European economy (Hahn 1991, 212; FRUS [1955–57], 16:9–10).

Eisenhower called Hoover back to the White House late that afternoon to discuss the letter. Hoover declared that the United States must move strongly or face a decline in the "whole Western position." Eisenhower, still feeling his way toward a position, stated that the situation was so troubling that Congress might need to be called back from summer recess. Its leaders must be told that "this development has the most serious implications for the Western world. If the movement of oil were interfered with, or if the pipelines were cut, we would be faced with a critical situation" (FRUS [1955–57], 16:11–12). That afternoon, Eisenhower sent a vague reply to Eden, telling him that he agreed with many of Eden's

---

[50]FRUS (1955–57), 19:123–25, 242–68, versus NSC 5501 of January 1955, ibid., 24–38.

points, but that other steps should be considered first, including consultations with affected maritime nations. Eisenhower's initial posture was to slow down British decision making to give diplomacy a chance, even as he kept the military option on the table. Over the next two days, however, as the costs of military action rose and risks of not acting began to appear slight, his perspective moderated substantially. Critical to Eisenhower's moderate stance by late July was his understanding that Nasser's action was not only legal but also that the Egyptians were signaling they would keep the canal open and operate it efficiently.

On Friday, a State Department legal adviser had written a memorandum underscoring that Nasser's nationalization decree agreed to provide compensation at full market value to the canal's European investors (ibid., 16:16). At a meeting the next morning (July 28), Eisenhower was informed that Egypt had agreed to abide by the 1888 convention guaranteeing states free use of the canal. Hoover also noted that Admiral Arleigh Burke, the Joint Chiefs of Staff's chief of naval operations, had said that piloting ships through the canal was not as difficult as had been previously reported. The president summarized the costs and risks of the two main options. It would not be difficult for Western states to retake the canal militarily. Yet there was no real basis for such action in terms of global public opinion. Accordingly, he agreed with the State Department that Egypt "was within its rights, and that until its operation of the Canal was proven incompetent, unjust, etc. there was nothing to do" (ibid., 16:26, 28).

Hoover quickly tried to back away from such an interpretation of State Department briefings, saying that he felt action was necessary or else the Western position would be gravely undercut. But the president had now arrived at the policy logic he would hold on to for the remainder of the crisis. The impact on global and especially Middle Eastern public opinion of any form of Western military action would be huge. Even if only Britain acted, the United States would likely be excused of aiding and abetting old-style European imperialism against a developing nation that was acting within its legal rights. And if the Egyptians were not only willing to keep the canal open but also proved more than capable of piloting the ships, then what was the real concern? Nasser was certainly a firebrand nationalist, but he had good self-interested reasons in keeping the canal open to maximize revenue for his Aswan project. As Eisenhower summarized his thinking in late July, the weight of world opinion was that Nasser had a legal right to nationalize the canal, and this right "could scarcely be doubted" as long as just compensation were provided. "The main issue at stake, therefore, was whether or not Nasser would and could keep the waterway open for the traffic of all nations, in accordance with the [convention] of 1888," Eisenhower (1965, 39) continues, and "This question could not be answered except through test."

Everything that happened over the next two months only reinforced for Eisenhower that a US "do-nothing" policy was the best of many distasteful options. A telegram from the US ambassador in Cairo arrived on July 30 describing his conversation with Nasser. Nasser underscored that he had only taken the action to finance the dam, and would have greatly preferred US and World Bank funding. The ambassador replied that Washington's main concern was whether the canal would remain open for international use. Nasser reassured the ambassador that he was committed to the canal's openness and had affirmed this in his recent declarations (*FRUS* [1955–57], 16:55–56).

This information may have helped Eisenhower relax somewhat, but his own military was proving a problem. The Joint Chiefs of Staff had submitted a study on July 28 specifying three options, from diplomatic support for British military action to actual US military participation (ibid., 16:21). At a White House meeting on the morning of July 31, the president and his advisers were told that Eden had made a firm decision to initiate hostilities to "break Nasser," probably after six weeks of preparation. Eisenhower opened the discussion by saying this was a unwise decision that was out of touch with present circumstances in the developing world. He and CIA director Dulles agreed that precipitous action would cause the whole Arab world to unite against the West, Middle East oil would "dry up," and the United States would have to divert oil to Europe, leading to rationing at home. Burke countered that it was the Joint Chiefs of Staff's opinion that Nasser must indeed be broken, and if diplomacy failed and Britain used force, Washington should support its action. The president gave no ground. Convinced that the British were making a deep error, he asked Dulles to go to London to explain his view. Asked what would happen if this caused a rift between London and Washington, Eisenhower agreed that this would a serious development, although "not as serious as letting a war start and not trying to stop it" (ibid., 16:62–68).

Later that day, a Special National Intelligence Estimate on the crisis was issued supporting Eisenhower's reasoning. While Nasser was committed to reducing Western influence in the Middle East, his decision to nationalize the canal was apparently taken on short notice in reaction to Washington's decision not to fund the Aswan Dam. But the action was legal, and should Egypt fulfill its promise to abide by current rules and practices, there was "little basis for legal action by the using powers" (ibid., 16:78–93). This seemed to seal it for Eisenhower. He immediately wrote Eden, telling him that despite the canal's importance, concerned nations could exert enough pressure on Egypt to assure "the efficient operation of the Canal . . . [into] the future." The canal's openness and efficiency were the key issues, not who controlled it, Eisenhower stressed.

Then came his warning. If the British went ahead with military action, "the American reaction would be severe," and most of the world would share that reaction (ibid., 16:69–71; Eisenhower 1965, appendix B).

The events of August to November can be covered in short order, given that Eisenhower never wavered from his fundamental position that a British-led attack would be disastrous for both Britain and the United States. He held to this in spite of the arguments of his advisers, including at times Secretary Dulles, that British action should be given at least implicit support.[51] In mid-August and again in mid-September, two separate multiparty conferences were held in London to coordinate the key maritime nations' response. The British were adamant that an international consortium of non-Egyptian states should assume control of the canal zone. During the August conference, Eisenhower told Dulles, who was acting as US envoy, that the group must not adopt a position that was impossible for Nasser to accept. Thus, instead of an international consortium assuming operational control of the canal, it should have merely a "supervisory" role (Fursenko and Naftali 2007, 104). This suggestion, similar to Moscow's proposal, was summarily rejected by London. After an eighteen to four vote in favor of the British position, Australian prime minister Robert Menzies traveled to Cairo with what amounted to an ultimatum: Egypt had to accept international control of the canal or face attack. As Eisenhower had predicted, Nasser rejected the terms as incompatible with Egypt's sovereign rights. A follow-up conference of the Western states in mid-September proved equally fruitless. The conference focused on Dulles's new proposal for a Suez Canal Users Association, a loose organization that would coordinate traffic through the canal, collect tolls, and pay Egypt its fair share of the revenues. Despite majority agreement in favor of this plan, it too was dead in the water, given lukewarm British support and Egyptian resistance (see Hahn 1991, 220–21).

Eisenhower himself saw little value in the Suez Canal Users Association by the end of the month. And yet he was still resolute in his opposition to the use of force. The events of September 14 proved decisive. That day, London and Paris ordered their canal pilots to leave the canal zone, hoping that this would expose the inability of Egypt to operate the canal. Over the next seven days, Egyptian pilots stepped in to guide 254 vessels safely through the canal—a new one-week record. This achievement not only showed the hollowness of the British and French arguments for action but also verified that Egypt was more than capable of running the

---

[51] On August 9, for example, Dulles contended at a NSC meeting that the United States should not restrain the British and French if they attacked Egypt. Eisenhower rejected such a policy, and by mid-August, Dulles was towing the president's line in discussions with London (Hahn 1991, 214–15).

canal by itself (ibid., 219). Eisenhower (1965, 51) in his memoirs states his reaction in no uncertain terms:

> As it [turned] out, not only were the Egyptian officials and workmen competent to operate the Canal, but they [demonstrated] that they could do so under conditions of increased traffic and with increased efficiency. . . . The assumption upon which the Users Association was largely based proved groundless. Furthermore, any thought of using force, under these circumstances, was almost ridiculous.

Positive trade expectations were playing their anticipated causal role. Eisenhower had no reason to push for force if the Egyptians were perfectly willing and able to keep commerce flowing through the canal zone and had every rational reason, including the funding of the Aswan Dam, for wanting to keep toll revenues flowing in. British fears of a cutoff might be driving them into war, but these worries were simply irrational from Eisenhower's perspective; they had no basis in fact, as the events of September 14–21 showed. Yet if Britain did go ahead, and if Washington was seen to be supporting such holdovers from a dying imperialist era, the United States' global position would suffer a dramatic decline.

Hence when Israel, Britain, and France ignored his warnings and entered the canal zone in late October–early November, Eisenhower knew that he had to stand symbolically against the "aggressors." The United States and Soviet Union, for the first time since the founding of Israel, stood together in the United Nations and condemned the attacks. Washington's subsequent unwillingness to provide oil to Western Europe or support the British and French currencies signaled to the world that European imperialism would no longer be tolerated, and that the United States stood on the side of progress in the developing world.

Trade expectations theory does a solid job explaining US moderation in the Suez Crisis. Unlike Iran 1953, there was little fear of Communism taking over in Egypt and little fear that the nationalist government in power would restrict the flow of oil. Economic realism cannot explain this moderation in the face of the West's high and growing dependence on Middle East oil. And it certainly cannot explain the variation in US behavior across the Iran and Suez cases. Economic liberalism might try to explain the moderation in 1956 through the fear of a widening war that might lead to even greater costs to US multinational oil firms and the US lifestyle back home. But the documents show Eisenhower carefully calculating the risks of Nasser severing oil traffic through the Suez Canal in terms of the larger issue of national security and Cold War struggle. In addition, he was more than willing to assume large risks of superpower war in 1953 given the security implications of losing access to oil. We can thus safely conclude that it was strategic dependence tied to trade expectations that drove his decision making, not domestic-level concerns.

TRADE EXPECTATIONS AND THE STRUGGLES
TO END THE COLD WAR, 1957–91

The last part of this chapter discusses the considerable efforts made by both superpowers after 1956, if not necessarily to end the Cold War, at least to reduce its intensity and the probability of nuclear war. By the mid- to late 1950s, it was perfectly clear to both sides that any major war would mean the destruction of their civilizations, if not the planet. Yet until the late 1980s, Washington and Moscow proved unable to secure a true peace that would keep their leaders' fingers far away from the nuclear button. Why did their efforts at peace initially prove fruitless and then by 1989–91 succeed? The first such attempt from 1957 to 1961 "ended" with the two most intense crises of the whole Cold War era. The puzzle to explain here is why the crises over Berlin 1961 and Cuba 1962 would occur despite efforts by both sides, but particularly Soviet leader Khrushchev, to establish a trade-based détente. The second try was from 1963 to the US-Soviet détente of 1972–74, and this one did have some limited successes, especially in moderating the risk of superpower war during the 1973 Middle East Crisis. Yet détente fell apart by 1975, leading to the so-called Second Cold War of 1979–83. What happened in 1974–75 to shift the superpower relationship back to one of tension and hostility? Finally, of course, we have the riddle of the end of the Cold War itself: the surprising about-face by both actors from 1984 to 1991 that led, even before the collapse of the Soviet Union, to a peace both countries knew would be truly a "new era" of stability and reduced mistrust.

This part differs from others in this chapter. Because liberals and economic realists both argue that when trade has been low for some time, it falls out as an important causal variable, there is little point in trying to test trade expectations theory against their assertions. My goal therefore is simply to demonstrate the surprising impact of changing trade expectations on great power behavior even in environments where trade is essentially nonexistent.

A Lost Opportunity? The Missing Détente of 1956 to 1962

In the late 1950s, the superpower competition over the third world was intensifying. In March 1956 Eisenhower approved Basic National Security Policy NSC 5602/1, which placed new emphasis on blocking Moscow's ability to draw developing nations into its sphere through offers of trade and aid (*FRUS* [1955–57], 19:242–68). In the struggle for the third world, the United States possessed some powerful tools. The main one was simply the continuation of severe restrictions on direct US-Soviet trade as well as trade between Western Europe and the East. By restraining Soviet economic development, Washington could hurt Moscow's ability to assist the third world or develop a strong base for its military.[52] Other tools included increased US trade and economic assistance to emerging nations, binding alliances, and military aid to combat internal Communist threats.

In a fundamental sense, Washington always retained the upper hand when it came to the economic side of the Cold War. The United States' economy and its global trade connections were always far stronger as well as more technically advanced, meaning that the Soviets were typically working against a stacked deck, both in their negotiations with Washington and their relations with emerging nations. But the dilemma facing Russia after 1956 was more complicated than merely the need for more power. Soviet decision making was pulled by two contradictory forces. On the one side, Khrushchev and his advisers knew that the high growth rates of the early 1950s could not be sustained without the creation of a stronger technological base, particularly in the chemical, electronic, and oil industries. To achieve his goal of catching up to the United States, Khrushchev needed the West to relax its restrictions on trade and issue trade credits in the process. CoCom's move away from pure economic warfare by 1954 had helped to build some trust with Western Europe. Yet constraints on high-tech exports from Western Europe remained. More important, because the United States was still clearly the world's most technologically advanced state and imposing near-total trade restrictions, to grow the Soviets needed to moderate the direct relationship to permit the purchase of high-tech exports from the United States itself (Parrott 1983, 1985; Fursenko and Naftali 2007).

Pulling from the other side was Moscow's precarious strategic situation. The United States had possessed military superiority since 1945. The Soviets needed to not only close the gap but also deter Washington during the transition. But actions to create a strong nuclear deterrent would work against the larger effort to relax tensions, increase trade, and improve economic growth. In the late 1950s, military technology was changing so fast that each side constantly worried about its ability to maintain a second-strike capability that would dissuade the other side from contemplating a first strike. To speed up his economic reform

[52] East-West trade had been devastated by the formation of CoCom in 1949, which blocked the sale of even the most basic products from Western Europe. By 1954, in the post-Stalin era of "peaceful coexistence," Western European capitals had been able to pressure Washington to halve the number of products restricted by CoCom, and further reductions were agreed on in 1958. But tight US restrictions on exports remained in place. The total US exports to Russia had fallen to a mere seven million dollars by 1959, and would hover between twenty and forty-five million dollars until the late 1960s—at a time when British and West German exports to Russia together averaged between seven and eight times this amount. See Mastanduno 1992, 93–118, including the table on 112.

program while protecting Soviet security, Khrushchev had decided in 1955 to reduce spending on conventional forces and increase funding for his missile program. The strategy worked. By the end of 1957, the Soviets appeared to be ahead on missile technology: they had successfully tested the first ICBM in August, and in October launched the world's first satellite (Sputnik). Knowing that B-52 bombers that could deliver an overwhelming strike ringed Russia, Khrushchev chose to encourage the perception that the USSR was rapidly turning out missiles that could hit not just Western Europe but the US homeland. As a result, fears of a "missile gap" that might give Moscow a first-strike opportunity dominated public discussions of US foreign policy from October 1957 to the end of 1961 (Ambrose 1984; Taubman 2003).

Eisenhower in late 1957 knew that the United States was ahead in deliverable nuclear weapons. Yet he worried that a future missile gap might arise if Washington was too complacent. At a November 4 meeting, he told his advisers that the true critical period was not now but rather five years hence (*FRUS* [1955–57], 19:621). To prevent a future gap, Eisenhower accelerated US missile programs while redirecting substantial resources to the training of more engineers and scientists. US superiority on deployed missiles was maintained because of these efforts—a fact John F. Kennedy learned only after assuming office. Still, the net result of this new arms buildup was that Washington was unwilling to provide any kind of trade that might accelerate Soviet economic power.

Ironically, this happened just as the Soviet need for US technology was rising and Eisenhower's desire for a superpower détente was peaking—that is, just as the opportunity for a trade-based peace was presenting itself. By 1958–59, Soviet agricultural and industrial reforms were losing momentum, and Soviet economic technology (if not military technology) was falling even further behind the United States (Parrott 1983, 1985; Zubok 2009). For his part, Eisenhower wanted to leave a legacy of peaceful superpower relations, including a slowing of the arms race. And he understood, as we will see, that the carrot of increased trade was one of the few levers that might help buy Soviet cooperation.

The period from January 1958 until the collapse of discussions in May 1960 thus constitutes a strange blend of acute arms racing and a genuine attempt on both sides to create a stable peace. Adding to the mix was Washington's fear that if Russia kept growing, third world states would see socialist planning as the wave of the future and gravitate toward Moscow's sphere. Eisenhower tried to square the circle by seeking détente even as he maintained the United States' dominant economic and military position around the world. But without a willingness to relax restrictions that were impeding Soviet economic development, this strategy was bound to fail.

In mid-February 1958, in discussing trade controls with the British, Undersecretary of State for Economic Affairs Douglas Dillon summarized the new significance of the global economic struggle. The relationship of trade controls such as CoCom to Russia's economic penetration of the underdeveloped areas was "the most serious aspect of our struggle with the Soviet Union at this time."[53] In his State of the Union speech of January 1958, Eisenhower had talked about the need to win "a different kind of war"—namely, the conflict set in motion by the "massive [Soviet] economic offensive" against free nations.[54] On March 3, Dillon explained to the Senate Foreign Relations Committee that this economic offensive was gaining momentum and the key issue was this: To what extent can Moscow use Soviet bloc economic power to advance the political objectives of international Communism? In this regard, the expanded Soviet aid program was "a new, subtle and long-range instrument directed toward the same old purpose": "drawing its recipient . . . into the Communist orbit."[55]

The Soviets by this point, however, were keen to improve US-Russian relations in order to moderate the arms race and secure high-tech goods. On June 2, 1958, Khrushchev sent a long letter to Eisenhower. It was of great importance that the two take advantage of "unused opportunities" to improve relations, Khrushchev wrote in the opening paragraph. For twenty-three of the next twenty-five paragraphs, his letter focused solely on the question of US-Soviet trade relations. With the Soviet people wanting increased consumer goods, opening trade would "further the cause of world peace." Khrushchev provided a long list of desired purchases—everything from chemical products to the equipment necessary to manufacture refrigerators and televisions. While Russia could export raw materials to buy these goods, Khrushchev indicated that some long-term trade credits and loans would be needed. He ended the letter by noting that a "positive solution" to the trade question would constitute "an important step toward a rapprochement between our two countries."[56]

Eisenhower's reply to Khrushchev on July 15—a short one-page letter that he made public—did not help matters. While expressing Washington's ongoing interest in trade, he disingenuously argued that the Soviets

---

[53] "Memorandum of Conversation," DDEL, February 18, 1958, US Council on Foreign Economic Policy, Records, 1954–61, Policy Papers Series.

[54] Quoted in a secretary of commerce memorandum to Clarence Randall, in DDEL, January 28, 1959, Council of Foreign Economic Policy (CFEP), Records, 1954–61, Policy Papers Series.

[55] "Statement," DDEL, March 3, 1958, CFEP, Records, 1954–61, Policy Papers Series.

[56] See letter with Dillon's note, in DDEL, June 4, 1958, US CFEP, Records, 1954–61, Policy Paper Series.

were free to sell their goods to the United States with few restrictions.[57] This ignored the thrust of Soviet complaints: that they were not free to *buy* US goods. A memorandum circulated at this time by Eisenhower's Council of Foreign Economic Policy—an organization with powerful influence over US-Soviet and third world trade policies—observed that many of the items listed in Khrushchev's letter were still under explicit "embargo"—things such as pumps and compressors, television equipment, and mining machinery. Sixteen of the eighteen other items, while not explicitly banned, required licenses from the US Department of Commerce and were under the "presumption of denial," including items as seemingly innocuous as air-conditioning equipment and pipes for city gas lines.[58]

Eisenhower had little choice but to continue restricting Soviet purchases of even relatively low-tech goods, though. Another Basic National Security Policy review had been completed in May 1958. Eisenhower's national security adviser Robert Cutler had told him on May 1 that as the Soviets moved toward strategic parity, there was not only increasing doubt among allies as to whether Washington would defend them but Moscow also was becoming bolder in its economic and political policies toward developing nations. The final policy document circulated on May 5 argued that the United States had to counter Russia's economic offensive against the developing world even as it maintained US nuclear superiority. So while Washington should remain open to negotiations, the United States should not make concessions "in advance of similar action by the Soviets" simply from a hope of inspiring Soviet compromises (*FRUS* [1958–60], 3:78–79, 98–116).

For the next two years, Eisenhower took this advice to heart. He did want a modus vivendi to reduce the risks of nuclear war. But he continually refused to make concessions, particularly on trade, until he had first seen large concessions or improved behavior from Moscow. This bargaining strategy differed substantially from the one adopted by Henry Kissinger in the early 1970s. Kissinger sought to link Soviet military and political concessions to US concessions on trade; that is, the two sets of concessions would occur *simultaneously* and be enshrined in written agreements to bind both sides. Eisenhower, however, remained unwilling to adopt such a "linkage" strategy. He wanted to see clear evidence of better Soviet behavior *prior to* accepting increased trade. As we will see, the adoption of this posture effectively sunk any hope for a détente before he left office.

[57] See letter released by James Hagerty, Eisenhower's press secretary, in DDEL, July 14, 1958, CFEP, Records, 1954–61, Policy Papers Series.

[58] See "Control Status of Categories Mentioned in Khrushchev Letter of June 2, 1958," DDEL, n.d., CFEP, Records 1054–61, Policy Papers Series.

It is hard to believe that a person of Eisenhower's intelligence and experience would not have seen the advantages of practicing such a tried-
and-true tactic as linkage. Something was clearly holding him back. This
something, in essence, was the strategic situation the United States faced
in 1958–60—a problem much more acute than the one confronting Kissinger and Richard Nixon in 1970–72. In the 1958–60 period, there was no
certainty that both sides could maintain a secure second strike to ensure
deterrence. There was also great uncertainty as to whether newly independent third world states would lean toward Moscow and start restricting
access to critical raw materials. Finally, it was unclear whether Russia
might indeed catch up to and even overtake the United States in total economic strength, given that its growth rates were twice the United States'
average. By the time Nixon assumed office, these concerns had been ameliorated: mutual assured destruction (MAD) was a reality, third world
alignments were clear, and the Soviet economic system was stagnating.

The United States of Eisenhower's era, in contrast, could not simply
begin free trading without expecting the Soviets to grab technologies that
might catapult them to predominance. This created a tragic feedback
loop: Washington could not afford to relax economic restrictions without first seeing major Soviet concessions. Yet continued restrictions only
hurt Soviet expectations of future trade, increasing Moscow's own fears
for the future. This in turn led to more hostile Soviet behavior, making it
even harder for Washington to offer substantial trade concessions.

Concern about Soviet economic catch-up permeated the key internal
analyses of the Eisenhower administration's last three years. On November 16, 1958, a report to Eisenhower from the CIA's deputy director
underscored that Moscow's new thrust was the "creation of the material-
technical basis" for Soviet power. Moscow was investing heavily in chem-
icals, but success depended on its ability to develop the petrochemical
industry. This would be difficult "unless substantial assistance [in] petrochemical technology and equipment is procured from the West."[59] This
report came right when Moscow was engaged in what Bruce Jentleson
(1986, 81–83) calls the "Soviet Oil Offensive" toward Western Europe.
Russian oil production had doubled from 1953 to 1958, and the country
had suddenly gone from a net importer to a net exporter of oil. Moscow
wanted to sell large quantities of oil to Western Europe in return for
higher-tech items still denied by the United States (see Mastanduno 1992,
109; Jentleson 1986, 80–87). US officials worried that the Soviets were

---

[59] "Memorandum for Director of Central Intelligence," DDEL, November 16, 1958,
Eisenhower, Dwight D., Records as President, White House Central Files (Confidential File),
1953–61.

using cut-rate oil prices to increase Western Europe's dependency, obliging it to realign eastward.[60]

These concerns coincided with Khrushchev's announcement in November 1958 that he would make Berlin a "free city" within six months if the wartime allies could not establish a new arrangement. Notwithstanding this unsettling development, Moscow kept pressing Eisenhower to reduce export restrictions. In December, Anatas Mikoyan, Russia's second in command and overseer of Soviet trade, asked if he could make an "informal" visit to Washington. This prompted Council of Foreign Economic Policy chair Clarence Randall to write Gordon Gray, Eisenhower's new national security adviser, to explain his evolving position on East-West trade. While there were government officials who wanted even harsher economic restrictions, Randall noted, US-Soviet strategic relations were "already too delicate" to take this risk. Hence "the time has come to let peaceful trade develop as it will."[61]

Randall's memo was the first to suggest a tension among Eisenhower's advisers. The Council of Foreign Economic Policy and the State Department had come to believe that increased trade might indeed moderate relations as well as help establish a détente. The Department of Commerce, however, was adamant that restrictions were critical to preventing US relative decline. The approaching Mikoyan visit exposed this interagency division. At the January 8, 1959 council meeting, Dillon emphasized that Eisenhower himself was now "very clearly in favor" of developing "peaceful trade" with Moscow. Randall pointedly asserted that "certain agencies" were dragging their feet here, even though trade "would help the cause the peace." Secretary of Commerce Lewis Strauss countered that even simple items like carbon black, used in tire production, could increase Russia's strength by helping it transport troops.[62] A follow-up State Department memorandum on "Peaceful Trade" with Russia outlined the competing arguments, but leaned toward trade. Although increased trade might help the Soviets convince "uncommitted countries" that Communism was the fastest route to industrialization, trade was also an "important way of avoiding war" and "relaxing tensions."[63]

[60] "Soviet Attempts to Penetrate West European Oil Market," DDEL, December 29, 1958, CFEP, Records 1954–61, Policy Paper Series.

[61] See "Randall's Memorandum for Mr. Gordon Gray," DDEL, December 16, 1956, CFEP, Records 1954–61, Policy Papers Series.

[62] "Extended Minutes of CFEP Meeting of January 8, 1959, with Attached Letter of January 9, 1959," DDEL, CFEP Records 1954–61, Policy Paper Series. See also FRUS (1958–60), 4:749–53.

[63] "Outline for a Study on Peaceful Trade Relations," DDEL, n.d., CFEP Records 1954–61, Policy Papers Series.

When Dillon met Mikoyan on January 19, he began by stating that his government understood that better commercial relations might help reduce tensions, but that "political complications" made it difficult to expand trade. Mikoyan quickly saw this as a statement that should Moscow improve its behavior, more trade would be forthcoming. He replied that while poor relations may not lead to greater trade, "trade expansion does contribute to good political relations," and US-Soviet trade was still very low. He went after the licensing system that restricted what Russians could buy. The meeting ended in a deadlock, with Dillon contending that the Soviets needed to resolve outstanding issues such as lend-lease payments, and Mikoyan maintaining that the sacrifices made by the Soviet people during World War II were payment enough.[64]

Despite the failure of the Mikoyan talks, the next nine months of 1959 showed promise. A new State Department memorandum sent to Eisenhower in early March stated that it was now an assumption of US economic defense policy that East-West commerce should be encouraged because "the benefits from peaceful trade" outweighed any impact it might have on Soviet economic, technological, and industrial growth.[65] Officials favoring trade still wanted to see concessions on Berlin and other issues before allowing Moscow to buy more goods.[66] But there was now for the first time in the Cold War a distinct possibility of using commerce and changing trade expectations to moderate the superpower conflict.

Eisenhower's strategy over the next five months was to dangle the possibility of future credits and relaxed trade restrictions to leverage the Soviets into concessions on Berlin and disarmament. He knew Moscow needed what Washington had to offer and was prepared to withhold all trade commitments until he got progress on security issues. By May, Eisenhower could see that the Soviets were already softening on the Berlin question; he was informed through British prime minister Harold MacMillan that Khrushchev did not view his original May 27 deadline as an ultimatum.[67] This deadline did indeed pass without incident, suggesting that the Soviets would not press the issue in the short term.

---

[64] See "Memorandum of Conversation, January 19, 1959, Attached to Letter from Dillon to Randall, January 23," DDEL, CFEP Records 1954–61, Policy Paper Series.

[65] "Outline for a Study of the Advantages and Disadvantages to Be Derived by the United States from Peaceful Trade with the Soviet Bloc," DDEL, March 5, 1959, CFEP Records 1954–61, Policy Paper Series.

[66] Even Randall, the individual most in favor of increased trade, understood the tension between buying peace and relative gains. Randall's briefing notes for a critical April NSC meeting indicated that despite trade's ability to reduce mistrust, there could be no major changes in policy as long as the Sino-Soviet bloc posed a "continued threat" to the West. "Memorandum for Mr. Randall," DDEL, April 29, 1959, CFEP Records 1954–61, Chronological File; *FRUS* (1958–60), 4:770–71.

[67] "Summary of Exchange of Communications between the President and Prime Minister MacMillan," DDEL, n.d., DDEL, CFEP Records 1954–61, Policy Paper Series.

The two sides restarted foreign minister talks in Geneva in May. The president believed these conversations might lead to a broad set of agreements on outstanding issues: not just Berlin and strategic disarmament, but also a test ban treaty, assurances against surprise attack, and perhaps even limitations on the deployment of intermediate-range missiles (Ambrose 1984, 524–25). Hopes therefore were high when, in late September, the Soviet leader arrived for a prearranged two-week tour of the United States, with direct talks with Eisenhower at the front and back ends.

State Department briefing papers for Eisenhower emphasized that trade would be high on Moscow's wish list. A September 8 paper reported that trade was a "major Soviet preoccupation" and Moscow wanted not just reduced restrictions but also loans to fund purchases. If Russia continued to threaten the United States, though, the "confidence" needed for long-term trade was not yet there.[68] Three days later, Eisenhower was told that Khrushchev would push for peaceful coexistence, using the argument that "expanded trade is the best road to improved U.S.-Soviet relations." The president was advised to tell the Soviet leader that history would see him as a great statesperson if he helped reduce the burden of the arms race.

> The U.S. and U.S.S.R. would then be able to confine their competition to peaceful fields. Of course, the ground rules would have to be agreed—and the competition, in ideas as well as the economic and cultural fields, would have to take place within the Communist as well as in the non-Communist world. The prospects for expanded economic relations . . . would then be bright.[69]

The repeated use of the word "then" in the above quotation is instructive. It underscores the overall orientation of the US bargaining strategy: trade could expand, but only *after* major shifts in Soviet behavior on arms and the "ground rules" of competition. Eisenhower, in short, should not enter summit negotiations with the intention of securing a quid pro quo deal. Moscow would have to move first to build the confidence needed for improved relations and trade.

Khrushchev arrived in Washington on September 15, and three hours later the two leaders held their first meeting. With both sides aware that the true give-and-take would come only after Khrushchev's ten-day tour, the first meeting was taken up with generalities about their mutual desires

---

[68] "Major Themes of Khrushchev's Public and Private Statements and U.S. Counter-Arguments," DDEL, September 8, 1959, Eisenhower, Dwight D., Records as President, White House Central Files (Confidential File), 1953–61, Subject Series.

[69] "U.S. Objective in Khrushchev Visit and Suggested Tactics for Conversation with Him," DDEL, September 11, 1959, Eisenhower, Dwight D., Records as President, White House Central Files (Confidential File), 1953–61, Subject Series.

to build trust (Ambrose 1984, 541–42; Eisenhower 1965, 435–37). When Khrushchev returned to Washington on September 25, he and Eisenhower left for Camp David for two days of talks. Once there, perhaps sensing Eisenhower's need for something concrete up front, Khrushchev quickly made a key concession: he agreed to withdraw his ultimatum on Berlin and allow the status quo to continue, at least for the near term. Eisenhower in return acknowledged that the current Berlin arrangements were abnormal and could not be maintained indefinitely. They also agreed to meet again in four-power talks that would include Britain and France (Taubman 2003, 437–38). On the second day of conversations, Khrushchev pushed hard on the trade issue. In a meeting with Dillon, when Dillon tried to encourage Russia to buy US machinery to make shoes and textiles, the Soviet leader angrily cut him off, saying he was not interested in discussing minor items. He wanted one thing and one thing only: an across-the-board end to discriminatory practices. If the United States refused to end these practices, "this would mean that it wants a continuation of the Cold War." Dillon replied that if Khrushchev wanted action on trade, he must realize that it depended on Congress along with "the general state of the relations between the U.S. and the U.S.S.R." The message was clear. There could be no progress on the trade question until there was a noticeable improvement in Soviet behavior.[70]

Other than the informal agreement on Berlin, the Camp David talks led to few concrete achievements. Yet for the next few months, a "spirit of Camp David"—the sense, at least, that the two superpowers could sit down as equals and work toward compromise—infused both sides with an optimism that an agreement on key issues might be possible by the time that the four-power summit convened in May 1960. Khrushchev in particular came away from Camp David energized and optimistic, telling advisers that the two sides had turned the corner and a peace deal could be reached (Fursenko and Naftali 2007, 241–42). Such a peace was critical to reducing the economic strain of the arms race. He knew from internal reports that the growth rate of the Soviet economy was slowing. Moreover, his US visit had convinced him that the United States was still far ahead in technology and industrial techniques. Much like Mikhail Gorbachev in the 1980s, Khrushchev understood that unless he got the arms race under control, Soviet economic performance would always lag considerably behind the United States. As he told his son, "If we are forced into [running this arms race], we will lose our pants" (quoted in ibid., 242–43).

Khrushchev's solution was a radical and bold one. He would dramatically cut the size of the Soviet conventional army, hold to a bare

---

[70] "Memorandum of Conversation, September 27, 1959, in Letter to Randall from Robert Brewster, October 8, 1959," DDEL, CFEP Records 1954–61, Policy Papers Series.

minimum the installations of first-generation ICBMs, and continue to seek to acquire technology from abroad. In January 1960, building on Camp David's afterglow, he publicly announced that the Soviet army would be cut by 1.0 to 1.2 million troops, or about a third of its active force. This would not only reduce costs but also signal the new Soviet spirit of cooperation and trust building—just the sort of thing the United States had said it was looking for (ibid., 246–47; Montgomery 2006).

The decision to forgo a massive ICBM buildup and wait for second-generation ICBMs to come online was a huge strategic gamble. Khrushchev knew better than anyone that Russia was still not equal in strategic military power, despite his well-publicized claims to the contrary. But he hoped that he could get through the interim period of inferiority without a war so that secure, second-generation missiles could establish a viable deterrent within three to four years. This move would save money and avoid redundancies. On the other hand, it entailed an enormous risk: it would leave the Soviets vulnerable to US blackmail and even war should Washington discover Russia's temporary inferiority.

The Soviets would also keep pushing for a relaxation in US economic restrictions. And to get it, they were now willing to change their negotiating tactics. Most important, for the first time Moscow stated its willingness to resolve the ongoing lend-lease debt accrued during the war. Formal talks on lend lease began in Washington on January 11, 1960. Even allowing such conversations to take place was a hugely symbolic concession. The Soviets had always found it insulting that despite having paid the highest blood price in the war, Russia was the only power asked to pay back a large percentage of the lend-lease loans—and without any compensating assurances of nondiscriminatory trade. Dillon's argument that resolving the lend-lease issue was critical to progress on trade had obviously bent Moscow to Washington's will. Yet the Soviets wanted something in return. In a February press release, they noted that any lend-lease agreement must be concluded "simultaneously" with a trade deal offering Russia most-favored-nation status and trade credits.[71] Moscow was countering Washington's bargaining strategy with good old-fashioned linkage politics.

For the first four months of 1960, Eisenhower remained hopeful that by the end of May, a peace deal could be secured at the Paris Summit. Then he made a fatal error of judgment. Despite the known risks, he allowed one more flight of a U-2 spy plane over Russia to help determine the true extent of the Soviet ICBM buildup. The U-2 plane was shot down on May 1, with the pilot captured alive. Khrushchev was in a quandary:

[71] "On Lend-Lease Negotiations," DDEL, February 4, 1960, CFEP Records 1954–61, Policy Papers Series.

he could not allow such flights to continue without exposing Soviet strategic inferiority, but if he pressed too hard for the flights' termination, the United States might become less inclined to compromise on the larger strategic and economic issues on the table. In the end, he decided to announce publicly that a US spy plane had been shot down and the pilot captured, apparently believing that Eisenhower wanted peace and would use the incident to chastise hawks within his administration. Eisenhower, however, refused to distance himself from the spy missions or agree to curtail them. In the first two days of the Paris Summit, Khrushchev kept pressing for a commitment to stop the flights, and when it was apparent that Eisenhower would not budge, the Soviet premier walked out of the meeting. The U-2 crisis was a classic example of an action-reaction spiral that produced a result that neither side had wanted or foreseen.[72]

Eisenhower quickly understood the implications. In late May, he told his main scientific adviser "with much feeling . . . how he had concentrated his efforts [over] the last few years on ending the cold war, how he felt that he was making big progress, and how the stupid U-2 mess had ruined all his efforts. He ended very sadly that he saw nothing worthwhile left for him to do now until the end of his presidency" (quoted in Ambrose 1984, 580). We will of course never know what might have occurred had the U-2 incident not destroyed the May talks. Yet the deeper dilemma hanging over Eisenhower's last two years in office was the problem of trying to engage in economic diplomacy during a period of strategic uncertainty. Because neither side had guaranteed second-strike capability, neither could relax its guard in a way that might allow positive expectations of future trade to do their work. The US government believed it could not offer trade until it had seen significant concessions. The Soviets, painfully aware of their strategic inferiority, believed that major concessions now—including allowing U-2 flights to continue— might increase the United States' perception of its advantage, leading to coercive diplomacy or worse. With MAD not yet in place, both sides feared that even minor shifts in the nuclear balance might give the other an incentive for a first strike.[73] Trade thus could not be expanded until Soviet behavior improved, yet Moscow had little incentive to improve its behavior if Washington was so mistrustful it would not sell even low-tech industrial goods. Both sides were trapped in a vicious conundrum that could not be resolved until MAD became a reality in the late 1960s.

---

[72] My short summary of the crisis is drawn from Fursenko and Naftali 2007; Beschloss 1988; Ambrose 1984.

[73] On the problem of adverse power oscillations in bipolarity, see Copeland 2000b, 25–27, 47–48, 186–206.

The Berlin Crisis of 1961 and Cuban Missile Crisis of 1962 under Kennedy's tenure arose out of the failure of the talks of 1959–60 to curb arms spending as well as achieve a preliminary trade-based détente. In the last six months of his tenure, Eisenhower continued to push forward with the US arms buildup. By the end of 1960, his administration had planned for eleven hundred ICBMs—a total that had been jumping each year since 1957 (Prados 1986, 114). The Kennedy administration, despite discovering the extent of US nuclear superiority in its first month, continued this buildup, given the worry that Moscow might still achieve temporary superiority before new US ICBMS were deployed in quantity.[74]

The same dilemma that plagued Eisenhower hung over the Kennedy administration. Kennedy wanted a reduction in the intensity of the Cold War. But given the possibility of a future strategic deficiency, Washington could not afford to offer economic concessions, or at least not without evidence of increasing moderation in Soviet foreign policy.[75] In the short term, it was clear to US officials that the Soviets wanted peace.[76] Unfortunately, an exogenous third-party problem was putting Khrushchev under intense pressure. In June 1961, Khrushchev announced that a new six-month deadline existed to solve the Berlin question. As I show elsewhere, the Soviet leader's move was driven primarily by fears that the exodus of refugees into West Berlin was causing the economic decline of his most important Eastern European ally, East Germany. If East Germany collapsed, the Soviet bloc's power and global image would be greatly undermined (Copeland 2000b, 181–86).

Although the Berlin Crisis was the immediate result of a fear of economic decline, the larger context is important. Had the United States and Russia been able to reach a deal in 1959–60 that would have promised increased US exports, Khrushchev would have had a stake in fostering future good relations. He would have worried that any new crisis over Berlin would have led to the hardening of Washington's position on trade restrictions (as his up-front concession on Berlin at Camp David suggests). Moreover, the promise of trade would have given him greater confidence in Moscow's ability to overcome East German economic decline through transfer payments. In a meeting with East German leader Walter Ulbricht in November 1960, for example, Khrushchev had agreed to "take over almost completely the East German economy . . . in order to

[74]See "Memorandum for Mr. Bundy," JFKL, January 30, 1961, NSF, box 275, folder "Department of Defense, Defense Budget FY 1963 1/61–10/61"; "Memorandum for the President," JFKL, NSF, January 31, 1961, box 313, folder 2; "Record of Actions by the National Security Council," JFKL, NSF, February 6, 1961, box 313, folder 2.

[75]For a detailed discussion, see Copeland, forthcoming.

[76]See "Notes on Discussion of the Thinking of the Soviet Leadership," written by Bundy on February 13, 1961, NSA (BC).

save it" (Harrison 1993, 28). Khrushchev knew that this would cost Russia in the short term. But had the Soviet economy itself not been slowing down, or at least had Khrushchev believed that US technology would give it a badly needed boost, he would have had more options and thus likely would have been more cautious in dealing with the exodus problem.

Such a counterfactual argument is, like all such claims, ultimately unprovable. Still, as I show in detail elsewhere, Kennedy's officials, especially in the State Department, were well aware from the get-go that continued trade restrictions were exacerbating tensions and limiting the chances for détente (Copeland, forthcoming). In late February 1961, for instance, Secretary of State Dean Rusk told Kennedy that it was of "great importance" to reduce restrictions to provide "a tangible demonstration of our desire to improve relations" during a time of high tension.[77] Rusk's assertion reinforced the findings of a task force appointed by Kennedy during his transition period and headed by George Ball, Kennedy's undersecretary of state. The so-called Ball Report, completed just before Kennedy took office, contended that a more relaxed approach to trade would give Washington a critical bargaining chip in future negotiations with Russia (Funigiello 1988, 125–26).

The State Department kept pressing this issue throughout 1961–62, and even in summer 1962, amid worrisome reports of a Soviet ICBM buildup, Rusk saw the dangling of trade carrots as a way to moderate Soviet behavior.[78] On July 10, he presented a memorandum to the NSC arguing that continuing to deny license applications worked at cross-purposes with efforts to improve relations. Because Moscow attached great significance to trade, US trade policy would shape whether it moved toward détente or increased pressure on the West.[79] In a follow-up memorandum, Rusk noted that he was "completely in accord with the often expressed premise" that trade was one of the few means to push Russia toward more peaceful behavior.[80]

When he wrote these words, Rusk was of course unaware that Moscow was already starting to deploy medium- and intermediate-range missiles in Cuba. The Cuban Missile Crisis, as I show elsewhere, arose from one overriding two-way dynamic. When the United States publicly exposed Soviet nuclear inferiority in late 1961 and then began to talk about a "no-cities" counterforce strategy in the first half of 1962, Khrushchev

---

[77] "Memorandum for the President," JFKL, February 26, 1961, NSF, box 176, folder: "U.S.S.R. General 2/21/61–3/1/61."

[78] "National Intelligence Estimate," 11–8–62, NSA (SE), July 6, 1962, doc. 372.

[79] "Memorandum for the National Security Council," JFKL, July 10, 1962, NSF, box 313, folder 35.

[80] "Memorandum for the National Security Council," JFKL, July 16, 1962, NSF, box 313, folder 35.

believed he needed a stopgap measure to provide basic deterrence until his second-generation missiles came on line. So he copied the US technique of deploying intermediate-range missiles near the Soviet Union by convincing the Cubans to accept Soviet missiles on the island. Yet the very act of deploying such missiles caused the United States to worry not only about a loss of superiority but also a potential short-term gap of inferiority—one that might tempt the Soviets to launch a first strike as the United States rebuilt its power. In short, the dynamics of adverse power oscillations were at the heart of the crisis (see Copeland 2000b, 186–208, 297n71; Copeland 1996b.).

Economic interdependence was not directly driving this process of fear, action, and reaction. As with Berlin 1961, though, we can pose the counterfactual: Would Khrushchev have been as concerned about a short-term Soviet position of inferiority had he been more confident that the United States was not seeking to drive Russia into the ground economically? I would contend that similar to the Berlin case, had Soviet trade expectations been substantially improved by a 1960 or early 1961 trade deal, Khrushchev would have felt more confident about Washington's willingness to accept peaceful coexistence as Russia built up its deterrent force. According to Alexandr Fursenko and Timothy Naftali (1997), Soviet leaders saw Kennedy's trumpeting of US nuclear superiority in late 1961 as a sign of the opposite intent: Washington would not allow Soviet growth and might even choose a preventive war to take advantage of short-term US strength.

As with Berlin, we can never know if a trade deal would have smoothed the waters enough to prevent the most dangerous crisis in world history. And I do not want to push the trade expectations argument too far: fears of losing one's second-strike capability were so strong on both sides that even with a new US commitment to trade, it is quite likely that the 1961–62 period would still have witnessed some form of existential crisis. But such a crisis would probably not have pulled the two actors so close to the edge of ultimate destruction. Had an initial détente been established by late 1960 or early 1961, both sides would have been more relaxed about the strategic balance. Greater caution during the transition period to MAD would likely have prevailed. Supporting this conclusion are Rusk's statements to the NSC showing that US officials were greatly aware of two things: the Soviets needed increased trade to remain confident about long-term growth, and trade was one of the few tools Washington possessed to influence Soviet behavior one way or the other.

What we can conclude from the above analysis is that the lack of progress on opening up US-Soviet trade and concomitant effect on Russian trade expectations played a far bigger role in the dynamics of Cold War politics during the Eisenhower and Kennedy eras than has been previously understood. Given Soviet need, trade was a powerful bargaining chip, and the United States was prepared to use it for good measure. But the fragility of the nuclear balance forced Washington to insist on Soviet concessions before trade restrictions would be relaxed. This strategic conundrum proved a constant roadblock to what Kissinger would later call a stable "structure of peace."

In the next section, I show that Nixon and Kissinger were willing to build such a structure through the negotiating strategy of linkage—mutual concessions that would move the superpower relationship forward across many issues simultaneously. The option of such a strategy was facilitated by the new reality of MAD and sense on both sides that with the Soviet economy stagnating, Russia was unlikely to catch up in overall economic power. This realization allowed the United States to feel more relaxed about providing the Soviets with limited relative gains through trade. And if Washington could get major concessions in return—concessions that would help the United States sustain its dominant position at a time when the Vietnam War was reducing the perception of US vitality—then the linked deal was more than worth it.

The Emergence and Breakdown of Détente, 1963–83

The theory of this book has stressed that actor behavior can be changed even when there is little real trade between them, as long as needy states have expectations that the future trade environment will improve and remain open for some time. This was clearly the case as the two superpowers maneuvered toward a true peaceful coexistence in the late 1960s. Variations in the Kremlin's trade expectations after 1965, combined with the increasing Soviet need for Western goods to overcome internal stagnation, directly shaped the peacefulness of Soviet behavior, even when actual trade levels did not change significantly. Since I have covered the period 1963–83 in some detail elsewhere, I will only summarize the basic findings here (Copeland 1999–2000).[81]

By the mid-1960s, the need to secure US trade to revitalize the flagging Soviet economy was becoming apparent. From average annual growth rates of 6 to 11 percent in the first decade or so after the war, the economy was registering only 5 percent growth from 1961 to 1965 (Aslund 1989, 15). At the root of this was what Soviet analysts were now labeling the "scientific-technological revolution"—the move away from heavy industry based on extensive production (increasing labor and capital inputs) to

---

[81] Table 2.7 treats 1963–83 as two separate case-periods, given that the years 1963–83 encompass both the arising of détente by 1972–73 and renewal of Cold War after 1974.

efficient, intensive development driven by computerization and miniaturization (see Hoffman and Laird 1982, chap. 1). After Khrushchev's ouster in 1964, Premier Alexei Kosygin led the charge toward technological improvement. By 1965–66, he was arguing that the scientific-technological revolution was now the crucial dimension of the superpower competition and Russia's "essential inadequacies" were having serious effects on economic growth (quoted in Parrott 1983, 186). For Kosygin, the easiest solution was more trade with the West, since foreign technology would save millions of rubles that would otherwise go into scientific research. Kosygin's efforts to encourage greater trade were initially resisted by the majority of politburo members, given their concern that trade dependence would leave the state vulnerable to Western political pressures. By 1969–70, however, Party Secretary Leonid Brezhnev came over to Kosygin's side. Internal economic reforms begun in 1965 were having little effect, and something had to be done. At the party congress of March 1971, a new orientation was formally codified in a "Peace Program" linking increased trade and the slowing of the arms race to Soviet long-term economic growth. The scientific-technological revolution must go forward, Brezhnev argued, and in this greater trade was essential.[82]

The Soviet need for trade gave Nixon and his national security adviser Kissinger the opening they were looking for. To build their structure of peace, trade would be offered in return for a moderation of Soviet behavior (including an arms control agreement, help in resolving Vietnam, and restraint in the third world) (Kissinger 1979, 152–53, 1203, 1254–55). The new US willingness to trade with Russia was signaled by a series of deals and agreements in 1971 and 1972. In November 1971, a grain deal and industrial contracts worth $261 million were worked out, and by February 1972, another $400 million in licenses for truck manufacturing equipment were approved. The Moscow Summit in May focused on the signing of the Strategic Arms Limitation Treaty, but the two sides also announced they would work actively to increase economic ties.[83] In October 1972, a formal trade agreement was signed, promising the Soviet Union most-favored-nation status and the extension of large trade credits. Both elements were important to the Russians: being short of hard currency, they could not afford to buy US goods unless they could both sell Soviet products and secure the short-term credit needed to expedite their purchases.

The impact of the new commercial spirit was felt quickly. Between October 1972 and May 1973, restrictions were removed on 477 of the 550 categories of banned exports. The Export-Import Bank extended a $202 million loan, and a trade council of three hundred US firms opened

[82] Anderson 1993, 127; Aslund 1989, 15; Volten 1982, 64–67; Parrott 1983, 243–49.
[83] FRUS (1969–76), 4:349–52; Stevenson 1985, 155; Jentleson 1986, 139.

a Moscow office. US companies, needed for their technology, became involved in joint plans to develop the vast Siberian oil and gas fields (Mastanduno 1992, 147; Jentleson 1986, 139–141, 147). Overall, the trend was definitely upward: total Soviet trade with United States grew from an annual average of $60–100 million in the 1960–1970 period to $649 million in 1972, and then $1577 million in 1973 (see Mastanduno 1992, 112, table 4; 158, table 5). Even more significant, however, was the impact of the new relationship on Soviet expectations for the future. In February 1973, Brezhnev wrote Nixon of his confidence that their upcoming June summit in Washington would lead to even more commercial agreements. An internal Central Committee report written on Brezhnev's return stated that the summit had provided "new prospects for the development of [US-Soviet] economic-trade relations . . . on a long-term large-scale basis" (quoted in Garthoff 1994a, 366–67, 389).

If anything, Brezhnev's expectations for future trade with the West during 1972–73 were, as Peter Volten (1982, 112) and Raymond Garthoff (1994a, 389) note, overly optimistic. The Soviets were slow to wake up to the implications of Watergate for Nixon's ability to control domestic opposition to US-Soviet trade. When the trade deal was signed in October 1972, both sides committed to a tripling of bilateral trade over next three years. Given that trade in 1972 had already reached $649 million, this effectively meant an anticipated jump to approximately $2 billion a year by 1975 (see Mastanduno 1992, 146; 158, table 5). But the Soviet expectation—never realized, of course—was for even more. A senior Soviet official during this time has revealed that Soviet leaders "expected that annual trade with the United States would reach $10 billion by the end of the decade."[84] Indeed, by 1973, Brezhnev was staking the very success of his revitalization program on the continuation of a stable US-Soviet relationship. Détente had to be made "irreversible," he argued through that year, since it was key to solving outstanding Soviet domestic problems (Volten 1982, 108–9, 111, 234).

As I discuss shortly, growing domestic opposition to détente inside the United States would ultimately destroy the prospects for future trade by January 1975. This led, as trade expectations theory would predict, to an abrupt shift toward a much more assertive Soviet foreign policy in the third world. But during the period when Soviet expectations were still positive (1972–73), there was clear moderation in Moscow's behavior. As Kissinger had hoped, the Soviets proved willing to sacrifice the periphery to gain the benefits of US-Soviet trade. Two examples stand out. Moscow used diplomatic pressure and the termination of military supplies to push North Vietnam to make the concessions that led to the Paris Accords

---

[84]Based on information given to Garthoff (1994a, 102n70) by this official.

of January 1973 (Parrott 1985, 38). Even more significantly, the Soviets proved accommodating during the 1973 Israeli-Egyptian conflict, thereby allowing Washington to control both the diplomatic process and final outcome.

The superpower crisis ignited by the Yom Kippur War in October 1973 might suggest that détente had not moderated Soviet behavior. Careful analysis leads to the opposite conclusion. The Soviets not only did not want a Middle East war and acted to prevent it; they also sought to end it quickly, before too much damage to détente was done. Kissinger acknowledges that he acted to exploit Moscow's evident caution in order to increase US influence in the region. In sum, the Middle East Crisis was provoked by the independent decisions of Egypt and Syria, despite Soviet efforts to dissuade them from war. Once under way, the economic incentives embedded in détente significantly moderated Soviet behavior—much to the delight of Kissinger and Nixon.

By spring 1973, Brezhnev could see that despite his entreaties, Egypt and Syria were preparing for war against Israel. Brezhnev told Nixon of this fact at the June summit. Over the next three months, notwithstanding repeated Russian pleas to deal with the situation, Nixon (1978, 884–86) and Kissinger kept shrugging them off (see Garthoff 1994a, 408–9). While they may have seen war as unlikely given Israeli superiority, it is also apparent, as Kissinger admits, that they viewed war, if it occurred, as a perfect opportunity to reduce Soviet influence in the Middle East. With détente serving as "a tranquilizer" for the Soviet Union and "cover" for the United States, Kissinger could draw the Middle East "into closer relations with us at the Soviets' expense."[85]

The Soviets did indeed find themselves trapped between their need for a trade-based détente and their obligations to Egypt and Syria. According to insider Victor Israelyan, Brezhnev and his politburo colleagues were unhappy that their effort to restrain Egypt and Syria had failed to prevent war. A few hours after Syria and Egypt's surprise attack on Israel, Brezhnev told the politburo that this action "would whip up international tensions and complicate the Soviet Union's relations with the West, especially with the United States" (quoted in Israelyan 1995, 31, 2). In a hurried note to Anwar el-Sādāt, Brezhnev wrote that Arab leaders were "interfer[ing] in the process of the development of political cooperation between the USSR and the USA," and asked for an immediate cease-fire (quoted in Lebow and Stein 1994, 201).

In essence, Kissinger's strategy during October was to "induce Soviet caution by threatening the end of détente," thereby enacting a regional

---

[85]Kissinger 1982, 594, 296, 299. Internal analyses at the time noted that Brezhnev's conciliatory posture reflected Moscow's stake in détente (Garthoff 1994a, 409–20, 434–41).

solution that best suited US interests.[86] Even Kissinger's dramatic move on October 25—the placing of US forces on temporary nuclear alert (DEFCON 3)—had little to do with fear of a superpower clash and almost everything to do with reducing Moscow's diplomatic standing. With Egypt's army on the ropes, Brezhnev had been warning that he might have to send Soviet forces to Egypt unilaterally should Washington reject his idea of a joint US-Soviet peacekeeping force. Kissinger (1982, 579, 584) worried that if Washington accepted a joint operation, it would legitimize a role for Moscow in Middle Eastern affairs, and thus he escalated the crisis to deter Soviet action.[87]

The above analysis shows the strong moderating effect of détente on Soviet behavior during October 1973.[88] Without the incentive of high expected US-Soviet trade, essential to Russia's reforms and continued superpower position, Moscow would have been more likely to have intervened actively in the Arab-Israeli dispute, and the probability of a dangerous superpower clash would have been that much greater. In the end, it is the US leadership that must bear most of the blame for the October crisis, since it was Nixon and Kissinger who, out of a desire for geopolitical gain, did so little to avert or moderate the conflict.

While positive trade expectations in 1972–73 were moderating Soviet behavior, trouble was brewing within the United States. Liberal and conservative critics of Nixon's presidency found a common ground on which to oppose his foreign policy: they would attack it as insensitive to human rights, particularly regarding Jewish emigration. In March–April 1973, Senator Henry Jackson formally introduced an amendment linking most-favored-nation status to significant increases in Jewish emigration as part of the 1973 Trade Reform Act (a similar amendment was introduced in the House by Representative Charles Vanik). Through 1973, the Jackson-Vanik Amendment slowly gathered momentum as the Nixon administration sank into the swamp of Watergate. In December, the House passed a bill containing the amendment, and in June 1974, Senator Adlai Stevenson III added a further amendment, limiting credits offered to Russia by the federal Export-Import Bank (see Jentleson 1986, 136–42).

The Soviets struggled hard to satisfy congressional critics at a price that would not damage Russia's global reputation. In April 1973, just as Jackson was introducing his amendment, Brezhnev rescinded the exit tax

---

[86]Kissinger 1982, 467–69; see also Lebow and Stein 1994, 210.

[87]Declassified documents support Kissinger's recollections (*KT*, 155).

[88]Kissinger would admit to his colleagues in a private meeting on March 18, 1974 that recent Soviet behavior had been "fairly reasonable all across the board. . . . Even in the Middle East where our political strategy put them in an awful bind, they haven't really tried to screw us" (*KT*, 225).

that was restricting Jewish emigration, and had so upset Jackson and his supporters. Jewish emigration rose from four hundred in 1968 to almost thirty-five thousand in 1973. For Jackson, however, this was not sufficient. In September 1974, he publicly indicated that he sought seventy-five thousand per year, and would press for at least sixty thousand. The Soviets made it known through back channels that they would go as high as fifty-five to sixty thousand, as long as the deal was kept private.[89] Yet Jackson, as Kissinger laments, "wanted an issue, not a solution." On October 18, 1974, just after Jackson and Vanik signed letters at the White House apparently resolving the dispute, Jackson used the occasion to trumpet his victory, arguing that the Soviets had completely caved to his demands (Kissinger 1982, 996; Garthoff 1994a, 509). The Soviets were outraged at this public humiliation. The trade bill with the Jackson-Vanik Amendment was passed on December 13. On January 3, 1975, President Gerald Ford reluctantly signed the Trade Reform Act into law. Ten days later, the Soviets signaled that the 1972 trade treaty was now null and void.

Hence by early 1975, as Garthoff (1994a, 512–13) summarizes, "the heart of the official American-Soviet trade component of détente had collapsed."[90] This domestic interference in the Nixon-Kissinger plan represented an exogenous blow to Soviet trade expectations.[91] Moscow now understood that there was little it could do, short of appearing to capitulate to ever-increasing demands, to save the 1972 trade treaty. And given the evident weakness of the US executive in the wake of Watergate, by December 1974 it was clear that further negotiations would serve no purpose.

What is significant is how quickly Soviet behavior on the periphery moved back toward the previous policy of "adventurism." Reversing its two-year policy of restraining North Vietnam, in December 1974 Moscow reinstated weapons shipments to Hanoi. Four months later, North Vietnam launched its decisive assault on South Vietnam, undoubtedly with at least the tacit approval of Moscow. In 1973–74, the Soviets had only provided the barest of aid to leftist forces in Angola, and only after US aid to antileftist groups grew. This restraint vanished in 1975, when Soviet support for Angola increased dramatically (Garthoff 1994a, chap. 15). By the late 1970s, Moscow made significant inroads in Somalia, followed by Ethiopia and Nicaragua. Then in 1979, with the invasion of Afghanistan, Russian forces for the first time in the Cold War invaded a country not formally part of the Soviet sphere.

Although the internal documents on politburo decision making for the 1975–83 period are still sketchy, it is surely no coincidence that Soviet

---

[89] Kissinger 1982, 249; Garthoff 1994a, 506; Jentleson 1986, 143.

[90] See also Mastanduno 1992, 150.

[91] This is the sixth of six types of exogenous factors shaping expectations; see chapter 1.

behavior changed so suddenly after the failure of the trade treaty.[92] As Bruce Parrott (1985, 38–39) observes, "Soviet willingness to accept implicit linkages between trade and Soviet political behavior depended on how the prospective economic benefits fitted into a larger balance of political opportunities and risks. . . . By 1975, however, the balance of benefits and costs had shifted." In sum, the end of the trade treaty represents a major reason for the collapse of détente and a return to a more conflictual superpower relationship.[93] Trade expectations theory supplies a simple but powerful explanation for this. Without the anticipation of a stream of increasing trade benefits accruing from US-Soviet cooperation, the Soviets no longer had the incentive to moderate their actions in the third world, as they had in 1972–73. While this explanation also may seem to align with liberal theory, note that it not current trade that constrained Soviet policy but rather the expectation of high trade in the future. Moreover, Moscow was propelled by purely power-political considerations. This again demonstrates the value of taking a dynamic approach to great power security within enduring rivalries.

Economic Relations and the End of the Cold War, 1984–91

For many, the end of the Cold War is rooted in one fundamental fact: the ascendancy of Mikhail Gorbachev along with his his new liberal vision for Soviet society and its place in the world. By this account, Gorbachev's belief that his country had to become an open and democratic society translated into a desire to integrate Russia into the Western liberal system, thereby ending nearly half a century of mistrust and tension. This section shows that to the extent that this interpretation emphasizes ideational epiphany over self-interested material calculation, it is inadequate.[94] Gorbachev's reforms, at least for the first two years, were not that new. They were extensions of the reform plan set down during the brief tenure of his mentor Yuri Andropov from 1982 to 1984. This plan in turn was based on the same goal that had driven the Kremlin toward reform in the late 1960s: the need to overcome economic and technological stagnation. Gorbachev's "new thinking" became progressively more

---

[92] For a few initial documents, see *CWIHPB*, nos. 8–9 (winter 1996–97).

[93] For scholars agreeing with this view, see Garthoff 1994a, 513; Njolstad 2010, 155–53; George 1983, 22; Jentleson 1986, chap. 5. Even right-of-center historian Adam Ulam (1983, 93–94, 134–35) notes that with the end of the trade treaty, Soviet behavior became more assertive.

[94] Stressing the former are Wendt 1992; Risse-Kappen 1994; Kydd 2005; Haas 2005. On the latter, see Jervis 1996, 224–25; Copeland 1999–2000; Brooks and Wohlforth 2000–2001.

radical only after 1986—that is, only after the failure of his initial reforms. But even here his actions were largely materially driven: only by democratization within along with greater peace and interdependence without did he believe that his country could reverse its decline and remain a superpower. The growing expectation that the United States—and after US approval, Europe—would offer the kind of trade and credits needed to further his reforms was an integral part of Gorbachev's larger strategy for peace.

While estimates vary, all accounts agree on one thing: by the late 1970s–early 1980s, the Soviet economy was in deep trouble. Annual GNP growth rates, which had been 5 percent in the 1960s, were now at best 0 to 2 percent. Productivity was flat, the quality of Soviet products far below the West, and inefficient factories were using up energy resources at rates many times greater than comparable Western figures.[95] Soviet leaders were not unaware of the problem. Before he came to power, while still head of the KGB, Andropov established a secret department within the KGB to study what was seen, according to one official, as "the coming economic catastrophe" (quoted in Kaiser 1991, 57, 59). A report in 1983 by the Soviet Academy of Sciences indicated that the centralized system was "incredibly . . . outdated" and the primary cause of Soviet decline.[96] In a June speech, Andropov emphasized the importance of reforms to increase technology-based productivity (Doder 1986, 182, 185).

Given Andropov's poor health, his protégé Gorbachev was primarily responsible for implementing the reforms. Gorbachev was fully supportive of Andropov's efforts, which at this stage were modest, focused mainly on greater workplace discipline. Gorbachev was well aware of the problem of relative economic stagnation. By 1982–83, he saw that "time was running out." The world was experiencing a sweeping scientific transformation. Yet while Western states were rising to the challenge, the Soviet system "spurned innovation." Not only was the West ahead, Gorbachev (1996, 135; 1987, 18–19) maintained, but the gap in advanced technology "[had begun] to widen, and not to our advantage." That Gorbachev's primary obsession was sustaining the Soviet Union as a superpower is revealed by his speech at a conference of party officials in December 1984. Outlining his strategy for economic reform, he argued that "we have to achieve a breakthrough. Only an intensive and highly developed economy can ensure the strengthening of the country's position on

[95] See Aslund 1989, 15; Doder 1986, 177–78; Gorbachev 1987, 18–19; Ellman and Kontorovich 1992.

[96] Doder, 1986, 111, 169–70, 186–87; Walker 1987, 47–48. Many similar studies were undertaken during 1983 (Oberdorfer 1991, 63).

the world scene and enable it to enter the next millennium in a manner befitting a great and prosperous country. . . . There is no alternative."[97]

By 1985, the question of decline was assuming overwhelming significance. On assuming power in March, Gorbachev was handed a top secret KGB report that alleged that unless the country began fundamental reform, "[it] could not continue as a superpower into the twenty-first century."[98] In late February 1986, Gorbachev told the Twenty-Seventh Party Congress that should technological trends continue, the capitalist world might achieve "social revenge"—"[its] recovery of what had been lost" (Walker 1987, 51).[99] To ensure Soviet economic and territorial security, Gorbachev had three priorities. First, he had to end the arms race to free up resources for consumer goods. Economic reform could not succeed if the Soviet Union continued to devote 20 percent of its GNP to the military.[100] Second, he needed to stop the US effort to build a space-based missile defense system. This system, even if not successful, would force Moscow to squander precious investment capital needed for economic growth. And if it did work, it would undermine deterrence and spark a new arms race.[101] Third, and increasingly important as his reforms progressed, Gorbachev had to convince the United States to relax restrictions on trade and economic credits. Like Brezhnev, Gorbachev understood that integral to overcoming economic decline was access to superior Western products and technology.

These three elements were essential to furthering a domestic reform program that was Leninist in its foundations, not liberal, as Gorbachev freely acknowledges. He sought not a revolution but rather an improvement of the existing socialist system, which he saw as having distinct moral and organizational advantages.[102] As with Lenin's effort in the early 1920s to use trade and diplomacy to rebuild Russian power, Gorbachev saw the importance of reestablishing good relations with the West. In May 1986, he spoke to six hundred foreign aid and trade officials from the Foreign Ministry. Soviet diplomacy "must contribute to the domestic development of the country." Thus the primary goal of foreign policy was to "create the best possible external conditions" for internal growth

[97] Quoted in Walker 1987, 58–59; see also Brown 1997, 79–81.
[98] For a summary of the document, see Coleman 1996, 224. For a similar report at this time, see Arbatov 1993, 322.
[99] On Eastern Europe's role in Soviet decline and revitalization, see *MH*, especially docs. 4–9, 39–42, 48.
[100] See *UECW*, docs. 19, 25, 32, 40, 52; Gorbachev 1996, 215, 401; Dobrynin 1995, 570.
[101] On Gorbachev's effort to counter the US Strategic Defense Initiative ("Star Wars"), see Gorbachev 1996, 407, 417–18, 455; Schultz 1993, 477–79, 577, 592, 768–69.
[102] Gorbachev 1996, 217–18, 250; *UECW*, docs. 44, 52; *MH*, 118.

(quoted in Oberdorfer 1991, 159–62). While Gorbachev's subsequent actions indicate that ending the arms race was the key initial step, securing trade was also critical. In his first meeting with Secretary of State George Schultz and Vice President George H. W. Bush immediately after assuming power, Gorbachev lamented the low level of contacts between the two countries. "Technology can be transferred only with the express approval of the president. Trade is not permitted" (quoted in Schultz 1993, 530). Two months later, in May 1985, Gorbachev told Secretary of Commerce Malcolm Baldrige that it was "high time" to improve economic ties—a theme he reiterated when the two met again in December (Garthoff 1994b, 218, 249).

The Soviets had reason to believe the United States was open to greater commerce. President Ronald Reagan had sent a personal letter to Andropov in July 1983 expressing hope for greater discussion on arms control and expanded trade. Five months earlier, Reagan had signaled that he believed the Jackson-Vanik Amendment was wrong and should be revoked. Beginning in late 1984, the commerce department had started to relax some intra-Western export controls—a crucial initial signal since much of the technology desired by the Soviets was being garnered through Western Europe.[103] But Gorbachev knew that much more was needed. In a statement of "fundamental principles" coming out of the Twenty-Seventh Party Congress in February 1986, the first principle in the economic sphere was the ending of "all forms of [trade] discrimination" (quoted in Gorbachev 1987, 231n1). In his book *Perestroika*, released in mid-1987, Gorbachev (ibid., 126, 222–23) offered a message to Western leaders: "don't be scared by perestroika [restructuring] . . . but rather promote it through the mechanism of economic ties." Such ties "[will help] build confidence between our countries."

Unlike the early 1970s, however, it was clear that the Reagan administration was unwilling to sign a quid pro quo deal linking arms control and better Soviet behavior to increased US trade commitments. Reagan and his associates were simply too mistrustful of Soviet intentions.[104] Consequently, the Soviets understood that they would have to make a number of dramatic gestures to show that the new leadership was different.[105] Gorbachev received a report in April 1985 from adviser Georgi Arbatov (1993, 321–22) arguing that the changing of the guard in Moscow opened up significant opportunities for better relations. Yet to avoid

---

[103] Dobrynin 1995, 531, 518; Mastanduno 1992, 300; Garthoff 1994b, 249, 198.

[104] For documents revealing the depth of these suspicions, see *RF*, especially 2–79, 176–284.

[105] These were "costly signals" too hard for traditional Soviet leaders to make. Fearon 1995; Kydd 2005; Glaser 2010; Copeland 1999–2000.

disappointment, "we [must] change our negotiating style and take unilateral measures," including the reduction of Soviet forces in Europe.

Gorbachev took this counsel to heart. In January 1986, he publicly proposed a three-stage plan for the elimination of nuclear weapons by the turn of the century. At the Reykjavik Summit in the fall, Gorbachev was willing to accept far-reaching reductions in strategic missiles in return for limitations on space-based weapons. While no agreement was reached, Schultz (1993, 775–80) saw the meeting as demonstrating Moscow's seriousness regarding fundamental change. This view was reinforced in late 1987, when Moscow agreed to a nuclear weapons treaty that entailed significantly disproportional cuts in intermediate-range missiles from the Soviet side (ibid., 1011–12).

These dramatic gestures led to some moderation of US trade policy. At a special CoCom meeting in January 1988, Washington accepted a relaxation of controlled items, including computers and telecommunications (Mastanduno 1992, 306; Garthoff 1994b, 342). Overall, though, the Soviets remained frustrated. At the Moscow Summit in May 1988, when Reagan asked about perestroika's progress, Gorbachev quickly turned to how the United States "persisted in maintaining a discriminatory trade policy towards the Soviet Union." Reagan's refusal to budge whenever Gorbachev raised the issue only led Gorbachev to believe that even more dramatic steps were needed to break the logjam.[106] In December, in a speech to the United Nations, Gorbachev took his most radical step yet. He stated that the Soviet Union would unilaterally reduce its troop presence in Eastern Europe over the next two years by five hundred thousand. The connection between this move and Gorbachev's economic goals was indirect but hard to miss. The global economy was becoming one organism, he told his audience, "and no state, whatever its social system or economic status, can normally develop outside it" (quoted in Oberdorfer 1991, 316–18). As Gorbachev (1996, 608) later described it, one of the primary themes of this speech was that "perestroika . . . required a change in the way we conducted our foreign trade, an organic integration with the world economy."

This speech, combined with the Soviet agreement to withdraw from Afghanistan, led Schultz to discuss further relaxations of controls with the defense department in the waning days of the Reagan administration (Mastanduno 1992, 308). Once George H. W. Bush assumed power, however, he decided to undertake a full review of US policy toward Russia. A number of his advisers were worried that Soviet concessions were simply a ploy to give Russia the breathing space needed to restore its power (see Beschloss and Talbott 1993, 17–25). For many months, aside from vague

---

[106] See Gorbachev 1996, 456–57; Garthoff 1994b, 358.

US statements applauding Soviet reforms, there was little concrete progress in normalizing relations. The Soviets were concerned. In September,
Foreign Minister Edvard Shevardnadze met with Secretary of State James
Baker and stressed that the Soviet Union was going through an important
stage and needed to overcome the incompatibility of its economic system with Western states. Moscow did not want aid but rather "economic
cooperation" to help perestroika succeed (quoted in Baker 1995, 144–
45). To further the negotiations, Shevardnadze offered two more critical
concessions: the Soviets would delink arms control talks (START) from
discussions on space-based weapons, and dismantle a radar station that
Washington saw as a violation of previous treaties (Garthoff 1994b, 384–
85; Beschloss and Talbott 1993, 117–21).

This additional evidence of Soviet cooperation seemed to do the trick.
By late 1989, the Bush administration made a definitive decision that
Gorbachev's reforms must be supported.[107] Baker made a major speech
in mid-October confirming that Washington was prepared to provide
technical assistance for Soviet reforms (Garthoff 1994b, 386–87; Baker
1995, 156). When Bush and Gorbachev met at Malta in December 1989,
the Berlin Wall was down and the Soviet position in Eastern Europe was
quickly unraveling. These developments gave new urgency to the need
to help perestroika succeed in order to keep Gorbachev in power. Bush
made the promise that Gorbachev had been waiting more than four years
to hear: the White House would seek to secure most-favored-nation status for the Soviet Union and end legislative restrictions on economic
credits. Bush also suggested that the two sides begin discussions on a new
trade agreement, to be signed at the next summit.[108] The atmosphere at
Malta turned optimistic, almost jubilant, with Gorbachev announcing,
"The world is leaving one epoch, the 'Cold War,' and entering a new
one" (quoted in Garthoff 1994b, 408). Positive Soviet trade expectations
were reinforcing the wisdom of the new peace program. A month later,
when Gorbachev submitted his report to the politburo, he welcomed the
US "readiness" to aid Soviet economic reforms, stressing the necessity of
cooperation as a "stabilizing factor" during this crucial stage of world
history (quoted in Dobrynin 1995, 634).

Despite the new atmosphere, when Bush and Gorbachev met for the
Washington Summit in late May 1990, no formal trade agreement had
yet been signed. The United States was still seeking to use Gorbachev's
desperate need for trade and technology as leverage in realizing US ends,
especially the unification of the two Germanies within the North Atlantic

---

[107] See Oberdorfer 1991, 376; Matlock 1995, 271–72; Bush and Scowcroft 1998, 41.
[108] See MH, 619–46; Garthoff 1994b, 406–7; Beschloss and Talbott 1993, 151–55; Bush
and Scowcroft 1998, 162–63, 173.

Treaty Organization alliance and a moderation of Russia's presence in Lithuania. Despite the great sensitivity for Russians of the first issue, Gorbachev chose the summit to make the dramatic move of allowing Germany to make up its own mind on which alliance to join. But he had a price. The next day, June 1, at a televised meeting with top congressional leaders, the Soviet leader stressed that the present trade relationship was "very primitive" and appealed for a "favorable gesture . . . on trade" from the US Congress. This gesture, he noted, was "very important . . . from a political standpoint."[109]

Both sides were up against the clock: they had committed to a signing ceremony late that day. When Bush met Gorbachev after the televised meeting, he told him that he was still unsure about the trade agreement. Gorbachev reiterated its critical importance (Bush and Scowcroft 1998, 283–84; Oberdorfer 1991, 419–20). The president kept Gorbachev hanging to the last minute. Just before entering the East Room for the signing ceremony at 6:00 p.m., Gorbachev asked, "Are we going to sign the trade agreement?" Bush replied that they would. Beaming, Gorbachev told the president, "This really matters to me." Bush also agreed that he would not explicitly link the deal to Soviet behavior on Lithuania (Beschloss and Talbott 1993, 223; Zelikow and Rice 1997, 280–81). Gorbachev thus came away with the deal he wanted. The United States was now committed to the normalization of trade relations in return for the Soviets' quiet acquiescence to the US position on Germany and private suggestions of moderation regarding Lithuania.[110]

It is clear that the Washington Summit of May–June 1990 was a significant moment in the unwinding of the Cold War. From Gorbachev's (1996, 542) perspective, the trade agreement of June 1 represented a "turning-point" in US-Soviet relations, in which the United States went "from verbal support for our perestroika to real action." On the day of the signing, he spoke of the body of agreements as a step toward a "new world." Bush's speech that day noted that while the two superpowers did not agree on everything, "we [do] believe in one great truth: the world has waited long enough; the Cold War must end" (quoted in Oberdorfer 1991, 423).[111]

Cooperation did indeed become the norm after this point. Most surprising and immediate was the way both sides worked together during

[109]Oberdorfer 1991, 415–19; Zelikow and Rice 1997, 276–79; Beschloss and Talbott 1993, 210–22; Baker 1995, 248–49.

[110]On the tie to subsequent Soviet moderation in the Baltic, see Matlock 1995, chap. 14; 380–81.

[111]As Baker recounts, the June agreements had an immediate effect on third world issues. "It was almost as if Gorbachev's acceptance of Germany in NATO, and the President's decision on the trade agreement, had moved our relations to a higher, more cooperative and personal plane." Baker 1995, 254.

the eight-month crisis to end Iraq's occupation of Kuwait, which began less than two months after the Washington Summit. By October 1990, the two Germanies were united, with the understanding that the new larger Germany would remain a part of the North Atlantic Treaty Organization. By spring 1991, East-West relations were hardly recognizable. Gorbachev received an invitation in June to the July G7 Summit of industrialized nations. On July 11, Gorbachev (1996, 612) sent a personal letter to the Western powers, stating that the Soviet people "feel that the time has come to take resolute steps . . . for a new type of economic interaction that would integrate the Soviet economy . . . into the world economy."

In one of the most remarkable events of the post-1945 period, the leader of the Soviet Union—still dedicated to the principles of socialism—arrived in London on July 16, 1991 to hold talks on international trade and investment with the seven leaders of the capitalist world. At a special meeting designed to represent the "7 + 1" formula, Gorbachev told the G7 leaders that the Soviet leadership now believed that "positive processes in the world could be sustained if the political dialogue we had established were to become rooted in the new economic cooperation." Of course, integration could be achieved only by "the lifting of legislative and other restrictions on economic and technical ties with the Soviet Union" (ibid., 613–14).[112] The G7 countries agreed to build a "special association" between the Soviet Union and International Monetary Fund/World Bank, while expressing their resolve to reestablish full access to trade and investment. From his perspective, Gorbachev came away from the G7 meeting "with a significant gain." He had achieved "a fundamental political agreement about the integration of our country [into] the world economy," thereby "fulfill[ing] the national and state interests of our country" (ibid., 617).

The above analysis demonstrates the profound importance of improving Soviet trade expectations on the winding down of the Cold War. Gorbachev recognized the need for trade and investment early on, and worked tirelessly to secure US and Western European agreement to a relaxation of existing restrictions. He understood that the probability of future trade was partly endogenous: unless he offered dramatic concessions in arms control and geopolitics, Reagan and Bush would be unlikely to use their political capital to press for the changes in CoCom along with domestic legislation. But he also used the promise of better behavior—and implicit threat of the reversal of new gains and a return to an intense Cold War—as a tool to secure Western commitments to future trade. As a result, a virtuous cycle of political concessions, signals of future Western trade, and further political concessions could be set in motion. The trade-security spiral that had initially been activated in 1945

[112]These are Gorbachev's own paraphrases from his actual speech.

had finally been reversed, leading to the ending of nearly a half century of intense cold war.

CONCLUSION

This chapter has reinforced a key theme of the book: across all eras, great powers, even those with access to nuclear weapons, are obsessed with access to markets, finance, and raw materials. As table 2.7 summarizes, for nine of the eleven case periods analyzed in this chapter, economic interdependence played a significant role in shaping the intensity of superpower conflict. And in eight of the nine positive cases, trade expectations theory beat economic realism and commercial liberalism hands down. Economic realism outshone trade expectations theory for Iran 1944, at least in explaining Washington's behavior, while liberalism proved inadequate across the board. Even in what should have been its "best cases"—Berlin 1948 and Korea 1950—liberalism could not explain the security- and power-driven calculations of the Soviet leadership.

Trade expectations theory also fell short for Berlin and Korea, even if its assumption that states are security maximizers worried about decline was upheld. Such contrary cases help us understand the conditions under which trade expectations may not have causal salience. When actors perceive their decline to be primarily the result of actions taken by the other to strengthen its sphere, such decline can overshadow trade concerns and push them into risky, destabilizing behavior. Yet as chapter 2 noted, we should not expect any single causal logic to be implicated in all events. For complex phenomena such as global conflict, the relevant question is how often a theory is right, as opposed to whether it is always right. And on this front, trade expectations theory does very well indeed.

CHAPTER SEVEN

European Great Power Politics, 1790–1854

THE PREVIOUS FOUR CHAPTERS showed that this book's theory could more than hold its own in the most hotly debated cases in international relations scholarship—those of the tumultuous twentieth century. I now turn to an exploration of the relative importance of economic interdependence and trade expectations on the policies of the European great powers from 1790 to the outbreak of the Crimean War in 1853–54. The following chapter takes the story up to 1899 and the start of the South African (Boer) War. Because of the more restricted availability of documents for the 1790–1899 period, I will not go into as much depth as I have in chapters 3–6. Moreover, since there are many cases where commerce had little or nothing to do with the outbreak of crisis or war, I will cover such cases briefly, highlighting their basic causes only to provide a complete survey of the origins of modern conflict and avoid charges of selection bias. Yet as we will see, economic interdependence and trade expectations played a far more significant role in the dynamics of nineteenth-century geopolitics than has been previously recognized.

In the first half of the nineteenth century, two conflicts in particular—the ongoing struggles of Britain, France, and Russia over the question of Turkish decline from 1820 to 1853, and start of the first Opium War with China in 1839—were both strongly driven by commercial concerns. Britain and France had been competing for control of the Levant trade for centuries, but this rivalry heated up after the Napoleonic Wars as both states sought new markets for their growing industries and control over traditional Middle Eastern transit points to the riches of Asia. Russian development of Black Sea grain production after 1815 and its forays into the export of cheap textiles after 1835 meant that it had an added interest in achieving protected access through the Turkish Straits and in penetrating Central Asian markets. Moves by Saint Petersburg against the Ottoman Empire and Persia thus took on new significance for London and Paris.

Most important, the British Empire, as the world's dominant industrial and naval power, saw Russian moves against Turkey, Persia, and Central Asia as a direct threat to its growing trade with these areas. And from a larger geopolitical perspective, Russian expansion left India, Britain's economic jewel in the crown, more vulnerable to Russian attack. Britain had to find a way to neutralize Russia as it simultaneously prevented Paris from exploiting Anglo-Russian conflicts to increase French regional trade. In the 1820s and 1830s, it did this by careful diplomacy and the occasional projection of naval power. In the 1840s, Russia and Britain reached a secret agreement to work together over the area. By 1852–53, however, this agreement proved unable to stop the rush of events that led to the Crimean War, the first large-scale conflict in Europe since 1815. Economic interdependence and shifting expectations of trade were critical to the contours of this three-decades-long competition as well as to why that competition eventually led to war.

The British-Chinese Opium War of 1839–42 has always been seen as more obviously linked to economic issues, since at the heart of it was the question of Britain's ability to penetrate China with its goods—most notoriously, opium, an addictive narcotic. It was China's efforts in 1839 to stamp out the opium trade through Canton—the only port in which foreign powers were allowed to trade—that triggered the war and led via British victory to the opening of five additional ports and the capture of Hong Kong. Because trade is so directly implicated in this particular war, the case provides an important comparative test of the relative explanatory power of the three main competing theories of the book as well as neo-Marxist logic. I demonstrate that trade expectations theory is much stronger than alternative arguments in explaining why Britain would divert valuable naval resources needed for the ongoing Mediterranean struggle to a large-scale war halfway around the world. The British understood that the opium trade was essential to the viability and growth of the whole empire, given its centrality to commerce with India and Asia overall. The threat to this trade implicated the long-term security of the British state, and as such, had to be countered.

This chapter covers many diverse cases, and scholars offer no theories that provide the 1790–1854 period with one overarching explanation. I therefore proceed by briefly noting specific explanations for the individual cases as I go along rather than summarizing a slew of theories up front. The main task at hand, though, as with our other chapters, is the testing of liberalism, economic realism, and trade expectations theory as possible explanations for fluctuating levels of conflict over time. Even when war is avoided, as it is in the 1830s, we must understand why great powers go from relative peace to the point where war is a strong possibility. Shifting expectations of long-term trade provide one (if not the only) powerful explanation for shifts in leaders' willingness to use hard-line policies to uphold their national security positions.

GREAT POWER POLITICS IN THE ERA
OF FRENCH EXPANSIONISM, 1790 TO 1815

The period from 1790 to 1815 was dominated by two distinct times of conflict: the wars of the French Revolution (1792–1801) and the Napoleonic Wars (1803–15). We can cover the wars of the French Revolution quickly since they have little root in economic variables. The war that began in 1792 between France, Prussia, and Austria, and drew in Britain the following year, was a true war of ideology. As Stephen Walt (1996) and Mark Haas (2005) have shown, the French Revolution introduced a liberal antimonarchical ideology into the European system that struck fear into the hearts of the elites of the established great powers. Simply by its existence, the new French state represented a challenge to the hierarchical monarchic and aristocratic order. If its ideology of liberty and equality was allowed to spread, it would lead to revolutions in neighboring states. In addition, a state as powerful as France, now professing a universal ideology, might later use force to impose its regime type on others. Prussia, Austria, and Britain thus cooperated to destroy revolutionary France before it was too late, and to restore a semblance of hierarchy and royal/aristocratic dominance. There is little need to invoke other causal variables to explain this war, and commercial factors in particular have almost no salience. This was a war to reestablish the system's ideological homogeneity, pure and simple.

The wars of Napoléon are much more complicated.[1] There is no doubt that Napoléon initiated the series of wars that began in 1803, and the rest of the system, weary of war, only sought peace. In terms of understanding the true origins of the wars, most historical accounts stop there. Almost invariably they assume that a mere detailing of the inner dimensions of Napoléon's personality—especially his presumed lusts for glory and power—is enough to explain his actions. Yet these personalistic accounts miss a key aspect of Napoléon the leader: namely, his acute geopolitical mind-set along with his deep knowledge of French history and France's tenuous position within the system. As I have discussed elsewhere, Napoléon saw that France by 1800 had lost the 150-year struggle with Britain for the domination of global trade, industry, and colonies (Copeland 2000b, 228–30). Through victories in the wars with Louis XIV and the Seven Years' War, Britain had accumulated a far larger colonial realm. It had used its superior naval power to defend its closed

---

[1] Because Napoléon launched his coup for power in 1799 in the midst of war, I follow convention and consider 1799–1801 as the tail end of the revolutionary war period versus part of the Napoleonic Wars per se. See table 2.7.

economic realm and facilitate specialization, trading manufactured goods for raw materials and foodstuffs.

Britain's mercantilist grand strategy was already well in place before 1750. But with the territorial gains of 1756–63—specifically the dominance of India, Canada, and the Caribbean—and its early start in the Industrial Revolution, Britain's global trade after 1770 skyrocketed. Even the loss of the US colonies did not slow Britain down; the new nation of the United States was simply reincorporated into the British system as a supplier of raw materials and major importer of British manufactured goods. Britain used its industrial superiority to undersell competitors as it dominated shipping. The results were startling. France's share of total European manufacturing from 1750 to 1800 fell from 17.2 to 14.9 percent, respectively, while Britain's rose from 8.2 to 15.3 percent. Britain's level of industrialization per capita by 1800 was twice that of France. Its total trade tripled from 1780 to 1800, while from 1773–74 to 1800 its merchant marine doubled in size (Kennedy 1976, 97–98, 106–20; 1987, 149). The implications were self-evident: if France failed to stop Britain's economic rise, it would be gradually excluded from the benefits of global commerce and would find its overall power position gravely endangered. Falling trade expectations and the way they reinforced French fears of long-term decline were thus critical propelling forces pushing Napoléon to launch an all-out war against the system.

The need to destroy Britain before it was too late was recognized by French leaders even before Napoléon assumed power.[2] Once Napoléon took power in late 1799, though, he immediately began planning for the reduction of British economic power and ultimate destruction of the rising British state. In March 1800, he issued a proclamation that Britain's goal was to divide Europe to seize its commerce and turn France into a second-rate power. Three months later, he told the British king that it was England, not France, that threatened the European balance of power because of its monopoly on global trade. He initiated an ambitious plan in September to rebuild French colonial strength. Napoléon also simultaneously ended the two-year naval war with the United States in the Caribbean and signed a secret treaty with Spain for the return of the Louisiana territory to France.[3]

His larger economic agenda became evident in 1801 when he sent a large expeditionary force commanded by his brother-in-law to the

[2]In early 1798, the Directory controlling France actively considered an invasion of Britain, but was convinced by Napoléon of its current infeasibility. To reduce British strength in another way, Napoléon was dispatched to conquer Egypt as preparation for a future attack on British India. Copeland 2000b, 230.

[3]See *CN*, 3:392, 376; Herold 1955, 51–52, 191; *DNL*, 124; *NL*, 65–67.

Caribbean to recapture Haiti from the rebel leader Touissant Louverture. Haiti had been the most valuable colony in the French Empire prior to the slave revolt in 1791, supplying France and Europe with sugar along with other key commodities. By reestablishing French control and using Louisiana to supply Haiti's population with food and raw materials, Napoléon hoped to counter Britain's mercantile realm with a revived mercantile empire of his own (see *CN*, 7:passim; Ross 1969, 241–42). But his overall vision was even more expansive than this. In spring 1802, he instructed Denis Decrès, his navy and colonial minister, to prepare a strategy to retake the French possessions in India that had been lost to the British in the Seven Years' War. Since Britain had defeated the French effort to get at India via Egypt in 1798–99, Napoléon now understood that he would have to do so the long way—around the Cape of Good Hope (*CN*, 7:435–36).

This elaborate plan to restore the vitality of the French Empire hinged on recapturing France's own former jewel in the crown—Haiti. Without Haiti, Louisiana would have little value and would become a net drain on the French treasury, and the British would continue to dominate Caribbean commerce. Britain could then use the surplus to reinforce its global naval superiority, making the reoccupation of parts of India next to impossible. By late 1802–early 1803, all reports showed that the French effort to retake Haiti had failed miserably. With disease and the population's fierce resistance devastating French forces, France had to withdraw. Given that his plan to rebuild France's global economic strength was now in ruins, Napoléon moved quickly to bring on war with Britain before it was too late. He publicly blamed Britain for wanting war, even as he repositioned forces toward the north in preparation for an invasion of the island. He sold Louisiana to the United States not only to raise cash for the invasion but also to avoid a war with Washington that would take funds away from his main objective of destroying Britain. This way, instead of having the United States as an enemy and potential ally of Britain, he could at least neutralize the United States and perhaps set it against Britain to reduce its naval presence in the North Atlantic (ibid., 8:326, 354–56, 288; Schom 1997, 321–22).

War with Britain was declared in May 1803. Napoléon spent the next two years preparing a massive invasion force. The plan was to divert the British navy to the Caribbean and then use temporary French naval superiority in the English Channel to protect France's army as it was ferried across open water. At the crucial moment, the admiral in charge of the operation deviated from the plan and went south with his fleet instead of north. He was defeated decisively off the coast of Spain at Trafalgar by Horatio Nelson in October 1805. This forced Napoléon to abandon any immediate plans to take the island and instead turn his huge army eastward. The new strategy was to defeat the continental states first in order to use Europe as a base for another attempted invasion of Britain. By fall 1806, Napoléon had beaten Austria, Russia, and Prussia in a series of decisive battles. In November, he announced the Berlin Decree, which closed Europe to British goods. This pronouncement along with the 1807 Milan Decree formed the basis of Napoléon's Continental System, an attempt to destroy the British economy by creating an exclusive French economic sphere in Europe.[4]

Destroying Britain remained Napoléon's main objective until the attack on Russia in 1812. In September 1807, he formulated plans for another invasion of Britain, and in early 1808 began rebuilding his strength in northern France for this purpose. Britain was still hanging on by 1810, but its economy was faltering. Yet the devastations of the continental system to Russia's economy was causing Czar Alexander to permit the British smuggling of goods into Europe through northern Russian ports. It was Alexander's refusal to stop this trade that led Napoléon to attack Russia in 1812—without a restoration of a tight blockade against Britain, Britain could not be weakened enough to allow a successful French invasion.[5]

The economic basis for Napoléon's larger strategy to destroy Britain was nicely revealed in a letter he sent to Foreign Minister Charles Maurice de Talleyrand in August 1803, soon after war with Britain had been renewed, but before his military moves of 1805. France and England, he argued, both had critical commercial interests in Asia and the Americas. But unless England was voluntarily willing to "limit its power" in these areas, France could not regain a competitive economic position. The fact that England refused to evacuate the island of Malta, as per the peace agreement of 1801–2, "made clear its intention to add the Mediterranean to its almost exclusive commercial sphere of the Indies, America, and the Baltic." Of all the problems that could arise, "there is none comparable to this." War was therefore necessary, since the French people refused to bow down before a nation that "makes a game of all that is sacred on the earth, and who have, especially in the last twenty years, assumed an ascendancy and temerity which threatens the existence of all nations in their industry and commerce, the lifeblood of states" (CN, 8:618–20; see also ibid., 616).

None of the above analysis denies that Napoléon might have had strong personal reasons for wanting a major war after 1801.[6] Nevertheless, it

---

[4]See CN, 11:87; DNL, 204; Carr 1941, 206–7; Schroeder 1994, 307–10; Seward 1988, 165, 173.

[5]NLN, 45–47; Schroeder 1994, 326, 405, 416–21; Tarle 1942, 5, 38–39; Schom 1997, 583–84.

[6]It is worth noting, however, that personalistic arguments are largely nonfalsifiable. Any leader who initiates a total war against the system can be said to "lust for power" by the sheer act of trying to destroy other great powers. Moreover, an egotistic sense of one's

shows that Napoléon put forward a geopolitical logic perfectly in line with established French thinking—one rooted in French fears for its position in the global economic system against its traditional rival, Great Britain. Britain's dominance of world trade, closed colonial system, and continued use of naval power to restrict others' access to markets meant that over time, France would decline as a major player in the European system. Contrary to economic realism, it was not dependence per se that caused France to go to war. It instead was the sense that Britain was using its naval and industrial dominance to restrict French access to the world economic system. Spirals of hostility between Britain and France over the previous century plainly underpinned Napoléon's pessimism about the future trade environment. Once he had failed to counter the British by rebuilding French colonial trade via Haiti and Louisiana, he knew that long-term decline for France was inevitable. The liberal argument could hold some sway here: the low levels of trade between France and Britain by the 1790s certainly meant that there was no material restraint on the internal drives for war that Napoléon himself seemed to possess. Yet the liberal logic has no propelling cause for war based on economic variables and thus must rely on unit-level pathologies to get war going. In this case, we do have a propelling economic force at work: the falling expectations for future trade that were shaping Napoléon's desire for war.

Of the three approaches tying commerce to war, trade expectations theory provides the best overall explanation of this complex case. It captures French concerns not only about France's need for access to markets and raw materials but also the elite belief that the viability of that access was deteriorating, given British policies. It also demonstrates that Napoléon's primary concern was with the development of British naval and commercial power rather than with continental threats per se. We might ask why British leaders, seeing that their policies were driving the French into another long war, did not try to open up global trade to French merchants, and indeed help the French to reconstitute their economic empire in Haiti and Asia. Irrationality on the part of London might be invoked. There nevertheless is a more plausible explanation at hand: the French commitment problem. Had France been allowed to reconstitute a vibrant economic empire and reverse its declining power position, there was no telling what it might do with its newfound power base. In British eyes, the French had proven over two centuries and particularly the last three decades (via aid to American revolutionaries and the revolutionary wars)

---

ability to shape world events is a prerequisite for any great statesperson, whether one is a Napoléon or a Roosevelt. In a case such as the Napoleonic Wars where domestic pressures are not propelling the leader, it seems entirely too easy to fall back on individual-level pathologies, especially when systemic forces are clearly at work.

that they could not be trusted. Britain, then, had good reasons to keep the French down economically. Yet this policy also inevitably pushed France into a preventive war for long-term survival.

Although trade expectations theory supplies the best trade-driven explanation for the Napoleonic Wars, it is not the whole story. French fears of decline versus Britain were not just a function of a deteriorating trade environment; they also were related to Britain's internal industrialization and high population growth. French efforts to replicate Britain's Industrial Revolution were being hampered by the entrenched practices of the ancien régime economy, particularly the French preference for small-scale agriculture and manufacturing. Without a massive shift of the rural population to the cities, the economies of scale for both farming and especially industrial mass production could not be achieved.[7] Napoléon's preventive motivations were thus also rooted in the relative stagnation of the French economy in the midst of British economic dynamism.

Given that the trade environment was only one of a number of key factors causing French decline by 1800, we cannot say that it alone caused Napoléon to initiate war against the system. But it certainly reinforced overall French pessimism: France could not maintain its position vis-à-vis Britain in a world where Britain controlled the economic prerequisites of great power growth and would not share its bounty. As such, the commercial environment can be seen as at least one propelling force that made war inevitable—a critical piece of the puzzle, if not the only piece.

THE POSTWAR INTERLUDE, 1815–30

The seven years after the end of the Napoleonic Wars in 1815 can be seen as a period of retrenchment and stabilization. All the great powers needed peace in order to rebuild their devastated economies and give their populations a well-deserved rest after almost a quarter century of general war. The concert system set up at the Congress of Vienna brought France back into a balance-of-power system as a restored monarchy, but it also sought to ensure coordinated solutions to great power and regional crises through the mechanism of periodic conferences. Four full-fledged congresses were held in the first six years after the war: at Aix-la-Chapelle in 1818, Troppau in 1820, Laibach in 1821, and Verona in 1821. The specific topics for discussion need not detain us, since they revolved around the question of France's status in the system and the prevention of liberal revolts in neighboring states, and had little or nothing to do with economic interdependence per se. Suffice it to say that the concert system

---

[7] For summary and references, see Copeland 2000b, 228–30.

proved fragile, largely because of the ideological divide at its core. The autocratic states of Austria, Prussia, and Russia were primarily interested in putting down any revolt that might trigger liberal revolutions in their homelands. This "Holy Alliance" supported Austrian moves into Italy in 1821 to restore monarchical rule in Piedmont and Naples, and France's intervention in Spain in 1823 to reverse Spain's liberal revolution against King Ferdinand. These actions were opposed by Britain, the most liberal state in the system. The principle of concerting to deal with specific crises would occasionally be invoked over the next thirty years, but after 1822 it was clear that the five-power commitment to maintain a collective response to European problems had ended.[8]

European geopolitics from 1822 to 1830 was largely driven by the selfish realpolitik calculations of the key actors, as Korina Kagan (1997–98) has effectively shown. Institutional "constraints," even when they existed, played almost no role in shaping their policies. Over the decade of the 1820s, Russia returned to its policy of cautiously expanding against the Turkish Empire without causing its complete collapse or the intervention of other powers. Austria continued to worry about Russian expansionism, seeking British naval support for a policy of containment. France, as it rebuilt its power, invoked its traditional policy of power projection in the Mediterranean and economic ties to the Levant. Britain reverted to its tried-and-true policy of maintaining balances of power between adversaries in every subregion of interest—a policy that left it free to reinforce its trade dominance in Latin America, Africa, and Asia (Schroeder 1994).

The first sign of trouble in paradise arose with the 1821 Greek insurrection against Turkish rule. Austria, despite hatred of the Ottomans, was dead set against any efforts to overturn the status quo, and found support for this view in London and Paris. The Russians were torn: on the one hand, they did not want to be seen as supporting rebellion, and on the other hand, helping fellow Christians might further Russia's goal of gaining secure access to the Mediterranean. Freer access to the Mediterranean Sea had been a long-held Russian dream, but its significance increased dramatically after the Napoleonic Wars as Russia began to actively develop the grain regions of the northern Black Sea coast. Economic realism captures one aspect of the Russian situation: as Russia's interest in trade grew, so did its drive to control the access routes that would facilitate it. As historian Matthew Anderson explains it,

[8] See Schroeder 1994; Kissinger 1959; Kagan 1997–98; Albrecht-Carrié 1973. See table 2.7, where the 1815–22 period is coded as one of the ten cases where economic interdependence had a negligible effect on great power behavior, especially compared to concerns for the stability of monarchical regime types.

Russia's material interest in the fate of the Ottoman Empire was increasing rapidly by 1821. The settlement and development of the fertile lands of the Black Sea steppe was bringing with it a spectacular growth in grain exports to western Europe. Odessa, by far the greatest center of this trade, was in the second decade of the nineteenth century the most rapidly growing port in the world. All this increased sharply for Russia the importance of free movement of her merchant ships through the Straits.

Yet for Russia the ultimate concern was ensuring that Turkey maintained a policy of openness with regard to the Turkish Straits, and here is where Istanbul's erratic decision-making process proved problematic. Anderson (1979, 82) continues: "[The concern] was driven home when, in the 1820s, the Turkish government began impeding that movement by administrative delays, by searching Russian vessels, and sometimes by preempting their cargos." Saint Petersburg had achieved the promise of free passage for Russian merchant ships through the straits after its short war with Turkey in 1809–10. And in the five years after the end of the Napoleonic Wars, Russia used this free passage to increase its grain exports almost 600 percent (Curtiss 1979, 11). But expanded agricultural trade was not the only thing that Saint Petersburg wanted. After 1815 Russia had also initiated an industrialization program to catch up with the Western powers, particularly Britain. By the early 1820s, the nation had some five thousand factories employing about two hundred thousand individuals. These factories, as Peter Hopkirk (1990, 102) relates, "were becoming desperate for new markets" on Russia's southern rim.

After 1820, then, the straits had a new level of importance, and Russian officials watched carefully for anything that would threaten the straits' openness to commerce. The Greek rebellion represented both a threat and opportunity. It was a threat if it destabilized the Istanbul government further, leading to additional restrictions on Russia's free passage rights. But it was also an opportunity if it allowed Russia to project more power into the region. Initially, Czar Alexander followed the lead of the other great powers and, beyond the restrained sending of supplies to the insurgents, refused to get actively involved in the Greek War of Independence. Things started to change in 1825 as brutal Turkish massacres in Greece raised the public opinion costs of noninvolvement. In April 1826, Russia under its new czar Nicholas I was able to draw Britain into an agreement that would offer a mediated solution, making Greece into an autonomous vassal-state of the Ottoman Empire. Significantly, if Turkey or Greece refused, the agreement allowed that the two great powers could intervene "jointly or separately" to resolve the situation. This clause gave the czar what he needed: the cover to act against Turkey to reestablish

Russia's open commercial access to the Mediterranean without immediately risking war with the one power—Great Britain—that could stop him. Nicholas proceeded to coerce the Turks into the Akkerman Convention (October 1826), an agreement that explicitly reaffirmed Russian privileges in the Turkish Danubian principalities and gave Russian merchant ships free navigation in the Ottoman Empire (Anderson 1979, 84–85; LeDonne 1997, 120–21).

Unfortunately, given its internal divisions, Turkey proved unwilling or unable to implement the deal. Russia was able to convince the British and French to increase their naval restrictions on Turkish resupply to troops in Greece. This led to the joint attack on the Turkish fleet at Navarino in 1827, a devastating action that convinced the sultan to abandon the Akkerman Convention and announce a "holy war" against the Russian state. War between Russia and Turkey began in April 1828. Britain honored its 1826 agreement and stayed out. Despite some initial setbacks, the Russians decisively defeated the Turks in summer 1829. In September the Treaty of Adrianople was signed, with Russia proving surprisingly moderate in its demands.

The details of this treaty reveal much about Russia's larger geopolitical aims and strategic thinking. Turkey was prostrate, and the European capitals were anticipating the collapse of its empire. French foreign minister Jules de Polignac even approached Russia to discuss the partition of Ottoman territory. Despite this great opportunity for territorial expansion, Saint Petersburg allowed the Danubian principalities to remain under nominal Turkish suzerainty. In the peace, however, Russia sought security for its burgeoning trade. Saint Petersburg was given authority over the Danube Delta, a critical commercial choke point for Austrian and Turkish trade out of the Balkan hinterland. It also obtained renewal of Turkey's 1826 guarantee of free access for Russian merchant ships through the straits.[9]

Given that Paris had already suggested dividing Turkey's empire, we cannot attribute such Russian moderation only to fears of European intervention. The Russians had a larger strategic vision. Coinciding with the negotiation of the treaty, the czar established a committee of high-ranking officials to examine the Turkish question. The committee's fundamental conclusion was that "the advantages of the preservation of the Ottoman Empire outweigh its disadvantages." Further Russian expansion was not necessary and would only cause other powers to pick off the best pieces of Turkey's Mediterranean possessions, bringing them closer to Russia's borders. A weak but stable Turkey, on the other hand, would provide a necessary buffer, and its policies could be shaped by Russia.

[9] For summary and references, see Anderson 1979, 85–86; Kagan 1997–98.

Keeping the Ottoman Empire alive was thus Russia's preferred outcome. Yet if Turkey were to fall apart, the committee argued, Russia should call an international conference to coordinate the peaceful partition of its empire. Most important, Russia must take "the most energetic measures" to ensure that the Turkish Straits "[are] not seized by any other power whatever." Given that the movement of warships through the straits had been outlawed for decades by previous agreements, this sentence was clearly a reference to the continued commercial movement of exports and imports through the Turkish choke point.[10]

This cautious policy view was to dominate Russian decision making for the next three decades, and as we will see, would shape the events that led to the Crimean War. But what is noteworthy at this point is that Russia was not simply a "revisionist" power constantly seeking opportunities to reduce its dependence, as economic realists would predict. Russia's anticipation of increasing southern trade did make Saint Petersburg wary about continued access to the Mediterranean. The first preference of Nicholas and his committee, though, was the continuation of Turkey as an empire. Only if this result could not be ensured and Turkey appeared likely to break apart would Russia fall back on its second preference: the division of the Turkish Empire by agreement of the key great powers. For Russia, the worst outcome was a free-for-all scramble for pieces of the dying Turkish state. And the czar's committee understood that Russia itself could bring about this result by seeming too aggressive in its foreign policy (Anderson 1979, 87). So the committee concluded, and the czar agreed, that moderation in the Near East was essential to both prevent a trade-security spiral and avoid a situation where other powers, by grabbing Turkish territories, blocked Russia's commercial access through the straits.

To conclude this section, we can see that both economic realism and trade expectations theory offer insights into the geopolitics of the "Eastern Question" of the late 1820s. Russia's growing dependence and need to trade through the Turkish Straits gave it an increased need to project power against Turkey as well as use war to ensure Istanbul's acquiescence to the free movement of goods. Yet it was Turkish interference with Russian merchants ships through the straits and the instabilities of the Greek rebellion that pushed Saint Petersburg to strong-arm the Turks into the 1826 Akkerman Convention that would reestablish unrestricted access. Russia's move to war in 1828 when Turkey proved slow to implement the convention's provisions reinforces that it was declining trade expectations more than just a fear of vulnerability that drove Russian decision

---

[10] Quoted in and summarized from Anderson 1979, 86–87. See also LeDonne 1997, 121–22; Schroeder 1994, 658.

making. Saint Petersburg's moderate peace terms in 1829, furthermore, show that assurances of open access were more important than grabbing opportunities to assert formal control.

Liberals might try to argue that growing Russian trade with the Western European powers, especially in grain, provided a restraint on both Russian and British/French tendencies toward warmongering. After all, aside from the Russo-Turkish War of 1828–29, great power war was avoided in the Mediterranean region. The liberal logic perhaps did give the great powers some reason for caution during the 1820s, although direct evidence is hard to come by. The main problem with this reasoning is a comparative one: it does not explain why war was not avoided in 1853–54 (Crimean War) when trade between Russia and the West had become even more significant. It also cannot explain the growing tensions and close calls of the 1830s as European trade continued to grow. It is to the 1830s that I will now turn.[11]

The Instability of Turkey and the Turbulent 1830s

Diplomatic relations during the decade of the 1830s, like the late 1820s, were dominated by third-party issues revolving around the viability of the Ottoman Empire and what its breakup might mean for the economic and geopolitical positions of the European great powers. Turkey was being undermined not by great power actions per se but rather the expansionistic desires of one of the sultan's vassals, the pasha of Egypt,

---

[11] A case straddling the 1820s and 1830s is the minicrisis over Belgium in 1830–31. This case can be discussed briefly, since the crisis was of low intensity and did not involve trade in any appreciable way. The crisis arose as a result of the Belgium people's efforts in 1830 to break from the Vienna settlement uniting the Dutch Netherlands and former Austrian Netherlands under the Dutch king. The king appealed to fellow monarchs to uphold the post-Vienna status quo. Prussia, Austria, and Russia offered verbal support but no direct aid. The French, however, moved to support Belgian independence, immediately triggering a reaction from Britain. As it became clear that Louis Philippe, the new "bourgeois king" of France, had no interest in occupying Belgium or controlling it through the coronation of his son as the future Belgian king, a great power solution was found. Negotiations from November 1830 until January 1831 (with loose ends tied up by November 1931) led to Paris and London's agreement to work together to realize Belgian independence, with Paris agreeing to forgo any territorial compensation as long as no great power intervened in Belgium. The crisis was fundamentally driven by London's concern for the security of the English Channel set against a low-level French desire to satisfy popular demands for changes in the 1815 settlement. Given the lack of evidence for the importance of either British or French trade interests, table 2.7 codes the case as one where commercial variables exerted no influence, meaning that none of the key theories of this book can explain the crisis. For overviews, see Albrecht-Carrié 1973, chap. 2; Bourne 1982, chap. 8. For documents, see Albrecht-Carrié 1968, 60–98.

Mohammed Ali. Ali's moves against the sultan led to two of the most significant crises of the decade. The first came in 1832–33 when Ali attacked Turkish possessions in Palestine and Syria on the way to a direct invasion of Asia Minor. His forces got within a few hundred miles of Istanbul itself before being convinced to pull back by a combination of the Turkish and Russians forces. The second crisis came in 1839–40 as the government in Istanbul prepared to push Ali out of Syria. The sudden death of the sultan just as the war was about to start led to the defection of the Turkish navy to Ali's side. Fear of the total collapse of the Ottoman state pushed Britain to intervene on the Turkish side, and call on the Russians and Austrians for help. The coalition that was created successfully neutralized the Egyptian threat to Turkey, yet in the process it isolated the pro-Egyptian French, effecting a diplomatic revolution that saw the final end of Anglo-French entente along with the formation of closer ties between Britain and Russia.

This section explores the relative salience of commercial issues for Russian, British, and French decision making in these two crises.[12] We have seen that in addition to the traditional objectives of secure buffer zones, Saint Petersburg's interest in the Ottoman Empire after 1820 was linked to the growing importance of trade through the Turkish Straits. For Britain and France, the significance of the territories that Turkey nominally controlled was even greater, for two reasons. First, since the time of Louis XIV, both states had competed for dominance of the Levant trade—the trade in cloth, spices, and other luxury items that flowed from the Far East through the Near East. Second, the overland communication routes through the Levant were critical to Britain's efficient management of its Indian and Asian Empire. Diplomatic dispatches could get to London from India in approximately three months, while going around the Cape of Good Hope took up to half a year—a difference that was essential to Britain's timely reaction to developments in Asia, including the growing crises brewing over China and Afghanistan (Marlowe 1971).

Through the 1820s, France sought to improve its economic and political ties to the Levant by supporting Ali. Although Egypt was still nominally a part of the Ottoman Empire, Ali had built up Egypt's power through a hasty modernization program, and by the early 1830s began to challenge the sultan for control of the empire. Britain's policy toward Ali remained consistent throughout the 1820s and 1830s: Turkey's survival was key to both contain Russia and negate French influence in the region. Given this, any efforts by Ali to undermine the Ottoman Empire were frowned on. The French, on the other hand, were torn between propping

---

[12] Each European power is treated as a separate case, given that each was separately propelled into assertive policies in the Near East.

up Turkey to contain Russia and using economic aid to Ali to increase their penetration of the area. Russia's victory over Turkey in the 1828–29 war convinced Paris that Turkey was unlikely to survive intact. Hence, after 1829, and consistent with economic realism's predictions, France supported Ali's territorial ambitions as a means of increasing overall French control of trade through the Near East.[13]

Ali attacked Palestine in 1832 and by early 1833 had moved through Syria to challenge the capital itself. Turkey called on Britain for support. British foreign secretary Lord Palmerston wanted to respond but the cabinet balked, constrained by parliamentary reform debates and the resolution of Belgium's bid for full independence from Holland. Lacking allies, the sultan turned to Turkey's historical enemy, Russia. In February 1833, Russia sent its fleet and landed five thousand troops on Turkish soil. Ali retreated to Syria, and proceeded to consolidate his control over Syria and Palestine (Webster 1969, 1:279–89; Anderson 1979, 88).

Russia and Turkey signed a formal treaty of alliance in July 1833—one that seemed to leave Turkey in a clearly subordinate position. Consistent with Nicholas's desire to maintain Turkey's viability, Russia promised military assistance to maintain the independence of the Ottoman Empire. Palmerston was worried, though. He was comforted to learn that the treaty reinforced previous agreements by closing the straits to all great power warships during peacetime. This implied Russia was continuing its defensive posture. Yet the very fact that the new treaty was an alliance meant that should Turkey find itself at war, Russian warships would likely be allowed through the straits even as the waterway remained closed to all other states (LeDonne 1997, 123).

The events of 1833 led Palmerston to shift Britain to a policy of active containment against Russia in the Near East—a policy that would stay in place for a century and a half. In 1834, the British navy increased its naval presence near the opening of the straits. In 1835–37, Palmerston began to prop up local rulers in Persia and Afghanistan—a move that led to the disastrous British intervention into Afghanistan in 1839. In 1837–38, London signed a free trade pact with Istanbul as part of Palmerston's strategy to revitalize Turkey while increasing Britain trade penetration of the Middle East. Turkey agreed to end most of the monopolies and high tariffs that had, in the British view, not only hurt trade but also impeded Turkey's modernization. The bolstering of Britain's overall presence in the eastern Mediterranean was obviously designed to warn Saint Petersburg that it must maintain its moderate stance toward the Ottoman state (Webster 1969, 1:338–39).

---

[13] The French occupied Algiers in 1830 as part of this larger effort to project power into the Moslem world. See Marlowe 1971, 173–76.

British and Russian leaders were perfectly aware that long-term trade dominance was at the crux of this new, intensified struggle over the Near East and Asia. In fall 1838, for example, the Russian foreign minister Karl Nesselrode wrote his ambassador in London that the British were attempting to subvert Russian influence in Central Asia and push out Russian goods, replacing them with British goods. "For our part," he argued, "we ask nothing but to be allowed to partake in fair competition for the commerce of Asia" (quoted in Hopkirk 1990, 202). Needless to say, there was not much hope that his ambassador could achieve this objective. Palmerston well understood that the economic policies of the continental great powers were driven by a combination of protectionism and state-sponsored export promotion, and he was determined to keep Russian and other European products from displacing British ones in the vast, growing markets of Asia. He revealed his larger strategic logic to George Auckland, governor-general in India, in a letter in January 1941 written before the disaster of his Afghanistan policy had become apparent. Riding high on his success with the 1839–40 Turkish Crisis (discussed below), he pressed Auckland to consolidate the gains made in Afghanistan up to that point, and find new markets for British goods in Arabia and Ethiopia. He continued:

> The rivalship [*sic*] of European manufactures is fast excluding our productions from the markets of Europe, and we must unremittingly endeavor to find in other parts of the world new vents [i.e., outlets] for the produce of our industry. The world is large enough and the wants of the human race ample enough to afford a demand for all [that] we can manufacture, but it is the business of the Government to open and to secure the roads for the merchant. Will the navigation of the Indus turn out to be as great a help as was expected for our commerce? If it does, and if we succeed in our China expedition, Abyssinia [Ethiopia], Arabia, the countries on the Indus and the new markets in China will at no distant period give a most important extension to the range of our foreign commerce. (quoted in Webster 1969, 2:750–51)

These are interesting words for someone who also apparently believed—at least when it came to relations with smaller powers—that it was "only by extensive Commercial Intercourse that a Community of Interests can be permanently established between the People of different Countries."[14] Any such liberal sentiments that Palmerston held as a Whig were clearly tempered in practice by his recognition that other states would resist the flooding of their markets by inexpensive British goods even as they sought to penetrate Britain's spheres of economic influence. As such, British

---

[14]Lord Palmerston to Lord Holland, May 1837, quoted in Bourne 1982, 552.

political and military power had to be projected into areas of economic competition to ensure open access.[15]

Returning to the Turkish question of the late 1830s, we see that both Britain and Russia by 1839 had acquired a new economic stake in Istanbul's future. Britain's free trade pact with Turkey in 1838 would lead to a major increase in British commerce in the region (see the analysis of the Crimean War below). Meanwhile, as Vernon Puryear (1965, 82–88) notes, Russia "was developing [its] southern export trade enormously" in the 1830s, not just in grain and raw materials, but also in cheap manufacturing goods. The supply of grain for export doubled in the decade. Even in unstable years such as 1839–40 when grain exports from Odessa fell, the losses were "more than made up in exports of cotton goods to the Trans-Caucasian provinces and China." Russia ran an overall trade surplus of some ninety-two million rubles by the end of the decade (see Webster 1969, 2:548–57, 581–82).

A crisis broke out in April–May 1839 when Turkey mobilized its military in a desperate effort by the aging sultan to push Ali out of Syria and consolidate the Ottoman realm before his death. By June the Turkish army had already suffered significant losses, and when the sultan died on July 1, the power vacuum at the top led to the defection of the Turkish fleet to Ali, further weakening the Ottoman state. Palmerston decided to act forcefully. Worried about losing the Turkish buffer against Russia, Palmerston sought to draw Russia into a multiparty response that would neutralize any Russian effort to exploit Turkey's desperate situation. France initially seemed to support such a move, but then threw its weight behind Ali.[16] Palmerston thus proceeded with his plan without French help. Significant opposition arose within the cabinet from lords Clarendon and Holland, who feared that military action would harm British commerce with the territories that Ali occupied and would interrupt communications with India.[17] In March 1840, Palmerston explained to Clarendon that while moving against Ali did risk British commercial connections with Egypt, Turkey had to be supported if it were to resist Russian encroachments. He was acting only "for the advantage of England, and to what offers the fairest prospect of extending her commercial relations and the sphere of her influence and power."[18]

---

[15] On the tie between power and economic interests, see Lord Palmerston's letter to Lord Melbourne, July 5, 1840, in *FPVE*, 243–46.

[16] Webster 1969, 2:625–43; *FPVE*, doc. 19 and page 38 (editor's discussion); Schroeder 1994, 737.

[17] See, for example, Lord Clarendon and Lord Holland's letter of protest to the queen, July 1840, in *FPVE*, doc. 24.

[18] Lord Palmerston to Lord Clarendon, March 14, 1840, in *FPVE*, doc. 22.

By July Britain was ready to finalize a four-power agreement with Austria, Russia, and Prussia to assist Turkey. Palmerston wrote a long note to Prime Minister Lord Melbourne to shape cabinet discussions. Joint action was necessary to uphold Turkey's integrity and the balance of power as well as preserve Britain's "commercial and political interests." If Britain did not act, Turkey would be divided into two states: one the dependency of France, and the other a satellite of Russia. In both cases, "our political influence will be annulled, and our commercial interests will be sacrificed."[19] On July 8, Palmerston's argument won the day. Britain soon signed the four-power convention and began to attack Ali's position in Syria, forcing his retreat to Egypt. Palmerston had saved Turkey from its most significant existential threat yet, allowing the Ottoman Empire to survive for another seventy-five years.

As for Russian decision making in the crisis, what is most notable is its moderation. Czar Nicholas and Foreign Minister Nesselrode in 1839 were able to restrain the hawks within the government and agree to allied action that left Britain playing the major military role in the war. They had agreed by May 1839 that cooperation with Britain was essential and Russia should not maintain its bilateral alliance with Turkey (Anderson 1979, 94). Russia also moderated its policy on Afghanistan and Persia to avoid a clash with Britain (FPVE, 42 [editor's discussion]). Such moderation reflected Nicholas and Nesselrode's long-standing agreement that Russia's first priority was to maintain Turkey's viability to ensure open commerce through the straits. Palmerston's policy therefore worked like a charm. By projecting naval power and yet insisting on multiparty action, he had kept Russia from exploiting the crisis to increase its control over Turkey. And by showing that his primary objective was Turkish survival, he had convinced Russia to align with London over Near East issues broadly defined.

As we will see, British-Russian cooperation would soon deepen, leading to the secret agreement of 1844 on Turkey's future. It is worth pausing to access the value of the competing theories for the period 1830–40. The liberal argument can explain some of Russia's willingness to cooperate in 1839–40: growing trade with Britain and the region made the status quo doubly attractive to Saint Petersburg. Yet trade expectations theory explains the specific reasons for Russian moderation. London was offering a compromise solution that would maintain Turkey's viability, thereby preserving Russian access through the straits while avoiding a scramble over the remains of a collapsed Ottoman Empire. Both economic realism and trade expectations theory do a good job explaining overall British decision making up to 1840. By the 1830s, British dependence on

[19]Lord Palmerston to Lord Melbourne, July 5, 1840, in FPVE, doc. 23.

commerce through the eastern Mediterranean was high and growing, and Palmerston was plainly worried about future threats to this trade. But it was the specific threats caused by Ali and the Egyptian army as well as fears of increasing Russian influence on Turkey that drove Palmerston's policy shifts. He was concerned that a weakened Afghanistan and Turkey would allow Ali to control Middle Eastern trade and communications routes, while furthering Russian economic and political penetration of the area. As these threats increased, he was able to convince his cabinet to support a more forceful British strategy in the Near East and Central Asia. This responsiveness to growing threats nicely aligns with the trade expectations argument. But because Palmerston sought to anticipate future threats to British commerce and not simply counter current threats, economic realism is also upheld.

Explaining French policy in the late 1830s is more difficult. By its support for Ali, Paris was needlessly endangering valuable trade links and political ties with Britain, contrary to the predictions of both liberalism and trade expectations theory. Economic realism has some descriptive value, since the French effort to build an alternative commercial realm in the Levant would help them reduce dependence on British-controlled trade routes. Still, French policy, insofar as it undermined the mid-1830s' entente with Britain, seems inherently counterproductive and thus at odds with realism's rational actor assumption.

Overall, the crisis of 1839–40 leaves us with mixed results. Liberalism and trade expectations theory captures Russia's moderation, economic realism wins by default with regard to France, and trade expectations theory edges out realism for British behavior. When put in the context of overall British policy in the Near East and Central Asia, the trade expectations approach is especially powerful: it explains why Palmerston and his colleagues would react so forcefully to what were seen as encroachments on British commerce. Britain's actions can be seen as defensive—a reaction to growing threats to its continued economic dominance in Asia.

THE ORIGINS OF THE CHINESE-BRITISH OPIUM WAR, 1939–42

Broad agreement exists among historians that Britain initiated a war against China in 1839 as a response to Chinese efforts to stop the British sale of opium into the country. Opium had become the linchpin of British trade with China, and so Beijing's new policy of enforcing bans on its importation wreaked havoc on overall East-West trade. This historical agreement means that we do not need to demonstrate that economic variables were critical to the outbreak of war. What is at question, however, is exactly how these variables led to war. The fact that the First Opium

War is perhaps the most clearly economically driven one over the last two hundred years makes it an ideal test of the relative explanatory power of all our competing theories, including neo-Marxism. Indeed, this is one of the few cases where any evidence exists linking domestic pressures from capitalist elites to war.

I show that both neo-Marxist and liberal arguments are quite weak relative to economic realism and trade expectations theory. Neo-Marxists contend that business interests affected by the Chinese opium ban pushed the British government into war to restore the profitability of their immoral ventures (see, in particular, Fay 1976). Despite surface plausibility, the neo-Marxist assertion falls flat on closer inspection. Most of the merchants lobbying the government did not want war (which they saw as bad for business) but rather only compensation for their initial losses. Foreign Secretary Palmerston convinced the cabinet to reject this demand and instead moved quickly to preserve Britain's overall Asian trade through force. So while the merchants eventually profited from increased trade with China after the war, this was an inadvertent side benefit of a policy driven by national interest and not a propelling cause of the war itself.

The liberal argument also seems to possess surface plausibility: the fall in trade after 1838 reduced constraints on individuals possessing non-economic reasons for war with China, such as glory, honor, or the ideology of empire. The main problem here is that British officials had been happy with informal control over the China trade for some time. In contrast with India, they did not see the necessity of formal imperial control over actual territory. Despite Britain's overwhelming victory in the war, then, London demanded only the opening of four additional ports and secession of Hong Kong. There was no push to colonize China itself.

Economic realism and trade expectations theory provide much stronger explanations for Britain's initiation of war. Realism captures the importance of Chinese-British trade to the overall British Empire. A triangular trade system between Britain, India, and China had been put in place by the early nineteenth century. British sales to India of textiles and other mass-produced goods depended on India's ability to purchase these goods. Yet India had surprisingly few things that Britain wanted to buy. The British did desire tea, silks, and ceramics, but these goods all came from China. Unfortunately, the Chinese wanted little from Britain except silver, a metal that was essential to the monetization of the Chinese economy. To avoid a massive drain on Britain's silver supplies—and concomitant reduction in Britain's domestic money supply—Britain required something it could sell to China to generate the cash needed to buy desired Chinese goods. The answer was Indian opium. In a complex triangular arrangement, British merchants centered in India would sell opium to China, use the bullion received to buy Chinese tea, silks, and ceramics, and then sell these products in Britain to acquire manufactured goods for sale in the Indian market.

To make the system work, British leaders understood that any two-way trade of Indian opium for British goods had to be kept to a bare minimum. Aside from the obvious societal implications, such trade would not solve the problem of obtaining Chinese goods without a drain on silver. But there was something else: Britain's treasury revenues were heavily dependent on the import duties from Chinese tea. So aside from the loss in economic strength that would accompany the ending of the opium trade, the very functioning of Britain's government and global empire would be put at risk. This was economic dependence of a unique but powerful kind, to say the least. London thus encouraged and supported the opium trade with China to sustain an arrangement that was the foundation of the whole imperial project. Britain had not been so reliant on triangular trade for its national security since its last venture in infamous cargo: the transatlantic slave trade of the seventeenth and eighteenth centuries.

Economic realism captures Britain's drive in 1839 to safeguard its economic power through the control of the sources of dependence. It confronts one key problem, however. The level of British dependence on this nefarious trade had been growing rapidly after 1810 (see below for statistics). Right up to 1839, though, the British government remained relatively complacent about this increased dependence and showed no signs of gearing up for war with China to ensure continued access, as economic realists would expect. It was only in 1839 when the Chinese government decided to strongly *enforce* previous laws outlawing the sale of opium into China that the British government stood up and took notice. That is, it was only when there was a direct threat to the continuation of the critical opium trade that the British government decided to go to war. As for the exogenous factor that made a negotiated solution impossible, this was nature of the opium trade itself. The Beijing government understood that as hundreds of thousands of additional Chinese citizens became addicted to the product, China would not only suffer huge productivity losses but also the outflow of silver to buy the opium would undermine China's monetary and taxation system. There was no jumping through the horns of this dilemma: China would decline precipitously if it did not stop the trade, and Britain would decline precipitously if it did not continue the trade. By the late 1830s, any bargaining space needed to avoid war had dried up (cf. Fearon 1995).

The origins of the 1839 crisis went back a century. British-Chinese trade took off in the early eighteenth century as tea grew in popularity with Britain's upper and middle classes. In 1760 Beijing restricted trade to just one port, the southern city of Canton. In the "Canton System," foreigners had to purchase tea, silks, and other goods from a few Chinese firms, or *hongs*, grouped into a larger mercantile body known as the Co-hong and overseen by the Chinese government. The East India Company, a government-sponsored monopoly, monopolized British trade with Canton. The trade proved highly profitable for the company and, because of a 100 percent duty on tea imports, the state itself.

Unfortunately, given China's large manufacturing sector, it did not need the goods Britain wanted to sell. Imbalances in trade were made up by "exports" of silver bullion to Chinese firms—that is, by British traders handing over silver to make up the difference between imports and exports. From 1710 to 1759, for example, Britain sold some nine million pounds sterling in goods to China, but paid out twenty-six million. As the supply of Spanish silver used by British merchants dried up during the American War of Independence, the East India Company turned to opium to keep the China trade going (Hanes and Sanello 2002, 20–21; Greenberg 1951, 8). In 1782, the first British ships carrying Bengali opium arrived in Canton. With China using opium mainly for medicinal not recreational purposes, the initial shipments found no ready buyer (Hanes and Sanello 2002, 19–21). A market therefore had to be created, not simply supplied.

Over the next sixty years, such a market was indeed developed. Annual opium shipments into China went from 4,570 chests in 1801–1 to 12,434 in 1824–25, to 20,486 in 1833–34, and over 40,000 chests by 1838–39. British traders regularly controlled about 40–60 percent of these shipments, with the Portuguese and other traders (including Americans selling Turkish opium) making up the rest (Greenberg 1951, 221; Fairbank 1953, 63–64). The doubling in opium imports in the 1830s reflected London's decision in 1833, under the banner of free trade and in recognition of popular pressures for lower tea prices, to end the East India Company monopoly on the China trade. British merchant firms such as Jardine Matheson Holdings and Dent, former conduits for the East India Company, jumped headlong into the opium business.

The increase in opium sales devastated China. Productivity dropped as hundreds of thousands of additional Chinese workers became addicted.[20] Perhaps even more significant was the net drain of silver for China's monetary system. Silver flowed out as China went from having a large trade surplus to a large trade deficit. From 1829 to 1840, China brought only $7 million in silver into the country, but sent out over $56 million in silver and other media of exchange (Greenberg 1951, 142). For a nation that had had the largest and most sophisticated industrial economy in the world during most of the eighteenth century, the trends

---

[20]Estimates vary, but the number of opium addicts in China rose to between one and four million (Hanes and Sanello 2002).

were ominous. The net loss in species meant dramatically reduced economic activity, just as Beijing was trying to modernize China to compete effectively with the European powers.[21] Beijing's need to stop the opium trade was completely understandable, and London could have avoided a war simply by recognizing Chinese concerns before it was too late. To understand why it did not, we need to explore in more detail the complex workings of Britain's triangular trade system.

The critical starting point of this system was Chinese exports—not of luxury goods such as silk and ceramics, but rather tea. Tea in the 1830s was only successfully grown in large quantities in China. The growth of tea consumption over the previous two centuries had been astonishing. From 1664 when the first two pounds of tea were imported into England until 1785 when the 100 percent import duty was reduced to 12.5 percent to reduce smuggling, annual sales had reached fifteen million pounds (in weight not currency). In 1833, the last year of the East India Company's monopoly on the China trade, the company imported some thirty million pounds. By the 1830s, even with reduced duty rates, tea taxes constituted one-tenth of the total annual revenue of the British government.[22]

Because of China's lack of interest in British manufactures, by the nineteenth century there were only two products that Britain could sell in large enough quantities to offset its massive tea purchases: opium and raw cotton. By the late 1820s–early 1830s, opium was clearly the dominant element of this mix, constituting over 50 percent of total British exports into Canton, with raw cotton and British-made products, including textiles, accounting for 30 percent and 10–15 percent, respectively, of export sales,. Sales of opium alone covered the total cost of the tea imports—the largest single item bought from Chinese firms (the value of the second-ranked imported item, raw silk, was less than one-seventh that of tea). The new trade surpluses of $8–10 million a year were made up by Chinese shipments of bullion abroad (Greenberg 1951, 10–15).

The second leg of the triangular system was the importance of opium sales for India itself. Without these sales, India could not play its role as Britain's economic jewel in the crown. The connection of India-China trade to Britain-India trade was understood as early as 1787, when Britain sent its first diplomatic mission to China. Instructions to the mission noted that India's prosperity depended on "procuring a secure vent for [Indian] products . . . [in] China, at the same time that the produce of such sales would furnish resources for the Investment (teas, etc.) to

---

[21] As the imperial edict of late 1838 put it, unless the opium ban was vigorously enforced, "the useful wealth of China will be poured into the fathomless abyss of transmarine regions" (quoted in Greenberg 1951, 143).

[22] Ibid., 3; Beeching 1975, 29.

Europe." After 1833, when the East India Company monopoly on British-Indian trade ended, inexpensive British textile exports flooded into India, destroying the Indian textile industry. British merchants residing in India needed something to sell to their homeland in order to buy British textiles. Tea and other Chinese products arriving from the Far East—bought with Indian opium and raw cotton—were critical to the process, allowing India to balance its payments with Britain. As T. C. Melville, the East India Company's auditor general, bluntly declared in 1830, "I am prepared to say that India does entirely depend upon the profits of the China trade" (quoted in ibid., 9, 14–15).

Manchester textile manufacturers certainly recognized China's significance to their overall livelihoods, notwithstanding China's low purchases of British cloth. In 1833, following the termination of the East India Company monopoly, the British navy became responsible for protecting India-China trade. The Manchester Chamber of Commerce sent a memorandum to the government on the "unprotected state of our trade with China." The memorandum stated that because the China trade provided an outlet for Indian products, this trade "enables our Indian subjects to consume *our* manufactures on a largely increased scale." If the Chinese government acted to restrict East-West trade, British industry would be paralyzed, and revenue losses could be upward of five million pounds sterling a year (ibid., 194–95). Moreover, British political rule in India was dependent on opium sales to China, since the Indian government's share of this revenue was the second most important source of its income overall. It is not surprising that Carl Trocki (1999, 59) calls the opium trade the "keystone of empire" for Britain in the nineteenth century.[23]

The immediate cause of the 1839 crisis was the appointment in late 1838 of Lin Zexu as commissioner to enforce a new imperial edict outlawing the sale and consumption of opium. Arriving in Canton in February 1839, Lin was determined to enforce past edicts against the sale of opium and punish corrupt officials who benefited from the opium trade. In March, he ordered the confiscation of all opium both in Canton and on outlying islands used by foreign merchants as trading bases. The chief superintendent of trade appointed by London to oversee British interests, Charles Elliot, convinced the British merchants to surrender opium chests worth upward of 10 million pounds sterling by promising that the British government would provide at least 2.5 million pounds in compensation. The opium was subsequently destroyed, and in May Lin expelled all opium traders from Canton.

Reports from the Far East took months to reach London. So when Palmerston and his colleagues gathered in late September to consider the

---

[23] See also Blue 2000, 45–47.

issue, they were unaware of the brief skirmish between Chinese war junks and British ships that had occurred earlier that month. They were thus making decisions for war or peace based only on the knowledge that Lin had kicked out British opium traders and would execute any that tried to return. At the time, the cabinet was already absorbed in the turmoil of the Turkish-Egyptian Crisis. The critical cabinet meeting on foreign policy on September 30 became so absorbed in the Eastern Question, in fact, that the China issue had to be postponed until the next day.

Details of the cabinet session on October 1 are few, but we do know, as Kenneth Bourne (1982, 588) relates, that the critical decision to endorse hostilities against China was taken. Elliot's dispatches to Palmerston had argued that the British response "should be made in the form of a swift and heavy blow unprefaced by one word of written communication." Palmerston used the meeting to read portions of Elliot's notes and employ maps supplied by opium merchant Jardine Matheson to make his case for war. He found support from Secretary of War Thomas Macaulay, and together their arguments won the day (Fay 1976, 192–93). The full extent of what the cabinet was taking on, given that Britain had entered Afghanistan earlier in the year and was preparing to support Turkey in its war with Ali, was made evident in the journal notes of one of the attendees, Arthur Hobshouse. He recorded that just before he left the meeting, he whispered to Macaulay that any opposition charge of idleness could hardly be sustained given that "we had resolved upon a war with the master of Syria and Egypt . . . and also on a war with the master of one third of the human race" (quoted in Bourne 1982, 588).

Palmerston moved quickly to implement the cabinet's decision. He accepted the Jardine Matheson firm's offer to deliver a message to Elliot by the fast schooner *Mor*, and on October 23, the schooner sailed with a letter that informed Elliot that British warships would be sent to China, likely arriving sometime in April 1840. Palmerston's discussions with Jardine Matheson prior to the cabinet meeting, the clamoring of business interests in August and September for action along with compensation for losses, and Palmerston's use of a Jardine Matheson ship to hurry his correspondence to his China envoy suggest that there might be something to the neo-Marxist claim that business pressure drove Britain into war. Yet three things indicate that national economic interests, not narrow merchant ones, were driving Palmerston and the cabinet to act. First, we have seen in our look at the Eastern Question and Afghanistan that the foundation of Palmerston's worldview was fundamentally a realpolitik one. He understood that British commerce around the world had to be promoted and protected to keep the state strong. And while we have no details on his thinking in September–October 1839 when the decision for war was made, an individual of his intellect could hardly have failed to recognize the importance of India-China trade to the general health of British Empire.

Second, Palmerston resisted all demands by Jardine Matheson and other opium merchants for immediate compensation for the confiscated opium, notwithstanding the fact that Elliot had used the promise of compensation to get them to turn over the opium in the first place. In the fall, he initially put them off with the excuse that Parliament had not yet voted for the money. But when parliamentary discussions on the government's already-deployed naval forces got under way in April 1840, Palmerston made it clear under questioning that he had no intention of asking Parliament for money for the merchants. The firms would have to wait until after the war for any compensation, meaning that, as Peter Fay (1976, 195) observes, a number of them "might not survive the test." The opium traders therefore failed to secure their one and only key demand, indicating the weakness of their lobbying effort. In terms of their causal role in the war, the merchants played more of a facilitating part than a propelling one. Palmerston effectively used Jardine Matheson's maps and ships to execute his plan for war, but there is no evidence that he felt pressured into war by their lobbying efforts.[24]

The third point weakening the neo-Marxist position is that Palmerston's China policy was only one part of a larger strategic response for Asia and the Mediterranean that he was unveiling at that time. Even as he pushed for a hard-line response in China, he was readying the British navy to push Ali back to Egypt as well as deploying the army to Afghanistan to contain Russia's political and economic penetration of Central Asia. During 1839–40, he also sent warships to the coasts of Portugal and Naples to force Lisbon to repay its debts plus convince Naples to maintain its most-favored-nation status with Britain (Bourne 1982, 588–89). To argue that business pressures drove all these largely simultaneous actions would require a conspiracy between firms of different sectors that boggles the mind. It is much more plausible, and more consistent with the evidence, to contend that Palmerston and the cabinet's understanding of national economic interests was the common root of these separate but coordinated policy actions.

The above conclusions on the minimal importance of domestic pressure politics are reinforced by the events of the parliamentary debates in March–April 1840. Through the winter, the majority of members in the

---

[24]During that fall, Palmerston often frustrated the merchants by failing to meet with them at appointed times, refusing additional requests to talk, and returning letters of protest regarding compensation unopened—with his clerks writing across the letter, "returned by Lord P. without observation" (see Fay 1976, 195; Collis 1946, 251–56). These are not the actions of someone in the pocket of the capitalist class.

House of Commons and House of Lords were unaware that the government had already decided on war with China, and had dispatched ships to implement the policy. Rumors were circulating, however, and public pressure led the government in January to promise the release of internal documents. The *Times* broke the story in March with a four-word headline: "War Declared on China." The opposition Tories demanded to know if a war decision had been made, and if so, why Parliament had not been consulted. Finally, in late March and early April, full-scale parliamentary debates began on the crisis—more than half a year since the cabinet's internal decision for war. Tory opposition members, led by John Graham and the leader of the Tory party, Robert Peel, chose for the most part not to challenge the notion that Britain must initiate war against China. As Maurice Collis (1946, 261) remarks, when a parliamentary committee had investigated the opium trade a few years before and "advised against interference with it on revenue grounds," the Tory party had raised no objections. The Tories decided to challenge only the government's handling of the China situation over the past six years that had "allowed a state of affairs to arise [where] a quantity of valuable property was endangered and [where] the whole future of a vast trade was clouded."

During the debates, the Tories pounded the Whig government on its incompetence rather than its immorality in overseeing the trafficking of such a debilitating drug. After they called for a motion of censure against the government, the House met for three straight days starting on April 7 to discuss the motion. Graham led the charge by arguing that significant national interests were at stake. By his estimates, one-sixth of the united revenues of Great Britain and India came from the China trade when one considered import duties of over four million pounds sterling on goods from China along with the two million pounds received by the Indian administration (he studiously failed to mention that this latter income was derived mostly from opium sales) (ibid., 262). Attacking Palmerston directly, Graham suggested that it was the foreign secretary's poor oversight that had now led to the threat to the tea trade from China. In the midst of a series of long Tory speeches reiterating the government's incompetence, a young William Gladstone—essentially alone among his Tory colleagues—spoke of the immorality of the opium trade itself and Britain's error in promoting it (ibid., 267–70). This appeal to liberal democratic values, however, was lost in the collective focus on Britain's material interests.

On the third and final night of debate, Palmerston rose to rebut the charges against him and the government. The Chinese people were demanding Indian opium, and if Britain stopped selling it, this would only lead other countries to fill the gap with Turkish and Persian opium. There were important economic interests at stake. Unless active measures were taken, the China trade could "no longer be conducted with security to life and property and with credit or advantage to the British nation" (quoted in ibid., 271–74; Fay 1976, 203–4). Beijing was acting not to help its citizens but instead only to stop the massive outflow of silver caused by the increased demand for opium. In the end, therefore, "[this] was an exportation of bullion question."[25] As he tried to reply, Graham was shouted down by weary parliamentarians, and a vote was called. The Whig government survived the motion of censure by nine votes. In a series of naval battles over the next year and a half, Britain won the first Opium War. By the treaty of Nanjing in 1842, China opened up four additional ports, gave up Hong Kong, and implicitly agreed to allow the continuation of opium sales into the country.

The Chinese-British War of 1839–42 strongly supports trade expectations theory while upholding aspects of economic realism. It was Britain's very dependence on the triangular trade system in Asia that made its leaders so concerned about the continuation of the opium trade. Without opium sales, two-way trade with India and the Far East would have suffered, and along with it the revenue of the state. Economic realism captures Britain's dependency problem, but it cannot explain why war happened in 1839 and not much earlier. The answer is straightforward. Beijing's decision in 1839 to enforce previous laws banning the sale of opium decisively undermined British trade expectations, forcing the government in London to react. By Lin's actions, it was apparent that this time, the Chinese government was serious. And with massive increases in opium sales destroying the social and economic foundations of the Chinese state, it could not have done otherwise. Yet because London could not end the trade without undermining its own long-term economic power, there was no room for a negotiated solution. Hence even in the midst of crises in the Middle East and Mediterranean, Palmerston and the cabinet decided to launch a large-scale war in Asia.

Liberalism has significant trouble with this case. Dependence on trade with China certainly did not help keep the peace. Recognition of opium's importance to the whole British economy had caused the British government to project naval power into the Canton region when the East India Company monopoly ended in 1833. Still, because the British did not seek formal control of China, it is hard to argue that the fall off in the opium trade in 1839 unleashed preexisting domestic pathologies such as glory seeking and the desire to spread Britain's ideology. More broadly, we see liberal democratic values playing little role as constraining forces pulling the nation back from war. Aside from Gladstone's famous speech against

---

[25] Quoted in Chambers 2004, 196–97; see also Hanes and Sanello 2002, 81.

the immorality of the opium trade, British leaders on both sides of the aisle focused almost exclusively on the material interests at stake. Well into the twentieth century, millions of Chinese citizens would continue to suffer the ravages of addiction as a result of their decisions.

The only unit-level counterargument to trade expectations theory that might offer some explanatory power is the neo-Marxist one. In the end, of course, it is hard to disentangle "national" economic interests from parochial ones: what's good for General Motors—or in this case opium merchants—is often good for the nation, and vice versa. Moreover, there is evidence of Palmerston's cooperation with Jardine Matheson and other merchant firms during the crucial months of September and October 1838. The evidence nevertheless indicates that Palmerston remained his own person during these months, and if anything, he was using the merchants to achieve his geopolitical goals rather than being used by them for their parochial ends. The year 1839 was a decisive one in British history as the country dealt with numerous crises across Europe and Asia, right at a moment when Britain's dominance over global commerce was being challenged by newly industrializing powers. Palmerston was not a man beholden to the interests of big business. Understanding, to paraphrase Napoléon, that commerce was the lifeblood of nations, Palmerston saw that unless threats to that commerce were met quickly and forcefully, the nation's long-term security would suffer.

The Origins of the Crimean War

The Crimean War of 1853–56 is one of the great neglected cases of the international relations field. Aside from discussions by James Richardson (1994), Jack Snyder (1991), Richard Smoke (1977), and Joseph Gochal and Jack Levy (2004), there are few theorists that give more than a passing aside to this fascinating war. This is unfortunate, since the war provides fodder for almost every theory of war out there, from diversionary war and domestic political arguments to inadvertent war theories concentrating on spirals of mistrust. Historians themselves are still deadlocked on the fundamental causes of the war, for two main reasons. First, while there is a great deal of documentary evidence on this case, there is no smoking gun revealing which of the three main actors—Russia, Britain, and France—was most responsible for the war or had the greatest interest in seeing it break out. Indeed, it seems on the surface like one of the few true examples in European history of a war that "nobody wanted." Second, the diplomatic events preceding the war are extremely complex, taking place among five key players over one of the longest periods of intense crisis in modern history (from January 1853 to March 1854). Such complexity makes it difficult to reach a clear judgment on causes in the absence of smoking gun documents.

In the face of such methodological difficulties, I proceed as follows. I begin with a short review of Russia's relations with Britain and France after the resolution of the 1839–41 Eastern crisis. This review will reveal not only the significant increases in economic dependence of both Russia and Britain on commerce through the Turkish Straits after 1840 but also both powers' continued worries about the free flow of this commerce given Turkey's ongoing instability and potential collapse. I then turn to the period from 1850 until late 1852 when France began to contest Russia's historically dominant role in the overseeing of Christian religious sites in the Holy Land, particularly Jerusalem. By December 1852, Turkish concessions to French demands, combined with revolts in Turkish-controlled Montenegro, led Saint Petersburg to worry that without strong action to restore the status quo, it would lose its influence with Orthodox Christians within the Ottoman Empire while Turkey would either fall apart or become dominated by a revisionist France led by the renegade emperor Napoléon III.

My subsequent analysis will make the strong claim that everything that follows from January 1853 on can be traced to one primary Russian fear: that a weakened or collapsed Ottoman Empire would lose control of the Turkish Straits to the upstart French or perhaps to Britain—a situation that would threaten critical Russian economic and political interests. Russia's loss of access through the straits would destroy its current trade into the Mediterranean while undermining the prospect of high future trade essential to its growth as a great power. The fact that Russia lacked an ice-free port in either the north or east made these concerns even more existentially salient. The czar thus provoked a crisis in order to coerce Istanbul into reversing its concessions to France and to reassert Russian dominance on Christian matters within the Turkish realm. He sincerely hoped that this would maintain Turkey's integrity as a state, allowing it to continue as the historical defender of the straits. This was Saint Petersburg's first preference, as it had been since the 1820s. Nevertheless, if the sultan failed to meet Russia's demands or commit to the upholding of his promises, the czar had to make sure that Russia would be positioned to execute his second preference: a military move to control the straits themselves. Diplomacy from January to October 1853 revolved around finding a deal that would meet Russia's minimal demands while assuring Turkey and its supporters that Saint Petersburg would not exert an overbearing influence on the Ottoman state. The failure to find this deal—driven by Russian fear of decline and made increasingly difficult by the overcommitment of reputations on both sides—was what led to the war itself.

This argument competes with three main explanations. Snyder (1991, chap. 5) contends that the war was fundamentally rooted in British and French responses to the destabilizing domestic changes caused by industrialization and democratization. In order to maintain social order and elite control, British and French leaders saw a war with Russia as a tool to whip up nationalist feelings as well as divert the masses attention from problems at home. This reasoning aligns with the overall liberal view that domestic pathologies are ultimately what drive nations into war.[26] Richardson (1994, chap. 5), Smoke (1977, chap. 7), and Gochal and Levy (2004) follow the lead of many traditional historians in asserting that the war was caused by the escalation process itself: by failing to take advantage of opportunities to end the war on reasonable terms during the crisis period, the three great powers fell into an unnecessary war. A third approach, adopted as a partial explanation by many historians, lays the blame on the individual personalities of the key leaders in Russia, Britain, and France. Had Napoléon III not been so driven to revise the system, or had Czar Nicholas not overreacted, or had Prime Minister Lord Aberdeen been more forceful with Russia from the beginning, war would not have occurred.

My argument does not reject all aspects of these contentions. Rather, it shows their limitations in explaining the deeper propelling forces for the war. Maintaining domestic control did push Napoléon III to initiate the dispute over the Holy Land sites. Once the crisis period got under way, though, Napoléon was more than anxious to make a deal to avoid war. It was the increasingly hard line of the British government, tied to the czar's beliefs that Turkey was disintegrating and only a formalized treaty between Russia and Turkey would save Russia's position, that led the states into war. French domestic politics and Napoléon's personality drop out as propelling factors that keep the actors moving toward the abyss. To understand the true causes of war, we must focus on British and Russian behavior. Yet Snyder's argument that Palmerston had a social-imperialist drive to roll back the Russian state is inadequate to explaining Britain's increasing intransigence. Palmerston's internal position during the critical

[26] See also Peterson 1996. Snyder does not bring in the trade dimension, but to the degree that British exports to Russia remained fairly low during 1845–52, Snyder's argument aligns nicely with commercial liberalism's logic. Britain's exports to Russia were about two-thirds of the exports to France and about a quarter of the exports to the German confederation, Britain's biggest European partner (*EHS*, 598; import figures unavailable). Unfortunately for the liberal argument, direct British-Russian trade had been consistently low since the 1820s, and yet the two states avoided conflict over Turkey, as we have seen. More important, as I will show, Britain and Russia both saw strong as well as increasing dependence on third-party trade that passed through the Turkish Straits. It was the future of this trade that drove the dynamics of the crisis.

year of 1853 was relatively weak, given that he was only the home secretary within a coalitional cabinet led by a member of the opposing party, Lord Aberdeen. To be sure, Palmerston along with three or four other individuals did help shift cabinet opinion toward the hard line. But the reasoning that swayed the majority had nothing to do with social order at home and everything to do with traditional British containment of Russian expansion—the very geopolitical logic that Palmerston had been pushing since the early 1830s.

Richardson, Smoke, and Gochal and Levy are correct to say that escalation dynamics made it hard for the powers to pull back from the brink. But the primary puzzle here is why the Russian czar was so willing to take the risks of an uncontrollable escalation in 1853 when he had been so cautious before. Specifically, why was Nicholas so determined to get a formalized treaty from the sultan confirming a return to the pre-1852 status quo—a stance that would likely guarantee that the crisis would spiral upward and bring on war? The answer to this puzzle lays in the difficulties in sustaining positive and stable expectations of the future. The czar had been given verbal promises throughout 1852 that Turkey would honor Russia's traditionally dominant role in the affairs of Christians in the Holy Land and Ottoman territories more generally. These promises had been broken when the Turks decided, under pressure, to meet the French demands for equal status for the Catholic Church in the Holy Land. Nicholas was rightly adamant that only a signed public document would have any hope of ensuring that the Orthodox Church's dominance and thus Russia's position in the region would be restored.

The dispute over control of churches in Jerusalem and Bethlehem may seem minor, but for Russia it was not. There were ten to twelve million Orthodox Christians living in the Ottoman territories. The czar understood that any perception that Russia could no longer protect them would lead to Christian revolts across the Turkish Empire and the disintegration of the Turkish state, creating a direct threat to the straits—a threat he had been fearing since the mid-1820s. A formalized treaty would give the czar greater confidence that Russia's authority with Turkey's Christians would be maintained. Far from wanting Turkey to fall apart, the czar believed that it was Russia's influence over Christians within the Ottoman Empire that would keep that empire together.[27] This meant that expectations of Russia's religious position within the Ottoman Empire were directly tied to Russian expectations of future commercial access through the straits—if the empire fell apart, then other powers might control this critical conduit into the Mediterranean.

[27] This point alone undermines any argument that religious, "pan-Slavic," or any other unit-level drives were pushing Saint Petersburg into a hostile posture.

The czar could not back down, therefore, on his main demand for a formal and public agreement. Yet this became the key sticking point for Britain's main diplomat in Constantinople, Stratford Canning, and his supporters back home. From their perspective, a formalized treaty would shift the balance of influence over the Ottoman realm, potentially making Turkey a vassal state of the Russian bear to the north. Stratford convinced the Turks to reject any such deal in late April 1853, leading to the breakdown of the first and most important of the negotiations held to avert war. Subsequent Russian moves to coerce the Turks to accept a formal treaty led to further negotiations that also fell apart over this fundamental point of disagreement. In short, while escalation dynamics did kick in by mid-1853, making it increasingly difficult to secure a deal, the larger problem was Russia's insistence on a credible commitment by Turkey to the restoration of the status quo. And because Britain convinced the Porte to resist such a commitment, war was inevitable after September 1853.

At the deepest level, then, this was a war driven by a single exogenous fact: the continued instability of the Ottoman Empire. As with so many of the wars studied in this book, Turkey played the role of a weaker third party that both provoked a larger great power crisis and made a negotiated solution impossible. It was Turkey's decision to grant France religious concessions in Palestine and its subsequent unwillingness to commit to reversing these concessions that forced Russia to act before things got worse. This action in turn forced Britain to resist Russian encroachments in the Balkans, further narrowing the bargaining space of deals that both states preferred to war. Both sides understood the risk of inadvertent escalation (indeed, this risk explains their mutual caution prior to 1853). Given Turkey's increasingly unstable empire, however, Saint Petersburg and London knew that such a risk would have to be accepted if an Ottoman collapse threatened their important trading interests in the region. A major crisis over Turkey was becoming increasingly likely by 1852–53, and all it needed was a spark.

Background to the Crisis, 1840–52

As we saw earlier, since the late 1820s Saint Petersburg had maintained a decided preference for a stable Turkey—one that could protect access to the Mediterranean as Russia commercialized its agriculture and tentatively began to industrialize. In 1833 Saint Petersburg had protected the Turkish homeland from Ali's attack, and in 1839–49 it had worked with the British to push Ali back to Egypt. Yet Czar Nicholas could see what all other European leaders could also see: Turkey was a shaky empire that might collapse from within at any moment. He had sat down at Münchengrätz in 1833 with his Austrian counterpart to agree that while the continuation of the status quo was preferred, if Turkey fell apart the two countries should consult about the division of its Balkan territories. Nicholas went one step further in 1844, accepting a secret agreement with Britain's Tory government confirming both Russia's desire to support Turkey's viability and its willingness to consult should the Ottoman Empire appear to be disintegrating. As a signal of his seriousness, Nicholas made the difficult journey to London himself (at a time when his daughter was seriously ill) to negotiate the agreement (Troubetzkoy 2006, 1–36).

The fact that both Britain and Russia were worried about French revisionism helped oil the wheels of diplomacy. France under King Louis Philippe had been trying to grab islands in the Pacific and had balked at London's requests to contain the emerging US threat. In light of this, Nicholas had a sympathetic ear when he sat down on June 4, 1844 with Lord Aberdeen, at that time Britain's foreign minister, to discuss closer ties. Louis Philippe was strengthening France at Russia's expense, Nicholas explained, particularly in the eastern Mediterranean. The key problem for both Britain and Russia in this regard was Turkey's declining health. Revealing his growing pessimism, he said that Turkey was a "dying man." Britain and Russia might try to keep the patient alive, but it was unlikely that they would succeed. When Turkey died, it would be a "critical moment" that would require Russia to put armies in the field, along with Austria. The shared British-Russian problem was the question of who would control Turkey's Mediterranean possessions after its collapse. "I fear nobody in this matter, but France. What will she require?" asked Nicholas. "I fear, much: in Africa, in the Mediterranean, in the East itself. Do you remember the expedition to Ancona? Why should she not undertake similar ones to Crete or Smyrna [a port in Asia Minor]? In such a case, must not England be on the spot with the whole of her maritime forces?"[28]

The czar's goal was to keep France out of the area while avoiding an inadvertent clash of British, Austrian, and Russian forces. The next day, Nicholas continued the discussions with Prime Minister Robert Peel. Nicholas highlighted his concern for the status of Constantinople (a concern that he would reveal in 1853 had almost everything to do with the security of the straits): "I do not want Constantinople [Istanbul]. But if the Ottoman throne falls by its own fault, if it succumbs as a result of its lack of vitality, in a word, if the empire is dissolved, never shall I permit Constantinople to fall into the hands of England, or France." To stress his point that Constantinople should remain a neutral city, Nicholas issued his first

---

[28] Quotations here and in next two paragraphs are from Puryear 1931, 45–50; Troubetzkoy 2006, 25–31.

hard-line warning of the talks, noting that if either Britain or France moved to take Constantinople, Russia would either expel them or preempt their attack. Such language implied a clear choice for the British: accept a deal to ensure Constantinople and the straits were kept out of the hands of any great power, or face a situation where Russia was the dominant player.

Peel remained calm during Nicholas's posturing. He told the czar that it was premature to specify exactly how Turkey was to be divided up, since Turkey was not yet dead. Nicholas quickly agreed, stating that any stipulations regarding what was to be done with Turkey "would only hasten [its] death. I shall, therefore, do all in my power to maintain the status quo," he explained. "But nevertheless we should keep the possible and eventual case of her collapse honestly and reasonably before our eyes. We ought to come to a straightforward and honest understanding on the subject . . . similar to that already existing between Russia and Austria." Nicholas was seeking to secure Britain's agreement to the logic of the Münchengrätz agreement that he had already worked out with Austria eleven years before. Each of the great powers would recognize the importance of trying to keep Turkey alive as long as possible. But if Turkey collapsed, which in Nicholas's mind it would probably do sooner rather than later, Britain, Russia, and Austria had to coordinate their responses to avoid a misunderstanding that might lead to an inadvertent war.

Nicholas left Britain with a verbal assurance from Peel and Aberdeen accepting the above logic. Because Britain had been Turkey's strongest supporter since 1837, London had to keep the agreement secret and informal. To ensure that there was complete agreement, however, Russian Foreign Minister Nesselrode visited Britain and then wrote up a long memorandum summarizing the key points of their "verbal agreement." The first eighteen paragraphs focused on one main point: how the two powers could realize their "common interest"—namely, the maintenance of Turkey's "independence" and "territorial possessions." Two things were seen as critical to achieving this end. First, because Turkey showed an ongoing tendency to break agreements with other powers, pressure had to be applied to stop this practice. Second, because the large Christian population within the Ottoman Empire was an ongoing source of "difficulty" (read: instability) for Turkey, it was essential that the sultan be convinced of the need to treat this population with toleration and respect. Nesselrode's memorandum emphasized that it was the duty of foreign powers "to exert all their influence to maintain the Christian subjects of the Porte in submission to the sovereign authority [of Turkey]."[29] Consistent with their thinking since the 1820s, Nicholas and Nesselrode had no interest in seeing these Christian subjects rise up to overthrow

---

[29] All quotations from Nesselrode's memorandum are from *FPVE*, doc. 32.

their Ottoman masters. As Nicholas had underscored in his talks with Peel, it was Austria that would become the "heir to European Turkey" should the Ottoman Empire fall apart (Puryear 1931, 48). The best outcome for Russia was indeed the status quo, since it would keep Austria from dominating the Balkans while protecting Russian commercial access through the straits.

It is critical to see this point, since Russia's clearly revisionist policy *after* Nicholas's death in 1856 can lead us to assume that Russian czars were always keen to cause trouble in the Balkans to advance their territorial interests. Nicholas's behavior after 1828 consistently shows that a stable status quo was his first choice, with the division of Turkey only a fallback option should Turkey collapse. This fact would come to have decisive significance, since in January–February 1853 the primary thing dividing Britain and Russia was a basic disagreement as to whether Turkey was actually falling apart or would survive as an important state. The Russians were convinced it was collapsing, and hence were anxious to act immediately to either save it one more time or act with Britain and Austria to divide it up peacefully. The British, conversely, believed Turkey was still a viable state. So they moved to protect it from Russian pressure and advances.

The so-called Nesselrode memorandum of 1844 undoubtedly helped convince the British that the Russians believed that maintaining Turkey's integrity was not only the top priority but also a more-than-achievable goal. After all, two-thirds of the memorandum focused on the steps that Britain and Russia, with Austrian assent, could take to keep Turkey's heart pumping. Aberdeen fervently approved of both Nesselrode's initial draft and the revised document he received in late 1844. In the final version, Nicholas had added a phrase indicating that the two powers should consult before Turkey's actual collapse if this seemed imminent. (This phrase would prove important in January 1853 when the czar, to show his fidelity, voluntarily broached the subject of Turkey's impending demise to avoid any Russian-British misunderstanding.) Aberdeen told the Russians that the document accurately captured the understanding between the two states and he hoped to continue to be in agreement "during all our negotiations with the Levant" (see *FPVE*, doc. 33). In stating this, Aberdeen was expressing London's fundamental view of the Turkish question. From the British perspective, both powers would work hard to keep Turkey alive, but only in the extreme situation of imminent death would they consult to discuss its division. At the core of the 1853 crisis, then, was a disagreement as to whether that imminent death had come.

Before turning to the crisis itself, we need to explore the degree to which Britain and Russia were dependent on trade through the Turkish

Straits—and to what extent they anticipated becoming even more dependent in the future. This will help us see exactly why the threat of the closure of the straits was so unnerving to both powers. Britain's trade through the straits increased dramatically after 1838 with the signing of the free trade pact with Constantinople and then jumped again when the Corn Laws that protected British agriculture from imports were revoked in 1846. The move to a free-trading posture was completed by the end of the 1840s, with British manufactures flooding into the non-European world in exchange for food supplies and raw materials. The trend lines were quite startling. In 1838, little grain from Turkish territories was imported into Britain. Within four years, almost a million bushels per year were imported. The figure by 1852 was fifteen million bushels, much of which came from the Danubian Principalities (modern-day Romania), over which Turkey still held nominal suzerainty.[30] As a result of this trade, but also due to the efficiency of British vessels, Britain shipping grew enormously. The number of British commercial ships passing through the Turkish straits increased 800 percent from 1842 to 1852 (from 250 to 1,741 ships) (Puryear 1931, 122–23). By 1852, the island nation controlled fully one-third of all trade out of the Danube River system—a fact that gave both Britain and Austria a huge interest in continued British access to the Black Sea (LeDonne 1997, 320; Puryear 1931, 123).

The growing need for free access to Ottoman grain had been reinforced by the disastrous harvests of the late 1840s and the Irish famine. Yet Turkey was also becoming critical as a market for British industrial goods. Because the rest of Europe was still in a decidedly protectionist mode, seeking to achieve the level of industrialization that Britain had already reached by the 1820s, Britain was finding it increasingly difficult to sell its manufactures to the European continent. As we saw in the discussion on the Opium Wars, British leaders were looking to Turkey, Persia, India, and China as increasingly important destinations for British exports. British exports to Turkey after the 1838 free trade pact rose even faster than imports, leaving the island with a valuable trade surplus that increased its reserves of foreign currency (Puryear 1931, 118–31).

British political leaders understood the net impact of this new trade. We have already seen that Palmerston was convinced that the European manufactured goods were crowding out British products from the markets of Europe and London had to act in support of British merchants

---

[30] Exact percentages from different regions are hard to come by, but Vernon John Puryear's (1931, 127n165) partial figures for 1853 suggest that one-third of Turkey's grain sales to England came from the Danubian Principalities alone, another 30 percent from its nominal possession, Egypt, and the rest largely from other Turkish dominions, including Bulgaria.

(Webster 1969, 2:750–51). Palmerston had of course been the force behind the 1838 free trade deal with Turkey. In 1849, with Russia maintaining its barriers to British manufactures as it built its own industrial base, Palmerston would tell the Commons, "If [from] a political point of view the independence of Turkey is of great importance, in a commercial sense it is no less important. . . . It is quite true that in no country is our trade so liberally permitted and carried on as in Turkey" (quoted in Curtiss 1979, 23–24). In March 1853, Colonel Hugh Rose, a British agent in Constantinople, would tell Foreign Minister Lord Clarendon that Turkey permits Britain to trade "on more advantageous terms than does any other Power," and the collapse of Turkey "would be the signal for the ruin of British trade and interests" (Puryear 1931, 127).

The significance of Turkey to Britain's commercial security came to the fore in an infamous exchange in the House of Commons between free trade radical Richard Cobden and Palmerston in August 1853, during one of the first major public debates of the emerging Crimean Crisis. Cobden adopted his traditional liberal line that war was not the way to further or protect British commerce, and free trade would spread only through the peaceful "conversion" of others to the benefits of exchange. Countering cabinet arguments that Britain had to project British power to protect British trade, Cobden stated,

> A great deal has been said about the necessity of maintaining the independence of Turkey on account of our commerce with her. Now, as a free trader, I must once [and] for all enter my protest against fighting for a market at all. . . . [L]et us not delude ourselves with any idea of danger resulting to the commerce of this country from Russian ascendancy. I maintain that all the commerce we have on the Black Sea is owing to [past] Russian invasions. We never had any commerce in the Black Sea until Russia took possession of the Crimea. (*FPVE*, doc. 62, 325–26)

Such an odd assertion was too much for Palmerston. Despite the fact that he had been privately critical of the moderate position that his prime minister had adopted up to that point, Palmerston rose to address the House. He honored Cobden as the individual who had done more to promote free trade than any other. Yet Cobden was forgetting, Palmerston contended, that "the commercial system of Russia is a restrictive and prohibitory one," while Turkey's was "the most liberal one that exists in any country" with which Britain had relations. Current and especially future commerce with the Ottoman Empire was critical to Britain. Already its products were as essential as those coming from Russia, he noted, "and as her natural and internal resources increase, her commerce will become more and more valuable." It was therefore "of great importance to the commercial interests of England that Turkey should remain independent, in order that a liberal system of commerce may exist." Turkey's modernization program had helped it revitalize. The British government, argued Palmerston, was determined to uphold Turkey's independence in the face of Russian actions—"an independence which we think it essential to maintain both for political and commercial purposes" (ibid., doc. 62, 328–332).

The above shows how crucial Turkey's continued existence was to Britain, not just as a buffer against Russian expansion, but also as a supplier of food and raw materials as well as a means to long-term British economic growth. It is thus not surprising that when Russian actions in early 1853 threatened the commercial and strategic status quo, Britain had to respond. Yet Russia's growing dependence on trade through the Turkish Straits after 1840 is also apparent. As mentioned earlier, Russia had begun to industrialize after 1815 to counter Britain's dominant economic position following the Napoleonic Wars. Russia's strategy was based on the classic infant-industry logic being adopted simultaneously in the United States, France, and Prussia. Agricultural goods would be sold abroad to raise the foreign currency and bullion needed to purchase the (mostly British) industrial and infrastructural goods needed for economic modernization. Under Nicholas's leadership, from 1825 to 1845 Russia increased its imports of heavy machinery by thirtyfold while more than doubling its number of industrial workers and factories. With Russia starting to push its cheap textiles into Central Asia and the Far East, imports of raw cotton from 1830 to 1842 quadrupled from 4 to 16 million pounds, and then doubled again from 1845 to 1850. Overall, Russian total industrial production from 1824 to 1854 more than tripled, from 47 to 160 million rubles, with half of that production in textiles. In Asian and North African markets, therefore, Russia was now competing directly against Britain's traditionally dominant export sector.[31]

To support this industrialization, Russia critically needed to export in its area of comparative advantage—agricultural products, particularly grain. From 1832 to 1840, grain exports were increasing by an astounding rate of 56 percent per annum. By the late 1840s, grain constituted approximately half of Russia's total exports. Improving agricultural techniques had made southwestern Russia the locomotive of this growth. Russian Black Sea ports, especially the modern port of Odessa, grew significantly as a result. By the mid-1840s, Odessa alone was handling one-tenth of all Russian external trade. Three-fifths of Odessa's commerce was in the form of wheat exports, with its major imports being the raw

---

[31] For these figures, see Fieldhouse 1973, 160; Troubetzkoy 2006, 52–53; Puryear 1931, 89n29.

cotton and silk needed for textile manufacturing and export. These up-ward trends were being reinforced over time. After the introduction of larger ships, the total trade tonnage out of Odessa doubled from 1850 to 1852, with 70 percent of its export trade now in grain.[32] Given the nature of the goods, almost all trade going through Russia's Black Sea ports had to pass through the Turkish Straits on the way to or from European destinations. This left Russian commerce highly vulnerable to any closure of the straits.

The czar and his officials were keenly aware of the growing impor-tance of this trade to Russia's long-term development and of Russia's dependence on a waterway controlled by a perpetually unstable regime. In 1844, following the agreement with London, a secret committee was established "to take into consideration the foreign trade of the empire and the best means of extending it." The committee soon discovered that Russian exports out of Saint Petersburg, historically the center of Russian trade with Europe, had not increased for forty years, even as the southern trade had grown enormously. The implication was clear: Russia's whole modernization program and ability to catch up to the established indus-trial powers of Europe now hinged around the effort to increase trade out of the Black Sea. Given this, the committee recommended steps to improve overall efficiency and expand total exports, including abolish-ing export duties, establishing state warehouses for the storage of grain, and improving infrastructure to facilitate the year-round transportation of goods. The British got wind of these reforms and sought to convince Saint Petersburg to do away with all import duties as well, but to no avail. Yet with Britain, Holland, Belgium, and other industrializing states ending import restrictions on grain after 1845 as part of their shift to "freer trade," the result was that Black Sea grain exports became even more critical to Russia's future (Puryear 1931, 97–102).

All this meant that any expected disruptions to trade through the straits took on even greater significance in the early 1850s than they had in the 1820s and 1830s. As Puryear (ibid., 136) summarizes it, Russia now had "a vast interest at stake. Her chief trade route had shifted to the Black Sea and the Straits. Commercial prosperity was possible only if that outlet for her produce were kept open. . . . [Russia's] infant industries, being given governmental support and encouragement, could grow only if their outlet were secure." It is not surprising, then, that Nicholas would be so ada-mant in his discussions with the British that no great power be allowed to control Constantinople should the Turkish state collapse. Of course, the best outcome of all would be Turkey's continued strong dominance of the straits. Back in 1838, as the Turkish dispute with Ali intensified, Nicholas

[32] For these figures, see Puryear 1931, 90n30, 96–97, 104–5; Troubetzskoy 2006, 52–53.

had contemplated sending two naval ships from the Baltic through the straits to demonstrate Russian power. Nesselrode had argued, with Nicholas agreeing, that this would provoke Britain and France, and "the real interests and the true needs of Russia" were "to maintain instead of shaking this political barrier that the Dardanelles establish between us and the maritime powers" (Curtiss 1979, 25). The Russians would continue this obsession with open access through the straits right into the crisis period of 1853. It is to that period that we now turn.

The Onset of the Crisis of 1853

The long crisis of 1853 that led to the Crimean War was triggered by what seems on the surface to be one of the most innocuous of disputes in European great power history: the French versus Russian standoff over which state should control the key religious sites in the Holy Land. For centuries the Ottoman Empire had allowed the Orthodox Church to have primary control over entry and religious observance for such important places as the Church of the Holy Selpuchre in Jerusalem and Nativity Church in Bethlehem. Because Russia was the main Orthodox great power, it had consequently seen itself as having primary influence over religious matters in the Holy Land, and this influence had been formalized by the Treaty of Kurchuk-Kainardji in 1774. In May 1850, however, the French government under Louis Napoléon initiated a challenge to Russia's dominance. Over the next two years, Napoléon pressed hard to undermine Russian dominance and establish at least equality for the Catholic Church—and by extension, France—in the Holy Land. The Turkish state was caught in the middle. It could not afford to offend France, since France now controlled the former Turkish territory of Algeria and had made naval demonstrations against other nominally Turkish North African holdings such as Tripoltania (Libya). Yet it also did not want to upset Russia, the Ottoman's traditional enemy, given the ten to twelve million Orthodox Christians living in Turkey's already-unstable Balkan territories. Giving the Catholic Church equality over religious sites could easily lead to war with Russia, especially if it sparked revolts within the Balkans against Turkish rule.

Turkey sought to square this circle by issuing separate and contradictory decrees in early 1852 that seemed to meet French demands, but also recognized Russian dominance. When Paris discovered the contradictions, it sent its envoy to Constantinople on a French warship—a clear violation of the 1841 straits treaty. Napoléon also menacingly deployed warships into the eastern Mediterranean. The Turks got the message, and in November 1852 arranged to make public only the decree favoring the

French. Going beyond simple equality, the keys to the Holy Sepulchre and Nativity Church were transferred from the Orthodox Church to the Latin (Catholic) Church in December. To make matters worse, in October–November 1852, new and dynamic officials within the Turkish government began to talk about an alliance with France against Russia in order to both reduce Russia's influence over Turkey's Orthodox Christians and dissuade France from using its warships for an attack on Syria and Palestine.[33]

For the czar and his officials, this was not only an underhanded betrayal of Turkey's original promises but also a direct threat to Russia's overall position in the larger eastern Mediterranean/Balkan region. Indeed, although one of the motives for Napoléon's challenge over the holy places had been to build support among conservatives within France, he also saw his move as part of an overall strategy to weaken Russia as France rebuilt its strength (see Ridley 1979, 355–61). As Napoléon's foreign minister wrote to the ambassador in Constantinople in 1850 at the beginning of the new policy (in a passage that was later crossed out), "Finally, there is another consideration of great weight in our eyes because it is connected with still higher interests yet, [namely,] that our influence in the Orient be adequate to counter-balance the always growing [influence] of Russia" (quoted in Saab 1977, 10). From Saint Petersburg's perspective, France had been Russia's main European threat since 1830. It was not only the leading proponent of liberal-nationalist revolutions; French leaders also had constantly sought to break the confines of the 1815 treaty and reassert France's position in the system (thus Nicholas's statement to the British in 1844 that "I fear nobody . . . but France) (Puryear 1931, 46). Napoléon's assumption of the presidency in France in December 1848 and subsequent coup in December 1851 did not assuage Russian fears. While his suppression of left-wing groups was applauded in European capitals, he also showed clear signs that he sought to walk in his uncle's footsteps and renew, if he could, France's dominant role in Europe. Most problematic from the czar's perspective was Napoléon's strong suggestions through 1852 that he would proclaim the Second Empire and turn himself into Napoléon III, emperor of France. For Nicholas, Napoléon's insistence on a hereditary empire and title was highly unnerving, since it meant a rejection of the 1815 ban on any Napoléon assuming power in France. As an internal Russian cabinet memorandum noted, this amounted to a complete overturning of the Vienna settlement (Curtiss 1979, 52). Nicholas tried strenuously through 1852 to convince Napoléon to forgo the empire and title, but he refused. In December 1852, Louis Napoléon was crowned Napoléon III, emperor of France,

---

[33] See Curtiss 1979, 45–48; Saab 1977, 9–12; Troubetzkoy 2006, 86–92.

in a ceremony replicating his uncle's coronation almost half a century earlier (see ibid., 48–57).

The timing could not have been worse—or more suspicious. The French victory in the Holy Lands dispute, coming at the same time as Napoléon's coronation, now seemed like much more than a minor loss in a faraway place. From the czar's point of view, France's victory would mean the collapse of Turkey's empire via the revolts of Orthodox Christians or France's control over the policy of a much weakened Turkish state. Either way, the status quo on the straits would be overturned, to Russia's disadvantage. The final piece of evidence reinforcing that Russia's situation was deteriorating came with the outbreak of a Christian revolt in Montenegro in late November 1852, contrary to the status quo wishes of Saint Petersburg. After initial Montenegrin successes in December, the Austrians sent a delegation to Istanbul to plead the case of Christians living not just in Montenegro but in Bosnia and Herzegovina as well. Austria's hard-line stance convinced the Turks to back down from all-out war against the Montenegrins, leaving the Montenegrins with a more autonomous position that enhanced Austrian influence (see Goldfrank 1994, chap. 7; Saab 1977, 19–22). For Nicholas, this was just one more indication that the "sick man of Europe" was now about to die or would survive only if propped up by another power. He had to act, either to reestablish the pre-1850 status quo, or more likely from his perspective, divide up the empire according to his 1833 and 1844 agreements with Austria and Britain.

It was this situation in December 1852–January 1853 that drove the czar to initiate the steps that eventually led to war in 1854. But when I say "initiate," it is critical to remember that Nicholas and his officials were reacting to a problem that was not of their making. Even in the midst of the negotiations in 1853, Nicholas still preferred the pre-1850 status quo to a division of Turkey with all its attendant risks of war. Nicholas simply no longer believed that the status quo could be preserved without strong action given what other powers were doing to undermine it. As Muriel Chamberlain (1983, 474) nicely puts it, "The situation in the East had suddenly deteriorated as a result of Austrian and French, not Russian, actions."

The growing sense of pessimism in Petersburg is shown by the notes that the czar made in December 1952 regarding how Russia could respond to the Near Eastern developments. Nicholas weighed various courses of actions, but saw all of them as excessively dangerous. Given the deteriorating reality within Turkey's Balkan territories, he observed in the notes, it seemed unlikely that Turkey's integrity could be salvaged. Acting in coordination with other powers for the peaceful partition of Turkey was now viewed as "the least bad of all bad possibilities" (quoted in Rich 1985, 22). Russia would get the Danubian Principalities, Austria the Adriatic coast, and Britain Egypt and perhaps Cyprus. France would probably have to be bought off with the island of Crete. Significantly, the czar's envisioned partition would leave Constantinople as a free city, with complete freedom of commerce through the straits (Curtiss 1979, 62).[34]

In January, Nicholas kicked off a series of talks with British ambassador to Saint Petersburg Hamilton Seymour. These conversations, which lasted until early March, were designed by the czar to achieve two main objectives: communicate to the British the determination on Russia's part to reverse the effects of French actions and hopefully preserve the status quo; and coordinate British-Russian actions according to the 1844 agreement should Turkey end up falling apart, as seemed increasingly probable, at least to the Russians. The irony, considering what ultimately happened, is that the czar believed Britain would be on his side against France and would appreciate his willingness to be forthcoming about his concerns. Russia's ambassador to Britain had written home in December that France was seeking to make trouble for Russia, and English ministers must be shown that "we want to defend the Sultan and not attack him, to sustain him in his rights. . . . [I]n short, to conserve Turkey, but not at all to hasten its fall" (quoted in Curtiss 1979, 60). Nicholas had reason to believe that Aberdeen, as the new prime minister, would be sympathetic to a coordinated response to the new developments. After all, Aberdeen had been foreign minister when the secret agreement of 1844 had been struck. The British themselves, moreover, were worried about Napoléon's intentions. In late 1852 Aberdeen had told Russia's ambassador in London, Philip Brunnow, that he feared Napoléon was gearing up for an invasion of Britain (and indeed the British spent much of the first three months of 1853 preparing their defenses against such an attack) (ibid., 33–34). Such information for Nicholas suggested that London and Saint Petersburg could actually work together to deal with Turkey's shaky status.

Nicholas's conversations with Seymour began informally on January 9, when Nicholas cornered Seymour at a soirée. Turkey was in a critical state, the czar argued. The country was "falling to pieces," and it was vital that Britain and Russia should come to a "perfectly good understanding on these affairs." Seymour replied that this was also his stance. Nicholas continued that the two states had a "very sick man" on their hands and

---

[34] Nesselrode, the czar's closest associate, shared his gloomy outlook. In December, Nesselrode wrote a memorandum indicating that Napoléon was trying to push Turkey into provoking Russia to initiate a war so that Russia, not France, would have to fight a European coalition alone. Out of this war, France would try to take Turkey's eastern Mediterranean possessions or use them as bargaining chips at a future peace conference (Ridley 1979, 359).

it would be a great misfortune if he were to die "before the necessary arrangements were made" (Troubetzkoy 2006, 104–5). Two weeks later, in a meeting at the czar's palace, Nicholas reassured Seymour that Russia had more than enough territory already and that in fact it would be dangerous to acquire more. Nevertheless, the czar stressed, he was responsible for the safety of millions of Orthodox Christians in Ottoman territories. Given Turkey's decrepit state, it was essential for Britain and Russia to have specific contingency plans in case Turkey should fall apart. Seymour responded with the traditional line that it was inappropriate for Britain to plan ahead for the death of an ally. Nicholas said he understood this, but that it was necessary to have at least a gentlemen's agreement so as not to be taken by surprise. Reiterating his long-standing obsession with Russia's commercial and naval access to the Mediterranean, Nicholas repeated his warning from 1844 that he would under no circumstances allow Britain to occupy Constantinople. Circumstances might require Russia to occupy it, yet this would only be on a temporary basis (see Troubetzkoy 2006, 105–7; Curtiss 1979, 67–68).

Seymour's subsequent correspondence with Lord Russell, Britain's foreign minister until the end of February, show that British officials were sympathetic to Nicholas's position. Seymour's note to Russell after the second meeting stated that the czar had been frank and honorable. But he noted that Nicholas was too certain that Turkey would collapse. Far from being outraged by Nicholas's ideas on partition, Seymour told Russell that it would be a "noble triumph" if a division of Turkish lands could be effected without a war, thanks to coordinated great power efforts. On February 8, Aberdeen wrote the queen that Nicholas's comments "were quite in conformity with his previous declarations" in 1844 (Curtiss 1979, 68–69). When Russell wrote back to Seymour the next day, however, he emphasized that Turkey's demise was not imminent, and an agreement on the division of its realm was not only premature but might hasten its death as well (Troubetzkoy 2006, 106–7).

Russell's comment exposed the key fault line between the two countries that would determine the subsequent course of the crisis. The czar was convinced that Turkey was truly tottering on the brink of death. The British believed that its demise, as Russell told Seymour, might not happen for "twenty, fifty, or a hundred years" (*FPVE*, 313–18; Troubetzkoy 2006, 107). Given the czar's fundamentally more pessimistic view of the situation, he saw strong action now as essential. In contrast, given their more relaxed assessment, the British thought moderation was the order of the day. The crisis would turn into a war precisely because these two sets of beliefs made a negotiated solution impossible to find. And given Turkey's truly deplorable state, it was impossible to know which side was right in its prediction.

When Nicholas and Seymour next met on February 20, Seymour informed him of the cautious, noncommittal response of the British cabinet. Seymour also stressed the British view that Turkey was not dying and that London might cause trouble by acting. Nicholas responded that Britain had false information; Turkey was certainly dying, and Britain and Russia should not let themselves be taken by surprise (Curtiss 1979, 69–70). Over the next two days, the two met again, and Seymour read Russell's dispatch of February 9 to Nicholas. In addition to highlighting the two countries' basic disagreement on the health of Turkey, Russell's memorandum spent five paragraphs responding to Nicholas's statement that Russia might have to temporarily occupy Constantinople. The power that controlled "the gates of the Mediterranean and the Black Sea," Russell wrote, would have a "great influence on the affairs of Europe." That influence "might be used in favor of Russia; it might be used to control and curb [Britain's] power." The British cabinet, he remarked, was pleased to hear that Nicholas had no need to extend his empire, and understood that should a "vigorous and ambitious State" (i.e., France) try to replace the Porte in the city, Russia would find war a "necessity." Russell warned, though, that a European conflict might arise should Russia try to permanently control Constantinople, since Britain, France, and probably Austria would oppose such a move. Yet Russell also stressed that his government was willing to renounce any intention of holding Constantinople and make no agreement with other powers regarding the division of Turkey without first talking to Russia (FPVE, 314–15).

In reply, Nicholas reiterated that the British were downplaying the threat to Turkey's internal stability resulting from recent events. The Montenegro crisis in particular was serious and a direct challenge to the sultan's sovereignty. Nicholas underscored that he "[would] not tolerate the permanent occupation of Constantinople . . . by the English, or French, or any other great nation [including Russia]." He nonetheless remained confident that if Britain and Russia worked together, they could neutralize French actions in the area. As for Austria, Nicholas claimed that he spoke for Austria since their larger interests were identical. In his follow-up report to Russell, Seymour told the foreign minister that he and the czar had had a direct discussion on the commercial implications of any new arrangement. He could not remember the exact terms used by Nicholas regarding "the commercial policy to be observed at Constantinople when no longer held by the Turks." But the purpose of the conversation "was that England and Russia had a common interest in providing the readiest access to the Black Sea and the Mediterranean" (Troubetzkoy 2006, 108–10; Curtiss 1979, 70–71).

In sum, Nicholas's language and behavior during this first set of talks had made clear that Russia's policy was one of determination but also moderation. Although he admitted having ordered a military demonstration, he assured Seymour that it was designed only "to prove I have no intention of being trifled with." The British understood the czar's reasonable need to respond to a deteriorating situation. Unfortunately, beliefs about that situation and its true seriousness kept them apart. In one discussion, Seymour reiterated that the key difference between Britain and Russia was that the czar wanted to focus on how to divide Turkey when it fell, while Britain sought to keep Turkey as it was. Nicholas replied that he kept hearing the British make this point, but that "the catastrophe" might soon occur and "will take us all unawares." For Nicholas, that day was almost on them, at least if they failed to work together (Troubetzkoy 2006, 109–10; Curtiss 1979, 73–75).

The Nicholas-Seymour meetings thus ended with no resolution of the fundamental issue. The British did not want to act in concert with Russia if Turkey was not likely to die, given that such action might actually cause its collapse. The Russians believed Turkey was gravely ill, and needed immediate attention either to save it or peacefully manage the division of its territory. Notwithstanding this divide—a divide, it must be emphasized, driven not by irrationality on either side but instead by the inherent uncertainty of the situation—Nicholas came away from the initial meetings feeling assured. He believed that Aberdeen and his cabinet did understand his dilemma, and would at least not oppose Russia if it acted to defend its position in the region. Nesselrode, on the other hand, worried that Nicholas had said too much. So he composed a memorandum for Seymour in early March stating that Nicholas had not proposed partition but rather was only seeking to find out what both sides did *not* want to occur. He noted that the French threats might cause Turkey to refuse to reverse its concessions to the Latin Church, and this in turn would outrage Turkey's large Orthodox majority. Fearing for their safety, revolts by Orthodox Christians might bring on a general insurrection. It was France's use of intimidation and threats, Nesselrode continued, that had led Turkey to break its promises and disregard Russia's interests. If Britain could convince the Turks to see reason and respect their Christian subjects, then the crisis that both sides wanted to avoid could be averted (Curtiss 1979, 74–75).

Nesselrode's memorandum mentioned that Nicholas was pleased with the talks, since both sides agreed that they would not let a strong power control Constantinople and each had renounced any interest in possessing it. Seymour wrote back to disagree with one main point. Contrary to the czar's impression, Britain had indeed acted to get France to moderate its demands and supported Russia's just claims. When Nesselrode and Seymour met on March 10, the foreign minister stated that Russia only wanted Britain to "strive towards opening the eyes of the French

Ministers" to the mistakes they had made. Seymour replied by reading from a late January dispatch from London to Paris in which the British told the French government that while Britain could not take sides in the dispute, it was clear that the French ambassador in Constantinople had been the first to disturb the status quo. Nesselrode expressed satisfaction with this (ibid., 75–76).

The generally positive tone of the talks led Nicholas to continue with his plan to push Turkey to return to the religious status quo ante. Back in January, Nicholas had commissioned Prince Aleksandr Menshikov to go to Constantinople with instructions to reestablish the Orthodox Church's pre-1852 position in the Holy Lands. Importantly, Menshikov was told to get a signed convention (*sened*) from the sultan to ensure his compliance with his promises. Menshikov was to declare categorically that Russia wanted no new concessions on religious matters, but only the rights and privileges that had existed for centuries. If the French should try to bully Turkey into resisting these demands, then Menshikov was given the authority to offer Turkey an alliance directed at France.[35]

Menshikov was ultimately unsuccessful in his talks with the sultan and his officials from March until early May. His harsh undiplomatic style had led a number of scholars to blame him for the failure of the talks and escalation to war that followed.[36] Yet a careful study of the points of contention shows that the Turks and Russians were almost fully in agreement on the concrete issues by the end of April. They got hung up on one and only one issue: the Russian demand that any agreement be formalized in a signed convention or treaty. By April 10, Menshikov could tell Saint Petersburg that Turkey had accepted the substance of his proposals, but a formal treaty had been far more difficult to secure. He asked for clarification on whether he should continue to press for a signed agreement (Curtiss 1979, 118; Rich 1985, 46–47). Nesselrode's telegram back to Menshikov reiterated the significance of securing a formal agreement, although whether it was called a convention, an explanatory decree, or something else was not critical. What mattered, the note stressed, was that the sultan was willing to sign the agreement to show his commitment to uphold it. The czar had felt betrayed by previous verbal promises and needed a signal of the sultan's willingness to meet his obligations (Rich 1985, 47; Curtiss 1979, 118–19).[37]

The fly in the ointment who undermined the emerging deal turned out to be the seasoned British diplomat Canning. Canning had returned

---

[35] Goldfrank 1994, 131; Rich 1985, 35–36; Troubetzkoy 2006, 112–13.

[36] For a review of the arguments and references, see Goldfrank 1994.

[37] In the language of game theory, the czar needed the sultan to make a costly signal of his willingness to uphold his promises.

to Constantinople in late March to take over the British side in the discussions. Despite Stratford's history of taking anti-Russian positions, he at first proved to be quite helpful. He encouraged the Turks to be accommodating, and as we see by Menshikov's April 10 dispatch, this encouragement was having its effect. Furthermore, he was able to mediate between the French and Russians to secure their basic agreement to the key Holy Land issues by April 22. Throughout April, however, Stratford made it plain to the Turkish officials that Turkey must resist any Russian demands for a formalized agreement. Stratford knew that the Russian demand for such an agreement was the only thing holding up a complete resolution of the crisis (Curtiss 1979, 119–20). Yet he was worried that any signed convention would greatly increase Russia's influence over Turkey and lead to a deterioration of Britain's position—a perspective he communicated to London. As the person on the spot, he was carving out his own policy and seeking to get his superiors' acquiescence to it. Still, the fact that the British cabinet did not force Stratford to bend on this final sticking point shows that the majority of its members shared Stratford's concerns.

On April 26, Menshikov reported to Saint Petersburg that he was still having trouble getting the formalized agreement, and it was the sultan's foreign advisers, with "Stratford at their head," who were "encourag[ing] the Ottoman Government to this resistance" (quoted in ibid., 120). On May 5, Menshikov received a reply from the Turks indicating that they would publish new decrees along the lines of the Russian-Turkish agreement. But he received no response to his request for a signed convention. Menshikov wrote back that if the Turkish government would merely agree to incorporate the decrees into a convention, the dispute would be resolved. He offered a draft agreement that moderated Russia's specific demands even as it stressed the importance of assuring Orthodox rights on the basis "of the strict status quo existing today" (quoted in ibid., 121).

Stratford immediately went into action. Over the next four days, he had extended talks with key Turkish officials, and on May 9 told the sultan that "in case of danger he was instructed to request the commander of [British] forces in the Mediterranean to hold his squadron in readiness." With British military support now apparently assured, on May 10 the Turks rejected Menshikov's latest request for a formal convention. Menshikov made a last-ditch effort to appeal directly to the sultan through Reshid Pasha, a Turkish statesman temporarily out of power. But Stratford was able to convince Reshid to delay any action until a vote could be taken in the Turkish Grand Council. In the meantime, Stratford lobbied the council members to convince them to vote against a convention. In the council meeting on May 17, the latest Russian proposal was rejected by a vote of forty-two to three. Menshikov made one final effort on May 20 to secure a deal. Scaling back his demands one more time, he asked simply for a signed note expressing the sultan's commitment to protect his Orthodox subjects. Even this was too much for Stratford. He wrote a memorandum to Reshid laying out reasons to reject this latest Russian suggestion. It would still have the spirit of a treaty, he contended, and would mean undue Russian influence in the internal affairs of the Turkish state. On May 21, Menshikov was informed of Turkey's refusal of his final suggestion and promptly left Constantinople to return to Saint Petersburg (quotation and summary from Rich 1985, 50–57).

The rest of the crisis can be told in short order. Russia's effort to achieve a return to the pre-1952 status quo in order to protect its access to the Mediterranean had failed. War became essentially inevitable, notwithstanding a number of strenuous efforts to keep the peace. By March the French had already deployed part of its navy into the Aegean Sea, but the British had held off from a similar deployment to avoid harming the talks. Once Menshikov left Constantinople and the Russian government heard of the talks' failure, the czar hoped he might still be able to coerce Turkey into accepting a signed convention by the occupation of the Turkish Danubian Principalities (two areas of modern-day Romania). The Danubian Principalities had been a Russian protectorate since the 1828–29 war, but Russian troops had remained outside the territory. In early 1853, the troops had been ordered to the border in case Nicholas needed to use them for coercive diplomacy. By May–June they were poised to enter, and in early July Russian forces crossed the Pruit River to occupy the principalities. The British fleet had been moved in June to Besika Bay just outside the Dardanelles to join the French navy.

The crisis of 1853 had now entered its militarized stage. The complicated diplomatic negotiations that ensued through various capitals over the next few months need not detain us. Suffice it to say that with clear British and French naval support, the Turkish government was even less inclined to accept any formalized agreement with Russia that might suggest Turkey was caving in under pressure. Russia proved relatively accommodating, accepting the terms of the so-called Vienna Note in August that the other European powers had cobbled together to save face for both sides. The Turks rejected its terms, however, and the powers were back to square one. In October, Turkey declared war on Russia for its continued occupation of the principalities, and in November the Turkish fleet was decimated by a surprise Russian attack on the port of Sinope in the Black Sea. Britain and France declared war on Russia in March 1954, and six months later their forces had landed in the Crimean. The war would last until early 1856 until the exhaustion of both sides convinced them to sign a peace accord in Paris. Russia lost its Bessarabian province (bordering the principalities) and agreed to a demilitarization of the

Black Sea. While these were relatively mild terms, Russia's humiliation created an interest in revisionism that would shape European diplomacy for the next half century, as we will see in chapter 8.

To round off this case study, let us briefly examine a key question for bargaining theory: why Britain and Russia through summer 1853 were unable to reach an agreement that both preferred to war (Fearon 1995). Of greatest interest to us here is the increasingly hard-line posture of Aberdeen's government after May 1853, since this stance not only encouraged Turkey to stand firm but also caused the Russians to believe that they had lost a partner they could count on to resist French penetration of the Turkish realm. In early spring 1853, the majority of the British cabinet had still been in favor of moderation. Aberdeen and Lord Clarendon (who had become foreign secretary in March), in particular, believed that Russia had made a reasonable case regarding French efforts to change the religious status quo. Moreover, with the British still worried about a French invasion, London and Saint Petersburg had reason to avoid a clash of arms. So why would Britain adopt an increasing hard line after May—a policy that made war largely inevitable?

One possible explanation is to assert that hard-liners within the cabinet had hijacked government decision making and were sending Britain into war. Snyder (1991), for example, has argued that Palmerston sought war because he was concerned about the rise of the working class and believed that war would divert attention from demands for reform at home. Palmerston was indeed one of two individuals who after April 1853 led the charge to stand up to the Russians, with the other being Russell, demoted from foreign secretary in late February but still a part of the cabinet. There is, however, no evidence to suggest that Palmerston or Russell had control over the cabinet or were in fact seeking war to avoid social reform at home. Russell for his part was the staunchest proponent of social reform within the cabinet and yet also its most consistent advocate of a hard-line posture. Diversionary war motives thus cannot be said to be driving this particular hawk. As for Palmerston, after the formation of the coalition cabinet in late 1852, he uncharacteristically found himself with little real power—as home secretary within a government led by a member of the opposing party, Aberdeen.

Given his experience in foreign affairs, Palmerston's views were no doubt taken seriously within cabinet debates. But influence is not power. Moreover, during summer 1853, far from wanting a war, Palmerston was trying to use his influence to save the peace by the timely deployment of naval power. We know this through the detailed diary notes of insider C. F. Grenville, a British official on intimate terms with almost every leading player of the day. Grenville's diary shows that Palmerston's position, consistent with his views for two decades, was that only a hard-line stance would convince Russia to back away from its coercive posturing. In modern terms, Palmerston's thinking was pure deterrence: the Russians only understood force, and as such, its timely application would make them back down before it was too late.[38] Aberdeen and Clarendon, the two most powerful figures in the cabinet, initially adopted something closer to spiral-model reasoning, believing that the overt use of British naval power would only provoke Russian into unwise military actions (Jervis 1976, chap. 3).

Grenville's private notes reveal that from April until August, British cabinet members were divided not on ends—they all wanted peace—but instead on means: whether deterrence or moderation would best avoid an escalation to war. When the Menshikov talks were showing promise in April and early May, the doves ruled the roost. But Menshikov's exit from Constantinople, combined with the negative spin on events provided by Stratford's reports, led to a distinct shift in opinion regarding Nicholas. It was this change, driven by a textbook increase in mistrust of Russian motives due to Nicholas's strong diplomatic stance, that fueled the spiral that took the nations into war.

Grenville's diary from May 30 notes the great alarm created within the cabinet by the approaching rupture between Russia and Turkey as well as the czar's apparent departure from his recent expressions of moderation. Clarendon was nonetheless still disposed to "give [Nicholas] credit for more moderate and pacific intentions than his conduct seem to warrant," holding that the Russian leader did not see how his actions might be interpreted in Britain (*GM*, May 30, 1853). Word of Russia's impending occupation of the principalities arrived in early June, increasing Clarendon's concerns. There might yet be time for negotiations, given that the czar was driven at least partly by "the exigencies of his position." London therefore might be able to help him "[get] honorably out of the scrap into which he has plunged himself and all Europe" (ibid., June 5 and 13, 1853).

By late June, Palmerston was pushing the cabinet to signal that additional Russian moves would lead to war with Britain. He was overruled by the majority. Contrary to his reputed tendency to dig in his heels, he gave way "with good grace." Indeed, throughout the crisis, Grenville observes, "Palmerston has behaved very well." The basis of the doves' position was straightforward. Clarendon believed that the country "would never forgive the Government for going to war, unless they could show that it was absolutely necessary and that they had exhausted every means of bring[ing] about a pacific solution" (ibid., June 22, 1853).

Aberdeen's attitude had shifted by July 9, however. Despite having spoken with conviction of a settlement ten days before, Aberdeen's

---

[38] See, for example, *GM*, June 22, 1853; July 12, 1853.

confidence in the czar was now "greatly shaken." At the heart of the internal debates was that classic problem of great power politics: uncertainty regarding the character and intentions of the adversary.

> The question resolves itself into this: what are the real wishes and views of the [czar]? If his present conduct is the execution of a long prepared purpose, and he thinks the time favourable for the destruction of Turkey, no efforts will be availing. . . . If, on the contrary, he is conscious that he has got into a dilemma, and he wishes to extricate himself from it by any means not dishonourable to himself . . . then, no doubt, diplomatic astuteness will sooner or later hit upon some expedient by which the quarrel may be adjusted. Which of these alternatives is the true one, time alone can show. (ibid., July 9, 1853)

In early August, Palmerston and Russell were able to draw Clarendon to the hawks' side (ibid., August 1, 1853). By month's end, however, the situation was worsening. Word was received that the Turks had rejected the latest diplomatic initiative (the Vienna Note). Istanbul also was requiring, as a condition for any deal, that Russia evacuate the principalities and guarantee that they would not be occupied again. Clarendon understood that the czar could not accept these terms. From Clarendon's perspective, the problem now lay with the Turks' unwillingness to accept a offer that gave them most of what they wanted, and he suspected Stratford was overly zealous in convincing Istanbul to maintain a hard line. With Napoléon signaling that he wanted out given poor harvests at home, Clarendon was now "almost in despair" at the situation facing Britain.[39]

By early September, even Aberdeen was accepting that Britain could not allow Turkey to be destroyed in a war that now looked increasingly likely. Reports in a German newspaper suggested that Saint Petersburg might be pushing for a general protectorate over the Orthodox Christians within the Ottoman realm. The effect on Aberdeen was shattering. It now seemed that perhaps the Russians did in fact want undue influence within Turkey's empire, as Stratford had been claiming since April (Chamberlain 1983, 485–86). Within the cabinet, Clarendon swung even more to the hawks' side, saying of himself that he was "the most warlike of the [group]" (GM, September 8, 1853). The cabinet was now united around the necessity of projecting military power into the region, either to deter Russia or fight effectively on the side of Turkey if and when war broke out. Dovish opinion had been crushed. By early October, even Grenville admitted to himself that the Palmerstonian position—namely, that using deterrent force early can convince the other to pull back before

---

[39]Through all these discussions, Palmerston had remained "extremely reasonable" (ibid., August 28, 1853; September 2, 1853; September 3, 1853).

things go too far—had probably been right all along. "As matters have turned out, it is impossible not to regret that we were perhaps too moderate and patient at first" (ibid., October 7, 1853).

From this point on, war was essentially inevitable. The Russians could not back away from their hard-line stance without accepting a return to the new status quo—one that threatened their long-term commercial and naval access through the Turkish Straits. The British could not allow the Russians to beat the Turks, since this would imperil their own ability to secure critical grain supplies and export their products into Eastern Europe. At the heart of the problem was the exogenous instability of a third party, the Ottoman Empire, and question of whether it could sustain itself as a cohesive unit into the future. The Russians by late 1952, given what had happened over the Holy Lands dispute, had good reason to think it would soon fall apart. The British disagreed, and believed that the very actions the Russians were taking to secure their position would cause Turkey to crumble. The tragedy of the Crimean War is that there were good arguments on both sides for their mutually antagonistic viewpoints. Given the uncertainty inherent is such a situation, no one could accurately predict how long Turkey would last (and the 1844 summit showed that even the British were not terribly optimistic). Unfortunately, that uncertainty fostered declining Russian expectations of future trade, leading to actions that caused London to worry about its own trade position. The result was a costly war that the agreement of 1844 was designed to avoid, but in the end could not.

CONCLUSION

This chapter has shown that shifting trade expectations played a surprisingly important role in many of the European great power crises and wars from 1790 to 1853.[40] Falling expectations of future trade were a critical, perhaps even predominant, factor for the start of the First Opium and Crimean wars. The liberal argument does poorly in both cases. In the Opium War, economic fears, not domestic forces, were driving British behavior. In the Crimean case, while direct trade between Britain and Russia was relatively low, both countries were strongly dependent on third-party trade that went through the Turkish Straits. When this trade became threatened by the potential collapse of the Ottoman Empire in late 1852, Saint Petersburg and London reacted. Economic realism in both instances can explain the general concern of leaders for their

---

[40] For summaries of the ten case periods covered in this chapter, see table 2.7.

economic vulnerability. But it fails to explain the shifting of behavior from peace to crisis and war.

Trade expectations were also strongly implicated in British, French, and Russian decision making regarding the eastern Mediterranean and Near East issues that hung over the geopolitics of the 1820s and 1830s. Napoléon I's assault on the European system after 1802 was at least partly driven by his fears of Britain's growing control of global trade and the implications of this for France's long-term power position. As is to be expected, some of the cases had nothing to do with changing levels of economic interdependence per se. The wars of the French Revolution were caused by the ideological divide between France and the other great powers along with the fear that this engendered throughout the system. The Austrian and French interventions in Italy and Spain in the early 1820s were likewise ideologically driven conflicts designed to put down liberal as well as nationalist threats to the (re)established monarchical order. Yet it is hard to explain the ebb and flow of great power politics *after* 1822 by reference to the domestic and ideological concerns of the main European protagonists. Russia alternated between encouraging nationalist revolt in Greece in the mid-1820s and efforts to shore up the Ottoman Empire as a protector of its commerce through the Turkish Straits. Britain maintained a highly geostrategic posture through the decades after 1815, obsessed as it was with countering any threats to its trade with the Levant and Far East. Only France could be said to be occasionally dominated by domestic forces that led to dysfunctional actions, as when it supported Ali against the British in the late 1830s and Catholic priests over the Orthodox Church in the Holy Lands dispute of 1850–52. Still, because of France's weak power position, its actions were far less critical than those of Britain and Russia to the ultimate resolution or escalation of the crises of the eastern Mediterranean.

Trade expectations theory outperforms its rivals on all the economically driven cases over the six decades examined, except perhaps for the period of the late 1830s. Neo-Marxism was the weakest theory overall. There is partial support for it in only one case: the First Opium War of 1839–41. Even here, however, pessimistic expectations regarding the China-India trade and its important connection to Britain's national power provide a better explanation for the behavior of Palmerston and the British cabinet during the key crisis months of late 1839–early 1840. Liberalism can account for Russian moderation in the 1839–41 Near East Crisis based on Saint Petersburg's desire not to hurt valuable trade with the Mediterranean region. As we saw, though, the Russians also had reason to be optimistic about the continued flow of trade through the straits—an optimism that underpinned their cooperative posture. Economic realism is at its best in capturing British fears of trade vulnerability during the late 1830s, especially after London committed itself to long-term trade with Turkey. Yet trade expectations theory can explain the growing willingness of the British to risk a clash with France given the increasing threat that the French-backed province of Egypt posed to Ottoman survival.

In the next chapter, I extend the historical analysis to the last half of the nineteenth century. We will see that falling trade expectations had a great deal to do with the rush into a new round of imperialism in the 1880s. Pessimism regarding the trade environment also shaped some of the key crises of the 1890s, most notably the British-German struggle over South Africa leading up to the Boer War of 1899. Some of the crucial developments of the period, including the wars of Italian and German unification, had little or nothing to do with economic interdependence. As with the first half of the nineteenth century, however, we will see trade and commercial factors playing far more important roles in great power politics than most political scientists would expect.

CHAPTER EIGHT

Great Power Politics in the Age of Imperial Expansion, 1856–99

THIS CHAPTER EXPLORES the forty-five-year period after the Crimean War when great powers of all stripes fell into an intense competition for formal political control over third-party territories. The competition greatly increased the level of tension in the system, even if most of the struggles stopped short of a direct great power war. Most significantly, of course, we see France, Britain, and Germany dive into a scramble for colonial territory after 1880 that drew most of Africa and large parts of Asia into the European orbit. On two particular occasions—the Austro-Prussian "Seven Weeks' War" of 1866 and the Franco-Prussian War of 1870—large-scale war between two great powers did break out. The purpose of the chapter is to uncover to what extent and in what manner economic interdependence shaped the struggles and wars of this almost-half-century period.

I show that interdependence and trade expectations were powerful forces for war or peace after 1870, but much less so during 1856–70. For the first fifteen years after the Crimean War, the diplomacy of the European system was driven almost exclusively by the unresolved questions of Italian and German unification. The consolidations of modern great powers out of smaller entities are rare events, but when they occur their potential implications are so revolutionary that they tend to force all other issues off the table. It is not surprising, then, that the four nation-building wars of this time—the Franco-Austrian War of 1859–60 and the three German wars of unification from 1864 to 1870—had little directly to do with changing levels of commerce between nations. As with other chapters, for sake of completeness and to provide a sense of the relative salience of systemic versus unit-level causes of conflict when economic factors are not at play, I will briefly discuss the origins of these wars. My focus is on 1870–99, when interstate economic variables rose once again to the fore. At issue, as always, is the degree to which any of our theories explain the outcomes for this thirty-year period relative to non-trade factors such as simple power accumulation and diversionary motives for conflict. I demonstrate that the trade expectations approach does a surprisingly good job of capturing the shift to a much more intensive phase of great power imperialism in Africa and Asia from 1880 to 1899.

The puzzling move to "new" or "high" imperialism after 1880 offers fertile ground for the testing of theories of international relations, given that practically every theoretical approach out there seems to have a dog in this fight. This chapter adopts the bold position that only trade expectations theory provides a solid across-case explanation for the new imperialist policies of France, Britain, and Germany after 1880. Alternative theories at both the domestic and systemic level prove to be quite limited in explanatory power: the factors they identify were almost always unimportant or merely reinforced the basic trade expectations logic driving the process. France, Britain, and Germany, each in their own way, were propelled into a new round of imperialism by a growing worry about being shut out of potentially valuable areas for raw materials, exports, and investment capital. France started the scramble for fear of losing trade to the more competitive economies of the other two. French actions in Tunisia and subsequent events in Egypt in turn forced Britain, quite reluctantly, into the game. As this preclusive spiral kicked in, Germany under Bismarck found itself compelled to respond to the other two to avoid being cut off from the current and future benefits of trade with the periphery.

Third parties again operate as critical conditional factors that trigger aggressive great power behavior. Italy's desire for control of Tunisia compelled French leaders in Paris to jump in and take the country first, even though domestic political conditions were acting as a restraint on French action. Internal turmoil within Egypt forced the hand of Prime Minister William Gladstone, known for his entrenched dislike of British imperial expansion. Germany's leap into imperialism in 1884 was largely a defensive response to French and British actions, but here too deteriorating local conditions in the Congo and Southwest Africa reinforced the significance of decisive and immediate action. Yet again it was an actor known for his aversion to colonialism—Otto von Bismarck—who found himself drawn into the imperial game to preserve trade access for his nation.

Liberalism and neo-Marxism, with their domestic political underpinnings, have difficulty grasping the rush to colonize Africa and much of Asia. Domestic-level drives for glory, ideological missions, or profits were not propelling the shift to the new imperialism. The French, British, and German governments were reluctant to act, and only did so because of anxiety over the trade door closing. Economic realism is much better on this score: it can tie growing dependence on external materials and markets to the greater need for secure access to third parties. Industrialization after 1860 had moved to a new stage. This so-called Second Industrial Revolution involved innovations in chemical processes and mass manufacturing that greatly expanded the variety of inputs and the ability to realize economies of scale. Any great power's desire to control the trade system will naturally intensify during such times (Barracough 1964). Yet realism once more has trouble explaining the timing of the new imperialism. Why was there a explosion of imperialist activity in the 1880s and not before? What changed the calculi of leaders to account for the new behavior? Falling trade expectations, rather than the arising of new opportunities for aggression, supply the answer.

I will end this chapter with a brief consideration of some of the key imperialist crises of 1890–99—most important, the outbreak of the South African or Boer War in 1899. These crises show that the maintenance of continued access to imperial resources, markets, and investment remained a critical cause of conflict after the initial scramble for territory from 1882 to 1885. Trade expectations were not fully stabilized by the formal imperialism of the 1880s. The crises of the 1890s, therefore, came out of the instability engendered by the preclusive scrambling of the previous decade.

A BRIEF LOOK AT THE WARS OF ITALIAN AND GERMAN UNIFICATION

The war that broke out between France and Italy in 1859 is easily explained. The northern Italian state of Piedmont, led by Camille de Cavour, sought to push Austria out of northern Italy and consolidate a larger Italian nation under Piedmont's leadership. Napoléon III of France saw an opportunity to reduce Austria's strength and grab some Italian territory for himself, so he agreed to help Piedmont achieve its goals. The war of 1859 succeeded in pushing Austria back, and by early 1860, despite Napoléon's defection from the offensive alliance, all of Italy except Rome and Venetia was brought together as a single nation-state.[1]

This was a war of nationalist fervor and (at least for Cavour and Napoléon) personal glory. Economic interdependence played no discernible role in its outbreak. But the war did lead to an important treaty that shaped the subsequent nature of global trade. France's behavior during the war greatly increased British apprehensions regarding Napoléon's perfidy and thus his future intentions. To help cool the rising tension between the two former Crimean allies, London and Paris agreed to a free trade pact in 1860 that was designed to have a self-consciously "liberal" effect on British and French behavior. Negotiated by Cobden, the arch supporter of the liberal vision in England, and Michel Chevalier, a French liberal economist, the so-called Cobden-Chevalier Treaty tore down many of the existing barriers to trade between the two states. Cobden in

---

[1] Albrecht-Carrié 1973, chap. 4; Ridley 1980, chaps. 33–36; Taylor 1954; Smith 1985.

particular believed strongly that the pact would give both sides an incentive to stay peaceful (Coutain 2009).

It is hard to judge the degree to which it kept Britain and France from war after 1860. Peace itself was overdetermined: both states were so obsessed with Prussia's moves to unify Germany in the 1860s that they had good reasons to avoid direct conflict with each other. Moreover, Britain and France continued to struggle for control of West African trade through the 1860s and 1870s, as I discuss below. Nevertheless, the fact that the British-French entente only fell apart in the early 1880s as trade expectations declined suggests that while these expectations remained positive, London and Paris had good security-driven rationales for cooperation.[2] The liberal argument, emphasizing trade's constraint on unit-level motives for war, also has value, at least with regard to Napoléon and the British-French entente of the 1860s. Napoléon's personal and domestic drives for expansion were certainly not tempered overall—in the early 1860s, he made a foolish bid to control Mexico as the United States was distracted by the Civil War. But he did avoid challenging British interests directly.[3]

The wars of German unification, like the Italian wars of unification, were also led by a single individual in pursuit of a larger national dream—Bismarck. Yet with Prussia already a significant state in the European hierarchy, relative power considerations played a much bigger role in the decision-making process. After all, any territorial extension of Prussia automatically increased its overall power in the center of Europe. Economic interdependence between the great powers had no perceptible causal role in the outbreak of wars in 1864, 1866, and 1870. Bismarck certainly understood that the control of the economic resources and markets of independent German states would greatly enhance Prussia's ability to survive against its larger neighbors, particularly Russia. Contrary to the economic realist approach, though, Prussia's dependence on these states did not create a drive to dominate them to reduce vulnerability. The military side of offensive realism prevailed instead: by absorbing these states through a series of opportunistic wars, Prussia would increase its potential power base manyfold. It could then use this base as a hedge against future threats arising from either east or west (Mearsheimer 2001).

---

[2] Positive trade expectations were also reinforced by France's extension of the provisions of the Cobden-Chevalier Treaty to most Western European states (but not Prussia) by 1863. This helped to create a zone of economic cooperation that may have moderated military concerns as well. See Coutain 2009.

[3] Because it is so hard to establish the cause of the British-French peace of 1860–70 through documentary sources, I do not consider this as a case period in table 2.7. British-French trade did more than double between 1860 and 1870 (*EHS*, 598–99), indicating that both the trade expectations and liberal arguments at least have the correlations right.

Bismarck initiated the Danish-Prussian War of 1864 to grab an opportunity to control the long-disputed Danish duchies of Schleswig and Holstein as well as to position Prussia for a future war with Austria. When Denmark's King Frederick died in late 1863, Bismarck used a feud over succession in the duchies to launch a joint Austrian-Prussian military intervention in April 1864. Austrian joined the attack largely to prevent Prussia from controlling the territory by itself. It was rewarded with control of the southern duchy of Holstein, with Prussia assuming control of Schleswig. As Stacie Goddard (2008–9) shows, Bismarck masterfully neutralized great power opposition by arguing that he was operating within the rules of the system, and that with its liberalizing constitution, Denmark was the true threat to European norms.[4]

Subsequent events reveal that Bismarck's sharing of the duchies with Austria was merely a tool to facilitate the next phase of his nation-building enterprise: ending Austria's control of the independent German states. Austria had dominated the pre-1815 Holy Roman Empire, and after 1815 was still the dominant player within the new German Confederation. To eliminate Austria's presence and increase Prussia's control of northern German states, Bismarck needed a war. In June 1866, Austria made the mistake of publicly calling for a final resolution of the status of Schleswig and Holstein. This gave Bismarck the excuse to charge Vienna with violating the 1865 Gastein Convention formalizing the division of the Austro-Prussian authority in the two duchies. He ordered troops to enter Holstein to reestablish Prussian "cosovereignty" over the duchies—a provocative move that led Austria to declare war on Prussia. In the Seven Weeks' War that followed, Prussia quickly defeated Austria in lightning strikes that surprised all of Europe. Bismarck then negotiated a moderate peace to secure Austria's friendship into the future. Austria lost no territory, although it was forced to relinquish any influence over the German states. A new Northern German Confederation was formed under Prussian hegemony. Wisely signaling his limited aims, Bismarck left the future status of southern German states unresolved.[5] The subsequent war with France four years later would bring these states into a new unified Germany.[6]

The Austro-Prussian War sowed the seeds for the 1870 war. The consolidation of Prussia's hold on northern German territories and ease with which Austria was defeated made it clear that Prussia would soon be the dominant force on the continent. The fact that Bismarck refused to

[4] See also Pflanze 1963; Mosse 1958; Steefel 1932; Carr 1991.
[5] Pflanze 1963; Albrecht-Carrié 1973; Pottinger 1966; Wawro 1997; Carr 1991.
[6] Because the 1864 and 1866 wars were both Bismarckian schemes to expand at Austria's expense, I consider1860–66 as one case period in table 2.7.

compensate France with territories along the Rhine, as he had promised in order to keep France neutral, only made French decline seem more real. As Napoléon's privy councillor warned on July 20, 1866, "Grandeur is relative. A country's power can be diminished by the mere fact of *new* forces accumulating around it" (quoted in Wawro 2003, 17). From 1866 to 1870, the French built their military strength while trying to bully their way to concessions. French demands for control of parts of Belgium and the Rhineland territory served Bismarck's purpose of isolating France. Britain, Russia, and even Austria by 1870 had begun to see France as potentially an even greater revisionist threat to the system than Prussia.[7]

Pervasive French fears of decline made it relatively easy for Bismarck to push France into striking the first blow. After a revolution in Spain overthrew Queen Isabella in September 1869, Bismarck lobbied to have Leopold of Hohenzollern, a direct descendant of the Prussian kaiser, assume the throne. If Leopold accepted, Bismarck knew that Paris would not tolerate the encirclement of French territory. He could thereby intensify French perceptions of decline as well as perhaps provoke the French to start a war at a moment when the political and military circumstances—France isolated and Prussia militarily strong—were optimal for Prussia. A reluctant Leopold, through Bismarck's cajoling, accepted the Spanish throne, and the decision was announced on July 3, 1870. Paris took the bait, with hard-line officials arguing for immediate preventive war. Foreign Minister Count Gramont told the legislature on July 6 that Germany's action would "upset to our disadvantage the present equilibrium in Europe" and France had to act (quoted in Wetzel 2008, 8). Gramont sent ambassador Edouard Benedetti to Bad Ems, a spa in southwestern Germany, with instructions to tell Kaiser Wilhelm that he must force Leopold to reject the Spanish offer within two days, "otherwise it is war" (quoted in Richardson 1994, 167). With news of French war preparations, Wilhelm caved, informing the envoy on July 11 that Leopold had withdrawn his candidacy.

The crisis seemed to be over. Yet Gramont and French prime minister Emile Ollivier were frustrated that France had been denied its necessary preventive war (Ridley 1980, 561). On July 13, Paris upped the ante in a clear effort to provoke a Prussian response. Benedetti was instructed to demand a public statement from Wilhelm that he would personally guarantee Leopold would never in the future be allowed to accept the Spanish Crown. Wilhelm rejected the demand, but did allow Benedetti to inform Paris of Wilhelm's "unreserved approval" of Leopold's renunciation of the Crown (Howard 1961, 53; Wetzel 2008, 10).

Bismarck was deeply troubled by Wilhelm's concessions. Seizing on a telegram summarizing the July 13 discussions, he edited out moderate

---

[7]Howard 1961; Pflanze 1963; Carr 1991.

phrases, leaving something that implied an unequivocal rejection of French terms. The altered "Ems telegram" was leaked to the press, and by the next day it was in newspapers across France and Prussia. The ploy worked. The French cabinet agreed that this was an unacceptable insult, and France declared war on Prussia on July 15 (Ridley 1980, 561–62). The French had played perfectly into Bismarck's hands: by making Napoléon appear the aggressor, he was able to isolate France, beat it quickly, and then complete the integration of the southern German states into the unified nation of Germany.

Although the Franco-Prussian War had little to do with economic interdependence per se, it shows just how propelling fears of decline can be in international relations, whether they come from deteriorating expectations of trade or, as in this case, straightforward power considerations. In fact, the Franco-Prussian War is one of those rare conflicts started because both sides perceive themselves to be in decline and want war sooner rather than later. The French understood that the Prussia that emerged out of the war of 1866 would eventually grow to menacing proportions. For his part, Bismarck knew that without the southern German states, the larger German state that he was creating would not have the economic and territorial base for future power against such giant empires as Russia and Britain. In short, while the French concern was of ongoing decline, Bismarck's worries centered on the imminent peaking of German power that would leave his nation vulnerable over the long term to non-French threats.

The period from 1856 to 1870, in sum, illustrates that when wars are being fought to consolidate the very foundations of nation-states, questions of economic interdependence tend to take a backseat. During these times, causal arguments drawn from offensive realism along with theories of preventive war and nationalism come to the fore. Yet by forging two new important states in the heart of Europe, the wars of Italian and German unification intensified the sense of industrial competition that would cause all great powers to look outward to the larger global economy. In particular, fears in Britain and France regarding the rise of Germany and (in the French case) the imperial strivings of Italy would push these two established states into a competition for the control of the periphery that would drive great power politics for the rest of the century. It is to this competition that I now turn.

EUROPE 1870–90 AND THE SHIFT TO THE NEW IMPERIALISM

The two decades after the Franco-Prussian War were a time of relative calm in the center of Europe, largely as a result of the diplomatic efforts of Bismarck, now chancellor of the new state of Germany. Having achieved his objective of uniting the German states under Prussian leadership, Bismarck smartly realized that he had to project relatively benign intentions in order to reduce European fears as well as buy time for Germany to consolidate its gains and develop its economic power. His overarching fear was what he called the "nightmare of coalitions"—other great powers uniting to fight a coalitional war against the rising German state. He thus worked tirelessly to ensure that no coalition against Germany would form, especially one that included France. His efforts were largely although not completely successful. Through the device of the Three Emperors' League—formed in 1872 and then renewed in 1881 after falling apart over the Eastern Question—he was able to bring together Russia, Austria-Hungary, and Germany in a pact that upheld their mutual desires for the status quo in eastern Europe. Through the Dual Alliance of 1879 with Austria-Hungary along with the subsequent Triple Alliance of 1882 with Vienna and Rome, he ensured that Austria-Hungary would rely on Germany to counter growing Russian power in the east (see Weitsman 2004). Above all, through these maneuvers and by encouraging France to take colonies in Africa, Bismarck was able to keep France from forming an alliance with Britain, Austria, or Russia. The nightmare of coalitions was thus temporarily averted.

Yet the so-called Bismarckian system saw its fair share of crises and intense struggles: the 1875 "War in Sight" Crisis, the 1876–78 Eastern Question Crisis that threatened war between Britain and Russia, and most significantly, the intense scramble for colonies that began after 1880. I cover the first two of these events quickly, since there is little historical debate about their causes. The bulk of this section will concentrate on the still hotly contested question of why France, Britain, and Germany (in that chronological order) jumped headlong into new, extensive imperialist programs after 1880—programs that led to the gobbling up of most of Africa and certain parts of Asia between the five short years of 1881 to 1886.

The War in Sight Crisis of 1875 was a direct result of France's remilitarization following its humiliating defeat of 1870–71. France lost Alsace-Lorraine in the peace, and as such, had strong reason for a war of revanche. As France rebuilt its military in 1873–74, German officials actively worried about Paris initiating war once the buildup was complete. As early as October 1873, Bismarck told his ambassador in Paris that "no government would be so foolish if, contrary to its wishes, war had to be considered unavoidable, to await the moment which would be the most agreeable to the enemy" (*GDD*, 1:2, quoted in editor's note). In April 1875, to gauge the opinion of European leaders, Bismarck leaked information to the newspapers that Germany was contemplating a short preventive war against France. As in 1870, Bismarck understood that he could not take on France if the other powers opposed him. Fortunately,

London and Saint Petersburg quickly lodged their objections. By July the crisis had dissipated, and Bismarck resigned himself to living with a revitalized French state.[8]

The 1875 crisis is easily explained by the anxieties engendered by France's quick recovery after 1871 and the threat its remilitarization posed to Germany. Given that Bismarck let the matter drop once other powers objected, it is unlikely he was using the crisis merely to build domestic support for his leadership (although with Bismarck, such internal objectives were often nice by-products of an assertive foreign policy, as we will see). Factors related to economic interdependence had no appreciable effect on the crisis or its resolution. Economic ends related to dependence were not part of Bismarck's decision making, nor was he deterred by the economic implications of war.

The Eastern Question Crisis of 1876–78 has a more direct connection to commercial issues. Revolts broke out across the Balkan territories still controlled by the Ottoman Turks in 1875–76. The Turkish government's brutal treatment of insurgents, particularly in Bulgaria, gave Saint Petersburg the excuse it had been looking for. Ever since the 1856 Peace of Paris, the Russians had been wanting to reestablish the position they had lost in the Balkans as a result of the Crimean War. In April 1877, Russia declared war on Turkey and launched a full-scale attack across the Danube, sending Turkish forces reeling. For the British government under Benjamin Disraeli, this was a replay of the crises of 1830s and 1850s over the Eastern Question, requiring a strong British response to deter a Russian takeover of the Turkish Straits, or worse.

Disraeli, like Czar Nicholas I in 1852–53, viewed the Ottoman Empire pessimistically, believing that it could not likely be preserved in its present form. The decisiveness of Russian military victories and extent of the revolts reinforced this perspective. Hence, he did not oppose limited territorial adjustments that led to independent states and greater Russian influence in the region. Yet Disraeli adamantly opposed, as all British leaders had before him, any form of Russian domination of Constantinople and the straits. When Russia imposed the Treaty of San Stefano on Turkey in February 1878—whose terms included the establishment a large Russian-dominated Bulgarian state with direct access to the Aegean Sea—the British thus responded with force. Disraeli moved naval forces into the Aegean and pointedly brought troops from India through the Suez Canal to suggest that Britain was willing to fight on land as well as sea. The Russians, not wishing a replay of the Crimean War, agreed to Bismarck's proposal for an all-European conference. The Congress of

---

[8]For documents, see *GDD*, 1:1–19. For summaries and references, see Langer 1950, chap. 2; Pflanze 1990, chap. 9; Seton-Watson 1972, chap. 1; Trachtenberg 2011.

Berlin in June–July 1878 led to the Russian acceptance of new terms that greatly altered the Treaty of San Stefano. The newly independent Bulgarian state would be half the size envisioned by San Stefano, have no access to the Aegean, and be hemmed into the south by a newly created province called Eastern Roumelia, a territory that would be administratively autonomous but under Turkish suzerainty. In a side deal, Britain convinced Turkey to hand over the island of Cyprus in return for Britain's defensive support of its remaining empire.[9]

The Eastern Question Crisis, then, ended without another Russo-British war in the Black Sea region. Russian motives for its attack on Turkey appear to be a mix of prestige (the reassertion of Russian influence in the area) and the traditional drive for assured access into the Mediterranean. The British aims were the long-standing ones of keeping Russia bottled up in the Black Sea while containing its overall geopolitical growth. This Palmerstonian strategy, as we have seen, was based on the protection of the commercial value of the Middle East and India to the British state. Disraeli's opposition to Russia was just another in a long line of British actions to defend its economic and political interests whenever they seemed to be threatened by the growing Russian bear.

Trade expectations theory does a good job explaining British behavior in this case, and why the Russians and British fell into a dangerous crisis in 1878. Economic and offensive realism as well as nationalist arguments do a better job with Russian decision making. Unlike 1852–53, Saint Petersburg faced no immediate threat, and was simply looking for an opportunity to recover territory and assure itself of commercial access to the Mediterranean.

COMPETING EXPLANATIONS FOR THE NEW IMPERIALISM

With this broad overview of European diplomacy after 1870 in place, we can turn to the most startling development of the last three decades of the late nineteenth century: the scramble by France, Britain, and Germany to gobble up most of the free territories remaining in the Southern Hemisphere. In understanding the surprising nature of this new imperialism of the 1880s, we need to remember that for two decades after the Crimean War, the European great powers had been largely disinclined to increase their formal control of large tracts of non-European land. For the most part, European states followed the British lead and focused on the building of "informal empires": they developed trading ports around Africa and

---

[9] For summaries and references, see Seton-Watson 1972; Pflanze 1990; Steinberg 2011; Albrecht-Carrié 1973; Taylor 1954.

Asia, and protected their trade rights via gunboat diplomacy, but generally refrained from absorbing independent African and Asian states as colonies. There were, of course, exceptions to this rule. Britain continued to annex princely states in India and in the early 1870s occupied Fiji while expanding control in Malaya. France under Napoléon III captured the southern part of Vietnam in the 1860s as it consolidated French colonial domination of Senegal. Both Britain and France, moreover, intensified their struggle to dominate the growing trade with West Africa. Yet compared to what happened after 1880, we cannot help but be struck by the relative restraint of the great powers in 1856–75. British officials in particular seemed relatively happy to keep costs down and profits high through "free trade imperialism," a term coined by Ronald Robinson and John Gallagher (1961), and even encouraged the formation of an independent Canadian dominion by 1867. With the signing of the 1860 Cobden-Chevalier Treaty, Napoléon also seemed convinced by liberal theory that open markets and trading posts were the best means to promote national economic power. Prussia/Germany for its part captured no colonies, and was led by a someone—Bismarck—who believed strongly (until 1882–83) that colonies were a losing venture that only sapped a nation's power and vitality.

In light of this, we have the puzzle that has animated historical debate since the late nineteenth century: Why did Britain, France, and Germany suddenly rush to annex almost the whole of Africa and large parts of Asia after 1880, to the point where by 1900, these three European powers dominated the non-Latin-American periphery? Needless to say, hundreds of different explanations have been offered to account for the changed behavior. These explanations can be lumped into five main groups, three at the domestic level and two at the systemic level. In what follows, I briefly summarize and critique these arguments before turning to the evidentiary record for each of the three great powers.

The first group of domestic claims includes any variant of the famous Hobson-Lenin thesis that the European great powers embarked on imperialism because of pressure from capitalist firms suffering from overproduction and underconsumption at home. The thesis contends that as the great powers entered a more advanced stage of capitalism, with finance capital concentrated in the hands of fewer and fewer firms and banks, there was insufficient demand from low-wage workers to absorb all the products turned out by highly efficient factories. Faced with unused capacity, powerful business classes after 1880 pushed leaders into grabbing colonies as markets for surplus goods and places to invest surplus capital (Lenin [1917] 1996; Hobson 1902).[10] Critical to this

---

[10] For summaries of other neo-Marxist theorists, including Hilferding, Luxenburg, and Kautsky, see Cohen 1973; Mommsen 1977.

"instrumental Marxist" logic is the idea that leaders are not autonomous but rather forced by the lobbying of capitalist firms and banks into imperialist policies (Krasner 1978).

The second group of domestic-level explanations captures those arguments stressing the desire of leaders to divert the population's attention from problems at home through the pursuit of imperial glory abroad. The development of modern urbanized states in the late nineteenth century created significant class conflict within the main great powers. Traditional agrarian and industrial elites, fearing revolts or electoral victories by the working and peasant classes, used imperial campaigns to unite the population around the glorious nation-state. In this way, traditional elites sought to maintain their hold on power and delay internal reforms threatening their dominant positions. Despite its neo-Marxist emphasis on class politics, this second group of reasons has an important difference from the first: here the political elites are seen as autonomous and acting simply to maintain the existing social order in the midst of significant industrial change, as opposed to trying to help capitalist firms maintain their profitability. Indeed, in the second approach, formal imperialism may be a money loser for most of the firms that do participate. But political leaders believe that it will nonetheless ensure elite dominance at home through the noneconomic appeal of the glorious empire.[11]

The third group of domestic contentions includes all arguments that emphasize the internalization of nonrational ideological or cultural belief systems, typically among the elite classes. Joseph Schumpeter (1951) famously asserted that late nineteenth-century imperialism reflected the atavistic holdover of aristocratic elites seeking glory through empire. Any claim stressing the use of imperial expansion to promote moral ends such as the civilizing of purportedly backward peoples or spreading of Christianity would be included in this third group (Doyle 1986a; Mommsen 1977). In terms of this book's main competing theories, it is worth noting that to the degree that factors within either the second or third groups of arguments kick in after we witness a drop in great power trade, the liberal thesis on trade and war is upheld.

The first group of systemic explanations captures reasoning underscoring imperialism's importance within the larger struggle for military power in the European core. Benjamin Cohen (1973), for example, offers the neorealist logic that under anarchy, states must grab territories to maintain their relative position in the system. Colonies provide direct access to raw materials, and are useful as leverage in the larger economic and political struggle back home. The new imperialism, in Cohen's view, resulted from the intensified competition within Europe after German

---

[11] See Wehler 1985; Snyder 1991; Mommsen 1977, chap. 4; Baumgart 1982, chap. 5.

unification in 1870. In terms of the theories from chapter 1, this position captures the basic economic realist logic of Waltz and Mearsheimer.

The second systemic approach builds on the first, but emphasizes that the main great powers, as security-seeking states, were worried about the declining possibilities for continued open trade after the mid-1870s. Tariff walls began to be erected in the European system in the 1877–81 period, leading France, Britain, and Germany to believe that it was essential to grab colonies now before the door closed, and they were then shut out of key markets and places for raw materials. A pervasive *Torschlosspanik* or "closing-door panic" took hold, creating a spiral of preemptive and preclusive actions that fed on each other, until almost all open territories were absorbed into formal imperial realms (Turner 1967).[12] This explanation aligns nicely with the trade expectations logic: the intense scramble for colonies was a defensive reaction to increasingly pessimistic expectations about the future trading environment.

In what follows, I show that the fifth approach provides a far better explanation for the shift to the new imperialism than the other four. Yet it was not merely the switch to protectionism in the core that provoked the new wave of colonial ventures. France, Britain, and Germany were also driven by the specific threats to their economic positions in places such as Tunisia, Egypt, West Africa, and South Africa. Hence, while a preemptive and preclusive cycle did break out as one great power's defensive moves set off defensive moves by others, new tariff barriers in Europe provided only the general context for great power concerns about the future. To explain the specific moves of the great powers, we need to look at the sequence of events and thinking of the leaders as those events unfolded. I show that among the great powers, France bears the largest share of responsibility for what followed. It was French moves to occupy Tunis in 1881 that started the preclusive ball rolling. Britain followed up these French actions with the occupation of Egypt in 1882. Both states in 1882–83 also began an intense struggle to dominate the river access to the Congo region. It was only after these initial forays by France and Britain that Bismarck reluctantly got into the game to protect Germany's growing trade with Africa.

In the process of supporting the trade expectations argument, I will also demonstrate the weaknesses of the alternative assertions. The first domestic approach has only limited applicability. The worldwide depression that hit Europe in 1873, and lasted on and off for two decades did leave many firms with excess capacity along with a desire to find places abroad to dump their surplus goods and investment capital, and some of these firms did call for colonial expansion to help improve their bottom

---

[12] See also Darby 1987; Fieldhouse 1973.

lines (see especially Darby 1987, chap. 3). But there is one major problem here: the lack of evidence showing that political leaders felt pressured into acting for business interests. Within all three great powers, leaders demonstrated that they were their own persons, and would only act when they saw a larger national interest at stake. The very timing of the imperialist scramble—the fact that it does not truly kick in until the early 1880s—suggests that leaders after 1873 were able to resist the call for colonies and something else intervened to shift their policies.

The second domestic argument seems to do better, especially in explaining Bismarck's surprising shift to a colonial strategy in 1884. There is evidence revealing that Bismarck believed a colonial policy might help right-of-center parties win the October 1884 elections. The argument, however, works poorly for France and Britain. The big French push for colonies came under the leadership of Jules Ferry in 1881 (the taking of Tunisia) and 1884 (the occupation of Madagascar). Yet Ferry understood, as all French leaders before him had, that a colonial policy was *not* popular with either the masses or French legislature. The reason was simple: following the defeat of 1870–71, the overwhelming majority of the population and legislators saw colonies as a wasteful venture that would divert attention from the main objective at hand: the reacquisition of Alsace-Lorraine. Ferry thus moved cautiously in adopting an imperialist stance, engaging the public only when he needed funding for his ventures. In the end, his colonial policy cost him his job: the efforts to acquire Madagascar and northern Vietnam led to his downfall in 1885 for what was widely seen as a disastrous waste of French blood as well as treasure.

The British case represents a decisive refutation of the second domestic contention. Britain's own scramble begins under the Liberal leadership of Gladstone. Gladstone entered into office in 1880 under an anti-imperialist banner that called for a renewal of cooperation via the concert system. He had been known for his personal aversion to imperialism ever since he stood alone against the moral outrages of the opium trade in 1839–40 (see chapter 7). Yet in 1882 he occupied Egypt, and then proceeded to project power into Sudan and West Africa to increase British control of key river systems. He undertook these actions with great reluctance, but felt that he had no choice given the harm French expansionism and local instability would cause to British trade and security.

The German case is the only one of the three that offers some support for the diversionary logic. In fact, other than perhaps the 1937 Sino-Japanese War, it is the only instance in this book where diversionary thinking has any plausibility as a cause of war.[13] As I will show, however,

---

[13] As I show elsewhere, concerns about domestic conflict were not only not driving Germany's hard-line behavior in July 1914, they were actually giving German leaders an incentive to avoid war (Copeland 2000b, chaps. 3–4). And as this book has demonstrated, such

winning the fall 1884 elections through colonial empire building was only a by-product of Bismarck's policy. He had already decided that he needed to protect German trade interests in Africa by the middle of 1883 given French and British actions. By winter 1883–84, he had taken the necessary steps to prepare Germany for a colonial grab. It was only in early summer 1884 that he began to consider using his colonial policy for electoral purposes. The primary propelling force behind his new policy was his declining trade expectations. Electoral politics was only a reinforcing factor, and not even a necessary one at that. In the absence of expected electoral gains, he would have gone ahead with the policy on national security grounds alone.

The third domestic argument—internalized moral and ideological values—is the weakest of all the explanations. Its main downside is that it cannot account for variation across time from low-key informal to all-out formal imperialism. Religious and moral reasons for imperialism were at best convenient justifications for policies as opposed to propelling or even reinforcing factors. They helped elites convince the masses that the destruction of independent societies in the south was for the latter's own good (a *mission civilatrise*) and probably helped the elites overcome the guilt associated with their brutal policies. There is little evidence, however, that some sudden shift in deep values occurred of the kind that would explain the jump into expansive imperialism after 1880.

The main problem with the first systemic explanation, as with offensive realism in general, is simply one of incompleteness. The argument captures a basic implication of anarchy: great powers may see colonies as tools to increase their power and ability to control their futures. But there is nothing that varies on the independent-variable side to explain why great powers would keep their formal imperialism within bounds prior to 1880, and then suddenly start subdividing the world. Declining trade expectations must be brought in to show how the level of perceived threat changed in the early 1880s, pushing the great powers into new behavior—the so-called new imperialism.

KICK-STARTING HIGH IMPERIALISM: THE FRENCH CASE

Because France was the first state to switch to more expansive imperialist policies, it is best to start our analysis there. The French sense of a hostile economic environment was triggered by the onset of the severe recession

---

concerns were not part of British decision making during the Crimean Crisis or Japanese decision making in 1941, the two other most-likely cases of diversionary war in the literature on great powers. (The diversionary argument may still have value for small states, however; see Chiozza and Goemans 2011.)

that swept the system in 1873. The French economy was especially hard hit by the global downturn given its technological inferiority and stagnating population levels versus its key rivals, Britain and Germany. Indeed, France's relative decline had set in prior to the economic crisis, but the crisis only made it worse. Consider some figures of relative power for the five key European states—Britain, France, Prussia/Germany, Austria, and Russia. France's share of iron and steel production had fallen from 15.4 percent in 1860 (versus Britain's 66.4 percent and Prussia's 6.8 percent) to 12.8 percent by 1870, with Britain holding its own at 65.8 percent and Prussia's share rising to 13 percent. By 1880 Germany would have 19 percent of the iron and steel production, while France's share was basically flat at 13.4 percent. Population levels were even more of a concern. In 1860 France's population was 37.4 million, increasing only marginally to 37.7 million by 1880. With Germany's population bounding ahead, the French population's portion of the five-power system fell from 19.4 percent in 1860 to 17.1 percent in 1870, and then to 14.6 percent by 1880, while Prussia/Germany's went from 9.3 percent in 1860 to 15.4 percent in 1870, and finally to 17.6 percent in 1880.[14] This demographic trend affected France's overall growth rates: national income, which had been growing at a modest 1.6 percent per annum in the 1850s–1860s dropped to 0.7 percent per annum by the 1875–85 period (Price 1981, 225).

The pervasive sense that France was becoming globally less competitive was exacerbated by two factors: significant political turmoil at home and the influx of cheap US grain. The establishment of a republic in 1873 only exacerbated preexisting domestic instability. French governments for the next fifteen years were notoriously fragile, often lasting only a few months, and rarely surviving for more than a year and a half. To make matters worse, by the late 1870s, falling transportation costs meant US grain was flooding into France, disrupting local markets in a country still dominated by small-scale agriculture. The deficit of wheat imports over exports, which in the two decades prior to 1878 had never been greater than 14 million hectoliters and had been as low as 971,000 hectoliters, rose to 18 million in 1878 and then 27 million by 1880 (Ashley 1910, 313). The overall trade balance went from a modest trade surplus of 191 million francs in 1872 to a trade deficit of 997 million by 1878, and a whopping 1,565 million by 1880. Given these trends, French agriculture and industry started pushing for an end to the post-1860 free trade system and return to tariff protection. Italy's and Russia's new protectionist policies, announced in 1877, reinforced the perception that France had to respond or be left behind. In early 1878, the French minister of commerce

---

[14] Figures from Copeland 2000b, appendix (based on Kennedy 1987 and the Correlates of War data set); Price 1981, 183.

introduced a plan for increasing import duties by an average of 24 percent. Domestic divisions held up passage of the plan, but by May 1881 his proposals became law with only slight modifications (ibid., 311–16).

By the late 1870s, this sense of decline helped convince French leaders of the need for a more neomercantilist policy in the south, thereby setting the stage for a full-blown push in the 1880s for colonies. If French products were having increasing trouble beating the British and German competition in Europe, perhaps with more governmental support they might secure new markets in Africa. Beginning in 1877, through discriminatory tariffs and increasing contact with inland tribes, France initiated a concerted effort to restrict British trade along the West African coast. This new policy was a reaction to the success of British products in free trade ports established by British merchants. It provoked a strong reaction in London, and by 1880–81, a spiral for control of West African trade was in full swing (Hargreaves 1966; Hynes 1979). As we will see, Bismarck watched all of this with growing concern, knowing that if Berlin did not act, the door to German trade might soon be closed.

In this environment of growing mistrust of other states' economic intentions, it didn't take much to trigger a full-blown scramble for formal colonies. The scramble began with Ferry's occupation of Tunisia in May 1881. Ferry turned out to be France's great champion of colonialism—a leader who during two short stints as prime minister (September 1880–November 1881 and February 1883–March 1885) did more than any other individual to set France on a course for imperial greatness. Like Bismarck, though, he had been a strong opponent of colonialism in the 1870s, seeing colonies as a wasteful distraction from problems at home (his particular interest being education reform) (Power 1944, chaps. 1–2).

This creates a puzzle that all theories must address: How do we explain his sudden "conversion" to a procolonial policy? There is little question that he became convinced by the early 1880s that those calling for greater protectionism and a more active colonial policy had it right, given France's need to compete for markets against the exporting giants, Britain and Germany. In a speech in July 1885, Ferry told the French chamber that for countries such as France, the colonial question was driven "by the very character of their industry, tied to large exports." From this point of view, "the foundation of a colony is the creation of a market." Five years later, in retirement, Ferry penned a more elaborate statement of his perspective. Colonial policy was "the daughter of industrialization." With so many states industrializing simultaneously, great powers must look south for markets for their manufactured goods. The growth of protectionism within Europe had "closed previous markets" and increased competition. Tariff policy might defend French markets, but it was not enough. Protectionism was "a steam-engine without a safety-valve" unless it was balanced by a sensible colonial policy. And with Europe's consumption "saturated," it was essential to find new markets abroad (quoted in Fieldhouse 1973, 22–25).

We might dismiss these statements as post hoc rationalizations of Ferry's colonial policy. But the unit-level explanations for his switch to imperialism have little value. The vast majority of the population and legislators was against colonialism, and both of Ferry's falls from power (November 1881 and April 1885) were the direct result of the perceived wastefulness of his colonial policy.[15] If anything, then, domestic politics should have predicted France's noninvolvement in the colonial scramble, yet the result was the exact opposite, with France being the primary driver of the process. Moreover, the fact that he had earlier opposed colonialism indicates that his push for imperialism in the 1880s was not arising from some personal drive for wealth or glory. Finally, there is no evidence that Ferry was the plaything of capitalist businesspeople; Ferry was an experienced and self-confident politician who remained his own person throughout the process (see especially Power 1944).

The Tunisian occupation of 1881 was provoked not by domestic pressure, or the pressure of French traders or investors in Tunisia, but instead by the fear that if France did not act, Italy would. In 1878, British officials informed the French that they could take Tunisia as a form of compensation for Turkey's ceding of Cyprus to Britain. Bismarck communicated his approval to Paris, saying that the Tunisian "pear" was ripe and ready to be plucked. Importantly, the French did not jump at this offer. For both republicans on the Left and monarchists on the Right, it seemed that Germany was only trying to divert France away from its primary task, the retaking of Alsace-Lorraine (Pakenham 1991, 110; Langer 1950, 221). Over the next three years, however, a problem emerged that could not be ignored. Italy was using its large and growing emigrant population in Tunisia to pressure the Tunisian bey—a leader nominally under Turkish suzerainty, but for all intents and purposes independent—to align with Italy and accept an Italian protectorate over his country. The Kingdom of Italy had cast hungry eyes on the Tunisian state since Italy's final consolidation in 1870. The territory was not simply of economic value; as part of the old Roman Empire, it appealed strongly to growing Italian nationalist fervor (Schuman 1969, 62–63; Power 1944, 33).

---

[15] One cannot argue that Ferry at least *believed* colonialism would help his domestic case. He did not use the Tunisian occupation for electioneering purposes in 1881, and the fact that he lost the October 1881 elections largely because of the Tunisian venture should have made him cautious when he reassumed the premiership in February 1883. It did nothing of the sort: he proceeded to work actively for further colonies, notwithstanding the public's reaction, and paid the price in spring 1885. See Power 1944, chaps. 2 and 7.

As early as October 1878, Italy was warned by the French ambassador to Rome to abandon any plans for a new conquest of Carthage (Power 1944, 38). Yet Italy continued its effort to dominate Tunisia through economic penetration. In July 1880, an Italian commander bought a bankrupt Tunisian railway for four times its value, with the Italian government guaranteeing earnings of 6 percent on the purchase price and on any additional capital investment. This upset even the mild-mannered French premier Charles Freycinet, who told the Italian ambassador that France's "great interests" in Algeria would not allow another power to establish its influence in Tunisia. Private Italian investments were fine. But when the Italian state involved itself in the development of Tunisian ports and railways, this constituted a "constant threat for us and an inevitable source of conflicts" (quoted in ibid., 41).

When Ferry assumed the premier's office in September 1880, he initially had no plans to occupy Tunisia; his focus was still on education reform, specifically the reduction of Catholic influence in the schools. Yet in the struggle for concessions in Tunisia, Thomas Power (ibid., 43) remarks, "Italian activities were becoming more menacing." Three concerns in particular dominated French thinking: the threat to future French investments and trade with Tunisia; the threat to Algeria, France's economic "jewel in the crown;" and the threat of Italian control of the straits between Sicily and Tunisia. France's envoy in Tunis acted strenuously throughout 1880 to defend French economic interests. But by early 1881, it was clear that the Tunisian bey was siding with Italian businesspeople and officials on almost every issue.[16]

As Power concludes, it was the combination of incidents that went against France—all of them seeming to indicate hostile Italian intentions—that finally moved the French government to act. Interestingly, Ferry himself was one of the last of his cabinet to come on board for a formal occupation of Tunisia. In March 1881, he told his foreign minister in a cabinet meeting, "An affair in Tunis in [an] election year, my dear Saint-Hilaire, don't think of it." Within three weeks, however, he was prepared to send troops in Tunisia. Ferry acknowledged in retirement that it was Italy's provocations that pushed him into acting (ibid., 49). In April, using raids by Tunisian tribespeople into Algeria to argue that France had to defend its interests, French troops crossed into Tunisia and proceeded to occupy the whole country. Italy had hoped to get English support to counter a French attack, but when London demurred, Italy wisely chose not to contest the occupation (Schuman 1969, 74–76).

---

[16] Of precedent-setting concern was a Marseille company's loss of its property rights in a local Tunisian court. When London supported the judgment, Paris responded angrily, and both countries dispatched warships to Tunisia. See ibid., 44–48.

The French move against Tunisia, as we have seen, cannot be explained by domestic-level arguments. Ferry and prior French governments had been reluctant to act on Bismarck's offer to grab the Tunisian pear. With no electoral upside and a potentially large downside, domestic factors were operating as a constraint on action rather than a propelling cause for it. One might contend that French investors and traders in Tunisia were pressuring Paris to act on their behalf. Yet this pressure had been a constant since the late 1870s and had been brushed aside by all French governments. It was only when the Italian state showed clear signs of seeking to absorb Tunisia itself, first economically and then politically, that Paris moved reluctantly to formal occupation. We may want to blame Italian nationalism—a domestic-level variable—for France's declining expectations and its provocative action. Yet this still means that it was a factor exogenous to French decision making that ultimately compelled France's response.[17] Trade expectations theory, especially when one brings in Ferry's retrospective points about the global trading system, is upheld and competing arguments disconfirmed.[18]

DEFENDING THE TRADE REALM: THE BRITISH REACTION

The British plunge into the new imperialism after 1880 can be covered more briefly, not only because it is more well known, but more important, because it is much more obviously a result of declining commercial expectations. British leaders under both parties understood that Britain in the 1870s was still the world's dominant industrial state, and so open trade (backed by gunboat diplomacy) was still the most profitable and cost-effective means to grow the national economy. While Disraeli's time in office (1874–80) did witness the acquisition of Cyprus, it was clear to all that he was acting only to safeguard the current empire, not enlarge it. Cyprus had almost no economic value, but it did serve to protect the Suez Canal along with the valuable trade routes to India and Asia. Britain's

---

[17] Conceptually, this is the third exogenous factor from chapter 1.

[18] The trade expectations logic works especially well for explaining Ferry's later land-grabs in 1883–85 during his second administration, such as his occupations of Madagascar and northern Vietnam. By that point, Britain had already taken Egypt (September 1882) and the struggle over West African trade had intensified. Given concerns about France's ability to compete without preferential access, Ferry felt he had to grab first and ask questions later. Domestic factors were constraining, not propelling. In taking Madagascar, for example, as Frederick Schuman (1969, 108) relates, Ferry moved with a minimum of publicity, acting from the realization, "already confirmed by painful experience," that his imperialistic policies, "if openly avowed, would not command the support of the Deputies." See also Power 1944, chap. 5.

battles with the inland Malay tribes in the 1870s also produced little reaction in European capitals. They were seen as actions required to prevent threats to the existing trading ports of Penang and Malaka.

Britain's true shift to the new imperialism came in 1882–84, starting with its occupation of Egypt, and this policy change was initiated by Gladstone, the individual who embodied the ideology of anti-imperialism more than any other British leader in the nineteenth century. Gladstone had begun his career as a Tory, yet in the 1860s jumped to the Liberal Party. By the late 1870s, he had joined the radical-liberal wing: Gladstone not only supported free trade but also believed, like Cobden, that a great power peace was possible only if states could reduce trade barriers and avoid exclusive colonial spheres. He had come out of retirement in 1876–77 to oppose what he saw as Disraeli's immoral neo-Palmerstonian policy—one that notwithstanding the horrific atrocities committed by Turkey in Bulgaria, supported Istanbul over Saint Petersburg. Gladstone's election victory in 1880 was itself directly a function of his radical liberal critique of Tory foreign policy (Seton-Watson 1972; Matthew 1997).

It is highly surprising and ironic, then, that it was Gladstone's administration from 1880 to 1885 that, quite reluctantly, led Britain into a scramble for the formal control of territories. The second and third domestic-level arguments outlined above plainly fall flat. Given his victory in 1880 on an anti-imperialist platform, Gladstone was obviously not shifting Britain to a formal imperialist policy to win elections. And his ideological predilections and moral outlook were constraints on an imperialist policy, not propelling forces. Indeed, his active colonial policy after 1881 can be seen as a crucial case against such unit-level explanations, since his behavior was exactly the opposite of what such assertions would have expected.

The first domestic argument, emphasizing the influence of capitalist elites on foreign policy, seems to have some value. As Philip Darby (1987, especially 55–59) shows, there were concerns among Britain's manufacturing elite that with the global downturn of the 1870s, new markets were needed to absorb the huge productive capacity of British industry. The growing protectionism on the continent reinforced these worries. Moreover, Peter Cain and Anthony Hopkins (2002) contend that Britain's large overseas investments by the late 1870s in such places as Egypt and South Africa made London's "gentlemanly elite" highly sensitive to threats to their capital abroad. The problem with such claims is the lack of evidence showing that Gladstone's imperialist shift was the result of either direct or even indirect pressure from the manufacturing and financial classes. Instead, the evidence reveals that British officials both during Gladstone's government and Lord Salisbury's subsequent Tory ministry (as of June 1885) operated independently of the business classes, and acted because of the overall threat to the nation's economy, not because of threats to particular interests.

It is telling, for example, that Phillip Darby (1987, 23–24, 60–65, 66–73)—one of the few historians to provide documentary support for the neo-Marxist position—ultimately understands where the bulk of the evidence points. British statespeople and officials, he concludes, saw the non-European world "largely through the lens of power politics." Their primary concerns in the 1880s, he notes, were defensive: to hold on to what Britain already possessed. By this period, Britain operated in an "uncertain world order" where "the increasing political discord and the growth of tariff barriers were seen to threaten the established international economic system and Britain's commercial pre-eminence." Chambers of commerce throughout Britain may have made strong public arguments that British firms needed exclusive markets in the face of continental competition. Yet in the end, "probably more influential than arguments about specific interests was the fear of future exclusion."

Gladstone's move into Egypt in 1882 powerfully illustrates the least-of-many-evils logic guiding British officials. The British and French had invested heavily in Egypt for decades. By the mid-1870s, the khedive of Egypt, nominally subordinate to Turkey but essentially independent, had fallen heavily into debt. Despite selling the khedive's shares in the Suez Canal to Britain in 1875, the Egyptian government still owed ninety million pounds to foreign creditors. Debt charges alone constituted two-thirds of the annual revenue (Robinson and Gallagher 1961, 81). In 1876, the khedive was forced to allow his revenues to be managed by an international body run by the English and French on behalf of the European powers. London and Paris directly supervised the running of Egypt's finance ministry under a system that became known as "Dual Control." Disraeli's cabinet was disinclined to act politically on behalf of European bondholders, but did so for the same reason that Britain had been intervening in Egyptian affairs since the 1790s: fear of France. As Foreign Minister Salisbury wrote to a colleague in 1879, Britain sustained its partnership with France to ensure France "[could not] acquire in Egypt any special ascendancy" (ibid., 84; see also Fieldhouse 1973, 113–14).

In 1879, Khedive Ismail fought back against great power interference and dismissed the European financial overseers. London and Paris convinced the Turkish sultan to dismiss Ismail and replace him with his son Tewfik. Unfortunately, the domestic situation in Egypt continued to deteriorate. This was largely the result of French efforts to extract the maximum in debt payments—a policy that overtaxed the peasants and left little for government functions. In September 1881, nationalist colonel Arabi Pasha gained control of the Egyptian state through a coup. Under the banner of Egypt for the Egyptians, he used nationalist sentiment against European officials to increase his domination of the government through winter and spring 1882. Gladstone initially sympathized with Arabi's nationalism and opposed intervention. If events required intervention, he believed, Turkey should do it, not France or Britain (Robinson and Gallagher 1961, 94–103; Pakenham 1991, 124–28).

The French government, under Léon Gambetta's ministry, argued for joint British-French action and the exclusion of the Turks. The French feared any Turkish action might inspire a pan-Islamic uprising in North Africa that would undermine their control over Tunisia and Algeria. In December 1881, Gambetta asked London to support a joint note drawn up to warn Egyptian nationalists that the two powers were determined to reestablish the power of the khedive and system of Dual Control. After much discussion, the cabinet convinced Gladstone that the note would compel changes in the Egyptian government, thereby averting the need for a British military intervention. The note was sent in January, but it had the opposite effect: it mobilized nationalist fervor around Arabi, and a nationalist ministry was formed in February with Arabi as the minister of war. London received reports in March–April 1882 from its envoys that Egypt was falling into anarchy, that the military was increasingly gaining the upper hand, and that European lives were now endangered (Robinson and Gallagher 1961, 96–98).

Gladstone was still seeking to avoid intervention, and the new French premier, Freycinet, who replaced Gambetta in February, was supporting him in this notion. Paris, however, was still against Gladstone's preferred fallback option—Turkish intervention—should things continue to deteriorate. Striving to preserve British-French cooperation, Gladstone agreed to a joint naval demonstration designed to show unified resolve. The French agreed that if the nationalist military officers failed to agree to a compromise with the khedive's faction, Turkish forces would land to restore order. On May 15, London and Paris announced their plan to the other great powers. But in late May, in the face of domestic opposition, Freycinet got cold feet and pulled out of the plan. Gladstone went ahead anyway and deployed the British navy off the Egyptian coast, yet once again the action only ended up consolidating Arabi's control. On June 11 and 12, fifty Europeans were massacred in Alexandra and the British consul was attacked.

Gladstone was now in a bind. British and French coercive diplomacy had only heightened instability in Egypt. Cabinet members were coming to see that military action was needed to protect the canal and that Turkey could not mobilize quickly enough, even if it wanted to. This view seemed confirmed in late June when Istanbul indicated its unwillingness to act to restore order in Egypt. By this time, Arabi was assembling shore batteries in Alexandria to counter any British naval attack. The admiral in charge of the British fleet off Egypt asked permission to bombard the facilities if work was not stopped. This set off another round of intense cabinet discussions, with a majority arguing for an ultimatum to Arabi, regardless of whether it led to an occupation. Gladstone and Foreign Minister Lord Granville held firm to their position that Britain had to maintain its wait-and-see policy.

By July 8, the deteriorating situation pushed Gladstone toward action. As Granville wrote a colleague that day, "Gladstone admitted to me yesterday for the first time that we were bound to protect the Suez Canal" (quoted in ibid., 111). The ultimatum was immediately approved, and when it expired on July 11 the fleet began its bombardment of Alexandria. This only produced additional anti-European riots and a call by Arabi for holy war. Egyptian officials still loyal to the khedive, including those in towns along the canal, were replaced by men from Arabi's camp. In response, on July 20 the cabinet agreed to send an expeditionary force into Egypt's interior and take Cairo if necessary. Four days later, Gladstone asked the House of Commons to support the operation via a 10 percent increase in the income tax rate.[19] He told the House of Commons that Egypt's internal anarchy posed a threat to the canal zone and it was up to Britain to impose the rule of law. Cabinet member Charles Dilke elaborated. Britain had "a predominant commercial interest" in acting given that 82 percent of the trade through the canal was British. The canal was also the principal highway to India and the Far East, where Britain had "vast interests" given its control over 84 percent of China's export trade. The House of Commons quickly approved support for the operation.[20]

In August General Garnet Wolseley landed forces on orders to secure the canal. By mid-September he had assumed control of the whole country. Gladstone promised radicals in his party that the occupation would be temporary, and Britain would leave once internal stability had been restored. Much to French anger, however, Gladstone kept refusing to specify an exit date, and by the time his government fell in June 1885, British forces still controlled Egypt.

The above analysis shows that it was the threat to the Suez Canal that had driven the British to take the country in 1882 (with investments in

[19] As Robinson and Gallagher (1961, 117) note, this was one of the few occasions when Gladstone relaxed his financial caution to support a foreign adventure—a clear sign of "the supreme importance which a restoration of order in Egypt had now assumed." See also Pakenham 1991, 134.

[20] In yet another instance of the risks of pursuing imperialism in France, Freycinet's government was soundly defeated in late July when it asked for money to back the limited plan of defending the canal. Such a move was seen as a diversion from the focus on the Rhine. Robinson and Gallagher 1961, 118–19.

Egypt a crucial reinforcing factor). Given the importance of the India-China trade, the impact on Britain's larger economy of losing the canal would have been huge. Such concerns would lead Britain to hold on to Egypt for another seventy years, and it would fully relinquish control only after yet another incursion to protect the canal zone (chapter 6).

The Egyptian question would come to dominate British-French relations over the 1882–85 period, greatly undermining the trust between the two countries. Perceived British unwillingness to give France a role in the running of Egypt and its finances would intensify Paris's interest in scrambling for trade in the Congo and West Africa. British responses along with London's effort to align with Portugal against the French over the Congo River system would cause Germany to jump into the imperial scramble in mid-1883. With the Tunisian and Egyptian landgrabs, the scramble for Africa, at least for France and Britain, was officially under way. Yet Germany was still not in the game. It is to Bismarck's surprising change of heart on colonial issues that I now turn.

SWITCHING GEARS: BISMARCK AND THE GERMAN CASE

In a very real sense, only Germany's move to the new imperialism remains a puzzle. French and British plunges into expansive formal imperialism in the 1880s reflected straightforward fears about future trade, and were taken despite the fact that domestic and ideological forces were pushing in the opposite direction. The same is not true for the German case. While there is powerful evidence that Bismarck was responding to declining trade expectations, there is also proof that he believed a new colonial policy might help bolster his position at home. Domestic drivers of this policy come in two possible forms: his apparent belief that an anti-British colonial posture would reduce the influence of the Anglophile crown prince Friedrich, and his view that such a posture might help pro-Bismarckian parties win the elections of October 1884. In what follows, I first briefly discuss the evidence for a domestic-level explanation of Bismarck's change of heart. I then show that any domestic force pushing Bismarck was at most only a reinforcing cause for his actions. Fear of having the door shut to German trade as France and Britain scrambled for Africa was the primary factor driving Bismarck. Domestic political gains were at best nice side benefits of his new policy.

The argument that Bismarck acted to reduced the influence of the crown prince goes as follows. Bismarck's relations with the reigning kaiser, Wilhelm I, were good, but by the early 1880s Wilhelm was in his eighties and expected to die soon. Crown Prince Friedrich had married Queen Victoria's daughter, and both greatly admired British-style liberalism. Bismarck thus feared that when Wilhelm died and Friedrich became kaiser, he would fire Bismarck and establish a "Gladstone ministry" that would reverse most or all of Bismarck's state-building policies. Jumping into a colonial empire would allow Bismarck to challenge Britain head-on, raise anti-British feelings within Germany, and make it harder for Friedrich to dismiss Bismarck once he assumed the imperial throne (Pakenham 1991, 204–11).

The main support for this view comes from two comments made after the new policy was already well under way. In September 1884 Bismarck told the czar in a one-on-one meeting, according to Friedrich von Holstein's diary, that "the sole aim of German colonial policy was to drive a wedge between the Crown Prince and England" (September 19, 1884, in HP, 2:161). The second comment is not from Bismarck, but from his son Herbert, one of his confidential envoys during the critical 1883–84 period. In March 1890, after both Wilhelm I and Friedrich had died, and Wilhelm's grandson Wilhelm II was now kaiser, Herbert was asked to explain Bismarck's sudden turn to colonies. He replied that when Germany began its colonial policy, "we had to reckon with a long reign of the Crown Prince" in which British influence would be strong. "To prevent this, we had to embark on a colonial policy, because it was popular and conveniently adapted to bring us into conflict with England at any given moment" (quoted in Kennedy 1980, 171).

This may seem like fairly definitive evidence. Nevertheless, there is good reason to doubt that this logic motivated or even influenced Bismarck's new policy. Holstein's diaries do document growing concerns within Bismarck's ministry about Friedrich's liberal tendencies and even more so his mercurial, unpredictable ways (HP, 2:passim). Yet Bismarck's behavior throughout the 1883–85 period when Gladstone was prime minister reveals that his "hostile" stance toward Britain was purely tactical and chosen only to help secure German colonies. After Gladstone proved accommodating in late 1884 when Bismarck needed London's support against France at the Berlin Conference on West Africa, Bismarck aligned with Britain to further his colonial ends and ensure German trade access to the Congo. If upsetting Britain to isolate Friedrich was his goal and colonial policy only a means, then he should have sacrificed territorial gains to maintain the British-German antagonism that arose through spring and summer 1884. The fact that Bismarck switched to accommodation with Britain shows that this mid-1884 antagonism was a tool to compel London into concessions—one that could be dropped once territorial and trade gains in Africa had been secured.

The contention that Bismarck sought to use colonial policy to win the October 1884 elections has more plausibility. By the late 1870s, there was growing support among right-wing parties for a colonial policy that would challenge Britain's historical domination of foreign markets. As he came to see the value of selective protectionism in the late 1870s, Bismarck parted ways with his former supporter in the Reichstag, the free trade National Liberal Party. The party itself imploded in 1879–80, with right-wing members aligning with conservative parties and the rest remaining committed to the original free trade platform (Wehler 1985, 74–75). In late 1878, Bismarck used two assassination attempts against the kaiser to push through legislation prohibiting agitation against the existing social order—legislation that allowed him to suppress socialist newspapers and organizing efforts. He then proceeded to ramp up his social welfare program to reduce working-class disaffection and the appeal of socialist parties (see Craig 1978, 144–57).

Despite these successes in neutralizing the parties that opposed him, scholars point to an unexpected event in March 1884 that greatly increased Bismarck's worry about the fall elections. This was the formation of a new party, the Deutschfreisinnige Partei, created as a fusion of the National Liberals and the Progressives. By this fusion, the new party was now the largest in the Reichstag. And as Paul Kennedy (1980, 171) notes, if it were able to do well in October, the new party might pose a huge threat to Bismarck's corporatist agenda. In the face of this threat, Bismarck did try to use the prospect of a larger colonial empire through summer and early fall 1884 as a way of increasing the electoral chances of the far-right and center parties, or at least hurting the explicitly anti-colonial Deutschfreisinnige Partei. According to Holstein's diary entry for September 23, 1884, Bismarck went as far as to tell future chancellor Georg Caprivi that "all this fuss about colonies was only being made because of the elections" (*HP*, 2:163).

Here is yet another statement from Bismarck regarding his motives that seems to confirm that internal objectives were primary and determinative, although two things indicate that winning the 1884 elections was neither. The first is the fact that Holstein's diary entry from four days earlier is the source for Bismarck's statement to the czar that the sole aim of colonial policy was to drive a wedge between the crown prince and Britain. So we see Bismarck giving two different statements about his "only" or "sole" aim in pursuing imperialism to two distinct audiences at essentially the same time. For someone of Bismarck's political smarts, it is unlikely that his use of the words "only" and "sole" were mere slips of the tongue. Rather, the contradictory nature of the statements suggests that Bismarck was following his typical pattern of anticipating what audiences wanted to hear and altering his words accordingly. Caprivi was at this point still in the old Bismarckian mode of seeing colonies as a wasteful diversion. As for the czar, we can imagine that he was highly suspicious of Bismarck's new turn to imperialism for simple geopolitical reasons. By telling these audiences he was acting only for domestic reasons, Bismarck could hide his larger strategic goal—the protection of German trade—while assuaging suspicions about his puzzling about-face on colonial acquisitions. If his new policy had been only a short-term domestic maneuver, he should have moderated his imperialism once those domestic goals had been achieved after the October elections. The very fact that he hosted a seminal conference on Africa from November 1884 to February 1885 and then worked diligently both during and after to affirm German colonial gains suggests that domestic ends were only a secondary side benefit of his new imperial policy (see Turner 1967, 52).

Yet there is a second, more decisive reason for doubting the "primacy of domestic politics" in this case. Bismarck showed an active interest in securing Germany's place in the West Africa scramble long before the formation of the Deutschfreisinnige Partei in March 1884, the key event that scholars believe led Bismarck to use colonial policy as a tool for electoral politics. As Henry Turner's detailed work has demonstrated, Bismarck began to be concerned about British-French competition in West Africa in early 1883, and by mid-1883 was actively inserting himself in the process to protect German trade. Tellingly, given his fears regarding the cost of formal imperialism, he initially hoped he could do this through German naval and diplomatic power. But by late 1883 and early 1884, in the face of French and British landgrabbing and resistance to his demands, he saw that formal colonies had become a necessary least-of-many-evils choice. As Turner summarizes it, Bismarck was a "reluctant convert" to imperialism. He was moved to reverse policy "not by the confident expectation of gaining concrete advantages but rather by a mounting concern about the possible adverse consequences of continued abstention." If Germany did not act quickly, the door to its future trade with Africa would be closed, at a point when the true value of this trade was unknown but projected to be potentially high. This closing-door panic led many German elites, including Bismarck, to grab now to avoid anticipated losses later. Declining trade expectations were the primary propelling reason behind Bismarck's radical shift of policy. Winning elections via this policy was a nice "add-on" that arose long after he had changed his mind on colonial acquisitions.[21]

German expectations of the future were shaped to a large degree by the reports of Heinrich von Kusserow, the most knowledgeable official on colonial affairs within the foreign office. In early April 1883, Bismarck received a memorandum from Kusserow on the secret Anglo-French Convention of June 1882, which had only been announced by Paris in March 1883. According to Kusserow's report, Britain and France had not only agreed to divide up territory around Sierra Leone but also had

[21] See Turner 1967, 50–52.

given each other immunity from any discriminatory duties that might be applied to foreign traders—an immunity that would apply to the whole west coast of Africa. As Turner (1967, 53) observes, had this been true, it would have been a foreboding development: "It would have meant the imperialist powers were safeguarding themselves from the effects of the growing protectionist movement in the colonial world by trading mutual privileges to the exclusion of noncolonial powers."

Only eighty years later did scholars show that Kusserow had got it wrong. The British and French agreement promised only to provide equal treatment regarding the protection of life and property (ibid., 53). But in an environment in which France had been imposing differential duties for five years and fighting Britain for direct control of key trading areas, Kusserow's report seemed more than plausible. Moreover, it came on the heels of a memorandum in early March to the German Foreign Office from Adolf Woermann, the head of a key Hamburg company involved in African trade. Woermann noted that the race to partition Africa was accelerating, and even the Portuguese and Spanish were jumping into the game. The British were trying to acquire territory in the Cameroons, an area where German firms had been heavily engaged. These developments, Woermann cautioned, would be "ruinous for German overseas trade, since all of the colonial powers were increasingly placing obstacles in the path of German merchants." He suggested the projection of German naval power into the region and acquisition of an island off the coast of the Cameroons.[22]

That Bismarck took these reports seriously is clear. On April 14, 1883, a German official in Hamburg was informed of the Anglo-French agreement and told to gather information to help Germany negotiate to ensure its merchants were not placed at a disadvantage in West African trade. Among the information Bismarck received back was a strongly worded report from the Hamburg Chamber of Commerce in July stressing the mistreatment of German traders in West African territories already controlled by the colonial powers. The report called for the acquisition by Germany of the Cameroons, remarking that if Germany hesitated, another power would grab its resources and rich interior markets. It was also in early summer 1883 that Berlin received reports that the British colony of Queensland had proclaimed ownership over eastern New Guinea, supposedly in response to rumors that Germany would grab the territory. German suspicions were heightened as well by London's lack of protection of German merchants stationed in Fiji, an island annexed by Britain in 1874. After a court ruled against the merchants, Bismarck asked in April 1883 for a British-German commission to investigate the

---

[22] The quotation is Turner's (1967, 54) paraphrase from the original document.

issue. Gladstone bluntly told Berlin that the matter was now closed—a posture that could only have reinforced perceptions that Britain was moving away from its traditional policy of protecting foreign traders (ibid., 55–57).

By late summer 1883, Bismarck was showing clear signs that his outlook regarding the role of the German state in Africa had changed. A Bremen trader, F.A.E. Lüderitz, had been pressing since November 1882 for official protection of a trading post he wanted to establish in southwest Africa. Bismarck's February 1883 dispatch to London had restated that Germany had no interest in "overseas projects" and indeed would only be too happy to have the British extend their "efficacious protection" to German merchants. In August, however, when Lüderitz reapplied for protection of the harbor of Angra Pequena (in modern-day Namibia), Bismarck wrote in the margin of the foreign office's report on the issue that Germany would "always seek to protect his lawfully acquired rights as long as he is a German subject." The chancellor also initiated a "cautious inquiry" by his embassy in London of British claims to the area near Angra Pequena. Then on August 18, he informed the German consul in Cape Town that he should extend consular protection to Lüderitz's establishment at the harbor. In early September Bismarck informed London that Lüderitz had bought land near the harbor, and he inquired as to any British claims to the bay. Any talk of wanting British protection of German merchants was now noticeably absent (quoted in ibid., 57–59).

This new active intervention did not yet mean Bismarck was convinced that Germany must create formal colonies in Africa. At this point Bismarck, rather than seeking a colony around Angra Pequena, was still interested more in getting London to disclaim any sovereign rights over unclaimed southwest African territory. When his inquiry in September on this issue went unanswered, he repeated it with more force in November. The British response was not comforting. Foreign Secretary Granville admitted to ambassador Georg Münster on November 17 that Britain had no specific claim to the southwest coast aside from Walfisch Bay and a few islands off Angra Pequena. Yet the British government, he continued, would see it as an infringement of British "legitimate rights" should any other state claim sovereignty or jurisdiction over the area from the Cape Colony to Angola (quoted in ibid., 62). London was plainly warning the Germans to stay out of an area that it considered an unofficial part of Britain's sphere of influence.

Bismarck pressed on. In late December 1883, he sent a long note to Münster detailing past British disavowals of sovereignty regarding the southwest coast. He asked pointedly whether the British had installations in the area that could ensure the protection of German citizens. Given that Britain obviously had none, Bismarck was trying to force London to acknowledge Germany's right to protect Angra Pequena itself. Münster presented Bismarck's concerns to the foreign office on December 31. London, though, did not reply for six months. To Bismarck, this silence indicated that Britain had decided to grab the coast for itself. His suspicions had foundation. By January 1884 the British foreign office had turned the affair over to the colonial office, which in turn invited the Cape Colony to annex the Namibian coast. That month a Cape official told the German consul of the Cape Colony's "rightful interests" regarding the coast, and that he hoped Lüderitz's supposed purchase of land would not conflict with these rights (quoted in ibid., 64).

In February, German merchants sent word that the British governor of the Gold Coast (modern-day Ghana) was preparing to annex neighboring Togo. It was learned later that month that Britain and Portugal had signed an agreement giving Portugal the mouth of the Congo River. Britain and France, along with Belgium's King Leopold, had been struggling for more than a year to determine who would control the river's vast potential trade. Since Portugal had long been considered a mere tool of British foreign policy, Bismarck could only have seen these developments as further examples of London's effort to restrict German and French access to prime trading areas. On March 9, an official responsible for Bismarck's communications from his country estate wrote to Berlin that London had dealt with Germany's reasonable concerns "not only with indifference but with severity and deliberate injustice." Bismarck's own anger was becoming apparent: by early April, his dispatches to his ambassadors were peppered with remarks about Britain's *Deutschfeinlichkeit*—its hostility to Germany (quoted in ibid., 64–65; Pakenham 1991, 206–7).

Bismarck's one remaining concern was the potentially high cost associated with formal colonies. This worry was alleviated by none other than Kusserow, who gave the chancellor a memorandum on April 8 outlining the solution: Berlin could use the old English model for India, granting charters to German companies to run new territories for the state. The state itself would only have to pay for the protection of the firms. That same day, a dispatch from Lüderitz was received again asking for protection, this time noting that based on information from his agent in Cape Town, the Cape Colony was about to annex Angra Pequena. Bismarck bluntly told Kusserow, by this point his closest adviser on the colonial question, "Now let us act" (quoted in Turner 1967, 66–69).

On April 19, Kusserow met with Lüderitz and asked him to draw up a plan for organizing the Angra Pequena region. Bismarck sat down two days later with the kaiser and received his approval to take whatever actions were considered appropriate. The next day, April 22, Lüderitz submitted a carefully worded memorandum—clearly shaped by Kusserow's knowledge of what Bismarck would accept—that asked for *Reichschultz* (government protection) for the Angra Pequena territory, but with the recognition that administration costs would be borne by his company. With an implicit agreement with Lüderitz now in place, Bismarck wrote to his consul in Cape Town on April 24 that he should "declare officially that [Lüderitz's Angra Pequena establishments] are under the protection of the Empire." Münster in London was told to inform British officials of this declaration (quoted in ibid., 69–70).

Bismarck's careful attention to the details of his new policy belies interpretations suggesting that he was acting only for domestic advantage. Even as he was plunging Germany into the territorial scramble in Africa, he was formulating a program to minimize the state's direct costs. This would ensure that the new German colonial empire could remain a going concern far into the future. The fact that the German state after 1884 would end up having to take on the formal administration of new acquisitions only reinforces the point. If Bismarck's plan in 1884 was simply to grab territory for short-term domestic gain, he would not have spent so much time establishing a base for a cost-effective German imperial realm, nor would he have reluctantly turned to formal empire after the October 1884 electoral victory. Rather, he would have proclaimed a formal empire in mid-1884 and then sought to minimize Germany's real costs after electoral success. Bismarck had been worried for some time that colonial empire would increase the Reichstag's power, given that it controlled the purse that would pay for it (Pakenham 1991; Craig 1978). The fact that he would willingly hand over more power to the Reichstag after the October elections in order to ensure the permanence of his colonial holdings shows that he was propelled by fear of the closing door, not by domestic concerns.[23]

In sum, this section has shown the power of the trade expectations argument relative to two apparently plausible but ultimately unsatisfying domestic interpretations of Bismarck's new imperialist policy. The most decisive point against the domestic arguments is that of timing. Bismarck embarked on a more forceful defense of Germany's trading rights in spring and summer 1883, long before we see any evidence that he thought a colonial policy would help him with internal problems. Domestic factors were therefore neither necessary nor sufficient conditions

[23] Bismarck's actions from April to August 1884 as well as at the Berlin Conference from November 1884 to February 1885 reinforce this interpretation. He spent May and June trying to keep Britain off the scent as he directed his navy to act preemptively against Togo, the Cameroons, and Angra Pequena (see his interchanges with London in *GDD*, 1:170–80). At the Berlin Conference, he worked with Britain to give the Congo to Belgium, thereby preventing France with its differential tariffs from dominating an area known to possess huge economic potential. He also used the conference to legitimate his new "protectorates" (Togo, Cameroon, and German Southwest Africa) and establish rules that would facilitate acquisition of what is now Tanzania (see Pakenham 1991; Stoecker 1986).

for his actions. Fear of the closing door had already forced a shift in policy before these factors came into play, and Bismarck almost certainly would have continued to solidify his colonial policy through 1884 and into 1885 without them. Domestic gains may have been nice side benefits of the new colonial policy. Who doesn't want to kill two birds with one stone when the opportunity arises? Yet Bismarck had picked up this stone quite reluctantly, and only because he knew that he had no other choice. For the sake of long-term German power, he could not afford to let Britain and France shut his country out from the future benefits of African trade.

THREE CRISES IN THE 1890s

This section examines three crises in the 1890s that brought the European powers of Britain, France, and Germany close to or into war: the Venezuelan border dispute in 1895, the Fashoda Crisis of 1898, and the crisis over South Africa after 1894 that led to outbreak of the Boer War of 1899. The first two crises can be covered briefly, not only because they have been covered well by other international relations theorists, but also because there is little real controversy over their causes. Scholars agree that economic factors played prominent roles in both, although issues of prestige and great power position in the system were also significant. The origins of the Boer War are much less clear, however, and perhaps because of this, it has been largely ignored by the security studies field. This is unfortunate, since it was the only crisis of the 1890s that actually led a European power into a costly and seemingly avoidable war. I show that Britain initiated the war to shore up a declining commercial position in southern Africa caused by the growth of the independent Transvaal Republic and its anticipated absorption of British colonies—developments that, significantly, were being facilitated by German capital and the Transvaal's ties to Berlin.

The Venezuelan Crisis of 1895 between Britain and the United States had straightforward economic roots. Britain and Venezuela had been disputing control of the mouth of the Orinoco River for decades. The area around the mouth was not only rich in raw materials but the river and its tributaries also offered access to the potentially valuable markets and resources of almost the whole of northern South America. That the river would be a nice prize for whatever power controlled it was reinforced in the early 1890s by the discovery of large gold deposits near the mouth. In 1894, the British began to extend their railways from British Guiana toward the goldfields. Rumors that London had claimed the region for Britain were confirmed in April 1894 when the British foreign minister,

Lord Kimberly, released a map showing British railway lines ending inside the river's delta.

With both Britain and the United States on the gold standard, and the United States in particular trying to pull itself out of depression through increases in its money supply and through export promotion, control of Venezuela's gold and markets were clearly of high importance to each. Executive and legislative leaders in Washington unanimously agreed that the British intrusion constituted a direct threat to US economic interests. US anger was fueled by the publication of a pamphlet by a former US minister to Venezuela, William Scruggs, stating that the Orinoco River "was the key to more than a quarter of the whole continent," and Britain planned "to work radical changes in the commercial relations and political institutions of at least three of the South American republics" (quoted in LaFeber 1963, 253).

In the face of this direct threat to US commercial interests, President Grover Cleveland, a leader known for his moderate foreign policies, had no choice but to take decisive action.[24] His secretary of state, Richard Olney, sent London a strongly worded message in July 1895, restating that the Western Hemisphere was in the United States' sphere and London had no right to encroach on US interests. Salisbury, the new British prime minister, was caught up in the affairs of South Africa (see below), but when he responded in early December, he bluntly rejected the universality of the Monroe Doctrine. By doing so, he indicated that Britain would continue to press its claims to the Orinoco. This led Cleveland to make his famous message to Congress on December 17 that the United States would resist by every means, "as a willful aggression against its rights and interests," the appropriation by Great Britain of any territory that rightfully belonged to Venezuela (quoted in LaFeber 1963, 268). Cleveland had taken his nation to the brink. Fortunately, a combination of British concern for South Africa and financial upheaval in the United States allowed cooler heads to prevail, and the crisis was resolved without war (see Kirshner 2007; McDonald 2009).

Scholars who have studied this crisis will accept the above synopsis without controversy. As Patrick McDonald (2009, 162–66) notes, the focus of their academic dispute lies only with the question of why the two sides were able to so quickly end the crisis without conflict (the role played by shared democracy, the capitalist natures of their economies, British concerns for South Africa, etc.). The scholarly agreement on the lead-up to the December crisis simplifies our task here. British encroachment in the Orinoco delta directly challenged US export and resource

---

[24]On Cleveland's full awareness of the economic importance of the Orinoco, see LaFeber 1963, 254. See also Campbell 1976.

interests in both Venezuela and the larger South American region. The harsh US reaction was the direct result of declining US trade expectations. Because Venezuela had been aligned with Washington and indeed had been seeking stronger US support for some time, the United States had no reason to seek a war with Britain prior to 1894. Thus while economic realism helps us understand the US interest in open access to South America, it cannot explain why Washington did not push for the formal control of Venezuela or why it reacted only in 1895. Liberals cannot explain why, given the high trade and financial flows between the United States and Britain, the two countries would come so close to war. Mutual dependence does perhaps capture why both sides in the end wished to avoid war (although British concerns about South Africa were a critical constraining factor) (see ibid., 155–82; Kirshner 2007).[25] Still, such dependence should have kept the peace from the outset, and it did not.[26]

Britain's behavior leading up to the crisis is better grasped by economic realism. Britain, as the world's financial center, was highly dependent on the flow of foreign currency and gold into London's financial district. The push into disputed territory in 1894–95 primarily reflected the desire to increase British control over global gold resources. Unlike in the South African case discussed below, there was no immediate and large-scale threat to Britain's commercial position in South America. The fact that Venezuela had handed out a large contract in the river delta to US companies and was trying to align itself more closely with Washington did suggest that Britain had to move fast to get in on the goodies (LaFeber 1963, 253). But economic realism would be correct to stress that this was Britain acting more on an opportunity for greater commercial control rather than reacting to a significant new threat.

The Fashoda Crisis of 1898–99 can be covered even more briefly, since the events leading up to it are not contested by international relations theorists. The French government clearly initiated the crisis by sending a band of soldiers under Jean Baptiste Marchand to the village of Fashoda in the Upper Nile Valley to dispute Britain's control of the Nile River. Fashoda was located exactly at the point where four major river systems out of French Congo, British Uganda, and Ethiopia came together to

---

[25] On the tie between the South African Crisis and Britain's backing down, see Layne 1994.

[26] Domestic-level arguments that liberals and neo-Marxists might make—that parochial groups that might benefit from war pushed Cleveland—are weak. Cleveland was known to be his own person, and had strongly resisted interest group pressure in the past (e.g., in the Hawaii annexation debate in 1894–95). Even those who contend that hawkish business interests played a role show little evidence that Cleveland was swayed by their arguments over the critical period from January to December 1895, and much proof that Cleveland was influenced by a Mahanian view emphasizing the importance of commercial access to long-term national power (see especially McDonald 2009, 166–82).

become the White Nile. It was also in the middle of territory London saw as part of the British lands needed to complete the "Cape to Cairo" colonial strip that once joined by a railway line, would ensure British economic dominance of the western half of Africa. Since France already controlled most of western Africa, French leaders knew that a move to Fashoda would be highly provocative. They did not expect to force the British to give up the southern part of Sudan to France. Instead, they wanted to use the Fashoda occupation to pressure London to reduce its economic and political hold on Egypt as well as agree to a boundary be-tween British Sudan and French Congo that would ensure French trade access to the headwaters of the Nile, and hence the Nile itself.[27]

The British government could not take such a challenge lying down. Salisbury had gained a reputation in Paris for moderation, but the French move threatened the whole British colonial position in Africa. If the French were allowed to control Fashoda and the surrounding territory, they would wreck the Cape-to-Cairo plan in one fell swoop. More im-mediately, the occupation would give France the opportunity to divert or dam up the key rivers feeding the White Nile. In parliamentary debates in 1895, it had become apparent that Egypt depended on the White Nile to supply summer water—water that was critical, among other things, to a cotton crop worth some ten million pounds sterling. The risk of France holding Egypt hostage over water was a real one. As Sir Edward Grey told the House of Commons in February 1899, building on remarks he had made in October, "The possibility of danger to the interests of Egypt in the Nile Valley, rendered possible by [innovations in] engineering sci-ence, is such as has never existed before, and the conditions are entirely altered" (quoted in Langer 1960, 559).

The new threat to Britain's African trade explains why Salisbury's government was willing to offer no concessions and instead mobilized the British navy for war. Given Britain's overwhelming naval superior-ity and the marked instability of the French polity in late 1898, it was not surprising that the French, after reducing their demands to the bare minimum (French commercial access to the Nile), decided to withdraw from Fashoda completely without securing any compensation.[28] Trade expectations theory therefore does a good job explaining Britain's hard-line stance. Like the United States in 1895, Britain had not sought a war, but was more than willing to fight one when its current and future

---

[27] See Langer 1960, 538–39, 554–68; Snyder and Diesing 1977, 67–68, 531–33; Schultz 2001, 178, 183–85.

[28] Kenneth Schultz (2001, 175–96) also shows that the support of Britain's opposition parties helped to convince the Paris government of Salisbury's willingness to go to war if necessary.

commercial interests were at risk. Economic realism is stronger for the French decision to go to Fashoda. The French government saw an opportunity to improve its access to commerce in eastern Africa and the Nile Valley, and reduce British control of this trade at the same time. No doubt London's decision to send Herbert Kitchener up the Nile to enforce Britain's claim to the Sudan reinforced the French belief that something must be done. The Fashoda scheme, however, had been kicked around for some three years by the time it was implemented; it was less a reaction to a threat than a plan to *create* a threat in order to make commercial gains at Britain's expense.

In sum, the Fashoda Crisis parallels closely the general format of the Venezuelan Crisis, with one power (Britain in 1894–95, and France in 1898) seeking an opportunity for gain and another power (the United States in 1895, and Britain in 1898) reacting fiercely to an emerging threat. The main difference, of course, is that Britain did not believe it was bringing on a crisis over Venezuela, meaning that it was up to Cleveland to bring the two sides toward the brink. France in 1898 was looking for a dangerous crisis precisely to compel Britain to make concessions. Trade expectations theory covers the behavior of the initiator of the first crisis and the defending state in the second, while economic realism does the opposite. Liberalism once again is disconfirmed: Britain and France were strong trade partners in 1898, and as such, should not have fallen into such a militarized dispute, let alone have moved so close to war. While liberal scholars may still claim that mutual dependence and shared democratic norms helped both sides pull back from the brink, the fact that the crisis occurred at all remains a mystery.[29]

THE ANGLO-GERMAN COMMERCIAL RIVALRY AND ORIGINS OF THE BOER WAR

The South African or Boer War is both an easy and difficult case. It is easy because almost all historians agree who started it and for what strategic objective. British officials brought on the war in fall 1899 in order to sustain British supremacy in southern Africa. Individuals such as Colonial Secretary Chamberlain and Prime Minister Salisbury as well as most of the cabinet saw war as the only way to prevent the gold-rich, growing Boer republic of Transvaal from overwhelming British possessions in South Africa in the future. Britain had to act, and act soon. Yet the case is difficult because the documents do not say explicitly *why* continued predominance was so important to these individuals—enough so

[29] For a review of these arguments and an important riposte, see Layne 1994.

as to justify a war that they knew would be costly and hurt relations with other powers, especially Germany. The leaders and officials who led Britain into war operated from the shared assumption that the territories of South Africa could not be allowed to go the way of the US colonies of 1775–83—that is, to become a Dutch-led independent republic united around the gold-rich state of Transvaal and aligned with Britain's primary adversary (in this case, Germany, rather than France as in the American Revolution). Due to the shared baseline, though, these leaders and officials rarely talked about the ultimate ends that made the loss of South Africa seem so critical to the empire.

Given this methodological roadblock, I will proceed as the best historians of the war do, and use inference and logic to both support my argument and show that the alternative explanations are inadequate. The focus of any account of the war must be on the thinking of Chamberlain, who supported the first effort to overthrow the Boer republic in December 1895—the failed Jameson Raid—and carefully managed events throughout the 1895–99 period to bring on war under the most optimal conditions. It was Chamberlain who in 1899 convinced a cautious British cabinet that war was necessary should Transvaal refuse to adopt reforms ensuring future British dominance of the Boer republic. It was Chamberlain who because of Salisbury's variable health and dual responsibilities as both prime minister and foreign minister, was given full control over British dealings with the non-European world. In what follows, then, I examine Britain's situation in the 1890s mainly through Chamberlain's eyes. I argue that the nation's declining global economic position made British leaders sensitive to anything that might make its already-bad situation worse, leading Chamberlain in particular to champion the revitalization of a strong colonial realm. The British colonies in southern Africa were critical to this plan. Given this, all threats to these colonies had to be resisted, especially when they implied direct economic gains for the German state and concomitant commercial losses for the empire.

As Aaron Friedberg (1988) shows, by the 1890s Britons of all stripes woke up to the profound relative economic decline that the country had been experiencing for some two decades. By almost all indexes, Britain after the 1870s was losing ground to the rising industrial powers of Germany and the United States. More than any other official, Chamberlain understood this decline and sought to do something about it. His desired solution was straightforward: use imperial preference tariffs to build tighter ties with Britain's vast imperial realm of colonies and self-governing dominions. This could protect Britain's manufacturing as well as export base from German and US competition as it supplied the island with cheap raw materials and food.

Southern Africa played a critical role in Chamberlain's overall plan in two main ways. First, the area's growing wealth, both in the British colonies and two independent Boer republics (Transvaal and Orange Free State), meant booming markets and cheap raw materials at a time when Germany had undermined Britain's traditional economic dominance in Europe. Second, the Transvaal's vast new discoveries of gold after 1886 had made South Africa increasingly important to the one realm Britain still dominated: global finance. London and its financial district ("the City") were the center of lending, insurance, and currency transfers for the international system. Control of South African gold would ensure confidence in the pound, backed as it was by British gold reserves (see Stephens 2003; Cain and Hopkins 2002).

The looming threat that obsessed British decision makers after 1893 was this: Should Transvaal absorb the British colonies and create a Boer-dominated United States of South Africa, the flow of exports, investments, and gold would be put at risk. In an open trade system, such a loss would mean little, since British firms dominated both the colonies' economy (the Cape Colony and Natal) and gold production in the Transvaal. Since the late 1880s, however, Transvaal had been trying to align with Germany to offset Britain's commanding role in the region. If Transvaal succeeded in uniting the region, the newly formed state would undoubtedly lean even more heavily on Germany. Moreover, the Transvaal regularly practiced economic discrimination against British products coming through the Cape Colony. Any new and independent Republic of South Africa controlled by Transvaal would likely do the same, but on a much larger scale. The impact on British economic power, already in decline relative to Germany, would be significant. Lower exports would mean reduced profits for British firms along with less gold and foreign currency flowing back to the home island. This would exacerbate Britain's historically large trade deficit while undermining confidence in the country's financial sector, all at a time when dominance in global banking and insurance was the only thing keeping the British pound strong (Friedberg 1988; Kennedy 1980, 1987). And the European power that would slip in to fill the gap would, of course, be Germany.

The figures on British decline after 1870 in areas other than finance are quite startling. Of the five-power European system of Britain, France, Germany, Russia, and Austria, Britain produced an amazing 61 percent of the system's total iron and steel in 1870, with Germany at 13 percent and Russia at only 4 percent of the total. But by 1900 Germany had overtaken Britain, producing 40 percent of system total and Britain only 30 percent (with Russia at 13 percent).[30] Britain's position in manufacturing

---

[30] Copeland 2000b, table A.2, calculated from the Correlates of War data set.

was also slipping dramatically. Its share of world manufacturing in 1870 was 32 percent and Germany's was 13 percent; thirty years later it was 20 percent to Germany's 17 percent, and by 1906–10, Germany would overtake Britain with a 16 percent share compared to Britain's 15 percent (Friedberg 1988, 26).[31] Britain's falling competitiveness took its toll on its trade balance. Through the latter half of the nineteenth century, Britain ran trade deficits that were offset by payments for its banking, shipping, and insurance services. When Britain's manufacturing was at its height, however, these deficits were relatively small. In 1872, the year when British exports peaked relative to imports, the trade deficit was approximately 11 percent of the total import bill. Over the next quarter century, as imports rose and exports leveled off or fell, the deficit ballooned, such that by 1898, it represented a staggering 38 percent of imports (Fieldhouse 1973, table 1).[32]

British politicians were keenly aware of these stark drops in Britain's competitive position, as the work of Friedberg (1988), Hoffman (1983), and Kennedy (1980, 1987) reveals. Especially worrisome was Germany's growing industrial might and competitiveness after 1890. The figures compiled by Hoffman show the trends. In 1892, German and British exports into Belgium/Holland and Russia were about equal, but by 1899 German exports were approximately 10 percent and 60 percent higher than Britain's, respectively. For Denmark, Norway, and Sweden as a group, Germany's export advantage over Britain doubled from 25 percent in 1892 to approximately 50 percent by 1899. Britain maintained its dominant position in Italy and on the Iberian Peninsula, but here too Germany was closing the gap. Of the countries Hoffman studies, it was only with France—a country that had significantly increased tariffs in 1892, partly out of fear of German growth—that Britain was able to hold its relative lead.[33]

Chamberlain needed no convincing that Britain was in decline. Since the late 1880s, he had been arguing that only an imperial preference system would save Britain from rising German and US productivity. By raising tariffs against states outside the empire, Britain would increase its manufacturing exports, allowing it to buy even more primary products from the colonies and dominions. Such a claim made some sense. Exports of manufactured goods to nonempire countries had fallen 57 percent

[31] The United States was the number one manufacturing power by the early 1880s, and by 1906–10, produced over 35 percent of the world's manufactured goods (ibid.).

[32] These figures actually understate the true fall in British trade competitiveness, since they include reexports of goods produced elsewhere, particularly from the colonies and dominions. If we take reexports out of the export total, the British trade deficit for the years 1895–98 is over one-half of the import bill.

[33] All figures are based on Hoffman's (1983, chap. 4) charts.

between the years 1870 and 1900, but exports of such products to the empire had increased 65 percent and indeed overtaken the nonempire exports in absolute terms (Cain and Hopkins 2002, 156). The growth markets, in short, were within the empire itself. The white-dominated dominions, which included the two South African states of Cape Colony and Natal, made up about half (49 percent) of all British exports to the empire by 1896–1900, up from 44.7 percent in the 1871–75 period (derived from ibid., table 5.3). The Cape Colony alone was already purchasing 13.6 million pounds worth of British goods by 1896, twice that of Canada and nearly one-half of India, a colony with many times the Cape's population (Hoffman 1983, 199).

The ongoing fear of British officials through the 1890s was that Germany would exploit its growing economic ties to Transvaal to pull this gold-rich republic out of the British sphere. Massive reserves of gold had been discovered in 1886 near the future town of Johannesburg, and German firms and miners quickly move in. The growth in Transvaal's wealth was nothing short of astonishing: by the end of the 1890s, its national income would increase twenty-five times the 1885 level. It was soon obvious to all that Transvaal would shortly become the center of the southern African universe. Railways were a key part of the emerging threat. In 1887, the Transvaal government gave a charter to the Netherlands South African Railway Company—a company that was nominally Dutch but financed by German money—to build a railway from the Portuguese port of Lorenzo Marques at Delagoa Bay (in modern-day Mozambique) to Pretoria and Johannesburg. Delagoa Bay was one of the few good harbors along the whole East African coast (Cape Town, the main port of the Cape Colony, was on the western tip of the continent). From the British perspective, a German-controlled railway line to Delagoa was a direct threat to the Cape Colony's plan to build its own railway into Transvaal to support British gold interests (Langer 1960, 218).

Chamberlain quickly saw the problem: Dutch Afrikaners in the Cape Colony, making up two-thirds of the white population in the self-governing colony, would cozy up to their Transvaal brethren and together align with Germany against Britain. In a speech in 1888, he stated that "sooner or later [the Dutch in the Cape Colony], with the sympathy of the Dutch in the Transvaal and of the Orange Free State, would stretch out their hands to the kindred nation (Germany), which is already established on the west coast of Africa" (quoted in ibid., 219). Such concern crossed party lines. It had been Liberal prime minister Gladstone in 1885 who had annexed the southern coastal region between Natal and the Cape Colony to forestall any similar German moves (Smith 1996, 37). When rumors arose in 1888 that Germany wanted Delagoa Bay, future Liberal foreign minister Lord Rosebery told the House of Commons that this was a "grave and pregnant matter." Germany's control of Delagoa would not only hurt Britain's South African dominions "but [also] may have an important bearing on our commerce as a country, and be the means of leading to the imposition of differential and hostile [tariff] rates" against British goods (quoted in Hoffman 1983, 203).

The German threat in southern Africa only grew through the 1890s. Paul Kruger, president of the Transvaal Republic, showed a preference for German companies as a way of offsetting the massive British investment in the gold mines near Johannesburg. German firms and German capital, including the national bank along with the lucrative dynamite and whiskey monopolies, dominated almost all the main government-controlled monopolies. As a result of this economic penetration, Germany's exports to the republic increased fivefold over the years 1889–94 (Langer 1960, 219).

The year 1895 became a time of decision. Salisbury's Conservatives had come back into office in June, with Chamberlain assuming the position of colonial secretary. Cecil Rhodes, prime minister of the Cape Colony, told Chamberlain of a plan to launch a raid on Transvaal that might stir British *uitlanders* (foreign residents) in Johannesburg to revolt against the government. What convinced Chamberlain to support it was the deteriorating trade situation between the Cape and Transvaal over 1895. The Cape's exports to Transvaal had increased 50 percent from 1892 to 1894 as a result of the booming gold business and recently completed Cape Town to Pretoria railway. But in early 1895, with the impending completion of the Netherlands South African Railway to Delagoa Bay, Kruger launched a boldly discriminatory economic policy to shift trade to the new route: he tripled the rate per mile charged to the Cape railway as it crossed the Vaal River into Transvaal. As the ensuing "Drifts Crisis" intensified, Kruger denied Cape goods passage across the Vaal. Salisbury and Chamberlain sent Kruger an ultimatum in November backed by the implied threat of military action. Kruger retreated and allowed goods to cross into Transvaal, but he did not revoke the exorbitant new railway charges. With the openings of the Delagoa Bay railway, the Cape Colony continued to see its exports to Transvaal plummet (Smith 1996, 62–66).

Back in London, Chamberlain was ready to go further. On December 26, he informed Salisbury that the raid from Botswana into Transvaal was imminent, and if the uitlanders rose up as expected and overthrew the Boer republic, "it ought to turn to our advantage" (quoted in ibid., 92–93). The Jameson Raid failed miserably, however, with all its members captured by early January. Notwithstanding the obvious diplomatic risks inherent in Rhodes's scheme, it was anxieties about growing German influence in Transvaal that convinced Chamberlain and Salisbury to support it. As Langer (1960, 228–29) observes, even after the Vaal River crossing was reopened, in British government circles there was a "growing feeling that the Germans were squarely behind Kruger." The British had been upset by the presence of German warships at the formal opening of the Netherlands South African Railway to Delagoa Bay in June. There were reports that many of the capitalists in Transvaal opposing Rhodes were actually agents of Germany. In November, Langer notes, an English agent in Pretoria informed the Cape government that the Germans were buying up as much land as they could around Delagoa Bay to strengthen their claims to the area. This news aligned with Chamberlain's warning to Salisbury two months before that Germany might try to take advantage of Portugal's financial difficulties to grab the bay. The possession of the railway to Delagoa by a "foreign power," meaning Germany, "would be disastrous and ought to be prevented if possible," Chamberlain argued (quoted in Robinson and Gallagher 1961, 428).

Perhaps most indicative of the state of British feelings by 1895 are comments made by Edward Malet, ambassador to Berlin, to German foreign minister Adolf Marschall in late October. Malet told Marschall that the Transvaal was the "black point" in Anglo-German relations due to Germany's continued support for the republic, and Berlin's behavior might eventually become intolerable and lead to "serious complications" (some German records indicate that Malet even used the word war).[34] Marschall replied that Germany only sought to support the status quo. But it would not let Transvaal collapse under Rhodes's schemes or permit the railway to Delagoa Bay to fall into his hands (Langer 1960, 228). This blunt discussion mirrored one from earlier in the year, when Malet told Marschall that the British were unhappy that Germany was "coquetting" with Transvaal leaders, making them believe that "whatever they did would have behind it the support of Germany." Marschall responded that Berlin's policy was simply aimed at defending the material interests Germany had developed with the Transvaal through the building of railways and trade connections. He charged Rhodes with wanting to absorb the Transvaal into a British-dominated South African state. Malet denied this, arguing that Rhodes merely wanted to create a commercial federation for all of South Africa. Marschall replied that this also would be contrary to German interests, since it meant "politically a [British] protectorate, and economically . . . the exclusion of German trade."[35]

When the Jameson Raid was reported in Berlin in late December 1895, the German government immediately authorized the landing of German troops from a cruiser in Delagoa Bay. Marschall warned London that Transvaal's independence must be maintained given important German economic interests as well as Berlin's sensitivity to public opinion. He

[34] See Kaiser Wilhelm to Adolf Marschall, October 25, 1895, in *GDD*, 2:368.
[35] Adolf Marschall, memorandum, February 1, 1895, in *GDD*, 2:366–67.

even contacted Paris to gauge its interest in a joint response.[36] By early January, as the failure of the raid became clear, Salisbury and Chamberlain distanced themselves from it by blaming Rhodes and forcing his resignation. With the publication of the "Kruger telegram," however, the downward slide in Anglo-German relations continued. In a one-sentence note sent on January 3, 1896, Kaiser Wilhelm expressed his "sincere congratulations" that President Kruger, supported by his people and "without appealing for the help of Friendly Powers," had emerged victorious against the armed bands that had invaded his country (*GDD*, 2:387). The British government and people exploded in anger. The German government was seen not only as intervening in British colonial matters but also as implying that had Jameson not been defeated, Germany might have been a "friendly power" that would have come to Transvaal's aid.

The Kruger telegram was a turning point in Anglo-German relations. Coming more than a year before Berlin officially embarked on Weltpolitik, it undermined the modicum of trust that the two countries had shared. London saw it as an effort to undermine the empire on which British strength was founded. Berlin for its part could not understand why the British would make such a fuss over a one-sentence telegram, suspecting that London was covertly setting out to contain and constrain German economic growth. The trade-security spiral that had been building in 1894–95 would now gain a momentum that would take the countries into war by 1914 (chapter 3). Salisbury's government was alarmed enough by the telegram to send three naval ships to Delagoa Bay in mid-January 1896, notwithstanding Germany's naval presence there. In March, the House of Commons authorized a naval program that included five new battleships and thirteen cruisers—a program ostensibly directed at the growing navies of France and Russia, but reinforced by deteriorating relations with Germany (ibid., 2:396).

For their part, the kaiser and his officials, now doubly wary of Britain's intentions, came out of the South African Crisis fully convinced that without a strong navy, Germany could not protect its growing global commerce against British high-handedness. On the day of the Kruger telegram, Admiral Alfred von Tirpitz, who was not yet Germany's naval secretary but had been asked for his opinion on naval construction, sent a memorandum to the kaiser calling for two squadrons of eight battleships each. In an early statement of his risk-fleet logic, Tirpitz argued that such a buildup would at least force Britain to be "more conciliatory" toward Germany. When the memorandum reached Wilhelm three days

---

[36] Smith 1996, 109; Adolf Marschall, memorandum, December 31, 1895, in *GDD*, 2:370–71; see also *GDD*, 2:378, 383. On the active consideration of a "continental league" against Britain, see *GDD*, 2:372–77.

later, the kaiser, frustrated by Germany's inability to project power during the Transvaal Crisis, was still focused on building cruisers to handle such regional tasks, and Tirpitz's suggestions were not taken up (Massie 1991, 169; Kelly 2011, 107–17). But when Tirpitz became state secretary of the navy in June 1897, he soon convinced Wilhelm and his colleagues that a balance of both battleships and cruisers was needed to give Germany a true naval presence opposite Britain. The Anglo-German naval race was on, with the dispute over South Africa providing one of the key triggers.[37]

Chamberlain recovered from the Jameson debacle with only minimal damage to his position. The raid itself only reinforced in his mind the significance of maintaining the dominance of Britain's position in southern Africa. Between 1896 and 1897, it became clear to him that there were only two ways the problem could be fixed: either the Boers in Transvaal would have to voluntarily relinquish control to the uitlanders through an expanded franchise or Britain would have to initiate war to force Transvaal into a larger British union of South African states. Chamberlain, unlike his future high commissioner to South Africa, Alfred Milner, was well aware of the likely costs and risks of an all-out war with Transvaal. As he told the House of Commons in May 1896, a war in South Africa "would be one of the most serious wars that could possibly be waged." It would "[have] the nature of a Civil War," a "long [and] costly war" that would leave resentment for generations, even if Britain won. Nonetheless, the first goal of British policy was to "preserve our position as the paramount State" and ensure that British authority "should be predominant in South Africa" (quoted in Smith 1996, 119–20). The tension between Chamberlain's larger objective and his recognition of the costs of war would haunt him for the next three years: he would seek to coerce the Boers to accept a peaceful transition to uitlander dominance even as he kept war in his pocket as the ultimate solution to the problem of decline.

The defining document of Britain's dilemma—one that would guide decision making for the next three years—was written in late March 1896 by Lord Selborne, Chamberlain's undersecretary at the colonial office and Salisbury's son-in-law. This long memorandum to Chamberlain on South Africa laid out the problems and possible solutions in stark detail. The overriding issue animating the whole report was whether British

[37]Tirpitz's naval buildup and the "world policy" (Weltpolitik) announced in mid-1897 fit together as two halves of a plan to protect German commerce around the world. As Smith (1986) shows, the idea of Weltpolitik originated in the foreign policy bureaucracy as a way to ensure German access to trade at a point when Germany was becoming increasingly dependent on overseas markets, raw materials, and investments for its continued economic growth. To be effective, a strong German navy was essential—a line of thinking that fit perfectly with the Mahanian logic that had swept Europe and earlier driven the US naval buildup of the early 1890s. See also my discussion in chapter 3 as well as Copeland 2011a.

possessions in South Africa would remain under London's control—as separate states or part of a Canadian-style confederation that would include the two Boer states—or be absorbed within a Dutch-dominated South African republic led by Transvaal. Selborne was pessimistic about London's ability to prevent a repeat of the American Revolution, this time with Transvaal leading the charge. Transvaal was now the "richest spot on earth" and thus was exerting a gravitational force on all its neighbors. "Transvaal will be the market for South Africa: the market for the manufactures of Cape Colony and Natal; the market for the agricultural products of those Colonies and of Rhodesia," proclaimed Selborne. "The commercial interest [in] the closest connection with the Transvaal will outweigh all other considerations." The British colonies would ultimately have to sue for closer commercial union, and Transvaal could demand as the price of admission that these states join a "United Republic of South Africa."[38]

Yet Transvaal had an ironic problem, Selborne observed. It was attracting so many English uitlanders that on its own, it could not permanently remain a Dutch republic—the uitlanders would eventually assume control by sheer numbers. Hence Pretoria had to draw the Cape Colony and Natal, with their large Dutch majorities, into a larger United States of South Africa. It could not do otherwise if it wanted to maintain internal Afrikaner dominance. This meant that even if London wanted to wait it out, uitlander population growth meant that the Dutch Boers could not—they needed a Transvaal-dominated Republic of South Africa just to survive internally. There was no jumping through the horns of this dilemma: Transvaal's declining domestic situation would force it to act in a way that would only exacerbate Britain's larger problem of decline. The report's pessimism did not end there, though. One and only one great power would benefit from all these developments—namely, Germany. The day after a united South African republic was declared, Selborne noted, Germany would swoop in and occupy Walfisch Bay, the strategic British port in the middle of German Southwest Africa. Then it would pressure the new republic to grant Germany favors to realize its larger ambition: "to connect her possessions on the West Coast of Africa with those on the East Coast."

To deal with the situation, Selborne suggested the immediate securing of Delagoa Bay and formation of a large Canada-like dominion for South Africa. If Britain took the bay from Portugal, this would allow the Cape Colony to achieve commercial and financial dominance over Transvaal. By convincing Transvaal that it was hemmed in, its leaders would

---

[38] All quotations in this and the next two paragraphs are from Robinson and Gallagher's (1961, 434–37) essentially complete version of the document.

be forced to "renounce their foreign intrigues" and come to terms with Britain. If, conversely, control of the railway passed to "a Foreign Power working with the Transvaal against British interests," then the results would be "very serious." The next sentence leaves little doubt as to which foreign power Selborne is referring. The Transvaal and this foreign power

> could then secure a monopoly of all Transvaal trade for the Delagoa Bay Railway with the effect not only of supplanting British imports by (say) German imports, and not only of inflicting grievous commercial injury on the trading classes of the Cape Colony and Natal, but they could also reduce [those classes] to the verge of financial bankruptcy, so dependent are they upon their railway revenue.

The loss of the railway would put added pressure on the British possessions to join a larger Transvaal-led union. It was therefore "a matter of vital importance" to prevent the railway from passing into the control "of any power whatever except the Portuguese or British Governments." Selborne ends the memo by stating that if Portugal could not hold on to Delagoa Bay, Britain should act to secure it.

British actions over the next three years closely followed Selborne's strategic logic, and the story can be told in short order. Through the remainder of 1896, Salisbury sought to convince Lisbon to transfer Delagoa Bay to Britain, but Portugal would not budge. In December, he considered sending part of the fleet to Delagoa Bay to impress Pretoria and Berlin with British concern for the port. The fleet was dispatched in March 1897 as a new crisis arose over Pretoria's restrictions on uitlanders (Robinson and Gallagher 1961, 440–43; Smith 1996, 136–39). In April, Chamberlain reminded a group gathered at a banquet for Milner, the Cape Colony and Natal's new high commissioner, that Britain was determined to maintain its position as "the paramount power in South Africa." But before Milner left, Chamberlain told him to remember that a war with the Transvaal would be unpopular at home unless started on "the utmost and clearest provocation." In the short term, then, Britain had to play a "waiting game" (quoted in Smith 1996, 150–51).

Both Chamberlain and Milner believed that the situation would probably be solved without war, since the Boer leadership would ultimately capitulate to London's demands for greater uitlander representation. Chamberlain nevertheless spent much of 1897 and 1898 establishing Britain's right to intervene militarily in the Transvaal should Kruger prove intransigent on the issue. In October 1897, Chamberlain prepared a note for Pretoria asserting Britain's claim to "suzerainty" over Transvaal—a word explicitly used in the British-Transvaal 1881 convention, yet left out of the 1884 convention at Pretoria's insistence. Selborne knew this note would outrage Kruger, but "it will be of great value as asserting our position before all the world." It was sent in December, although Kruger did not respond until April 1898, rejecting the suzerainty claim outright. He correctly saw it as a tool to justify interference in Transvaal's internal affairs and prevent it from appealing for aid from interested foreign states (most obviously, Germany) (quoted in ibid., 174–76).

After Kruger won reelection by a large margin in February 1898, it seemed much less likely that the uitlanders would gain control of Transvaal through Boer capitulation. On February 23, Milner wrote Chamberlain that the solution to Britain's troubles was by reform or war, but the chances for reform now were "worse than ever." Hence, he was "inclined to work up to a crisis" by pressing for a redress of injustices. British needed an "active policy"—supported by a large army—that insisted on British rights (quoted in ibid., 185). Chamberlain reminded Milner that a war would be unpopular and costly, and if it were to come, it was "most important that Transvaal should be the aggressor" (quoted in Langer 1960, 607).

To avoid conflicts on too many fronts at once, Chamberlain approached Germany in early 1898 to try to resolve issues over Africa and China, but the initial meetings proved unproductive.[39] London restarted talks in May 1898 with Lisbon over Delagoa Bay. With Portugal in bad financial shape, Salisbury and Chamberlain hoped they could convince Lisbon to transfer the bay and the Portuguese section of the railway to Britain, or at least agree to use Portuguese colonies as collateral for any British loan. This would give London strong leverage should Portugal be unable to repay its loan. When Berlin got wind of the talks in June, it immediately pushed London to include Germany in any loan arrangement and agree secretly to the distribution of Portuguese colonies should Lisbon default. By mid-June, the British seemed willing to at least discuss the issue. But it quickly became apparent to the Germans that the primary British goal, above all else, was to grab Delagoa Bay.[40] Despite suspicions regarding British plans, negotiations continued, and on August 30, London and Berlin reached a secret agreement to partition Portugal's African colonies should Lisbon default on a joint British-German loan. Caving to British demands, Germany gave Britain the southern half of Mozambique, the area that included Delagoa Bay, in return for northern Mozambique, the territory that bordered on German East Africa.[41]

The Anglo-German agreement seemed to resolve the issue of which great power would control access routes into the Transvaal. Unfortunately, it became a dead letter in late 1898 when Portugal, understandably wary

---

[39]Joseph Chamberlain, memorandum, March 29, 1898, in *FPVE*, 453–54; Massie 1991, 245–46.

[40]See Paul von Hatzfeldt, telegram to the German Foreign Office, June 14, 1898, in *GDD*, 3:28–29.

[41]See Smith 1996, 208–9; documents in *GDD*, 3:36–41.

of both Britain and Germany, accepted a less constraining loan offer from France. For some authors, the simple fact that Berlin had agreed to relinquish Delagoa Bay meant that Germany no longer posed a problem for Britain in South Africa (Smith 1996, 39, 208–9). In situations of anarchy, however, leaders know that others can change their minds. And given the intense decade-long concern shown toward Germany's increasing commercial and political ties to Transvaal, it is hard to believe that any British official would think Germany would avoid exploiting a future united South African republic merely because of a secret dead letter agreement. The very fact that Germany wanted northern Mozambique would have reminded the British that Berlin was still greatly interested in linking its western and eastern colonial possessions into a commercially valuable *Mittelafrika*. So with the August 30 deal negated by the French loan, all the problematic implications of Transvaal's continued growth identified in Selborne's 1896 memorandum, including the worry about Germany's ties to a future Dutch Republic of South Africa, remained in play.

With the Delagoa Bay question still unresolved by late 1898, events began to move quickly. The Boer leadership was alerted to British plans through a remarkable meeting between Jan Smuts, Transvaal's attorney general, and British envoy Edmund Fraser on December 22. According to Smuts's record, written that day, Fraser told him that the British government had done nothing for two years because of the Jameson Raid, but "the time had now . . . come for her to take action." Smuts asked what he meant, and Fraser replied that Gladstone had made "a great mistake" in giving Transvaal its full independence back in 1881. Afrikaners throughout South Africa had an "aspiration for a great republic," and Gladstone had by his action "encouraged this aspiration." London had in the interim allowed this situation to continue, but had "now come to make an end of this by 'striking a blow.'" London, Fraser went on, would be happy if Transvaal remained a richer version of the Orange Free State, yet it knew that Pretoria would not accept such a humble role. Transvaal had rejected Britain's "paramount influence" and "always coquetted with the European powers." It was therefore time to show the Boers "that England was master in South Africa."[42] Five months later, Smuts wrote that Fraser had also stated that day that "the position and influence of the [Transvaal] . . . had filled all Dutchmen with the idea that a great Afrikaner republic would be established in South Africa. The longer England waited, the stronger would this separatist aspiration become and the weaker [England's] own position; and it was now a question whether she would sit still any longer."[43]

---

[42] Quoted from Smuts's memorandum on the day of the meeting, in Smith 1996, 205.

[43] Quoted from Smuts's letter to the head of main Dutch political organization in the Cape Colony, in Smith 1996, 205–6.

These strikingly blunt admissions not only reveal British perceptions of the core problem—namely, that Transvaal would use its growing strength to organize a larger Dutch republic. They also show that London was indeed concerned about Transvaal's ongoing policy of coquetting with foreign powers. The fact that this phraseology—the same one used by Ambassador Malet in discussions with German officials in 1895—comes four months *after* the August 1898 agreement (and just after its subsequent negation) indicates that British officials were still very much worried about Transvaal's ongoing ties to Germany.

Following this meeting, Pretoria understandably sought to avoid war by preventing the uitlander issue from being used as a pretext. In March 1899, Kruger offered the foreign mining interests in Johannesburg a "Great Deal": if they would allow certain monopolies to continue, he would grant them concessions in other areas, including the ability to appoint advisers to oversee the state's financial administration. He also announced that he would reduce the residency time required for an uitlander to achieve full citizenship from fourteen years to nine (Meredith 2007, 394–95). But the uitlanders balked, and the Great Deal fell through. In late May, High Commissioner Milner met Kruger to discuss the possibility of a deal. Kruger offered Milner a "reform bill" reducing the residency requirement to a maximum of seven years, with gold-mining districts receiving five new seats in the Transvaal Parliament. Milner insisted on a maximum of five years of residency and seven new seats. When Kruger showed reluctance to go further, arguing that he could not hand his country over to strangers, Milner abruptly ended the talks and returned to Cape Town (ibid., 405–8; Smith 1996, 278–87). The British were at a point where they felt only significant concessions could avert war. A week before the summit, Milner had told London that if Kruger failed to accept British demands, "it would better to fight now than in 5 or 10 years hence," when the Transvaal "will be stronger and more hostile than ever" (quoted in Smith 1996, 289).

In mid-July, Kruger announced that six new seats had been added to Parliament for the gold-mining districts. Such concessions, Selborne told Chamberlain, were just efforts to buy time and prevent the consolidation of British public opinion (Meredith 2007, 410). Chamberlain decided to up the ante. In a speech to the House of Commons on July 28, he argued that British-Boer "race antagonism" was spreading from Transvaal into neighboring states, creating "a constant menace to the [region's] peace and prosperity." After detailing uitlander grievances, he asked Parliament to back the government and help Kruger see the necessity of yielding.[44]

---

[44] Quoted in Smith 1996, 321–22; Meredith 2007, 410–11. See also Pakenham 2001, 79–80.

Chamberlain was seeking to mobilize public opinion behind one last effort at coercion—and if that should fail, for war.

Seeing where things were going, Kruger proposed one last set of concessions. In mid-August, he offered to meet Britain's demand for a maximum five-year waiting period for citizenship and give the mining areas ten seats in the Parliament, or a full one-quarter of the total. In return, Britain would have to end its claim to suzerainty over Transvaal and agree not to interfere in its internal matters. On August 26, Chamberlain spoke publicly of Kruger's delaying tactics, and argued that Britain was now free to establish the conditions for determining once and for all which state was the paramount power in South Africa. Two days later, he sent a note to Pretoria accepting Kruger's concessions while rejecting his two additional conditions (Smith 1996, 358; Meredith 2007, 414).

Chamberlain had clearly decided that the crisis would now end either in a last-minute capitulation or war. He spend most of September bringing the cabinet on board for the final push. On September 6, he provided the cabinet with a memorandum reiterating that Britain's position in South Africa and the world was now at stake. The threat came from the Dutch, who were trying "to get rid altogether of the connection to Great Britain" and "substitute a United States of South Africa" (quoted in Robinson and Gallagher 1961, 454–55). When the cabinet met two days later, Chamberlain's call for the buildup of ten thousand British soldiers in the area was accepted. His report to Milner later that day indicated that the cabinet was united on every key point. Prime Minister Salisbury himself was firmly on board for the final gambit. Chamberlain wrote Queen Victoria on September 23 that given Transvaal's rejection of British demands, it was "impossible to avoid believing that the Boers really aim at setting up a South African Republic, consisting of the Transvaal, the Orange Free State and Your Majesty's [colonies]." In early October, in a letter to Lord Courtney, he indicated that the conduct of not just Pretoria but also the Afrikaner leaders in the Cape Colony had led him to the belief "that there is an understanding among [Dutch] leaders . . . and their aspiration is the restoration of South Africa to the Dutch race" (quoted in Langer 1960, 616–17).

The Boers of Transvaal obliged the British by rejecting London's final ultimatum and, with their Orange Free allies, launching a preemptive attack on Natal in late October 1899. Chamberlain had his war to maintain British "paramountcy" in South Africa. Yet as we have seen, from the perspective of Chamberlain and his associates, British supremacy in South Africa was intimately tied to the overall economic and political power of the British Empire. At a time when British trading strength was on the wane, the nation could not allow the Transvaal to stay independent and ultimately absorb the rest of South Africa into a powerful

Dutch-led republic. Even without considering the possible domino effect on other possessions, including India, the British had to worry that this new republic would align with Germany, destroying British trade, investments, and gold production in the region.

In sum, by 1898–99, it was evident that the future of the British Empire's global economic position was at stake, and something had to be done soon before things got worse. Declining commercial expectations were bolstering British fears of overall decline, making preventive action necessary. Alternative explanations prove quite weak. Chamberlain and Salisbury were cautious men who would have been happy if the Boer leadership had simply agreed to allow the uitlanders to control Transvaal's domestic politics. They were certainly not plunging Britain into what was expected to be a costly, unpopular war to win elections or satisfy capitalist parochial interests back home. Liberal and neo-Marxist arguments that see unit-level forces as propelling are inadequate. As Selborne's memorandum made apparent to all, the South African situation was fundamentally about Britain's larger place in a global economic struggle that had Germany as the empire's main European competitor. And yet this war was not just about Britain's rising dependence on trade with South Africa, as economic realists would have to contend. Something was causing a fall in British trade expectations, and that something was Transvaal's continued growth, its recognized need to absorb the British colonies, and its long-standing ties to the German state and German capital—exogenous realities that were not going to be altered by diplomacy alone. In an environment of overall economic decline, the British leadership could not afford to see the South African region slip from its grasp, only to land in the hands of its main economic rival in Europe.

Conclusion

This chapter has demonstrated the important role of falling trade expectations in the explanation of the imperialist struggles of the great powers from 1880 to 1900. For cases such as the French, British, and German scrambles for Africa and the Boer War, the trade expectations argument strongly outperforms realist and liberal explanations linking trade to conflict. In these cases, leaders were reluctant to embark on new imperial campaigns, and only did so once they suspected that other great powers were seeking to deny them access to vital raw materials, investments, and markets. The French after 1880 began to feel squeezed out of West Africa and Tunisia by the British and Italians, respectively. They responded by grabbing Tunisia in 1881–82, in an action that increased British mistrust and led Gladstone to occupy Egypt in 1882 during a period of domestic unrest in Egypt. These moves in turn made the previously anti-imperialist Bismarck realize that unless he acted quickly, the closing door would shut Germany out of Africa, just at the moment when the continent's potential value for industrializing economies was becoming more self-evident. The British maneuvers to bring on war with the Boer republics of Transvaal and Orange Free State also reflected fears that if London did not act, South Africa would fall under the domination of Transvaal, a state with strong economic and political ties to Germany.

Pessimistic trade expectations plus economic dependence also played crucial roles in other great power conflicts between 1890 and 1900. The Venezuelan and Fashoda crises were clearly tied to the larger US, British, and French struggles for control of and access to materials and markets. Economic realism does a good job by itself in explaining British action over Venezuela and French behavior in the Sudan. But falling expectations of future trade must be brought in to understand Washington's reaction regarding Venezuela and British policies at Fashoda. Interestingly, these cases also show that democracies can sometimes get close to war over economic matters, notwithstanding the normative and institutional constraints on their behavior. My short review of these two crises omits consideration of some of their more purely geopolitical and prestige dimensions. And the cases of Italian and German unification demonstrate that interdependence is sometimes completely overshadowed by noneconomic factors: neither dependence nor trade expectations had any discernible role in Cavour's decision to unite Italy through war in 1859–60 or Bismarck's wars to unite Germany from 1864 to 1870. In the latter case, however, systemic variables—particularly the need to build Germany's long-term potential power base—were likely more important than more purely unit-level variables such as social stability, greed, or ideological drives. In this sense, systemic realism still does a better job than liberalism in explaining the pressures for war, even if trade expectations are not a salient systemic factor in such instances.

Chapters 7 and 8 together build our overall confidence in the trade expectations approach. Going beyond the well-known twentieth-century cases, these chapters highlight that across a wide variety of geopolitical and ideological settings, a broad assortment of great powers were often driven by one common obsession: the maintenance and enhancement of their access to raw materials, investments, and markets in the face of perceived threats. Notwithstanding differences in domestic type, great powers as diverse as Britain, France, Germany, the United States, and Russia were more than willing to initiate coercive diplomacy as well as war when they saw economic access to be under threat. In the next chapter, I extend the trade expectations approach to such contemporary issues as the rise of China and growth of Sino-American economic relations.

CHAPTER NINE

Implications of the Argument

THIS BOOK has sought to demonstrate the significant deductive and explanatory power that can be realized through building a theory that accepts the insights of liberalism and realism but corrects for their limitations. Liberals are right to argue that trade can sometimes provide an important constraint on actors who might otherwise be inclined to aggressive and competitive actions. Yet liberals as a group assume that states are propelled into expansionist behavior by underlying unit-level drives such as greed, glory, and the pursuit of ideological or religious dominance. To borrow from Plato, economic interdependence for liberals is not a force for action, only a restraint on the black horse of domestic politics and leader pathology.[1] Yet as we saw in previous chapters, there are few cases where war could be explained as the unleashing of unit-level pathologies after a significant drop in trade and commerce. The Korean War and World War II in Europe and the Pacific are the three cases that come the closest, but even they do not work terribly well on closer inspection.

Economic realists correctly contend that trade and commerce can be forces for conflict as dependent actors, worried that others might cut them off from access to vital raw materials, investments, and markets, seek to reduce their vulnerability through the extension of military power abroad and direct occupation of crucial trading partners. Yet such realists, because they underplay the risks of overly hard-line policies while overplaying the risks of trading in the first place, cannot explain why great powers might exist within a cooperative economic relationship for years without falling into war. Moreover, although the stress on actors' opportunistic grabs for more economic control occasionally explains shifts to new and more aggressive policies (most notably, Japan against China 1894 and Britain over Venezuela 1895), in the broad swath of cases, states typically make those shifts only after threats to their established trade relations have emerged.

Trade expectations theory resolves the problems for established liberal and realist theories in three main ways. For one, it offers a new

[1] See Plato's *Phaedrus*, in Hamilton and Cairns 1961.

variable—a dependent state's expectations of the future economic environment—as a way to link liberal theory's emphasis on the benefits from trade and investment with realism's concern for the potentially significant costs of adjustment that a state would face were it to be cut off after becoming dependent on such commerce. This variable, depending on its value, will determine a state's assessment of its future. If the state remains optimistic about the economic environment, it will not only want the trade to continue but also will be aware of the opportunity costs of disrupting it through overly hard-line behavior. If the state's evaluations of the trading environment turn pessimistic, however, vulnerability to the costs of adjustment will kick in, causing leaders to fear long-term decline unless more assertive policies are undertaken. The expectations variable thus helps establish the conditions under which liberal and realist predictions are likely to hold. Yet by starting with the assumption that states are primarily interested in maximizing their security, trade expectations theory avoids the liberal problem of having to dip down to the unit level to explain why wars may actually break out. States in trade expectations theory are seeking trade to build their long-term power positions, and accordingly will see restrictions in access to trade and investment as direct threats to their future security. The case studies show that security concerns more than unit-level drives were determinative in the key great power crises and wars over the last two centuries.

Yet to fully transcend the limits of economic realism, a second new dimension—the notion of a trade-security dilemma—must be incorporated into the theory. Economic realism, given its offensive realist roots, is a theory of opportunism. Dependent states, always on the lookout for ways to reduce their vulnerability to cutoffs, will grab any and all opportunities to increase their control over valuable markets and sources of vital goods, at least as long as the costs of doing so are low. Yet one of the key potential "costs" that economic realists ignore is the possibility that hard-line behavior designed to protect economic access will end up leading to hostile counterbalancing behavior by other great powers, including those that provide markets and help to supply vital goods either directly or indirectly. Economic containment by these great powers can feed back into the original state's assessment of its future trade environment, creating a pessimism that then leads to even more hard-line behavior. A spiral of economic restrictions and increasingly aggressive behavior can result that pushes the system into crisis as well as war, with the lead-up to the Pacific War providing the most dramatic example.

The notion of a trade-security dilemma builds on the defensive realist insight that hard-line actions can create positive feedback loops of mistrust and hostility. Unfortunately, the security dilemma within defensive realism has always remained a purely military concept, focusing on the impact of military buildups and alliance behavior that create direct threats to a state's existence. The trade-security dilemma brings in the economic side of a great power's security calculation. Dependent states that seek to protect their access to raw materials, investments, and markets can inadvertently hurt this access if they cause less dependent states to impose economic restrictions and carve out spheres for themselves. This simple fact, when actors are aware of it, goes a long way to explaining why great powers are often so cautious in their behaviors toward one another. Both sides want to avoid sparking a trade-security spiral that might lead to crisis and war. Moreover, both will have an incentive to project a character of reasonableness and moderation in order to solidify positive expectations in the adversary: for the dependent state, an expectation that the other is committed to the long-term economic openness; for the less dependent state, an expectation that the other will restrain the desire to act like an offensive-realist state—that is, to use its military power to enhance its control of its economic future.

Once we realize that rational actors will be aware of the trade-security dilemma and thus inclined toward moderation, the puzzle of conflict and war becomes this: Why would states ever switch to hard-line policies that undermine the confidence of others in their overall "reasonableness"? This is where the third contribution of the theory comes in: the specification of exogenous factors that shift actor calculations of the cost, benefits, and risks of staying with past moderate behavior versus shifting to more assertive policies. Within any bargaining situation between two great powers, there is an incentive to find a peace that provides benefits to both sides while avoiding the costs and risks of war. The fact that great powers can be trading peacefully for many years is prime facie evidence that they have found a bargain that is better than war for both sides. Hence to explain the shift to hard-line policies, we must look for changes in certain key exogenous factors that lie "outside" the bargaining relationship—changes that alter the actors' view of its value. The most important of these, as we have seen confirmed in the historical chapters, are the role of third parties and the level of growth of the dependent state. When third-party actors threaten a dependent state's ability to access raw materials, investments, and markets, this can cause the state to increase its military commitment to a region or simply occupy the territory of value. Such third-party concerns come in a variety of forms: small states undergoing revolts that endanger present trade or encourage other great powers to absorb them into their spheres (e.g., Turkey in 1852–53, Egypt in 1882, or Western Europe in 1945); domestic political factors in a third party that give it an incentive to attack a territory of significance to both state X and state Y (e.g., Italy toward Tunisia in 1881 or Egypt toward the Ottoman Empire in 1833–39); the role of a third party in reshaping the economic parameters of the X-Y relationship (e.g., Russia for Japan and the United States in 1939–41); and so forth.

Yet state X's willingness to continue to trade with the more dependent state, state Y, will also crucially depend on the growing size of state Y and threat it might pose in the future, simply because of its power. The most obvious case of this is the early Cold War, where the United States practiced severe economic containment against the Soviet Union in order to prevent the Soviets from making economic gains that would increase their long-term power base. But as a result, the Soviets felt pushed into a more assertive policy toward the third world than they might otherwise have thought prudent. Concerns about Germany's growing preponderance in Europe led to increasing economic restrictions by Britain and France after 1895—actions that fueled German fears that over the long term, Germany would decline relative to new economic powers such as Russia and the United States.

The economic environment can also be undermined by domestic forces that operate independently of the executive branches of the two main states. We saw this most clearly with the destruction of Nixon and Kissinger's carefully constructed détente of the early 1970s. The Soviets began to act with notable caution in 1972–73 once they believed that trade and technology benefits from the United States would be forthcoming. Yet when the US Congress after Watergate pulled the economic rug out from under the administration's linkage strategy, the Soviets quickly reverted to more assertive policies around the world. Domestic factors within Russia may have also played a role in hurting Japan's expectations of future trade over Manchuria and Korea in 1903. To be sure, there were good strategic reasons for the Russians to want to maintain a strong forward position in Manchuria in order to penetrate the emerging Chinese market. From the Japanese perspective, however, domestic pressure groups were steering the czar's policy toward the hard line, preventing the negotiation of a reasonable agreement that could define economic spheres of influence in the area and thus keep the peace.

The empirical chapters of this book, in covering pretty well every important case period since 1790 involving two or more great powers, show just how powerful an expectations approach to interdependence can be. Falling expectations of future trade and commerce played a prominent or decisive causal role in explaining the shift to crisis and war or peace in almost two-thirds of the case periods (twenty-six out of forty, or 65 percent). And when we consider just the cases where economic interdependence was directly implicated in the conflict, the trade expectations argument explained close to nine out of ten cases (twenty-six of thirty, or 87 percent). Economic realism scored a number of successes, but it did considerably less well than the trade expectations argument. The economic realism logic played an important or decisive role in a quarter of all the cases (eleven of forty, or 28 percent), or over a third of the cases involving economic interdependence (37 percent). Liberal economic explanations rooted in the unleashing of domestic pathologies as trade levels fall performed poorly overall. The liberal logic played a decisive role in none of the forty cases.[2] In conjunction with trade expectations or economic realist factors, it covered only three cases: Russia's moderation in the 1839–41 eastern crisis, some reinforcing aspects of Bismarck's decision to turn to imperialism in 1883–84, and Japan's relative restraint over Manchuria in the late 1920s. These three amount to just 7 percent of the total number of cases, or 10 percent of those involving economic interdependence.[3] Even for what should have proven to be its "best cases"— Germany and Japan leading up to World War II, the Berlin Crisis of 1948, and the outbreak of the Korean War in 1950—the liberal argument could not explain the primary drives for conflict.

The rest of this chapter will be taken up with two main tasks. I will first consider the implications of the argument for international relations theory. The focus will be on its broader importance for thinking about liberal and realist theories that are not focused on economic interdependence per se. I will then turn to an examination of the contemporary US-China relationship. I contend that China's growing dependence on external raw materials and markets along with its expectations for the future are critical to predicting the likely shape of the relationship over the next two or three decades. No issue aside from perhaps Taiwan obsesses the Chinese leadership like the economic dependence question. Yet there are strong reasons to believe that China will stay peacefully engaged in the system over the long term, at least as long as the United States proves willing to maintain an open and free-flowing global economic system.

Broader Implications of the Theory

The empirical chapters have shown, both through quantitative and qualitative methods, the superior explanatory power of trade expectation theory over its rivals. Chapter 2 demonstrated that the new variable, leader expectations of the future economic environment, supplies a simple but powerful explanation for a wide variety of quantitative large-N results over the last two decades. It explains, among other things, why

---

[2] Domestic and psychological factors independent of commerce but part of the larger liberal paradigm, on the other hand, were important in cases such as the Sino-Japanese War of 1937–45 and wars of Italian reunification.

[3] These statistics are drawn from table 2.7 in chapter 2.

authoritarian states might become more hostile as trade levels increase (such actors generally have less of a commitment to open commerce) and why states with contract-intense legal structures tend toward greater levels of peace (their leaders have greater confidence in the stability of current trade). In addition, the trade expectations logic explains the recent discovery in the quantitative literature of a "capitalistic peace": the possibility that it is the capitalist nature of states rather than their trade levels per se that helps reduce the likelihood of militarized conflicts and war. Capitalist states are generally more committed to long-term trade openness and unrestricted financial flows. From the perspective of this book, then, it is not surprising that such states are correlated with lower levels of militarized conflicts, given that such actors, at least with each other, are likely to have positive expectations about the future. Furthermore, as McDonald's (2009) statistical work confirms, even when trade levels are currently low, falling levels of protectionism are associated with lower risks of conflict. This result is consistent with the view that positive expectations of future trade can help keep the peace even when current trade is essentially nonexistent, given actors' anticipation of future benefits if they stay peaceful.

The review in chapter 2 of the quantitative literature only provided correlational support for trade expectations theory. The qualitative historical chapters went further, confirming that it is indeed the expectations variable that is doing the causal heavy lifting in the vast majority of case periods where economic interdependence is implicated in the outbreak of war or peace. Now that we can see how powerful commercial expectations are in world history, we can go beyond economics as such, and explore trade expectations theory's implications for liberalism and realism as general approaches to international relations.[4] Liberals as a group assert that international institutions and the presence of democratic dyads should also enhance the probability of peace: the former by reducing actor uncertainty about others' probability of cheating on agreements, and the latter largely through normative and legislative constraints on leaders who might contemplate war with another democracy.[5]

The trade expectations logic offers some straightforward insights regarding the value of institutional and democratic peace arguments. To the extent that institutions between actors have been designed to enhance positive expectations and reduce leader uncertainty about being cut off from valuable trade and investments, liberals are exactly right to

---

[4] I am again using the labels liberalism and realism as shorthand for groups of theories with common sets of assumptions regarding actor ends and the salience of certain variables.

[5] For summaries and references, see especially Doyle 1986b; Owen 1994; Oneal and Russett 2001; Maoz and Russett 1993; Russett 1993; Keohane 1984, 1990.

maintain that institutions can help keep the peace. In correlational terms, we have already seen this effect in the role that preferential trade agreements and regularized high-level meetings have had in moderating the likelihood of a militarized interstate dispute since 1945 (chapter 2). Yet the historical case studies show that institutions are neither a necessary nor sufficient condition for peace between actors. For the vast majority of great power cases, peace was maintained for many years without any formalized institutions or even agreement on regular meetings between top officials. And when crises and war did break out, it was rarely because of the deterioration of preexisting institutional mechanisms. Hence, while international institutions can certainly help bolster positive trade expectations, they typically operate only as supporting or reinforcing factors within the larger context of great power politics. A more powerful set of forces is found historically in the judicious use of diplomacy by rational actors aware of the deleterious effects of overly assertive behavior and in the ability of these actors to show that they are committed to open trade into the future, even when institutional mechanisms are weak or nonexistent. US leaders did this effectively in 1972 and again in the late 1980s, signaling to the Soviets that the United States would be a more reliable trade partner as long as Moscow moderated its foreign policies. To be sure, institutionalizing any diplomatic deals can help to reinforce each side's commitment to open trade and reasonable military behavior. But trade expectations can be improved prior to such institutionalization, and institutionalization itself will probably not become entrenched without these prior diplomatic efforts.

The trade expectations approach also helps us understand exactly what is at stake in the ongoing debate about the democratic peace. As we saw in chapter 2, it may well be the case that the correlation between mutual democracy and peace is really reflective of an economic peace as opposed to a political one. Democracies are unlikely to fight each other, in other words, not because they respect each other's normative values or because their legislatures pull illiberal leaders back from the brink, but rather because democracies generally have open liberal economic foundations and thus are able to signal their commitment to open-door economic policies into the future. This does not mean, of course, that democracies are not often prone to raise tariffs and restrict monetary flows, especially during economic downturns (as we saw in the early 1930s). Nevertheless, leaders of democracies should expect other democracies to want to return to freer trade once their economies lift themselves out of recession. The longer-term outlook of democracies toward each other should be quite positive then—a fact that should make them more sanguine about their ability to access vital goods and markets, and so support their future security.

Yet what our case studies have clearly revealed is that democracies can be just as aggressive as authoritarian states when they believe they are facing actors who are not committed to open trade and commerce in the future. Britain in the nineteenth century is our most obvious example. British leaders regularly initiated crises or wars when they believed other great powers were trying to restrict Britain's access to raw materials, investments, and markets, as we saw in the struggles with France and Russia over the Near East in the 1830s, the initiation of the First Opium War in 1839, the response to Russian moves against Turkey in 1853 and 1878, and the worries over Africa in the 1880s and again in the Boer Crisis of 1895–99. We also saw the US state become much more hard line in 1945 when confronted with the economic challenges of global Communism. The US-British standoff over Venezuela in 1895 also suggests that even two democracies can get close to war when one of the sides starts to feel the other encroaching into its economic sphere.

The biggest challenge to the overall liberal perspective, however, comes from the new understanding of why authoritarian states might launch themselves into costly wars. The liberal argument for the outbreak of war is rooted in the view that external pressures alone are not enough, that unit-level pathologies must be at work. The presumption of liberalism—indeed, the thing that most differentiates it from the realist perspective—is that a state's systemic situation cannot be the primary driving force for war. In almost all our cases, even those seemingly domestically driven ones such as World War II in Europe and Asia, we nonetheless find that the initiators of war felt strong systemic pressures to resort to war to uphold their security. These systemic pressures were not always the direct result of falling expectations of trade. Yet in cases such as Berlin 1948 and Korea 1950 where we might expect domestic variables to have the most salience, we still see fears of long-term decline due to the economic rise of the other to be a critical component of the initiator's reasons for war.

If these case studies show anything, it is that unit-level forces are not nearly as powerful a cause of war in world history as liberal theory believes them to be. Domestic variables can still be important, of course. But their main role is typically in the shaping of an actor's expectations of its adversaries' future willingness to keep commerce open, and if the actor is declining, its estimates of the adversaries' desire to attack later once they are more powerful. In other words, if unit-level variables play any role in the outbreak of crisis and war, it is usually the unit-level characteristics of the *other*—not the unit-level characteristics of the initiating state—that best explains why the latter might change its policy and initiate conflict. The empirical evidence of this book thus forces a fundamental reorientation of liberal thinking. Liberals must move away from the perspective that the crises and wars of history are generally started by pathological states toward a view that shows how the domestic politics of state X shape the security calculations and behavior of state Y, the state whose hard-line behavior we are trying to explain.

This discussion also indicates where realism in its various strands needs to be reformulated. Offensive realism can do a good job explaining the universal *desire* of great powers for more control over future events, but by ignoring the downsides of hard-line politics, economic or military, it does a less than satisfactory job of understanding their *behavior*. Once we bring in the defensive realist point regarding variations in the intensity of the security dilemma, we can see why most great powers for the most of their histories are relatively cautious in their policies. Nevertheless, defensive realism's understanding of the security dilemma ignores the economic side of the equation. Incorporating the trade-security dilemma and tying it to varying expectations of future trade allows us to see why actors may be both more cautious and more aggressive than defensive realism allows. They will be more cautious when expectations are positive, given fears that a turn to hard-line behavior will cause not just increased arms spending and alliance buildups by other states (the counterbalancing of the traditional security dilemma) but also the imposition of economic restrictions and even cutoffs that could greatly damage long-term economic power as well as security. Yet when exogenous factors, including domestic factors in other states, push either dependent or less dependent states toward policies to protect their economic access and restrict the access of other powers, a spiral of mistrust and hostility can occur more quickly and intensely than defensive realism would otherwise predict. Moreover, the offensive realist insight that actors do have a desire to hedge against future problems can easily be kicked in under such circumstances, leading both sides to start scrambling for control of third-party resources, investments, and markets.

PRACTICAL IMPLICATIONS: THE UNITED STATES AND THE RISE OF CHINA

The argument of this book has important practical implications for one of the most, if not the most, pressing issues of our time: the future of US-Chinese relations in the face of China's phenomenal rise in economic and technological power. China's GDP growth over the last three decades has been nothing short of spectacular, rising an average of at least 7–9 percent per annum (with many years in the double digits). This has led to a steady doubling in China's absolute size every eight to ten years, and a quadrupling every sixteen to twenty years. Given the much lower growth rates of the Western states and Japan, China has now passed Japan as the world's second-largest economy and is poised to overtake the US economy in total GDP in fifteen to twenty-five years, if it can sustain these trends.[6] The rise of China in economic terms has led to ongoing debate over whether there is a growing "China threat," and if so, what the United States can and should do about it. This section will use the trade expectations argument to show that China's increasing economic dependence is the one factor, other than perhaps Taiwan, that is likely to lead to a deterioration of Sino-American relations and yet, paradoxically, also the factor that is most likely to keep the peace. Over the next two decades, everything will depend on how the two sides play their cards and the impact of their policies on their respective views of the future economic environment.

The biggest problem China faces is the same one that plagued the United States after World War II: the very speed of its economic growth has greatly increased the raw material demands of its economy, particularly in energy. For the sake of space, I will focus on China's burgeoning dependence on foreign oil, given oil's vital importance to almost every sector of a modern economy. In 1993, China went from being a net exporter of oil to being a net importer. Over the next decade and a half, even as domestic production increased by a third, China's demand for oil increased almost more than two and a half times, to the point where China now relies on outsiders for more than 55 percent of its oil needs. Domestic production is expected to soon peak, even as consumption races ahead. By 2025 to 2030, according to most estimates, China will have to import over 75 percent of its consumed oil from abroad.[7] We saw

[6] The above statistics are on the conservative side and reflect the broad consensus opinions of China scholars. See especially the following edited volumes: Shambaugh 2005; Womack 2010; Ross and Feng 2008; Collins et al. 2008; see also Kang 2007; Jacques 2009; Friedberg 2011. A scholar's particular predictions will depend on which Chinese historical government statistics are employed and the way the undervalued Chinese yuan is adjusted to capture the true size of China's economic output. Many have argued that to sustain its phenomenal growth, China will have to reduce its reliance on exports while building domestic markets through increased consumption and lower overall savings rate (after the 2008 financial crisis, Chinese leaders seemed to take this advice to heart). This section assumes that China will continue its strong growth, even if at somewhat-lower levels than in the past. Of course, if China should start to stagnate due to environmental degradation and traditional S-curve determinants (Gilpin 1981), we should expect Beijing to be less inclined to moderation and more likely to initiate hard-line policies to prop up its waning regional position (see Copeland 2000b, 15–27, 240–45).

[7] These figures are drawn from the *Washington Post*, September 18, 2011, A1 (based on the International Energy Agency's World Energy Outlook report, 2010); *People's Online Daily*, February 5, 2013, english.peopledaily.com.cn/90778/8122545.html; Pietz 2008; Downs 2010; Freeman 2008.

in chapter 6 that growing US oil dependence after 1943 greatly increased US willingness to project military power around the world and occasionally use hard-line measures to maintain access to it. One of the key questions that must be addressed is whether China's growing dependence will force it over the two decades to follow a similar route—that is, switch to a power projection strategy that could only be seen in Washington as a challenge to US military dominance around the world.

The problem of increasing dependence has been the focus of the Chinese leaders for more than a decade. Their main concern boils down to this: Would the US government ever use its vast superiority in naval and conventional power to block China's access to its historically most important oil suppliers—the states in the Middle East and Africa? China faces what its leadership calls "the Malacca problem." More than four-fifths of China's foreign oil comes through the narrow Malacca Strait between Malaysia and Indonesia. The US navy, ostensibly to deter pirates, has overseen the protection of this critical sea lane of communication for the last half century. From the Chinese perspective, however, the strait constitutes a potential choke point that Washington could use as leverage to deter China from adequately addressing its foreign policy concerns (e.g., Taiwanese talk of independence) or to contain or even reverse China's overall industrial and technological growth.[8]

The United States has shied away from using China's oil dependence as a direct tool in the two states' diplomatic relations. As an economic realist might point out, though, this has not stopped Chinese leaders from becoming obsessed with their growing dependence on oil-rich states and reliance on the United States for continued access to them. Where economic realism goes wrong is in its insistence that dependence on vital raw materials necessarily leads actors to adopt hard-line aggressive policies to maintain their access. Over the past two decades, China has been remarkably unwilling to seriously challenge the naval status quo in the Indian Ocean and Malacca Strait (see Collins et al. 2008). This cooperative attitude can be traced directly to one overarching fact: the US willingness to avoid practicing any form of economic containment against China reminiscent of the old Cold War days. There are a number of reasons for this US reticence, as I discuss below, but the effect has been a straightforward one. Chinese leaders have maintained a positive view of the long-term global economic environment, and given this, have had a strong incentive to avoid the kinds of actions that might set off a trade-security spiral with highly dangerous consequences. Both sides seem to have learned from the spiraling US-Japanese conflict of the 1930s and have no wish to repeat

[8] See Collins and Murray 2008; Kaplan 2010; Pollack 2008; Holmes and Yoshihara 2008; Collins, Erickson, and Goldstein 2008.

that experience. China has in fact gone to great lengths to demonstrate that it is committed to an open door in Asia—that it is not in any way trying to re-create a restrictive coprosperity sphere for its own benefit—and that it is more than willing to bind itself to institutional arrangements that demonstrate its peaceful intentions.

Both actors can be seen to be behaving in highly rational ways given the economic realities they both face. The United States is now highly dependent on Chinese investments in American treasury bills to cover the ongoing deficits of the US government. China need the continued US purchase of Chinese goods to keep growth going and supply the foreign currency reserves that give China financial leverage on the world stage. In fact, China's strategy over the last three decades can be seen as nothing short of brilliant. Deng Xiao-ping noted in his famous "24-character" internal policy statement in the early 1990s that China should bide its time, hide its capabilities, and not appear to be seeking to assert a leadership position in international politics.[9] By not rocking the diplomatic boat, China could build its economic power in peace, using its growing ability to produce inexpensive quality products to beat others at their own game. That strategy had a downside: it would necessarily increase China's dependence on others for raw materials, investments, and markets. But like Japan after 1870, this was a trade-off that China was more than willing to make in order to catch up to the established industrial powers. Joining hundreds of international institutions, participating in world forums and G20 summits, and demonstrating a willingness to cooperate on trade and finance issues of global significance has proved a great way to ease US and neighboring states' fears that China's growth would ever constitute a threat in the Asian theater, let alone around the world (Johnston 2003, 2004, 2007, 2013).

The situation as it now stands is significantly different from the one that arose in the aftermath of World War II. As we saw in chapter 6, US leaders by 1945 were very worried about the postwar rise of the Soviet Union, despite seeing Stalin as a largely moderate and reasonable geopolitician. Their concerns, aside from the fear of long-term Soviet growth and changing intentions of future Soviet leaders, were twofold: first, that small states on the periphery would have Communist revolutions that would make them fall into the Soviet economic and political sphere; and second, that the Soviet ideology of the time called for closed economic spheres, meaning that the United States would not have access to the resources and markets of these peripheral states after their revolutions. In the last three decades, however, China has gone to great lengths to show that it is a different fish from the old Soviet Union. China is not seeking

[9] Sutter 2005, 293; Jacques 2009, 348; Jiang 2008, 31–32.

to support revolutions or ideological dominance abroad; instead, it is a highly pragmatic state, wanting only sound economic deals that enhance the penetration of Chinese products and Chinese access to raw materials. Moreover, by adopting the Western approach to trade relations, including the joining of the World Trade Organization and pursuit of most-favored nation status with its trade partners, it is demonstrating that any smaller states that do gravitate toward China for straightforward economic reasons will not in any way be closed off from trade or investment with the Western powers.[10]

This all means a muting of American worries that China will cut the United States off from access to resources, investments, and markets once China catches up to the United States in total GDP.[11] Given that intentions can change, of course, there will always be a concern that once China is on top, it will switch to a more closed economic strategy that serves to exacerbate US decline. Yet in the short term, the downside risks of sparking a destabilizing trade-security spiral will likely continue to overshadow any long-term fears of the future for all but the most extreme US government officials and analysts. Neither party in the United States is thus likely to switch to a CoCom-like economic containment policy against China to reduce its growth rate.

Still, China's strategy of economic engagement with the world also contains a subtle hedging dimension—one that may be understandable within the anarchic context of international politics, but that could have destabilizing consequences for long-term US-Chinese relations. For one thing, China is trying its best to diversify its energy imports away from its primary reliance on Middle East and African oil. Over the last decade, China has built oil and gas pipelines to Kazakhstan, Turkmenistan, and Russia, and increased oil exploration in the East and South China seas. A pipeline that would go from Iran into Pakistan and over the Karakorum mountains into western China has been actively discussed, too.[12] Such

---

[10] See Copeland 2003; Johnston 2007, 2013; Goldstein 2003, 2005; Rotberg 2008.

[11] Nuclear weapons and satellite reconnaissance, furthermore, make it highly unlikely that China would ever think of launching a surprise attack on the US homeland or against major US allies.

[12] Lo 2008; Kozyrev 2008; Kaplan 2010. Recently there has been much talk about China's increased "assertiveness" in defending, for example, its territorial claims in the East China Sea as well as its energy exploration and access rights in the South China Sea. Yet in such disputes, Beijing has been acting largely reactively, seeking to counter claims to sovereignty over islands in these seas by Japan, the Philippines, Vietnam, and other states. Moreover, it has been willing to moderate its posture when other powers object, and has continued its broader policy of cooperation across almost every other policy issue. (For a incisive analysis showing that China's new assertiveness is neither new nor terribly assertive, see Johnston 2013.) Overall, it must be said that US analysts often judge China by standards they do not apply to either recent US behavior (e.g., in the Middle East) or the

pipelines not only give China more control over its access to oil; over the long term they would reduce US leverage over Chinese foreign policy as well. Beijing is also implementing plans to build up a three-month strategic reserve of oil to lessen any shock caused by a cutoff, and give suppliers and the United States less of an incentive to implement oil sanctions. Finally, China has solidified relations with Pakistan and Burma, and is helping both nations construct deepwater harbors that once the necessary pipelines are constructed, would allow China to bring Middle Eastern and African oil into the country without having to go through the Malacca Strait.[13]

All this makes good strategic sense, notwithstanding the up-front economic cost. With oil consumption expected to rise from eight to fifteen million barrels a day over the next two decades, the pipelines from Central Asia, Russia, and Iran will give China additional suppliers to help fill any supply shortfalls.[14] The proposed pipelines from harbors in Pakistan and Burma can provide China with alternative routes that would undercut any US threats to refuse passage of oil tankers bound for China through the Malacca Strait. Yet the question that hovers over US-China relations is this: Just how long can China maintain such a strategy without having to build up a power projection capability needed to protect the pipelines and trade routes (not to mention its allies and oil suppliers) from emerging threats? The United States found itself after 1943 having to actively project its naval and conventional power into the Middle East in order to deter threats, and from Eisenhower onward, respond to them by occasionally putting boots on the ground. Will Chinese leaders eventually be forced to project significant naval power into the Indian Ocean, or perhaps intervene in the affairs of Central Asian states, just to maintain their sense of secure access to energy?

The theory of this book would predict that Chinese leaders will continue to be cautious about turning to such strong power projection options, at least as long as they remain confident that the United States is willing to sustain the free flow of oil. To build a large navy and start sending it into the Indian Ocean might seem to make sense from an economic realist perspective. But this is not the multipolar environment of the 1880s and 1890s when new powers such as Italy, Japan, and Germany could build up their naval forces to protect their trade without

United States' own history as a rising power (e.g., over twenty military interventions in Latin America and the Caribbean from 1898 to 1930).

[13] Western analysts have dubbed this policy as China's "string of pearls" strategy for the Indian Ocean. See Holmes and Yoshihara 2008; Collins, Erickson, and Goldstein 2008; Kaplan 2010; Myint-U 2011.

[14] *Washington Post*, September 18, 2011, A1; Downs 2010, 186.

automatically provoking the dominant naval power (Britain) into a hard-line reaction.[15] In the current situation of clear US naval and conventional hegemony, no American administration would take kindly to a significant change in Chinese naval policy. Officials in Beijing understand this. They know that a new Chinese power projection policy would almost certainly set off a trade-security spiral, with US economic sanctioning and alliance efforts likely forcing China to pressure neighbors to become part of a Chinese economic sphere. The undermining of three decades of economic progress—not to mention a rise in the risk of actual war—would follow as a result. Until trade expectations take a downturn, then, Chinese leaders will probably play it smart, and continue Deng's policy of building economic power and not rocking the geopolitical boat.

What all this depends on, of course, is a US willingness not to change *its* policy—that is, not to initiate a turn toward the economic or political containment of China. Rising states have obvious incentives to avoid rocking the boat to keep the economic benefits of engagement flowing. For relatively declining states such as the United States, however, there is an incentive to initiate a switch to hard-line policies to slow the other's economic growth before it is too late (see Copeland 2000b, 35–53, 240–46). Fortunately for world peace, there are three good reasons for Chinese leaders to believe that the United States, even under future Republican administrations, will not return to the kind of tight economic sanctions regime imposed on the Soviet Union (and China) during the Cold War. The first and probably the weakest of the three is the ideological orientation of the United States as a liberal free trade state. US leaders who find themselves inclined to raise economic restrictions will likely also find themselves pressured by legislators and multinationals to maintain generally open policies with Beijing as long as Beijing reciprocates. Still, Chinese officials cannot count on ideology alone to keep trade and investment flowing in the decades ahead as their country starts to overtake the United States in total GDP. After all, during the Cold War a "liberal" United States proved able to implement one of the most severe peacetime sanctioning regimes in world history in the face of another rising great power threat.

The second reason for Chinese optimism is more powerful: US leaders of both parties have shown that they understand well that a containment policy would not only cost the United States absolutely (in lost loans and less trade) but also would lead to a risky trade-security spiral that could, in turn, lead to a new Cold War or worse. Before George W. Bush came

---

[15] Britain of course did participate in a major naval race with Germany after 1897 (see chapters 3 and 8). Up to that point, however, its focus had been on the naval growth of its traditional rivals, France and Russia.

into office in 2001, for example, he denied any strategic partnership with China and instead spoke of a new Sino-US strategic competition. Yet through his eight years in power, he maintained the economic engagement policies established by his predecessors. Future hard-line leaders from either party will likely also find themselves sobered by the implications of a CoCom-like trade-sanctioning regime for the stability of US-Chinese relations.

If in another two decades China does indeed seem on the verge of overtaking the United States in total GDP, there may be great domestic pressure to switch to at least a moderate economic containment policy to keep the United States on top. This is where a third reason for optimism comes in—one that is frequently overlooked by analysts. China has been doing such a good job in establishing strong commercial connections with Japan, the European Union, and its Asian neighbors that the United States will have an increasingly hard time over the coming decades *implementing* a new CoCom program—at least if China continues to appear fully committed to an open global economic system. In the early Cold War era, the Europeans, Japanese, and other US allies went along with the US-led CoCom program because they agreed on the reality of the Soviet threat, and had economies that were highly dependent on the US market and American capital. Such is not the case today. These states have strong and growing economic ties with China that they would be loath to break just because some hard-line US administration argued that it was time to contain the rising Chinese colossus. Moreover, they would likely disagree that China was enough of a future threat to warrant strong—and economically costly—sanctions now, especially with the populations of these countries clamoring for more jobs and low-cost products. If even by the 1950s the Europeans were pressing for a relaxation of CoCom in the face of Khrushchev's peaceful coexistence campaign, it is close to certain that American allies across the board would reject a renewal of a CoCom-like sanctions regime against China or would skirt its provisions in order to make individual gains. And if a sanctions regime had significant leakage, it would end up hurting the United States even more than continued engagement. China could make up for lost US-China trade through trade with other states, and such trade diversion would lead the United States to decline even more steeply in relative terms.

For all these reasons, the Chinese leadership should have continued confidence in the American willingness to sustain a policy of free trade and open investment flows into the foreseeable future. Given the downside risks of provoking a trade-security spiral, Beijing will therefore be likely to maintain its low-profile posture for some time to come. If there is one major caveat to this rosy picture, it lies with that pervasive bugbear of great power politics: the role of third parties. We have seen in previous chapters just how often third parties can interrupt a great power peace by forcing one or both sides to take a hard-line position in a crisis that they are otherwise loath to adopt. If Taiwan, for example, made a major push for full independence, China might have to turn to military options that might in turn lead to US economic sanctions as a first-cut response. If Chinese leaders believed these sanctions were part of a long-term economic containment program, they might have to move to harder-line policies in the region, and a trade-security spiral to a Cold War would not be out of the question. US leaders might also find themselves under great pressure to move toward sanctions if they found that China's economic allies in Africa, Asia, and Latin America were adopting highly repressive policies with Beijing's support, or simply aligning so tightly with China that the United States' "open access" to these countries seemed questionable. What might appear to be China's increasingly closed sphere might trigger a shift to sanctions that could set a new Cold War in motion, especially if growing US and China resource needs seem to foreshadow a scramble for nonrenewable raw materials in developing nations.

Overall, though, the reasons for optimistic economic expectations in both China and the United States should outweigh the reasons for pessimism for at least a couple more decades. Both countries not only do well absolutely from the current trade and investment relationship, but leaders on both sides are highly inclined to avoid a repeat of either the disastrous 1930–41 period or the dangerous Cold War era. Peace is never a certainty, of course, and triggers caused by third parties or overly fearful estimates of the future could lead to an action-reaction cycle of sanctioning and military buildups that ends up undermining the decades-long cooperative relationship between Beijing and Washington. Still, in the nuclear age, the risks of spiraling between great powers are self-evidently high. If actors can learn from history (and perhaps international relations theory?), they should be able to take steps to solidify each other's positive expectations as well as avoid the missteps that can lead to crisis and war.

Epilogue: The Path Forward

This book has demonstrated the explanatory and predictive value of approaching the question of economic interdependence and war from a dynamic perspective. By incorporating into its deductive causal logic a sense of how leaders think about future dependency and future commercial access, the theory of trade expectations is able to explain significantly more of the diplomatic-historical evidence and quantitative scholarship than its two main competitors, liberalism and economic realism along with their subsidiary theories. This suggests that the new research agenda on commerce and conflict should be guided by three main priorities. First, any deductive theories that rely on liberal and realist assumptions should move away from comparative-static models based on snapshots of current levels of interstate trade and investment. Since leaders are driven more by their expectations of the future commercial environment than by whether current trade and investment flows are low or high, deductive theories need to be built on this foundation. With this change in place, empirical analysis will adjust accordingly.

Second and related, there is still theoretical work to be done specifying the conditions under which states will likely believe that the future commercial environment will be stable and open, rather than unstable and restrictive. Chapter 1 laid out a number of exogenous factors that should determine a leader's sense of optimism or pessimism regarding the future, including third parties, power trends, raw material reserves, and internal constraints on an adversary's executive branch. We saw these factors play important roles in the shifting levels of great power conflict from 1790 to 1991. Yet more theoretical study is needed on the ways such factors interact with one another and the conditions under which some factors are likely to be more causally salient than others.

Third and finally, research must delve more deeply into the nature of trade-security dilemmas as well as the forces that set off destabilizing trade-security spirals of mistrust and increasingly hard-line behavior. This book has examined some of the most obvious factors that drive intense trade-security dilemmas, including concerns for the other's internal stability and future type, the degree to which geography and industrialization lead actors to project military power to protect access routes, and the types of vital goods that third parties possess (e.g., oil) that may force great powers to get involved in regional disputes. Yet our understanding of trade-security dilemmas and how they differ from more traditional military-security dilemmas is still at an early stage. The problem of making credible commitments to peaceful behavior in environments of uncertainty has been widely explored over the last two decades, for example. But we still know little about how states build reputations for economic openness and for being disinclined to set trade-security spirals into motion.

I end this book with a call for the proper integration of realist and liberal insights into the development of sound theories. The realist concern for economic power along with the security implications of being cut off from vital goods and markets has provided the foundation of the alternative theory of this study. And once we bring in the fears leaders have regarding their economic environments and long-term relative power, we can see why so much of world history is the tragic result of intense security competitions that all sides seem incapable of ending. Yet unit-level variables can still play important subsidiary roles in the outbreak of historical conflicts, if not necessarily for the reasons liberals argue. We have seen that domestic factors in "the other" often drove security-seeking actors to pursue hard-line policies by increasing these actors' pessimism about their ability to sustain access to trade and investments over time. So while unit-level factors may rarely be the primary propelling reasons for great power conflict, they can still serve as parameters shaping the likelihood that security-seeking states will pursue aggressive policies against states they believe are hostile to their economic interests. In this way, we can maintain a focus on the security fears that drive so much of great power behavior in history, and yet also recognize that unit-level factors external to our primary actors can sometimes lead them into wars and destabilizing conflicts that they would otherwise want to avoid.

Bibliography

SECONDARY SOURCES

Albrecht-Carrié, René. 1968. *The Concert of Europe, 1815–1914*. New York: Harper and Row.

———. 1973. *A Diplomatic History of Europe since the Congress of Vienna*. Rev. ed. New York: Harper and Row.

Ambrose, Stephen E. 1984. *Eisenhower the President, 1952–1969*. London: George Allen.

Anderson, Matthew. 1979. "Russia and the Eastern Question, 1821–41." In *Europe's Balance of Power 1815–1848*, edited by Alan Sked. London: Macmillan.

Anderson, Richard D. 1993. *Public Policy in an Authoritarian State*. Ithaca, NY: Cornell University Press.

Angell, Norman. 1933. *The Great Illusion*. 2nd. ed. New York: Putnam's Sons.

Arad, Ruth, Seev Hirsch, and Alfred Tovias. 1983. *The Economics of Peacemaking*. New York: St. Martin's Press.

Arbatov, Georgi. 1993. *The System: An Insider's Life in Soviet Politics*. New York: Random House.

Armstrong, Charles K. 2003. *The North Korean Revolution, 1945–50*. Ithaca, NY: Cornell University Press.

Ashley, Percy. 1910. *Modern Tariff History: Germany, United States, France*. 2nd ed. New York: John Murray.

Aslund, Anders. 1989. *Gorbachev's Struggle for Economic Reform*. Ithaca, NY: Cornell University Press.

Backer, John H. 1983. *Winds of History*. New York: Van Nostrand Reinhold.

Baker, James A. 1995. *The Politics of Diplomacy*. New York: Putnam's Sons.

Baldwin, David A. 1980. "Interdependence and Power: A Conceptual Analysis." *International Organization* 34 (4): 471–506.

———. 1985. *Economic Statecraft*. Princeton, NJ: Princeton University Press.

———, ed. 1993. *Neorealism and Neoliberalism*. New York: Columbia University Press.

Barbieri, Katherine. 1996. "Economic Interdependence: Path to Peace or Source of Interstate Conflict." *Journal of Peace Research* 33 (1): 29–49.

———. 2002. *The Liberal Illusion: Does Trade Promote Peace?* Ann Arbor: University of Michigan Press.

Barkin, Kenneth D. 1970. *The Controversy over German Industrialization, 1890–1902*. Chicago: University of Chicago Press.

Barnhart, Michael. 1987. *Japan Prepares for Total War: The Search for Economic Security, 1919–41*. Ithaca, NY: Cornell University Press.

Barraclough, Geoffrey. 1964. *An Introduction to Contemporary History*. Harmondsworth, UK: Penguin.

Basso, Cristina, Barry J. Maron, Domenico Corrado, and Gaetano Thiene. 2000. "Clinical Profile of Congenital Coronary Artery Anomalies with Origin from the Wrong Aortic Sinus Leading to Sudden Death in Young Competitive Athletes." *Journal of the American College of Cardiology* 35 (6): 1493–1501.

Baumgart, Winfried. 1982. *Imperialism*. Oxford: Oxford University Press.

Bearce, David H. 2001. "The Commercial Institutional Peace: Commerce, Institutions, or Both?" Paper prepared for the International Studies Association annual convention, Chicago, February 20–24.

———. 2003. "Grasping the Commercial Institutional Peace." *International Studies Quarterly* 47 (3): 347–70.

Bearce, David H., and Sawa Omori. 2005. "How Do Commercial Institutions Promote Peace?" *Journal of Peace Research* 42 (6): 659–78.

Beasley, W. G. 1987. *Japanese Imperialism, 1894–1945*. Oxford: Oxford University Press.

Beeching, Jack. 1975. *The Chinese Opium Wars*. New York: Harcourt Brace.

Behr, Edward. 1989. *Hirohito*. New York: Vintage.

Bennett, Andrew, and Colin Elman. 2006. "Complex Causal Relations and Case Study Methods: The Example of Path Dependence." *Political Analysis* 14 (3): 250–67.

Benson, Michelle. 2007. "Trade Expectations: The Trend in Trade and Dyadic Disputes." Typescript, State University of New York at Buffalo.

Beschloss, Michael R. 1988. *Mayday: Eisenhower, Khrushchev, and the U2 Affair*. New York: Harper and Row.

Beschloss, Michael R., and Strobe Talbott. 1993. *At the Highest Levels: The Inside Story of the End of the Cold War*. Boston: Little, Brown.

Bix, Herbert P. 2000. *Hirohito and the Making of Modern Japan*. New York: HarperCollins.

Blue, Gregory. 2000. "Opium for China: The British Connection." In *Opium Regimes: China, Britain, and Japan, 1839–1952*, edited by Timothy Brook and Bob Tadashi Wakabayashi. Berkeley: University of California Press.

Booth, Ken, and Nicholas J. Wheeler. 2008. *The Security Dilemma: Fear, Cooperation, and Trust in World Politics*. New York: Palgrave.

Bourne, Kenneth. 1982. *Palmerston: The Early Years, 1784–1841*. London: Allen Lane.

Brady, Henry E., and David Collier, eds. 2010. *Rethinking Social Inquiry*. 2nd ed. Lanham, MD: Rowman and Littlefield.

Braumoeller, Bear F. 2004. "Hypothesis Testing and Multiplicative Interaction Terms." *International Organization* 58 (4): 807–20.

Braumoeller, Bear F., and Anne Satori. 2004. "The Promise and Perils of Statistics in International Relations." In *Models, Numbers, and Cases: Methods for Studying International Relations*, edited by Detlef F. Sprinz and Yael Wolinsky-Nahmias. Ann Arbor: University of Michigan Press.

Brooks, Stephen G. 1997. "Dueling Realisms." *International Organization* 51 (3): 445–47.

———. 2005. *Producing Security: Multinational Corporations, Globalization, and the Changing Calculus of Conflict*. Princeton, NJ: Princeton University Press.

Brooks, Stephen G., and William C. Wohlforth. 2000–2001. "Power, Globaliza-tion, and the End of the Cold War: Reevaluating a Landmark Case for Ideas." *International Security* 25, no. 3 (Winter): 5–53.

Broszat, Martin. 1981. *The Hitler State.* London: Longham.

Brown, Archie. 1997. *The Gorbachev Factor.* Oxford: Oxford University Press.

Bruck, W. F. 1938. *Social and Economic History of Germany from William II to Hitler, 1888–1938.* Cardiff: Oxford University Press.

Bueno de Mesquita, Bruce, James D. Morrow, Randolph M. Siverson, and Alastair Smith. 1999. "An Institutional Explanation of the Democratic Peace." *American Political Science Review* 93 (4): 791–807.

Bueno de Mesquita, Bruce, Alastair Smith, Randolph M. Siverson, and James D. Morrow. 2003. *The Logic of Political Survival.* Cambridge, MA: MIT Press.

Bullock, Alan. 1964. *Hitler.* Rev. ed. New York: Harper and Row.

Bush, George, and Brent Scowcroft. 1998. *A World Transformed.* New York: Knopf.

Buzan, Barry. 1984. "Economic Structure and International Security." *International Organization* 38, no. 4 (Fall): 597–624.

Cain, Peter J., and Anthony G. Hopkins. 2002. *British Imperialism, 1688–2000.* 2nd ed. Harlow, UK: Longman.

Campbell, Charles S. 1976. *The Transformation of American Foreign Relations, 1865–1900.* New York: Harper and Row.

Carr, Albert, ed. 1941. *Napoleon Speaks.* New York: Viking.

Carr, William. 1991. *The Origins of the Wars of German Unification.* London: Longman.

Carroll, Berenice A. 1968. *Design for Total War: Arms and Economics in the Third Reich.* The Hague: Mouton.

Cashman, Greg. 2013. *What Causes War?* 2nd ed. Lanham, MD: Rowman and Littlefield.

Cecil, Lamar. 1967. *Albert Ballin: Business and Politics in Imperial Germany.* Princeton, NJ: Princeton University Press.

Chamberlain, Muriel E. 1983. *Lord Aberdeen.* London: Longman

Chambers, James. 2004. *Palmerston.* London: John Murray.

Chan, Steve. 1997. "In Search of Democratic Peace: Problems and Promise." *Mershon International Studies Review* 41:59–91.

Chiozza, Giacomo, and H. E. Goemans. 2011. *Leaders and International Conflict.* Cambridge: Cambridge University Press.

Chouchri, Nazli, and Robert North. 1975. *Nations in Conflict: National Growth and International Violence.* New York: Freeman.

Christensen, Thomas J. 2011. *Worse than a Monolith: Alliance Politics and Problems of Coercive Diplomacy in Asia.* Princeton, NJ: Princeton University Press.

Christensen, Thomas J., and Jack Snyder. 1990. "Chain Gangs and Passed Bucks: Predicting Alliance Patterns in Multipolarity." *International Organization* 44 (Spring): 137–68.

Clark, Alan. 1965. *Barbarossa: The Russian-German Conflict, 1941–45.* New York: Quill.

Clubb, O. Edmund. 1971. *China and Russia: The "Great Game."* New York: Columbia University Press.

Cohen, Benjamin. 1973. *The Question of Imperialism*. New York: Basic Books.

Coleman, Fred. 1996. *The Decline and the Fall of the Soviet Empire*. New York: St. Martin's Griffin.

Collier, David, and James Mahoney. 1996. "Insights and Pitfalls: Selection Bias in Qualitative Research." *World Politics* 49, no. 1 (October): 56–91.

Collier, David, James Mahoney, and Jason Seawright. 2004. "Claiming Too Much: Warnings about Selection Bias." In *Rethinking Social Inquiry: Diverse Tools, Shared Standards*, edited by Henry E. Brady and David Collier. Lanham, MD: Rowman and Littlefield.

Collins, Alan. 1997. *The Security Dilemma and the End of the Cold War*. Keele, UK: Keele University Press.

Collins, Gabriel B., Andrew S. Erickson, and Lyle J. Goldstein. 2008. "Chinese Naval Analysts Consider the Energy Question." In *China's Energy Strategy*, edited by Gabriel B. Collins, Andrew S. Erickson, Lyle J. Goldstein, and William S. Murray. Annapolis, MD: Naval Institute Press.

Collins, Gabriel B., Andrew S. Erickson, Lyle J. Goldstein, and William S. Murray, eds. 2008. *China's Energy Strategy*. Annapolis, MD: Naval Institute Press.

Collins, Gabriel B., and William S. Murray. 2008. "No Oil for the Lamps of China?" In *China's Energy Strategy*, edited by Gabriel B. Collins, Andrew S. Erickson, Lyle J. Goldstein, and William S. Murray. Annapolis, MD: Naval Institute Press.

Collis, Maurice. 1946. *Foreign Mud: The Opium Imbroglio at Canton in the 1830s and the Anglo-Chinese War*. New York: W. W. Norton.

Coox, Alvin D. 1985. *Nomohhan: Japan against Russia, 1939*. Stanford, CA: Stanford University Press.

Copeland, Dale C. 1996a. "Economic Interdependence and War: A Theory of Trade Expectations." *International Security* 20 (4): 5–41.

———. 1996b. "Neorealism and the Myth of Bipolar Stability: Toward a New Dynamic Realist Theory of Major War." *Security Studies* 5 (3): 29–89.

———. 1999–2000. "Trade Expectations and the Outbreak of Peace: Détente 1970–74 and the End of the Cold War 1985–91." *Security Studies* 9 (1–2): 15–58.

———. 2000a. "The Constructivist Challenge to Structural Realism: A Review Essay." *International Security* 25 (2): 187–212.

———. 2000b. *The Origins of Major War*. Ithaca, NY: Cornell University Press.

———. 2003. "Economic Interdependence and the Future of U.S.-Chinese Relations." In *International Relations Theory and the Asia-Pacific*, edited by G. John Ikenberry and Michael Mastanduno. New York: Columbia University Press.

———. 2011a. "Rationalist Theories of International Politics and the Problem of the Future." *Security Studies* 20 (3): 441–50.

———. 2011b. "A Tragic Choice: Japanese Preventive Motivations and the Origins of the Pacific War." *International Interactions* 37 (1): 116–26.

———. 2012a. "Realism and Neorealism in the Study of Regional Conflict." In *International Relations Theory and Regional Transformation*, ed. T. V. Paul. Cambridge: Cambridge University Press.

———. 2012b. "Trade Expectations and the Grand Strategies of Germany and Japan in the Interwar Era." In *The Grand Strategies of the Great Powers in the Interwar Era*, edited by Steven Lobell, Norrin Ripsman, and Jeffrey Taliaferro. Cambridge: Cambridge University Press.

———. 2014. "IR Theory and the Three Great Puzzles of the First World War." In *The Outbreak of the First World War: Structure, Politics, and Decision-Making*, edited by Jack S. Levy and John Vasquez. Cambridge: Cambridge University Press.

———. Forthcoming. *Commerce, War, and American Foreign Policy, 1790–2003*.

Coutain, Brian. 2009. "The Unconditional Most-Favored-Nation Clause and the Maintenance of the Liberal Trade Regime in the Postwar 1870s." *International Organization* 63 (1): 139–75.

Craig, Gordon A. 1978. *Germany, 1866–1945*. Oxford: Oxford University Press.

Crescenzi, Mark J. 2005. *Economic Interdependence and Conflict in World Politics*. Lanham, MD: Lexington.

Crowley, James. 1966. *Japan's Quest for Autonomy: National Security and Foreign Policy, 1930–38*. Princeton, NJ: Princeton University Press.

Cumings, Bruce. 1990. *The Origins of the Korean War*. Vol. 2. Princeton, NJ: Princeton University Press.

———. 1997. *Korea's Place in the Sun: A Modern History*. New York: W. W. Norton.

Curtiss, George B. 1912. *The Industrial Development of Nations*. Vol. 1. Binghamton, NY: Curtiss.

Curtiss, John Shelton. 1979. *Russia's Crimean War*. Durham, NC: Duke University Press.

Dafoe, Allan. 2011. "Statistical Critiques of the Democratic Peace: Caveat Emptor." *American Journal of Political Science* 55 (2): 247–62.

Dallek, Robert. 1979. *Franklin D. Roosevelt and American Foreign Policy, 1932–1945*. Oxford: Oxford University Press.

Darby, Phillip. 1987. *Three Faces of Imperialism*. New Haven, CT: Yale University Press.

Davis, Christina L. 2008–9. "Linkage Diplomacy: Economic and Security Bargaining in the Anglo-Japanese Alliance, 1902–23." *International Security* 33 (3): 143–79.

Davis, James W. 2000. *Threats and Promises*. Baltimore: Johns Hopkins University Press.

Davis, Lance E., and Douglass C. North. 1971. *Institutional Change and American Economic Growth*. Cambridge: Cambridge University Press.

Davis, Lynn Etheridge. 1974. *The Cold War Begins: Soviet-American Conflict over Eastern Europe*. Princeton, NJ: Princeton University Press.

Dickinson, G. Lowes. 1926. *The International Anarchy, 1904–1914*. New York: Century.

Dixon, William J. 1994. "Democracy and the Peaceful Settlement of International Conflict." *American Political Science Review* 88 (2): 14–32.

Dobrynin, Anatoly. 1995. *In Confidence*. New York: Random House.

Domke, William J. 1988. *War and the Changing Global System*. New Haven, CT: Yale University Press.

Doder, Dusko. 1986. *Shadows and Whispers: Power Politics inside the Kremlin from Brezhnev to Gorbachev*. Harmondsworth, UK: Penguin.

Dobbs, Charles. 1982. *The Unwanted Symbol: American Foreign Policy, the Cold War, and Korea*. Kent, OH: Kent State University Press.

Dorussen, Hans. 2006. "Hetereogenous Trade Interests and Conflict: What You Trade Matters." *Journal of Conflict Resolution* 50 (1): 87–107.

Dower, J. W. 1979. *Empire and Aftermath: Yoshida Shigerua and the Japanese Experience, 1878–1954.* Cambridge, MA: Harvard University Press.

Downs, Erica S. 2010. "China's Energy Rise." In *China's Rise in Historical Perspective*, edited by Brantly Womack. Lanham, MD: Rowman and Littlefield.

Doyle, Michael W. 1986a. *Empires.* Ithaca: Cornell University Press.

———. 1986b. "Liberalism and World Politics." *American Political Science Review* 90 (4): 1151–69.

Dueck, Colin. 2006. *Reluctant Crusaders.* Princeton, NJ: Princeton University Press.

Duus, Peter. 1984. "Economic Dimensions of Meiji Imperialism: The Case of Korea, 1895–1910." In *The Japanese Colonial Empire, 1895–1945*, edited by Ramon H. Myers and Mark R. Peattie. Princeton, NJ: Princeton University Press.

Duus, Peter, Ramon H. Myers, and Mark R. Peattie, eds. 1989. *The Japanese Informal Empire in China, 1895–1937.* Princeton, NJ: Princeton University Press.

Earle, Edward Mead. 1924. *Turkey, the Great Powers, and the Baghdad Railway: A Study in Imperialism.* New York: Macmillan.

Eisenberg, Carolyn Woods. 1996. *Drawing the Line: The American Decision to Divide Germany, 1944–1949.* Cambridge: Cambridge University Press.

Eisenhower, Dwight D. 1963. *Mandate for Change, 1953–1956.* Garden City, NY: Doubleday.

———. 1965. *Waging Peace, 1956–1961.* Garden City, NY: Doubleday.

Ellman, Michael, and Vladimir Kontorovich, eds. 1992. *The Disintegration of the Soviet Economic System.* London: Routledge.

Fairbank, John King. 1953. *Trade and Diplomacy on the China Coast.* Cambridge, MA: Harvard University Press.

Farber, Henry S., and Joanne Gowa. 1995. "Politics and Peace." *International Security* 20 (2): 123–46.

Fay, Peter Ward. 1976. *The Opium War, 1840–1842.* New York: W. W. Norton.

Fearon, James D. 1995. "Rationalist Explanations for War." *International Organization* 49 (3): 379–414.

———. 1998. "Commitment Problems and the Spread of Ethnic Conflict." In *The International Spread of Ethnic Conflict*, edited by David A. Lake and Donald Rothchild. Princeton, NJ: Princeton University Press.

Feis, Herbert. 1931. *Europe, the World's Banker, 1870–1914.* New Haven, CT: Yale University Press.

Fenby, Jonathan. 2004. *Chiang Kai-Shek.* New York: Carroll and Graf.

Fieldhouse, David. 1973. *Economics and Empire, 1830–1914.* Ithaca, NY: Cornell University Press.

Fischer, Fritz. 1967. *Germany's Aims in the First World War.* New York: W. W. Norton.

———. 1975. *War of Illusions: German Policies from 1911 to 1914.* New York: W. W. Norton.

Freeman, Chas W., Jr. 2008. "Energy as China's Achilles' Heel?" In *China's Energy Strategy*, edited by Gabriel B. Collins, Andrew S. Erickson, Lyle J. Goldstein, and William S. Murray. Annapolis, MD: Naval Institute Press.

Freiberger, Steven Z. 1992. *Dawn over Suez: The Rise of American Power in the Middle East, 1953–1957.* Chicago: Ivan R. Dee.

Friedberg, Aaron L. 1988. *The Weary Titan: Britain and the Experience of Relative Decline*. Princeton, NJ: Princeton University Press.

———. 2011. *A Contest for Supremacy: China, America, and the Struggle for Mastery in Asia*. New York: W. W. Norton.

Friedrich, Robert J. 1982. "In Defense of Multiplicative Terms in Multiple Regression Equations." *American Journal of Political Science* 26 (4): 797–833.

Fuller, William C. 1992. *Strategy and Power in Russia, 1600–1914*. New York: Free Press.

Funigiello, Philip J. 1988. *American-Soviet Trade in the Cold War*. Chapel Hill: University of North Carolina Press.

Fursenko, Aleksandr, and Timothy Naftali. 1997. *"One Hell of a Gamble": Khrushchev, Castro, and Kennedy, 1958–64*. New York: W. W. Norton.

———. 2007. *Khrushchev's Cold War*. New York: W. W. Norton.

Gaddis, John Lewis. 1972. *The United States and the Origins of the Cold War, 1941–1947*. New York: Columbia University Press.

———. 1983. "The Emerging Post-Revisionist Synthesis on the Origins of the Cold War." *Diplomatic History* 7 (3): 171–90.

———. 1997. *We Now Know: Rethinking Cold War History*. Oxford: Oxford University Press.

Gardner, Lloyd C. 1972. *Architects of Illusion: Men and Ideas in American Foreign Policy, 1941–49*. New York: Quadrangle.

———. 1993. *Spheres of Influence: The Great Powers Partition Europe from Munich to Yalta*. Chicago: Ivan Dee.

———. 2009. *Three Kings: The Rise of an American Empire in the Middle East after World War II*. New York: New Press.

Garthoff, Raymond L. 1994a. *Détente and Confrontation*. Rev. ed. Washington, DC: Brookings.

———. 1994b. *The Great Transition: American-Soviet Relations and the End of the Cold War*. Washington, DC: Brookings.

Gartzke, Erik. 2003. "The Classical Liberals Were Just Lucky: A Few Thoughts about Interdependence and Peace." In *Economic Interdependence and International Conflict*, edited by Edward D. Mansfield and Brian M. Pollins. Ann Arbor: University of Michigan Press.

———. 2007. "The Capitalist Peace." *American Journal of Political Science* 51 (1): 166–91.

Gartzke, Erik, and Joseph Hewett. 2010. "International Crises and the Capitalist Peace." *International Interactions* 36 (2): 115–45.

Gartzke, Erik, and Quan Li. 2003. "War, Peace, and the Invisible Hand: Positive Political Externalities of Economic Globalization." *International Studies Quarterly* 47 (4): 561–86.

Gartzke, Erik, Quan Li, and Charles Boehmer. 2001. "Investing in the Peace: Economic Interdependence and International Conflict." *International Organization* 55 (2): 391–438.

Gatzke, Hans W. 1950. *Germany's Drive to the West*. Baltimore: Johns Hopkins University Press.

Gasiorowski, Mark. 1986. "Economic Interdependence and International Conflict: Some Cross-national Evidence." *International Studies Quarterly* 30 (1): 22–38.

Gasiorowski, Mark, and Solomon Polachek. 1982. "Conflict and Interdependence: East-West Linkages in the Era of Detente." *Journal of Conflict Resolution* 26 (4): 709–29.

Gavin, Francis J. 1999. "Power, Politics, and U.S. Policy in Iran, 1950–1953." *Journal of Cold War Studies* 1 (1): 58–89.

Gelpi, Christopher, and Joseph M. Grieco. 2003a. "Democracy, Interdependence, and the Sources of the Liberal Peace." Manuscript, Duke University, Durham, NC.

———. 2003b. "Economic Interdependence, the Democratic State, and the Liberal Peace." In *Economic Interdependence and International Conflict*, edited by Edward D. Mansfield and Brian M. Pollins. Ann Arbor: University of Michigan Press.

———. 2008. "Democracy, Interdependence, and the Sources of the Liberal Peace." *Journal of Peace Research* 45 (1): 17–36.

George, Alexander L. 1983. "Détente: The Search for a Constructive Relationship." In *Managing the U.S. Soviet Rivalry*, edited by Alexander George. Boulder, CO: Westview.

George, Alexander L., and Andrew Bennett. 2005. *Case Studies and Theory Development in the Social Sciences*. Cambridge, MA: MIT Press.

George, Alexander L., and Richard Smoke. 1974. *Deterrence in American Foreign Policy*. New York: Columbia University Press.

Gholz, Eugene, and Daryl G. Press. 2001. "The Effects of Wars on Neutral Countries: Why It Doesn't Pay to Preserve the Peace." *Security Studies* 10 (4): 1–57.

———. 2010. "Protecting 'The Prize': Oil and the U.S. National Interest." *Security Studies* 19 (3): 453–85.

Gilpin, Robert. 1975. *U.S. Power and the Multinational Corporation*. New York: Basic Books.

———. 1977. "Economic Interdependence and National Security in Historical Perspective." In *Economic Issues and National Security*, edited by Klaus Knorr and Frank N. Trager. Lawrence, KS: Allen.

———. 1981. *War and Change in World Politics*. Cambridge: Cambridge University Press.

———. 1987. *The Political Economy of International Relations*. Princeton, NJ: Princeton University Press.

Glaser, Charles. 1994–95. "Realists as Optimists." *International Security* 15 (3): 50–90.

———. 1997. "The Security Dilemma Revisited." *World Politics* 50 (1): 171–201.

———. 2010. *Rational Theory of International Politics*. Princeton, NJ: Princeton University Press.

Gleditsch, Nils Petter. 2008. "The Liberal Moment Fifteen Years On." *International Studies Quarterly* 52 (4): 691–712.

Gochal, Joseph R., and Jack S. Levy. 2004. "Crisis Management or Conflict of Interests? A Case Study of the Origins of the Crimean War." In *Multiple Paths to Knowledge in International Relations*, edited by Zeev Maoz, Alex Mintz, T. Clifton Morgan, Glenn Palmer, and Richard J. Stoll. Lexington, MA: Lexington Books.

Goddard, Stacie E. 2008–9. "When Right Makes Might: How Prussia Overturned the European Balance of Power." *International Security* 33 (3): 110–42.

Goemans, H. E. 2000. *War and Punishment*. Princeton, NJ: Princeton University Press.

Goldfrank, David M. 1994. *The Origins of the Crimean War*. London: Longman.

Goldstein, Avery. 2003. "An Emerging China's Emerging Grand Strategy: A Neo-Bismarckian Turn?" In *International Relations Theory and the Asia-Pacific*, edited by G. John Ikenberry and Michael Mastanduno. New York: Columbia University Press.

———. 2005. *Rising to the Challenge: China's Grand Strategy and International Security*. Stanford, CA: Stanford University Press.

Goncharov, Sergei, John Lewis, and Litai Xue. 1995. *Uncertain Partners: Stalin, Mao, and the Korean War*. Stanford, CA: Stanford University Press.

Goralski, Robert, and Russell W. Freeburg. 1987. *Oil and War: How the Deadly Struggle for Fuel in WWII Meant Victory or Defeat*. New York: William Morrow.

Gorbachev, Mikhail. 1987. *Perestroika*. New York: Harper and Row.

———. 1996. *Memoirs*. New York: Doubleday.

Gowa, Joanne S. 1989. "Bipolarity, Multipolarity, and Free Trade." *American Political Science Review* 83 (4): 1245–56.

———. 1994. *Allies, Adversaries, and International Trade*. Princeton, NJ: Princeton University Press.

Gowa, Joanne S., and Edward D. Mansfield. 1993. "Power Politics and International Trade." *American Political Science Review* 87 (2): 408–20.

Greenberg, Michael. 1951. *British Trade and the Opening of China, 1800–42*. New York: Monthly Review Press.

Grieco, Joseph. 1988. "Anarchy and the Limits of Cooperation: A Realist Critique." *International Organization* 42 (3): 485–529.

———. 1993. "Understanding the Problem of International Cooperation: The Limits of Neoliberal Institutionalism." In *Neorealism and Neoliberalism*, edited by David A. Baldwin. New York: Columbia University Press.

Griswold, A. Whitney. 1938. *The Far Eastern Policy of the United States*. New Haven, CT: Yale University Press.

Haas, Mark. 2005. *The Ideological Origins of Great Power Politics*. Ithaca, NY: Cornell University Press.

Haftel, Yoram. 2007. "Designing for Peace: Regional Integration Arrangements, Institution Variation, and Militarized Interstate Disputes." *International Organization* 61:217–37.

Haggard, Stephan, and Robert R. Kaufman. 2012. "Inequality and Regime Change: Democratic Transitions and the Stability of Democratic Rule." *American Political Science Review* 106 (3): 495–516.

Hahn, Peter L. 1991. *The United States, Great Britain, and Egypt, 1945–1956*. Chapel Hill: University of North Carolina Press.

Hamilton, Edith, and Huntington Cairns, eds. 1961. *The Collected Dialogues of Plato*. Princeton, NJ: Princeton University Press.

Hanes, W. Travis, and Frank Sanello. 2002. *The Opium Wars*. Naperville, IL: Sourcebooks.

Harbutt, Fraser J. 2010. *Yalta 1945*. Cambridge: Cambridge University Press.

Hargreaves, John D. 1966. *Prelude to the Partition of West Africa.* New York: St. Martin's Press.

Harriman, Averell, and Elie Abel. 1975. *Special Envoy to Churchill and Stalin, 1941–1946.* New York: Random House.

Harrison, Hope M. 1993. "Ulbricht and the 'Concrete Rose': New Archival Evidence on the Dynamics of Soviet–East German Relations and the Berlin Crisis, 1958–61." Working paper no. 5. Washington, DC: Cold War in International History Project.

Hearden, Patrick J. 2002. *Architects of Globalism.* Fayetteville: University of Arkansas Press.

Heckscher, Eli F. 1933. *Mercantilism*, 2 vols. London: George Allen.

Hegre, Havard. 2000. "Development and the Liberal Peace." *Journal of Peace Research* 37 (1): 5–30.

Heinrichs, Waldo. 1988. *Threshold of War: Franklin D. Roosevelt and American Entry into World War II.* New York: Oxford University Press.

Herold, J. Christopher, ed. 1955. *The Mind of Napoleon.* New York: Columbia University Press.

Herring, George C. 1973. *Aid to Russia, 1941–1946: Strategy, Diplomacy, the Origins of the Cold War.* New York: Columbia University Press.

Herwig, Holger H. 1976. *Politics of Frustration: The United States in German Naval Planning, 1889–1941.* Boston: Little, Brown.

Herz, John H. 1950. "Idealist Internationalism and the Security Dilemma." *World Politics* 2 (2): 157–80.

Hildebrand, Klaus. 1973. *The Foreign Policy of the Third Reich.* Berkeley: University of California Press.

Hillgruber, Andreas. 1981. *Germany and the Two World Wars.* Cambridge, MA: Harvard University Press.

Hirschman, Albert O. 1977. *The Passions and the Interests.* Princeton, NJ: Princeton University Press.

———. (1945) 1980. *National Power and the Structure of Foreign Trade.* Exp. ed. Berkeley: University of California Press.

Hitler, Adolf. 1925. *Mein Kampf.* Translated by Ralph Manheim. Boston: Houghton Mifflin.

Hobson, J. A. 1902. *Imperialism.* London: Allen and Unwin.

Hoffman, Erik P., and Robbin F. Laird. 1982. *"The Scientific-Technological Revolution" and Soviet Foreign Policy.* New York: Pergamon.

Hoffman, Ross J. S. 1983. *Great Britain and the German Trade Rivalry, 1875–1914.* New York: Garland.

Holmes, James R., and Toshi Yoshihara. 2008. "China's Naval Ambitions in the Indian Ocean." In *China's Energy Strategy*, edited by Gabriel B. Collins, Andrew S. Erickson, Lyle J. Goldstein, and William S. Murray. Annapolis, MD: Naval Institute Press.

Hopkirk, Peter. 1990. *The Great Game: The Struggle for Empire in Central Asia.* New York: Kodansha.

Howard, Michael. 1961. *The Franco-Prussian War.* London: Routledge.

———. 1986. *War and the Liberal Conscience.* New Brunswick, NJ: Rutgers University Press.

Hull, Cordell. 1948. *The Memoirs of Cordell Hull*. 2 vols. New York: Macmillan.

Hynes, William G. 1979. *The Economics of Empire: Britain, Africa and the New Imperialism*. London: Longman.

Iriye, Akira. 1967. *Across the Pacific: An Inner History of American–East Asian Relations*. New York: Harcourt, Brace, and World, Inc.

———. 1990. *After Imperialism: The Search for a New Order in the Far East, 1921–31*. Chicago: Imprint.

Israelyan, Victor. 1995. *Inside the Kremlin during the Yom Kippur War*. University Park: Pennsylvania State University Press.

Ito, Yukio. 2007. "The Emperor Meiji and the Russo-Japanese War." In *Rethinking the Russo-Japanese War: Volume II, The Nichinan Papers*, edited by John W. Chapman and Inaba Chiharu. Kent, UK: Global Oriental.

Jäckel, Eberhard. 1981. *Hitler's World View*. Cambridge, MA: Harvard University Press.

Jacques, Martin. 2009. *When China Rules the World*. New York: Penguin.

Jentleson, Bruce. 1986. *Pipeline Politics: The Complex Political Economy of East-West Energy Trade*. Ithaca, NY: Cornell University Press.

Jervis, Robert. 1976. *Perception and Misperception in International Politics*. Princeton, NJ: Princeton University Press.

———. 1978. "Cooperation under the Security Dilemma." *World Politics* 30 (2): 167–214.

———. 1996. "Perception, Misperception, and the End of the Cold War." In *Witnesses to the End of the Cold War*, edited by William C. Wohlforth. Baltimore: Johns Hopkins University Press.

———. 1997. *System Effects: Complexity in Political and Social Life*. Princeton, NJ: Princeton University Press.

Jiang, Shixue. 2008. "The Chinese Foreign Policy Perspective." In *China's Expansion into the Western Hemisphere*, edited by Riordan Roett and Guadalupe Paz. Washington, DC: Brookings.

Johnston, Alastair Iain. 2003. "Socialization in International Institutions." In *International Relations Theory and the Asia-Pacific*, edited by G. John Ikenberry and Michael Mastanduno. New York: Columbia University Press.

———. 2004. "Beijing's Security Behavior in the Asia-Pacific: Is China a Satisfied Power?" In *Rethinking Security in East Asia*, edited by J. J. Suh, Peter J. Katzenstein, and Allen Carlson. Stanford, CA: Stanford University Press.

———. 2007. *Social States: China in International Institutions, 1980–2000*. Princeton, NJ: Princeton University Press.

———. 2013. "How New and Assertive Is China's New Assertiveness? *International Security* 37 (4): 7–48.

Jones, Howard, and Randall B. Woods. 1993. "Origins of the Cold War in Europe and the Near East." *Diplomatic History* 17 (2): 251–310.

Kagan, Korina. 1997–98. "The Myth of the European Concert: The Realist-Institutionalist Debate and Great Power Behavior in the Eastern Question, 1820–1841." *Security Studies* 7 (2): 1–57.

Kaiser, David E. 1980. *Economic Diplomacy and the Origins of the Second World War*. Princeton, NJ: Princeton University Press.

Kaiser, Robert G. 1991. *Why Gorbachev Happened*. New York: Simon and Schuster.

Kang, David C. 2007. *China Rising*. New York: Columbia University Press.

Kaplan, Robert D. 2010. *Monsoon: The Indian Ocean and the Future of American Power*. New York: Random House.

Kehr, Eckart. 1970. *Economic Interest, Militarism, and Foreign Policy*. Berkeley: University of California Press.

Kelly, Patrick J. 2011. *Tirpitz and the Imperial German Navy*. Bloomington: Indiana University Press.

Kennedy, Paul. 1976. *The Rise and Fall of British Naval Mastery*. London: Ashfield.

———. 1980. *The Rise of Anglo-German Antagonism, 1860–1914*. London: Ashfield.

———. 1987. *The Rise and Fall of the Great Powers*. New York: Random House.

Keohane, Robert O. 1984. *After Hegemony*. Princeton, NJ: Princeton University Press.

———. 1990. "International Liberalism Revisited." In *The Economic Limits to Modern Politics*, edited by John Dunn. Cambridge: Cambridge University Press.

———. 1993. "Institutional Theory and the Realist Challenge after the Cold War." In *Neorealism and Neoliberalism*, edited by David A. Baldwin. New York: Columbia University Press.

Keohane, Robert O., and Joseph Nye. 1977. *Power and Interdependence*. Boston: Little, Brown.

———. 1989. *Power and Interdependence*. 2nd ed. Glenview, IL: Scott, Foresman.

Kershaw, Ian. 1993. *The Nazi Dictatorship*. 3rd ed. London: Arnold.

Kimball, Warren F. 1991. *The Juggler: Franklin D. Roosevelt as Wartime Statesman*. Princeton, NJ: Princeton University Press.

———. 1997. *Forged in War: Roosevelt, Churchill, and the Second World War*. New York: William Morrow.

King, Gary, Robert O. Keohane, and Sidney Verba. 1994. *Designing Social Inquiry: Scientific Inference in Qualitative Research*. Princeton, NJ: Princeton University Press.

King, Gary, and Langche Zeng. 2001a. "Explaining Rare Events in International Relations." *International Organization* 55 (3): 693–715.

———. 2001b. "Logistic Regression in Rare Events Data." *Political Analysis* 9 (2): 137–63.

Kinzer, Stephen. 2003. *All the Shah's Men*. Hoboken, NJ: John Wiley and Sons.

Kirshner, Jonathan. 2007. *Appeasing Bankers: Financial Caution on the Road to War*. Princeton, NJ: Princeton University Press.

Kissinger, Henry A. 1959. *A World Restored: Metternich, Castlereigh, and the Problems of Peace, 1812–1822*. Boston: Houghton Mifflin.

———. 1979. *White House Years*. Boston: Little, Brown.

———. 1982. *Years of Upheaval*. Boston: Little, Brown.

Knorr, Klaus E. 1973. *Power and Wealth: The Political Economy of International Power*. New York: Basic Books.

———. 1975. *The Power of Nations: The Political Economy of International Relations*. New York: Basic Books.

Kolko, Gabriel. 1990. *The Politics of War.* New York: Pantheon.

Kozyrev, Vitaly. 2008. "China's Continental Energy Strategy: Russia and Central Asia." In *China's Energy Strategy*, edited by Gabriel B. Collins, Andrew S. Erickson, Lyle J. Goldstein, and William S. Murray. Annapolis, MD: Naval Institute Press.

Krasner, Stephen D. 1978. *Defending the National Interest: Raw Materials and U.S. Foreign Policy.* Princeton, NJ: Princeton University Press.

Kuniholm, Bruce R. 1980. *The Origins of the Cold War in the Near East.* Princeton, NJ: Princeton University Press.

Kupchan, Charles. 1994. *The Vulnerability of Empire.* Ithaca, NY: Cornell University Press.

Kuznets, Simon. 1967. "Quantitative Aspects of the Economic Growth of Nations: X. Level and Structure of Foreign Trade: Long-Term Trends." *Economic Development and Cultural Change* 15, no. 2 (part II): 1–140.

Kydd, Andrew. 1997a. "Game Theory and the Spiral Model." *World Politics* 49 (3): 371–400.

———. 1997b. "Sheep in Sheep's Clothing: Why Security Seekers Do Not Fight Each Other." *Security Studies* 7 (1): 114–54.

———. 2005. *Trust and Mistrust in International Politics.* Princeton, NJ: Princeton University Press.

LaFeber, Walter. 1963. *The New Empire: An Interpretation of American Expansionism, 1860–1898.* Ithaca, NY: Cornell University Press.

Lake, David A. 2011. "Why 'Isms' Are Evil: Theory, Epistemology, and Academic Sects as Impediments to Understanding and Progress." *International Studies Quarterly* 55 (2): 465–80.

Landes, David S. 1961. "Some Thoughts on the Nature of Economic Imperialism." *Journal of Economic History* 21 (4): 496–512.

Langer, William L. 1950. *European Alliances and Alignments, 1871–1890.* New York: Knopf.

———. 1960. *The Diplomacy of Imperialism, 1890–1902.* New York: Knopf.

Lascurettes, Kyle. 2008. "Trading for Intentions: Relative Gains, Potential Adversaries, and the Prospects for Cooperation." Paper presented at the American Political Science Association annual meeting, Boston, MA, August 28–31.

Layne, Christopher. 1994. "Kant or Cant: The Myth of the Democratic Peace." *International Security* 19 (2): 5–49.

———. 2006. *Peace of Illusions: American Grand Strategy from 1940 to the Present.* Ithaca, NY: Cornell University Press.

Lebow, Richard Ned. 1981. *Between Peace and War.* Baltimore: Johns Hopkins University Press.

Lebow, Richard Ned, and Janice Gross Stein. 1994. *We All Lost the Cold War.* Princeton, NJ: Princeton University Press.

LeDonne, John P. 1997. *The Russian Empire and the World, 1700–1917.* New York: Oxford University Press.

Lee, Steven Hugh. 1995. *Outposts of Empire: Korea, Vietnam, and the Origins of the Cold War in Asia, 1949–54.* Montreal: McGill-Queen's University Press.

Leffler, Melvyn P. 1984. "The American Conception of National Security and the Beginnings of the Cold War." *American Historical Review* 89 (2): 346–81.

Leffler, Melvyn P. 1992. *A Preponderance of Power: National Security, the Truman Administration, and the Cold War*. Stanford, CA: Stanford University Press.

———. 1994a. "Interpretative Wars over the Cold War, 1945–50." In *American Foreign Relations Reconsidered, 1890–1993*, edited by Gordon Martel. London: Routledge.

———. 1994b. *The Specter of Communism*. New York: Hill and Wang.

———. 1996a. "Inside Enemy Archives: The Cold War Reopened." *Foreign Affairs* 75 (4): 120–35.

———. 1996b. *The Struggle for Germany and the Origins of the Cold War*. Occasional paper no. 16. Washington DC: German Historical Institute.

Lenin, V. I. (1917) 1996. *Imperialism, the Highest Stage of Capitalism*. London: Pluto Press.

Levitsky, Steven, and Lucan A. Way. 2010. *Competitive Authoritarianism*. Cambridge: Cambridge University Press.

Levy, Jack S. 1989. "The Causes of War: A Review of Theories." Vol. 2, *Behavior, Society, and Nuclear War*, edited by Philip E. Tetlock, Jo L. Husbands, Robert Jervis, Paul C. Stern, and Charles Tilly. New York: Oxford University Press.

———. 2008. "Preventive War and Democratic Politics." *International Studies Quarterly* 52 (1): 1–24.

Levy, Jack S., and Philip Streich. 2008. "Time Horizons, Discounting, and Intertemporal Choice." *Journal of Conflict Resolution* 51 (2): 199–226.

Levy, Jack S., and William R. Thompson. 2010. *Causes of War*. New York: Wiley-Blackwell.

Levy, Jack S., and John A. Vasquez, eds. 2014. *The Outbreak of the First World War: Structure, Politics, and Decision-Making*. Cambridge: Cambridge University Press.

Li, Quan, and Rafael Reuveny. 2009. *Democracy and Economic Openness in an Interconnected System*. Cambridge: Cambridge University Press.

Liberman, Peter. 1996a. *Does Conquest Pay? The Exploitation of Occupied Industrial Societies*. Princeton, NJ: Princeton University Press.

———. 1996b. "Trading with the Enemy: Security and Relative Economic Gains." *International Security* 21 (1): 147–75.

———. 1999–2000. "The Offense-Defense Balance, Interdependence, and War." *Security Studies* 9 (1–2): 59–91.

Lieber, Keir A. 2007. "The New History of World War I and What It Means for International Relations Theory." *International Security* 32 (2): 155–91.

Lipson, Charles. 2003. *Reliable Partners: How Democracies Have Made a Separate Peace*. Princeton, NJ: Princeton University Press.

Lloyd, T. O. 1993. *Empire, Welfare State, Europe: English History 1906–1992*. 4th ed. Oxford: Oxford University Press.

Lo, Bobo. 2008. *Axis of Convenience: Moscow, Beijing, and the New Geopolitics*. Washington, DC: Brookings.

Lobell, Steven E., Norrin M. Ripsman, and Jeffrey W. Taliaferro. 2009. *Neoclassical Realism, the State, and Foreign Policy*. Cambridge: Cambridge University Press.

MacDonald, Douglas J. 1995–96. "Communist Bloc Expansion in the East Cold War: Challenging Realism, Refuting Revisionism." *International Security* 20 (3): 152–88.

Mackie, John L. 1980. *Cement of the Universe: A Study of Causation.* Oxford: Oxford University Press.

Maddox, Robert James. 1988. *From War to Cold War.* Boulder, CO: Westview.

Mahan, Alfred T. (1890) 1987. *The Influence of Sea Power on History, 1660–1783.* 5th ed. New York: Dover.

Mahoney, James. 2010. *Colonialism and Postcolonial Development: Spanish America in Comparative Perspective.* Cambridge: Cambridge University Press.

Mahoney, James, and Gary Goertz. 2006. "A Tale of Two Cultures: Contrasting Quantitative and Qualitative Research." *Political Analysis* 14:227–49.

Malozemoff, Andrew. 1958. *Russian Far Eastern Policy, 1881–1904.* Berkeley: University of California Press.

Mansfield, Edward D. 1994. *Power, Trade, and War.* Princeton, NJ: Princeton University Press.

Mansfield, Edward D., and Jon Pevehouse. 2000. "Trade Blocs, Trade Flows, and International Conflict." *International Organization* 54 (4): 775–808.

Mansfield, Edward D., Jon Pevehouse, and David H. Bearce. 1999–2000. "Preferential Trading Arrangements and Military Disputes." *Security Studies* 9 (1–2): 92–118.

Mansfield, Edward D., and Brian M. Pollins. 2001. "The Study of Interdependence and Conflict: Recent Advances, Open Questions, and Directions for Future Research." *Journal of Conflict Resolution* 45 (6): 834–59.

———, eds. 2003. *Economic Interdependence and International Conflict.* Ann Arbor: University of Michigan Press.

Mansfield, Edward D., and Jack Snyder. 2005. *Electing to Fight.* Cambridge, MA: MIT Press.

Maoz, Zeev, and Bruce Russett. 1993. "Normative and Structural Causes of Democratic Peace, 1946–1986." *American Political Science Review* 87 (3): 624–38.

Marini, Carmine, Rocco Totaro, Federica De Santis, Irene Ciancarelli, Massimo Baldassarre, and Antonio Carolei. 2001. "Stroke in Young Adults in the Community-Based L'Aguila Registry: Incidence and Prognosis." *Stroke* 32:52–56.

Marlowe, John. 1971. *Perfidious Albion: The Origins of Anglo-French Rivalry in the Levant.* London: Elek.

Maron, Barry J., Thomas E. Gohman, and Dorothee Aeppli. 1998. "Prevalence of Sudden Cardiac Death during Competitive Sports Activities in Minnesota High School Athletes." *Journal of American College of Cardiology* 32 (7): 1881–84.

Marshall, Jonathan. 1995. *To Have and Have Not: Southeast Asian Raw Materials and the Origins of the Pacific War.* Berkeley: University of California Press.

Martel, Leon. 1979. *Lend-Lease, Loans, and the Coming of the Cold War.* Boulder, CO: Westview.

Mason, Tim. 1995. *Nazism, Fascism, and the Working Class.* Cambridge: Cambridge University Press.

Massie, Robert K. 1991. *Dreadnought: Britain, Germany, and the Coming of the Great War.* New York: Random House.

Mastanduno, Michael. 1991. "Do Relative Gains Matter? America's Response to Japanese Industrial Policy." *International Security* 16 (1): 73–113.

———. 1992. *Economic Containment: CoCom and the Politics of East-West Trade.* Ithaca, NY: Cornell University Press.

Matlock, Jack F. 1995. *Autopsy of an Empire*. New York: Random House.

Matthew, H.C.G. 1997. *Gladstone, 1809–98*. Oxford: Oxford University Press.

McDonald, Patrick J. 2004. Peace through Trade or Free Trade? *Journal of Conflict Resolution* 48 (4): 547–72.

———. 2007. "The Purse Strings of Peace." *American Journal of Political Science* 51 (3): 569–82.

———. 2009. *The Invisible Hand of Peace: Capitalism, the War Machine, and International Relations Theory*. Cambridge: Cambridge University Press.

———. 2010. "Capitalism, Commitment, and Peace." *International Interactions* 36 (2): 146–68.

McFarland, Stephen L. 1980. "A Peripheral View of the Origins of the Cold War: The Crisis in Iraq, 1941–47." *Diplomatic History* 4 (4): 333–52.

McJimsey, George. 1987. *Harry Hopkins*. Cambridge, MA: Harvard University Press.

McLellan, David. 1976. *Dean Acheson*. New York: Dodd, Mead.

McMillan, Susan M. 1997. "Interdependence and Conflict." *Mershon International Studies Review* 41 (suppl. 1): 33–58.

Mearsheimer, John. J. 1992. "Disorder Restored." In *Rethinking America's Security*, edited by Graham Allison and Gregory F. Treverton. New York: W. W. Norton.

———. 1994–95. "The False Promise of International Institutions." *International Security* 15 (3): 5–56.

———. 2001. *The Tragedy of Great Power Politics*. New York: W. W. Norton.

Meredith, Martin. 2007. *Diamonds, Gold, and War: The British, the Boers, and the Making of South Africa*. New York: Public Affairs.

Miller, Aaron D. 1980. *Search for Security: Saudi Arabian Oil and American Foreign Policy, 1939–1949*. Chapel Hill: University of North Carolina Press.

Mommsen, Hans. 1979. "National Socialism: Continuity and Change." In *Fascism*, edited by Walter Laqueur. Harmondsworth, UK: Penguin.

Mommsen, Wolfgang J. 1977. *Theories of Imperialism*. Translated by P. S. Falla. Chicago: University of Chicago Press.

Montgomery, Evan Braden. 2006. "Breaking Out of the Security Dilemma: Realism, Reassurance, and the Problem of Uncertainty." *International Security* 31 (2): 151–86.

Montgomery, Michael. 1987. *Imperialist Japan*. London: Christopher Helm.

Moravcsik, Andrew. 1997. "Taking Preferences Seriously: A Liberal Theory of International Politics." *International Organization* 51 (4): 513–53.

Moriarty, Thomas. 2007. "Third Party Market Competition and War: The Anglo-Dutch Rivalry." Master's thesis, University of Virginia.

Morrow, James D. 1999. "How Could Trade Affect Conflict?" *Journal of Peace Research* 36 (4): 481–89.

———. 2003. "Assessing the Role of Trade as a Source of Costly Signals." In *Economic Interdependence and International Conflict*, edited by Edward D. Mansfield and Brian M. Pollins. Ann Arbor: University of Michigan Press.

Mosse, William E. 1958. *The European Powers and the German Question, 1848–71*. Cambridge: Cambridge University Press.

Mousseau, Michael. 2000. "Market Prosperity, Democratic Consolidation, and Democratic Peace." *Journal of Conflict Resolution* 44 (4): 472–507.

———. 2003. "The Nexus of Market Society, Liberal Preferences, and Democratic Peace: Interdisciplinary Theory and Evidence." *International Studies Quarterly* 47 (4): 483–510.

———. 2009. "The Social Market Roots of the Democratic Peace." *International Security* 33 (4): 52–86.

Mousseau, Michael, Havard Hegre, and John R. Oneal. 2003. "How the Wealth of Nations Conditions the Liberal Peace." *European Journal of International Relations* 9 (2): 277–314.

Mueller, John. 2010. "Capitalism, Peace, and the Historical Movement of Ideas." *International Interactions* 36 (2): 169–84.

Munck, Geraldo L. 2004. "Tools for Qualitative Research." In *Rethinking Social Inquiry: Diverse Tools, Shared Standards*, edited by Henry E. Brady and David Collier. Lanham, MD: Rowman and Littlefield.

Myint-U, Thant. 2011. *Where China Meets India: Burma and the New Crossroads of Asia*. New York: Farrar, Straus and Giroux.

Nagaoka, Shinjiro. 1980. "Economic Demands on Dutch East Indies." In *The Fateful Choice: Japanese Advance into Southeast Asia, 1939–41*, edited by James W. Morley. New York: Columbia University Press.

Narizny, Kevin. 2007. *The Political Economy of Grand Strategy*. Ithaca, NY: Cornell University Press.

Ninkovich, Frank. 1994. *Modernity and Power: A History of the Domino Theory in the Twentieth Century*. Chicago: University of Chicago Press.

Nish, Ian. 1985. *The Origins of the Russo-Japanese War*. London: Longmam.

Nixon, Richard M. 1978. *RN: The Memoirs of Richard Nixon*. New York: Grosset and Dunlap.

Njolstad, Olav. 2010. "The Collapse of Superpower Détente, 1975–1980." In *The Cold War*, vol. 3, *Endings*, edited by Melvyn P. Leffler and Odd Arne Westad. Cambridge: Cambridge University Press.

North, Douglass C., and Robert P. Thomas. 1973. *The Rise of the Western World*. Cambridge: Cambridge University Press.

Oberdorfer, Don. 1991. *The Turn: From Cold War to a New Era*. New York: Poseidon.

O'Brien, Patrick. 1999. "Imperialism and the Rise and Decline of the British Economy, 1688–1989." *New Left Review* I (238): 48–80.

Offer, Avner. 1989. *The First World War: An Agrarian Interpretation*. Oxford: Oxford University Press.

Okamoto, Shumpei. 1970. *The Japanese Oligarchy and the Russo-Japanese War*. New York: Columbia University Press.

Oneal, John R., Frances H. Oneal, Zeev Maoz, and Bruce Russett. 1996. "The Liberal Peace: Interdependence, Democracy, and International Conflict, 1950–1985." *Journal of Peace Research* 33 (1): 11–28.

Oneal, John R., and Bruce M. Russett. 1997. "The Classical Liberals Were Right: Democracy, Interdependence, and Conflict, 1950–1985." *International Studies Quarterly* 41 (2): 267–94.

———. 1999. "The Kantian Peace: The Pacific Benefits of Democracy, Interdependence, and International Organization, 1885–1992." *World Politics* 52 (1): 1–37.

———. 2001. *Triangulating Peace*. New York: W. W. Norton.

Oneal, John R., Bruce M. Russett, and Michael L. Berbaum. 2003. "Causes of Peace: Democracy, Interdependence, and International Organizations, 1885–1992." *International Studies Quarterly* 47 (3): 71–93.

Oneal, John R., Bruce M. Russett, and David R. Davis. 1998. "The Third Leg of the Kantian Tripod for Peace: International Organizations and Militarized Disputes, 1950–85." *International Organization* 52 (3): 441–67.

Owen, John M. 1994. "How Liberalism Produces the Democratic Peace." *International Security* 19 (2): 87–125.

———. 2012. "Economic Interdependence and Regional Peace." In *Regional Orders and International Security*, edited by T. V. Paul. Cambridge: Cambridge University Press.

Painter, David S. 1986. *Oil and the American Century*. Baltimore: Johns Hopkins University Press.

Pakenham, Thomas. 1991. *The Scramble for Africa*. New York: Avon.

———. 2001. *The Boer War*. New York: Perennial.

Papayoanou, Paul. 1996. "Interdependence, Institutions, and the Balance of Power." *International Security* 20 (4): 42–76.

———. 1999. *Power Ties: Economic Interdependence and War*. Ann Arbor: University of Michigan Press.

Parrott, Bruce. 1983. *Politics and Technology in the Soviet Union*. Cambridge, MA: MIT Press.

———. 1985. "Soviet Foreign Policy, Internal Politics, and Trade with the West." In *Trade, Technology, and Soviet-American Relations*, edited by Bruce Parrott. Bloomington: Indiana University Press.

Paterson, Thomas G. 1973. *Soviet-American Confrontation: Postwar Reconstruction and the Origins of the Cold War*. Baltimore: Johns Hopkins University Press.

Pelz, Stephen E. 1974. *Race to Pearl Harbor*. Cambridge, MA: Harvard University Press.

Peterson, Susan. 1996. *Crisis Bargaining and the State*. Ann Arbor: University of Michigan Press.

Pflanze, Otto. 1963. *Bismarck and the Development of Germany: The Period of Unification, 1815–1871*. Princeton, NJ: Princeton University Press.

———. 1990. *Bismarck and the Development of Germany: The Period of Consolidation, 1871–1880*. 2nd ed. Princeton, NJ: Princeton University Press.

Pietz, David. 2008. "The Past, Present, and Future of China's Energy Sector." In *China's Energy Strategy*, edited by Gabriel B. Collins, Andrew S. Erickson, Lyle J. Goldstein, and William S. Murray. Annapolis, MD: Naval Institute Press.

Plokhy, S. M. 2010. *Yalta: The Price of Peace*. New York: Vintage.

Polachek, Solomon W. 1980. "Conflict and Trade." *Journal of Conflict Resolution* 24 (1): 55–78.

———. 1992. "Conflict and Trade: An Economics Approach to Political International Interactions." In *Economics of Arms Reduction and the Peace Process*, edited by Walter Isard and Charles H. Anderton. Amsterdam: North Holland.

Polachek, Solomon W., and Judith McDonald. 1992. "Strategic Trade and the Incentive for Cooperation." In *Disarmament, Economic Conversions, and Peace*

Management, edited by Manas Chatterji and Linda Rennie Forcey. New York: Praeger.

Pollack, Jonathan D. 2008. "Energy Insecurity with Chinese and American Characteristics: Realities and Possibilities." In *China's Energy Strategy*, edited by Gabriel B. Collins, Andrew S. Erickson, Lyle J. Goldstein, and William S. Murray. Annapolis, MD: Naval Institute Press.

Posen, Barry R. 1993. "The Security Dilemma and Ethnic Conflict." *Survival* 35 (1): 27–47.

Pottinger, E. Ann. 1966. *Napoleon III and the German Crisis, 1865–1866*. Cambridge, MA: Harvard University Press.

Powell, Robert. 1999. *In the Shadow of Power: States and Strategies in International Politics*. Princeton, NJ: Princeton University Press.

———. 2002. "Bargaining Theory and International Conflict." *Annual Review of Political Science* 5 (1): 1–30.

———. 2006. "War as a Commitment Problem." *International Organization* 60 (1): 169–203.

Power, Thomas F. 1944. *Jules Ferry and the Renaissance of French Imperialism*. New York: King's Crown.

Prados, John. 1986. *The Soviet Estimate: U.S. Intelligence Analysis and Soviet Strategic Forces*. Princeton, NJ: Princeton University Press.

Prange, Gordon W. 1981. *At Dawn We Slept: The Untold Story of Pearl Harbor*. Harmondsworth, UK: Penguin.

Press-Barnathan, Galia. 2009. *The Political Economy of Transitions to Peace*. Pittsburgh: University of Pittsburgh Press.

Price, Roger. 1981. *An Economic History of Modern France, 1730–1914*. New York: Palgrave Macmillan.

Puranik, Rajesh, Clara K. Chow, Johan A. Duflou, Michael J. Kilborn, and Mark A. McGuire. 2005. "Sudden Death in the Young." *Heart Rhythm* 2:1277–82.

Puryear, Vernon John. 1931. *England, Russia, and the Straits Question, 1844–1856*. Hamden, CT: Archon.

Ragin, Charles C. 1987. *The Comparative Method: Moving Beyond Qualitative and Quantitative Strategies*. Berkeley: University of California Press.

———. 2000. *Fuzzy-Set Social Science*. Chicago: University of Chicago Press.

———. 2008. *Redesigning Social Inquiry: Fuzzy Sets and Beyond*. Chicago: University of Chicago Press.

Ray, James Lee. 1995. *Democracy and International Conflict*. Columbia: University of South Carolina Press.

Read, Anthony, and David Fisher. 1988. *The Deadly Embrace: Hitler, Stalin and the Nazi-Soviet Pact, 1939–1941*. London: Michael Joseph.

Reed, William. 2003. "Information and Economic Interdependence." *Journal of Conflict Resolution* 47 (1): 54–71.

Reiter, Dan. 2003. "Exploring the Bargaining Model of War." *Perspectives on Politics* 1 (1): 27–43.

———. 2009. *Why Wars End*. Princeton, NJ: Princeton University Press.

Reuveny, Rafael, and Quan Li. 2009. *Democracy and Economic Openness in an Interconnected System*. Cambridge: Cambridge University Press.

Rich, Norman. 1985. *Why the Crimean War? A Cautionary Tale*. Hanover, NH: University Press of New England.

Richardson, James L. 1994. *Crisis Diplomacy*. Cambridge: Cambridge University Press.

Ridley, Jasper. 1980. *Napoleon III and Eugenie*. New York: Viking.

Ripsman, Norrin M., and Jean-Marc F. Blanchard. 1996–97. "Commercial Liberalism under Fire." *Security Studies* 6 (2): 4–50.

Risse-Kappen, Thomas. 1994. "Ideas Do Not Float Freely: Transnational Coalitions, Domestic Structures, and the End of the Cold War." *International Organization* 48 (2): 185–214.

Robinson, Ronald, and John Gallagher. 1961. *Africa and the Victorians*. Garden City, NY: Anchor.

Robst, John, Soloman Polachek, and Yuan-Ching Chang. 2007. "Geographic Proximity, Trade, and International Conflict." *Conflict Management and Peace Science* 24 (1): 1–24.

Roett, Riordan and Guadalupe Paz, eds.. 2008. *China's Expansion into the Western Hemisphere*. Washington, D.C.: Brookings.

Rosecrance, Richard. 1986. *The Rise of the Trading State*. New York: Basic Books.

Rosecrance, Richard, and Peter Thompson. 2003. "Trade, Foreign Investment, and Security." *Annual Review of Political Science* 6:377–98.

Rosato, Sebastian. 2003. "The Flawed Logic of Democratic Peace Theory." *American Political Science Review* 94 (4): 585–602.

Ross, Robert S., and Zhu Feng, eds. 2008. *China's Ascent: Power, Security, and the Future of International Politics*. Ithaca, NY: Cornell University Press.

Ross, Stephen T. 1969. *European Diplomatic History, 1789–1815*. Garden City, NY: Anchor.

Rotberg, Robert I., ed. 2008. *China into Africa: Trade, Aid, and Influence*. Washington, DC: Brookings.

Rubin, Barry. 1980. *Paved with Good Intentions: The American Experience and Iran*. Oxford: Oxford University Press.

Russett, Bruce. 1993. *Grasping the Democratic Peace*. Princeton, NJ: Princeton University Press.

———. 2010. "Capitalism or Democracy? Not So Fast." *International Interactions* 36 (2): 198–205.

Saab, Ann Pottinger. 1977. *The Origins of the Crimean Alliance*. Charlottesville: University Press of Virginia.

Sagan, Scott. 1986. "1914 Revisited: Allies, Offense, and Instability." *International Security* 11:151–75.

———. 1989. "The Origins of the Pacific War." In *The Origins and Prevention of Major Wars*, edited by Robert I. Rotberg and Theodore K. Rabb. Cambridge: Cambridge University Press.

Samuels, Richard J. 1994. *"Rich Nation, Strong Army": National Security and the Technological Transformation of Japan*. Ithaca, NY: Cornell University Press.

Schimmelpenninck van der Oye, David. 2005. "The Immediate Origins of the War." In *The Russo-Japanese War in Global Perspective: World War Zero*, edited by John W. Steinberg, Bruce W. Menning, David Schimmelpenninck van der Oye, David Wolff, and Shinji Yokote. Boston: Brill.

———. 2007. "An Invitation to the Aquarium: Sergei Witte and the Origins of Russia's War with Japan." In *Rethinking the Russo-Japanese War, 1904–5*, edited by Rotem Kowner. Kent, UK: Global Oriental.

Schom, Alan. 1997. *Napoleon Bonaparte*. New York: Harper.

Schroeder, Paul W. 1994. *The Transformation of European Politics, 1763–1848*. Oxford: Oxford University Press.

Schultz, George. 1993. *Turmoil and Triumph*. New York: Scribner's Sons.

Schultz, Kenneth. 1999. "Do Democratic Institutions Constrain or Inform? Contrasting Two Institutional Perspectives on Democracy and War." *International Organization* 53 (2): 233–66.

———. 2001. *Democracy and Coercive Diplomacy*. Cambridge: Cambridge University Press.

Schuman, Frederick L. 1969. *War and Diplomacy in the French Republic*. New York: Howard Fertig.

Schumpeter, Joseph A. 1951. *Imperialism and Social Classes*. Cambridge, MA: Harvard University Press.

Schweller, Randall L. 1996. "Neorealism's Status-Quo Bias: What Security Dilemma?" *Security Studies* 5 (3): 90–121.

Seawright, Jason, and John Gerring. 2008. "Case Selection Techniques in Case Study Research." *Political Research Quarterly* 61 (2): 294–308.

Seton-Watson, R. W. 1972. *Disraeli, Gladstone, and the Eastern Question*. New York: W. W. Norton.

Seward, Desmond. 1988. *Napoleon and Hitler*. New York: Touchstone.

Shambaugh, David, ed. 2005. *Power Shift: China and Asia's New Dynamics*. Berkeley: University of California Press.

Sheffrin, Steven M. 1996. *Rational Expectations Theory*. 2nd ed. Cambridge: Cambridge University Press.

Sherry, Michael S. 1977. *Preparing for the New War*. New Haven, NJ: Yale University Press.

Sherwood, Robert E. 1950. *Roosevelt and Hopkins*. Rev ed. New York: Harper and Brothers.

Simmons, Beth. 2003. "Pax Mercatoria and the Theory of the State." In *Economic Interdependence and International Conflict*, edited by Edward D. Mansfield and Brian M. Pollins. Ann Arbor: University of Michigan Press.

Smith, Denis Mack. 1985. *Cavour: A Political Biography*. New York: Knopf.

Smith, Iain R. 1996. *The Origins of the South African War*. London: Longman.

Smith, Woodruff D. 1986. *The Ideological Origins of Nazi Imperialism*. Oxford: Oxford University Press.

Smoke, Richard. 1977. *War: Controlling Escalation*. Cambridge, MA: Harvard University Press.

Solingen, Etel. 1998. *Regional Orders at Century's Down*. Princeton, NJ: Princeton University Press.

Snyder, Glenn H. 1984. "The Security Dilemma in Alliance Politics." *World Politics* 36 (4): 461–96.

Snyder, Glenn H., and Paul Diesing. 1977. *Conflict among Nations: Bargaining, Decision Making, and System Structure in International Crisis*. Princeton, NJ: Princeton University Press.

Snyder, Jack. 1984. *The Ideology of the Offensive*. Ithaca, NY: Cornell University Press.

———. 1991. *Myths of Empire: Domestic Politics and International Ambition*. Ithaca, NY: Cornell University Press.

Snyder, Jack, and Robert Jervis. 1999. "Civil War and the Security Dilemma." In *Civil Wars, Insecurity, and Intervention*, edited by Barbara F. Walter and Jack Snyder. New York: Columbia University Press.

Souva, Mark. 2000. "Types of Trade and International Conflict: A Response to the Manchester School." Working paper no. 12, Political Institutions and Public Choice, Michigan State University.

Steefel, Lawrence D. 1932. *The Schleswig-Holstein Question*. Cambridge, MA: Harvard University Press.

Stein, Arthur A. 1993. "Governments, Economic Interdependence, and International Cooperation." In vol. 3, *Behavior, Society, and Nuclear War*, edited by Philip E. Tetlock, Jo L. Husbands, Robert Jervis, Paul C. Stern, and Charles Tilly. New York: Oxford University Press.

———. 2003. "Trade and Conflict: Uncertainty, Strategic Signaling, and Interstate Disputes." In *Economic Interdependence and International Conflict*, edited by Edward D. Mansfield and Brian M. Pollins. Ann Arbor: University of Michigan Press.

Steinberg, Jonathan. 2011. *Bismarck*. Oxford: Oxford University Press.

Stephens, John J. 2003. *Fuelling the Empire: South Africa's Gold and the Road to War*. Chichester, UK: Wiley.

Stevenson, Richard W. 1985. *The Rise and Fall of Détente*. Urbana: University of Illinois Press.

Stoakes, Geoffrey. 1986. *Hitler and the Quest for World Domination*. Leamington Spa, UK: Berg.

Stoecker, Helmuth. 1986. *German Imperialism in Africa*. Translated by Bernd Zöllner. London: Hurst.

Stolberg, Eva-Maria. 2007. "'The Unknown Enemy': The Siberian Frontier and the Russo-Japanese Rivalry." In *Rethinking the Russo-Japanese War, 1904–05*, edited by Rotem Kowner. Kent, UK: Global Oriental.

Stoler, Mark. 2000. *Allies and Adversaries: The Joint Chiefs of Staff, the Grand Alliance, and U.S. Strategy in World War II*. Chapel Hill: University of North Carolina Press.

Streich, Philip, and Jack Levy. 2011. "The Role of Preventive Logic in the Japanese Decision for War against Russia in 1904." Paper prepared for American Political Science Association annual meeting, Seattle, September 1–4.

Sun, Youli. 1993. *China and the Origins of the Pacific War, 1931–1941*. New York: St. Martin's Press.

Sutter, Robert. 2005. "China's Regional Strategy and Why It Might Not Be Good for America." In *Power Shift: China and Asia's New Dynamics*, edited by David Shambaugh. Berkeley: University of California Press.

Taliaferro, Jeffrey. 2005. *Balancing Risks*. Ithaca, NY: Cornell University Press.

Tang, Peter S. H. 1959. *Russian and Soviet Policy in Manchuria and Outer Mongolia, 1911–1931*. Durham, NC: Duke University Press.

Tang, Shiping. 2010. *A Theory of Security Strategy for Our Time: Defensive Realism*. New York: Palgrave Macmillan.

Tarle, Eugene. 1942. *Napoleon's Invasion of Russia, 1812.* New York: Oxford University Press.

Taubman, William. 2003. *Khrushchev.* New York: W. W. Norton.

Taylor, A.J.P. 1954. *The Struggle for Mastery in Europe, 1848–1918.* Oxford: Oxford University Press.

Taylor, Jay. 2009. *The Generalissimo: Chiang Kai-Shek and the Struggle for Modern China.* Cambridge, MA: Harvard University Press.

Tester, David J., and Michael J. Ackerman. 2007. "Postmortem Long QT Syndrome Genetic Testing for Sudden Unexplained Death in the Young." *Journal of the American College of Cardiology* 49 (2): 240–46.

Tooze, Adam. 2006. *The Wages of Destruction: The Making and Breaking of the Nazi Economy.* New York: Penguin.

Trachtenberg, Marc. 1999. *A Constructed Peace: The Making of the European Settlement, 1945–1963.* Princeton, NJ: Princeton University Press.

———. 2006. *The Craft of International History.* Princeton, NJ: Princeton University Press.

———. 2011. "Audience Costs: A Historical Analysis." *Security Studies* 21 (1): 3–42.

Trebilcock, Clive. 1981. *The Industrialization of the Continental Powers, 1780–1914.* London: Longman.

Trocki, Carl A. 1999. *Opium, Empire, and the Global Political Economy.* London: Routledge.

Troubetzkoy, Alexis. 2006. *A Brief History of the Crimean War.* New York: Carroll and Graf.

Truman, Harry S. 1955. *Year of Decisions.* Garden City, NY: Doubleday.

Tsunoda, Jun. 1980. "The Navy's Role in the Southern Strategy." In *The Fateful Choice: Japanese Advance into Southeast Asia, 1939–41,* edited by James W. Morley. New York: Columbia University Press.

———. 1994. In *The Final Confrontation: Japan's Negotiations with the United States, 1941,* edited by James W. Morley. New York: Columbia University Press.

Turner, Henry. 1967. "Bismarck's Imperialist Venture." In *Britain and Germany in Africa: Imperial Rivalry and Colonial Rule,* edited by Prosser Gifford and W. Roger Louis. New Haven, CT: Yale University Press.

Ulam, Adam. 1983. *Dangerous Relations: The Soviet Union in World Politics, 1970–1982.* New York: Oxford University Press.

Van Evera, Stephen. 1999. *Causes of War: Power and the Roots of Conflict.* Ithaca, NY: Cornell University Press.

Venn, Fiona. 1986. *Oil Diplomacy in the Twentieth Century.* New York: St. Martin's Press.

Volten, Peter. 1982. *Brezhnev's Peace Program.* Boulder, CO: Westview.

von Stein, Jana. 2001. "Interdependence and Militarized Conflict: Toward a Signaling Theory of Trade and War." Paper presented at International Studies Association annual meeting, Chicago, February 20–24.

Wagner, R. Harrison. 2000. "Bargaining and War." *American Journal of Political Science* 44 (3): 469–84.

———. 2007. *War and the State.* Ann Arbor: University of Michigan Press.

Walker, Martin. 1987. *The Waking Giant: The Soviet Union under Gorbachev.* London: Abacus.

Walt, Stephen M. 1996. *Revolution and War*. Ithaca, NY: Cornell University Press.

Waltz, Kenneth. 1970. "The Myth of Interdependence." In *The Multinational Corporation*, edited by Charles P. Kindleberger. Cambridge: Cambridge University Press.

———. 1979. *Theory of International Politics*. New York: Random House.

Ward, Patricia Dawson. 1979. *The Threat of Peace*. Kent, OH: Kent State University Press.

Warner, Denis, and Peggy Warner. 1974. *The Tide at Sunrise: A History of the Russo-Japanese War, 1904–05*. New York: Charterhouse.

Wawro, Geoffrey. 1997. *The Austro-Prussian War*. Cambridge: Cambridge University Press.

———. 2003. *The Franco-Prussian War*. Cambridge: Cambridge University Press.

Webster, Charles. 1969. *The Foreign Policy of Palmerston, 1830–1841*. 2 vols. New York: Humanities Press.

Weeks, Jessica L. 2008. "Autocratic Audience Costs: Regime Type and Signaling Resolve." *International Organization* 62 (1): 35–64.

Wehler, Hans-Ulrich. 1985. *The German Empire, 1871–1918*. Translated by Kim Traynor. Providence, RI: Berg.

Weinberg, Gerhard L. 1970. *The Foreign Policy of Hitler's Germany: Diplomatic Revolution in Europe, 1933–36*. Chicago: University of Chicago Press.

———. 1980. *The Foreign Policy of Hitler's Germany: Starting World War II*. Chicago: University of Chicago Press.

Weisiger, Alex. 2013. *Logics of War: Explanations for Limited and Unlimited Conflicts*. Ithaca, NY: Cornell University Press.

Weitsman, Patricia A. 2004. *Dangerous Alliances*. Stanford, CA: Stanford University Press.

Wendt, Alexander. 1992. "Anarchy Is What States Make of It." *International Organization* 46 (2): 391–425.

———. 1999. *Social Theory of International Politics*. Cambridge: Cambridge University Press.

Westwood, J. N. 1986. *Russia against Japan, 1904–05: A New Look at the Russo-Japanese War*. London: Macmillan.

Wetzel, David. 2008. "The Origins of the Franco-Prussian War." Paper presented to the International Studies Association annual meeting, San Francisco, March, 26–30.

Whealey, Robert H. 1989. *Hitler and Spain: The Nazi Role in the Spanish Civil War, 1936–1939*. Lexington: University Press of Kentucky.

White, John Albert. 1964. *The Diplomacy of the Russo-Japanese War*. Princeton, NJ: Princeton University Press.

Williams, William Appleman. 1962. *The Tragedy of American Diplomacy*. Rev. ed. New York: Dell.

Womack, Brantly, ed. 2010. *China's Rise in Historical Perspective*. Lanham, MD: Rowman and Littlefield.

Yegorova, Natalia I. 1996. "The 'Iran Crisis' of 1945–46: A View from the Russian Archives." Working paper no. 15. Washington, DC: Cold War in International History Project.

Yergin, Daniel. 1991. *The Prize: The Epic Quest for Oil, Money, and Power*. New York: Simon and Schuster.

Zacher, Mark, and Richard Matthews. 1995. "Liberal International Theory: Common Threads, Divergent Strands." In *Controversies in International Relations Theory*, edited by Charles W. Kegley. New York: St. Martin's Press.

Zelikow, Philip, and Condoleezza Rice. 1997. *Germany Unified and Europe Transformed*. Cambridge, MA: Harvard University Press.

Zubok, Vladislav. 2009. *A Failed Empire: The Soviet Union in the Cold War from Stalin to Gorbachev*. Chapel Hill: University of North Carolina Press.

Index

GPSR Authorized Representative: Easy Access System Europe - Mustamäe tee
50, 10621 Tallinn, Estonia, gpsr.requests@easproject.com

www.ingramcontent.com/pod-product-compliance
Ingram Content Group UK Ltd.
Pitfield, Milton Keynes, MK11 3LW, UK
UKHW041915310325
456954UK00004B/165